# Evolving Practice in EU Enlargement

# Studies in EU External Relations

*Edited by*

Marc Maresceau, Ghent University



VOLUME 4

# Evolving Practice in EU Enlargement

## With Case Studies in Agri-Food and Environment Law

*By*

Kirstyn Inglis

MARTINUS NIJHOFF PUBLISHERS

LEIDEN • BOSTON
2010

This book is printed on acid-free paper.

Library of Congress Cataloging-in-Publication Data

Inglis, Kirstyn.
Evolving practice in EU enlargement : with case studies in agri-food and environment law / by Kirstyn Inglis.
p. cm. — (Studies in EU external relations ; 4)
Includes bibliographical references and index.
ISBN 978-90-04-18166-3 (hardback : alk. paper) 1. European Union. 2. European Union—Membership. 3. Environmental law—European Union countries. 4. Food industry and trade—European Union countries. I. Title.

KJE5091.I54 2010
341.242'2—dc22

2009051751

ISSN 1875-0451
ISBN 978 90 04 18166 3



PRINTED IN THE NETHERLANDS

# CONTENTS

PART TWO

CASE STUDIES ON EU ENVIRONMENT AND AGRI-FOOD LAW

## LIST OF ABBREVIATIONS

| | |
|---|---|
| ADNS | Animal Disease Notification System |
| AJEM | Access to Justice in Environmental Matters |
| BIPs | Border Inspection Posts |
| SCFCH | Standing Commitee on the Food Chain and Animal Health |
| BSEC | Black Sea Co-operation |
| BSE | Bovine spongiform encephalopathy |
| CAP | Common Agricultural Policy |
| CFSP | Common Foreign and Security Policy |
| CMO | Common Market Organisation |
| COM | Common Market Organisation |
| DABLAS | Danube-Black Sea Task Force |
| DIS | Decentralised Implementation System |
| EMU | Economic and Monetary Union |
| EFTA | European Free Trade Association |
| ESA | EFTA Surveillance Authority |
| GMO | Genetically Modified Organism |
| HACCP | Hazard Analysis Critical Control Points |
| IPPC | Integrated Pollution Prevention and Control (IPPC) |
| LIFE/LIFE+ | EU funding instrument for environment and conservation |
| PCBs | Polychlorinated Biphenyls |
| PCTs | Polychlorinated Terphenyls |
| VOCs | Volatile organic compounds |
| EAGGF | European Agricultural Guarantee and Guidance Fund |
| EBRD | European Bank for Reconstruction and Development |
| EDIS | Extended Decentralisation Implementation System |
| EEA | European Economic Area |
| EEAg | European Environment Agency |
| EFSA | European Food Safety Authority |
| EIB | European Investment Bank |
| ENP | European Neighbourhood Policy |
| ENPI | European Partnership Neighbourhood Instrument |
| FADN | Farm Accountancy Data Network |
| FVO | Food and Veterinary Office |

| | |
|---|---|
| ICTY | International Criminal Tribunal for the former Yugoslavia |
| IPA | Instrument for Pre-accession |
| NPAA | National Plan for the Adoption of the *Acquis* |
| PEPA | Priority Programme for Pre-accession |
| RASFF | Rapid Alert System for Food and Feed |
| REC | Regional Environment Center |
| RCC | Regional Co-operation Council |
| SAAs | Stablisation and Association Agreements |
| SEECP | South East European Co-operation Process |
| SIS I | Schengen Information System I |
| SIS II | Schengen Information System II |
| SISone4ALL | Temporary IT solution for enlargement of the SIS |
| TACIS | Technical Assistance to the Commonwealth of Independent States |
| TFEU | Treaty on the Functioning of the European Union |
| TSE | Transmissible spongiform encephalopathies |

## LIST OF CASES

## LIST OF TABLES

ACKNOWLEDGEMENTS

This book is a selective, simplified and updated version of the findings of the PhD thesis entitled *European Union Enlargement: Pre-accession and Transitional Arrangements with Case Studies in Agri-food and Environment Law*, successfully defended at Ghent University. It has been revised to incorporate the written and oral comments of the promoter of the PhD, Professor Marc Maresceau, as well as those of the members of the jury, namely Professors Marise Cremona, Johan Erauw, Inge Govaere and Frank Hoffmeister and Sir Francis Jacobs, to whom I am sincerely grateful for their precious time and input into my research.

I would also like to recognise the confidence and financial support of the *Fonds voor Wetenschappelijk Onderzoek* (FWO Vlaanderen), the Flemish Scientific Research Fund, for my current position as Post-doc Research Fellow, a mandate that has made this book possible as much as my ongoing research in other areas of EU external relations law.

All my colleagues here at the European Institute, Ghent University, deserve a special mention too, most important among them being Professor Marc Maresceau for his unfailing support. I would also like to thank a few key individuals who have been instrumental in my career to date – John Berridge, Sir Bill Nicol, Janice Webster and Sir Alexander Stone, Eric Beaume and Judge Koen Lenaerts – as well as the Law Society of Scotland.

As for all of my friends and family, and you know who you are, a very big thank you for your patience, especially Andrea Ott.

I dedicate this book to my folks, Helen and John.

# INTRODUCTION

Almost continuously since the six original Member States founded the first Communities,[1] in parallel with its integration process, the Union has been preparing its enlargements and negotiating with the applicant or candidate countries the terms of their accession, and then integrating them as new Member States after their accession using a combination of arrangements to ease the transition after the enlargement date itself. Today the Union comprises twenty-seven Member States. The first four enlargements brought in Denmark, Ireland and the United Kingdom on 1 January 1973, followed by Greece on 1 January 1981, then Spain and Portugal on 1 January 1986, and then Austria, Finland and Sweden on 1 January 1995.[2]

Even before signing the fourth Accession Treaty on 24 June 1994, the twelve Member States had committed to eastwards enlargement at the famous 21/22 June 1993 Copenhagen European Council.[3] Next, in two separate waves, ten Central and Eastern European countries as well as Malta and Cyprus became EU Member States. The fifth Accession Treaty entered into force on 1 May 2004 and sets out the terms of the accession of eight of the CEECs, being the Czech Republic, Estonia, Hungary, Latvia, Lithuania, Poland, Slovakia, Slovenia, together

---

[1] The Treaty of Rome, signed by Belgium, France, Germany, Italy, Luxembourg, the Netherlands on 25 March 1957, establishing the European Economic Community (EEC) and came into force on 1 January 1958. The European Atomic Energy Community (Euratom) was signed on the same day and entered into force on the same day. The Treaty of Paris was signed on 18 April 1951 and established the European Coal and Steel Community, which expired on 23 July 2002.

[2] The first Accession Treaty was signed with Denmark, Ireland and the United Kingdom on 22 January 1972 and entered into force on 1 January 1973, *OJ* 1972 L 73/1. The second Accession Treaty was signed with Greece on 28 May 1979 and entered into force on 1 January 1981, *OJ* 1979 L 291/1. The third Accession Treaty was signed with Spain and Portugal on 12 June 1985 and entered into force on 1 January 1986, *OJ* 1985 L 302/1. The fourth Accession Treaty was signed with Austria, Finland and Sweden on 24 June 1994 and entered into force on 1 January 1995, *OJ* 1994 C 241/1.

[3] European Council, Declaration of Copenhagen of 21/22 June 1993, *Bull. EU* 6/1993 p. 13.

with Cyprus and Malta.[4] The Sixth Accession Treaty brought in Bulgaria and Romania on 1 January 2007.[5]

Generally speaking, EU enlargement to the east and now to the south east, has been a foremost driving force in democratisation in the new CEEC Member States and the actual and potential candidate countries of the Western Balkans and Turkey. Preparations are underway for further expansion to include the countries of the Western Balkans as well as Turkey[6] although the actual time frames for their ultimate accession is not certain. The countries of the Western Balkans include Albania, Bosnia and Herzegovina, Croatia, the Former Yugoslav Republic of Macedonia, Kosovo, Montenegro and Serbia.[7] The Former Yugoslav Republic of Macedonia was recognised as a candidate for accession in December 2005 but accession negotiations have not been opened with this country. Croatia is the only Western Balkans country to be recognised by the Council as a candidate, in October 2005, with which accession negotiations have been opened. Accession negotiations were opened with Croatia on 4 October 2005 although no date has been fixed by the EU Council for its eventual accession. While Croatia hopes to sign an accession treaty in the course of 2009, and then become a Member State in 2010, Serbia applied on 22 December 2009 and Iceland on 23 July 2009.[8]

The Union's strategic approach to preparing third countries for their eventual accession to the European Union has been devised to enable them to take on the full rights and obligations of membership as well as to enable the continued application and evolution of the *acquis* in an enlarging Union. Enlargements have always proved a major challenge both to the 'old' and the 'new' or aspiring Member States. Enlargement always involves institutional reforms in order to include new Member

---

[4] The fifth Accession Treaty was signed with the Czech Republic, Estonia, Latvia, Lithuania, Hungary, Cyprus, Malta, Poland, Slovenia and Slovakia on 16 April 2003, *OJ* 2003 L 236/1, as amended.

[5] The sixth Accession Treaty was signed with Bulgaria and Romania on 25 April 2005, *OJ* 2005 L 157/1, as amended.

[6] Turkey was officially recognised as a 'candidate' country by the 1999 Helsinki European Council: see Council mandate of December 2004, loc. cit. n. 9. Significantly, accession negotiations were expressly not opened with Turkey.

[7] See the Presidency Conclusions of the June 2000 Feira European Council and subsequent European Councils of December 2002 in Copenhagen, March 2003 in Brussels, June 2003 in Thessaloniki.

[8] In January 2008, Slovenia threatened to put a Croatian Accession Treaty to national referendum because of a maritime and territorial borders dispute. They resolved the issue in the September of 2009, before the International Court of Justice, see http://news.bbc.co.uk/2/hi/europe/8250441.stm.

States in decision-making and institutional structures for example. In every enlargement, new Member States have had to take on the full breadth of their rights and obligations under the Treaties to the letter and prior to their entry. Each Accession Treaty states in the very first provisions on Principles, that upon accession the incoming Member State is in the 'same situation' with every other Member State. It is an established point of principle that the provisions of Community law apply *ab initio* and *in toto* to new Member States, derogations being allowed only insofar as they are expressly laid down by transitional measures.[9] Incoming Member States have always had a preparatory or pre-accession phase during which the terms of the eventual Accession Treaty have been 'negotiated', although the room for actual negotiation is limited because the founding Treaties themselves cannot be revised: it is only possible for the incoming country to negotiate transitional arrangements in order to enable more gradually to adjust to the full rights and obligations of membership. Even then, however, these arrangements are limited to what is necessary. Accession Treaties have always involved flexibility mechanisms: the legal clauses that differentiate between groups of Member States or that single out different legal provision for one single Member State compared to the rest, such as the temporary derogations from specific measures of the *acquis* which are included in accession treaties.

## Part 1: Evolving practice in European Union enlargement

The first half of this book is concerned with the legal implications of past and future EU pre-accession and accession treaty practices. It covers the Union's strategy for European Union enlargement, for candidate countries and the receiving Member States alike, both before enlargement as well as the legal arrangements that apply after an enlargement in order to smooth the transition of enlargement on the 'old' and 'new' Member States. This book introduces the reader to the preparatory phase leading up to the fifth and then the sixth enlargements. The first Chapters begin by putting the general pre-accession strategy in its historical context and trace its evolution and influences. These first five chapters highlight the particular problems facing today's pre-accession

[9] See ECJ, Case 258/81, *Metallurgiki Halyps A.E.* v. *Commission* [1982] *ECR* 4261.

strategy. They then look at Accession Treaty practice and how to smooth the entry of the incoming countries into the Union post-enlargement: the legal framework for the transitional arrangements. The transitional arrangements that have applied since the accession of the twelve new Member States in 2004 and 2007 introduce a fresh layer of legal complexity in the *acquis communautaire* in an enlarged European Union.

The first Chapter traces how the Union has developed the criteria that apply to countries aspiring to membership as well as the procedural steps to follow. This involves a brief comparative analysis of the relevant accession treaty practice and procedure on accession generally. In terms of eligibility and procedural steps for accession, uncertainty arises in various ways. In particular, there is the 'wild card' unpredictable hurdle of national referendums which are increasingly likely to scupper the ratification at the level of the Member States even if further accession treaties should be concluded.

Chapter 2 explores the content and implications of the Copenhagen criteria, adopted by the June 1993 Copenhagen European Council.[10] Since 1993, the approach to preparing applicant or candidate countries for accession has changed and the Union programmes the preparations of incoming Member States through a variety of new legal tools and changing conditions and incentives. The nature and purpose of the legal and financial 'conditionality' instruments, including the accession negotiations and the 2006 Instrument for Pre-accession Assistance,[11] which now apply to the countries of the Western Balkans and Turkey, are also explored briefly.

The vast approximation exercise required under the pre-accession strategy that was formally set out in the European Commission document of 1997 *Agenda 2000: for a stronger and wider Union*,[12] was intended to further limit the use of transitional arrangements in the Accession Treaty itself. Chapter 2 sets out the evolution of the pre-accession strategy. In addition to preparing candidates for accession, the motivation behind this approach is to preserve the entire body of the *acquis communautaire* and avoid systematic recourse to long transitional arrangements, which could jeopardise the indivisibility of

---

[10] Op. cit. n. 3.

[11] See Regulation 1085/2006, *OJ* 2006 L210/82, corrigendum *OJ* 2007 L18/11.

[12] See *Agenda 2000*, COM(97) 2000 of 15 July 1997.

the *acquis* and the cohesion of the Union as a whole, even leading to a backlash against new Member States.[13] Equally important to the pre-accession strategy therefore is the concern that the new Member States not only continue to apply and enforce the laws in the future but also that they will contribute to the evolution of the *acquis* in an enlarging Union: hence the concentration of 30% of the pre-accession assistance allocated by the Union to assisting candidates in building up their governmental, judicial and administrative capacity as of 1998.[14]

For the CEECs, however, this ever moving target for approximation had to be approached from the very different socio-economic and political backgrounds and cultures of public administration of the Communist era. Their accession to the European Union is all the more remarkable an achievement given the extent of the effort required. Under the pre-accession strategy conditionality devised by the Union to prepare the candidates for EU entry, approximation with every single piece of the *acquis communautiare*, extending to some 80,000 pages, was non-negotiable: each law had to be transposed into national law, implemented or given effect in national law and then complied with and enforced. In particular, it meant giving effect to a raft of laws that the new Member States had not participated in drafting, which presented considerable challenges, not least of which included the translation of the *acquis* and establishing entirely new judicial and administrative structures to implement and enforce the new laws, and especially in the case of the environment *acquis*, required enormous capital investment.

Chapters 3 to 5 make a synopsis of the pre- and post-accession conditionality that applies to the new Member States. This highlights the enormous workload in terms of transposition of laws, their implementation and enforcement, including the considerable investment and administrative hurdles involved. Chapter 4 lays out the standard forms of transitional arrangement and other flexibility mechanisms that have been contained in accession treaties to date. All accession treaties provide the legal basis for the adjustment or adaptation of measures of the *acquis*, or for derogation therefrom. They have all also contained exceptional safeguard measures to protect a given sector of

---

[13] See *Agenda 2000*, Vol. 2, at A-11.

[14] See Chapter 3.

the economy in any one country or area as a direct result of enlargement (the economic safeguard clause).

Before moving on to researching the application of the pre-accession strategy and the Accession Treaty transitional arrangements in the context of the agri-food and environment *acquis* in the second half of this volume, Chapter 5 briefly discusses the entirely new 'flexibility' means introduced into the Accession Treaties of the fifth and sixth enlargements. What has been entirely new under the fifth and sixth accession treaties is that on the date of their accession, the twelve new Member States did not fully participate in certain core areas of Union activities, namely the Schengen *acquis*, the CAP *acquis* and the Eurozone. There is also the nebulous solution to integrating Cyprus into the EU, which remained a divided island on the date of its accession in 2004. For the fifth enlargement, the Union had also to push ahead with the reforms in other areas, notably in the Common Agricultural Policy (CAP), before the new Member States joined. For the fifteen 'old' Member States, in order to proceed with the 2004 enlargement, new means had to be found to enable the newcomers to accede to the Union without participating in all areas of Community activity immediately on the date of their accession. Significantly, the full participation of the new Member States in the CAP will only be completed in 2013 when they will access CAP funding programmes, which are in any case diminishing due to the CAP reforms.

The fifth and sixth Accession Treaties also provide for exceptional safeguard measures, in various forms, to protect a given sector of the economy in one country as a direct result of enlargement (the economic safeguard clause) for example, or to bring a new Member State into compliance with Community law concerning the Internal Market or the Justice and Home Affairs *acquis*. The two safeguard clauses relating to the Internal Market and the JHA *acquis* are entirely new to enlargement practice and are considered 'trust mechanisms' because they were necessary in order to convince the Member States that their new partners would continue to meet their obligations under the Treaties after they had acceded. These trust mechanisms were necessary before the Member States would agree to the fifth and sixth enlargements. The safeguard clauses of the accession treaties have not been reverted to and will likely expire unused with only one example of their use: the Commission Regulation concerning air safety in the case of Bulgaria.[15] The Chapter on the agri-food *acquis* in particular, suggests instances where the Internal Market safeguard clause would have been justified, such as where a new Member State has failed to transpose legislation upon the date of the accession. Such situations would not have been entertained in accession negotiations and are blatant breaches of the new Member State's pre-accession commitments.

Chapter 5, at section 3, also explores the new means that have be devised to deal with manifest failings in the preparation of both Bulgaria and Romania to meet the commitments during the negotiations, in order to enable their accession. The introduction of the new Verification and Co-operation Mechanism was specifically designed by the Commission and approved by the Member States in Council of course, in order to enable the 2007 enlargement to proceed despite serious reservations as to their actual state of preparedness in the Justice and Home Affairs *acquis* and concerning corruption in these countries.

Exceptionally in the case of the sixth Accession Treaty with Bulgaria and Romania, a special clause was included to postpone enlargement by one year should either country prove manifestly unprepared to accede to the Union. There are significant differences in the wording of the clause as concerns Romania and Bulgaria. In spite of the very critical remarks of the European Commission in its evaluation of the preparedness of these countries on the eve of their accessions, in September 2006, this clause was not used. Use of the postponement clause would arguably have been preferable to the Internal Market or the JHA safeguard measures, principally because it would not have undermined the solidarity between Member States and it would have given Bulgaria and Romania a little more time – with the carrot of accession driving it on – to reach the same footing as its partner Member States so that it did not enter at a disadvantage. However, as becomes clear in Chapter 5, three years on, serious problems persist in both of these new Member States in precisely the same problem areas, which makes the one-year postponement clause seem toothless also.

Instead of opting for postponement, a more 'co-operative' approach has been taken: a Co-operation and Verification Mechanism has been

---

[15] See Chapter 5 at 2 and 3.

devised in order to help these two countries bring themselves into line with measures in the agri-food and the JHA *acquis*. It transpires from the Commission's reports to the European Parliament on the progress made under this mechanism in June 2007,[16] that both of these countries needed more time. Certain safeguards have been introduced under core EU food safety provisions for Romania, not under the Internal Market safeguard clause of the 2005 Accession Treaty.

## Part 2: Case studies on EC environment and agri-food law

The second half of this book concentrates on the implications of the pre-accession strategy and the transitional arrangements provided for in the fifth and sixth Accession Treaties for a number of reasons.

### *Why choose these two chapters of the* acquis communautaire *for research?*

Apart from the author having a personal expertise in these areas, the longest and most numerous temporary derogations are in the existing environment *acquis* compared to those on the freedom of movement of workers, persons, services, capital, company law, transport and a few other chapters of the *acquis*. While the *Agenda 2000* document insisted on the indivisibility of the *acquis* and expressly intended that the pre-accession preparations would keep transitional arrangements generally to a minimum, it was recognised that numerous transitional arrangements in the environment *acquis* would be inevitable, even if kept to a minimum.

In the case of the environment *acquis*, the main reason for this is the problem of attracting the external investment necessary to bring infrastructure into compliance with the *acquis*. A particular challenge for new and aspiring Member States is not only building up the necessary administrative and judicial capacity to apply the environment *acquis*, but also finding the necessary financing in order to build the infrastructure for waste and water plants for example, or adapting

[16] See Report from the *Commission on Bulgaria's progress on accompanying measures following accession*, COM(2007) 377, and also *Report from the Commission on Bulgaria's progress on accompanying measures following accession*, COM(2007) 377, both 27 June 2007.

existing energy installations. The massive investment required, which could not be met by Community pre-accession funding alone, explains the lengthy transitional arrangements referred to earlier. Following the *Agenda 2000*, rough estimates for the CEECs' compliance with the environment *acquis* was anywhere between EUR 120 billion and Community financing could not meet more than 10 percent of this.[17] In the post-accession phase the new Member States must press on with plans for fully complying with the environment *acquis*, and their success in meeting their commitments to the timeframes of the transitional arrangements is therefore dependent on their success in securing the financial resources.

By comparison at this time, the radical overhaul of the agri-food *acquis* meant that this chapter of the *acquis* was not settled at that time, although the Commission's concern with food safety was apparent from the outset, and throughout pre-accession the Commission insisted on full approximation with the agri-food *acquis*. In the end the number of transitional arrangements in the agri-food chapter, which are more limited in time and number compared to those in the environment chapter, relate only to structural requirements relating to food processing establishments for example, and which in no way must threaten food safety.

Allowing temporary derogations from a particular piece of legislation to give the new Member States time to adjust or to enable the existing Member States to adjust to the enlargement, is nothing new to enlargement practice. However, because the transitional arrangements allow so many new Member States different temporary derogations from different EU directives and regulations, the fifth and sixth Accession Treaties have introduced a new complexity to the *acquis*. In the cases of the agri-food and environment *acquis*, this complexity is compounded by other factors, such as important evolutions in both of these chapters of the *acquis* since previous enlargements and the governance challenge of actually enforcing the *acquis* coherently in so many different countries. Additionally, the transitional arrangements

[17] As will be seen however, the environmental benefits in terms of human health alone have been estimated to have a cumulative value of between EUR 134 and 681 billion by the year 2020, see further; Commission External Service Contract 'The benefits of compliance with the environment *acquis* for the candidate countries and their preparations for accession', Ecotec Research and Consulting Limited, 2000. The 2003 Kok Report, at p. 57, quotes the Commission and the EBRD estimates of anything between EUR 80 and 110 billion.

in the fifth and sixth Accession Treaties are being updated during the first three years after the fifth/sixth enlargements, especially in the case of the agri-food *acquis*. Further adding to the complexity, a whole range of food products originating in the new Member States were restricted from the Internal Market and may be sold only on the national markets and under special marketing provisions.

Another distinguishing factor of the agri-food chapter compared to any other chapter of the *acquis* subject to transitional arrangements, is that different clauses in the Accession Treaties allow for the adaptation and adjustment of certain of veterinary and phytosanitary measures (Art. 42, 2003 and 2005 Acts of Accession). Exceptionally in the case of the 2005 Accession Treaty, this clause also provides for adoption of additional derogations in the food safety legislation. Further derogations from other measures of the agri-food *acquis* would have to be introduced according to the general legislative procedure set out in the accession treaty for doing so (Art. 55, 2003 and 2005 Acts of Accession).

It is also interesting to research the pre-accession strategy and transitional arrangements in these two chapters of the *acquis* because food and the environment are intimately linked: both of these chapters fall under the Treaty on the Functioning of the Union, have an Internal Market dimension and concern the trade in goods. By their nature, these chapters of the *acquis* are very different. Member States decide the policy, regulations and directives at the level of the European Community in different ways. While the environment *acquis* includes a raft of product-related laws that have been adopted under the legal basis for the adoption of Internal Market legislation, the environment *acquis* at the same time straddles other legal bases including, of course, that for the protection of the environment. By contrast the legal bases for the agri-food *acquis* are predominantly trade and product-related, falling under the legal bases for the Internal Market and external trade policy as well as the Common Agricultural Policy, and of course have a strong consumer and human health dimension.

The agri-food and environment chapters of the *acquis communautaire* are no exception to the requirement that the new Member States must fully transpose, implement and enforce these laws upon their accession. While the Union's agri-food and environment *acquis* has undergone far reaching policy and regulatory change and development in recent years, the unprecedented recent enlargement of the European Union has accentuated the challenges facing the future evolution of the agri-food and environment *acquis*. The remarkable progress in policy co-ordination and regulatory integration that the Member States have undertaken since the fourth enlargement can be seen in both the environment and the agri-food chapters of the *acquis*. The Union's fifth and sixth enlargements brought in twelve new Member States at a time when the agri-food and environment *acquis* has been changing rapidly, requiring considerable efforts by the receiving Member States as much as the newcomers. Apart from the general questions of reforming the institutions and decision making procedures, the radical and comprehensive overhaul of the agri-food *acquis* in the aftermath of the BSE crisis of the mid-nineties introduced a whole new dimension of consumer protection and scientific risk assessment to EC agri-food law. By comparison, the heaviest and most expensive laws of the environment *acquis*, such as Directive 96/61 on Integrated Pollution Prevention and Control (IPPC),[18] were adopted with the full participation of the countries that joined in the first four enlargement waves.

Under the pre-accession strategy that was reinforced by the *Agenda 2000* approach, the challenge of enlargement in both of these fields of the *acquis communautaire* has been tackled according to an overall template, or rationale and structure, during pre-accession and in the first years after accession, referred to as the pre-accession strategy. The strategy that was progressively worked out for the incoming countries of the fifth and sixth enlargements and which will also be the operational template for the preparations for the future enlargements, is the starting point. However, each chapter has its own particular challenges both in the pre-accession phase and the post-accession phase. While the strategic approach to preparing accession is essentially the same for both the EU agri-food and the environment *acquis*, there are important differences between the two.

## The implications of pre-accession and accession treaty practice for the environment and agri-food *acquis*

In order to explore the implications of enlargement for these two chapters of the *acquis*. It is useful to introduce Chapters 6 and 7 briefly.

[18] See Council Directive 96/61 concerning integrated pollution prevention and control (IPPC), *OJ* 1996 L 257/26 ('IPPC Directive').

In the case of the fifth and sixth enlargements in the context of the agri-food and environment *acquis*, it would seem that to a certain extent the political will to go ahead with the 'big-bang' enlargement has prioritised the inclusive nature of the project over: the concern of the Union to differentiate between the new Member States in terms of their progress towards membership, and; the actual readiness of the new Member States to meet the legal conditions set out under the pre-accession strategy, and; perhaps most significantly, over the readiness of the Union itself to take in so many new countries.

### *The environment* acquis: *pre-accession and practice under the 2003 and 2005 Accession Treaties*

The inevitably lengthy lead times for full compliance with the environment *acquis*, with far longer gestation periods for compliance compared to the agri-food *acquis*, give rise to many uncertainties for the future functioning and evolution of this important chapter of the *acquis communautaire*. This general introduction to the post-accession framework for the new Member States highlights the legal complexity of the transitional regime that applies to the environment *acquis* since the fifth and sixth enlargements. In some cases these transitional arrangements extend to many years, such as in the case of Directive 88/609 on Large Combustion Plants[19] where Poland[20] has until 2017 to bring existing installations into compliance with the full breadth of the Directive's provisions, while Bulgaria and Romania have deadlines for compliance with the same Directive between 2009 and 2014.[21]

As to the future evolution of the environment *acquis* in an enlarging Union, section 3 of Chapter 6 first explores the feasibility of the new Member States pre-accession commitments in respect of the environment *acquis*. A certain lack of preparedness of certain among the new Member States in both the agri-food and environment chapters of the *acquis* is revealed, which in itself suggests the precedence afforded the political commitment to enlargement over the legal and strategic preparations.

---

[19] See Council Directive 88/609 on the limitation of emissions of certain pollutants into the air from large combustion plants, *OJ* 1988 L 336/1 ('Large Combustion Plant Directive).

[20] See the Fifth Accession Treaty, Annex XII (Poland), 13.A-E, pp. 911–901.

[21] See the Sixth Accession Treaty, Annexes VI (Bulgaria) and VII (Romania), pp. 292–301 and 330–631 respectively.

It is also too early, five years since the 2004 enlargement and two years since the 2007 one, to predict whether the new Member States will be able to keep to their timetables for fully complying with the environment *acquis* under their transitional arrangements. Since the 2004 enlargement, the Commission has published annual reports on the transposition, implementation and compliance with the *acquis* from 2004 to 2007, although many transitional arrangements in the environment *acquis* especially will last for a longer time frame. An analysis of these initial reports is also embarked on in the Chapter 6 case study in the environment *acquis* and reveals that 'informal transitional arrangements' have arisen in core areas of the environment *acquis* where the Union has expressly ruled out any formal transitional arrangements: transposition of framework legislation for example, was not even to be considered for transitional derogations but the Commission's reporting in the aftermath of the 2004 enlargement tells a different story. Also, it transpires that various of the new Member States were not ready to apply the agri-food *acquis* on the day that they acceded to the EU. Various instances of legal uncertainty in the agri-food and environment *acquis* have arisen as a direct result of weaknesses in the pre-accession strategy or the lack of rigour in its application. The Commission's *2008 Report on the Application of Community Law*[22] covers the year preceding - 2007, when Bulgaria and Romania had acceded - and so as yet there is little information on these countries' compliance.

In the context of the environment *acquis*, certain instances arise where no transitional arrangements are contained in the accession treaty but amendments to the relevant regulation or directive have been agreed among the Member States in order to delay the application of these laws to the new Member States. These are not transitional arrangements such as those contained in an accession treaty for example. However, the end result is that new Member States are treated differently from the 'old' Member States in the substantive provisions of a given piece of legislation. In the context of the third enlargement to take in Austria, Finland and Sweden, certain interesting situations arise where they were able to maintain higher standards than the EC average. Chapter 6 also shows how the new Member States of the fourth enlargement were only allowed to keep their higher 'green'

[22] COM (2007) 398, 17 July 2008.

standards by political will rather than by a specific legal safeguard to this effect in their Accession Treaty – these case studies concern cadmium in fertilisers, dangerous preparations and pesticides, lead in petrol, sulphur in liquid fuels and benzene in petrol. The different treatment of new and old Member States can also be explained by the political sensitivity or differences between Member States concerning certain topics, such as in the case of taxation of energy products[23] or also in the case of the nuclear *acquis* for example, which do not strictly speaking form part of the environment *acquis*, but which have a decidedly 'green' dimension.

Importantly also, the pre-accession strategy conditionality has included a raft of conditions concerning nuclear installations in the CEECs. This is an area where pre-accession conditionality (see Chapter 6 at 1.2.3) and post-accession conditionality (see Chapter 6 at 2.1.3) has been imposed in the absence of Community standards. This is not an area of the environment *acquis* strictly speaking, although there have been recent legislative developments, such as the common binding framework on nuclear safety adopted by the Council on 25 June 2009.[24] However, there has been a marked absence of measures generally speaking at Community level, under the Euratom or the Community Treaties, due to the Member States' inability to agree. The transitional arrangements on nuclear installations in the fifth and sixth Accession Treaties, were negotiated under the energy chapter of the *acquis*.[25] But the decommissioning of nuclear power plants in new Member States holds obvious implications for human health and the environment.

---

23 Council Directive 2003/96 restructuring the Community framework for the taxation of energy products and electricity, *OJ* 2003 L 238/51.

24 See Commission Press Release IP/09/1039, 25 June 2009. The adopted measure is Directive giving binding legal force at EC level to the safety fundamentals established by the International Atomic Energy Agency and the obligations resulting from the Convention on Nuclear Safety.

25 Strictly speaking there is no Energy Title in the EC Treaty but the Member States have taken various concerted actions in this field using other legal bases. The Lisbon Treaty would introduce a new Title on Energy. See K. Inglis, 'Anticipating New Union Competences in Energy' in Maastricht Journal of European and Comparative Law, 2008, Vol. 15, N° 1, pp. 125–134. See *Commission Guide to the Negotiations Chapter by Chapter*, December 2002, published on the Internet without publication reference. See also *Commission Report on the Results of the negotiations on the Accession of Bulgaria and Romania to the European Union*, February 2005, published on the Internet under the reference 5859/05.

In fact the pre-accession conditionality of the Union in relation to nuclear installations has gone beyond the actual *acquis* measures. Nuclear installations are considered in Chapter 6 in order to show how the fifth and sixth Accession Treaties have been framed in order to impose human health and environment protection conditionality on incoming Member States in the absence of measures taken by the EU Member States under the Euratom or EU Treaties.

To all intents and purposes, having acceded to the EU, the new CEEC Member States are now subject to de facto 'transitional arrangements' under the fifth and sixth Accession Treaties for dismantling nuclear reactors and meeting safety standards. This situation is made all the more complex by the fact that the future evolution of the Euratom Treaty in an enlarged Union is still not clear today. With the Treaty of Lisbon now inforce, a few articles of the Euratom Treaty have been deleted and the European Parliament points out that Protocol 2. ToL would 'make the text illegible and very complicated' and emphasises the need for a consolidated version.[26]

As for the evolution of the environment *acquis* in an enlarging Union, Chapter 6 concludes with a comment on the benefits and drawbacks of the pre-accession strategy for the continued evolution of the environment *acquis* in an enlarging Union. This concluding section looks at enlargement of the environment *acquis* in the broader context of achieving economic development that is sustainable from an environmental perspective and notes the need for continued efforts by the EU Twenty-Seven.

On the one hand, it can be said that EU enlargement holds very significant benefits for Europe's environment and that it has introduced a body of laws in the new Member States – where previously there was a general vacuum in environmental protection measures – aimed at least at curbing the negative environmental effects of the economic development that membership inevitably implies. At the same time it is also true that in some ways accession to the EU limits the Member States' ability to take action both at home and abroad, whether to improve the environment or to simply do nothing. Because the environment knows no borders, the behaviour of third countries necessarily affects

[26] See EP Report on the Lisbon Treaty, Report 2007/2286 (INI) of 29 January 2008 at points 12 and 13. The text of Protocol 2 can be found at *OJ* 2007 C 306/199.

Europe's environment. At the same time of course, national environmental policy and law is crucial to sustainable development in new and aspiring Member States.

While the appropriateness of the environment *acquis* to the needs of the new Member States was questioned by the European Environment Agency (EEAg)[27] from the outset, the wholesale approximation with the environment *acquis*, as an integral part of the *acquis communautaire*, has simply been the approach taken under the pre-accession strategy. All new Member States have had to develop their own national environment policies and laws, which will require investment in itself. Implementing the *acquis* alone cannot replace local and national environment law. On top of this, the new Member States are concentrating on a wide range of other, parallel priorities, notably the economic reforms necessary to introduce the EURO, and this will continue for many years after their accession.

Chapter 6 explores all of this as well as the governance challenge of enlarging the environment *acquis*. It is still too early to predict the 'greenness' of the voting of the new Member States in future Union environment laws and ultimately, the positive or negative effects of enlargement on the state of Europe's environment. In future, however, certain innovations in governance within the EU promise to improve compliance and enforcement of the environment *acquis*. New plans for improving the implementation of the environment *acquis* promise to improve the situation[28] of serious lacks in making the environment *acquis* effective throughout the twenty-seven Member States. Should it enter into force, the Treaty of Lisbon will add some welcome innovations, see Chapter 6 at section 3.

### *The agri-food* acquis: *pre-accession and practice under the 2003 and 2005 Accession Treaties*

Turning to the agri-food *acquis*, Chapter 7 on the agri-food *acquis* also begins by exploring the task facing the new Member States compared to the countries that acceded in the first four enlargements. *Agenda 2000* made clear there would be no compromise of the food safety *acquis* in the pre-accession strategy. The agri-food *acquis* straddles

---

[27] See *Europe's Environment; The Second Assessment*, (Copenhagen, EEAg 1998) at p. 7.

[28] See Chapter 6 at 3.2.1, and particularly COM(2008) 2852 of 18 November 2008.

various chapters of the *acquis*, including the Internal Market and the Veterinary and Phytosanitary standards under the CAP. The overhaul of the agri-food *acquis* throughout the pre-accession phase proved a considerable challenge to old and new Member States alike of course. This chapter portrays the state of the food laws in these countries prior to the pre-accession strategy, looks at the shift in their obligations under the Europe Agreements compared to their obligations as Member States, during the pre-accession strategy and then under the post-accession transitional arrangements specified in the fifth and sixth Accession Treaties. The Kok Report – see Chapter 7 at section 1.1 – highlights the considerable demands on acceding countries in raising their national food safety standards to the Community level and that the EU makes no compromise on the safety of the food chain. The particular approximation challenge for the new Member States involved the structural upgrade of food establishments and the administrative capacity building of inspection bodies and other competent authorities in order to guarantee the food chain.

Chapter 7 on the agri-food *acquis* in Part 2, in particular, presents the Union's approach to food safety in the context of the transition of the new Member States. At section 1.2.3 it transpires that the new Member States had heavier approximation work to do under the pre-accession strategy for the food safety and hygiene *acquis* than did the countries of the European Economic Area, which only provided for the provisional application of the food hygiene package on 26 April 2008.

The fifth and sixth Accession Treaties contain only minimal temporary derogations from the agri-food *acquis* and they are far shorter than those under the environment *acquis*. In the main, they relate to structural changes to food producing establishments and do not allow for food safety or hygiene standards to be compromised. Also, certain special provisions in the fifth and sixth Accession Treaties allow for new transitional arrangements to be introduced after enlargement, in given circumstances.

Various – not all – of the new Member States of the fifth enlargement acceded without having complied with a raft of agri-food laws. It had long been apparent that not all of the new Member States would be ready to accede to the agri-food *acquis* on the date of their accession. As a direct consequence, nearly fifty laws were the subject of 'informal' transitional arrangements, which are inherently illegal given that they were not formally agreed during the negotiation of the fifth Accession Treaty. The emergence of such informal transitional arrangements goes against the very purpose of the lengthy and laborious pre-accession strategy. After all, it was intended precisely to prevent such lesions in the *acquis* and strictly limit and manage any transitional periods that were in any case, absolutely minimal and necessary.

Chapter 7 at section 3 researches the reports of the European Commission's Food and Veterinary Office (FVO) in order to assess the compliance by the new Member States with their transitional arrangements. Certainly the pre-accession input of the FVO has been instrumental in keeping track of problems in the new (and old) Member States and in reacting speedily to potential threats to the safety of the food chain. The FVO was active throughout the pre-accession strategy but increasingly so in the last year leading up to the 2004 enlargement. Its inspection role is key to anticipating problems and reacting speedily to them so as to curb threats to the safety of the food chain.

Also on the topic of the agri-food *acquis* it is clear that full compliance is as much a challenge for the 'old' and 'new' Member States alike. The agri-food reform has gradually been entering into force since the end of 2002, although the general requirements relating to food and feed as well as responsibilities of food and feed operators only came into force on 1 January 2005, after the fifth enlargement and before the sixth. Even before the agri-food reform, the fifteen Member States were being sued by the European Commission for failure in the same areas of the agri-food *acquis* where the new Member States were striving for compliance, such as in the area of the Border Inspection Posts.

This section also explores whether the typical safeguard mechanisms under the Treaties and specific agri-food laws are adequate in order to guarantee the integrity of the food chain. It advocates that the Internal Market safeguard clause should indeed have been used, despite the fact that it risks discriminating against 'new' Member States. This would be consistent with maintaining the integrity of the food chain as well as to shame any other recalcitrant Member State into compliance. They would be especially appropriate where such informal transitional arrangements give unfair advantages to the new Member States' businesses and nationals.

The research for this book was completed in June 2009. A few updates have been made to refer to the Treaty of Lisbon (ToL) and new applications for membership. The revised Treaties are referred to as follows: the Treaty on European Union by the abbreviation TEU and the Treaty on the Functioning of the European Union, previously the EC Treaty, by the abbreviation TFEU.[29]

---

[29] For consolidated versions, see respectivley *OJ* 2008 C115 and 306.

PART ONE

# EVOLVING PRACTICE IN EUROPEAN UNION ENLARGEMENT

CHAPTER ONE

# ELIGIBLE CANDIDATES AND PROCEDURAL STEPS TO ACCESSION

## 1. An introduction to understanding European Union enlargement

Enlargement as a means of uniting the peoples of Europe, must be seen as a core goal of the Union from even before the signature of the founding Treaties in order to further peace on the European continent but, importantly, without diluting progress already made before enlarging. The preamble to the European Coal and Steel Community Treaty, which was signed in Paris on 18 April 1951, had little to say about coal and steel but, rather, spoke of safeguarding peace, establishing an economic community and substituting for age-old rivalries and bloody conflicts the merging of essential interests.[1] The premise of the later European Economic Community Treaty was that of an ever closer union of the peoples of Europe.

### 1.1 *An open Community*

Since the inception by the original six Member States of the first Communities – the foundations of today's European Union – six Accession Treaties and accompanying Acts of Accession have been signed to bring a total of nineteen new Member States into the Union[2] bringing the total number of Member States to twenty-seven today. For most

[1] See W. Nicoll and A. Salmon, *Understanding the European Communities* (Worcester, Philip Allan 1990) at p. 7.

[2] The first Accession Treaty was signed with Denmark, Ireland and the United Kingdom on 22 January 1972 and entered into force on 1 January 1973, *OJ* 1972 L 73/1. The second Accession Treaty was signed with Greece on 28 May 1979 and entered into force on 1 January 1981, *OJ* 1979 L 291/1. The third Accession Treaty was signed with Spain and Portugal on 12 June 1985 and entered into force on 1 January 1986, *OJ* 1985 L 302/1. The fourth Accession Treaty was signed with Austria, Finland and Sweden on 24 June 1994 and entered into force on 1 January 1995, *OJ* 1994 C 241/1. The fifth Accession Treaty was signed with the Czech Republic, Estonia, Latvia, Lithuania, Hungary, Cyprus, Malta, Poland, Slovenia and Slovakia on 16 April 2003, *OJ* 2003 L 236/1, as amended. It took effect on 1 May 2004. The sixth Accession

of the nearly fifty years of the existence of the EEC – the EC – the European Union, the Union has been preparing to widen. Considering that new members continue to adjust to membership in the first years after they accede – through 'transitional arrangements' and other flexibility mechanisms – the Union has been almost continuously 'in pre-accession' since the first enlargement to take in the UK, Denmark and Ireland in 1973.

At the time of the first of the Communities, the European Coal and Steel Community, the aim of reuniting Germany and bringing it into the fold was apparent. The Convention on Relations between the Three Powers and the FRG of 26 May 1952 (the Bonn Agreement), signed by France, the United States of America, the United Kingdom and the Federal Republic of Germany expressed the Parties' aim of a reunified Germany integrated within the European Community and in the negotiation of the original Treaties (although in the end the Bonn Agreement fell, unratified).[3] The German delegation together with the other delegations specifically declared it possible to amend the Treaties should Germany reunify. Moreover, in legal terms the reunification of Germany and the subsequent extension of the Union's borders has not been treated as 'enlargement' of the Union as such.[4]

Treaty was signed with Bulgaria and Romania on 25 April 2005, *OJ* 2005 L 157/1, as amended and took effect on 1 January 2007.

[3] The last recital to the preamble reads; 'WHEREAS the Three Powers and the Federal Republic recognise that both the new relationship to be established between them by the present Convention and its related Conventions and the Treaties for the creation of an integrated European community, in particular the Treaty on the Establishment of the European Community for Coal and Steel and the Treaty on the Establishment of the European Defence Community, are essential steps to the achievement of their common aim for a unified Germany integrated within the European Community'. The Bonn Agreement never entered into force because the French National Assembly refused to ratify them in August 1954. They were replaced by the Paris Agreements of 23 October 1954, which did not mention this same aim. See J. Charpentier, 'L'est déjà plus? Le cas de l'Allemagne' in Slobodan Milacic, ed., *L'intégration européenne et la révolution de l'europe de l'est* (Luxembourg, Institut Universitaire International Luxembourg 1991) p. 62, at p. 67. See also J.-P. Jacqué, 'German unification and the European Community', 94 *Revue générale du droit international public* (1990) pp. 997–1018.

[4] Although nothing in the treaties allowed the inference that it could apply *ipso facto* to the whole of united Germany without amendment. The extension of the territorial area of application of Community law was in the end achieved without Treaty revision and raised problems for the application of Community law to the territory of the ex-GDR with existing instruments. See Jacqué, ibid.

Certainly, the United Kingdom remained outside the ranks of the founding Member States for its own reasons,[5] most notably being its resistance to the federalist momentum of the founding Six and not forgetting its concerns to maintain its US and Commonwealth ties and preferences even.[6] Once the UK had made its application for membership on 10 August 1961, however, actual negotiations began only two months later – an indication of just how receptive the Six were to such an enlargement,[7] despite the British refusal to participate from the outset in the Communities.

Indeed, enlargement of the common market was already under consideration by the founding Member States not even three years after the entry into force of the EEC Treaty on 1 January 1958. Already in 1959 the Intergovernmental Conference was preoccupied with the trade problems arising inter alia from relations with the EFTA trading block and the means of UK participation in any political union.[8] The European Commission's *Communiqué* of 1 August 1961[9] stated that it 'regards [the UK application] as a fresh recognition of the economic and political value of the work of European integration undertaken since 1950'. In the same *Communiqué* the Commission 'resolved to bring its full support to a positive solution of these problems [anticipated to arise during the negotiations] in order to contribute to the

[5] See in G. Wilkes, ed., *Britain's Failure to enter the European Community 1961–1963: The enlargement negotiations and crises in European, Atlantic and Commonwealth relations* (London-Portland Oregon, Frank Cass 1997). In that volume, see in particular R. Griffiths 'A slow one hundred and eighty degree turn: British policy towards the Common Market, 1955–60' pp. 35–50.

[6] This was also the concern of the US and the Commonwealth countries, see for example the National Security Action Memorandum N° 76 of 20 August 1961 on the subject of UK membership in the Common Market sent by J.F. Kennedy, the President of the US, to the then Under Secretary of State, George Ball. The President requested a 'realistic detailed study' on the subject because he 'had been informed that the effect will be extremely serious' for the US despite the fact that the US had been 'encouraging the Common Market for political reasons', see McGeorge Bundy, John F. Kennedy Library (NLK), Boston, MA, Columbia Point, Boston, MA 02125. NLK. NSF. MM. NSAM. 10DDDK, ARC Id. 193 472. Moreover, 'virulent' attacks were reported against UK accession by the Commonwealth Prime Ministers; see the Letter from A. Wapler to M. Couve de Murville, London, 12 September 1962, Eleventh Conference of Commonwealth Prime Ministers 10–12 September 1962, to examine the UK accession to the Common Market, *Political Yearbook, 1962,* pp. 537–539.

[7] These first negotiations failed in 1963, see Wilkes, op. cit. n. 5.

[8] See European Commission, *The First Stage of the Common Market: Report on the execution of the Treaty, January 1958 to January 1962* (Brussels, EEC Commission 1963) pp. 94–98.

[9] See *Bull EC* 9/1961 at pp. 9–10.

realisation of the new step in the economic and political unification of Europe, and thereby to tighten the bonds which link the free world on both sides of the Atlantic'.

Moreover, when the Council referred the UK application, together with those of Denmark and Ireland, to the Commission according to the relevant Treaty procedure, the Commission replied that 'it would render its Opinion only as the negotiations proceeded and in the light of their outcome' and expressed 'satisfaction' at the UK readiness to accept the objectives set out in Articles 2 and 3 of the EEC Treaty together with the institutional provisions, the Common Customs Tariff and the European Coal and Steel Community Treaty as well as the European Atomic Energy Community Treaty. The Commission also emphasised that the negotiations with Ireland and Denmark were dependent on the outcome of the negotiations with the UK.[10]

While attempts at bringing in the United Kingdom failed in the Sixties, this was for particular reasons that by no means detracted from the goal of enlargement. General de Gaulle's veto of the UK accession aspirations in the January of 1963[11] was not shared by the other Member States[12] at the time, nor by the negotiators.[13] Paul-Henri Spaak even referred to the exclusion of Great Britain from Europe 'without valid reasons' as 'doing grave violence to [...] our solemn promises'

[10] See European Commission, *The First Stage of the Common Market,* op. cit. n. 8 at para. 79.

[11] See 'Press Conference by President de Gaulle, Paris, 14 January 1963' in *Western European Union Assembly-General Affairs Committee: A Retrospective view of the political year in Europe, 1963,* March 1964, WEU Secretariat General at pp. 20–22.

[12] See 'Speech by Gerhard Schröder, minister for Foreign Affairs of the Federal Republic of Germany, Brussels, 29 January 1963' in *Western European Union Assembly-General Affairs Committee: a retrospective view of the political year in Europe 1963,* March 1964, ibid. at pp. 34–35. Mr. Schröder highlighted the 'deep disappointment' of all EEC Member States, see *Bulletin de documentation,* 31 January 1963 at p. 6. The ministers regretted the block to proceeding with UK enlargement and as a result the enlargements to take in Ireland and Denmark. Gerhard Schröder emphasised the intention to enlarge; 'Allow me to take up again an idea expressed earlier on, namely, that the Rome Treaty, in Article 237 and in the preface, issues a general and open invitation to European countries to join the Six. And allow me to point out also that it was only possible to get the Bundestag to adopt the Treaty instituting the European Economic Community a few years ago by promising (and the Government which made this promise has remained almost unchanged) to try to widen the circle of members.'

[13] The President-in-Office of the Ministerial Conference, Henri Fayat, announcing that the negotiations could no longer be continued, did so with 'very much regret'. See 'Concluding Statement by Henri Fayat, 29 January 1963', *Western European Union Assembly-General Affairs Committee, 1963,* ibid. at p. 40.

and emphasising this to be against the nature of the open Community written into the text of the Treaty.[14]

De Gaulle exercised the veto over UK accession a second time in 1967 but when Georges Pompidou replaced him at the head of the French Republic, the Six were able to push on with the enlargement project. The summit of 1 and 2 December 1969 in The Hague, commonly known for the launch of the European Political Co-operation, set out a triptych for action:[15] completion (to lay down a definitive financial arrangement for the Common Agricultural Policy (CAP)); deepening (or consolidation), and; widening (or enlargement). Significantly, the 'Europeanisation' of Greece and Spain and Portugal consolidated and reinforced democracy in these countries. Since the accession of Greece the European Commission has expressly stated in all of its Opinions on the readiness of the applicant to join the Union, that the enlargement in question 'will help to preserve and strengthen peace and liberty in Europe'.

Enlargements have always been inspired by the will of the Member States to end the division of the European continent[16] and to continue the process of creating an ever closer union among the peoples of Europe.[17] The failed Constitutional Treaty expressly mentioned the notion of the openness of the European Union, although the Treaty of Lisbon omits such terminology in the legal basis for enlargement.[18] The will to do so[19] is reiterated in the preamble to the fifth Accession Treaty. The Treaty establishing a Constitution for Europe[20] (hereafter 'the Constitutional Treaty') reflected this same inspiration but spoke

[14] See 'Speech by Paul-Henri Spaak, minister for Foreign Affairs of Belgium (Brussels, 29 January 1963)' in *Western European Union Assembly-General Affairs Committee, 1963*, op. cit. n. 12 at pp. 32–33.

[15] See *Bull. EC* 2/70.

[16] Second Recital to the Treaty on European Union, consolidated version, taking into account the amendments introduced by the Treaty of Nice and in force as of 1 February 2003.

[17] See the Twelfth Recital to the Treaty on European Union prior to the Treaty of Lisbon.

[18] Art. I-58 of the Treaty establishing a Constitution for Europe stated that 'The Union shall be open to all European States which [...].' The equivalent provision currently is Art. 49 TEU.

[19] See also the Joint Declaration 'One Europe' on 'the continuous, inclusive and irreversible nature of the enlargement process', annexed to the final act of the fifth Accession Treaty at p. 971, agreed between the European Union and the acceding States agreed, at the December 2002 Copenhagen European Council, at Conclusions 21 of the Presidency Conclusions, *Bull. EU* 12-2002.

[20] See *OJ* 2004 C 310/1.

of an already 'reunited Europe', of the peoples of Europe 'determined to transcend their ancient divisions and, united ever more closely, to forge a common destiny', a Europe 'united in its diversity', 'the great venture which makes of it a special area of human hope'.

This is not to say that enlargement of the Union is now complete. It is, rather, a recognition of the progress made so far. The same rationale as has always applied is still the starting point for the strategy for enlargement that continues today. The introduction to the European Commission's *2004 Strategy Paper on Progress in the Enlargement Process* begins:

> The enlargement of the EU to ten new Member States on 1 May 2004 has further strengthened the unity of the European continent. The historical and political arguments in favour of this enlargement are compelling: it enhances peace, prosperity, stability and security and has also produced substantial economic benefits.

In the fifth Accession Treaty the twenty-five Member States underscored the 'continuous, inclusive and irreversible enlargement process' in their Joint Declaration *One Europe*,[21] declaring the accessions of Bulgaria and Romania in 2007 an 'objective' and 'welcoming' the next stage in Turkey's candidature.[22] Since then, the matter of Union's 'absorption capacity' – see Chapter Two at 1.3 – has come to the fore and the debate surrounding it has left some question marks as to the feasibility of future enlargements. Moreover, the Treaty of Lisbon does away with the reference to the 'openness' of the Union.

Bulgaria and Romania then acceded on 1 January 2007. Other official candidates include Turkey and Croatia with which accession negotiations have been launched following the European Council's decision to do so on 3 October 2005 – see Table 1. Also waiting in the wings are other countries of the Western Balkans. While accession negotiations have not begun with Macedonia, it is an official candidate and are all recognised as 'potential candidates' but have still to attain formal candidate status. Serbia, Kosovo, as defined by United Nations Security Council Resolution 1244, Montenegro, Bosnia and Herzegovina, Albania are all potential candidates. There is even talk of enlargement to

[21] See Declarations adopted by the Plenipotentiaries, annexed to the Final Act of the Accession Treaty, op. cit. Introduction, n. 2.

[22] This was confirming the decisions taken by the Informal European Council in Athens on the same day as the signature of the fifth Accession Treaty on 16 April 2003.

take in Ukraine and Moldova. In response to the Ukrainian crisis over the disputed elections of 21 November 2004, Commissioner Ferrero-Waldner made it clear at one and the same time that 'the question of Ukrainian entry into the EU is not on the agenda' but also that 'it is clear that we are not closing any doors'.[23]

### 1.2 *Evolution in pre-accession practices*

There are many political, economic and legal requirements, procedures and practices that have been common to all preparations in advance of the enlargements.[24] Measures have also been taken after the date of accession itself in respect of each enlargement in the form of legal provisions as well as financial instruments, to smooth the transition from applicant or candidate status to full Member State status, in the interests of the incoming as much as of the receiving Member States.

As concerned the first four enlargements, the organisation and execution of preparations for accession were predominantly made at the prerogative of the acceding country itself. However, in the case of the fifth enlargement, the Member States and the Commission and European Parliament have been instrumental and directly implicated in the preparations made by each of the twelve new members and this

---

[23] www.euractiv.com/Article?_lang=EwN&tcmuri=tcm:29-133155-16&type=News Site visited on 7 December 2004.

[24] General literature of relevance include: M. Maresceau, 'Pre-accession' in M. Cremona, ed., *The Enlargement of the European Union* (New York, Oxford University Press, 2003) pp. 9–40, F. Hoffmeister 'Earlier enlargements' and 'Changing requirements for membership', K. Inglis on 'Pre-accession and the accession partnerships' and L. Maurer 'Progress of the negotiations' all contained in A. Ott and K. Inglis, eds., *Handbook on European Enlargement. A commentary on the Enlargement process* (The Hague, TMC Asser Press 2002) pp. 87–129, M. Maresceau, 'The EU Pre-accession Strategies: a Political and Legal Analysis' in M. Maresceau and E. Lannon, eds., *The EU's Enlargement and Mediterranean Strategies: a comparative analysis* (Basingstoke, Palgrave 2001), M. Maresceau, 'On Association, Partnership, Pre-accession and Accession' in M. Maresceau. ed., *Enlarging the European Union: relations between the EU and Central and Eastern Europe* (London and New York, Longman 1997), pp. 3–22. P.-C. Müller-Graff, ed., *East Central Europe and the European union: from Europe Agreements to a Member Status* (Baden-Baden, Nomos Verlagsgesellschaft 1997), C. Preston, *Enlargement and Integration in the European Union* (London and New York, Routledge 1997), J.-C. Gautron, ed. *Les relations communauté européenne europe de l'est* (Paris, Economica 1991), See W. Nicoll and A. Salmon, *Understanding the European Communities*, (Worcester, Philip Allan 1990), J.-P. Puissochet, *L'élargissement des Communautés européennes* (Paris, Editions techniques et économiques 1974).

can also be said of the preparations for future enlargements. From the first enlargement, the Union has taken an inclusive-yet-differentiating approach towards countries on track for accession in terms of the conditions that must be met prior to accession as well as in the first years after accession. Nevertheless, an increasingly refined pre-accession conditionality has emerged with the fifth and future enlargements. Enlargement is now an instrument of the Union's foreign policy in its relations with neighbouring countries.[25]

The original founding Member States, at the time of the very first enlargement negotiations, had established that the point of departure for negotiating the terms and conditions to be contained in an accession treaty with an applicant country was that the founding Treaties themselves would not be substantively amended or revised, and membership of all three Communities would be sought after conclusion of the EEC membership negotiations.[26] In particular, at that time the six founding Member States and the Commission insisted on preserving the 'Community's integrity at all costs' and that 'the Community could never agree to schemes that might, by means of protocols or otherwise, introduce exceptions to the Treaty's rules which would be permanent or on so large a scale as to make the application of these rules an exception in itself'.[27] Thus it has never been the case that Accession Treaties give incoming Member State permanent derogations from the *acquis* in any fields of its activities.[28]

The fact that Member States or contingents of the Fifteen had opted-out of sections of the *acquis* has not been accepted as an excuse for non-participation of an applicant in those same sections. Quite the contrary, and as will become clear later, the possibility of opt-outs has

---

[25] See M. Cremona, 'Enlargement: a Successful Instrument of Foreign Policy?' in Trimidas and Nebbit, eds., *European Law for the Twenty-First Century Vol. II* (Hart Publishing 2004) pp. 397–413.

[26] See European Commission, *The First Stage of the Common Market,* op. cit., n. 8 at paras. 80 and 81. See also D. Booss and J. Forman, 'Enlargement', 32 *CML Rev.* (1995) at p. 95, n. 19. Booss and Forman do, however, point out that in fact permanent derogations were introduced.

[27] See European Commission, *The First Stage of the Common Market,* op. cit. n. 8 at para. 81.

[28] While Sweden is not participating in the Euro, it is country effectively with a derogation. It did arise in the case of two incoming countries of the first enlargement wave, namely Denmark and the United Kingdom, that permanent opt-outs or opt-ins (derogations) were later negotiated from EMU. Denmark and Austria and now also Malta secured specific permanent derogations concerning the purchase of second residences.

been categorically refused to the twelve new Member States of the fifth and sixth enlargement waves.

That is not to say, however, that under the founding Treaties, the Union advances as one block in all policy fields of the present and future *acquis*. Far from it. Once a country has become a member of the Union, it may act in its capacity as a Member State to contribute to shaping the evolution of the *acquis communautaire*. Alternative means of closer integration and co-operation in entirely new spheres for EU activity had already been sought by the Union of Twelve for the introduction of the Euro. The insertion into the Treaties of different mechanisms for flexible co-operation between a majority of Member States is an indication of potential future developments of a Union proceeding on different planes of activity, in layers of 'concentric circles'[29] so to speak.

For accession treaties however, incoming countries are obliged to accede to the entire *acquis* as it stands at the time of that enlargement. In the 2003 Accession Treaty, Article 53 expressly deems the new Member States to have been notified of and subject to EU directives and decisions, while Article 54 of the Act of Accession expressly obliges the new Member States to comply with those measures, excepting only where the limited derogations are provided for in the country annexes (transitional arrangements) to the Accession Treaty. The equivalent provisions in the 2005 Accession Treaty are contained in Articles 52 and 53, see Chapter 4.3 of this volume.

In every enlargement, the accession negotiations have centred on the adjustment to be undertaken by the acceding country. Acts of accession set out the means to smooth their entry into the Union. In line with the premise that the *acquis communautaire* is non-negotiable, the room for amending the *acquis* has been very limited. Acts of accession have only ever provided for amendments to the founding Treaties as well as to secondary measures of the *acquis* referred to as adjustments in the form of technical adaptations. Such adjustments may, for example, alter references to the competent authorities or add the language of the incoming Member State to annexes of a directive.

[29] See Preston, *Enlargement and Integration in the European Union*, op. cit. n. 24 at pp. 230–235, discussing how the receiving Member States use the enlargement process to pursue their own interests and collectively to externalise internal problems.

Additionally, it has been the practice within accession negotiations to allow some flexibility in the timeframes for full implementation and enforcement of the *acquis* in the early years of membership. Transitional arrangements or temporary derogations have been used to enable the newly acceded country more time to bring itself into compliance with the *acquis* but only for good, substantiated reason. They are also typically used to delay, actually or potentially, the application of the *acquis* to an incoming Member State's workers or to protect against speculative purchases of agricultural land in the new Member State or to make the adjustments to the Common Market Organisations in the event of disturbances, for example. Spanish temporary derogations/transitional arrangements on fisheries were extremely long. This was not an opt-out but necessary to avoid the stalemate in the negotiations. Moreover, an economic safeguard clause has always been inserted in each Accession Treaty in order to protect certain industries or regions against the aftershocks of enlargement and available to all Member States alike.

The shock events of 1989 that presented the then European Economic Community with the possibility of truly guaranteeing peace on the European continent and thus meeting its declared ideals of the Nineteen-fifties, presented the twelve Member States with a major headache. The CEECs had come from vastly different political, economic and legal (as well as social and cultural) backgrounds to that of the Union and were as different amongst themselves as they were from the EU Member State. Austria had applied for membership in the July of 1989 and there was a strong prospect of Nordic expansion. The Member States did not immediately jump at the chance of embracing the CEECs back into the fold with the their western neighbours. This would take some three years.

However, the German Democratic Republic was able to unify with its other half on 3 October 1990 and thus also, to be included within the European Union as Germany, which had never accepted to recognise the east-west split in the first place.[30] As already noted, this was an exceptional situation and was dealt with as such.[31] Debating the

[30] *OJ* 1990 L 353/1.

[31] The division of Germany had not been set down in international law and the FRG had always considered itself representative of the entire German people, threatening to sever diplomatic relations with any country recognising the Soviet zone. See Charpentier and Jacqué, op. cit. n. 3.

rationale behind the exceptional incorporation of GDR territory into the Union upon reunification would be going off the point. It suffices to say here that a three-month period of grace, until 31 December 1990, was granted Germany to maintain in force those national provisions that were already in force in the territory of the former German Democratic Republic and which did not comply with Community acts, pending the entry into force of the transitional measures proposed on 21 August 1990 by the Commission to the Council.

This was because the Community legislature had not been able to act as fast as would have been required of it in order to have introduced interim measures before the date of unification, which preceded the adoption of transitional measures themselves. However, it was expressly mentioned within the body of the Council Regulation[32] and the implementing Directive[33] adopted under it, that this was 'the result of exceptional circumstances and may not be subsequently cited as a precedent'. The interim measures took the form of derogations from a range of *acquis* measures in various chapters of the *acquis*.[34] It is an exceptional case that could not be compared to an enlargement situation. No treaty revision was required because the new German Länder became part of the Federal Republic by economic and monetary union and then unification itself, so that the Community Treaties could apply immediately throughout the unified Germany.[35] This was not an enlargement situation.

However, the preparations for the fifth enlargement of the European Union to take in eight Central and East European countries (CEECs) together with Cyprus and Malta (initially including Bulgaria and Romania), took on a whole new dimension in legal and administrative practice in the preparations of the Member States-to-be. The challenge of incorporating the CEECs demanded a new and more considered approach in the political, economic and legal practice of preparing

---

[32] Council Regulation 2684/90 on interim measures applicable after the unification of Germany, in anticipation of the adoption of transitional measures by the Council either in co-operation with, or after consultation of, the European Parliament, *OJ* 1990 L 263/1.

[33] Council Directive 90/476 on interim measures applicable after the unification of Germany in anticipation of the adoption of transitional measures by the Council in co-operation with the European Parliament, *OJ* 1990 L 266/1.

[34] Commission Decision 90/481 of 27 September 1990 introducing interim measures relating to the unification of Germany, *OJ* 1990 L 267/37.

[35] See C. Timmermans. 'German unification and Community law', 27 *CML Rev.* (1990) at p. 437.

the fifth enlargement. The pre-accession strategy formulated to do so has been innovative and driven by the will of the Member States and acceding countries alike. Pre-accession practice evolved again further in respect of the sixth Accession Treaty, bringing in Bulgaria and Romania in 2007, although fundamentally the same tools were used as under the pre-accession strategy for the fifth enlargement, with some important differences. This continues to be the case for future accession practice and treaties, notably those for Turkey, Croatia, the Former ex-Yugoslav Republic of Macedonia and other potential candidates from the Western Balkans.

### 1.2.1 *'Pre-accession' and the Copenhagen criteria*

The word 'pre-accession' has long been used as an adjective in EC/EU circles. Key to the emergence of 'pre-accession' as a noun, formally appearing for the first time in the Conclusions of the December 1994 Essen European Council,[36] was the statement by the June 1993 Copenhagen European Council of the Copenhagen criteria,[37] supplemented by the 1994 Essen European Council condition of good neighbourliness and the December 1995 Madrid European Council requiring administrative and judicial capacity for the effective implementation of the *acquis*. This statement of the comprehensive conditions required of aspiring Member States conditions which broadly existed already – see Chapter Two – were addressed specifically to the CEECs, rather than to Malta and Cyprus. Malta was only brought on to the pre-accession train in 1999.[38] As for Cyprus, its perspective of accession was directly linked to progress in the inter-communal talks and the settlement of the Cyprus question. Malta and Cyprus fell within the inclusive-yet-differentiating approach of the pre-accession strategy that would be built upon them. These Copenhagen criteria guided political, economic and legal relations between the Union and the aspiring Member States. And it has been on the basis of the 1993 Copenhagen criteria that the

---

[36] See Maresceau 'Pre-accession' in Cremona, ed., *The Enlargement of the European Union*, op. cit. n. 24, at p. 9. See Inglis 'The Europe Agreements compared in the light of their pre-accession re-orientation' in 37 *CML Rev.* (2000) pp 1173–1210.

[37] European Council, Declaration of Copenhagen of 21/22 June 1993, *Bull. EU* 6/1993, p. 13.

[38] See Chapter 3, Table 2. While Malta applied for membership in 1990, it froze its application in 1996 due to a change in government only to 'defrost' it in 1998 following the return of the socialist government to power.

strategy and processes for preparing their entry have been progressively established through legal and financial instruments or worked out by the European Commission in administrative practice.

With the fifth enlargement of the European Union, 'pre-accession' has come to denote a state of being that is the metaphorical preparatory waiting room for countries preparing their accession to the Union. Of course, it is the receiving European Union as much as the incoming countries that are 'in pre-accession'. Thus, the Union has been in pre-accession on many occasions but consistently so since 1 February 1993 when accession negotiations were opened with Austria, Finland and Sweden or since July 1989 if the date of Austria's application is considered the starting point, see Table 1 for an indication of the time frames for the first six enlargements. The Union declared its willingness to undertake a fifth enlargement in the June of that year when, simultaneously, it adopted the famous 1993 Copenhagen criteria that were to form the basis of the pre-accession strategy as we know it today. For those CEECs that had signed association agreements in the form of Europe Agreements with the Union prior to that date, namely Poland, Hungary and Czechoslovakia,[39] their aspirations to join the Union were clear from before 1993 and their political, economic and legal reforms were autonomously directed at membership.

Pre-accession in the context of the fifth enlargement can be taken to comprise any number of elements. The relevant Europe or association agreement with an applicant, the Copenhagen criteria and subsequent legal and financial instruments, provide the yardsticks against which to measure and evaluate progress towards accession. Pre-accession denotes the continuous activity of preparing a candidate country for accession. In some cases the term pre-accession itself is not used and alternative adjectives or nouns serve to convey the meaning more precisely in a given context. The Union's institutions, for example, do not always stick to the term and phrase the same process and strategy as 'Accession Process'[40] or the 'Enlargement Strategy' or to the notion of

[39] The EA Czechoslovakia was replaced by separated Agreements with the two separate states of the Czech and Slovak Republics after Czechoslovakia's dissolution in 1993.

[40] See for example, Commission information note: 'Croatia becomes a candidate for EU Membership', to be found at www.europa.eu.int/comm/enlargement/negotiations/index.htm

the preparatory period in advance of accession as 'the pre-enlargement phase' or the 'accession preparation strategy' as it was referred to in the preambles to the Europe Agreements Baltic States and Slovenia, for example.

The strategic approach that was used for the most recent enlargements continues to serve as the template for future enlargements. Moreover, due to the number and extent of transitional arrangements, temporary derogations and institutional arrangements, it seems also that elements of the pre-accession status of the twelve new Member States will continue to apply for some years after their actual accession and that future new members also face the prospect of retaining certain elements or an impression of their pre-accession status once they have acceded.

As was the case with previous enlargements, certain situations arise whereby the new Member States continue to find themselves in the pre-accession waiting room despite their formal accession to the Union due to the use of certain 'transitional arrangements' or 'temporary measures', which were negotiated prior to their accession. Contrary to the approach taken in previous enlargements, in the case of the fifth enlargement the approach has been to not fully include the new Member States temporarily in certain (key) realms of Union activity (Schengen and Economic and Monetary union (EMU)) while at the same time to oblige them to participate in those realms at some unspecified date in the future, which will depend on a variety of factors. These provisions are included in the titles 'Principles and Adjustments to the Treaties' of the fifth Accession Treaty. Also, participation in the CAP is staggered over time.

These are particular inventions of the pre-accession strategy or process that has driven the fifth enlargement. This same approach has been taken in the drafting of the fifth and sixth Accession Treaties given that the countries that acceded on 1 May 2004 and on 1 January 2007 were not fully incorporated into these same areas of Union activity at that time. This approach sets a precedent for future enlargements and holds far-reaching implications for the very notion of membership of the European Union as much as for the evolution of the Union's activities and the *acquis communautaire.*

Of course the new Member States are referred to as Member States. But their capacity to act as full Member States or to benefit on a par with the Fifteen, is already limited, raising serious constitutional questions and purely practical issues of differentiation in the *acquis* and in decision-making.[41] Moreover, the December 2004 Brussels European Council paved the way for the permanent exclusion of Turkish workers from free movement rights but also from benefiting under the Union's Common Agricultural Policy (CAP) or regional policy instruments. Specifically as concerns Turkey, the Presidency Conclusions[42] made clear when establishing the basis for the Commission's negotiating framework, the following:

> Long transitional periods, derogations, specific arrangements or permanent safeguard clauses, i.e. clauses which are permanently available as a basis for safeguard measures, may be considered. The Commission will include these, as appropriate, in its proposals for each framework, for areas such as freedom of movement of persons, structural policies or agriculture. Furthermore, the decision-taking process regarding the eventual establishment of freedom of movement of persons should allow for a maximum role of individual Member States. Transitional arrangements or safeguards should be reviewed regarding their impact on competition or the functioning of the Internal Market.

Precisely the same wording has been reproduced in the Commission's negotiating framework, which was adopted 3 October 2005.[43]

This brings us to another novelty of the fifth Accession Treaty. In addition to the economic safeguard clause that has been common to all accession treaties, which is available to all Member States, the fifth Accession Treaty contains two entirely new safeguard clauses that can be used against the new Member States only (not the fifteen 'old' Member States) in order to protect the Internal Market and the Justice and Home Affairs *acquis*. Even after having acceded to the Union, the new Member States must continue to pursue their pre-accession commitments, made during the accession negotiations, to meet their obligations under their Accession Treaty in order to accede to every area of the Union's activities. The pre-accession conditionality that characterised the pre-accession strategy post-enlargement, to a certain extent, continues to apply to the new Member States after their accession. The continuation of this pre-accession conditionality after their formal accession to the Union raises important questions concerning

---

[41] See M. Cremona, 'EU enlargement: solidarity and conditionality' in 30 *ELRev.* (2005) pp. 3–22.

[42] See *Presidency Conclusions*, Council Press Release 16238/1/04 REV I, 17 December 2004, under Title I. Enlargement at p. 7.

[43] See point 12 of the negotiating framework adopted by the European Council for the Commission on 3 October 2005.

the focus of the members resources and priorities as well as insights into the future evolution of the *acquis* in the Union of twenty-five and more Member States.

From the view point of the agri-food and the environment *acquis*, the new Member States remain bound by various pre-accession commitments. The environment and particularly the agri-food *acquis* form part of the internal Market *acquis* generally speaking. There are no examples of the Internal Market safeguard clause having been used under the fifth Accession Treaty. The safeguard measures could not be taken after 30 April 2007 for the ten countries that joined in 2004. The safeguard clauses in the sixth Accession Treaty can still be used until the end of 2009. There is one example of their use under the sixth Accession Treaty, in the air transport sector – see Chapter Five. For the environment *acquis* in particular, there are very long-term transitional periods. The transitional arrangements in the agri-food *acquis* are changing and there are examples of the emergence of an undergrowth of 'informal' transitional arrangements, which are to all intents and purposes illegal because they were not agreed upon during the accession negotiations.

## 2. Eligibility to apply for membership, admissibility criteria and procedural steps

The Treaties have given scant insight into what is required of any country aspiring to membership of the European Union. The conditions have been worked out progressively depending on the situation in hand and therefore, this chapter must be read alongside the brief comparative analysis of practice, past and future made in the subsequent chapters on the Copenhagen criteria and the instruments of the pre-accession strategy.

These chapters will show how the gestation period from application for membership to full membership have increased with the fifth enlargement in particular. The Copenhagen criteria and conditionality were devised in 1993 specifically with the countries of central and eastern Europe in mind. The strategy for future enlargements to bring in Turkey and the countries of south eastern Europe carries its own conditionality which builds upon the Copenhagen criteria and the pre-accession process devised for the fifth and sixth enlargements. The strategy for the Western Balkans and the Eastern and Southern neighbours is built on similar structures based on pre-accession instruments.[44] It is a different path to reach the same goal: ultimately their accession to the Union. Nevertheless, the relatively minimal yet all embracing Copenhagen criteria that have been devised for the fifth and sixth enlargements continue to provide the foundations for the Union's pre-accession conditionality for future enlargements also. As is seen in Chapter 2 on the Copenhagen criteria, future enlargements face new hurdles: new leanings towards national referendums on accession treaties, notably the increasing concern of various Member States about the capacity of the Union to absorb new members in the wake of the failure of the Constitutional Treaty and now it seems, the Treaty of Lisbon too.

### 2.1 *Article 49 TEU establishes eligibility conditions and procedural steps*

One single Article in the Treaties establishes the conditions of eligibility to apply for EU membership as well as the procedure for becoming a member of the Union: Article 49 TEU. The procedural steps specified in the Treaties for acceding to the Union run as follows: before an accession treaty may be signed, the aspiring country makes an application to the Council, the European and national parliaments are notified, Council takes a Decision unanimously after it has received the Opinion of the Commission and the consent of the European Parliament acting by majority of its component members, upon each application for membership. These documents introduce the Accession Treaty in the preamble to the Treaty of Accession. There is no specific reference to the participation of the Community Institutions – notably the European Commission – but their participation is not excluded.[45]

From the time of the very first enlargements, the Commission drew up preliminary opinions on an application but this is not to be confused with the formal Opinion that introduces an accession treaty and which closes the negotiations. As for the conditions of admission and adjustments to the Treaties which might be required in the first years after a new member's accession, the second paragraph of Article 49

[44] See M. Cremona, op. cit. n. 25 at pp. 411–413.

[45] See P.J.G. Kapteyn and P. VerLoren van Themaat, *Introduction to the Law of the European Communities* (Dordrecht, Kluwer Law International 1998) at pp. 93–94.

leaves this to 'an agreement between the Member States and the applicant State' and provides that such 'agreement be submitted for ratification by all the contracting States in accordance with their respective constitutional requirements'.

In practice, once a country applies for membership, the Commission issues its opinion on the application.[46] Interestingly, Morocco applied on 20 July 1987. In an Exchange of Letters, the Council rejected the Moroccan application without requesting a Commission Opinion, which are not published. The Council took its decision on 1 October 1987. Morocco's application never reached the procedural stage of requiring a Commission Opinion. This is not the final Commission Opinion required under Article 49 TEU and which introduces the final Accession Treaty itself. In this first Opinion, the Commission assesses the challenge for the applicant as well as for the Union. The actual launch of accession negotiations is not automatic. Also, since the fifth enlargement, the preparations undertaken by the applicant must be well advanced before, in the first place, the country is formally recognised as a 'candidate', and before actual accession negotiations can be opened. Negotiations have always been bi-lateral between the EU and each applicant in turn, even though the Accession Treaties provide for multiple entries.[47]

### 2.1.1 *Referendums: a wild card in accession treaty procedure*

The practice of putting an accession treaty to referendum by the candidates served to thwart the accession of Norway after it had signed the fourth Accession Treaty[48] as the result of the negative vote of its own people. In the case of the fifth and sixth enlargements, only one

---

[46] Morocco applied on 20 July 1987. From a response to a European parliamentary before that the time, it is clear that the Commission did not consider Morocco to be 'European' for the purposes of Article 237 EEC and did not consider Morocco's accession to the Union possible, see Réponse donnée par M. Delors au nom de la Commission le 19 février 1985 au Question Ecrite 1404/84 de Karel Van Miert à la Commission des Communautés européennes, *JO* 1985 C 97/26. However, in a response to a parliamentary question of October 1987, the Commission advised the MEP concerned that it would examine the problem of how to interpret Article 237 in its Opinion to the Council, see Réponse donnée par M. Cheysson au nom de la Commission le 3 décembre 1987 au Question Ecrite 1423/87 à la Commission des Communautés européennes, *JO* 1988 C 61/45.

[47] All except for the second Accession Treaty which was with Greece alone.

[48] Norway had signed the fourth Accession Treaty along with Austria, Finland and Sweden only to fail to ratify due a negative national referendum thereon.

of the ten acceding countries - Malta - held a national referendum, which was consultative rather than required by its constitution and every referendum was affirmative. For the rest, the result was positive and in some cases overwhelmingly so.

None of the receiving Member States in any enlargement have rejected an accession treaty after its signature and no national referendum has been used in the receiving Member States in any of the first six enlargements, whether before or after signature of an accession treaty. Of course, they have all ratified the accession treaties in accordance with their own national constitutional requirements, which have not required any referendum. However, (ex-)President Chirac announced that France would hold a referendum on the accession of Turkey, although this amendment was subsequently withdrawn on 25 June 2008.[49] Both France and Cyprus spoke out against a Turkish accession in November 2007. In any case, the Commission will submit an Accession Treaty with Turkey to an Intergovernmental Conference, see p. 48 further. Moreover, the new CEEC Member States have more of a tradition of using referendums and in some cases the 'souverainist' character of their constitutions requires a referendum in respect of any treaty amendment that is of primary relevance to their national constitutional procedures.[50] Also, in January 2009 Slovenia expressly mentioned the possibility of a referendum on an accession treaty for Croatia if it does not get its way in an ongoing dispute with Croatia of land and maritime borders.[51]

However, for future enlargements, taking as an example the ratification method for the Constitutional Treaty, more Member States may

---

[49] On 2 March 2005, the French Congrès adopted LOI constitutionnelle n° 2005-204 du 1er mars 2005 modifiant le titre XV de la Constitution, amending Art. 88-5 thereof to read; 'Tout projet de loi autorisant la ratification d'un traité relatif à l'adhésion d'un Etat à l'Union européenne et aux Communautés européennes est soumis au référendum par le Président de la République.' See 'Chirac considering referendums on future EU enlargements', www.euobserver.com/?aid=17408, visited on 4 October 2004. This amendment was withdrawn: see 'La France supprime le référendum pour l'adhésion de la Turquie', www.EurActiv.com, visited 25 juin 2008.

[50] See A. Albi, 'Referendums in Eastern Europe', *EUI Working Papers RSC* (2002) p. 65. See by the same author, *EU Enlargement and the Constitution of Central and Eastern Europe* (Cambridge, Cambridge University Press 2005).

[51] Slovene foreign minister Samuel Zbogar, quoted in Euobserver.com, visited on 8 January 2009.

choose to use a national referendum as a pre-condition to ratification of an accession treaty. Among them may well be the CEEC Member States but potentially also the fifteen Member States. The fact that Denmark, France, Ireland, Luxembourg, the Netherlands, Portugal, Spain and the United Kingdom, in addition to the new Member States of the Czech Republic and Slovenia, decided to hold referendums on the Constitutional Treaty[52] indicates the political concerns of these countries. The political reasons included for example:[53] making a genuine commitment to the Constitution and renewing the expression of its legitimacy; resolving splits between a national parliament and its electorate; to act as arbiter between national political parties of opposing views; to resolve divisions between anti and pro-integrationist groups within one and the same political party.

While Ireland has held referendums on all Treaty amendments in the form of the Single European Act, the Treaties of Maastricht, Amsterdam and Nice, it has not so far held referendums on the Accession Treaties *per se*. In Ireland, a referendum is obligatory when the there is an additional transfer of sovereign power to the EU.

#### 2.1.2 *Only 'European' States may apply: expanding geographical limits of the Union*

In terms of eligibility to make an application for membership, Article 49 TEU specifies that '[a]ny European State which respects the values referred to in Article 2 TEU and is committed to promoting and applying them, may apply', see 2.2 and 2.3 further. 'European' remains undefined – neither the Commission nor Council have fixed the geographical boundaries of the Union.[54] So the debate continues as to the geographical, historical and cultural elements that constitute 'European'. The fact that the association agreements signed with the CEECs were called 'Europe Agreements' was certainly recognition by the

[52] See 'Slovenia ratifies EU Constitution', www.euractive.com visited 9 February 2005. See the European Commission's interactive map of the ratification of the Constitutional Treaty, dated July 2005 to be found at www.europa.eu.int/constitution/ratification_en.htm

[53] See C. Closa, 'Ratifying the EU Constitution: referendums and their implications', *US-Europe Analysis Series* (November 2004), to be found at www.brookings.edu

[54] See Commission Communication *Europe and the Challenge of Enlargement*, *Bull. EU*, Suppl. 3/92 at p. 11. See M. Maresceau in 'Association, partnership, pre-accession and accession' in Maresceau, ed., *Enlarging the European Union. Relations between the EU and Central and Eastern Europe,* (London and New York, Longman, 1997) at p. 13.

Union of their 'Europeaness'. Although at the time of the first Europe Agreements, eastwards enlargement was not the Union's expressed intention[55] these association agreements did differ from ordinary or qualified trade agreements such as Partnership and Co-operation Agreements concluded with Russia, Ukraine, Belarus and Moldova.[56]

It seems of little use to explore the meaning of 'European' in abstract terms in the context of today's pre-accession strategy. In concrete terms, included among the actual and potential candidates for accession to the Union, are countries that do not fall wholly within the European continent (for example, Turkey) and countries for which the very prospect of accession to the Union had not been contemplated in the early Nineteen-nineties (for example, Albania[57]). Turkey's inclusion in the pre-accession strategy is now a reality in spite of the fact that not all of its territory lies on the continent of Europe while Morocco was expressly excluded on the basis of the geographical criterion alone.

Also in concrete terms, changes in the geopolitical situation have been accompanied by an inclusion of the western Balkans as eligible[58] and they are now even recognised as 'potential' candidates for accession to the Union, including Albania.[59] The Commission refers to the

[55] See M. Maresceau and I. Montaguti, 'The relations between the European Union and central and eastern Europe: a legal appraisal', 32 *CML Rev.* (1995) p. 1328.

[56] See P.C. Müller-Graff, 'Legal Framework for Relations between the European Union and Central and Eastern Europe: General Aspects' in M. Maresceau, ed., *Enlarging the European Union. Relations between the EU and Central and Eastern Europe*, op. cit. n. 24 at pp. 27–40.

[57] The June 2000 Feira European Council stated that all the SAP countries are 'potential candidates' for EU membership and the Thessaloniki Summit of June 2003 reconfirmed this prospect. Albania had signed a Trade and Co-operation Agreement with the Union in 1992, *OJ* 1992 L 343/1 but still in 1996 the Union's approach was more to foster a regional approach in its co-operation with and amongst the Balkans countries, namely Bosnia-Herzegovina, Croatia, the Federal Republic of Yugoslavia (prior to the launch of the regional approach the Union had no contractual links with these three latter countries), Albania and the Federal Republic of Macedonia. See two reports from the Commission to the Council and Parliament, the first on Prospects for the development of regional co-operation for the countries of the former Yugoslavia and what the Community could do to foster such co-operation, SEC(96) 0252 and the second, on Common principles for future contractual relations with certain countries in South-Eastern Europe, *Bull. EU* 1/2-1996, point 1.4.108. See also the European Parliament Resolution A4-0127/97 on said reports, *OJ* 1997 C 167/143.

[58] See Maresceau, 'Association, partnership, pre-accession and accession', op. cit. n. 24, at pp. 4–5. Indeed, in the later 1980's and early 1990's Yugoslavia was 'usually regarded as an impossible applicant', see Nicoll and Salmon (Eds.), op. cit. n. 1 at p. 36.

[59] Namely, Serbia including Kosovo, as defined by United Nations Security Council Resolution 1244, Montenegro, Former Yugoslav Republic of Macedonia, Bosnia and

Western Balkans as having a 'European vocation',[60] and states clearly that the June 2000 European Council's objective of enlargement to the South East 'is a promise which the EU will honour when each country fulfils the criteria'. In any case, the SAAs unambiguously frame the intent of the Union to extend its borders to the Western Balkans, pursuant to the June 2000 Feira European Council's Conclusion, and make express reference to the Copenhagen criteria.[61] Then again, this is not to say that the Union was not reticent at all and the adjective 'potential' in this context could not be interpreted as a legally enforceable right to membership.[62]

Consequently, the eligibility of these SEE countries for membership is now beyond question and the Union's will to enlarge further to the south-east is a commitment, which is the single most important incentive for the countries of South Eastern Europe.[63] This seems logical from a geographical viewpoint alone – once Romania and Bulgaria joined the Union, these Balkan countries, will be entirely surrounded by Union Member States.

The geographical criterion seems superfluous in the context of possible future applications from the Ukraine and Moldova as both of these countries are situated wholly on the continent of Europe. As concerns Ukraine in particular, it is the political and economic factors

---

Herzegovina, Albania. See the Presidency Conclusions of the June 2000 Feira European Council and of the December 2002 Copenhagen European Council, the March 2003 Brussels European Council and the June 2003 Thessaloniki European Council. Conclusion 40 of the Presidency Conclusion to the June 2003 Thessaloniki European Council reads: 'The European Council, recalling its conclusions in Copenhagen [December 2002] and Brussels [March 2003], reiterated its 'determination to fully and effectively support the European perspective of the Western Balkan countries, which will become an integral part of the EU, once they meet the established criteria".

[60] See Commission Report on *The Stabilisation and Association process for South East Europe*, COM(2004) 202, 30 March 2004. The Commission referred to the 'ultimate vocation' of membership for these countries in 1999 in its Communication on the Stabilisation and Association Process, COM(99) 235, 26 May 1999.

[61] The final recital in the SAA FYROM reads: 'Recalling the European Union's readiness to integrate to the fullest possible extent the former Yugoslav Republic of Macedonia into the political and economic mainstream of Europe and its status as a potential candidate for EU membership on the basis of the Treaty on European Union and fulfilment of the criteria by the European Council in June 1993, subject to successful implementation of this Agreement, notably regarding regional co-operation'.

[62] See S. Blockmans, 'EU conflict prevention in the Western Balkans' in V. Kronenberger and Jan Wouters, eds., *The European Union and Conflict Prevention: Policy and Legal Aspects* (The Hague, T.M.C. Asser Press 2004).

[63] See Cremona, op. cit. n. 25. See also M.A. Vachudova, 'Strategies for Integration in the Balkans' in Cremona, op. cit. n. 24, pp. 141–160 at p. 143 and p. 160.

that militate against tentative approaches made by Ukraine concerning a possible application.[64] The reluctance of the European Union to draw firm geographical boundaries emerges in the New Neighbourhood Policy where the Union dissociates[65] itself from the question of membership. Membership is not promised to neighbouring countries but it is not dismissed outright either. In this way the Union refuses to limit its scope of manoeuvre in its external relations with the wider Europe and avoids compromising the ultimate incentive that potential membership provides in relations with neighbouring countries.

### 2.2 *Innovations of the Amsterdam Treaty*

Article 49 TEU has evolved over time, first with the Treaty of Amsterdam and then with the Treaty of Lisbon, which took effect on 1 December 2009.[66] Following Amsterdam, by reference to (ex-) Article 6(1) EU, any aspiring Member State had to respect the principles upon which the Union 'is founded' and 'which are common to the Member States', namely, 'the principles of liberty, democracy, respect for human rights and fundamental freedoms and the rule of law.' However, this was no more than a codification of an unwritten constitutional principle common to all Member States.[67] The full range of principles and rights that make up the fabric of the Union included even the terminology used in the European Convention on Human Rights and its Protocols or the 1990 OSCE Copenhagen

---

[64] See Joost Lagendijk MEP and Marinus Wiersma MEP, 'The ultimate borders of the European Union' on www.euobserver.com, visited on 17 December 2001.

[65] See Cremona, 'Enlargement: a successful instrument of foreign policy?', op. cit. n. 25 at p. 12.

[66] Originally, Art. 237 EEC was the relevant provisions and its was amended by Art. 8 SEA before being repealed by Art. G(83) TEU and replaced by Art. O TEU and then renumbered by the Amsterdam Treaty as Art. 49 EU. A second important revision should also be noted however. The European Parliament, as a result of the 1986 Single European Act, effectively held a veto in respect of an application for membership Ex-Art. 6(1) EU is now Art. 2 TEU. See F. Hoffmeister, 'Earlier enlargements' and 'Changing requirements for membership' in Ott and Inglis, eds., *Handbook on European Enlargement. A commentary on the Enlargement process*, op. cit. n. 24 at pp. 87–102. Also a slightly different procedure applied as concerned the ECSC Treaty whereby the Council decided on an application by unanimity upon the recommendation of the Commission, unilaterally establishing the conditions of admission. For the situation prior to Amsterdam but nevertheless relevant today, see also Maresceau, 'On Association, Partnership, Pre-accession and Accession', op. cit. n. 24, at pp. 13–21.

[67] See Hoffmeister, op. cit. n. 24, at pp. 93–96.

Declaration on minorities. The Treaty of Lisbon amended ex-Article 49 EU and also expands the list of pre-requisites for aspiring Member States.[68]

### 2.3 *Implications of the Treaty of Lisbon*

The Constitutional Treaty, which failed in the wake of the negative referendums in France and the Netherlands in 2005, has influenced the Treaty of Lisbon drafting of Article 49 TEU. It is useful to note that there are subtle differences between the changes that the Constitutional Treaty would have made and those introduced by the Treaty of Lisbon.

The equivalent of Article 49 TEU in the Constitutional Treaty was Article I-58. Article I-58 belonged under Title IX on Union Membership in Part I of the Constitutional Treaty, alongside the provisions for the suspension of a Member State or for a Member State's voluntary withdrawal. The change of title was intended, by the Convention, to reflect the constitutional nature of an enlargement, although initially this Article had been proposed under its own specific heading. This 'constitutional' aspect to Accession Treaties could also be seen in the use of the instrument of an 'Accession Protocol' rather than the Accession Treaty that has been used to date.

Also significantly, by incorporating the legal basis for enlargement alongside the provisions for the suspension or voluntary withdrawal of a Member State, the Constitutional Treaty arguably[69] distanced this legal basis from the legal basis for a major treaty revision under Article 48 TEU, which would require an intergovernmental conference to be convened. Article I-58 of the Constitutional Treaty could thus be looked on as a means of calming the blur between ex-Articles 49 and 48 EU. It sought to ease the procedural uncertainties that might ensue in the event that a Member State was faced with accusations of introducing institutional reforms 'through the backdoor'.

The first paragraph of Article I-58 differed only slightly from ex-Article 49 EU. Article I-58(1) declared the Union to be 'open' to all European States that respect the values set out in Article I-2 (ex-Art.

---

[68] See n. 66.

[69] See P. Manin, 'Article I-58' in L. Bourgorgue-Larsen, A. Levade and F. Picod, (eds.), *Traité établissant un Constitution pour l'Europe*, (Bruxelles, Bruylant 2007) at p. 718.

6 EU) and required a commitment to promoting them together. This 'openness' was not really new given previous practice. As has already been pointed out, it has always been the case that once the Union opens accession negotiations, it commits itself enlarging.

The reference to 'openness' was not really new either as it shows the inclusiveness of the Union, emphasising the Union's enlargement goals and the common values that underpin this widening. Article I-58(1), by reference to Article I-2, added to the list of explicit values upon which the Union is founded and required that the newcomer be 'committed to promoting [these values] together'. The list of values upon which the Union is founded expressly required:

> respect for human dignity, liberty, democracy, equality, the rule of law and respect for human rights, including the rights of persons belonging to minorities. These values are common to the Member States in a society of pluralism, non-discrimination, tolerance, justice, solidarity and equality between men and women prevail.

This wording built on the principles set out in ex-Article 6(1) EU and reflects the broader 'values, rights and principles' enshrined in the Charter on Fundamental Rights of 2000. It is fair to say that all of these themes arise in the various legal instruments of the pre-accession strategy, worked out under ex-Article 49 EU, starting with the June 1993 Copenhagen European Council in particular. However, Article I-2 was not intended to be exhaustive, otherwise, like ex-Article 49 EU, Article I-2 would also have included the need to respect the principles of a market economy for example.

As for the procedural dimension of Article I-58 of the Constitutional Treaty, Article I-58(2) established 'Conditions of eligibility and procedure for accession to the Union'. It provided that the European Parliament and the Member States' national parliaments would have to be 'notified' of any application for membership and the European Parliament would have to reach a majority of its MEPs voting in plenary, in order to give its consent to an application. The notification of national parliaments was taking account of the practice of the European Parliament in any case, so it would not have been all that novel a provision in any case. For the rest, the Constitutional Treaty would have changed little in terms of procedure and the interplay between Member States/EU institutions/candidates.

Accession Protocols were to be the instrument of accession, replacing the Accession Treaty as such. This was foreseen in the Constitutional

Treaty and indeed we already have a working example of this because the Accession Treaty with Bulgaria and Romania was accompanied by an Accession Protocol when published in the *Official Journal*. This was because the sixth Accession Treaty was signed after the conclusion of the Constitutional Treaty but before the latter's ratification. If however, the Constitutional Treaty had been ratified, then the Accession Protocol and not the Treaty of Accession, incorporating the Act of Accession, would have taken effect. Also important to note for practical purposes, all previous Accession Treaties would also have been incorporated in the Constitutional Treaty in the form of Accession Protocols having the same legal value as provisions contained within the body of the treaty itself. Finally, under the Constitutional Treaty, the Accession Protocol would have remained an agreement between the receiving Member States acting by unanimity on the one hand, and the incoming Member States on the other. Thus, an accession would remain an international treaty, assuring against any fears of a possible 'federal' orientation.

This brings us to the Treaty of Lisbon itself. It was clearly inspired by Article I-58 of the Constitutional Treaty as regards changes to the legal basis for enlargement. Under the Treaty of Lisbon there will be no Accession Protocols but the traditional Accession Treaty format will still be used, which as just mentioned removes any shadow of a 'federal' orientation.

As a first practical comment, any lawyer working with the revised Treaties will also have to work with the Accession Treaties. Since the fifth and sixth enlargements this not only means working with the transitional arrangements that have been limited to the first years after these two enlargements: it also means arrangements whereby the new Member States do not participate in Schengen, the CAP or the Eurozone for indefinite periods of time.

The amendments introduced into Article 49 TEU clearly reflect the substantive and procedural amendments intended by the Constitutional Treaty. In terms of procedure:

- the Member States agree by unanimity, as they have always done;
- the European Parliament and national parliaments have to be 'notified' of any application for membership, and;
- the European Parliament has to reach a majority of its component MEPs voting in plenary, in order to consent to an application, as it has always done.

Article 2 TEU is worded in the same way as Article I-2 of the Constitutional Treaty and reflects its concerns by additionally referring, for example, to human dignity and equality between men and women. Moreover the new Article 6(1) TEU provides for the Union's accession the European Convention on Human Rights and expressly recognises the 'rights, freedoms and principles' of the Charter on Fundamental Rights as primary EU law. Thus, Article 49 TEU has updated and expanded the pre-requisites for aspiring Member States, a list that is not exhaustive and includes the need for respect of the market economy too, for example. It also requires that aspiring members commit to promoting those values. Breach of these same values as set out in Article 2 TEU, may trigger the procedure for the suspension of the Member State concerned (Art. 7 TEU), in one way or another.

Finally, the new Article 8(1) TEU expressly states the Union's own obligation to develop a 'special relationship' with its neighbours, building in the concern of good neighbourliness, and again founded on the 'values' of the Union. Article 8(2) TEU provides for the conclusion of international agreements with neighbouring countries, based on reciprocal rights and obligations.

There are noticeably differences between the Constitutional Treaty and the Treaty of Lisbon. First is the entirely new sentence that reads: 'The conditions of eligibility agreed upon by the European Council shall be taken into account'. The European Council, as progressively becomes clear in this book, has always been active in setting pre-accession conditionality. This reference undoubtedly refers to the Copenhagen criteria but also appears to leave a door open for the continued introduction of new 'conditions of eligibility'.

The Treaty of Lisbon makes no reference to the 'openness' of the Union to all European States that respect the given values of the Union. When compared to the Constitutional Treaty, this omission implies a certain political reticence to further enlargements. The notification of national parliaments takes account of the practice of the European Parliament in any case, so it is not that novel a provision in reality. For the rest, the Constitutional Treaty would have changed little in terms of procedure and the interplay between Member States/EU institutions/candidates.

The next thing to note is that the equivalent of Article 49 TEU will remain among the Final Provisions but it will sit alongside the entirely new provisions allowing for the voluntary withdrawal of a Member State from the Union, Article 50 TEU. Certainly for future enlargements the question of whether an enlargement will involve major treaty revision requiring an IGC can be expected to arise again. Suspension of membership is now provided for in Article 7 TEU. The sensitive issue of Turkey for example, will raise serious institutional questions given the rapid growth in population there. The European Commission 2004 Report on Turkey expressly called for an IGC on an accession treaty with Turkey in any case.

Under today's Treaties, future enlargements may well be more difficult in a number of ways, perhaps most importantly and most unpredictably because of the likelihood of national referendums. Such a procedural step is not a requirement of the Treaties themselves however, but would result from the phrase contained in Article 49 TEU guaranteeing the respect for national constitutional arrangements.

The ToL is a treaty of 'continuity', enabling an enlarged Union to continue to function, rather than consolidating and finalising the foundations for the future of the Union. For the future, the use of existing and even new clauses of flexibility are being seen as the only way of defusing future institutional crises and the knock-on constitutional crises that have become ever more pressing with each enlargement wave.

However, all of these themes arise in the various legal instruments of the pre-accession strategy that work out Article 49 TEU. In particular, the June 1993 Copenhagen European Council, dealt with in Chapter 2, set down the general criteria for enlargements and the subsequent working out of a strategy to prepare for the fifth and sixth enlargements which brought in the ten Central and Eastern European Member States, as well as Cyprus and Malta.

## 3. Primary law limits on accession treaties and transitional arrangements

There are limits to the changes that can be introduced through an act of accession. In the founding Treaties themselves, certain limits are put on the changes or transitional arrangements that can be agreed in an accession treaty.

### 3.1 *Article 49 TEU: 'adjustments'*

Article 49 TEU is the relevant legal basis for an accession treaty, and it only provides for 'adjustments' to be agreed by this procedure. In 1993 the Copenhagen criteria consolidated and comprehensively stated the political, economic and legal foundations that had been worked out with the first three enlargements and has been further refined since.

In the first place, Article 3 TEU sets the objective for the Union of maintaining the *acquis* and building on it and requires the consistency and continuity of all activities in order to do so. The principle of the equality of rights and obligations of the Member States also dramatically limits the scope for derogations from the *acquis*.[70] This same rationale underlies the third Copenhagen criterion, dealt with in the next chapter, which requires the acceptance of the rights and obligations, actual and potential, of the Community system and its institutional framework.[71] A candidate country is always limited in terms of what it can negotiate because in joining the Union it must accept its rights and obligations of membership that have been instituted prior to their entry. Any transitional arrangements must be seen as no more than an exception to this equality of rights and obligations of the Member States and only to a limited extent and for a fixed time frame. Such partial and restricted non-application of the *acquis* was designed so as not to constrain the development of the Union and the *acquis*. Transitional arrangements are not a re-negotiation of the substance of the Treaties and the *acquis*.

Each Accession Treaty states in the very first provisions on Principles, that upon accession the incoming Member State is in the 'same situation' with every other Member State. It is an established point of principle that the provisions of Community law apply *ab initio* and *in toto* to new Member States, derogations being allowed only insofar as they are expressly laid down by transitional measures.[72] This has been consistent in the Court's judgments since and the same applies to the 2003 and 2005 Accession Treaties.[73] In the fifth Accession Treaty this was contained in Article 5(3).[74] In the sixth it is contained in Article 3(2).

---

[70] See Commission Communication, *Enlargement of the Community: transitional period and the institutional implications of enlargement*, 20 April 1978, *Bull EC* 2/78 at p. 7, para. 6.

[71] See European Commission *Europe and the challenge of enlargement*, 1992.

[72] See ECJ Case 258/81, *Metallurgiki Halyps A.E.* v. *Commission* [1982] *ECR* 4261.

[73] Latterly in relation to the fourth Accession Treaty, see for example ECJ, Case C-233/97 *KappAhl Oy* [1998] *ECR* I-8069.

[74] The new Member States are in the same situation as the present Member States in respect of declarations or resolutions of, or other positions taken up by, the European

### 3.2 *Permanent derogations from the* acquis *are extremely rare*

Permanent derogations from the *acquis* are extremely rare. Denmark has a permanent derogation[75] to prevent non-Danes from buying secondary residences there, a restriction which would normally fall foul of the Article 18 TFEU ban on discrimination based on nationality. This derogation is now contained in Protocol 1 to the Treaty on European Union of 1992. Finland's Åland Islands also have a permanent derogation, contained in Protocol 2 to the fourth Accession Treaty, to the effect that the relevant national competent authorities must authorise the acquisition of real property there. Malta now also has a derogation to restrict the purchase of secondary residences there by non-Maltese EU nationals. This is contained in Protocol 6 to the fifth Accession Treaty,[76] which sets out the limits to these restrictions. Malta is allowed to maintain restrictions under its Maltese Immovable Property (Acquisition by non-residents) Act, Chapter 246. Non-Maltese nationals from other Member States are only allowed to buy secondary residences there after they have been resident in Malta for five years and they must pay a certain price. Other discrimination is not allowed

Council or the Council and in respect of those concerning the Community or the Union adopted by common agreement of the Member States; they will accordingly observe the principles and guidelines deriving from those declarations, resolutions or other positions and will take such measures as may be necessary to ensure their implementation.

[75] Protocol 16 to the first Accession Treaty.

[76] Bearing in mind the very limited number of residences in Malta and the very limited land available for construction purposes, which can only cover the basic needs created by the demographic development of the present residents, Malta may on a non-discriminatory basis maintain in force the rules on the acquisition and holding of immovable property for secondary residence purposes by nationals of the Member States who have not legally resided in Malta for at least five years laid down in the Immovable Property (Acquisition by Non-Residents) Act (Chapter 246). Malta shall apply authorisation procedures for the acquisition of immovable property for secondary residence purposes in Malta, which shall be based on published, objective, stable and transparent criteria. These criteria shall be applied in a non-discriminatory manner and shall not differentiate between nationals of Malta and of other Member States. Malta shall ensure that in no instance shall a national of a Member State be treated in a more restrictive way than a national of a third country. In the event that the value of one such property bought by a national of a Member State exceeds the thresholds provided for in Malta's legislation, namely 30 000 Maltese lira for apartments and 50 000 Maltese lira for any type of property other than apartments and property of historical importance, authorisation shall be granted. Malta may revise the thresholds established by such legislation to reflect changes in prices in the property market in Malta.

and any authorisation procedures must be published, objective, stable and transparent. Moreover, third country nationals cannot be treated more favourably than EU nationals.

However, with the fifth enlargement, the staggered participation of the incoming Member States in key areas of Union activity[77] calls into question to true equality of the rights and obligations of membership. The Internal Market and JHA safeguard measures that are contained in both the fifth and sixth Accession Treaties potentially clash with core principles enshrined in the Treaties. The tension between solidarity on the one hand, and differentiation/conditionality on the other, is striking.[78] These issues are explored further in Chapters Three and Four.

Certainly, there is a strong case against any derogations from primary law that might eat into the hard core of EU principles,[79] that there can be no negotiation of the fundamental freedoms, human rights, democracy, the rule of law and liberty, such as laid out in Article 2 TEU nor the other values on which the Union is founded. While an Accession Treaty is an international treaty and in itself primary law, no provision of an accession treaty could be interpreted as validating measures in contradiction of the Treaties, no matter their form.[80] Moreover, it is established case law that any derogation that has been sanctioned by an accession treaty, must be interpreted in such a way as to facilitate the achievement of the objectives of the Treaty and the application in full of its procedures[81] and must be interpreted restrictively.[82] Chapter Four deals with the legal scope and content of the various transitional arrangements and flexibility mechanisms.

While permanent derogations are not the subject of this work, it is worth mentioning that accession negotiations begin from the premise that requests for permanent derogations will not be entertained. It was also the case, although far from standard practice, to allow certain of

[77] Arts. 3 and 4 of the fifth Accession Treaty and Arts. 4 and 5 of the sixth.

[78] See Cremona, 'EU Enlargement: solidarity and conditionality', op. cit. n. 41.

[79] See A. Ott, 'The Pinciple of Differentiation in an Enlarged European Union: Unity in Diversity?', in Inglis and Ott (eds.) *The Constitution for Europe and an Enlarging Union: Unity in Diversity?*, Groeningen, Europa Law Publishing 2005, p. 103 at p. 122 *et seq*.

[80] See ECJ Case 185/73, *Hauptzollamt Bielefeld/König*, [1974] *ECR* 607.

[81] ECJ, Joined Cases 194/85 and 241/85 *Commission* v. *Greece* [1988] *ECR* 1037, para. 20.

[82] ECJ, Case 77/82 *Peskeloglou* v. *Bundesanstalt fur Arbeit* [1983] *ECR* 1085, para. 12.

the newcomers certain permanent derogations in order to extend the *acquis* where it was otherwise silent.[83] This also occurred in previous accessions: for example Articles 100, 102 and 103 of the 1994 Act of Accession lays down a regime for fisheries in order to adapt the *acquis* to the sea-faring nature of Austria, Finland and Sweden. Thus also the 1994 Act of Accession had to take account of the specific geographical and climatic conditions of the Nordic countries: see in particular, Article 142 on Nordic agriculture, Protocol No. 3 on the Sami people and Protocol No. 6 on a new structural fund 'objective 6'. Another example of how the *acquis* was extended to take account of an incoming country is that of cotton, which was included in the CAP by Protocol No. 4 in the 1976 Act of Accession as, within the Community, cotton is grown only in Greece.

Protocol 7 to the fifth Accession Treaty[84] was sought by Malta as a guarantee that it would not be obliged to legalise abortion, although strictly speaking this cannot be interpreted as a permanent derogation because the EU has no laws on abortion as such and the choice of whether to prohibit, legalise or restrict abortion remains the preserve of the Member States. The Maltese Protocol can be seen as a pre-emptive response to the legislative Resolution of the European Parliament of July 2002[85] which was interpreted by the Maltese Bishops and the European Catholic Bishops as calling for the legalisation of abortion. Previously, Ireland had insisted on a Protocol to the Maastricht Treaty[86] following a case referred by the Irish Supreme Court

[83] See Booss and Forman, op. cit. n. 26, at n. 19.

[84] Said Protocol 7 reads; 'Nothing in the Treaty on European Union, or in the Treaties establishing the European Communities, or in the Treaties or Acts modifying or supplementing those Treaties, shall affect the application in the territory of Malta of national legislation relating to abortion.'

[85] European Parliament legislative resolution on the proposal for a European Parliament and Council regulation on aid for policies and actions on reproductive and sexual health and rights in developing countries, *OJ* 2004 C43 E /34-350. Regulation 1567/2003 of the European Parliament and of the Council on aid policies and actions for reproductive and sexual health and rights in developing countries, *OJ* 2003 L 224/1, was then adopted in July 2003.

[86] See Protocol No. 17 to the Maastricht Treaty, which reads; 'Nothing in the Treaty on European Union, or in the Treaties establishing the European Communities, or in the Treaties or Acts modifying or supplementing those Treaties shall affect the application in Ireland of Article 43.3.3. of the Constitution of Ireland'. That sub-paragraph in the Constitution of Ireland reads; 'The State acknowledges the right to life of the unborn and, with due regard to the equal right to life of the mother, guarantees in its laws to respect, and, as far as practicable, by its laws to defend and vindicate that

to the ECJ for preliminary ruling[87] on the matter of the application of the Irish Constitution concerning the protection of the unborn child which brought to light certain potential tensions between the right to free expression and the right to life of the foetus in the context of Article 66 TFEU on freedom to provide services.[88] This was felt to highlight a potential clash between Article 66 TFEU and Article 40.3.3. of the Irish Constitution.

### 3.3 *Accession treaties cannot be used for major treaty revision*

Another important question – highlighted in the previous section on the Lisbon Treaty – arises about the limits to the scope and content of an accession treaty. Could an accession treaty spill over into a major treaty revision that goes beyond mere conditions and adjustments? Article 49 TEU only allows for 'adjustments' to be made. Article 48 TEU provides its own legal basis for the revision of the Treaties. Procedurally, this is a matter for the Member States in consultation with the European Parliament and requires that an intergovernmental conference be convened. Otherwise, as with Article 49 TEU, the unanimous support of the Member States is required and their ratification of the reforms must be done according to national constitutional arrangements. Article 48 TEU is itself restricted in how far it can be used to revise the Treaties.[89]

---

right. This subsection shall not limit freedom to travel between the State and another state. This subsection shall not limit freedom to obtain or make available, in the State, subject to such conditions as may be laid down by law, information relating to services lawfully available in another state.'

[87] ECJ, Case 159/90, *Society for the Protection of Unborn Children Ireland Ltd (SPUC)* v. *Grogan*, 8 *ECR* [1991] I-4685.

[88] See D. Binder, 'The European Court of Justice and the Protection of Fundamental Rights in the European Community; New Developments and Future Possibilities in Expanding Fundamental Rights Review to Member State Action', *Jean Monet Working Paper* 4/1995.

[89] Especially as concerns 'supra'-constitutional principles, see F. Snyder, *General Course on Constitutional Law of the European Union*, Academy of European Law, Volume VI, Book I, 1998, at p. 76, A. Ott, Unity in Diversity? – *Differentiation in EU Law and policy in an Enlarged European*, EUI Working Paper. 2004/16. J.L. Cruz Vilaca and N. Picara, 'Y a-t-il des limites matérielles à la révision des traités instituant les CE?, *Cahiers du droit européen*, 193, p. 29, J. Wouters, 'Constitutional Limits of differentiation: the principle of equality', in B. de Witte, D. Hanf and E. Vos (eds.), *The Many Faces of Differentiation in EU law*, (Antwerp, Oxford, New York, Intersentia 2001) at p. 326.

In the cases of the first four enlargements, the institutional adaptations were incorporated within the accession treaties themselves. There was of course, much discussion among the Member States on the institutional provisions. However, for the fifth and sixth enlargements, the institutional 'adjustments' raised questions concerning the traditional balance between equality of States and equality of citizens because the new Member States are predominantly small countries. The approach taken was to address institutional reform through a separate Treaty reform under Article 48 TEU. While the Amsterdam Treaty failed to live up to expectations in this regard,[90] the Nice Treaty established the institutional landscape for the fifth and sixth enlargements. Thereafter, the fifth and sixth Accession Treaties only had to make slight adjustments to take account of the fact that the Bulgaria and Romania were not ready to join along with the other ten new Member States on 1 May 2004.

The accession of Turkey, because of its size, would potentially give this incoming country a dominant role in the legislative decision-making procedures. The exclusion of Turkey from core areas of 'Community' activities however, would be unprecedented and would pose an obvious threat to the fabric of solidarity of Member States, not least because this would involve an unprecedented exception to the notion of equality of Member States in terms of their rights and obligations under the Treaties. It would be difficult to argue in such circumstances that such a treaty is a pure accession treaty involving 'adjustments' to the Treaties only and would not substantially alter the Treaties.

Moreover, it has always been clear from enlargement preparations practice that any transitional non-application of the *acquis* is severely limited – only partial application for pre-determined periods of time has been the approach. Requests from candidates for permanent non-application or derogations from the *acquis* are most unlikely to be entertained, including in areas like Schengen or EMU where certain receiving Member States do not participate. Already the situation where new Member States of the fifth and sixth enlargements do not participate in EMU and Schengen and the CAP is unprecedented and while this is not intended to be 'exclusive' or 'permanent', the divid-

[90] See P. Van Elsuwege and Vermeersch A., 'Institutional Reform in the European Union: A Difficult Balancing Act', in Ott & Inglis (eds), *The Constitution for Europe and an Enlarging Union: Unity and Diversity?*, Groningen, Europa Law Publishing, 2005, pp. 57–84.

ing line between the legal basis for accession to the Union and that for major Treaty revision is tested.

Finally, the Treaty of Lisbon would not resolve the niggling doubt about the possibility that an accession treaty spills over the boundaries of Article 49 TEU into Article 48 TEU.

CHAPTER TWO

# THE COPENHAGEN CRITERIA: EFFORTS REQUIRED BEFORE AND AFTER ACCESSION

## 1. The Copenhagen criteria

Throughout its enlargements, the substantive criteria and conditionality applied by the Union to applicant countries have evolved both:

- to take account of the specificity of the incoming Member States with a view to preserving the values, objectives and the practical functioning of the Union as it enlarges, as well as to guarantee its own continued progress on all fronts of its activities, and;
- to take account of the Union's own stage in growth.

The same can be said of the pre-accession strategy for the fifth enlargement, the core of the pre-conditions, conditions and incentives that programmed all relations between the Union and the candidates was the June 1993 European Council of the famous Copenhagen criteria.[1] In 1997, the Commission set out its proposals for a strategy based upon these criteria in its *Agenda 2000* document. The Council set out four criteria in the following terms:

> The associated countries in Central and Eastern Europe that so desire shall become members of the Union. Accession will take place as soon as a country is able to assume the obligations of membership by satisfying the economic and political conditions. Membership requires:
>
> - That the candidate country has achieved stability of institutions guaranteeing democracy, the rule of law, human rights and respect for and protection of minorities;
> - The existence of a functioning market economy, as well as the capacity to cope with competitive pressures and market forces within the Union;

[1] European Council, Declaration of Copenhagen of 21/22 June 1993, *Bull. EU* 6/1993 p. 13. On the additions made by the 1994 Essen and the 1995 Madrid European Councils, see L. Maurer, 'Negotiations in Progress' and M. Maresceau, 'Pre-accession', both op. cit. Chapter 1, n. 24.

- The ability to take on the obligations of membership, including adhering to the aims of political, economic and monetary union;
- The Union's capacity to absorb new Members, while maintaining the momentum of European integration, is also an important consideration in the general interest of both the Union and the candidate countries.

While any possibility of an enlargement to bring in certain countries in the Balkans was beyond the Union's sights when the Copenhagen criteria were adopted, the same pre-accession strategy tools and legal instruments as were used in the fifth enlargement – including the Copenhagen criteria – are now being successfully transposed in the same inclusive-yet-differentiating way; to the situational specificity of the Balkans under the auspices of the Stabilisation and Association Process (SAP).

The ongoing elaboration and minutiae have been worked out with the countries of South Eastern Europe and Turkey in sight. In the case of the political Copenhagen criteria in particular, pre-accession conditionality has come to mean different things for different candidates. The addition of the criteria of good neighbourliness by the December 1994 Essen European Council and the criteria of having adequate administrative capacity to apply the *acquis* added by the December 1995 Madrid European Council, are cases in point. They have been used as a lever to insist upon intra-regional co-operation between the applicant CEECs and huge investment in administrative and judicial capacity. Since the Treaty of Lisbon, Article 8(1) TEU provides for good neighbourliness in the Union's relations with its neighbours. In the context of the Stabilisation and Association Process, the regional approach is one of the very first building blocks even for meeting the Copenhagen criteria and opening negotiations for a Stabilisation and Association Agreement.

### 1.1 *The precedents for the Copenhagen criteria were already in place*

As becomes increasingly evident below, the precedents for these criteria were already firmly in place. Before the actual, formal adoption of the Copenhagen criteria, however, their political and legal foundations as well as the practice of the Commission, Council and Parliament and Member States' practice in relation to them, were clearly perceptible in the Union's behaviour towards future members. Precedents for the Copenhagen criteria were already perceptible particularly in terms of the:

- formulation of the Union's policy in anticipation of an application for membership;
- reaction to applications for membership;
- conduct of the negotiations, and;
- imposition of the early pre-accession conditionality during those negotiations.

They were then formally adopted in the form of 'the Copenhagen criteria' in 1993[2] – in advance of the fourth enlargement when Austria, Finland and Sweden joined. The December 1994 Essen European Council supplemented the Copenhagen criteria, adding the condition of good neighbourly relations[3] and the December 1995 Madrid European Council added a further requirement that the incoming country had the necessary administrative and judicial capacity for the effective implementation of the *acquis*.[4]

The matter of the administrative and judicial capacity of an applicant had not proved a particular area of focus during the negotiations preceding the first four Accession Treaties. The four Copenhagen criteria, in one form or another, were applied by the Union in its pre-accession conditionality from the very first enlargement. In the first enlargement, the political, economic and legal conditions applicable to the candidate were all concretely applied as well as in the next two

---

[2] See Hoffmeister, 'Changing requirements for membership', op. cit. Chapter 1, n. 24, and Boss and Forman 'Enlargement: legal and procedural aspects', op. cit. Chapter 1, n. 26 at pp. 100–103.

[3] 'Being aware of the role of regional co-operation within the Union, the Heads of State and Government emphasise the importance of similar co-operation between the associated countries for the promotion of economic development and good neighbourly relations. The Council has therefore approved a programme to promote such co-operation. That programme will also contribute to the objectives of the Stability Pact.' See also U. Sedelmeier and H. Wallace, 'Eastern Enlargement: Strategy or Second Thoughts?' in H. Wallace and W. Wallace, eds., Policy Making in the European Union (Oxford, Oxford University Press 2000) at p. 443. See also Maresceau, 'Pre-accession', op. cit. Chapter 1, n. 24 at pp. 17–18.

[4] 'The European Council also confirms the need to make sound preparation for enlargement on the basis of the criteria established in Copenhagen and in the context of the pre-accession strategy defined in Essen for the CEE; that strategy will have to be intensified in order to create the conditions for the gradual, harmonious integration of those States, particularly through the development of the market economy, the adjustment of their administrative structures and the creation of a stable economic and monetary environment.'

enlargements, to take in Greece, Portugal and Spain. The criteria of good neighbourly relations and of governmental capacity were not apparent in the earlier enlargements. The matter of administrative and judicial capacity is of crucial importance to the ability of the new Member States to apply the agri-food and environment *acquis* as much as to the evolution of these chapters of the *acquis communautaire*.

The essential elements of these criteria have progressively been worked out in greater detail and even re-stated with each application for membership in the Commission's reports and opinions on the applicants, including its final (favourable) Opinion under Article 49 TEU, as well as by the European Council. Nevertheless, the criteria that apply to accession to the Union are generally referred to as the Copenhagen criteria and in today's pre-accession process are no longer thought of as conditions addressed to the CEECs alone but to any country aspiring to accede.

Thus, the Copenhagen criteria are the result as much of the Union's own deepening and widening as the specific character of the acceding country and its relationship with the Union. While certain of the Copenhagen conditions must be referred to as the consolidation of the conditions of previous enlargements, the Copenhagen criteria have certainly been supplemented in entirely new ways, stated in precise terms and even supplemented by the Council during the process of the fifth enlargement. Today, the Copenhagen criteria are the membership conditions that determine eligibility for membership of the Union. This is not to say that they are exhaustive. The Copenhagen criteria have grown in detail, they have been supplemented, they act as a lens through which to evaluate the specific circumstances and needs/obligations of the (aspiring) applicant country concerned. To properly understand their substantive content, it is necessary to briefly trace their evolution.

### 1.2 *Absorption capacity: the increasing importance of the fourth Copenhagen criteria*

The fourth Copenhagen criteria expressly links the Union's widening agenda with its deepening agenda. No enlargement has been easy and enlargements have always presented a challenge to the Union in terms of the cohesion and vitality of the Union, its institutional balance of and decision-making in the Union, democratic representation and decision-making, the integrity of the *acquis* and its enforcement, the development of core policy fields.[5] The fourth Copenhagen criterion is often given more cursory attention that the other three when reference is made to the Copenhagen criteria in the context of the pre-accession strategy. The European Commission's 1992 report *Europe and the Challenge of Enlargement* highlighted this aspect of enlargement preparations before the Copenhagen criteria existed.[6] In 1994, at the Essen European Council, the German Presidency insisted that the institutional conditions for the proper functioning of the Union must be created at the 1996 Intergovernmental Conference, even before the launch of accession negotiations.

In practice however, the fourth criteria can be seen more as a pre-condition to the conclusion of accession negotiations rather than the opening of accession negotiations. The fourth Copenhagen criteria comes to the fore increasingly nowadays – especially in the light of the outcomes of the French and Dutch referendums on the Constitutional Treaty, which have been signalled as votes against further enlargements and as fears over the loss of national identity in particular, although not against further European integration as such.[7] German[8] rumours that it would not ratify the sixth Accession Treaty for national reasons

[5] Preston, op. cit. Chapter 1, n. 24, questions whether the classical method of enlargement, in which the receiving Member States collectively external their internal problems, can continue pp. 230–231. He notes that the Union traditionally: creates new policy instruments to overlay existing ones rather than undertake necessary fundamental reforms of existing inadequacies of instruments. The Member States promise to make a more fundamental review after enlargement and this results in the 'incrementalisation of the classical method'.

[6] *Bull. EC* Supp. 3/92 at 12.

[7] See the Eurobarometre Flash survey, 'Le "non" à la Constitution n'est pas un "non" à l'Europe', 15 June 2005, to be found at http://europa.eu.int/comm/public_opinion/index_fr.htm subsequent to the negative referendums in the Netherlands and France provides some keys to understanding the French and Dutch votes. These were not votes against membership of the Union. The support in France for membership of the EU still amounts to 88% of the population and in the Netherlands it stands at 82% of the population. Moreover, among the 'no' votes, 83% of the population in France and 78% of the population in the Netherlands remain supporters of their EU membership. In the same Flash the reasons for the negative votes are outlined and were motivated by dissatisfaction with socio-economic concerns and the actual results achieved by the EU in the case of the French. For the Dutch the reasons were primarily the lack of information and fears over the loss of national sovereignty.

[8] In the context of the election contest in Germany, on 26 May 2005, Germany's Christian Democrats announced that if the French voted 'No' [concerning the Constitutional Treaty'] then the Bulgaria and Romania accession would have to be put off, see www.euractiv.com visited on 29 May 2005. The Accession Treaty however will go ahead as planned, having already been signed and undergoing ratification now, see the

underlined 'new' preoccupations with the fourth Copenhagen criteria. France's President Chirac had called for the enlargement schedule to be revisited as late as 17 June 2005 – after signature of the sixth accession Treaty – in the fresh light of the negative French vote on the EU Constitutional Treaty: 'In this new situation, can the Union continue to expand without us having the institutions capable of making this enlarged union work efficiently?'[9] This is an additional source of uncertainty – see Chapter 1.

Already in 1962, concerning the opening of negotiations with the UK and Denmark, the Commission was emphatic on the need for incomers to adhere to the objectives of the Community and institutional provisions as well as the need to accede to all three Communities (that is, including the ECSC and EURATOM) and the institutional provisions. The attitude of the six receiving Member States and the Commission in the first negotiations was to:

> preserve the Community's integrity at all costs and in particular to maintain the balance established by the Treaty between the several elements of the economic Union and between one Member State and another [...] the Community could never agree to schemes that might, by means of protocols or otherwise, introduce exceptions to the Treaty's rules which would be permanent or on so large a scale as to make the application of these rules an exception in itself. By thus setting the limits within which negotiations may proceed, the Community is making sure that its vital interests are respected.[10]

The Commission highlighted the difficulties and risks as well as the potential advantages of the accession of new members again in 1967 concerning the first enlargement.[11] Apart from the internal jostling between the internal legislative organs of the Community, setting their political and legislative competences and boundaries, in the Sixties too the Member States were experiencing difficulties in terms of the decision-making as well as in terms of their visions of their collective

---

Commission: enlargement schedule will remain on track, www.euractiv.com visited on 27 May 2005.

[9] See 'Chirac proposes emergency summit on the pace of enlargement' www.euractiv.com visited on 17 June 2005.

[10] See *The First Stage of the Common Market*, op. cit. Chapter 1, n. 8.

[11] See the *Commission Opinion on the applications for membership received from the United Kingdom, Ireland, Denmark and Norway*, COM(67) 750, 29 September 1967.

identity.[12] Indeed, this was de Gaulle's declared motivation behind his initial rebuff of the United Kingdom's initial overtures for accession in 1963.[13] Not long after, the Member States agreed the 'infamous' Luxembourg Compromise of 28–30 January 1966,[14] which meant that the Member States sought consensus in all voting and in turn served to progressively delay and stall decision-making in the then EEC and would not be done away with properly until the Single European Act of 1986. The *Second General Report on the Activities of the Communities* was already concentrating on the need to improve and strengthen the institutional machinery.

Institutional and decision-making reforms have never been easy for many reasons, as much logistical as political. Thus, the matter of the Union's own state of readiness to enlarge has been a major preoccupation even before the time of the first application to accede. The pros and cons of enlarging in terms of the necessary institutional reforms and compromises that necessarily have had to be made by the receiving Community and now the Union, have always proved tricky.[15] Enlargement from six to the nine members with the first enlargement involved a 'numerical' change in that the only changes made reflected the new Member States in the institutions of the newly enlarged Union. The changes to the Treaties by virtue of the Accession Treaty of 1972 were done by means of 'adjustments'. A more creative approach was required in the second and third enlargements,[16] which would double the number of participating Member States compared to the original six Member States, in order to reflect the consequent shift in the balance of power in terms of population size and other political considerations as well as to enable the Community to operate properly. For example, as a result of the Accession Treaties for the

[12] See J.L. Torreblanca, 'The Enlargement acquis and external strategy: a prelude to deliberative foreign policy?', CPA ESTUDIOS, 4/2003, at p. 10, www.uned.es/depa/estudios.html at p. 10.

[13] See J.L Torreblanca, ibid. at p. 9.

[14] See W. Nicoll, 'The Luxembourg Compromise', 23 *Journal of Common Market Studies* 1984, pp. 35–43.

[15] See Commission Opinion of 29 September 1967, op. cit. n. 11. See also, See Commission Opinion 'The Applications for Membership from the United Kingdom, Ireland, Denmark and Norway of 1 October 1969', *Bull. EC.* Supp. 9/10, 1969 at pp. 31–43. See also Commission Opinion 'on Greek application for membership', COM(76) 30, 29 January 1976 at p. 9. See also *Bull. EC* 2/76.

[16] See also *Commission Communication Transitional period and the institutional implications of enlargement*, COM(78) 190, 24 April 1978, *Bull. EC*, Supp. 2/78.

accessions of Greece, Spain and Portugal, the Southern Member States formed a blocking minority in qualified majority voting in Council, which had not previously been the case.

The fifth enlargement, however, called for institutional responses of 'unprecedented sophistication' due to the unprecedented number of states and the fact that the Union has been suffering a 'crisis of legitimacy'.[17] In terms of the Union's growth in all respects and most relevantly in political, economic and legal terms, the context of the first four enlargements compares dramatically with the context of the fifth enlargement. The fifth enlargement has been the biggest and most difficult in terms of the size of the incoming countries and their difference from the fifteen Member States. The fifth and sixth Accession Treaties themselves underlines the question marks overhanging the preparedness of the Union itself to enlarge. The fact that full-participation in the CAP, Schengen and EMU has been staggered over time begs some reflection on whether enlargement has become a political imperative that has prevailed over and in spite of the fourth Copenhagen criteria.

At the same time, however, the fact that such safeguard clauses exist in an accession treaty begs certain questions. If the Fifteen were not willing to trust the long term capabilities and willingness of the twelve new Member States, was the Union truly ready to enlarge? And if a new Member State is open to safeguard measures in respect of a breach of its pre-accession commitments while another (fifteen) Member State that has infringed its obligations is not subject to safeguard measures, would those measures prove discriminatory and untenable on the basis of the Treaties?

Previous attempts at treaty revision, notably the Nice Treaty, failed to reform the institutions and their decision-making capacity sufficiently in preparation for enlargement. The Union's capacity to absorb new countries while maintaining the momentum of European integration was only touched on in the Convention on the Future of the

---

[17] For a full background to these failures and consideration of the outstanding issues to be resolved see B. de Witte 'The Impact of Enlargement on the Constitution of the European Union' in M. Cremona, ed., *The Enlargement of the European Union*, op. cit. Chapter 1, n. 24 at pp. 211–227 and on the inadequacies of the Nice Treaty at 250–251. See also N. Walker 'Constitutionalising Enlargement, Enlarging Constitutionalism', 8 *European Law Journal* (2003) pp. 365–385. See also F. Cameron, 'The European Union and the Challenge of Enlargement' in Maresceau, ed., *Enlarging of the European Union*, op. cit. Chapter 1, n. 24 at pp. 241–251.

Union while the pre-accession strategy went ahead with preparing the fifth and sixth enlargements. In the meantime however, the Accession Treaties had to be read in conjunction with the Protocol on Enlargement attached to the Nice Treaty, which implemented the Nice Protocol and also revises the weightings of the countries' votes – the Nice Treaty was based on the hypothesis of twenty-seven Member States[18] whereas the fifth Accession Treaty has only extended the Union to twenty-five. So the Nice Treaty amendments that entered into force on 1 January 2004 were amended in turn by the provisions of the Act of Accession as of 1 May 2004.[19] The permanent changes to the European Parliament, the Council,[20] the Court of Justice, the Economic and Social Committee, the Scientific and Technical Committee under the Euratom Treaty and the European Central Bank were set out there.[21] The Union had only made some inroads into tackling the reforms required for it to function in the longer term.[22]

However, revision of institutional and decision-making provisions after enlargement failed successively to go far enough. The Constitutional Treaty would have introduced a new institutional architecture.[23]

[18] Including Bulgaria and Romania, which are now set for accession in 2007.

[19] The provisions that will enter into force on the day of accession concerning institutions, decision-making and the applicability of acts of the institutions can be found in Parts Two and Four of the Act of Accession entitled 'Adjustments to the Treaties' and 'Temporary Provisions' respectively.

[20] As of 1 November 2004, under Art. 12 Act of Accession, the new weightings of votes for qualified majority decision-making apply. The difference between the transitional arrangement and the permanent provision is that qualified majority percentage of the total vote is higher in the permanent provision (72.27%) than in the transitional arrangement (70.97). However, the percentage of the total vote is lower than the 74.78 % foreseen in the Protocol on Enlargement annexed to the Treaty on European Union, which had been introduced by the December 2000 Nice European Council. Thus, the Accession Treaty is more favourable to qualified majority voting than the Protocol on Enlargement because it will be easier for coalitions of Member States to reach 72.27% of the total vote than to meet 74.78%.

[21] Arts 11–17 Act of Accession, fifth Accession Treaty. The temporary provisions contain transitional measures concerning seats in the European Parliament and also votes in Council. Arts. 25 and 26 Act of Accession.

[22] See H. Wallace, *Adapting to Enlargement of the European Union: Institutional Practice since May 2004*, TEPSA Conference Paper, 16 November 2007.

[23] Arts. 19–20 thereof. See P. Craig, 'The Treaty of Lisbon: Process, architecture and substance', (2008) *CML Rev.*, pp. 137–166. See also M. Dougan, 'The Treaty of Lisbon 2007: Winning Minds, Not Hearts', 2008 *CML* Rev., pp. 617-703. See A. Ott, 'The European Union, its Constitution and institutional future' in N. Neuwahl, ed., *European Union Enlargement: Law and Socio-Economic Changes* (Montréal, Editions Thémis 2004) pp. 237–254. See P. Van Elsuwege and A. Vermeersch, op. cit. Chapter 1, n. 91. According to the Nice Protocol, the Council must decide the final

Already since the accessions of Bulgaria and Romania, the Commission has functioned on a rotating basis. The Treaty of Lisbon's entry into force in 2009 does extend qualified majority voting to make decision-making more efficient. However, the new method of calculating the qualified majority will not become operational until 2014: representing the dual legitimacy of the Union, that of the Member States and people, qualified decisions will be taken by 55% of the Member States and 65% of the Union's population.

Moreover, the fourth Copenhagen criterion requires that the Union also maintains the momentum of European integration. In the run up to the fifth enlargement the fourth Copenhagen criterion seemed more of a declaration of intent rather than a truly indispensable prerequisite to enlargement. This calls into question the Union's readiness itself to enlarge as prescribed by the 1993 Copenhagen European Council. As Pernice puts it, 'enlargement of the European Union without substantial changes in its institutional settlement would come close to suicide for the European Union'.[24] To his mind, the entry into force of the Constitutional Treaty in November 2006 was crucial in a way that past treaty revisions have never been.

The perspective of Turkey becoming a Member State will of course accentuate again the uncertainties facing the Union. In its Staff Working Document *Issues Arising From Turkey's Membership Perspective*,[25] the Commission highlights the effects of Turkey's integration into the Union. The issues raised are central to the capacity of the Union to absorb new members – the fourth Copenhagen criteria. It is emphasised that the 'considerations in the present paper do not constitute additional criteria or conditions to be fulfilled'[26] by Turkey but it is

arrangements based on the principles that all Member States must be treated on a strictly equal footing as regards determination of the sequence of, and the time spent by, their nationals as members of the Commission. Each successive College should be composed so as to reflect satisfactorily the demographic and geographical range of all Member States.

[24] See I. Pernice, 'Institutional Settlements for an Enlarged EU' in G.A. Bermann and K. Pistor, eds., *Law and Governance in an Enlarged European Union: essays in European Law* (Oxford and Portland, Hart Publishing 2004) pp. 3–36 at p. 32. In the same contribution Pernice advocates even more ambitious reforms than would have come into force with the Constitution, see p. 34.

[25] SEC (2004) 1202, 6 October 2004.

[26] Ibid. at p. 1.

also clear that it is too early to reliably predict the problems likely to arise during the negotiations.

Not least among the uncertainties is the possibility of earlier accessions of countries in the Western Balkans, further EU policy development, the special arrangements made for Turkey (including transitional arrangements) and the fact that the current financial perspective will change. The ability of the Union to go on deepening integration among the Member States and even to continue with what has already been achieved is brought into question. With every new candidate, enlargement become less a question of the ability of a candidate to meet the membership conditions set down by the Union and more one of the fourth Copenhagen criteria: the capacity of the Union to absorb new members. In other words, how the Union functions and how it sees itself as much as its future vision of an enlarging Union. At stake is the effectiveness of the Union's stability and security ambitions in the wider European continent.

The fact that Turkey, in the event of its accession to the Union, may find itself outside of the freedom of movement of workers, the CAP or regional policy instruments[27] for very long transitional periods and subject to 'permanent safeguard measures' would not only add to the overall complexity in the *acquis*: it necessarily implies a shift in what is understood by the notions of solidarity among Member States and the reciprocal rights and obligations of Member States.

With the failure of the Constitutional Treaty, the need for a renewed consensus[28] among the Member States becomes clear. At the request of the June 2006 Brussels European Council,[29] in August 2006 the Commission issued a Communication addressing the future challenges for future enlargements, in which it identifies certain elements of evaluating the Union's capacity to absorb new members at a given moment or in a given period, without jeopardising the political and policy objectives established by the Treaties.[30] For EU integration to keep up its momentum, institutional changes are necessary, as well as budgetary adjustments revised. Also, the common policies must be pursued even with the transitional arrangements and derogations or safeguard

[27] See Presidency Conclusions, 17 December 2004, op. cit. Introduction, n. 43.

[28] Agreed at the December 2006 European Council.

[29] See Presidency Conclusion, 15/16 June 2006.

[30] Commission Communication *Enlargement strategy 2006–2007: challenges and integration capacity*, COM(2006) 649, 8 November 2006.

clauses. The Commission specifically highlights the need to assess the impact of enlargement on, in particular, the CAP, on cohesion policy, on energy policy and common foreign and security policy (CFSP).

As for the fulfilment of rigorous conditions by the candidates, this is more akin to the first three Copenhagen criteria than an element of the fourth Copenhagen criteria. A final element is to ensure better communication of the democratic legitimacy of the pre-accession process in order to prepare citizens for future enlargements and gain their support, particularly by communicating the advantages of enlargement. In response to the Commission's report, Parliament stressed that any failure to ensure that the EU's integration capacity matches its enlargement agenda, would weaken the Union internally and externally and reduce the benefits of increased membership for all its members, and that this effect would not be compensated by increased external size.[31]

It is not surprising that the European Parliament and the Committee of the Regions[32] found the Commission's document inadequate. It fails to provide details of the current negotiations from the integration capacity point of view, nor does it state the principles that ought to underpin such a definition. Still today, the annual strategy reports of the Commission concentrate avoid any detailed evaluation of the Union's absorption capacity and concentrate on the progress of the (potential) candidates, although the 2007 strategy dedicated a page to ensuring public support for enlargement.[33]

While the Member States can be said to have muddled along to a certain extent in the past without making the necessary agreements on time, making limited headway in agreeing institutional or budgetary reforms, this has not prevented the enlargements from going ahead. The Union has grown and the political climate has changed, and the pre-condition of the readiness of the EU can be expected to take a more prominent role in the rationale underlying future accession negotiations. This is the case especially as regards Turkey but also as regards the countries of the Western Balkans.

[31] See European Parliament resolution on the Commission's communication on the enlargement strategy and main challenges 2006–07, *Bulletin EU* 12-2006 at 1.25.2.

[32] *OJ* 2007 C 197/7.

[33] See Commission *Enlargement Strategy and Main Challenges 2006–2007*, COM(2007) 663, 6 November 2007.

The Member States failed to undertake sufficient reforms in advance of the fifth enlargement and the possibility of reform remains open still today. The receiving countries do not have the same incentive to makes reform nor are they subject to any threat of censure or legal redress for failing to meet the fourth Copenhagen criteria. The fulfilment of the fourth criteria by the Member States (and Council) is evaluated and undertaken by they themselves, so the carrot of accession is no longer an incentive in itself. The Commission's Directorate-General for Enlargement, responsible for the programming, monitoring and implementing the pre-accession strategy in the candidate countries, does not have the same tools at its disposal for programming, monitoring and evaluating the progress of the receiving Member States in meeting their pre-accession conditionality.

## 2. The political criteria and good neighbourly relations

While this book focuses on agri-food and environment *acquis*, it is relevant to briefly mention the prerequisite that accession negotiations will only be opened once certain political prerequisites are satisfied.

The political condition that an acceding country must commit to the political objectives of the Union has always been non-negotiable in accession negotiations. In the first round of negotiations that failed in 1961[34] the candidates accepted the political objectives of the Community from the outset of negotiations – at this stage in the Union's enlargement practice, the Commission envisaged giving its Opinion only as the negotiations proceeded and in the light of their outcome. The Commission was careful to exclude the possibility of accession unless the candidate were to 'show that it is in a position to accept without restriction the political aims of the Community as these appear from the Preambles to the Treaties.'[35]

The Commission's favourable Opinion[36] on the British, Irish and Danish applications, which introduced the first Accession Treaty,

[34] See *The first report on the Common Market*, op. cit. Chapter 1, n. 8 at paras. 80 and 81.

[35] See Commission Opinion op. cit. n. 15 at para. 6.

[36] Commission *Opinion of 19 January 1972 on the applications for accession to the European Communities by the Kingdom of Denmark, Ireland, the Kingdom of Norway and the United Kingdom of Great Britain and Northern Ireland, OJ* 1972 L 73/3. The preamble reads, in part: 'Whereas in joining the Communities the applicant States

insisted on the incomers' acceptance 'without reserve' of the political objectives of the Communities and the essential nature of the legal system set up by the Treaties. The same wording has introduced the Accession Treaties with Greece and has since appeared in subsequent accession treaties. Moreover, the European Court of Justice (ECJ) made clear in it its decision of 29 May 1974 that the Act of Accession has the essential object of extending the entirety of Community law in force upon the date of accession to the new Member States.[37] Also, no provision of an accession treaty, according to the Court, could be interpreted as validating measures in contradiction of the Treaties, no matter their form. Article 49 EU cannot be interpreted as allowing changes to the *acquis* as would weaken – or go in the direction of weakening, the Communities.[38]

However, it is also relevant here that a number of the incomers of the first four enlargements were able to negotiate, in their capacity as Member States, opt-outs from participating in key fields of EU activity that were elaborated after their accession, namely Schengen and EMU. Within a few years of the existence of the Community, its institutions were already elaborating the political conditions of membership in preparation for the very first accession negotiations. The European Commission worked along the same lines for the political criteria. The 1962 Birkelbach Report,[39] insisted that the rule of law and respect for human rights featured among the political conditions:

---

accept without reserve the Treaties and their political objectives, all decisions taken since their entry into force, and the action that has been agreed in respect of the development and reinforcement of the Communities; Whereas it is an essential feature of the legal system set up by the Treaties establishing the Communities that certain of their provisions and certain acts of the Community institutions are directly applicable, that Community law takes precedence over any national provisions conflicting with it, and that procedures exist for ensuring the uniform interpretation of this law; And whereas, accession to the Communities entails recognition of the binding force of these rules, observance of which is indispensable to guarantee the effectiveness and unity of Community law'.

[37] Judgment of 29 May 1974 in Case 185–73, *Hauptzollamt Bielefeld / König*, [1974] ECR. 607. On the interpretation of Art. 237 EEC Treaty (now Art. 49 EU), including this case, see I. Jalles, *Implications juridico-constitutionelles de l'adhésion aux Communautés européennes; le case de Portugal* (Bruxelles, Bruylant 1981), at pp. 46–50.

[38] See I. Jalles, ibid., at p. 49, referring to G. Olmi 'L'impact de l'élargissement sur les institution et le droit des Communautés européennes' in A Community of Twelve? The Impact of Further Enlargement on the European Communities (College of Europe, Semaine de Bruges 1978) p. 76.

[39] Rapport de la Commission politique de l'Assamblée Parlamentaire Européenne sur les aspects politiques et institutionnels (15 January 1962), Document 122 (Archives

> Les Etats dont les gouvernements n'ont pas de légitimation démocratique et dont les peuples ne participent aux décisions du gouvernement ni directement par des réprésentants élus librement, ne peuvent prétendre être admis dans le circle des peuples qui forment les Communautées européennes.

The European Commission also demonstrated such an interpretation of the political conditions to be met by aspiring Members. In its Opinion sent to Council on 1 October 1969 on the Danish, Irish and UK applications,[40] at paragraph 7, it stated that:

> On the plane of principles, the accession of States whose traditions of political equilibrium and democracy are as old-established and deep-seated as are those of the candidate countries would be of great value to the Community, both as regards its internal development and the exercise of increased responsibilities in international life.

The Birkelbach Report has had a strong impact on the Commission's approach to working out the political criteria that it has applied in all enlargements. The European Parliament – still then an assembly – and Commission concurred actively on this,[41] stressing that the Community and its Member States are based on parliamentary democracy and respect for human rights and public freedoms and that only those European countries having regimes, institutions, ideals and political goals comparable to those of the Member States could conclude association agreements that might allow for their accession to the Union.[42]

---

of the European Communities, Janvier 1962, 07.515:32;X3.075.15). See in particular para. 25, at p. 4.

[40] See Commission Opinion of 1 October 1969, op. cit. n. 15, p. 25 at para. 36. It reads: 'The countries of southern Europe, which are at a stage of economic development that rules out any idea of immediate membership of the Community, should be able to establish with an enlarged Community preferential relations so conceived that their development would benefit. Such relations could not take the form of association proper except *in the case of those countries whose institutions and regimes are comparable to those of the founder states.* [emphasis added]'

[41] Referring to various previous reports and resolutions expressing the same views, the EP stated that, 'Seul le dernier type d'association [soit, les accords d'association avec un pays européen] peut ouvrir la voie à l'adhésion à part entière à la Communauté. C'est pourquoi il est entouré de certaines conditions économiques et politiques précises', Rapport fait au nom de la commission des relations économiques extérieures sur les consequences de l'élargissement de la Communauté européenne sur les relations avec les pays du bassin mediterranéen, Parlement Européen, *Documents de Séance* (1972–1973) PE 29.993, para. 13 at p. 13.

[42] See Resolution 10 of the Resolution of the European Parliament contained in *Documents de Séance du Parlement Européen*, 1972–1973, Document 302/72, 28 February 1973.

However, the political criterion was properly tested for the first time with the accession application of Greece and then again by the applications of Spain and Portugal, due to their recent pasts under dictatorships. As already noted, the goal of enlargement of the Communities as a means to help preserve and strengthen peace and liberty on Europe has, since the Greek enlargement, been stated expressly in all of the European Commission's Opinion's introducing accession Treaties since the Accession Treaty Greece. The April 1978 Copenhagen European Council then adopted a Declaration on democracy to the effect that 'respect for and maintenance of representative democracy and human rights in each Member State are essential elements of membership.'[43] Thereafter, the Commission would evaluate an application for membership accordingly in its opinions on an application for membership. The wording of the subsequent Opinions introducing the Accession Treaties specifically state that the principles of pluralist democracy and respect for human rights form part of the common heritage of the Peoples of the Member States and are therefore essential elements of membership.[44] Also in the statutes of the European Bank for Reconstruction and Development (EBRD) 31 May 1990,[45] adopted before the Copenhagen criteria, two conditions of eligibility for financing were set out; transition to a market economy and principles of a pluralist democracy.[46]

---

[43] *Bull. EC* 3/1978 pp. 5–6.

[44] Commission Opinion of 19 January 1972, op. cit. n. 36. Commission Opinion of 23 May 1979 on the application for accession to the European Communities by the Hellenic Republic, *OJ* 1979 L 291/3. Commission Opinion of 31 May 1985 concerning the applications for accession to the European communities by the Kingdom of Spain and the Portuguese Republic, *OJ* 1985 L 302/3. Commission Opinion of 19 April 1994 on the applications for accession to the European Union by the Republic of Austria, the Kingdom of Sweden, the Republic of Finland and the Kingdom of Norway, OJ 1994 C 241/3.

[45] See J.C. Gautron, 'La problematic politique des relations entre la communauté européenne et l'europe de l'est' in S. Milacic, ed., *L'integration européenne et la révolution de l'europe de l'est*, op. cit. Chapter 1, n. 24 at pp. 124–126.

[46] The first sentence of the Agreement Establishing the European Bank for Reconstruction and Development reads: 'Committed to the fundamental principles of multiparty democracy, the rule of law, respect for human rights and market economics' while the first article reads 'Purpose. In contributing to economic progress and reconstruction, the purpose of the Bank shall be to foster the transition towards open market-oriented economies and to promote private and entrepreneurial initiative in the central and eastern European countries committed to and applying the principles of multiparty democracy, pluralism and market economics.'

As of the fifth enlargement, the Commission restates word for word the first three Copenhagen criteria (political, legal and economic) as applicable to the incoming ten countries in its Opinion in the fifth Accession Treaty. *Agenda 2000* addressed the content of the Copenhagen criteria:[47] the Commission found that all of the candidates except Slovakia[48] met the political criterion. In the country opinions accompanying *Agenda 2000* the Commission looked beyond a formal description of the political institutions in the country. It was concerned with: the conduct of free and fair elections; whether the party in Opposition played a normal part in the operation of the institutions; the stability of institutions in order to enable public authorities to function properly and democracy to be consolidated and guaranteeing the rule of law and human rights.

When endorsing *Agenda 2000* and opening the first round of accession negotiations in December 1997, the Luxembourg European Council stated:[49]

> Compliance with the Copenhagen political criteria is a prerequisite for the opening of any accession negotiations. Economic criteria and the ability to fulfil the obligations arising from membership have been and must be assessed in a forward-looking, dynamic way.

Long after the adoption of the Copenhagen criteria, the Treaties of Amsterdam and Lisbon specified the political values, including legal principles, on which the Union is founded and thus codifying the unwritten constitutional practice common to all Member States.[50] Also today, Article 8 TEU provides that the Union develop special relations with its neighbours, aiming for prosperity and good neighbourliness based on those same values. In practical terms, the nitty-gritty of the Copenhagen criteria is worked out separately for each country in the Accession Partnerships,[51] which guide the overall accession process and act as bench marks by which the candidate and the

---

[47] Commission Communication *Agenda 2000: for a stronger and wider Union*, COM(1997) 2000 of 15 July 1997, Part 2 at pp 42–43. The country reports also treat the political criteria of course.

[48] *Agenda 2000*, ibid. at p. 45.

[49] See Presidency Conclusion 24.

[50] See Art. 2 TEU, ex-Art. 6(1) EU. See Chapter 1, n. 24 at p. 93.

[51] See further at Chapter 3 at 2.

Commission/Council/Parliament may gauge their progress in meeting the Copenhagen criteria.

While the Commission identified weaknesses in the functioning of the judicial system and fight against corruption, it did not consider this as an impediment to recommending that the Council open accession negotiations. In its 1998 report[52] the Commission identified a variety of weaknesses which did not amount to impediments to the opening of accession negotiations – see Table 1.

Table 1. Non-impediments to the opening of accession negotiations with the applicant countries of the fifth and sixth enlargements

- inherent weakness in the judiciary from the training of judges through to the need for procedural reforms;
- a lack of 'determination' to confront corruption and root it out;
- the need for strengthening the independence of radio and television;
- for Romania specifically, the need to improve the protection of 100,000 children kept in orphanages;
- the need for citizenship laws in Estonia to allow stateless children to become citizens;
- the need for improvement in the right of the Roma in Hungary, Slovakia, Bulgaria, the Czech Republic and Romania;
- the need for better rights for the Hungarian minorities in Slovakia and Romania.

Source: *1998 Composite Paper of the European Commission*, at pp. 3–4.

Bulgaria and Romania continued to fulfil the Copenhagen political criteria[53] but they had still to push on with reforming the judiciary, the fight against organised crime, anti-corruption efforts and discrimination against the Roma. Each had their own specific problems.[54] The Copenhagen political criteria include the respect for and protection of minorities as a political prerequisite but these instances of lacks in the respect for and protection of minorities were not considered

[52] 1998 Composite Paper of the European Commission, *Reports on the Progress towards accession by each of the candidate countries*, at pp. 3–4.

[53] Commission *Communication Strategy Paper of the European Commission on progress in the enlargement process*, COM(2004) 657, 6 October 2004 at p. 3.

[54] Bulgaria had to address libel and defamation by journalists, the trafficking of human beings and prison conditions, the placement of mentally disabled people or inadequacies in child welfare. Romania had to improve policy making, the management of court cases and judicial judgements, and introduce standards for child protection services, as well as trafficking in human beings and prison overcrowding.

an impediment to opening accession negotiations[55] with the twelve countries of the fifth and sixth enlargement waves.

For Croatia, accession negotiations could begin[56] because it could demonstrate stable democratic institutions, including that the 2000 and 2003 elections were free and fair and that the opposition plays a normal part in the operation of the institutions. There were no major problems over assuring the rule of law and respect for fundamental rights. However, it still had to make considerable improvements in protecting minorities' rights, particularly the Serb minority. The judicial system and corruption were also singled out for attention. While co-operation with the ICTY had improved, delivery of indicted war criminals to the ICTY in The Hague was still a bone of contention. Maritime border disputes were also highlighted for action.

### 2.1 *Increasingly precise political preconditions*

On the theme of actual candidates for the moment, Turkey and the countries of the Western Balkans are facing increasingly precise political conditionality both in advance of the opening of accession negotiations and during the negotiations themselves. These preconditions must be met for formal accession negotiations to begin.[57] These conditions are outlined neatly in the Annex to Council Conclusions of 29 April 1997 on the principles of conditionality governing the development of the European Union's relations with certain countries of

[55] Hoffmeister, op. cit. Chapter 1, n. 24, refers to the minimum standards of Art. 27 of the International Covenant on Civil and Political Rights (1996) and the fact that Arts. 31 and 32 of the OSCE Copenhagen Declaration of 1990 specifies the sort of rights that a minority should enjoy in a candidate country and since OSCE states that canted to conclude a Partnership Agreement with the EC had to accept these provisions as binding, that same standards must apply a fortiori for all candidate countries. Hoffmeister also refers to the Council of Europe Framework Convention for the Protection of National Minorities, 1995.

[56] See *Commission Opinion on Croatia's Application for Membership of the European Union*, COM(2004) 247, undated and not published in the *Official Journal.*

[57] Already in 1997, Turkey was refused accession negotiations alongside the CEECs, Malta and Cyprus because of anomalies in the functioning of public authorities, persistent human rights violations and major shortcomings in the treatment of minorities. The lack of civilian control over the army was a cause for concern. See *Agenda 2000*, op. cit. n. 47, Part 2 at pp. 67–68. The means of taking relations with Turkey forward were dealt with separately in order to take the relationship beyond the customs union in the light of the decision of the April 1997 Association Council. The Commission's Communication on how to proceed was issued the same day as *Agenda 2000*. See Commission Communication on the further development of relations with Turkey, COM(97) 394, 15 July 1997, *Bull. EU* 7–8/1997, at 1.4.110.

South East Europe.[58] For the countries of the Western Balkans, certain of the political preconditions must be met before the Stabilisation and Association Agreement can be signed – contractual relations were never so bound up with the pre-accession process in prior enlargements.[59] As for the political criteria of the good neighbourly relations and good neighbourliness, while it had been apparent in the Union's approach to Turkey already in 1998,[60] these criteria have truly come into their own in the case of the Western Balkans.

A full exploration of the political arm of the Copenhagen criteria is not fully relevant to the agri-food and environment *acquis*, other than to emphasise that the candidate and potential candidate countries are first concerned with these issues in order to then be able to focus on the economic and legal Copenhagen criteria. In practice, however, the aspiring countries already set about the transposition, implementation and enforcement of the *acquis*, aware of the long term challenge of such a vast approximation exercise. They also begin participating in the Community agencies and other bodies. Since the adoption of the 2006 Instrument for Pre-accession Assistance,[61] this focus becomes all the more coherent and structured, having learned much from the example of the fifth and sixth enlargements.

To be brief, the political reforms and far reaching constitutional and legislative changes require strong efforts of all of today's candidates and potential candidates. Indeed the Member States' concern is to ensure that these reforms are sustainable and that they are not reversed during the negotiations[62] or after the eventual accession. The Commission proposes to make use of the relevant tools available to it to recommend the suspension of the negotiations in a case of serious

[58] *Bull. EU* 4/1997.

[59] See Chapter 1 at 3.3.

[60] In 1998 the Commission insisted that Turkey make a constructive contribution to the settlement of all disputes with the various neighbouring countries by peaceful means in accordance with international law.

[61] See Chapter 1 at 3.3.

[62] Additional means of keeping up the pressure on Turkey during the negotiations under Article 4 of Regulation 390/2001, *OJ* 2001 L58/1. This gives the Council the power (acting by a qualified majority on a proposal from the Commission) to suspend assistance to Turkey '*an element that is essential for continuing to grant pre-accession assistance is lacking, in particular when the commitments contained in the EC-Turkey Agreements are not respected and/or progress towards fulfilment of the Copenhagen criteria is insufficient*'.

and persistent breach of the principles of liberty, democracy, respect for human rights and fundamental freedoms and the rule of law.[63]

The good neighbourly relations requirement was established first by the 1994 Essen European Council but then reiterated in Helsinki in 1999.[64] Already the Commission cited the situation in Cyprus as a reason, alongside economic and political reasons and the negative effects of the Turkey/Greece dispute, for not opening accession negotiations with Turkey back in December 1989.[65]

### 2.2 *Potential candidates: the specificity of the Stabilisation and Association Process*

Looking at the remaining potential candidates, the Copenhagen political criteria are evident in precise and comprehensive terms in the countries of the Stabilisation and Association Process. In the early Nineteen-nineties the CEECs were not subject to such a rigorously specified conditionality in terms of their eligibility for financial and technical assistance under the PHARE instrument – its political and financial conditioning was only progressively reoriented after the 1993 Copenhagen European Council Under the pre-accession strategy for the fifth and sixth enlargements, the Copenhagen political criteria were a prerequisite to the opening of accession negotiations. For the SAP countries, these criteria have been rigorously specified in general, regional and country specific terms and then prioritised according to the nature of the relationship in order to benefit from assistance, from autonomous trade preferences and in advance of the establishment of any bi-lateral contractual relations, the Stabilisation and Association Agreements.

---

[63] See *Presidency Conclusions*, op. cit. Chapter 1, n. 43. See also 'Turkey Could face permanent safeguard clause', www.EurActiv.com visited on 30 November 2004.

[64] Turkey has been keen to emphasise her pursuit of a peaceful foreign policy and in her National Plan for the Adoption of the *Acquis*. Turkey was keen to emphasise in the very first introductory paragraphs the significance of the principle of a peaceful foreign policy, how she will to continue to develop her relations with neighbouring countries on the basis of peace-seeking foreign policy and to undertake initiatives and efforts towards settlement of the bilateral problems through dialogue with Greece. See A. Sozen 'Turkey's democratisation in light of its EU candidate status; EU enlargement at a crossroads' in Inglis and Ott, eds., *Unity in Diversity*, op. cit. Chapter 1, n. 80, pp. 279–306.

[65] See Commission Communication *Opinion on Turkey's request for accession to the Community* SEC(89) 2290, 20 December 1989 at para. 11. See also, L. Maurer in Ott and Inglis, *Handbook on European Enlargement*, op. cit. Chapter 1, n. 24, at p. 113.

This tells of the level of development of the countries of the SAP. Most countries of the Western Balkans will take longer than the CEECs did to develop functioning market economies due to the conflicts of the last decade. The economic situation is still precarious in large parts of the region, although FYROM is on the way to establishing a functioning market economy. The resources required of the Union in financial and technical assistance terms are considerable but the Union recognised the necessity of providing a high level of support and deepening involvement in the region if it is to achieve a true shift from the post-crisis situation to a feasible pre-accession situation.[66]

The foundations must be in place before the negotiation of contractual relations will even be considered. The conditionality attaching to contractual relations are specific to the region as well as to each country in turn. In advance of bilateral contractual relations, the SAP countries have had to make do with limited concessions and autonomous trade preferences.[67] For the purposes of understanding the political conditionality applied in the context of the SAP, a lower level of compliance is insisted on for the start of negotiations for an Stabilisation and Association Agreement (SAA) than for the conclusion of an SAA. This paves the way for reaching a higher level of compliance with the Copenhagen criteria in order to open accession negotiations. The conclusion of an SAA becomes the first significant incentive – on the way to the ultimate incentive of accession – for compliance with the Union's pre-accession conditionality.

For FYROM, while it has an SAA in place,[68] it has not proceeded to opening accession negotiations, although this was up for consideration before Council in early 2009. The main reason for this is that there is

---

[66] See Commission Report, *The Stabilisation and Association process for South East Europe*, COM(2004) 202 of 30 March 2004, at section 1.3.

[67] In the case of Croatia, see Regulation 2007/2000 introducing exceptional trade measures for countries and territories participating in or linked to the European Union's Stabilisation and Association process, amending Regulation No 2820/98, and repealing Regulations 1763/1999 and 6/2000, *OJ* 2000 L 240/1. See also the Textiles Agreement, in force as of 1 January 2001 and the technical forum for bilateral discussions in the EU/Croatia Consultative Task Force set up January 2000. Council Decision 2001/55 on the signing and the provisional application of the Agreement on trade in textile products between the European Community and the Republic of Croatia initialled in Brussels on 8 November 2000, *OJ* 2001 L 25/1.

[68] On 17 May 2005 the Council asked the Commission to provide an opinion on FYROM's application for membership of 22 March 2004, delivered on 9 November 2005, recommending that it be formally recognised as a candidate country, which was granted on 17 December 2005.

'frequent tension and insufficient co-operation between political actors [which] has affected the normal functioning of institutions and slowed down reforms. The dispute between the government and an opposition party about a constitutional matter led to that party boycotting parliament'.[69] Its Accession Partnership highlights eight short term priorities, or benchmarks, to be reached first.[70] Moreover, FYROM signed and ratified the Bilateral Immunity Agreement with the US authorities, granting, inter alia, citizens of that country exemption from the jurisdiction of the International Criminal Court in The Hague, which flouts the EU common position on the integrity of the Rome Statute of that Court.

### 2.3 *Good neighbourly relations and good neighbourliness*

Good neighbourly relations in pre-accession conditionality did not arise in the first four enlargements. For example, Greece was not obliged to settle its differences with either Turkey or Cyprus. 'Good neighbourly relations' are established in terms of ten universally recognised principles deriving from the Charter of the United Nations of 24 October 1945, the Helsinki Final Act of 1 August 1975 and the Paris Charter for a New Europe of 21 November 1990.[71]

---

[69] See 2007 Report of the Commission on FYROM, COM(2007) 663, undated and not published in the *Official Journal*, at pp. 6 and 36.

[70] Council Decision 2008/212/EC on the principles, priorities and conditions contained in the Accession Partnership with the former Yugoslav Republic of Macedonia and repealing Decision 2006/57/EC, *OJ* 2008 *L 80/32.*

[71] The short term priorities are: Ensure proper implementation of all commitments undertaken in the Stabilisation and Association Agreement; Promote a constructive and inclusive dialogue, in particular in areas which require consensus between all political parties, in the framework of the democratic institutions; Ensure effective implementation of the law on police; Establish a sustained track record on implementation of judiciary reforms and strengthen the independence and overall capacity of the judicial system. Implement the reform of the prosecution and finalise the appointment of the Judicial Council; Establish a sustained track record on implementation of anti-corruption legislation; Ensure that recruitment and career advancement of civil servants is not subject to political interference, further develop a merit-based career system and implement fully the law on civil servants; Reduce impediments to employment creation and address in particular youth and long term unemployment; Enhance the general business environment by further improving the rule of law, strengthening the independence of regulatory and supervisory agencies, speeding up legal procedures and continuing registration of property rights.

Sovereign equality; Respect for rights inherent in sovereignty; Refraining from the threat of use of force; Inviolability of frontiers; Territorial integrity of States; Peaceful settlement of disputes; Non-interference in internal affairs; Respect for human rights and fundamental freedoms, including freedom of thought, conscience, religion

In the context of pre-accession, as noted earlier, the demand that candidates pursue good relations with their neighbouring countries takes root in the 1994 Essen European Council. Regional co-operation and good neighbourly relations were *fostered*. In the context of the fifth enlargement, the candidates concluded bilateral agreements between each other and co-operated with the fifteen Member States on a wide range of issues including fostering economic relations. The 1995 Treaties on Good Neighbourly Relations between Hungary and Slovakia or Hungary and Romania provide examples, as does the Black Sea Economic Co-operation (BSEC) which extended Romania's and Bulgaria's co-operation beyond the future EU borders to Moldova and Ukraine. The EAs Baltic States gave special attention to fostering intra-Baltic co-operation with other CEECs and countries bordering the Baltic, with a view to integrated development of the region.[72] Before *Agenda 2000* even, the Europe Agreements that followed the 1994 Essen European Council (those with the Baltic States and Slovenia) specifically mentioned the Bonn Conference on Economic Co-operation in their preambles as 'the basis for the domestic and external policies of the Parties' in the definition of their essential elements. These EAs also expressly provided that political dialogue 'shall take place within the multilateral framework',[73] reflecting the hopes instilled in the multilateral (structured) dialogue as a mechanism to advance and intensify relations throughout the region. While this component was discontinued following *Agenda 2000*, it was replaced by the European Conference, also a regional forum.

Good neighbourliness really came into its own as a deeper, regional and political conditionality in the strategy devised for the Balkans[74] in a way that distinguishes it from the comparatively weaker regional conditionality applied to the ten CEECs. The result of the complexity of the regional jigsaw that followed the break-up of the former Yugoslavia, the regional conditionality established in 1997 is further reaching and more specific when it comes to South Eastern Europe

---

or belief, equal rights and self-determination of peoples; Co-operation among states; Fulfilment in good faith of obligations under international law.

[72] EAs with Estonia (Art. 71(4)), Lativa (Art. 72(4)) and Lithuania (Art. 72(4)).

[73] See Art. 5 of the EAs with Estonia, Latvia, Lithuania, Slovenia.

[74] See Cremona, 'The Union as a global actor: roles, models and identity', 41 *CML Rev* (2004) pp. 553–573 at pp. 560–562.

as a region.[75] The Stability Pact for South Eastern Europe of 10 June 1999, adopted by the EU and the Western Balkans countries concerned together with the full force of international institutions and financial institutions in the objective of bringing about stability and growth in the region.[76] The Parties declared their solemn commitment to promoting good neighbourly relations as the first principle of the stability pact, while bilateral and multilateral agreements on good neighbourly relations between the Western Balkans countries was declared an 'essential element' of the Stability Pact. It co-ordinates the input of the relevant international organisations and financing institutions and fosters regional initiatives and institutions in the region. The Stability Pact provided for the set up of the South Eastern Europe Regional Table to carry forward the Stability Pact by acting as a clearing house for all questions of principle relating to the substance and implementation of the Stability Pact as well as a steering body in the Stability Pact process. The regional table was supported by Working Tables, which are responsible for maintaining and improving good-neighbourly relations in the region by constructively addressing and facilitating the resolution of the issues entrusted to them. The Regional Table guides the Working Tables.

Once the prospect of EU membership by the countries of the Western Balkans had been acknowledged, by the June 2000 European Council,[77] as the only means of bringing lasting peace in the region, regional co-operation became equally important in pre-accession conditionality as rapprochement with the Union. In its January 2006 Communication on the Western Balkans, the Commission reported

[75] See Commission Report *The Stabilisation and Association Process for South East Europe; First Annual Report*, COM(2002) 163, 4 April 2003.

[76] Which was adopted by Member States of the European Union, the European Commission, the Foreign Ministers of Albania, Bosnia and Herzegovina, Bulgaria, Croatia, Hungary, Romania, the Russian Federation, Slovenia, the former Yugoslav Republic of Macedonia, Turkey, the United States of America, the OSCE Chairman in Office and the Representative of the Council of Europe representing the participants in the Conference on South Eastern Europe; and the Foreign Ministers of Canada and Japan, Representatives of the United Nations, UNHCR, NATO, OECD, WEU, International Monetary Fund, the World Bank, the European Investment Bank and the European Bank for Reconstruction and Develoment, acting within their competences, representing the facilitating States, Organisations and Institutions of today's Conference, as well as the Representatives of the Royaumont process and the South Eastern European Co-operation Process.

[77] June 2000 Feira European Council and December 2000 Nice European Council.

significant progress in regional co-operation in the Western Balkans, with tangible results beyond progress towards accession.[78]

The South East European Co-operation Process (SEECP) – the Zagreb Process, named after the Zagreb Summit[79] of 24 November 2000 – provided a multilateral forum for broader regional participation in bringing about stability in the Western Balkans. It was a process that was launched on the initiative of the SEE countries themselves. This annual forum[80] was intended to discuss issues of common concern and review progress towards stability, democracy and economic recovery as well as regional co-operation and good neighbourly relations, in the objective of acceding to the EU. It is conducted in the presence of the Secretary General/High Representative for the CFSP, the Special Representative of the United Nations Secretary General, the Special Co-ordinator of the Stability Pact for South East Europe and the High Representative for Bosnia and Herzegovina. Ultimately the aim is to enhance co-operation between the South East European countries where a regional approach is required. However, the SEECP has not been designed to prepare the Western Balkans countries to work within the Union's political and institutional structures.

In the course of 2007 and 2008, the Stability Pact was phased out and transformed into this more 'regionally owned co-operation structure' under the framework of the South East Europe Co-operation Process (SEECP). This was decided upon at the 30 May 2006 meeting of the Regional Table of the Stability Pact, endorsing the Roadmap Toward a Regionally-Owned Co-operation Framework in South Eastern Europe. The 10th summit of the SEECP in May 2007 moved to establish a new Regional Co-operation Council (RCC) with a Secretariat – the Regional Co-operation Coucil (RCC) – and a Secretary General from the region.[81] The RCC took over the responsibilities of the Regional Table and the Working Tables of the Stability Pact on 27 February

[78] See Commission Communication *The Western Balkans on the road to the EU: consolidating stability and raising prosperity*, COM(2006) 27 of 27 January 2006.

[79] The Zagreb Final Declaration was signed there by the heads of state or government of European Union Member States and countries covered by the Stabilisation and Association process.

[80] See Joint Press Statement 'EU-Western Balkans Forum, Second Foreign Ministers meeting Brussels 22 November 2004,' PRES/04/318, November 2004. See also the Commission Press Release 'EU-Western Balkans Summit Thessaloniki 21 June 2003', PRES/03/163, 21 June 2003.

[81] See http://www.rcc-see.org

2008.[82] This approach is seen as a means to 'enhance local ownership in regional co-operation in South East Europe'.[83] Like the Stability Pact, ultimately the aim is to enhance co-operation between the South East European countries where a regional approach is required. Significant initiatives concern the environment *acquis*.

The Stabilisation and Association Process works from the premise that integration within the EU is only possible if future members can demonstrate that they are willing and able to interact with their neighbours as EU Member States do.[84] Specific conditions for each country are listed in terms of their behaviour towards other countries in the region. Good neighbourliness is *rigorously fostered* not only in the SAP but as a guiding principle of the bilateral SAA relationship between the EU and the associate.[85] Thus, certain additional and generally applicable political conditions are also specified for the region. In addition to the right to return for refugees and displaced persons and the readmission of any of their nationals that are illegally present in the Union, the general conditions in the regional approach require the implementation of the Dayton Peace Agreements and 'proven readiness to enter into good neighbourly and co-operative relations with [...] neighbours'.

On top of the foregoing general conditions, each country must meet its own conditions,[86] and this is recognised in the body of the preamble to that country's association agreement. None of the countries within this regional approach had a bi-lateral contractual relationship with the Union at the time of the regional approach. As is seen in Chapter Three at 3.5, EU funding to these countries is also subject to regional and country specific conditions. To be eligible for financial and technical assistance or begin negotiations, a lower level of compliance is required that for the conclusion of an association agreement. Conclusion of the agreement itself requires compliance with the 'verifiable elements' of the general political and economic conditions that are, in

---

[82] See website of the Stability Pact, *Meeting of the Regional Rable of 27 Feburary 2008*, to be found www.stabilitypact.org/rt/ last visited on 28 February 2008.

[83] See Commission Press Release IP/07/622 of 8 May 2007, *Zagreb Summit for more regional cooperation in South-East Europe*.

[84] See Commission *Report The Stabilisation and Association Process for South East Europe; First Annual Report*, COM(2002) 163, op. cit. n. 75, at p. 11.

[85] See for example Art. 3, SAA Croatia.

[86] These 'specific conditions' are listed in the same Council Conclusions of 29 April 1997, *Bull. EU* 4/1997. No specific conditions are specified for Albania.

basic terms, the Copenhagen criteria. An overview of the pre-accession strategy for South Eastern Europe is outlined in Chapter 3.

## 3. The economic, legal and administrative capacity criteria

As the December 1997 Luxembourg European Council had already made clear, the economic criteria and the ability to fulfil the obligations arising from membership have been and must be assessed in a forward-looking, dynamic way.[87]

### 3.1 *... to be assessed in a 'forward looking and dynamic way'*

The Copenhagen economic and legal criteria are more flexible than the political criterion in that accession negotiations may already begin, provided that a candidate has taken first steps in their direction and can be expected to meet the requirements in advance of their accession. There is a political dimension to these criteria. Take the example of the SAP countries, being the countries of the Western Balkans, where the need for market reform is as much a political pre-condition to the opening of negotiations for establishing contractual relations.[88] Central to the market reforms is:

- the creation of macroeconomic institutions and policies necessary to ensure a stable economic environment;
- comprehensive liberalisation of prices, trade and current payments;
- setting-up of a transparent and stable legal and regulatory framework;
- demonopolisation and privatisation of State-owned or socially-owned enterprises;
- establishment of a competitive and prudently managed banking sector.

[87] See Presidency Conclusion 24, *Bull. EU* 12–1997.

[88] Annex to Council Conclusions of 29 April 1997 on the principles of conditionality governing the development of the European Union's relations with certain countries of South East Europe, *Bull. EU* 4/1997.

Such market reforms can be measured by various indicators,[89] notably that significant barriers to market entry (establishment of new firms) and exit (bankruptcy) are absent and that economic rights and contracts are legally enforceable. These indicators prove the country's capacity to cope with competitive pressures and market forces once a member. Also important is that infrastructure and the financial climate together with education and research must be sufficiently developed, and that the role of the State in the economy should be modest and the trade integration with the Union advanced.

The use of such indicators as conditions for membership was not so readily apparent in the Commission's country opinions concerning the first three enlargements. While Austria, Finland and Sweden were not even evaluated on economic grounds because they clearly had functioning market economies, were undoubtedly competitive and participation in the EEA Agreement meant that legal arrangements of a transitional nature had been dealt with so that their accession to the Union did not even require a general transitional period.[90] In the early years, the European Parliament emphasised the need for a candidate for accession to fulfil the economic condition of being sufficiently large both structurally and in competitive terms,[91] as did the Commission.

This compared dramatically with the fifth enlargement. At the time of the applications from Austria, Finland and Sweden,[92] the applications from Cyprus, Malta and Turkey were still outstanding while a number of other countries: at that time Poland, Hungary, Czechoslovakia, Bulgaria and Romania were eager to apply. The December 1991 Maastricht European Council invited the Commission to

---

[89] See the Commission's Opinions on all applicants contained in part 3 of *Agenda 2000*, op. cit. n. 47.

[90] Austria was considered to form part of the group of member countries that were the most stable and strongest economically at the time, see Commission Opinion on *Austria's application for membership*, SEC(91) 1590, 1 August 1991, *Bull. EU*, 4/92, at 8. Sweden had pegged the Swedish Krona to the ECU in 1991 which had brought it close to the Union in monetary terms, see Commission Opinion *on Sweden's application for membership*, SEC(92) 1582, 31 July 1992 at 5–11. Finland had reached a standard of living on a par with the richest Member States, see Commission Opinion on *Finland's application for membership*, SEC(92) 2048, 4 November 1992 at 6–10.

[91] See para. 13 of the Exposé des motifs, accompanying the Resolution of the European Parliament contained in Documents du séance du Parlement Européen, 1972–1973, Document 302/72, 28 February 1973.

[92] After a negative national referendum in Switzerland, the treatment of the Swiss application was discontinued. Norway too had a negative referendum and Norway had to be written out of the fourth Accession Treaty.

examine the questions arising in those applications, always with an eye on the Union's future development too. The Commission noted that 'the question is thus posed of a Community of 20, 30 or more members, even without the new independent States of the former Soviet Union'[93] but declined to address such a possibility even in scant terms.

For the first time, in *Europe and the challenge of enlargement of 1992,*[94] the Commission highlighted the need for a functioning and competitive market economy together with an adequate legal and administrative framework in both public and private sectors. Otherwise not only could a country not be effectively integrated but membership would more likely harm that country's economy and disrupt the functioning of the Union.[95] The Commission, in the same document, recommended that negotiations begin with Austria, Finland and Sweden immediately after the ratification of the Maastricht Treaty because they required no period of preparation to adopt the Community system.[96]

As of the fifth enlargement, the candidates have had to be willing to enter into EMU and adopt Stage II EMU, requiring central bank independence, co-ordination of economic policies and respect of the Stability and Growth Pact. This obligation applies despite the fact that Member States that have acceded previously (Denmark, the United Kingdom and Sweden) do not participate However, it is important to emphasise that the need to fulfil the Maastricht convergence criteria and the Stability and Growth Pact objectives are not accession conditions to be met prior to accession.[97] To proceed to stage III EMU a Member State needs to meet the convergence criteria in order to introduce the EURO single currency and thus the new Member States were not obliged to fulfil their obligations under the EMU *acquis* completely upon accession.[98] This stage cannot be reached until after accession to the Union.

---

[93] Commission Communication Europe and the challenge of enlargement, 24 June 1992, *Bull. EU*, Suppl. 3/92 at p. 9.

[94] Ibid.

[95] Ibid. at p. 11.

[96] Ibid. at p. 18.

[97] See Dziechciarz, 'Candidate countries and economic and monetary union' in *Handbook on European Enlargement*, Chapter 1 at n. 26, at p. 710.

[98] See F. Amtenbrink, 'Economic and Monetary Policy in the Framework of EMU' in Ott and Inglis, *Handbook on European Enlargement*, op. cit. n. 24, at pp. 701–702.

After accession, Convergence Reports are prepared, every two years, by the European Commission and the European Central Bank. These are based on Article 122(2) EC, which requires the Commission and the ECB to report to the Council, at least once every two years, or at the request of a Member State with a derogation, on the progress made by the Member States in fulfilling their obligations regarding the achievement of economic and monetary union. They examine whether Member States satisfy the conditions for adopting the single currency and form the basis for the decision on whether a Member State may join the Euro zone. They are issued every two years but more frequently if an aspiring entrant requests one. They are useful to aspiring members because they provide a detailed analysis of how well the criteria have been met by all countries assessed.[99]

### 3.2 *The Copenhagen legal criteria*

That an applicant must have the capacity to take on the *acquis* and all obligations of membership was also non-negotiable in the 1972 enlargement. The Commission specified that 'accession to the Communities entails recognition of the binding force of these rules, observance of which is indispensable to guarantee the effectiveness and unity of Community law'.[100] It was referring to the *acquis communautaire*. This phraseology has followed in all Accession Treaties since.

As already seen, the acceding country accepts 'without reserve' the political objectives of the Communities and the essential nature of the legal system set up by the Treaties. Opt-outs in the form of those currently enjoyed by Denmark and the UK were not imagined at the time of their accession negotiations. These opt-outs were the result of the negotiation of later Treaties which were to go far further that the original Treaties to which they had acceded in 1973. Exceptionally, in the fourth enlargement, the incomers were already well advanced in approximation to the Internal Market *acquis* under the EEA Agreement.

---

[99] See for example the 2008 Convergence Report, COM(2008) 248 final of 7 May 2008, COM(2006) 762 of 5 December 2006. The first such report after enlargement was issued in October 2004. All convergence reports can be found at www.ecb.int/pub/convergence/html/index.en.html. *A specific Convergence Report was issued in 2006 at the request of Slovenia and Lithuania, on the strength of which Slovenia was able to adopt the Euro on 1 January 2007.*

[100] See the Commission Opinion, COM(97) 750, op. cit. n. 11.

For the purposes of the comparison with the approach taken in the fifth enlargement, there has been no relaxation of the requirement that an incoming country must meet the entire *acquis*. The close relationship between the Copenhagen criteria and the *aquis communautaire* is apparent. The third criterion obviously refers directly to the acceptance of the rights and obligations, actual and potential, of the Community system and its institutional framework as described by the Commission in its preparations for the last enlargement.[101] The Commission made clear that following the entry into force of the Maastricht Treaty, future enlargements would require the candidates to take on the *acquis* in the field of common foreign and security policy (CFSP) and fulfil the criteria for economic convergence if economic and monetary union was to be successful.

Nowadays the word '*acquis*' is also used to denote the broader European Union activities.[102] The obligation of membership extends to the application of the entirety of the *acquis* as it stands on the date of accession regardless of whether a receiving Member State does not apply the entire *acquis*. It will be interesting to see how this criterion might develop in future enlargements should the Member States of the European Union have made use of the various mechanisms for enhanced co-operation. If a majority of the Member States should decide to push ahead with legislative measures, the question arises as to whether such a flexibility measure would be considered an obligation of membership. Leading on from this question is that of whether the flexibility measures would continue to be legitimate if, after an enlargement, there would no longer be a majority of Member States participating.

How this criterion has been met in practice for the environment and the agri-food chapters of the *acquis*, is explored in Chapter 6 and 7.

### 3.3 *The Madrid criteria: administrative and judicial capacity*

As for administrative capacity, the demands of membership required in the first enlargements did not involve such a considerable body of the *acquis* as in the case of the fifth enlargement. In the case of Greece,

---

[101] See European Commission *Europe and the challenge of enlargement*, op. cit. n. 93.

[102] See C. Delcourt, 'The *Acquis Communautaire*: Has the Concept had its Day?', 38 *CML Rev.* (2001) pp. 829–870.

the Commission had not identified the problem of low standards in public administration and the civil service in its initial findings.[103] Austria, Finland and Sweden, while they had a considerable approximation exercise, were able to cope with the demands on their administrative and judicial structures relatively quickly: within five years as concerns Austria and three years as concerns Finland and Sweden. The accession of the Sweden and Finland also brought higher standards in public administration.

By comparison, the CEECs came from entirely different backgrounds. The December 1995 Madrid European Council requirement could be implied by reference to the Copenhagen criteria that the applicant have the 'ability to take on the obligations of membership, including adhering to the aims of political, economic and monetary union'. The Madrid conclusions stated simply that the applicants should 'adjust their administrative structures' which was made in the context of the broader reform and modernisation of public administrations that had to be undertaken in the transition economies that were emerging from the entirely different political, judicial and administrative structures of their Communist pasts.

It was most useful to specify this criterion. Indeed, PHARE funding was concentrated on the adoption of the *acquis* under the pre-accession strategy of 1997 (see Chapter Three), which meant in concrete terms thirty per cent of PHARE funding was allocated to capacity building of public administration as well as the judiciary, while investment projects for adoption of the *acquis* would account for the remaining seventy per cent.[104] In any case, these two guiding objectives for the pre-accession strategy devised for the fifth and sixth enlargements are interdependent. The ability to take on the obligations of membership necessarily includes the ability to correctly transpose, implement and then enforce the *acquis communautaire*. In practical terms, institution-building involved budgetary implementation, decentralisation of management of PHARE and other pre-accession funding and long-term secondment of experts from ministries of the Member States and semi-public organisations ('twinning').[105]

---

[103] See Dagtoglou, 'The Southern Enlargement of the European Community', 1984 21 *CML Rev*. 149–162.

[104] See *Agenda 2000*, op. cit. n. 47, Vol. 2 at pp. A-5.

[105] See European Commission, *Twinning News*, 13 November 2009 for example. See the Court of Auditors' criticism of over reliance on twinning, Chapter 6 at 1.2.1.

The June 2002 Seville European Council Conclusions stressed the importance of continued progress in implementation and effective application of the *acquis* generally.[106] The Council was particularly concerned to see progress before it would consider finalising as planned the accession negotiations in the December of that year. In 2002 the Commission issued action plans[107] designed to take more decisive action and enable the Commission to monitor the commitments given by the candidates in the accession negotiations. These plans covered all twelve candidate countries with which negotiations had been opened.[108] Moreover, for the first years after the fifth enlargement, the fifth Accession Treaty allocated through the Transition Facility,[109] continued support for institution building in the new Member States for 2004, 2005 and 2006 to the value of EUR 200 million, EUR 120 million and EUR 60 million respectively. For Bulgaria and Romania, the sixth Accession Treaty provided a temporary financial assistance of € 82 million (Article 31) and for the period between the date of accession and the end of 2009 a Cash-flow and Schengen Facility of EUR 239 million (in total) for Bulgaria and EUR 560 million for Romania, to finance actions at the new external borders of the Union for the implementation of the Schengen *acquis* and external border control and to help improve cash-flow in national budgets (Art. 32).

Intimately linked with the Madrid criterion is the matter of trust between Member States. Trust and reciprocity are not specified. Nicolaides points out that the issue of implementation of the *acquis*, while important to the enlargement process, also has the potential to obstruct it.[110] The Commission has been criticised for its approach to capacity building, in the main because it has consistently recommended that the accession countries follow the 'M&M solution' (meaning men

[106] See *Bull. EU* 6–2002, Conclusion 24.

[107] See Commission Communication on the *Action Plans for administrative and judicial capacity, and the monitoring of commitments made by the negotiating countries in the accession negotiations*, COM(2002) 256, 5 June 2002, not published in the *OJ*. A Food Safety Action Programme dated 23 July 2002 and contained in a Note from Commissioner Byrne to E. Landaburu, the Director General for Enlargement, outlines the joint initiative of DG Enlargement and DG Health and Consumer Protection as part of the last 18 months of the pre-accession effort.

[108] Thus, there was no action plan Turkey.

[109] Art. 35 Act of Accession, fifth Accession Treaty.

[110] See P. Nicolaides, 'Preparing for Accession to the European union: How to Establish Capacity for Effective and Credible Application of EU rules' in Cremona, ed., *The Enlargement of the European Union*, op. cit. Chapter 1, n. 24 at p. 46.

and money),[111] which fails to take account of the willingness of those responsible for applying and enforcing the *acquis*. Nicolaides advocates an approach of 'credible commitments' in order to establish the core of integration and to do so by means of an institutional approach. Credible commitments involves the accession countries demonstrating to the Union their commitment to apply the *acquis* and assign the task of implementation to sufficiently empowered and accountable institutions that have both considerable decision-making independence and are subject to performance obligations.

Trust and reciprocity become a 'radical challenge' to the system of co-operative regulatory relations and trust at the heart of the Common Market.[112] The pre-occupation of the Union with the matter of governance[113] at the turn of the Century largely focussed on the institutions and regulatory environment of the fifteen Member States but certainly came under more strain in a Union of twenty-five and more Member States. Establishing co-operative relations among national administrations of the Twenty-seven has been served to an extent by twinning projects and vast exercises of technical assistance in the new Member States. Although, an anarchic web of national regulatory relations certainly posed a greater headache compared to that of the revision of the Union's institutional decision-making and functioning, which is only the tip-of the iceberg of guaranteeing the effectiveness of the *acquis* in an enlarged Union.

With the fifth enlargement the acceding countries have had to prove both that they have adequate administrative capacity and can guarantee their continued administrative capacity as Member States. The concerns of the Fifteen on this point led to the insertion of the safeguard clauses into the fifth Accession Treaty, so that in the event of the failure by the incoming Member States to maintain their compliance and enforcement of the *acquis*, 'appropriate measures' may be taken by the Union against the country concerned. A certain amount of

[111] See Nicolaides, ibid. at p. 44.

[112] See F. Bignami, 'The Challenge of Co-operative Regulatory Relations' in George. A. Berman and Katharina Pistor, *Law and Governance in an Enlarged European Union* (Oxford and Portland, Hart Publishing, 2004), pp. 97–140 at 99. See also Cremona's discussion of solidarity and conditionality in 'EU Enlargement: solidarity and conditionality', op. cit. Chapter 1, n. 41.

[113] See the Commission's *White Paper on European Governance*, COM(2001) 428, 25 July 2001. Consultation was launched in December 2000, see www.europa.eu.int/comm/governance/whats_new/consultation_report.pdf

suspicion of the readiness of the new Member States to meet the Madrid criteria was obvious even at the time of the signature of the Accession Treaty. The approach of the Fifteen was to continue with the Union's pre-accession conditionality[114] in the first years after accession.

Indeed, for the first time in its Opinion of February 2003 on the applications for accession,[115] required under Article 49 EU,[116] unlike previous accession treaties, the Commission;

> [called] on the acceding States to pursue vigorously the improvements that still [need] to be made in the context of the political and economic criteria for membership and in relation to the adoption, implementation and enforcement of the acquis; the Commission will continue to monitor the implementation of the commitments and obligations taken on by the acceding States, and will assist them with the available instruments.

The new Member States must continue to build administrative capacity. Two financial instruments were introduced to this end: the Transition and Schengen Facilities. The new safeguard clauses in the Accession Treaties are an added conditionality tool as is the new postponement clause in the sixth Accession Treaty with Bulgaria and Romania. Chapter 5 however, reveals significant lessons in governmental capacity since the sixth enlargement.

Administrative capacity of the new Member States in the fields of the environment an agri-food *acquis* is discussed in Part Two. Different considerations arise in relation to these two chapters of the *acquis*. The Union had been uncompromising in its insistence that the new Member States be able to fully apply the agri-food *acquis* from the date of accession, although this cannot be taken for granted. The integrity, first and foremost in terms of food safety, underlies the Union's uncompromising stance. As will be seen, the Transition Facility specifically allocates funds for capacity building of veterinary services as well as food safety. Moreover, food produced in the new Member States where administrative capacity cannot be guaranteed has been restricted to ensure that food in circulation on the Internal Market meets EU agri-food standards. However, the fact that so many of the

[114] All efforts of the new Members' during pre-accession have been focused entirely on approximation to the *acquis communautaire* and building sufficient administrative capacity to apply it in preparation for membership.

[115] Commission Opinion of 19 February 2003, *OJ* 2003 L 236/3.

[116] Title IX, Art. I-58, Constitutional Treaty.

new Member States show an implementation deficit in even transposing certain laws of the agri-food *acquis* raises important doubts as their preparedness to fully participate in the Internal Market for food on the date of accession.

In the case of the environment *acquis* however, it was accepted from long before even *Agenda 2000* that while much considerable progress could be made by the new Member States in approximating with this chapter of the *acquis*, it would simply be impossible for them to reach the required level of administrative capacity to enforce the entire chapter upon enlargement. This is discussed also in Part 2 of this volume.

CHAPTER THREE

# INSTRUMENTS OF THE PRE-ACCESSION STRATEGY: FROM *AGENDA 2000* TO DATE

## 1. Growing significance of bilateral contractual relations in pre-accession instruments

The Treaties give no indication of the mechanics of the preparations undertaken between the application for membership put to the Council and the signature and entry into force of the first four Accession Treaties. No treaty amendments have attempted to introduce a strategy for pre-accession. However, all enlargement preparations share certain core similarities.[1]

Table 2 presents a comparative snap shot of the gestation periods for accession after each application for membership has been made. This gives an overall picture and shows that not only has 'pre-accession' increased in time but it has increased in complexity and transparency. For Turkey, the gestation period may be over twenty years due not only to the fact that it has had its application on the EU table since 1987 but also for other reasons expanding upon briefly below, although this case must be treated as exceptional for those same reasons. Finally, among the Balkans countries, in particular Croatia and Macedonia, which applied on 21 February 2003 and 22 March 2004 respectively, Croatia has already been recognised as an official candidate since 18 June 2003 and was included alongside Bulgaria and Romania in the Commission's strategy paper of October 2004.[2] Official

[1] See in particular, Preston, op. cit. Chapter 1 at n. 24. Concerning the first four enlargements, Preston identifies 'the classical method of enlargement' as an integral component of the Community integration method in terms of the formal accession procedures adopted, the implicit assumptions and principles that have shaped the expectations of the participants and the progress of the negotiations, at pp. 8–9, pp. 18–22 and 227–235. Preston further sets out key principles of the classical method and points to the fact that in the forty years of enlargement experience, it has been impossible to recast the Union and that the 'rules of the game' have become more entrenched.

[2] See Commission Communication Strategy Paper of the European Commission on progress in the enlargement process, COM(2004) 657, 6 October 2004 at p. 2.

negotiations began with Croatia 4 October 2005. Albania applied for membership on 28 April 2009, although this is not reflected in Table 2 below because Albania's application has not been formally responded to in Council and it has not been granted candidate country status so far.[3] The fact that association agreements are concluded with (potential) candidates in advance of their applications and that these are key components in the pre-accession strategy nowadays, means that the true length of pre-accession preparations is far longer.

### 1.1 *Previously, contractual relations were not a pre-requisite for accession negotiations*

In the cases of the first three enlargements, association or preferential agreements were not seen as a legal basis for pre-accession work and the negotiations were the forum for discussions. The drawbacks of concluding association or preferential agreements with countries that were likely full members – being sufficiently developed economically with the necessary institutions and regimes comparable to those of the founding Member States – meant that the Community tended to contemplate entering into such agreements only with third countries that could not become full members because of international circumstances.[4] Among the drawbacks identified were that commitments made within the association and the multiplicity of special arrangements would make for inextricable complications upon eventual membership. However, all of the countries that acceded to the Union with the first four enlargement waves, except for Ireland, had prior contractual relations with the Union in one form or another. The *coup d'état* in Greece of 1 November 1967 brought an end to the 'Rule of the Colonels' there, which lasted until 24 July 1974. The Association Agreement Greece of 1961 had been frozen during these seven years prior to its application. For the purposes of preparing Greece's accession, however, it was considered a contractual relationship that covered not only trade policy but a whole series of steps that were to be undertaken to ensure Greece's progressive integration into the entire fabric of Community life.[5]

[3] See EUObserver, http://euobserver.com/?aid=28009 visited on 28 April 2009.

[4] See Commission Opinion 'The Applications for Membership from the United Kingdom, Ireland, Denmark and Norway of 1 October 1969', *Bull. EC*. Supp. 9/10, 1969, at para. 36, p. 26.

[5] Commission Opinion on Greek application for membership, COM(76) 30, 29 January 1976 at p. 7, para. 4. See also *Bull EC* 2/76.

Table 2. Time frame from application for membership to full membership

| Country | First application | Commission's first Opinion(s) on application (not the final Commission Opinion required under Art. 49 EU) | Official negotiations | EP Assent* | Council Decision + signature of Accession Treaty + entry into force |
|---|---|---|---|---|---|
| Denmark<br>Ireland<br>UK | 10/8/61 & 11/5/67<br>30/7/61 & 11/5/67<br>31/7/61 & 11/5/67 | On all applicants together:<br>29/9/1967<br>2/4/1968<br>1/10/1969 | 30/6/1970<br>30/6/1970<br>30/6/1970*** | NA | 22/1/1972<br>+ 22/1/1972<br>+ 1/1/1973 |
| Greece | 12/6/1975 | 29/1/1976 | 27/7/1976 | NA | 24/05/1979<br>+ 28/5/1979<br>+ 1/1/1981 |
| Portugal<br>Spain | 28/03/1977<br>28/07/1977 | 23/05/1978<br>29/11/1978 | 06/06/1978<br>05/02/1979 | NA | 30/03/1985<br>+ 12/06/1985<br>+ 1/01/1986 |
| Austria<br>Finland<br>Sweden | 17/07/1989<br>18/03/1992<br>01/07/1992 | 1/08/1991<br>4/11/1992<br>31/07/1992 | 1/2/1993 | 04/05/1994 | 16/05/1994<br>+ 24/06/1994<br>+ 01/01/1995 |
| Czech<br>Estonia<br>Latvia<br>Lithuania<br>Hungary<br>Poland<br>Slovenia<br>Slovakia<br>Cyprus<br>Malta | 17/1/1996<br>24/11/1995<br>13/10/1995<br><br>08/12/1995<br>31/03/1994<br><br>05/04/1994<br>10/06/1996<br>27/06/1995<br>03/07/1990<br>03/07/1990°<br>°defrosted 10/09/98 | On CEEC applicants<br>15/07/1997<br><br><br><br><br><br><br><br><br>30/06/1993<br>30/06/1993 | 31/03/1998<br>31/03/1998<br>15/02/2000<br><br>15/02/2000<br>31/03/1998<br><br>31/03/1998<br>31/03/1998<br>15/02/2000<br>31/03/1998<br>15/02/2000 | 09/03/2003 | 14/4/2003<br>+ 16/04/2003<br>+ 01/05/2004 |
| Bulgaria<br>Romania | 14/12/1995<br>22/06/1995 | 15/07/1997<br>15/07/1997 | 15/02/2000<br>15/02/2000 | 13/04/2005<br>13/04/2005 | 31/03/2005<br>+ 24/04/2005<br>+ 01/01/2007 |
| Turkey<br>Croatia<br>Macedonia | 14/04/1987<br>21/02/2003<br>22/03/2004 | 20/12/1989<br>20/04/2004<br>09/11/2005 | 04/10/2005**<br>04/10/2005<br>17/12/2005** | | |

Source: author. Note that Iceland applied on 17 July 2009 and Serbia on 22 December 2009
** Candidate without accession negotiations
* Not required prior to the 1986 Single European Act
*** UK negotiation first began 10 October 1961

As concerned the fourth enlargement negotiations with Austria, Finland and Sweden in particular, the existence of a prior association was a welcome factor in the smooth conduct of the negotiations. The fact of their familiarity and trading or association relationship facilitated their rapid transition to full-membership status. The negotiations with Austria, Finland and Sweden were helped by the fact that they had been operating under Free Trade Agreements (FTAs) with the Union and had enjoyed free trade with the EU before the FTAs were signed even.[6] Under the later EEA Agreement, they were already meeting food and environment standards of the Union – the preparatory work that Austria, Finland and Sweden had done prior to the entry into force of the EEA Agreement in approximating to and implementing the Internal Market and competition *acquis* was equally valid for their accession to the Union.

The first four enlargements were necessarily less daunting than the fifth because the deepening and widening of the Union was far less advanced.[7] In particular, the first three enlargements of Denmark, Ireland and the United Kingdom in 1973, of Greece in 1981, Spain and Portugal in 1986 occurred before some of the most ambitious deepening actions of the EEC as it evolved into the European Union, such as the introduction of the Treaty on European Union or even the completion of the Internal Market. The evolution in conditions for membership is explored in Chapter 2, while the pre-accession process is outlined and the transitional arrangements past and present is considered in Chapters 4 and 5.

In the case of the previous four enlargements, the time frame between the third country's application and the signature of the Accession Treaty was at best two years in the cases of Finland and Sweden and at longest just over seven years in the case of Spain (see Table 2). In some cases, the gestation period between the date of a country's application and the date of accession have been short. For Finland and Sweden, the whole time frame from application to full membership was just over thirty-three months in the case of the former and

[6] See Peers, 'An ever closer waiting room?: the Case for Eastern European Accession to the European Economic Area', 32 *CML Rev.* (1995) pp. 187–213 at pp. 190–191.

[7] At the outset of the changes in central and eastern Europe, see B. Soret, 'Réforme Institutionelle et Elargissmenet de l'Union Européenne aux PECOs' in Müller-Graff, ed., *East Central Europe and the European Union: from Europe Agreements to a Member Status,* op. cit. n. 24 at pp. 369–376.

only thirty months in the case of the latter. Generally, however, the road from application to membership has been far longer. The first countries to apply (Denmark, Ireland and the United Kingdom) had made initial applications in 1961 that had resulted in the opening of accession negotiations that had later failed in 1963. It was only after fresh applications in 1967 and fresh negotiations picking up from previous accession negotiations, that these countries joined in January 1973. For Greece, keeping in mind the Union's eagerness to forge ahead with this enlargement in the interests of peace and liberty in the Europe, it was a four and a half year time-frame between application and actual membership (rather than just signing an accession treaty), while for Austria it was a five and a half year time-frame and for Portugal and Spain it took over nine years.

The pre-accession strategy that is in operation today is an integral part of the strategy for the future of the Union as a whole. This gives an insight into the magnitude of the work to be done by both the Union and the candidates in advance of enlargement and therefore the longer gestation period is not surprising. The Commission document of 1997 *Agenda 2000: for a stronger and wider Union*[8] considered the challenge of enlargement in its Part Two. Part One addressed the internal policies of the Union, economic and social cohesion, the CAP and the external dimension. The gestation period between application for membership and signature of the fifth Accession Treaty lasted between the thirteen-year time frame as concerned Malta[9] and Cyprus,[10] the first of the new Member States to apply, and eight years

[8] COM(97) 2000, 15 July 1997.

[9] Although Malta froze its application in October 1996 only to defrost it in September 1998 when a new labour government took office. Malta was excluded from the pre-accession strategy, including the structured dialogue. With the subsequent change in government following a general election on 5 September 1998, the Maltese government reactivated the application and the Commission updated its 1993 Opinion on Malta in its 1999 annual report on Malta, recommending that screening begin for Malta with a view to beginning accession negotiations.

[10] As for Cyprus, which made its application on 3 July 1990, the Commission Opinion was issued only in 1993 due to a number of difficulties encountered by the Commission, notably the refusal of the Turkish Cypriot authorities to co-operate with the Commission in the technical preparation of the Opinion. See Commission Opinion of 30 June 1993, *Bull. EC*, Suppl. 3/92, para. 12 at p. 9. Moreover, the perspective of Cyprus' accession was directly linked to the progress in inter-communal talks in the January of 1995 and the eventual accession of Cyprus was made conditional on the prior settlement of the Cyprus question. See M.A. Gaudissart, 'Cyprus and the European Union. The Long Road to Accession', 8 *The Cyprus Review* Spring 1996 pp.

in the case of Slovenia. Slovenia was the last to apply for membership, on 10 June 1996 and the Commission's positive opinion on the Slovenian application of July 1997 was followed by the opening of bi-lateral accession negotiations with Slovenia in March 1998 and accession on 1 May 2004. But the speed of Slovenia's treatment was due to the preoccupation of the Union with the inclusiveness of the project rather than any easier or fast-tracking of negotiations with Slovenia. Generally speaking, looking at the cases of the largest countries in terms of population and size, the time between the application for membership and the actual signature of the fifth Accession Treaty was considerably longer than in any previous enlargement. Poland and Hungary waited ten years from the date of their applications to become Member States. For Bulgaria and Romania the accession negotiations lasted seven years but overall, since their applications in 1995, these two countries waited twelve years.

The accession strategy of today is essentially the same for each of the candidates and has used the association as the bilateral legal foundation for the pre-accession strategy. The Union has shown itself anxious to assure candidate countries of the inclusive nature of the accession process while at the same time to ensure that there is sufficient differentiation between the candidates according to their particular progress or problems. The Association Agreement Turkey[11] made explicit reference to its use in preparing for ('facilitating') possible membership of the Community.[12] The PHARE Regulation of 18 December 1989[13] was initially for Poland and Hungary but was later extended to all

13–22. On 6 March 1995, the General Affairs Council Conclusion gave the go ahead for Cyprus' membership and advocated that accession negotiations should begin with Cyprus six months after the end of the Intergovernmental Conference (IGC). The 1997 Luxembourg European Council confirmed that accession negotiations would begin in spring 1998. The Turkish Cypriots were invited to participate in the Cypriot delegation and accession negotiations started on 30 March 1998.

[11] Signed in Ankara on 12 September 1963 and in force on 1 December 1964, see *OJ* 1964 217/3702.

[12] See the Preamble to the Ankara agreement; 'reconnaissant que l'appui apporté par la Communauté économique européenne aux efforts du peuple turc pour améliorer son niveau de vie facilitera ultérieurement l'adhésion de la Turquie à la Communauté'. But no mention of such an intent or purpose was made in the Association Agreements Malta or Cyprus.

[13] Council Regulation 3906/89 on economic aid to the Republic of Hungary and the Polish People's Republic, *OJ* 1989 L 375/11.

the CEECs and then to South-East Europe.[14] It pre-dated the Europe Agreements and was demand driven so that funds were allocated in response to the needs and requests of the CEEC. It did not apply to Turkey nor tied to the CEECs performance under their Europe Agreements. Nor did the European Bank for Reconstruction and Development (EBRD), established on 15 April 1991, link loans for productive investment in the CEECs to the Europe Agreements (EAs).[15] The first Europe Agreements[16] of 1990 did not contain any declaration of intent on the part of the EU to enlarge although the CEECs did themselves declare their hopes of accession to the Union in their respective EA preambles. Their use as pre-accession vehicles was not intended initially.[17] The Europe Agreements had not been devised to prepare the partner country for accession to the Union. The same applies to the Association Agreements Cyprus, Malta and Turkey. These agreements were later built into the matrix of other economic, political and legal instruments of the pre-accession strategy that was developed with the *Agenda 2000* document of 1997. For the rest, the European or Accession Partnerships and other pre-accession instruments are of the EU and the candidates working in tandem: they are mutually complementing and work in parallel rather than bilaterally.

The EAs were only recognised by the European Union as a vehicle for accession following their political reorientation by the June 1993

---

[14] Albania, Bosnia-Herzegovina and the former Yugoslav Republic of Macedonia, the Federal Republic of Yugoslavia (Serbia and Montenegro) and Croatia.

[15] The Bank invested in private and entrepreneurial initiatives throughout Central and Eastern Europe also active in the CIS (and in South Eastern Europe).

[16] All EAs were published in the L series of the Official Journal of the European Union. They are all preceded by a Decision of the Council and the Commission on the conclusion thereof, while they are followed in the same Official Journal by the Final Act and the Information regarding their respective dates of entry into force. The ten EAs entered into force on four separate dates over a period of five years beginning 1 February 1994. The last to enter into force, on 1 February 1999, was that with Slovenia (1999 OJ L 51/1), with which accession negotiations had already been opened on 30 March 1998. The EA Poland (*OJ* 1993 L 348/1) entered into force 1 February 1995. The EA Hungary (*OJ* 1993 L 347) entered into force 1 February 1994 together with the EAs Bulgaria (*OJ* 1994 L 358), Romania (*OJ* 1994 L 357), Czech Republic and Slovakia (*OJ* 1994 L 359). The EA Estonia (*OJ* 1999 L 68) entered into force 1 February 1998 together with the EAs Latvia (*OJ* 1998 L 26) and Lithuania (*OJ* 1998 L 51).

[17] See P.-C. Müller-Graff 'The framework for EU-CEEC relations' in Maresceau (Ed.), *Enlarging the European Union*, op. cit. Chapter 1, n. 24 at p. 34. On the politics of the struggle between the Visegrad countries (Czech and Slovak Republics, Hungary and Poland) and the Commission and the Member States on this point see Torreblanca, *The reuniting of Europe: promises, negotiations and compromises* (Aldershot, Ashgate 2001) at pp. 309–312.

Copenhagen European Council.[18] Since the 1993 Copenhagen European Council, numerous strategy documents of the European Commission together with the necessary added driving force of the many European Council's thereafter, have served to work out and give shape to this strategy for the 'European family'. Following the Commission's 1997 *Agenda 2000* recommendations,[19] the accession process was launched 30 March 1998 and accession negotiations opened with twelve of the then thirteen candidates (excepting Turkey). The following sections explore the emergence and evolution of a strategy in pre-accession, putting the Copenhagen criteria in context as well as the financial and legal tools used.

Key to any understanding of all pre-accessions preparations are two themes: an inclusive approach to the region and treating all (potential) candidates on an equal footing, while always keeping an eye on possible future enlargements, and; the particular characteristics of a (potential) candidate and its readiness for membership.

For the countries of the Western Balkans at that time, it was clear that contractual relations insofar as they did exist in the early to mid-nineties were not ever intended as accession vehicles. The 1980 Co-operation Agreement and 1991 Transport Agreement with the Former Socialist Federal Republic of Yugoslavia were terminated by a decision of the Council of Ministers in November 1991. PHARE was extended to FYROM on 18 March 1996.[20] The Yugoslav Republic of Macedonia signed a Co-operation Agreement with the Union in April 1997, which entered into force on 1 January 1998 only to be partially suspended on 1 December 2000 in order to allow the application of a more favourable regime of trade measures granted by Council Regulation 2007/2000.[21] An earlier agreement in the field of transport had

[18] On the evolution and substance of the Europe Agreements, see M.A. Gaudissart, "L'association des pays d'Europe centrale et orientale", Chapter VII of *L'association: un mode de co-opération privilégié et les Etats tiers*, PhD Thesis, Ghent European Institute, University of Gent, Faculteit Rechtsgeleerdheid, 1999–2000. See also K. Inglis, 'The Europe Agreements Compared in the Light of their Pre-accession re-orientation', 37 *CML Rev* (2000) pp. 1173–1210.

[19] Approved by the December 1997 Luxembourg European Council.

[20] Council Regulation 463/96 amending Regulation 3906/89 with a view to extending economic assistance to the Former Yugoslav Republic of Macedonia, *OJ* 1996 L 65/3.

[21] Council Regulation 2007/2000 introducing exceptional trade measures for countries and territories participating in or linked to the European Union's Stabilisation and Association process, amending Regulation 2820/98, and repealing Regulations 1763/1999 and 6/2000, *OJ* 2000 L 240/1.

been in force already since 28 November 1997 and a textiles agreement was in force as of 1 January 1997.

In the case of Croatia, while the EU had recognised it in the January of 1992, the Union made any possibility of contractual relations with Croatia conditional on its observance of a 'code of democratic conduct' and, due to the political situation, contractual relations did not get off the ground. Continuity in trade relations was enabled only by the Union's annual grant of autonomous preferential trade measures on a renewable basis. Negotiations for a Trade and Co-operation Agreement together with a transport agreement began in March 1995 but soon failed, in the August of 1995, when military operations began in former UN sectors. The Union had granted Croatia humanitarian aid and democratisation assistance between 1991 and 1995, when PHARE was extended to Croatia,[22] but as of 1996 the assistance was once again restricted to the return of refugees and displaced persons.

### 1.2 *Opening accession negotiations: a real commitment to enlarge?*

Once accession negotiations have been opened, the Union commits itself to successfully completing those negotiations in order to sign an accession treaty and close the negotiations within the politically agreed timeframe.[23] To do otherwise would be grossly prejudicial to both the interests of the Member States and the Union[24] and would certainly affect the Union's credibility in its foreign policy generally, whether in

[22] On 20 June 1995. See Regulation 1366/95 amending Regulation 3906/89 in order to extend economic aid to Croatia, *OJ* 1995 L 133/1.

[23] In all of the first four enlargements, however, the initial Commission Opinions formed the basis for the initial treatment of an application for accession and have heralded the opening of accession negotiations within six months to a year, except for Ireland and Denmark when the opening of their accession negotiations was dependent on the decision to open accession negotiations with the United Kingdom – in its Opinion of 1 October 1969, the Commission commented that 'the candidature of the United Kingdom cannot be considered in isolation from the other three countries [at that time Norway had also applied]....on the other hand, these other three countries could hardly contemplate joining the Community independently of the United Kingdom because of the links uniting them with that country, particularly as EFTA members, and it would also be difficult for them to remain outside a Community enlarged by the accession of the United Kingdom alone', op. cit. Chapter 2, n. 15.

[24] The European Parliament highlighted this fact in its Explanatory Statement accompanying its Resolution of the European Parliament of 14 March 1985 on the results of the negotiations on the enlargement of the European Community, *OJ* 1985 C94/78, see European Parliament Working Documents, A2–20/85, 24 April 1985 at paragraph 21.

terms of its international commitments to and its negotiating position with third countries or in negotiating any future accession treaties or relations under the ENP.[25]

Enlargement negotiations are always contentious due to the specificities of the incoming country as well as the state of development of the Union itself. Accession negotiations have always proved contentious because of conflicting interests of incoming and existing Member States and the compromises sought. For example, the accession negotiations with Spain and Portugal had reached stalemate in the last months leading up to the signature of the relevant Accession Treaty[26] particularly because of the objections of the existing Member States (notably the United Kingdom) concerning the access of Spanish boats to EC waters and the transitional period, licences, quotas and territorial limits to be set as adjustments to the Treaties within the body of the relevant Act of Accession of the Accession Treaty.

So far the process of enlargement has always been an irreversible process. The 'inclusive and irreversible nature' of the process of enlargement once accession negotiations have been opened has always been considered the main driving incentive of the pre-accession preparations in the candidate countries, encouraging them to meet their own specific catalogue of performance based criteria. This was recognised – being one of many examples – by the October 2002 Brussels European Council when referring to the readiness of Bulgaria and Romania and the outstanding work that they had still to achieve before their accession on 1 January 2007. The time-frame between the opening of accession negotiations and the actual date of accession was considerably longer in the cases of the fifth and sixth enlargements, but the Union's commitment to enlargement was beyond question. The lengthy time

[25] Press articles have portrayed the EU Foreign Ministers decision on 16 March 2005 not to open accession negotiations as 'the first time in the EU's history [that] Member States have put off a previously set date for accession talks with a candidate state'. See the press article 'EU shelves Croatia talks', www.EurActiv.com visited on 16 March 2005. This is not strictly true because it was only in 1999 that the Helsinki European Council introduced the distinction between a candidate with which accession negotiations would begin and a candidate with which accession negotiations would not begin. This distinction was introduced in order to maintain the incentive of enlargement, and therefore also the momentum of reform, in Turkey.

[26] See Resolution of the European Parliament of 14 March 1985 on the results of the negotiations on the enlargement of the European Community, op. cit. n. 24, and Resolution of the European Parliament of 14 March 1985 on the accession negotiations with Spain in the fisheries sector, also at *OJ* 1985 C94/78.

taken between accession negotiations and actual enlargement was in order strategically to prepare the 'big-bang' fifth and sixth enlargements properly and in no way undermined the Union's commitment to bringing these countries into the EU. With Croatia, however, while an accession treaty is planned for 2010, no date for accession has been set for Croatia's accession and nor has any political commitment been given by the Member States to Turkey for a specific date for its accession.

With the December 1999 Helsinki European Council, Turkey was not brought within the negotiating block – although it was included in the list of official candidates – on the grounds that it did not meet the political criterion fixed by the June 1993 Copenhagen European Council as a pre-condition to membership. This introduced a nuance to the status of candidate, distinguishing for the first time in enlargement practice the difference between a 'candidate' and 'a candidate with which accession negotiations have not been opened'. It is also important to emphasise the fact that having recognised Turkey as a candidate alongside all other candidates the EU was careful, initially, to refuse to open accession negotiations with Turkey. In previous practice, the opening of accession negotiations heralded the Union's true commitment to enlarging. The singularity in treatment of Turkey was the result of its need to improve the situation with regards to human and minorities' rights.[27]

Given that Turkey has been treated separately in the pre-accession strategy leading up to the opening of accession negotiations in October 2005,[28] the frequent and consistent commitment of the European Council and the European Commission to Turkey's accession is a necessary reassurance not only of the incentive of accession but also that Turkey is not being discriminated against compared to other candidates.[29] Picking up again the emphasis of the European Council

---

[27] See Conclusion and Recommendation 6 of the European Commission *1998 Composite Paper on progress towards accession by each of the candidate countries*, at p. 31.

[28] See E.T. Fakiolas and N. Tzifakis, 'Transformation or Accession? Reflecting on the EU's Strategy Towards the Western Balkans', 2008 *European Foreign Affairs Review* pp. 377–398.

[29] See December 1999 Helsinki European Council, the December 2002 Copenhagen European Council, the June 2004 Brussels European Council. See also the various Commission reports under the pre-accession strategy, elaborated on below, and most recently the Commission *Regular Report on Turkey's progress towards accession*, COM(2004) 656 of, 6 October 2004.

in October 2005 on the 'open-ended' nature of accession negotiations 'the outcome of which cannot be guaranteed beforehand' and combining this with the resistance of the December 2004 European Council to commit to a projected date for Turkey's actual accession to the Union having opened accession negotiations with Turkey, puts a strain on the inclusive and irreversible nature of the enlargement project. Such uncertainty could be expected to dilute support in Turkey but potentially also other candidate countries for the reforms and efforts required of them. Section 2.3 below explains the special conditionality that has been introduced, since 2004, for the launch of accession negotiations with the SEECs. Indeed, the absence of the incentive of accession proved to be a dilemma in the wider European Neighbourhood Policy from the time of its nascent conditionality approach, which after all, was self-evidently a transposal of the pre-accession strategy instruments and conditionality.[30]

Keeping to the topic of accession negotiations, the introduction of new means during the accession negotiations phase to suspend accession negotiations, points to the possibility of a weaker commitment to actual enlargement by the Member States. The removal of the phrase 'open Community' also implies a reticence on the part of the Member States to enlarge further and this applies to all candidates and potential candidates. Turkey is looking at a far longer timeframe for accession negotiations and is not included within a group of negotiating candidates as such, despite the fact that the October 2005 European Council decided to open accession negotiations with Turkey alongside Croatia. The prospect of the Turkish accession raises a plethora of new considerations for the functioning of the Union in terms of its institutions and decision-making in addition to its geo-political and economic dimensions, the Internal Market and related fields, the agriculture sector as well as veterinary and phytosanitary issues (of direct relevance to the agri-food *acquis*) and the fisheries sector, regional and structural policy and the justice and home affairs *acquis*.[31]

Turkey is expected to have a population the size on a par with Germany by 2015. Its accession will significantly affect the allocation of

---

[30] See C. Hillion, 'The EU's Neighbourhood Policy Towards Eastern Europe', in A. Dashwood and M. Maresceau (eds.), *Law and Practice of EU External Relations: Salient Features of a Changing Landscape*, pp. 309–333.

[31] See Commission Staff Working Document *Issues arising from Turkey's Membership Perspective*, COM (2004) 656, 6 October 2004, pp. 1–53.

seats for MEPs in the European Parliament. It would enable a blocking minority of countries with large populations to be more easily reached in qualified majority voting in Council under the system introduced by the Treaty of Lisbon. It would also have a significant impact on the budget but available estimates are to be treated with 'extreme caution' given the timetable for accession and the uncertainties involved. It is, however, clear that Turkey's accession will affect most expenditure areas of the EU budget significantly. For example, Turkey would be eligible for significant support under the CAP as it stands today and also from the rural development funds.

The fact that new means have been devised for suspending accession negotiations and for introducing safeguard clauses for Turkey emphasises the Union's commitment to its pre-accession conditionality in advance of actual accession. In particular, the implications of the German elections of September 2005 were broad[32] and German support for Turkey's accession was not strong when negotiations began. Austria insisted at the October 2005 European Council to move towards more of a 'special relationship' with Turkey as opposed to Turkish accession. While this did not curry the full support of the Member States, the negotiating framework for Turkey nevertheless includes the proviso that 'if turkey is not in a position to assume in full all the obligations of membership, it must be ensured that Turkey is fully anchored in the European structures through the strongest possible bond.'[33]

However, in the specific case of Turkey, the European Parliament took the stance in 2004 that accession is not the automatic consequence of the start of accession negotiations.[34] Resolution 55 reads:

> [the European Parliament] stresses that the opening of negotiations will be the starting point for a long-lasting process that by its very nature is an open-ended process and does not lead 'a priori' and automatically to accession: emphasises, however, that the objective of the negotiations is

[32] See 'German elections: implications for EU policymaking' www.euractiv.com visited on 15 September 2005.

[33] See Principle 2 of the negotiating framework adopted by the European Council for the Commission on 3 October 2005, which takes up the wording and conclusions of the *Presidency Conclusions*, Council Press Release 16238/1/04 REV I of 17 December 2004, under Title I, Enlargement at p. 7.

[34] See Resolution 55 of European Parliament Resolution on the 2004 regular report and the recommendation of the European Commission on Turkey's progress towards accession, contained in European Parliament Report A6–0063/2004 of 3 December 2004.

> Turkish EU Membership but that the realisation of this ambition will depend on the efforts of both sides; accession is thus not the automatic consequence of the start of the negotiations.

The negotiating mandate given the Commission by the European Council on 3 October 2005 reflects this same approach. The second principle governing the negotiations reads;

> As agreed at the European Council in December 2004, these negotiations are based on Article 49 of the Treaty on European Union. The shared objective of the negotiations is accession. These negotiations are an open-ended process, the outcome of which cannot be guaranteed beforehand. While having full regard to all Copenhagen criteria, including the absorption capacity of the Union, if Turkey is not in a position to assume in full all the obligations of membership it must be ensured that Turkey is fully anchored in the European structures through the strongest possible bond.[35]

All this, compared to the irreversible intent declared in the previous four enlargements, marks hesitation on the EU's part, with all that this implies for the Union's credibility on the world stage and in the broader region.

### 1.3 *The Association Agreement becomes a contractual yardstick of pre-accession progress*

The first legal instruments of the new, enhanced pre-accession strategy to refer to the mutual goal of accession for both parties were the Accession Partnerships, see 2 below. They became the key legal instrument of the pre-accession strategy. They were, just as they are in today's pre-accession strategy, instruments unilaterally adopted by the Council in respect of each candidate separately, after consultation with each candidate separately. By comparison, the Accession Partnerships are based on the TFEU but are instruments of the Council of the European Union as they include areas that lay outside the old EC Treaty, such as political competences and justice and home affairs. With the accession process, the distinction between EC and EU competences has become increasingly blurred.

However, as a result of the strategy launched by *Agenda 2000*, the association agreement became the sole legal instrument that was bilaterally agreed by the EC and its Member States and the partner CEEC. Each EA with the CEECs was a mixed agreement of the EU and of the

[35] See Council Press Release 16238/1/04, op. cit. n. 33.

Member States giving the Commission provisional competence to act beyond the competences set down in the EC Treaty at the time. Thus, the *Agenda 2000* strategy raised the significance of the EAs in legal, political and economic terms and speeded up the accession train. The CEECs' progress in implementing their Europe Agreements became a core gauge of progress for the purposes of their accession negotiations. Likewise the Association Agreements Cyprus, Malta and Turkey have been used as bilateral contractual yardsticks in these countries' pre-accession efforts, although their substantive context was/is limited compared to the Europe Agreements. It was logical to use the same strategy and its instruments in respect of the association agreements with the countries of the Western Balkans.

The combined effect that surfaces from the interaction of the many political, economic and legal instruments of the pre-accession strategy is a far-reaching and powerful enlargement conditionality policy in its own right. The Union's pre-accession or membership conditionality shapes a partner's policy and actions to take account of the obligations of membership of the Union and it does so in project conception and implementation, in terms of training officials, in terms of drafting or adapting laws and establishing the administrative and judicial structures to enforce it.

Today, the SAAs have been drafted to incorporate the pre-accession reorientation that was wrapped around the Europe Agreements. The pre-accession strategy that is in place today is specifically built upon the association agreement with the candidate and, as is seen in the next section, short, medium and long-term priorities are established by the Accession Strategy (in particular by the Accession Partnerships) as defined unilaterally by the Union. The current Association Agreement Turkey continues to provide the sole bilaterally agreed legal instrument of today's pre-accession strategy for Turkey. The association agreements with the Balkans countries, the Stabilisation and Association Agreements have been specifically designed to prepare these countries' membership and by comparison, play a more prominent role in the Stabilisation and Association Process. The Stabilisation and Association Agreements (and the European Partnerships, in the first place and then Accession Partnerships once the country is granted candidate status) have been devised and framed with the sights of both partners firmly upon preparing the EU partner for membership.

The pre-accession strategy for the Western Balkans has relied more heavily on the contractual relationship established between the Union and the (potential) candidate. They are a sort of Europe Agreement redesigned and are a new form of contractual relationship.[36] As a result of the Thessaloniki Agenda,[37] they are incorporated in the Stabilisation and Association Process, which is to all intents and purposes a (pre) accession strategy for the Western Balkans.[38] The Stabilisation and Association Agreements have purposefully been drafted as 'potential' accession vehicles for 'potential candidates'. A multilateral forum had already been put in place by the November 2000 Zagreb summit.[39] The SAAs are now used by the Union as a conditionality incentive in their own right and in advance of the opening of accession negotiations in a way that the EAs were not.

The SAAs serve generally to intensify the integration efforts of their partners at multi-country level but also at sub-regional level. They guide the work to be done by the (potential) candidate. The contractual relationship also specifies the association and is the bilateral legal basis for the overarching pre-accession strategy. The association agreement provides the basis for continuity in the relations between the candidate and the EU while they undergo the necessary, extensive and progressive reforms. While the European Integration Partnerships (referred to hear as European Partnerships) and Accession Partnerships provide the single framework for the accession strategy, the SAAs provide for efforts of the Parties to focus on their implementation.

The influence of the Copenhagen criteria in particular can be seen in their main elements:

- provision for political dialogue;
- provisions on enhanced regional co-operation, including the perspective of establishing free trade areas between the countries of the region;
- the perspective of the establishment of a free-trade area;

[36] See Commission Communication on the Stabilisation and Association process for countries of South Eastern Europe, *COM* (1999) 235, 26 May 1999. See J. Marko and J. Wilhelm, 'The Balkans and the NIS' in Ott and Inglis, *Handbook on European Enlargement*, op. cit. Chapter 1, n. 24 at p. 167. See also D. Phinnemore, 'Stabilisation and Association Agreements: Europe Agreements for the Western Balkans?', 8 *EFA Rev.* (2003) pp. 77–103.

[37] Adopted by the June 2003 Thessaloniki European Council.

[38] On the Union's integrated approach to the Western Balkans generally, see S. Blockmans, *Tough Love: the European Union's Relations with the Western Balkans*, The Hague, T. M. C. Asser Press 2007.

[39] See Chapter 2.2.

- provisions on the movement of workers, freedom of establishment, supply of services, current payments and movement of capital;
- the commitment to approximate its legislation to that of the EC, in particular the Internal Market;
- co-operation in a wide range of fields, including justice, freedom and security;
- the establishment of a Stabilisation and Association Council which supervises the implementation of the Agreement, of a Stabilisation and Association Committee and a Stabilisation and Association Parliamentary Committee.

An SAA is both an association agreement and at the same time a mixed agreement adopted under Article 217 TFEU. A mixed agreement takes full effect only once the last party to the agreement has ratified it.

The SAA Croatia was signed 29 October 2001 and was concluded 13 December 2004.[40] The SAA Former Yugoslav Republic of Macedonia was signed 9 April 2001[41] and entered into force 1 April 2004.[42] These two countries are formal candidates alongside Turkey, although accession negotiations have not yet been opened with FYROM. All of the other potential candidates under the Stabilisation and Association Process have signed SAAs with the Union. The SAAs with Albania,[43]

[40] See Council Decision 2005/40/EC of 13 December 2004 concerning the conclusion of the Stabilisation and Association Agreement between the European Communities and its Member States and the republic of Croatia on behalf of the European Community. *OJ* 2005 L 26/1. Its Interim Agreement entered into force March 2002. In accordance with Article 6(2) of the fifth Accession Treaty 2003, a protocol to the SAA Croatia was agreed in December 2004 (*OJ* 2005 L 26/222) together with a Council Decision concerning the signature and provisional application of this new protocol to the SAA Croatia by the ten new Member States. Council Decision 2005/41/EC, *OJ* 2005 L 26/221.

[41] The Interim Agreement was signed the same day and entered into force 1 March 2002.

[42] Council and Commission Decision 2004/239 of 23 February 2004 concerning the conclusion of the stabilisation and association agreement between the European Communities and their Member States, of the one part, and the former Yugoslav Republic of Macedonia, of the other part, *OJ* 2004 L 84/1.

[43] Signed on 22 May 2006. The SAA Albania has not yet been published in the *Official Journal*. Regulation 1616/2006 applies the interim agreement and certain of provisions pending its ratification, see *OJ* 2006 L 300/1.

Bosnia and Herzegovina,[44] Montenegro[45] already apply partially pending their final ratification because Interim Agreements have been agreed or letters have been exchanged between the Parties, which give effect to trade provisions for example, and include these countries in EU programmes. There is no Interim Agreement with Serbia nor Kosovo, yet.[46] Pending the ratification of an SAA, interim agreements have been adopted for the application of certain provisions and the inclusion of these countries in EU programmes as part of the pre-accession strategy.

The focus of the contractual relationship is clearly accession driven. The SAA FYROM applies a general ten-year transitional period for FYROM and a six-year period for the SAA Croatia. Article 68 of the SAA FYROM even provides for a timetable for the approximation of laws in two stages, the first being for competition law, intellectual property law, standards and certification law, public procurement law and data protection law as well as other areas of the Internal Market *acquis*. The second stage of the SAA transitional period will be used for all other areas of the *acquis*. Entirely new areas of co-operation are introduced into these agreements reflecting the evolution of the *acquis* and helping to specify means and areas for approximation. Moreover, the economic co-operation takes place within the regional framework of the regional approach under the SAP.

Nevertheless, the needs of these countries and the efforts required of them during pre-accession are different in many ways to those faced by the ten CEECs, Malta and Turkey. It is also clear that the focus of the pre-accession strategy in the first place, is on regional conditionality and good-neighbourliness and the political criteria and preparing the ground for the adoption of the *acquis* and administrative and judicial capacity building. In the earlier stages the *acquis* is adopted and implemented in the general interests of the Union and the partner country

[44] Signed on 15 October 2007. As it January 2009, the SAA Bosnia and Herzegovina has still to be concluded by the EU. The Interim Agreement was applied, on 30 June 2008, by Regulation 594/2008, *OJ* 2008 L 169/1, as amended by *OJ* 2008 L 233/1.

[45] Signed on 16 June 2008. As it January 2009, pending ratification of the SAA Montenegro, Regulation 140/2008, *OJ* 2008 L 43/1, applies the interim agreement as of 10 March 2008. A Council Decision 2008/127, *OJ* 2008 L 43/9, and an Exchange of Letters applies provisions on the participation of Montenegro in EC programmes, *OJ* 2008 L 43/11.

[46] The SAA Serbia was signed on 30 April 2008. As it January 2009, it remains to be concluded by the EU, COM(2007) 743 of 20 November 2007. No interim agreement is in place, see proposal therefor COM(2007) 744 of 20 November 2007.

rather than on the wholesale adoption of the *acquis* and its implementation, which necessarily demands longer term and ambitious investment and support. Regional co-operation occupies a prominent place in the SAAs. For example, the SAAs Croatia and FYROM, Articles 3 and 4, declare the regional approach as the framework for the relationship and prescribe co-operation and good neighbourly relations.

Having signed an SAA, taking the example of Article 12 in the SAA Croatia, the partner undertakes to conclude, within two years, conventions on regional co-operation in order to enhance the scope of the co-operation with other countries that have also signed an SAA. In these conventions they undertake to address political dialogue, establish an FTA consistent with the WTO, make mutual concessions concerning the movement of workers, establishment, services, currency payments and capital at a level equivalent to that of the SAA. Such conventions must also cover Justice and Home Affairs, something which was not tackled in the EA Poland for example. In Articles 13 and 14 SAA, Croatia there is also an obligation to co-operate with the other countries of the SAP as well as the other candidate for accession, Turkey. The SAAs cannot be considered in isolation from the other instruments of the (pre-)pre-accession strategy as the latter are constantly updated and directly impact on the relationship between the Union and SAA partners.

## 2. European/Accession Partnerships: autonomous instruments in so many ways

European or Accession Partnerships are autonomous instruments that are rooted in the bilateral contractual relationship but which, all the same, work out the specifics of the principles and objectives set out there. The title of 'European Partnership' was introduced for the SEECs and is now used for countries that have formally been recognised as potential candidates. They will be renamed Accession Partnerships when the country becomes a candidate, as was done with the Macedonian European Partnership. Yet they are not bilaterally agreed and are adopted by the Council, albeit upon the proposal of the European Commission.

Through the Accession and European Partnerships, the increasingly precise conditionality is tailored within the differentiating-yet-inclusive approach. In the case of the fifth enlargement all candidates in the region were treated on an equal footing but could progress faster in the negotiations if they progressed faster in their preparations. However, to hold back one country that is ready to accede because of another's failure to reach the same progress would run against the grain of the Union's pre-accession conditionality. With the SEECs and Turkey too, it is not at all certain, if not unlikely – for reasons already outlined – that the Union would aim for another mass enlargement. This is the challenge: to find new ways of keeping the pre-accession conditionality inclusive, keeping the candidates on an equal footing until they and the Union are ready for accession/enlargement.

### 2.1 *Legal basis and relationship with the association agreement*

The legal basis for today's European or Accession Partnerships is Article 212 TFEU. Article 212 TFEU expressly provides a legal basis for economic, financial and technical co-operation measures of the Union with third countries that are not developing countries. Such measures must be carried out consistently with Union development policy.[47] It is also the legal basis that has been used for the adoption of the 2006 Instrument for Pre-accession Assistance (IPA) – see 3.2. below. Moreover, Article 212 TFEU requires that these measures be consistent with development policy and within the framework of the principles and objectives of the Union's external action. This is a direct reference to Article 21 TEU, which clearly echoes the wording of Article 2 TEU values and the Charter of Fundamental Rights. It lists the principles of democracy, the rule of law, the universality and indivisibility of human rights, respect for human dignity, the principles of equality and solidarity and respect for the UN Charter and international law.

This removes any doubts as to the scope of Union competence in relation to the instruments adopted. Unanimity in the Council is required for association agreements based on Article 217 TFEU and for

[47] The explanatory memorandum to the Commission's proposal for the IPA makes clear the choice of legal basis, previously Art. 181a EC: 'The legal basis of the proposal is *Art. 181(a) TEC*, and not *Art. 179 TEC* [now Art. 207 TFEU], despite the fact that a number of the beneficiary countries listed in the Annexes are considered developing countries by the International community. However, the simple fact that some of the beneficiary countries may be considered developing countries does not automatically permit the proposal to be based on Article 207. That Article is used to adopt measures to promote Community policy in the area of development policy.'

agreements to be concluded with the candidates for accession. Implementing measures are adopted by qualified majority in the Council and the European Parliament has a right of consultation only.

European Partnerships for potential candidates have been adopted separately: Croatia[48] and FYROM[49] as well as Albania,[50] Bosnia and Herzegovina,[51] and Serbia and Montenegro[52] and Kosovo.[53] These have been described by the Commission as a means to 'enrich current policies towards the region with elements taken from the enlargements process, reinforcing the ultimate goal of extending membership of the EU to the Western Balkans.'[54] They identify the short and medium-term reforms that countries need to carry out, to serve as a check list against which to measure progress, and to provide guidance for assistance

[48] Council Decision 2004/648 on the principles, priorities and conditions contained in the European Partnership with Croatia, *OJ* 2004 L 297/19, repealed and replaced by Council Decision 2006/145 on the principles, priorities and conditions contained in the Accession Partnership with Croatia and repealing Decision 2004/648/EC, *OJ* 2006 L 055/30.

[49] Council Decision 2004/518 on the principles, priorities and conditions contained in the European Partnership with the former Yugoslav Republic of Macedonia, *OJ* 2004 L 222/20. Council Decision 2006/57 on the principles, priorities and conditions contained in the European Partnership with the former Yugoslav Republic of Macedonia and repealing Decision 2004/518, *OJ* 2006 L 35/57.

[50] Council Decision 2004/519 on the principles, priorities and conditions contained in the European Partnership with Albania, *OJ* 2004 L 223/20, repealed and replaced by Council Decision 2006/54 on the principles, priorities and conditions contained in the European Partnership with Albania and repealing Decision 2004/519/EC, *OJ* 2006 L 35/1.

[51] Council Decision 2004//515 on the principles, priorities and conditions contained in the European Partnership with Bosnia and Herzegovina, *OJ* 2004 L 221/10. Council Decision 2006/55 on the principles, priorities and conditions contained in the European Partnership with Bosnia and Herzegovina and repealing Decision 2004/515/EC, *OJ* 2006 L 35/19.

[52] Council Decision 2004/520 on the principles, priorities and conditions contained in the European Partnership with Serbia and Montenegro, *OJ* 2004 L 227/21. Council Decision 2006/56 on the principles, priorities and conditions contained in the European Partnership with Serbia and Montenegro including Kosovo as defined by the United Nations Security Council Resolution 1244 of 10 June 1999 and repealing Decision 2004/520, *OJ* 2006 L 035/32.

[53] As defined by United Nations Security Council Resolution 1244 of 10 June 1999. While taking account of the sovereignty and territorial integrity of this state, the UN has placed the province of Kosovo under an interim international civil and military administration following the 1999 conflict.

[54] See Commission Press Release 'European Commission proposes new European Integration Partnerships for the Western Balkans', IP/03/721, 21 May 2003.

under the financial and technical assistance given.[55] FYROM's European Partnership was renamed an Accession Partnership[56] by the General Affairs and External Relations European Council on 10 March 2008, denoting its formal candidate status once accession negotiations have been formally opened.

The Accession Partnerships and the European Partnerships do not give rise to any rights or obligations for the parties. They are not binding on the partners as such but are implemented voluntarily and they provide the yardstick for evaluating progress with the Copenhagen criteria. As concerns the countries of the Western Balkans, which have had to begin from a lower starting point than the CEEC counterparts, the fact that the European Partnerships have been adopted in advance even of the contractual relations gives the impression of a sort of 'pre' pre-accession process.

The annual reporting of the Commission of the progress made by the Western Balkans countries are treated, like the progress reports for Bulgaria, Romania and Turkey, as the basis for the elaboration of the European Partnerships. The potential candidates, with or without a Stabilisation and Association Agreement, are expected to mirror the objectives and priorities set down by the Council within the European Partnerships in their national planning. At the outset, the priorities and objectives are broad-based and concentrate on challenges such as crisis management, reconstruction and rehabilitation. In the longer term, the priorities focus on the same priorities of the transposition, implementation and enforcement of the *acquis* as well as on administrative capacity building, and speed up progress towards EU membership.[57]

As was made clear by the feasibility report on Albania, for example, its starting point is 'so low'[58] that it has a very ambitious programme to implement due in particular to its political problems as well as to

---

[55] See Commission Communication The Western Balkans and European Integration, COM(2003) 285, 21 May 2003 at p. 3.

[56] Council Decision 2006/57/EC on the principles, priorities and conditions contained in the European Partnership with the former Yugoslav Republic of Macedonia and repealing Decision 2004/518/EC, *OJ* 2006 L 35.

[57] See Commission Report *The Stabilisation and Association process for South East Europe*, COM(2004) 202, op. cit. Chapter 2, n. 66 at section 3.1.

[58] See Commission Staff Working Paper *Albania Stabilisation and Association Report*, SEC(2002) 339, 4 April 2002, at p. 4.

lacks in its implementation capacity, political culture and its judicial and administrative cultures.[59] The 2004 European Partnership Albania reflected this in the short and medium term priorities, aiming at what is possible in real terms rather than setting the targets beyond the country's reach. Under the SAP, while there were no contractual relations in the form of SAAs with Albania, Bosnia and Herzegovina as well as Serbia and Montenegro,[60] these countries benefited from preferential trade concessions, financial and technical assistance and have the possibility of concluding an SAA.

A concrete prospect of actually acceding comes only with the formal launch of accession negotiations. The European/Accession Partnerships are expressly mentioned in the SAAs, providing for the Stabilisation and Association Council's review of progress under the partnership, such as Article 8 in the SAA Bosnia and Herzegovina.

After the *Agenda 2000* document, the progressive reorientation of the Union's conditionality in its relations with the CEECs was underpinned by the Accession Partnerships in the pre-accession strategy. This increased the coherence and specificity of that conditionality generally, gave a considerable role to the Commission in the formulation and implementation of the pre-accession strategy and accession negotiations, and ultimately served to depoliticise the process.[61]

The conditionality, which takes the form of preconditions, conditions and incentives,[62] is being rigourously applied by the Union in its relations with the SEECs in this pre-accession phase. The reinforcement of the pre-accession strategy and, in particular, the reliance on an increasingly precise conditionality extending into all areas of current and even future EU policy, can be seen in the working out of conditions and how to apply them in a systematic and all-inclusive, non-discriminatory way. Both the European and Accession Partnerships

[59] See Commission Staff Working Paper Albania Stabilisation and Association Report 2004, COM(2004) 203, undated, at pp. 2–4. See Marko and Wilhelm in Ott and Inglis, eds., *Handbook on European Enlargement*, op. cit. Chapter 1, n. 24 at pp. 169–170.

[60] See Commission Staff Working Paper Serbia and Montenegro Stabilisation and Association Report COM(2004) 206, undated.

[61] M. Maresceau, 'The pre-accession strategy: a political and legal analysis', in Maresceau and Lannon (eds.), op. cit. Chapter 1, n. 24.

[62] See E. Lannon, K. Inglis and T. Haenebalcke, 'The many faces of EC conditionality in pan-Euro-Mediterranean Relations' in M. Maresceau and E. Lannon, eds., *The EU's Enlargement and Mediterranean Strategies* (London and New York, MacMillan 2000).

are designed to put all the candidates on equal footing in terms of what is expected of them in order to fulfil the Copenhagen criteria. This helps to take the heat out of the political jealousies between aspiring members, removing any impression of the preferential treatment of countries in the pre-accession train.

The central role given to the Commission in the formulation and implementation of pre-accession strategies and negotiations and in the co-ordination of the financing instruments has enabled the pre-accession preparations to progress. The introduction of the specific legal mechanisms for the suspension of Union assistance should a candidate flout fundamental elements of the Copenhagen criteria, is a considerable stick. And it is the Commission who must first propose the suspension of Union assistance before the Council can take 'appropriate measures' or 'appropriate steps'[63] to suspend pre-accession assistance acting by qualified majority. At the same time, this helps to depoliticise, to some extent, the relations between the EU and the candidates in the run up to accession. Moreover the weakening of the multilateral, structured dialogue dimension to the accession process has served to underline this trend and the greatly expanded role of the Commission, the executive arm of the Union's institutions, in the accession process adds to this impression.

Despite this apparent 'depoliticisation', the accession process nevertheless remains essentially political. The decision to open accession negotiations with Croatia in spite of its failure to deliver war criminals to the ICTY smacked of political bargaining rather than a to-the-letter application of the pre-accession conditionality that the Union itself had set. This highlighted the fact that in the end, any decision to suspend assistance must always be political because it is taken by a qualified majority of the Member States. Ultimately, once the candidates have shown themselves to have completed the whole process, it is for the Member States to decide whether the accession conditionality has indeed been met.

The Member States are under no obligation to take a favourable decision on a candidate's eventual accession, which they must do by unanimity in any event, even if a candidate fulfils all that has been required of it under the Accession/European Partnerships and the European Commission has given its favourable opinion. The pre-

[63] Art. 4 of Regulation 622/98, *OJ* 1998 L 85/1.

accession strategy maintains the Union's room to manoeuvre according to its own (political) circumstances as well as those of countries aspiring to membership. The broad differentiation of the pre-accession train has been devised in the context of the regional and sub-regional situations of the candidates in order to avoid diminishing the incentive that accession provides to candidate countries.

Given the enormity and complexity of the project of enlarging the Union and given the extent of the transformation required of the incoming countries, it is not surprising that the fifteen 'old' Member States sought guarantees in the fifth and sixth Accession Treaties that they would continue to fulfil their pre-accession commitments and meet the Copenhagen criteria after their accession. Also, innovative means were used to allow the gradual entry of the new Member States in key areas of the *acquis*. Chapters 4 and 5 deal with the reach of pre-accession conditionality into the first years of accession, and potentially longer term, for the new Member States and the use of transitional flexibility mechanisms to ease their entry into the European Union.

The AP is the core component of the matrix of political, financial and legal instruments that make up the pre-accession strategy. These guide this overall re-orientation in the EU-candidate relations. They set out the specific principles, priorities, intermediate objectives and conditions for each candidate, specify the significant adjustments required of each of them and, last but not least, programme their Union and international assistance (financial and technical) accordingly. The Accession Partnerships reflect the recommendations and finding of the European Commission in its annual country reports on each candidate's progress under the pre-accession strategy. In direct response to the Accession Partnership, the candidate adopts the legal instruments and structures in line with the Accession Partnership.[64] In this way, it is more of a parallel and mutually complementing strategy than a bilateral one. The Accession Partnerships have provided a means of reinforcing the pre-accession strategy without impairing the legality and effectiveness of the bilateral association agreements. The

---

[64] Indeed, the enthusiasm of the CEECs to follow the political, economic and legal order of the then European Communities was apparent even before the existence of formal agreements and facilitate that re-orientation. See Müller-Graff, 'General Report' in Müller-Graff (ed.), *East Central Europe and the European Union: from Europe Agreements to a Member Status*, op. cit. Chapter 1, n. 24, at pp. 14–15.

Union devised this matrix of interrelated legal and economic instruments that were practical and expedient at the time. In particular, this approach also avoided involving time-consuming decisions within the Association Councils under the relevant association agreement due to constitutional problems that had held up integration efforts in the past.[65] It therefore avoided revision of the bilateral contractual relationship.

The European/Accession Partnerships guide the work of the EA partners in meeting their commitments under the association agreements. In direct response to the European/Accession Partnerships, typically the candidates will, for example: adopt their own National Plans for the Adoption of the Acquis (NPAAs); make joint assessments of medium-term economic policy priorities; participate in the Pact against organised crime; adopt National Development Plans and other sectoral plans for the participation of the candidate in the Union's structural funds after membership and for implementation of additional assistance for agriculture and rural development and for structural policies in the field of environment and transport infrastructure. They will also begin to participate in EC programmes and agencies.

The candidates commit to their respective programmes through ratification of their own parliaments. With the accession negotiations underway, screening of the candidates' progress in adopting and being able to implement the *acquis communautaire* can begin. This is an ongoing process clearing the way for negotiations on outstanding matters and problems arising, or on the future transitional arrangements, which are kept to a minimum. The screening also necessarily affects the drafting of the European/Accession Partnerships.

Even more detailed Road Maps – working documents akin to the Commission's annual progress reports – were used for Bulgaria and Romania, to supplement their Accession Partnerships and included timetables and increased financial assistance, giving them precise milestones and benchmarks to work towards and to use in order to gauge their progress. The Commission would propose to Council the revi-

[65] Various issues arose in the context of the Association Council under the Europe Agreements, such as in the case of the EA Hungary in the adoption of implementing competition rules.

sion of the Accession Partnerships on the basis both of its the regular, annual country reports[66] and the roadmaps.

The pre-accession strategy has therefore continued to evolve in a dynamic way, in line with the inclusive-yet-differentiating approach of the Union towards the potential candidates. The SAAs are drafted to reflect the commitments of the partners in the same optic (that of meeting the Copenhagen criteria) and include time frames for approximation and capacity building work to be completed. Like the Accession Partnerships, the European Partnerships require fulfilment of SAA objectives and programme all Community funding as well as programmes third party lending through the World Bank, the EBRD and the EIB through framework agreements.

The bodies established under the Association Agreement with Turkey and the SAAs are used for the implementation of the overall strategy and are key in the examination and implementation of the European/Accession Partnerships. Due to the political volatility and institutional fragility in the region, the SAP had to begin from a level of preparation in the SEE region that was far lower than that of the CEECs at the time of the launch of the pre-accession strategy. This explains the 'concept of steps' approach under the SAP; the gradual approach beginning with trade preferences, the extension of financial assistance and economic co-operation as well as the establishment of contractual relations, such as the Stabilisation and Association Agreement, all subject to different degrees of conditionality.[67]

It is for this reason that the Union opted to transpose certain of the instruments of the pre-accession strategy into the body of the SAAs themselves, including administrative capacity building and twinning

[66] See Commission 2003 Regular Report on Bulgaria's progress towards accession and 2003 Regular Report on Romania's progress towards accession, both contained in COM(2003) 676, 5 November 2003. See Commission Communication Roadmaps for Bulgaria and Romania, COM(2002) 624, 13 November 2002 at p. 5. The relevant APs Bulgaria and Romania: Council Decision 2003/396/EC on the principles, priorities, intermediate objectives and conditions contained in the Accession Partnership with Bulgaria, *OJ* 2003 L 145/1, and; Council decision 2003/397/EC on the principles, priorities, intermediate objectives and conditions contained in the Accession Partnership with Romania, *OJ* 2003 L 145/21.

[67] Council conclusions on the principle of conditionality governing the development of the European Union's relations with certain countries of south-east Europe, 29 April 1997, *Bull. EC* 4–1997, point 2.2.1.

projects and management.[68] The Union expressly referred to these agreements as central components of the Stabilisation and Association Process and of the Cologne Stability Pact as well as the pre-accession strategy.[69] As described already, the Stability Pact was transformed into the more 'regionally owned co-operation structure' – the Regional Co-operation Council (RCC) – in February 2008.

The priorities and objectives in the European/Accession Partnerships differ according to the country and include political conditions, institutional and administrative capacity building, additional Internal Market measures, justice and home affairs, and the environmental *acquis*. Article 2 of the AP Turkey provided that the bodies established under the Association Agreement Turkey. The appropriate Council bodies examine the implementation of the Accession Partnership and the Commission reports regularly to the Council thereon. Progress is examined by the Council which relies on the Commission for Annual progress Reports in order to assess those areas where further work is required.

### 2.2 *The pre-accession tools for Turkey*

The difficulties faced in the accession negotiations with Turkey were touched on briefly above. This section deals with the pre-accession instruments that apply to Turkey. The pre-accession strategy that was devised for the fifth and sixth enlargements has obviously influenced the form and content of the preparations for the pre-accession of Turkey. In the case of Turkey, Council Regulation 390/2001 was adopted in 2001[70] and is the basis for the current (2005) Accession Partnership for Turkey[71] and is virtually identical to Regulation 622/98, which was used for the CEECs. The first AP Turkey was adopted in 2001

[68] See Commission Report on the Stabilisation and Association process for South Eastern Europe, COM(2002) 163, 4 April 2004 at p. 14.

[69] See the second recital of the SAA Macedonia which reads: 'Considering the importance of this Agreement, in the framework of the Stabilisation and Association process with the countries of south-eastern Europe, to be further developed by an EU Common strategy for this region, in the establishment and consolidation of a stable European order based on co-operation, of which the European Union is a mainstay, as well as the framework of the Stability Pact.'

[70] See Council Regulation 390/2001 on assistance to Turkey in the framework of the pre-accession strategy and in particular on the establishment of an Accession Partnership, *OJ* 2001, L 58/1.

[71] See Council Decision 2006/35/EC on the principles, priorities and conditions contained in the Accession Partnership with Turkey *OJ* 2006 L 22/34. Its predecessor

after the December 1999 Helsinki European Council recognised it as a candidate.[72]

A single financial framework was adopted for Turkey to focus on helping it meet its AP priorities and objectives.[73] In the same wording as Regulation 622/98, Article 4 of Regulation 390/2001 provides the Council with the legal basis to take 'appropriate steps with regard to any pre-accession assistance granted to an applicant State' should Turkey fail to respect elements essential to continued pre-accession assistance. As a result of the December 2004 Brussels European Council, within the framework of the negotiations, further conditionality has been introduced.[74]

This was new at the time. It is a procedure whereby accession negotiations will be suspended rather than Community assistance being harmed or other 'appropriate measures' being taken. The possibility to so suspend the negotiations is limited to the breach – which has to be serious as well as persistent – of human rights, fundamental freedoms and the rule of law. Thus, the negotiations could not be arbitrarily suspended in respect of other Copenhagen or Association Agreement obligations or commitments made during the negotiations and as part of the pre-accession strategy. Also new was that a third of the Member States could take the initiative to stall the negotiations, which at the same time limited the possibility for a lone Member State to act

was Council Decision 2003/398, *OJ* 2003 L 145/40. The first AP Turkey was published in Council Decision 2001/235, *OJ* 2001 L 85/13.

[72] See Council Decision 2001/235/EC on the principles, priorities and intermediate objectives and conditions contained in the Accession Partnership with the Republic of Turkey, *OJ* 2001 L 85/13.

[73] Council Regulation 2500/2001 concerning pre-accession financial assistance for Turkey and amending Regulation 3906/89, 1267/1999, 1268/1999 and 555/2000, *OJ* 2001 L 342/1. See also Corrigendum to Council Regulation 2500/2001, *OJ* 2002 L 285/26.

[74] Presidency Conclusion 23, bullet point 5, which reads: 'in the case of a serious and persistent breach in a candidate state of the principles of liberty, democracy, respect for human rights and fundamental freedoms and the rule of law on which the Union is founded, the Commission will, on its own initiative or on the request of one third of the Member States, recommend the suspension of negotiations and propose the conditions for eventual resumption. The Council will decide by qualified majority on such a recommendation after having heard the candidate State, whether to suspend the negotiations and on the conditions for their resumption. The Member States will act in the IGC in accordance with the Council decision, without prejudice to the general requirement for unanimity in the IGC. The European Parliament will be informed.'

autonomously to block a positive decision by the receiving Member States at the end of the negotiations.

Looking forward to how or when the negotiation may be concluded, it is useful the keep in mind that the twelve new Member States all recognised each other as legal entities under international law. This raises the situation of Turkey. At the time of the 1997 Luxembourg European Council, Turkey had refused to recognize the EU as a legitimate third party to negotiations on issues such as the Cyprus issue or Turkish–Greek disputes.[75]

The Declaration by the European Community and its Member States of 21 September 2005, goes as far as to state that;

> Recognition of all Member States is a necessary component of the accession process. Accordingly, the EU underlines the importance it attaches to the normalisation of relations between Turkey and all EU Member States, as soon as possible.

However, the European Council has held back from insisting on the resolution of the Cyprus problem as a pre-condition to accession.[76] It is hard to imagine how an accession treaty could be signed by a receiving Member State that has not been recognized by the acceding country because unanimity is required among the receiving Member States for signature of an accession treaty. As Hoffmeister points out, the above drafting is intended 'itself to open to potential progress towards finding a comprehensive settlement under UN auspices'. The full recognition of the Republic of Cyprus in advance of a Cyprus settlement would strengthen its position in the UN talks.[77] To date, Turkey has refused to recognise as the Government of the Republic of Cyprus, which is the only authority recognised by international law. The resolution of the Cyprus problem itself cannot be brought about by Turkey acting alone and the EU recognises the UN as the forum for a comprehensive settlement.

---

[75] See Ahmet Sozon 'Turkey's Democratisation in Light of its EU Candidate Status' in Inglis and Ott, eds., *The Constitution for Europe and an enlarging Union: Unity in Diversity?* (Groningen, Europa law Publishing 2005). The Turkish government even announced that it would start integrating Turkish Republic of Northern Cyprus with Turkey in the same way the EU proposed to integrate the Republic of Cyprus.

[76] See F. Hoffmeister, *Legal Aspects of the Cyprus Problem: Annan Plan and EU Accession*, Leiden/Boston, Martinus Nijhoff Publishers 2006 at p. 231.

[77] See ibid.

The December 2004 Brussels European Council 'welcomed'[78] Turkey's willingness to extend the Ankara Agreement to the ten new Member States, some time after the entry into force of the fifth Accession Treaty.[79] The negotiating framework adopted by the European Council on 3 October 2005 lists Copenhagen criteria alongside Turkey's continued support for a comprehensive settlement of the Cyprus problem, Turkey's commitment to good neighbourly relations and its fulfilment of its obligations under the Ankara Agreement. The 2005 AP for Turkey reiterates this position[80] and expressly refers to the declaration by the European Community and its Member States of 21 September 2005. Due to some ambiguity under general international law as to the need for the recognition by Turkey of Cyprus, treaty relations may be established but this in itself does not amount to implied recognition. Therefore, Turkey agreed to the enlargement Protocol to the Ankara Agreement in order to ensure the proper application of the Customs Union with Turkey.[81]

In November 2005, the Commission's Enlargement Strategy Paper was based on three principles: the consolidation of existing commitments; applying a fair and strict conditionality, and; improving communication. This Strategy Paper was drawn up as an accession strategy for Turkey and Croatia but also outlined the further steps necessary to realise the European perspective of the Western Balkans.

---

[78] See Council Press 'Conseil européenne – Conclusions de la présidence' DOC/04/6, 17 December 2004. The relevant passage reads: 'The European Council welcomed Turkey's decision to sign the Protocol regarding the adaptation of the Ankara Agreement, taking account of the accession of the ten new Member States. In this light, it welcomed the declaration of Turkey that 'the Turkish Government confirms that it is ready to sign the Protocol on the adaptation of the Ankara Agreement prior to the actual start of accession negotiations and after reaching agreement on and finalising the adaptations which are necessary in view of the current membership of the European Union'.

[79] Which was signed by Turkey on 28 July 2005.

[80] Op. cit. n. 72. The AP specifies that Turkey should; 'Ensure continued support for efforts to find a comprehensive settlement of the Cyprus problem within the UN framework and in line with the principles on which the Union is founded, whilst contributing to a better climate for a comprehensive settlement. Implement fully the Protocol adapting the Ankara Agreement to the accession of the 10 new EU Member States including Cyprus. Take concrete steps for the normalisation of bilateral relations between Turkey and all EU Member States, including the Republic of Cyprus, as soon as possible.'

[81] See Hoffmeister, ibid. at pp. 223–29.

### 2.3 *The Western Balkans: the Council's conditionality checklist of April 1997*

To conclude contractual relations, the checklist[82] is evaluated and substantial progress must be shown in the field of political and economic reforms and a credible commitment of the government concerned to continue on this path, as well as proven readiness to co-operate and entertain open, good neighbourly relations with the countries in the region. The Copenhagen criteria guide the negotiations, which can be suspended by qualified majority in Council, in the event of a serious and persistent breach of liberty, democracy, respect of human rights and fundamental freedoms.

Thus, the Copenhagen political criteria have evolved beyond a precondition to the opening of accession negotiations and that, together with the good neighbourliness criterion, is the main tool of conditionality in Union's contractual relations with these potential candidates, aimed at building long-term stability on the European continent. While the political criteria are the principal prerequisites to opening accession negotiations, the economic and legal criteria are taking on more importance in the minds of the Commission and the Council. Unlike any previous enlargement, the conclusion of contractual relations (in the form of the SAA) has become the first port of call on the way to fulfilling the entirety of the Union's pre-accession conditionality.

For example, Croatia had to prove that *credible headway* had been made to fulfilling these conditions prior to opening negotiations on its Stabilisation and Association Agreement as did the Federal Yugoslav Republic of Macedonia. There are obvious elements of crisis management, reconstruction and rehabilitation and co-operation with the International Criminal Tribunal for the Former Yugoslavia (ICTY) within this conditionality that were not specifically evident in the political criteria that guided the Commission's *Agenda 2000* evaluation of candidates' readiness to proceed to accession negotiations in the case of the fifth enlargement.[83] This can be attributed to the lower

[82] Council Conclusions of 29 April 1997, op. cit. n. 68, at point 2.2.1.

[83] See above. To recap for ease of reference, in Agenda 2000 the Commission considered the following as indicators or benchmarks against which to mark the readiness of the candidates: the conduct of free and fair elections; whether the party in Opposition played a normal part in the operation of the institutions; the stability of institutions in order to enable public authorities to function properly and democracy to be consolidated and guaranteeing the rule of law and human rights.

political (including economic) point of departure for the integration efforts of the SAA countries, only recently emerging from conflict and political/economic disintegration.

Croatia was successful in opening negotiations for a SAA with the EU following the positive opinion of the Commission, contained in a Feasibility Study on the matter,[84] on its application of 24 May 2000. The Commission was satisfied in particular with the parliamentary and presidential elections.[85] Rather than being a rigid pre-condition to opening negotiations on the SAA, the Commission was moved to its favourable opinion because of 'the encouraging steps undertaken by Croatia to fulfil the EU conditionality' and it was convinced Croatia 'has the capacity ultimately to fulfil the obligations of a SAA'.[86] Accession Protocols were not need for those SAAs that proceeded the fifth and/or sixth enlargements. The benchmarks are the same as those identified in the Commission's positive opinion for opening accession negotiations with nine of the candidates of the fifth enlargement in its *Agenda 2000*. Following signature and conclusion of the SAA Croatia it entered into force 1 February 2005.[87]

The actual launch of accession negotiations is a different matter. In the case of the CEECS, the Commission recommended[88] the opening of accession negotiations based on the political pre-conditions as it outlined in its 1997 country opinions, in which it recommended the opening of accession negotiations with nine of the CEECs. By comparison, for Croatia, within the frame of the Copenhagen criteria are also included: the SAP conditionalities; the fact that Croatia is now a functioning market economy; the fact that Croatia should be able to meet the other economic and legal Copenhagen criteria in the medium term (although full compliance with the *acquis* was highlighted as a long term project).

---

[84] See Report of the Commission on the feasibility of negotiation a Stabilisation and Association Agreement with the Republic of Croatia, COM(2000) 311, 24 May 2000.

[85] The Commission's negotiating mandate, given by the European Council on 20 November 2000, saw the process of negotiation of the SAA begin 24 November 2000 and the initialling of the agreement on 14 May 2001.

[86] See the Commission's explanatory memorandum to its proposals for a Council Decision concerning the signature of the SAA, COM(2001) 371, 9 July 2001 at p. 2.

[87] The Accession Protocol to the SAA Croatia was adopted by Council decision of 13 January 2005, *OJ* 2005 L 26/222.

[88] See for example the Commission's *Opinion on Croatia's Application for Membership of the European Union*, COM(2004) 257, 20 April 2004, pp. 117–12, at pp. 119–120.

The anticipated date for opening accession negotiations with Croatia on 17 March 2005 lapsed principally due to its failure to meet its SAP conditionality to deliver General Gotovina, an indicted war criminal to the ICTY. The opening of accession negotiations with Croatia alongside Turkey by the European Council on 3 October 2005 seems inconsistent with, even to fly in the face of, this same conditionality. In particular, Ante Gotovina – the suspected war criminal indicted for war crimes before the ICTY – had not been handed over to the court in The Hague for actual trial. It had been made clear repeatedly by both Council and Commission that 'full and unconditional co-operation with the ICTY remains an essential requirement for further movement towards the EU'.[89] After all it is very much a matter of the rule of law.

After their launch, *progress* in the negotiations is determined by the measure of: the sustainability of political reforms and Croatia's fulfillment of regional co-operation with the other countries of former Yugoslavia and other international obligations such as co-operation with ICTY, and; the correct transposition and implementation of the *acquis* including effective and efficient application through appropriate administrative and judicial structures.

The EU Foreign Ministers at the January 2005 General Affairs and External Relations Council at least emphasised that negotiations would be slowed or blocked by failure to deliver the indicted war criminals. To have formally opened accession negotiations before indicted war criminals have been physically handed over to the ICTY threatens legal and political weight of the conditionality. The Commission refused to open negotiations with Serbia even for its SAA, on the grounds that it failed to deliver the indicted war criminal Radko Mladic to the ICTY. In January 2005, the General Affairs and External Relations Council added to the list of indicted Serbs (Mr Karadzic and Mr Mladic) that had to be delivered to the ICTY as a prerequisite to negotiations beginning. FYROM has not proceeded to opening accession negotia-

---

[89] See General Affairs and External Relations Council Conclusions of 31 January 2005 referring to similar statements made at previous Councils, including the General Affairs and External Relations Council Conclusions in October 2004. The Council has insisted that accession negotiations will not go ahead without the delivery of General Gotovina.

tions due the slow down in reforms as a result of, interference in the normal functioning of institutions under the current government.[90]

## 3. Financial and operational support and inclusion

### 3.1 *Beginning with Phare…*

Phare[91] had been in place since 1989, initially targeting Hungary and Poland. It was extended over time to all candidates, except Turkey, the last of which to be included in Phare funding being Croatia,[92] before it was repealed and replaced by the Instrument for Pre-accession, which is dealt with in the next section. The Commission's latest report on PHARE, ISPA and SAPARD, was published in 2008.[93] Initially Phare was demand driven in that the recipients decided their own priorities and allocated the funds accordingly.

Back in 1997, *Agenda 2000* kick started the new approach to financing the pre-accession strategy alongside the reorientation of the Europe Agreements to make them proper accession vehicles. To make rapid, useful and quantifiable progress, an innovative approach to financing was needed. All financing, Community and IFI, became accession-driven. Phare remained the main pre-accession financing instrument but two further instruments were added to the mix:

- the ISPA instrument[94] providing structural support for environmental and transport projects, comparable to the Union's Cohesion Fund Regulation 1164/1994, and;
- SAPARD,[95] which provided structural support for agricultural and integrated rural development, comparable to the structural part of the Union's European Agricultural Guarantee and Guidance Fund.

---

[90] See Chapter 2 at p. 79.

[91] Council Regulation 3906/89, op. cit. n. 13.

[92] Council Regulation 2257/2004 amending Regulations 3906/89, 1267/1999, 1268/1999 and (EC) No 2666/2000, to take into account of Croatia's candidate status, *OJ* 2004 L 389/1-4.

[93] See Commission Communication COM(2008) 880 of 22 December 2008. The earlier report was contained in Commission Communication COM(2007) 3 and its annex, COM(2007) 11, both of 12 January 2007.

[94] Regulation 1267/99, *OJ* 1999 L 161/73.

[95] Regulation 1268/99, *OJ* 1999 L 161/87.

The various funding instruments had to be sufficiently flexible to accommodate changes in the priorities for action in line with the progress made by the candidates. Pre-accession aid had to be effective in the medium term and not only in the longer term, as in the case for traditional development aid. However, Regulation 622/98 and the APs could not have financial implications as such.[96] As regards the financing of the strategy, therefore, Council Regulation 1266/99[97] was adopted, to tie the various pre-accession funding instruments to the association agreements, the Copenhagen criteria and to the APs as well as providing for their co-ordination.

The conditionality attaching to Turkey's financing instruments was dealt with at 2.2 above. Between 1991 and 2000, over EUR 5 billion has been provided by the EU to the countries of the Western Balkans.[98] Most of the Community assistance had previously been provided under the 1996 OBNOVA[99] and the 1989 PHARE[100] programmes. Under the CARDS programme for the period of 2000 to 2006, a budget of EUR 4.65 billion was agreed, in addition to the benefits of the trade preferences awarded these countries. The CARDS programme,[101] is the equivalent of the co-ordinating Regulation 1266/99 used in support of the priorities and actions undertaken within the SAP and under the SAAs.

Under the specific pre-accession conditionality set out by the Council for south eastern Europe in April 1997[102] access to Union assistance under PHARE as well as the Obnova Regulation,[103] was also subject

[96] This Regulation, adopted by unanimity, was based on Art. 235 EC Treaty, which in the absence of any other appropriate Treaty Articles, enables the Community to take 'appropriate measures' to 'attain one of the objectives of the Community'. Art. 235 could only be used where no other Treaty Article provided the legal basis for appropriate measures. Aid programmes are provided for in the Treaties and the programming of financial resources is, rather, dealt with in the financial instruments and programmes adopted under the pertinent Treaty provisions.

[97] Regulation 1266/99 on co-ordinating aid to the applicant countries in the framework of the pre-accession strategy and amending Regulation 3906/89, *OJ* 1999 L 161/68.

[98] See Annex B to the *First Commission Report on the Stabilisation and Association Process for South East Europe*, COM(2002) 163 final, 4 April 2002, p. 23.

[99] Council Regulation 1628/96 of 25 July 1996 relating to aid for Bosnia and Herzegovina, Croatia, the Federal Republic of Yugoslavia and the Former Yugoslav Republic of Macedonia, *OJ* 1996 L 204 /1 ('Obnova').

[100] Regulation 3906/89, op. cit. n. 13.

[101] Contained in Council Regulation 2666/2000.

[102] Op. cit. n. 67.

[103] Council Regulation 1288/96, op. cit. n. 95.

to the regional and country specific political pre-conditions. Obnova was repealed and replaced as the Community's main assistance programme for the Western Balkans by the CARDS programme on 7 December 2000.[104] CARDS amended PHARE to extract the countries of the region from its scope and established the single financial framework for the region.

As of the Council's 1997 Conclusions, PHARE assistance in support of democracy would be measured by 'evidence of a country's credible commitment to democratic reforms and progress in compliance with the generally recognised standards of human and minority rights'. General PHARE assistance required 'compliance with obligations under the peace agreements, including those relating to co-operation with the International Tribunal in bringing war criminals to justice'. Compliance includes an undertaking to make the Federation/Croatia as well as the Republica Srpska/Federal Republic of Yugoslavia agreements compatible with the Dayton Peace Agreements, the General Framework Agreement for Peace (GFAP), under the guidance of OHR (Office of the High Representative and the EU Special Representative).

An equally important part of the equation is human and minority rights and the offer of real opportunities to displaced persons (including so called "internal migrants") and refugees to return to their place of origin. A 'credible commitment' was needed to economic reforms. Moreover, significant steps had to be shown towards co-operation with its neighbours and the establishment of open relations, including the free movement of people and goods. General PHARE assistance also requires a credible offer of a real dialogue on the status of Kosovo by the SEE countries concerned. PHARE assistance to Bosnia that did not meet this demand, were limited to projects in direct support of the peace agreements, in particular the building of cross-entity links and refugee return.

For the Western Balkans countries there is no specific clause in the European Partnership for the express suspension of assistance in the event of a breach of the European Partnership. But the CARDS financing

[104] Council Regulation 2666/2000 on assistance for Albania, Bosnia and Herzegovina, Croatia, the Federal Republic of Yugoslavia and the Former Yugoslav Republic of Macedonia, repealing Regulation 1628/96 and amending Regulations 3906/89 and 1360/90 and Decisions 97/256 and 1999/311/, *OJ* 2000 L 306/1, as amended by Regulation 2415/2001, *OJ* 2001 L 327/3.

regulation[105] had its own specific essential elements clause (Art. 5 thereof). However, the conditionality being applied is increasingly specified for the Western Balkans and harder than the conditionality applied in respect of the CEECs – harder because the concrete conditions on human rights and minority rights and fundamental freedoms are *preconditions* to assistance. Where these essential elements were found lacking, the partner was no longer eligible for assistance and this did away with the need for a Council decision. This gives the executive more powers at an earlier stage in the proceedings. In the case of Regulation 622/98, the lack of an essential element was not a pre-condition to funding as such and concerned the fulfilment of obligations under the Europe Agreement or the Copenhagen criteria and commitments made during the negotiations. Also under the CARDS Regulation, the country-specific conditions (which are not referred to as pre-conditions) of the Council Conclusions of 29 April 1997 (Art. 5(2) of the CARDs Regulation) applied to Community assistance in advance of a country joining the ranks of the candidate countries.

### 3.2 *The Instrument for Pre-accession Assistance*

This conditionality is taken up again in the reform of the financing rules under the new Council framework Instrument for Pre-accession Assistance (IPA) Regulation.[106] The IPA is one of the six external relations instruments that apply for the 2007 to 2013 timeframe, introducing an overall coherence and structure to the Communities financial perspectives for external aid and development instruments. The other instruments include two regional instruments – the European Neighbourhood and Partnership Instrument (ENPI), the Development Cooperation and Economic Co-operation (DCEC) – and three thematic instruments – the Stability Instrument, the Humanitarian Aid Instrument, the Macro-financing Instrument (MFA). The MFA will provide exception additional support to the IPA: according to the European Commission's website, such support will normally be in the context of an IMF programme, the Commission launches EC macro-financial assistance in favour of a particular third country. There is currently one ongoing macro-financial assistance operation in the Western Bal-

[105] Contained in Council Regulation 2666/2000, ibid.
[106] Regulation 1085/2006, *OJ* 2006 L 210/82.

kans, in favour of Kosovo, in the form of up to EUR 50 million grants for budget support.[107]

The IPA has recast the 'preconditions for eligibility for Community assistance' of human rights, minority rights and fundamental freedoms, conform to Article 5 CARDS Regulation, as 'essential elements'. According to the wording of Article 17 of the IPA Regulation, Community assistance will be subject to these 'essential elements' and also the 'conditions' of the Council Conclusions of 29 April 1997. Article 21 of the IPA sets down a *clausula rebus sic stantibus* (to take account of a material or serious change in circumstances) for the granting of Community assistance, giving the Council acting by qualified majority – on a proposal of the Commission – the competence to make the adaptations it considers necessary should a beneficiary country violate fundamental principles of democracy, rule of law, human rights, minority rights or where progress with a view to the European Partnerships or the Accession Partnerships is insufficient. For the Western Balkan countries, this repeats the special conditionality set out in Article 5(2) of the CARDS Regulation. Failings by a potential or actual candidate in meeting either the essential elements or the preconditions may attract suspension of Community assistance, again by Council decision acting by qualified majority on a Commission proposal. Once a country becomes a candidate proper, the above clause on the suspension of the negotiations will also apply.

The IPA entered into force on 1 January 2007. It is based entirely upon Article 212(1) TFEU, see page 114 above. These articles concern development co-operation and economic, financial and technical co-operation with third countries. It repealed the Regulation 2500/2001 on pre-accession financial assistance for Turkey[108] and replaced the CARDS Regulation, which did not require repeal because it came to an end on 31 December 2006, although prior commitments may remain open still. It has a total budget of EUR 4,118.9 million for the period 2007–2009, the bulk of which is used in the national programmes, while 10% of the budget under the Multi-Beneficiary Programmes is EUR 401.4 million. The Multi-Beneficiary Programme is expressly

[107] See European Commission Europa website, visited on 30 June 2009, http://ec.europa.eu/economy_finance/int_economic_issues/non_eu_economies211_en.htm.
[108] Regulation 2500/2001 op. cit. n. 73.

designed to complement the national programmes where there is a clear advantage to be gained through harmonised regional approaches, such as facilitating networks of experts.[109] The Multi-Beneficiary Programme also expressly provides for the co-ordination of all financing of International Financing Institutions, just as the Memorandum of Understanding (MoU) had provided in respect of the fifth and sixth enlargements, and is specific as to the expected results and activities for such financing. The MoU of 20 May 2003 concerns the co-operation and financing by the EBRD, the World Bank, the European Investment Bank and the Council of Europe Development Bank and the German Kreditanstalt für Wiederaufbau (KfW).

Further financial commitments to the new Member States under PHARE, the CBC Regulation, for Malta and Cyprus under Regulation 555/2000 or under other pre-accession funding were no longer possible after 31 December 2003 (Art. 32(1) of the fifth Accession Treaty). Two funds were directly concerned by this: ISPA,[110] the old pre-accession fund for structural policies in the field of the environment and transport infrastructure, and; SAPARD,[111] the pre-accession funds for agriculture and rural development. The equivalent provisions in the sixth Accession Treaty, Article 28 and 29. These funds can still be used after the actual enlargement. This is so that funds that have not been used pre-accession can still be allocated or applied if they have already been allocated. As will be seen in Chapter 5, Bulgaria and Romania face serious difficulties in taking up and absorbing outstanding pre-accession funding and risk losing millions of Euro as a result.

However, the IPA Regulation, at Article 25, enables these rules to continue to apply in respect of legal acts and commitments implementing the budget years preceding 2007. Otherwise, once the IPA took effect it replaced the financing procedures that applied under these instruments. Global budget commitments made before accession, which include individual legal commitments and payments made after accession, continue to be governed by the rules and regulations of the pre-accession financing instruments and are charged to the corre-

[109] See Commission Decision C(2007)2205 of 29 May 2007, establishing a Multi-Beneficiary Multi-annual Indicative Planning Document (MIPD) 2007–2009, which has been adopted on the basis of Art. 6 of the IPA.

[110] Op. cit. n. 94.

[111] Op. cit. n. 95.

sponding budget chapters until closure of the programmes and project concerned (Art. 33(2), 2003 Act of Accession).

The IPA is a housekeeping and improvement exercise. Such a framework approach is consistent with the inclusive nature of the pre-accession strategy. Introducing such a unified system is logical for other reasons too. All eligible countries are governed by the same regime, improving transparency and ensuring coherence with earlier Community assistance, allocated under the CARDS or Turkey Regulations, by globally targeting the same objectives set down there. It also limits the possibility for political jealousies to arise between countries as they progress towards membership, albeit with their different status of candidate and potential candidate. It remains a parallel and mutually complementing approach effectively requiring all target countries to adopt these objectives, principles and priorities into their own national planning and by means of their own procedures. While it is a Council Regulation, the Commission will continue to monitor and evaluate the implementation and enforcement in the candidate and potential candidate countries just as it has always done.

The regulation builds on the main lessons learned in the context of the pre-accession process, in particular through:[112]

- streamlining pre-accession assistance by enhancing co-ordination between the different components, through the creation of a single framework for assistance. This single framework will integrate the Phare/ISPA/SAPARD structure and complete the framework with other Structural Funds and Rural Development Funds Components. It will aim at harmonising implementation rules, where possible taking into account the specificity of the Structural Funds and Rural Development Regulations, and create a Comitology system which will ensure a maximum of co-ordination among the components,
- aiming at better preparation for Structural and Rural Development Funds implementation after accession, through further enhancing emphasis on institution building as well as progressive emulation of Structural Funds rules in the run-up to accession.

The Accession Partnerships with the candidate countries and the European Partnerships with the potential candidate countries will continue to provide the single framework and will guide the Commission in its allocation of assistance under each component and country. There are

[112] See Explanatory Memorandum to the IPA proposal in the General Introduction, COM(2004) 627, 29 September 2004.

Table 3. Entitlement components under the proposed Instrument for Pre-accession Assistance (IPA)

The five components are set out in Title II of the proposed IPA Regulation and components are set out in Article 3(1), namely:

(a) Transitional assistance and institution building;
(b) regional and cross-border co-operation;
(c) regional development;
(d) human resources development;
(e) rural development.

five components, see Table 3. Candidate countries have access to all five components. Potential candidate countries are limited to the first and second component.

These components address the (potential) candidates' need for support of wide-ranging institution building measures, including investment, and the need to vigorously support their preparations for implementing the Unions structural and cohesion policy. The rationale of three separate components tackling regional, rural and human development is that candidate countries are confronted with exactly this situation in the Union's agricultural and cohesion policy after accession. As the enlargement process for the fifth and sixth enlargements has shown, the early familiarisation with this complex system is of primary importance for the proper implementation and management of structural and rural development funds after accession. Mastering this complex system requires an intensive and sustained learning process. Candidate countries thus have the opportunity to 'practise' the Union rural and cohesion policies by applying rules as closely as possible to the structural and rural development funds before accession.

A core objective of the pre-accession strategy is to build the candidates' capacity to manage EU funds in preparation for their inclusion in the various forms of structural funds at Union level. All candidates are required to move towards being accredited to participate in the Extended Decentralised Implementation System – or the partially Decentralised Implementation System (DIS) in the interim – so that they are able to do this. Having done so, they are ready to participate in the 'shared management environment' along with the Member States for managing the structural funds when they eventually do accede. For the countries of the 2004 enlargement wave, this was completed in 2005. For Bulgaria and Romania, while they were both fully EDIS accredited in 2007 although problems have been identified there.[113] As for the Balkans countries, only Croatia operated under the partial DIS but problems persist there also. Turkey, also operating under the partial system, was also highly criticised for failings in the administration of the Community funds.

### 3.3 *Incorporating the candidates at an operational level in EU programmes and agencies*

Another factor in the lengthened lead-time for the accession of the CEECs must be that of mutual trust between the receiving and entering Member States. For the purposes of accession to the Union this has been more a matter trust of the receiving Member States in the abilities of the incoming Members not only that they would truly meet the Copenhagen criteria upon their accession but that they would continue to be able and willing to do so as Member States. This can be said because in some cases the demands made of the candidates have gone further than the standard applied in the Union.[114] Preparing (potential) candidates for taking part in the every day workings of the Union has been part of the overall trust building exercise. Participation of the candidates in Union programmes, agencies and committees was anticipated by the Copenhagen European Council of 1993. The December 1994 Essen European Council specifically mentioned that the pre-accession strategy was designed to encourage mutual trust through structured dialogue[115] and the Europe Agreements signed thereafter would highlight this purpose in their preambles.[116] Trust is a rather elusive concept to quantify and therefore also to anticipate. It implies the need of one party for assurance from the other

[113] See European Commission *2007 Annual Report on Phare*, etc., COM(2008) 880 of 22 December 2008.

[114] See C. Hillion 'Enlargement of the European Union – The discrepancy between membership obligations and accession conditions as regards the protection of minorities', 27 *Fordham International Law Journal* (2004) pp. 715–740.

[115] 'The [pre-accession] strategy adopted by the European Council is being politically implemented by the creation, between the associated States and the institutions of the European Union, of 'structured relations' which encourage mutual trust and will provide a framework for addressing topics of common interest.'

[116] For example, the Europe Agreement Latvia uses the same wording as the Essen European Council in its preamble.

of the latter's integrity, veracity, justice, friendship, or other sound principle, including confidence, reliance, hope, belief.[117] In the case of the CEECs, the obvious example of their transition from non-market economies to functioning market economies in the 1990s, which has been a painful leap, compares dramatically with the situations of previous enlargements. The Balkan countries begin from an even lower starting point. The concrete criteria attaching to membership that are explored in the following chapters, are the means by which the candidates give credence to their commitments to the receiving Member States. They must justify the belief of the Union in their ability and willingness, present and future, to meet their obligations as Member States and participate in the future development and reinforcement of the Union's activities.

Many of the programmes and agencies are also open to third countries. For example, in the cases of the agri-food and the environment *acquis*, the countries of the EEA participate in the Food and Veterinary Office (FVO) and neighbouring countries also participate in the European Environment Agency (EEAg), including other European countries as well as, for example, those bordering the Mediterranean and Russia.

A Commission Communication[118] on the matter in 1999 outlined the approach for the fifth enlargement to incorporating the candidates, following *Agenda 2000* and the 1997 Luxembourg European. It has become standard practice for the Union to agree with each candidate, and now also potential candidates, the specific terms for that third country's participation in Union programmes and agencies. Participation requires that the candidates forward part of their pre-accession funding allocation to the programme in question, giving them the full administrative backup of the Union agencies and bodies. Participation in Union bodies is decided on a case-by-case basis but is a fundamental step towards familiarising the candidates with the *acquis communautaire*. Again, the European or Accession Partnerships specify priorities for reinforcing administrative and judicial capacity as well as the funding allocations for participation in the Sixth Research and Technological Development Framework Programme for

[117] Definitions taken from *Merriam Websters Collegiate Dictionary*, 11th edition.

[118] Communication from the Commission to the Council on *Participation of candidate countries in Community programmes, agencies and committees*, COM(1999) 710, 20 December 1999, *Bull. EU* 12/99 at 1.3.16.

example. Under the Seventh Research and Technological Development Framework Programme,[119] Turkey and all the candidates and potential candidates are also associate members. This further deepens the overall process of familiarising the candidates with practical aspects of becoming a Member State. As had been the practice with Cyprus and Malta, a Framework Agreement was agreed between the European Union and Turkey for its participation in Union programmes.[120]

According to the 'Thessaloniki Agenda for the Western Balkans: moving towards European integration', endorsed at the June 2003 Thessaloniki European Council, '[Union] programmes are opened to SAP countries along the lines established for the participation of candidate countries' and 'SAP countries could be allowed to participate in Union agencies, in ways similar to those established for candidate countries.' A Communication was adopted in 2003,[121] preparing the Western Balkans countries for their gradual participation in Union programmes. Priority areas for the opening of programmes include education and training, culture, research, energy, environment, civil society, SME support, and anti-fraud co-ordination. A Council Decision was adopted in June 2005 for the signing of a Protocol to the SAA FYROM on general principles for the FYROM's participation in Union programmes.[122]

---

[119] See http://cordis.europa.eu/fp7/. See the Memorandums of Understanding to this effect signed 1 June 2007 (Turkey), 13 June 2007 (Croatia, FYROM, Serbia), 17 December 2007 (Albania), 25 January 2008 (Montenegro), 1 January 2009 (Bosnia & Herzegovina).

[120] Framework Agreement between the European Community and the Republic of Turkey on the general principles for the participation of the Republic of Turkey in Community programmes, *OJ* 2002 L 061/29. Council Decision 2002/179 concerning the conclusion of a Framework Agreement between the European Community and the Republic of Turkey on the general principles for the participation of the Republic of Turkey in Community programmes, *OJ* 2002 L 061/27. The general terms and conditions for the participation of Bulgaria and Romania when they were candidates, were agreed under the auspices of the Europe Agreements in the EU-Romania and EU-Bulgaria Association Councils, see Decision 1/2002 of the EU-Bulgaria Association Council of 5 June 2002 adopting the general terms and conditions for the participation of the Republic of Bulgaria in Community programmes, *OJ* 2002 L 317/27 and Decision 1/2002 of the EU-Romania Association Council of 18 February 2002 adopting the general terms and conditions for the participation of Romania in Community programmes, *OJ* 2002 L 91/20.

[121] Communication, Preparing for the participation of the Western Balkan countries in Community programmes and agencies, COM(2003) 748, 3 December 2003.

[122] Commission Proposal for a Council Decision concerning the signing of a Protocol to the Stabilisation and Association Agreement between the European Communities and their Member States, of the one part, and the former Yugoslav Republic of Macedonia, of the other part, on a Framework Agreement between the European

Framework Agreements were also concluded in June 2005 with the other Western Balkans countries to the same end.[123]

There are obvious advantages to incorporating (potential) candidate countries in pre-accession within the bodies and programmes before their actual membership, including familiarising them with the practicalities of participating in such bodies and the multiplier effect of investing Union resources in the region. However, neither the multilateral component of the SEECP nor its predecessor the European Conference, nor even the inclusion of the new members in Union programmes and agencies, can fully prepare future Member States for the breadth of institutional decision-making expertise and know-how that had been hoped of the structured dialogue[124] in the early days of the association with the Europe Agreement countries. Chapters 6 and 7 touch on how candidates are incorporated into the Union programmes and agencies in the specific context of the agri-food and environment *acquis*.

Community and the former Yugoslav Republic of Macedonia on the general principles for the participation of the former Yugoslav Republic of Macedonia in Community programmes, COM(2004) 729, 27 October 2004. It was adopted by the Justice and Home Affairs Council on 2 June 2005, see Council document 9568/05 of 1 June 2005 (it was adopted as an 'A' point), to be found on the Council website at www.register.consilium.eu.int/pdf/fr/05/st05/st05532.fr05.pdf.

[123] Including Albania, Bosnia and Herzegovina, Croatia and Serbia and Montenegro, all contained in COM(2004) 809, 16 December 2004. These were formally adopted by Council on 2 June 2005, see Council Decision OJ 2005 L 92/84. A Protocol to the SAA Montenegro, Protocol 8, has also been adopted and is being implemented on a provisional basis, see Council Decision 2008/127, *OJ* 2008 L 43/9.

[124] See *Agenda 2000*, COM(1997) 2000 of 15 July 1997, Vol. 1 at p. 62. Torreblanca talks of political dialogue having become 'flexibility without substance' leading to general retrenchment of a majority of the Member States and even the Commission services from the principles written into the Europe Agreements. See Torreblanca, op. cit. n. 17, at pp. 287–296. See also M. Maresceau, 'Pre-accession: the legal approach' op. cit. Chapter 1, n. 24.

CHAPTER FOUR

# ACCESSION TREATIES: TRANSITIONAL ARRANGEMENTS AND OTHER MEANS TO EASE THE IMPACT OF ENLARGEMENT

## 1. Flexibility mechanisms in accession treaties and their negotiation

Various new means have been introduced into accession treaty practice used in the fifth and sixth Accession Treaties to allow a certain flexibility to smooth the entry of the incoming countries but without allowing permanent derogations from the *acquis communautaire*.

Typical devices[1] in accession treaties to ease the newcomers' entry, as much for the receiving Member States, are conceived as flexiblity mechanisms.[2] Transitional arrangements allow for the temporary derogations from provisions of the *acquis*. They have to be set out in the Act of Accession. Certainly, where no transitional arrangement is set out in an Accession Treaty – although perhaps it is to state the obvious – the reciprocal rights and obligations of membership demand compliance with the *acquis* in its entirety.

The vast approximation and capacity building exercise of the fifth, sixth and future enlargements was explicitly designed to reduce the margins for transitional arrangements and the Commission was keen

[1] Peculiar to the Fourth enlargement, certain transitional arrangements had to be agreed in the form of a Transitional Arrangements Agreement to enable Austria, Finland and Sweden to move from the EFTA pillar of the EEA Agreement to the EC pillar. See the Agreement on the transitional arrangements for a period after the accession of certain EFTA States to the European Union of 28 September 1994. On this Agreement, see Tichy and Dedicehm, 'Securing a smooth shift between the two EEA Pillars: prolonged competence of EFTA institutions with respect to former EFTA states after their accession to the European Union', 32 *CML Rev.* (1995) at pp. 131–156. However, generally speaking the Union took no role in the adaptation and approximation exercise undertaken by the incoming countries. It was for the applicant alone to set about adopting the entirety of the *acquis communautaire* and it was for the applicant to evaluate and guarantee its ability to take on the obligations of membership prior to their accession.

[2] See Commission Communication *Enlargement of the Community: transitional periods and the institutional implications of enlargement*, 20 April 1978, *Bull. EC* 2/78 at p. 7, para. 12.

throughout to grant only the most worthy of requests for transitional arrangements. While transitional arrangements are a possibility in limited circumstances, it is certain that any request by a candidate for a transitional arrangement in the transposition of mundane but nevertheless necessary legislation for example, would have been rejected by the Commission services. As is addressed in Part Two, however, there are examples of such informal transitional arrangements in the agri-food and environment *acquis*.

This Chapter first looks at how transitional arrangements are negotiated, see 1.1 below. The structure of the Accession Treaties is briefly outlined at 1.2. The scope and content of transitional arrangements are dealt with at 2. This Chapter ends by considering the scope for emergency economic safeguard measures under an accession treaty, which are open to 'old' or 'new' Member States or both, depending on the circumstances, see 3 below. Chapter 2, at 3.2, has already emphasised the extreme unlikelihood of permanent derogations from the *acquis*. Where a new Member State has not transposed, implemented or complied with other measures, this would be illegal. Examples of such 'informal transitional arrangements' are looked at in the context of the EU agri-food and environment *acquis* in Part 2.

The next Chapter explores the new flexibility mechanisms that were introduced in the fifth and sixth Accession Treaties, which should be distinguished from transitional arrangements as such. Perhaps most novel of all is the partial or non-participation of the new Member States of the fifth and sixth enlargements in EMU, Schengen and the Common Agricultural Policy. There is also the special situation of Cyprus, which remains a divided island. The approach to the integration of the new (and future) Member States in these areas of the *acquis* is to gradually include them while the fifteen Member States continue to make their own progress in these fields. This marks a new era of differentiation between Member States, with all the legal complexity that this involves,[3] and raises important broader questions for the future of the Union, including for example, solidarity among Member States and European identity.

---

[3] See also A. Ott, 'Unity in Diversity? Differentiation in EU law and policy in an enlarged European Union', Zeszyt 15 EUI *Research Laboratory Centrum Europejskie Natolin* (2004).

Additionally, new forms of safeguard measure – or 'trust mechanisms' – have been included in the fifth and the sixth Accession Treaties. Chapter 5 also looks at the new Co-operation and Verification Mechanism that was devised to keep up the pressure on Bulgaria and Romania to improve their implementation of and compliance with the certain sensitive chapters of the *acquis* after their accession in 2007. Finally, Chapter 5 will comment on the postponement clause contained in the sixth Accession Treaty, to postpone the application of that Treaty, which was not used in the end.

Looking to the future, further accessions will bring new accession treaties containing their own transitional arrangements together with, no doubt, similar (perhaps even new) safeguard clauses or means of delaying full participation in EU policies and programmes, while the transitional arrangement contained in the fifth and sixth Accession Treaties run their course. If the same approach is taken as under the sixth Accession Treaty, much of the work adjusting the *acquis* will not be done by means of the Accession Treaty but will be done progressively by special amendment of the laws concerned.

### 1.1 *Negotiating transitional arrangements*

The fact that a transitional arrangement was granted one applicant has never stood as a precedent for granting transitional arrangements requested by another. This is evident from the accession treaties, which are drafted so as to treat the specific provisions and transitional arrangements of relevance to each of the applicants in turn.

In previous practice, a Community procedure[4] was followed at all levels and on all matters. For the very first enlargement negotiations, the Member States, with the help of the Commission, would speak only through the Council. The Member States would be present at the negotiating session as silent observers, on hand to caucus consensus should the session require their input.[5] The Council decided on a

[4] See also Kapteyn and VerLoren van Themaat on 'Scope and revision of the Treaty' in Gormley, ed., *Introduction to the Law of the European Communities,* (London, The Hague, Boston, Kluwer Law International 1998) at p. 94. Introducing the negotiating process for the first four enlargements, see Preston, op. cit., Chapter 1 at n. 24 at pp. 10–11. See also Puissochet op. cit., Chapter 1, n. 24 at pp. 19–30, covering also the negotiations according to the Arts 98 ECSC Treaty and 205 EURATOM Treaty.

[5] See W. Nicoll and A. Salmon, *Understanding the European Communities,* (Worcester, Philip Allan 1990) at pp. 28–29.

common position for the negotiations and invited the Commission to make the necessary proposals to that effect. COREPER prepared the discussions in Council and the President in office put forward the common position in the negotiations and defended that common position. The Council would decide in certain cases, particularly as concerned Community policies, to devolve the task of negotiating to the Commission, in some cases even to the extent of discussing the solution with the third country before reporting back to the Council. The terms that were agreed upon were then inserted into the agreement in the form of a treaty of accession and an act of accession and, as already noted, the bulk of the approximation work of the incoming Member States would be undertaken before accession.

The rationale behind the negotiation of the transitional arrangements for the fifth and sixth enlargements emphasised the Union's insistence on full approximation prior to accession. Between the signature of the fifth Accession Treaty and its entry into force on 1 May 2004, the candidates had considerable work to complete. It was already clear that more transitional arrangements would be added to the country annexes contained in the Act of Accession after closure of the negotiations for the 2003 Accession Treaty, see 4.3 below.

In its Opinion of 19 February 2003 on the applications for accession,[6] required under Article 49 EU, in the fifth recital the Commission[7] found the Ten to 'fulfil the political criteria for membership and that they will have fulfilled the economic and *acquis* criteria and will be ready for membership from the beginning of 2004'. No mention was made of the actual readiness of the Ten. Unlike previous accession treaties, the Commission;

> [called] on the acceding States to pursue vigorously the improvements that still [need] to be made in the context of the political and economic criteria for membership and in relation to the adoption, implementation and enforcement of the *acquis*; the Commission will continue to monitor the implementation of the commitments and obligations taken on by the acceding States, and will assist them with the available instruments.

---

[6] Commission Opinion of 19 February 2003, *OJ* 2003 L 236/3.

[7] It made this recommendation on the basis of its *2002 Strategy Report*, COM(2002) 700 of 9 October 2002.

This eleventh recital[8] is entirely new to previous Commission Opinions introducing the Accession Treaties and clearly referred to the fact that the candidate must continue to make substantial efforts *after* their accession. The same wording can be found in Recital 10 to the Commission's Opinion introducing the sixth Accession Treaty. A considerable programme of work faced the twelve new Member States even having signed their Accession Treaties,[9] on top of the timetables for complying with the transitional arrangements written into the fifth and sixth Accession Treaties.

It was clear from the Commission's strategy as early as 1997[10] that while transitional arrangements were inevitable, they were to be the exception rather than the rule and to be avoided insofar as feasibly possible. Obvious central themes underlying this approach were the indivisibility of the *acquis* and a concern to avoid a protectionist backlash against the future new Member States, and the consequent disunity that this might provoke. In its *Enlargement Strategy Paper*[11] in 2000 the Commission framed its approach: transitional arrangements would be exceptional, 'limited in time and scope, and accompanied by a plan with clearly defined stages for application of the *acquis*. They must not involve amendments to the rules or policies of the Union, disrupt their proper functioning, or lead to significant distortions of competition. In this connection, account must be taken of the interests of the Union, the applicant country and the other applicant states.' The Commission went on to note that:

> for those areas linked to the extension of the single market, regulatory measures could be implemented quickly. Any transition periods should therefore be few and short. For those areas of the *acquis* where considerable adaptations are necessary and which require substantial effort, including important financial outlays in areas such as environment, energy and infrastructure, transitional arrangements could be spread

[8] For the sixth Accession Treaty, the equivalent statement is contained in the ninth recital of the Commission Opinion of 22 February 2005 on the applications for accession to the European Union of Bulgaria and Romania, *OJ* 2005 L 153/3.

[9] See the Commission's ten country reports, Cyprus SEC(2002) 1401, Czech Republic SEC(2002) 1402, Estonia SEC(2002) 1403, Hungary SEC (2002)1404, Latvia SEC(2002) 1405, Lithuania SEC(2002) 1406, Malta SEC(2002)1407, Poland SEC(2002) 1408, Slovakia SEC(2002)1410 and Slovenia SEC(2002)1411, all of 9 October 2002.

[10] See *Agenda 2000*, op. cit., Introduction n. 14 at p. 56.

[11] Enlargement Strategy Paper, Report on progress towards accession by each of the candidate countries (for 2000), pp. 225–28 to be found at www.europa.eu.int/comm/enlargement/report_11_00/index.htm

> over a definite period of time, provided candidates can demonstrate that alignment is under way and that they are committed to detailed and realistic plans for alignment, including the necessary investments.

Each request for a transitional measure (a pre-determined transitional measure) was assessed on a case-by-case basis, taking account of that country's interests and the likely impact of each request on the functioning of the Union and the interests of the other applicant states. That one country secured a transitional arrangement was not taken as a precedent for the other countries and nor was that fact that transitional measures had been granted in a previous accession treaty.

Requests for transitional arrangements were divided into three types:

*Acceptable*: being transitional measures of a technical nature that pose no significant problem. Acceptance of this type of request had advanced negotiations in certain chapters from early on the negotiations. The Commission had, since September 2000, been examining favourably requests for transitional measures that were limited in time and scope, and were considered not to have a significant impact on competition or the functioning of the Internal Market.

*Negotiable*: being those requests with a more significant impact, in terms of competition or the internal market, or in time or space. Such transitional measures were acceptable subject to set conditions and a time-limit. Account was taken of their relationship to other transitional arrangements or areas of the *acquis* without transitional measures or of the country's commitment to well-defined plans for implementation and investment. Necessarily, implications for competition and the single market were a decisive factor in the final grant of the transitional arrangement, as were effects on the economy, health, safety, the environment, consumers, citizens, other common policies and the Union budget.

*Unacceptable*: being requests for transitional measures posing fundamental problems.

Thus, in the negotiation of the fifth and sixth Accession Treaties, the Union was careful to limit transitional arrangements and to ensure that the incoming countries complete their work under the pre-accession strategy in advance of accession. In this regard, the main point of comparison between the first four enlargements and the most recent enlargement has been the extent and detail of pre-accession assistance and conditionality used. The vast, wholesale approximation exercise of the new pre-accession for the fifth enlargement was specifically designed to reduce the need for transitional arrangements. No picking and choosing of bits and pieces of the *acquis* was considered; a 'take it or leave it' approach has characterised the fifth and sixth enlargements' accession negotiations. The new Member States have been denied the possibility of derogating permanently from any chapter of the *acquis*, even where certain of the Fifteen do not participate, such as Schengen or Economic and Monetary Union. The rationale underlying the negotiation of the transitional arrangements for the fifth enlargement has reflected this. Examples of how this applied in practice in the environment *acquis* are given in Chapter 6.

### 1.2 *The structure of accession treaties*

Little has changed in the content of an Accession Treaty, which typically contain only three articles. The sixth, which was signed during the national ratification procedures for the Constitutional Treaty, contained three extra articles to take account of the possibility of the Constitutional Treaty having been ratified.

An *Accession Treaty* typically has three articles. The first lays down the conditions of admission and the adjustments to the treaties and provides that its accompanying acts of accession form an integral part of that treaty. The second provides for the ratification of the Treaty by the High Contacting Parties in accordance with their respective constitutional requirements, together with the date of entry into force of the Treaty and the details of the deposit of national instruments of ratification, and makes provision for a situation where a signatory fails, for whatever reason, to do so. The third establishes which languages are 'equally authentic' for the Treaty. With the 2005 Accession Treaty Bulgarian and Romanian became official languages, Bulgarian being the first official language in Cyrillic script, bringing the total number of official languages to twenty-three.

Malta secured temporary derogation measures for the drafting in Maltese of the acts of the institutions of the European Union, which lifted the obligation to publish secondary legislation in the Maltese language for 30 months, potentially extendable for a further year.[12]

[12] Regulation 930/2004, *OJ* 2004 L 169/1. Also, the Irish language is also now recognised as an official language, see Regulation 920/2005 amending Regulation No. 1 of

However, this did not apply to the 2003 Accession Treaty or its Act of Accession and nor does it apply to regulations of the European Parliament and Council.

The conditions of accession are fleshed out in the accompanying *Act of Accession*, under the following headings.

*Principles* These principles place the new Member States on the same footing as the existing Members. In the 2003 Act of Accession, Article 3 (to be read in conjunction with Annex I), the new Members are not fully included in Schengen, see further, and according to Article 6(10) the new Members are obliged in certain circumstances to withdraw from prior international commitments should they 'encounter difficulties' in adjusting the (free trade) agreement.

*Adjustments to the Treaties* This title makes the necessary adjustments to the institutions and bodies.

*Adaptations to acts adopted by the institutions* This Title makes technical adaptations only to the *acquis*. The Court of Justice, in Joined Cases 31–35/86, *LAISA and Another* v. *Council*, took the view that the conditions of admission and the adjustments to the Treaties include adjustments to the secondary legislation agreed by the Member States upon accession.[13]

---

15 April 1958 determining the language to be used by the European Economic Community and Regulation No. 1 of 15 April 1958 determining the language to be used by the European Atomic Energy Community and introducing temporary derogation measures from those Regulations, *OJ* 2005 L 156/3. Thus, as of 1 January 2007 there are twenty-one official languages but neither Maltese or Irish are fully operational languages. The Irish derogation will be five-years renewable subject to the unanimous review of the Council. Until 1 May 2007, the EU institutions were not obliged to draft all acts in Maltese and to publish them in that language in the *OJ*. After a review of the operation of Regulation 930/2004, following improvements in translation from and into Maltese, and the Council Decision of 24 October 2006 chose not to extend the derogation so that this transition period ended on 30 April 2007. However, for all those acts that had not already been published in the Maltese language, the institutions were given an extension of the deadline to end 2008, see Council Regulation 1738/2006 amending Regulation 930/2004 on temporary derogation measures relating to the drafting in Maltese of the acts of the institutions of the European Union, *OJ 2006 L 329/1*.

[13] ECJ, Joined cases 31–35/86, [1988] *ECR* 2285, paras 9–12, with a critical note by Vandersanden, (1998) *CML Rev.* 551–561.

In the 2003 Act of Accession, this title is replaced by '*Permanent provisions*', although it contains two sub-headings. The first, 'Adaptations to acts adopted by the institutions', is to be read in conjunction with Annexes II and III. The second sub-heading reads '*Other provisions*', which is new to accession treaty practice, provides the legal bases (Art. 22) for additional provisions in the fields of the free movement of capital, company law, competition policy (including state aid), agriculture and the customs union. Article 23 is also new and contained in the second sub-heading and enables the Fifteen to adapt the 2003 Act of Accession insofar as concerns the CAP in order to take account of modifications in the EU rules, see Chapter 5.

A major difference in approach has been taken in the drafting of the sixth (2005) Act of Accession for Bulgaria and Romania compared to previous accession treaties. Most of the technical adaptations to the *acquis* were not included in the relevant act attaching to the Accession Treaty or Constitutional Treaty. These technical adaptations were adopted by the EU institutions closer to the date of accession. Only amendments to the *acquis* that have been discussed in the negotiations are included in the sixth Act of Accession.

*Transitional measures* This title introduces temporary derogations from particular regulations or directives for example. These are typically listed in Annex I to an act of accession (Annex II in the 2003 Act of Accession). In the 2003 Act of Accession, this title is replaced by '*Temporary provisions*' which is split up into two subtitles of '*Transitional measures*' and '*Other provisions*'. The first subtitle provides the legal basis for the ten separate annexes for each of the incoming Member States, Annexes V to XIV. Article 24 of the 2003 Act of Accession provides for the application of these country annexes.

Innovations in this second sub-title in particular, include new forms of safeguard clause contained in Articles 38 and 39 – see Chapter 5 in this volume.

This Title begins with two Articles emphasising that the new Member States take on the full rights and obligations of membership from the very date of their accession. In the 2003 Act of Accession, Article 53 provides that:

> Upon accession, the new Member States shall be considered as being addressees of directives and decisions within the meaning of [Article 288 TFEU] and of Article 161 of the Euratom Treaty, provided that those

> directives and decisions have been addressed to all the present Member States. Except with regard to directives and decisions which enter into force pursuant to [Articles 297 and 298 TFEU], the new Member States shall be considered as having received notification of such directives and decisions upon accession.

Article 54 of the 2003 Act of Accession continues:

> The new Member States shall put into effect the measures necessary for them to comply, from the date of accession, with the provisions of directives and decisions within the meaning of [Article 288 TFEU] and of Article 161 of the Euratom Treaty, unless another time-limit is provided for in the Annexes referred to in Article 24 or in any other provisions of this Act or its Annexes.

The equivalent provisions in the 2005 Accession Treaty are found in Articles 52 and 53 of the Act of Accession. However, Article 53 in the 2005 Act of Accession is even more explicit in that it requires Bulgaria and Romania to communicate to the Commission, their national measures designed to implement these Union laws, including any amending directives.

*Provisions relating to implementation of the Act of Accession* Finally, in addition to their Annexes, Acts of Accession are followed by the Protocols and then the Declarations annexed to the final acts of the Conferences, which are treated in the same way as the Declarations annexed to the original Treaties and successive Treaties revising them. Article 56 of the 2003 Act of Accession was used as the legal basis for implementing Protocol 4 on the closure of the Ignalina nuclear power plant in Lithuania and granting it an extra EUR 837 million to that end.[14] A different approach was used for granting a further EUR 437 million to Slovakia concerning the decommissioning of the Bohunice nuclear power plant, where the extra funding was granted using the Euratom financial Regulations[15] in order to further stipulate conditions to the use of the money.

---

[14] Council (Euratom) Regulation 1990/2006, first published in *OJ* 2006 L 411 and then published again in full as a corrigendum in February 2007, in *OJ* 2007 L 27/7. See Chapter 6.

[15] See Council Regulation (Euratom) 1605/2002, *OJ* 2002 L 248/1 and Commission Regulation (Euratom), *OJ* 2002 L 657/1. See Chapter 6.

### 1.3 *Information and consultation provisions*

All Accession Treaties provide for the standard practice of informing and consulting the incoming Member States on the adoption of certain decisions and other measures to be taken during the period between the date of signature of the Accession Treaty and its entry into force.[16] For example, the consultation and information applied to all proposals and communications from the Commission to the Council and in preparation for the fourth enlargement. It also applied to draft common positions as well as joint positions and joint actions and conventions under the Treaty on European Union. In practice, having signed the Accession Treaty, the incoming Member State is represented in Council meetings at all levels and at committee meetings chaired by the Commission and they are also entitled to receive all documentation.[17]

An interesting question arose here in the context of three cases concerning the fifth Accession Treaty.[18] Where derogations are concerned, because the candidate is not a member until the date of enlargement, once they have applied to the Commission for the measure, the only way for them to participate in such a legislative procedure is as observers, through the information and consultation procedure. This is agreed by an Exchange of Letters accompanying the Final Act. In the period between the signature and conclusion of an agreement the Union discussed all important decisions liable to affect the acceding countries and the latter would even play quite a large part in Council deliberations. The acceding countries have to consult the Commission

---

[16] See the Information and consultation procedure contained in the first Accession Treaty, *OJ* 1972 L73/203, for the second Accession Treaty, *OJ* L 1979 L 291/191, for the third Accession Treaty, *OJ* 1985 L 302/497, and for the fourth Accession Treaty see the Exchange of Letters between the European Union and the Republic of Austria, the Republic of Finland and the Kingdom of Sweden together with the Annex on the Information and consultation procedure for the adoption of certain decisions and other measures to be taken during the period preceding accession, both of which are annexed to the 1994 Accession Treaty, op. cit., Chapter 1, n. 2 at pp. 399–401. This arrangement took effect on the conclusion of the enlargement negotiations, namely the signature of the Accession Treaty in question.

[17] In the case of the sixth Accession Treaty, see Final Act – III. Exchange of Letters between the European Union and the Republic of Bulgaria and Romania on an information and consultation procedure for the adoption of certain decisions and other measures to be taken during the period preceding accession, *OJ 2005 L 157/393–395.*

[18] ECJ, Case C-413/04 *European Parliament* v. *Council* [2006] *ECR* Page I-11221, ECJ, Case C-414/04 *European Parliament* v. *Council* [2006] *ECR*-I-11279 and ECJ, Case C-273/04 [2007] *ECR* I-08925.

in advance on any national legislative or other measure that might affect the functioning of the Union. They do not have a right to vote in Council nor through their observer-MEPs in the European Parliament.

In these cases the Court defends the use of the information and consultation procedure for precisely such a situation. The Court holds in favour of the use of the relevant TFEU procedure. Not only, to the Court's mind, can an accession treaty not prevent the adoption of EU measures in anticipation of enlargement.[19] The Court heralds the information and consultation procedure[20] as a means by which the special interests of the incoming Member States can be "appropriately balanced against the general interests of the Community and that the considerations relating to the principles of equality, good faith and solidarity among current and future Member States [...] will be called into play."[21]

As will be seen at 2.3.3, the Court prefers the use of the ordinary legislative procedures under the then EC Treaty, which involve the incoming countries through the information and consultation procedure, over the special legislative procedures contained in the accession treaties for adjusting, adapting and amending accession conditions. In the context of ECJ, Case C-173/04 the comments of Advocate General Maduro question the limits to the information and consultation procedure. In particular he identifies a lack in provision for an effective right to judicial remedy for incoming members after they have signed their accession treaty but before becoming a Member State a year or more later.

## 2. Scope and content of transitional arrangements

### 2.1 *General transition periods and approximation with the* acquis

Previously a general timeframe was set within which the various transitional arrangements must end. The bulk of the adaptations that had to be undertaken by the incoming Member States were undertaken after the signature and entry into force of the relevant accession treaty.

[19] The Court's judgment in Case C-413/04, at para. 65.

[20] See para 72, refering to Joined Cases C-39/81, 43/81, 85/81 and 88/81 *Halyvourgikiand Helleniki Halyvourgia* v. *Commission* [1982] *ECR* 593, para. 10.

[21] At para. 68.

Transitional periods were already used in the original Treaty of Rome but were experimental and in practice they were shortened – they had been dictated by caution during the negotiation of the founding Treaties but were not needed in the end and some were never used at all.[22]

General transitional periods were used in the cases of the enlargements of 1973 and 1981. Bringing in the UK, Ireland and Denmark involved a general transitional period of five years beginning on the date of accession, 1 January 1973.[23] The 1981 accession of Greece also involved a general five-year transition period.[24] As regards the UK, Ireland and Denmark, the purpose of the transition was to reduce progressively and eventually eliminate, tariff barriers and quota systems and to adapt the Common Agricultural Policy and the same applied to Greece.[25]

The situation became much more complicated with the third enlargement to bring in Spain and Portugal and this complexity is reflected in the range of flexibility mechanisms used in the third Accession Treaty. The use of temporary or exceptional transitional measures was more

---

[22] For example, Art. 8 EEC Treaty provided for a twelve-year transitional period for the common market, which came to an end 31 December 1969, see Commission Communication *Enlargement of the Community: transitional periods and the institutional implications of enlargement*, op. cit., n. 2 at para. 7. The twelve year period could be extended to 15 years but this was not necessary because the Council decided that the first of the three stages had been complete on 31 December 1961, See Council Decision of 14 January 1962, *JO* 1964/62. Moreover, the 'acceleration decisions' of Member States of 12 May 1960 and 15 May 1962 served to introduce the customs union earlier than foreseen. In the end however, the common market was not instituted before the end of the transitional period 'due to technical complications and political sensitivities [...] to secure the right of establishment and liberalise capital movements. The accession of new Member States, budgetary disagreements and economic recession produced euro-sclerosis, bringing the achievement of the common market to a standstill. Admittedly the Court of Justice has given broad interpretation to the provisions on free movement, but residual disparities between national legislation could be harmonised only in so far as they directly affected the establishment or functioning of the common market, and this required unanimous vote in the Council (EEC Treaty, Art. 100).' See K. Lenaerts and P. Van Nuffel, *Constitutional Law of the European Union* (London, Sweet and Maxwell 2005) at pp. 367–368.

[23] Art. 9(2) thereof, *OJ* 1972 L 73/15, which provided 'Subject to the dates, time limits and special provisions provided for in this Act, the application of the transitional measures shall terminate at the end of 1977'.

[24] See Art. 9(2) thereof, *OJ* 1979 L 291/18, which reads 'Subject to special provisions in this Act laying down different dates or shorter or longer time limits, the application of the transitional measures shall terminate at the end of 1985.'

[25] European Parliament Resolutions 1980/703, *OJ* 1980 C 346/29, 1980/688, *OJ* 1980 C 346/28, and 1979/399, *OJ* 1979 C 289/51.

extensive and these temporary or exceptional transitional arrangements in respect of the movement of workers was longer than had been the case in respect of Greece (as well as Ireland, the UK, Austria, Finland and Sweden). For workers, these systems of temporary or exception transitional arrangements have been accompanied by their own special safeguard clauses. Such clauses have typically allowed the receiving Member States to take safeguard measures in the form of re-introducing work permits temporarily in respect of workers from the incoming Member States in the event of: unexpected disturbance in their labour markets, or; disturbances in a given region or profession. However, these worker safeguard clauses were not reverted to in any of the first four enlargements.[26]

The fourth enlargement required the least flexibility mechanisms because Austria, Finland and Sweden had advanced far in economic and legal approximation under framework of the European Economic Area Agreement.

The temporary derogations agreed in the accession negotiations have been kept to a minimum and the pre-accession strategy of the fifth and subsequent enlargements can be thanked for this situation. Flexibility mechanisms used in all six Accession Treaties include:

- delaying the entry into force of the *acquis*, which may combine safeguard clauses together with temporary derogations from the *acquis* (temporary or exceptional transitional arrangements);
- allowing for the introduction of derogations from the *acquis*, after closure of the accession treaty negotiations, or allowing for adaptations and adjustments to the *acquis* (additional transitional arrangements), or;
- allowing for the possibility of introducing emergency safeguard measures within tightly framed procedural and substantive requirements (emergency economic safeguard measures).

Although the fifth and sixth Accession Treaties did not establish a general transition period as such, the transitional arrangements are precise in their timeframes and can be complicated because they are

[26] See also Commission *Practical Guide for an enlarged European Union*, of August 2002 and revised 14 November 2002, at p. 4.

different for different chapters of the *acquis*, as well as for different Member States.

A particularly complicated system is that governing the free movement of workers in the fifth and sixth Accession Treaties.[27] Exceptional transitional arrangements had always been used for given sectors of the *acquis*. For Greece an exceptional pre-determined transitional period for the free movement of workers applied for seven years from the date of accession until 1 January 1988.[28] A ten-year pre-determined transitional period applied to the free movement of Spanish – not Portuguese – workers, which was subsequently shortened,[29] as well as for the common agricultural policy – but only in exceptional circumstances – and fisheries. Generally speaking however, institutional or temporary measures were minimal in the chapters of the *acquis* on customs union convergence, agriculture, fisheries, services and capital, workers and budgetary provisions.

The transitional arrangements for the freedom of movement of workers in the fifth and sixth Accession Treaties apply for seven years but, in very limited circumstances, may last longer. They are complicated and differentiate not only between the new Member States, but also between the 'old' Member States. The result of all this is that, under the fifth Accession Treaty, the eight CEEC Member States' workers and their families are open to (differing) restrictions in the Fifteen Member States and vice versa until the end of April 2011. This system applies to Bulgarian and Romanian nationals, on the one hand and the Twenty-five Member States (including the eight CEECs that joined in 2004), until end 2013. Malta may institute safeguard measures against the other twenty-four Member States (plus Bulgaria and Romania since 1 January 2007) to limit access to its labour market. No transitional arrangement applies for Cyprus.

---

[27] On the negotiations see G. Zeigler, 'the Accession Negotiations on the free movement of workers' in *Handbook on European Enlargement*, op. cit., pp. 131–142. See also K. Inglis 'Treading the tightrope between flexibility and legal certainty: enlargement and temporary derogations from the workers *acquis*' in D. Hanf, ed., *La libre circulation 10 ans après '1993'*, Brussels, Peter Lang 2007, pp. 99–122.

[28] See Art. 45, Act of Accession Greece.

[29] See Declarations by the EEC on Spanish and Portuguese workers taking up employment in the [then] Member States, *OJ* 1985 L 302/492 and Joint Declarations on workers already established *OJ* 1985 L 302/480 or on the free movement of workers, *OJ* 1985 L 302/480.

Curiously, therefore, only Cypriot (from areas over which the Government of Cyprus exercises effective control) and Maltese citizens were entitled to move unrestricted as of 1 May 2004 throughout the entire Union. Most remarkable is that more beneficial rules apply to EEA and Swiss (being third country) nationals compared to the eight new CEEC Member States' as well as Bulgarian and Romanian nationals.

The CEEC Member States are entitled only to mirror the national restrictions maintained by the Fifteen against them. So, nationals of the current Fifteen Member States may very well also find themselves subject to differing regimes in the CEEC Member State although potentially also in Malta but not in Cyprus. With the introduction of the sixth Accession Treaty, the ten new Member States are also able to maintain national measures and take safeguard measures against Bulgaria and Romania, if they existed at the time of signature of the sixth Accession Treaty. Under the fifth Accession Treaty, the eight CEEC Member States may only adopt safeguards in respect of the other seven CEEC Member States where they undergo or foresee disturbances on their labour markets that could seriously threaten the standard of living or level of employment in a given region or occupation – not in respect of the Fifteen nor Cyprus and Malta. Bulgaria and Romania are only able to do so in respect of each other.

### 2.2 *Temporary or exceptional transitional arrangements*

The key provision introducing the bulk of the transitional arrangements in the fifth Accession Treaty is Article 24 of the Act of Accession, and Article 23 in the sixth. The transitional arrangements referred to here are worked out in the ten country Annexes and provide for technical adaptations to various laws in order to apply the transitional arrangements correctly to each of the candidates. The annexes specify the content of the European Commission's *Guide to the Negotiations*, published almost immediately after the 'closure' of the negotiations.[30] In no circumstances may the enforcement of national rules during the

[30] Art. 54, 2003 Act of Accession, expressly allows for the application of the time limits set out in Annexes V–XIV. Art. 53 is the equivalent in the 2005 Act of Accession.

transitional periods, referred to in the new Member State annexes, lead to border controls between the Member States.[31]

Accession Treaties are drafted to allow temporary transitional arrangements to be extended up to the general transitional period and that their time-frames might vary according to the programme or sector to which they apply.[32] However, the rationale behind the extension of transitional arrangements to the full length of the general transitional period was intended to cover situations 'where the adjustments were so complicated or so extensive as to need the full transitional period'.[33] It is for this reason that temporary transitional arrangements are intended to be exceptional. Temporary transitional arrangements set specific objectives and in the case that these objectives are not met, the transitional arrangements may be extended up to the end date of the general transitional period.

In the case of Denmark, Ireland and the UK, for the reasons outlined earlier, transitional arrangements were relatively few by comparison with the Southern enlargements. An exceptional transitional arrangement involved a special fisheries regime applied to the UK until 1983.[34] Greece, Portugal and Spain proved more problematic due to their lower levels of development compared to the Community average. A significant, exceptional derogation for Greece involved promises by the European Commission to refrain from instituting proceedings against infringements of the then Article 95 EEC concerning taxation. The Commission also promised, in Protocol 7 to the Act of Accession Greece, that it would take a flexible approach towards Greece when applying the rules on state aids.[35] For Portugal and Spain significant and numerous transitional arrangements were put in place, notably

[31] Art. 40, 2003 Act of Accession reads: 'In order not to hamper the proper functioning of the internal market, the enforcement of the new Member States' national rules during the transitional periods referred to in Annexes V to XIV shall not lead to border controls between Member States.' This is the basically the same as Article 153 Act of Accession for Austria, Finland and Sweden.

[32] See Commission Communication *Enlargement of the Community: transitional period and the institutional implications of enlargement*, op. cit., n. 2 at p. 7, para. 12.

[33] See ibid.

[34] See Art. 100 first Act of Accession. Art. 103 reads; 'Before 31 December 1982, the Commission shall present a report to the Council on the economic and social development of the coastal areas of the Member States and the state of stocks. On the basis of that report, and of the objectives of the Common Fisheries Policy, the Council, acting on a proposal from the Commission shall examine the provisions which could follow the derogations in force until 31 December 1982.'

[35] *OJ* 1979 L291/177.

covering the customs union,[36] and other core areas of Community competence.

As concerns the customs union, the transitional arrangements were designed, for example, to stagger the alignment of Spain's basic customs duties on imports from the receiving Member States with the Common Customs Tariff and the Unified ECSC tariff and this state of affairs continued in effect until 1 January 1993.[37] A transitional arrangement also applied to Spain's revision of its unified tariff applying to third countries and lasted until 1 January 1993.[38] Charges having equivalent effect on imports and exports were not allowed but quantitative restrictions on certain imports were allowed Spain for a time after their accession.[39] The receiving Member States enjoyed reciprocal tariffs and quantitative restrictions.

The fourth enlargement is noteworthy for the specific temporary predetermined derogations that were given Austria, Finland and Sweden allowing them to maintain higher standards in the chemicals, environmental and sanitary standards and which lasted four years beginning 1 January 1995. An exceptional fisheries regime also applied for Finland while Sweden and Finland had derogations in transit traffic. Austria too secured a derogation for transit traffic.[40]

### 2.3 *The legal nature of transitional arrangements*

As for the legal nature of such provisions contained in acts of accession, it has long been settled case law that provisions of Acts of Accession are not acts of the institutions the validity of which can be challenged before the ECJ.[41] The Court has also made clear that new Member States are bound to meet their full Treaty obligations and comply with all of the operative *acquis* as of their date of accession unless they have a derogation, in which case they must apply the derogation by the agreed end-date. As said in Chapter 1 at 3.1 already, it is an established point of principle that the provisions of Community law apply *ab initio* and *in toto* to new Member States, derogations being allowed

[36] See Art. 30, 31, 75(1), 173(1) and (2) Act of Accession Portugal and Spain.
[37] See Art. 31, Act of Accession Portugal and Spain.
[38] See Art. 37, Act of Accession Portugal and Spain.
[39] See Art. 43, Act of Accession Portugal and Spain.
[40] See Chapter 6 on the environment *acquis*.
[41] See ECJ, Joined Cases 31 and 35/86 *LIASA* v. *Council* [1988] *ECR* 2285, at para. 18. See also ECJ, Case C-313/89 *Commission* v. *Spain*, [1991] *ECR* I-5231.

only insofar as they are expressly laid down by transitional measures.[42] This has been consistent in the Court's judgments since and the same applies to the fifth and sixth Accession Treaties.[43]

The Spanish midwives case illustrated this.[44] Spain attempted to rebut the Commission cases against it for failure to comply with a Directive on the training of midwives. Spain argued that the rules were too complicated to be enacted by the date of accession and that it was having difficulty in transposing them, in particular because no transitional provision had been provided those persons that had begun their professional training before accession and had yet to complete their course. Spain also attempted to argue, basically, that in any case Spanish midwives were not trained to an inferior level. The ECJ rejected all of these arguments insisting on the new Member State's Treaty obligation to comply with the Community law.

Moreover, any transitional arrangements, including additional transitional arrangements, will be interpreted restrictively by the Court. In relation to the Greek accession, the Court provided that any provision contained in an Act of Accession that constitutes a derogation from the free movement of goods must be interpreted restrictively.[45] The Court then clarified further that any derogations permitted by an Act of Accession must be interpreted in such a way as to facilitate the achievement of the objectives of the Treaty and application in full of its rules of procedure.[46]

### 2.3.1 *The fifth and sixth Accession Treaties*

Taking an example from the Annex XII to the fifth Accession Treaty, this means that Poland was entitled to maintain certain existing national certificates for medical devices or authorisations for pharmaceuticals until December 2005 or 2008 respectively, contrary to the terms of the relevant Directives. However, other Member States, including the new Member States, were not obliged to recognise those authorisations or

---

[42] See ECJ, Case 258/81 *Metallurgiki Halyps A.E.* v. *Commission* [1982] *ECR* 4261.

[43] Latterly in relation to the fourth Accession Treaty, see for example ECJ, Case C-233/97 *KappAhl Oy* [1998] *ECR* I-8069.

[44] Case C-313/89, op. cit., n. 41.

[45] ECJ, Case 77/82 *Peskeloglou* v. *Bundesanstalt fur Arbeit* [1983] *ECR* 1085, para. 12.

[46] ECJ, Joined Cases 194/85 and 241/85 *Commission* v. *Greece* [1988] *ECR* 1037, para. 20.

certificates and could therefore prevent the products concerned from being placed on their markets.[47]

Transitional arrangements in the 2003 Act of Accession concerned the following fifteen chapters (out of a total of thirty-one chapters) of the *acquis*:

- free movement of goods;
- freedom of movement of persons;
- freedom to provide services;
- free movement of capital;
- company law;
- competition policy;
- agriculture, including veterinary and phytosanitary;
- fisheries;
- transport policy;
- taxation;
- employment and social policy;
- energy;
- telecommunications, IT and postal services;
- culture and audio-visual policy, and;
- environment.

Transitional arrangements concerned eleven chapters of the *acquis* under the sixth Accession Treaty with Bulgaria and Romania, namely:

- freedom of movement of persons;
- freedom to provide services;
- free movement of capital;
- competition (Romania only, not Bulgaria, and only relating to fiscal aid, state aid for regional investments and steel restructuring;)[48]
- agriculture, including veterinary and phytosanitary;
- transport policy;
- taxation;
- (Bulgaria only[49] social policy and employment);

[47] See Annex XII, 1.1.–1.5., 2003 Act of Accession p. 875.

[48] See Annex VII, 2005 Act of Accession, pp. 316–322.

[49] See Annex VI.7, 2005 Act of Accession, p. 291. Bulgaria has a derogation from Directive 2001/37, *OJ* 2001 L 194/26, on the approximation of the laws, regulations

- energy;
- telecommunications and information technology, and;
- environment.

In some cases, the derogations are minimal and relatively short. For example, Malta could allow certain collective agreements on working time to remain in force until 31 December 2004 in contravention of Directive 93/104. Where derogations in the chapter on the free movement of goods have been introduced in the fifth Accession Treaty, these are minimal.[50] There are no derogations from this chapter of the *acquis* in the sixth Accession Treaty.

Other derogations are far longer in duration and involve considerable continued efforts after accession, including financial, such as in the case of the environment *acquis* where Poland will benefit from a derogation in respect of large combustion plants until 2017. Poland has also been granted limited derogations from the state aid *acquis* to support necessary investments in meeting the environment, see Chapter 6.

### 2.3.2 *Derogations, adjustments and adaptations to the* acquis *after signature of an accession treaty*

Only a very few clauses in an accession treaty allow the receiving Member States to add to this list of derogations, adaptations or adjustments beyond what has been specifically agreed and specified in the Accession Treaty itself. They are intended to deal with new legal developments that had not been anticipated during the accession negotiations. Until an Accession Treaty enters into force, all the Parties are still in "pre-accession". These clauses provide for special legislative procedures for the Member States to go ahead and adopt such measures, whether by qualified majority or unanimity, upon a proposal from the

and administrative provisions of the member States concerning the manufacture, presentation and sale of tobacco products. Bulgaria has until 2011 to reduce the tar yield of cigarettes.

[50] And relate only to licensing of medical equipment and the marketing authorisations for pharmaceutical products as described earlier, concerning Malta, Cyprus, Lithuania, Poland and Slovenia. Estonia had an exceptional derogation from Commission Regulation 466/2001 setting maximum levels for certain contaminants in foodstuffs, *OJ* 2001 L 077/1, specifically as concerns the dioxin limits in fish until end 2006. Malta has a special derogation concerning the chocolate directive, Directive 2000/36, *OJ* 2000 L 197/19. See Chapter 7.

Commission. They are an exception to the ordinary legislative procedure, notably not involving the European Parliament.

Given that the *acquis* is constantly evolving, candidates are approximating to a moving target and the references of the *acquis* legislation may well change between signature of the Accession Treaty and the date of accession. A few clauses allow for new temporary derogations to be added between the date of signature of an accession treaty and its entry into force. Other clauses allow for adaptations and adjustments to be made after the signature of an accession treaty and even after its entry into force.

Certain clauses are used to allow for the adoption of additional transitional measures for the functioning of the common organisations of the markets in agriculture (COMs) or to update the list of transitional measures in order to take account of legislative developments between the date of signature or closure of negotiations for an accession treaty. For example, Article 378 of the Act of Accession for Spain and Portugal[51] provided for the introduction of new transitional measures derogating from directives or regulations adopted in the period leading up to the entry into force of the Accession Treaty, at the 'duly substantiated request' of either incoming Member State before the date of their accession. While various temporary derogations applied for Denmark, Ireland and the UK until end 1977,[52] the Council was able to adopt the rules necessary to ensure the proper functioning of the CAP and the COMs in particular, in accordance with the decision making procedure for working out and implementing the CAP.[53] Also, the Act of Accession Greece provided for the introduction of new temporary derogations in state aids in agriculture, for example.[54]

[51] Paragraph 2 reads 'At the duly substantiated request of the Kingdom of Spain or the Portuguese Republic, the Council, acting unanimously on a proposal from the Commission may, before 1 January 1986, take measures consisting of temporary derogations from acts of the institutions of the Communities adopted between 1 January 1985 and the date of signature of this Act' [namely 12 June 1985].

[52] See Art. 9 Act of Accession Denmark, Ireland and the UK.

[53] Art. 43 of the EEC Treaty 1957.

[54] Art. 69 of the Act of Accession Greece. National aids could be maintained until 31 December 1985 'on a transitional basis and in a degressive manner' but a derogation to the 'principle of degressivity' could be made for Greek national aids taking into consideration the scope for certain specified socio-structural directives. Implementing measures could be adopted by qualified majority in Council acting a proposal from the Commission setting detailed rules, including timeframes, and always allowing equal access to the Greek market.

In both the 2003 and 2005 Accession Treaties, Article 41 Act of Accession, concerns transitional measures in relation to the common market organisations (COMs) under the CAP. These new measures may be extended beyond the three-year cut-off, subject to the unanimous decision of Council in consultation with the European Parliament. Article 41 foresees the possibility of extending this transitional system beyond the three years but only in accordance with a decision-making procedure that involves consultation of the European Parliament. The relevant comitology procedure applies to the adoption of such transitional measures. The equivalent clause in the fourth Accession Treaty was contained in Article 149 Act of Accession, and was extended by means of Council Regulation 2596/97[55] for one year to end December 1998. This same Regulation extended the transitional arrangement by two years for the fat content of milk in particular and was last extended to end April 2009, when in any case it became obsolete as a result of the 2003 CAP Reform.

Such measures in the case of the fifth enlargement concern for example, implementation of the EAGGF until 30 April 2007 or to avoid deflection of trade in certain agricultural products,[56] or single area payments during 2004 and specifying a reduction in eligibility for certain aid schemes where minimum good agricultural and environmental conditions of agricultural land are not respected,[57] or transitional measures to avoid speculative disruption in the sugar sector.[58]

In the veterinary and phytosanitary chapter of the *acquis*, Article 42 of the 2003 Act of Accession enabled the Commission to adopt further transitional arrangements in accordance with the comitology procedure set out in the relevant *acquis* measure, until end April 2007, which may not be extended beyond the first three years after enlargement. The equivalent in the sixth Accession Treaty is also Article 42 but the deadline is end December 2010. It is interesting to note that Article 42 of the sixth Accession Treaty extends to the food safety rules in addition to the veterinary and phytosanitary rules, while Article 42 of the fifth Accession Treaty is worded to cover only the veterinary

[55] Council Regulation 2596/1997, *OJ* 1997 L 351/12, last amended by Council Regulation 1805/2003, *OJ* 2003 L 265/5, to extend the transitional arrangement to end April 2009 and the repealed as obsolete by Council Regulation 72/2009, *OJ* 2009 L 30/1.

[56] Commission Regulation 1972/2003, *OJ* 2003 L 293/3.

[57] Commission Regulation 2199/2003, *OJ* 2003 L 328/21.

[58] Commission Regulation 60/2004, *OJ* 2004 L 9/8.

and phytosanitary rules. Examples of such measures are set out in Chapter 7.[59]

Article 55 Act of Accession, is generally applicable and allows, at the 'duly substantiated request' of a new Member State, additional 'temporary derogations' to be added to those agreed in Council in December 2002 but only in respect of new *acquis* measures that were adopted between 1 November 2002 and the date of signature of the Accession Treaty on 16 April 2003, which took effect upon accession (Art. 2(3), 2003 Act of Accession). However, further transitional derogations, apart from Article 55, may be adopted in respect of specific legislation, such as in the case of the Directive on waste electrical and electronic equipment. Various examples also exist in the agri-food *acquis*, see Chapter 7 at 2.3.1. There are important differences in the drafting of some of these clauses in the fifth and sixth Accession Treaties, (Arts. 55 in bother the 2003 and 2005 Acts of Accession). In particular, the 2005 Act of Accession provides that the applicable voting procedure is that contained in the piece of EU legislation being derogated from, which the 2003 Act of Accession provided that a special legislative procedure applied, where the Council adopted the derogation by unanimity and the European Parliament was not included. The European Court of Justice has ruled on the scope and substance of certain of these clauses in the fifth Accession Treaty.

Three cases before the ECJ have dealt with the distinguishing features of these three special procedures. The first two cases were brought by the European Parliament against the Council and concerned changes to *acquis* to take account of the needs of two incoming countries, Estonia and Slovenia. The third case was brought by Poland to challenge changes to the Act of Accession in order to take account of changes in the EU regime for the Common Agricultural Policy.

Before commenting on the three cases, it is interesting to note that Advocate General Geelhoed made a useful suggestion[60] that Article 27 TFEU, previously Article 15 EC, could be relied on as a legal basis for a temporary derogation in such circumstances as these. It allows for temporary derogations to take account of differences in development between the economies of the Member States and like Article 55 of the

[59] On the agri-food *acquis* at 2.2.

[60] See para. 64 of his Opinion in ECJ, Case 413/04, which will become Art. 27 TFEU if the Lisbon Treaty takes effect. See K. Inglis, annotation on these cases, (2009) *CML Rev.* 641–663.

fifth Accession Treaty, it also provides for the adoption of such a measure by the Council, acting by qualified majority on a proposal from the European Commission.[61] This procedure might better accommodate the Council's concerns to act swiftly to address serious social and economic consequences for new Member States immediately after signature of the accession treaty.

The case of *Parliament* v. *Council*, ECJ Case C-413/04, concerned the use of a special legislative procedure provided for in the legal basis of the fifth Accession Treaty – Article 57, Act of Accession – in order to allow Estonia an extended derogation from the Community regime to open up electricity markets as of 1 July 2007.[62] The Court annulled the 'temporary derogations' granted in favour of Estonia on the basis of that Article 57, which is the legal basis for adopting 'adaptations' to the Act of Accession. The appropriate legal basis in that Act of Accession for adopting temporary derogations is Article 55, which was no longer available to the Council in these circumstances. Here the Court has clarified certain differences between 'derogations' and 'adaptations' to the *acquis communautaire* in accession treaty practice. This clarification calls into question previous practices under former accession treaties and sets a precedent for the use of such special procedures in future accession treaties. Importantly, the Court has demonstrated its preference for the ordinary legislative procedure for the introduction of derogations and adaptations after the date of signature of an accession treaty. The Court follows the same approach in its Judgment concerning ECJ, Case C-414/04, where it annulled certain 'temporary derogations' in favour of the Republic of Slovenia concerning the application of Regulation 1228/2003 on conditions for access to the network for cross-border exchanges in electricity.

In these cases the Court and the Advocate General take issue with the chosen legal basis only and the use of special legislative procedures that effectively side-step the ordinary legislative procedures provided for in Article 263 TFEU. In the Estonia case for example, the incoming Member States had been involved in the formulation of the 2003 Directive, which had been in the legislative pipeline long before the closure of the accession negotiations on 1 November 2002. Estonia had applied for this transitional derogation some seven months before

[61] See Art. 14(3) EC.

[62] Council Directive 2004/85, *OJ* 2004 L 236/10.

the date of enlargement but the Commission issued the proposal for the temporary derogation only four days before the date of enlargement, using the relevant legal bases of the EC Treaty. In this case, the newly enlarged Council adopted the measure some two months after enlargement, by qualified majority according to Article 57 of the Act of Accession, fifth Accession Treaty. On a strict interpretation of Article 57, there is no onus on the Commission to make the proposal within a time frame that would allow the Council to use this special procedure. The Council could have adopted the measure using Article 57 in all legality before the date of enlargement but not after it.

By comparison, Article 55 enables the Council to introduce 'temporary derogations' by means of a special procedure, acting by unanimity on a proposal from the European Commission.

In its Judgments of 28 November 2006, the Court is setting some important limits on the extent to which 'adaptations' or 'temporary derogations' can be introduced to the *acquis* between the closure of accession negotiations and the subsequent signature of the Accession Treaty itself, or after its entry into force.

The Court held that the special procedure contained in Article 55 could be used for introducing *temporary derogations* but that it:

- is only available in respect of *acquis* measures adopted between the date of the closure of negotiations and the date of signature of the accession treaty, and;
- only allows for those temporary derogations to be adopted before the date of enlargement.

Therefore, the wording of the fifth Accession Treaty does not make provision for new temporary derogations to be introduced for a law that was adopted between its date of signature and its entry into force. It only applies to regulations and directives adopted between closure of the accession negotiations and the signature of the Accession Treaty. This seems a logical extension of the pre-accession approach to the negotiation of transitional arrangements.

At paragraphs 31 to 38 the Court follows settled case law and the Advocate General goes on to give guidance as to the difference between the '*derogations*' and '*adaptations*' for the purposes of determining which procedure applies, if at all. 'Adaptations' should be thought of more as measures that are intended to integrate the new Member State into the *acquis*: they are 'indispensable for the purpose of ensuring the full applicability of that [EU measure] as regards that new Member State'.[63] Article 57 is excluded for other purposes, such as derogations.[64]

For the Court, at paragraph 60, a '*temporary derogation*' has the sole object and purpose of postponing EU act temporarily, and the adoption of which involves a political assessment.

The later judgment of 23 October 2007[65] deals with the definition of '*necessary adaptations*' to the Common Agricultural Policy under the fifth Accession Treaty. The legal basis in the fifth Accession Treaty for the "necessary adaptations" to the CAP is Article 23 of the 2003 Act of Accession (2005 Accession Treaty: Art. 22 Act of Accession). This was the legal basis for the contested decision. It is the equivalent of Article 57 for the other chapters of the *acquis*. However, whereas the latter procedure is adopted by qualified majority in Council, the special procedure for adopting necessary adaptations to the CAP requires unanimity in Council.

Six months after signing the Accession Treaty, the Member States adopted the CAP reform contained in Regulation 1782/2003, expanded the phasing-in to cover energy crops, nuts and dairy products ('the 2003 Regulation').[66] It amended a raft of CAP regulations in order to do so, including the 1999 Regulation establishing common rules for direct support to farmers under support schemes in the framework of the CAP.[67] However, in this case, the Act of Accession had introduced the phasing-in mechanisms into the 1999 Regulation.[68] Thus, the Council introduced the CAP reform into the fifth Accession Treaty using the Article 23 procedure to adopt Decision 2004/281, repealing and replacing the 1999 Regulation. The Council adopted Council Decision 2004/281 on 22 March 2004,[69] just over a month before the fifth enlargement.

---

[63] See para. 60 of the Court's judgment in ECJ, Case C-413/04.

[64] Regulation 96/2004, *OJ* 2004 L 15/13. Other such technical adaptations concerning the common organisation of the markets in agriculture include Regulation 498/2004 (products processed from fruit and vegetables), *OJ* 2004 L 80/20, Regulation 406/2004 (olive oil), *OJ* 2004 L67/10, Regulation 323/2004 (rice seed and seed other than rice seed), *OJ* 2004 L58/14.

[65] ECJ, Case C-273/04, [2007] *ECR* I-08925.

[66] Regulation 1782/03, *OJ* 2003 L 270/1, as amended.

[67] See Regulation 1259/1999, *OJ* 1999 L 160/113, as amended.

[68] At Annex II, Chapter 6.A.27.

[69] *OJ* 2004 L17/23.

### 2.3.3 *The right to effective judicial remedy prior to entry into force of an accession treaty*

ECJ, Case C-273/04 highlights the moving target for regulatory approximation by incoming Member States up to the last minute before accession. It also puts the spot light on the enduring dilemma of balancing the limits to admissibility with the fundamental principle of the right to effective judicial protection for the incoming countries between signature and entry into force of an accession treaty. Quite a debate surrounded the admissibility of Poland's challenge of measures that the Council took to adapt the 2003 Accession Treaty after signature of that Treaty. The Court, however, chose first to explore the substance of the case on the basis of the compatibility of the 2004 Decision with Article 23 of the Act of Accession. Because Poland failed on substance, the Court was able to avoid the matter of admissibility altogether. The fact that the Court addressed the substance of the case however, should lay to rest any claims that the Council 'got off on a technicality', so to speak. Nevertheless, certain unresolved questions of judicial protection linger for future accession treaties and are explored by the Advocate General in paragraphs 22 to 60 of his Opinion.

Strictly speaking, Poland's case was lodged out of time[70] but it would not have been out of time if the date of accession itself had been taken as the starting point for the admissibility clock rather than the date of publication in the *Official Journal*. However, Article 58 of the fifth Accession Treaty provides that, '[t]he texts of the institutions [...] shall, from the date of accession be authentic under the same conditions as the texts drawn up in the present eleven languages.'[71]

Normally an annulment case should be lodged within 2 months of the date of publication. Advocate General Maduro identified the potential for the institutions to adopt measures under the Act of Accession more than two months before the entry into force of the Treaty of Accession, without threat of challenge. For the Advocate General this deprives the future Member States of any possibility of a remedy. The question is: should such cases be admissible because 'the candidate States must be allowed to defend their rights as future Member States under the balance of benefits and burdens agreed on signature of the

---

[70] Opinion of Advocate General Maduro in ECJ, Case C-273/04 [2007] *ECR* I-08925 at paras. 14 to 20.

[71] The Court ignored Article 58 altogether.

accession documents, they must be recognised as having the capacity to bring annulment proceedings under the principle of effective judicial protection of community law rights'?[72]

He considers the redress channel of observer status insufficient protection for an incoming country in respect of measures that clearly affect them.[73] As things stand, the existing Member States can both vote on measures that are of direct relevance to the waiting-to-be Member States, and sue for the annulment of the same measures, regardless of whether those measures are of direct relevance to them. The waiting-to-be Member States are neither able to vote in Council nor bring actions for annulment.

The Advocate General expresses his preference for a certain access for future Member States after the signature of an accession treaty: he proposes limited access[74] to bring annulment proceedings against measures adopted between signature and entry into force of an Accession Treaty without having to demonstrate interest for the purposes of Article 263 TFEU, i.e. outside of Article 263 TFEU altogether. To this end he relies on ECJ, Case C-70/88 *Parliament* v. *Council*[75] for the need for judicial protection of the Parliament's prerogatives as an aspect of institutional stability. Although he realises the potential for constant challenges that could result, and the negative impact on legal certainty also, what persuades him is that;

> [most] of all, it does not seem to me to be acceptable that the effectiveness and even the existence of the fundamental right to judicial protection in the Member States should be dependent on the arbitrary selection by the [EU] institutions of the date of publication of the contested measure.[76]

One wonders whether Advocate General Maduro would have been so inclined to explore this avenue in a case where the Member States had met their own timetable for their own internal reforms when they signed the fifth Accession Treaty. Perhaps the reasoning of the Advocate General, anticipates – even pre-empts – any temptation that the Member States may have to over-stretch the limits of transitional arrangements in future accession treaties. After all, already in 2004, the

---

[72] See the Opinion of A.G. Maduro at para. 55.
[73] See the Opinion of A.G. Maduro at paras. 67–68.
[74] See the Opinion of A.G. Maduro at paras. 56 and 57.
[75] Case C-70/88, at paras. 22, 24 and 25.
[76] See the Opinion of A.G. Maduro at para. 47.

European Council made clear in establishing the Commission's negotiating framework for Turkey, that long transitional periods, derogations, specific arrangements or permanent safeguard clauses, should be considered in freedom of movement of persons, structural policies or agriculture.[77]

The *acquis* must be able to continue to evolve in the interim between signature and effect of an accession treaty but the Member States 'must not be allowed to upset the balance of rights and obligations for future Member States stemming from the *acquis* as it existed on the date of signature of an accession treaty without the future Member States being able to defend their interests by way of access to the [EU] Courts.'[78]

Indeed, it would seem legally dubious that the only right of defence of the future Member State would be to refuse to ratify or apply the accession treaty: 'retaliation on that scale is so disproportionate that its use and therefore its effectiveness would in the end be entirely nugatory'.[79] Advocate General Maduro is advising that the principle of solidarity should prohibit existing Member States from "arbitarily upsetting the balance of benefits and burdens established by the accession instruments in favour of new Member States". Moreover, in international law terms, he argues – on the basis of the principle of legitimate expectations in Community law – that the principle of good faith demands an opportunity for the incoming countries to test whether such measures destabilise the balance of rights and obligations.[80]

Additionally, in both the fifth and sixth enlargements, there were various instances of incomplete measures published in the *Official Journal* – presumably to have the publishing date before enlargement – and which were subsequently corrected by corrigendum, in some cases a long time after the fifth enlargement.[81] The example of the workers'

---

[77] See op. cit., Chapter 1, n. 42.

[78] See the Opinion of A.G. Maduro, at paras 51 and 53. He relies on the reasoning of the Court in ECJ, Cases C-39/72 *Commission* v. *Italy* [1973] *ECR* 101 para. 68 and C-128/78 *Commission* v. *United Kingdom* [1979] *ECR* 419, para. 12, thus extending the principle of solidarity in the context to an accession treaty situation.

[79] See the Opinion of A.G. Maduro at para. 49.

[80] See the Opinion of A.G. Maduro at para. 52. He relies on Art. 18 of the Vienna Convention on the Law of Treaties, requiring States to refraining from acts that defeat the object and purpose of a Treaty.

[81] Directive 2004/38 on the right of citizens of the Union and their family members to move and reside freely within the territory of the Member States amending Regu-

*acquis* comes to mind. Directive 2004/38 on the right of EU citizen, which amended a swathe of directives, is a prime example. Reporting and transposition dates were omitted in the original version and the final completed versions followed in subsequent corrigenda, notably introducing the reporting and the transposition dates in the June of 2004. Ten days prior to Bulgaria's accession, the Council adopted Council Regulation 1990/2006 concerning the grant of EUR 837 million to Lithuania for the decommissioning of its nuclear power plant. It was first published in the *Official Journal* on 30 December 2006 and then again in full, in corrigendum, on 2 February 2007.

## 3. Emergency economic safeguard measures

Measures designed to protect against the serious deterioration of a given sector of the economy or a given region are incorporated into the 2003 Accession Treaty in Article 37 of the Act of Accession. The same clause was inserted into all previous Accession Treaties. The equivalent in the 2005 Accession Treaty is contained in Article 36 of the Act of Accession. In both cases the clause is the same as the emergency economic safeguard clause contained in all previous accession treaties.

### 3.1 ... *to protect a given area or sector of the economy*

Article 37 of the 2003 Act of Accession provides for safeguard measures to protect a given sector of the economy or a given area. It is an emergency procedure carried out by the Commission at the request of the Member State seeking the protective measures. Such emergency measures may involve derogations from the TFEU or derogations from the Act of Accession but are restricted to the first three years following accession. All twenty-seven Member States may apply to the Commission for protective measures, subject to certain conditions. Serious difficulties must arise and be liable to persist in a sector of the economy and they must bring about a serious deterioration in the economic situation of a given area. Any protective measures taken must be necessary, must aim to rectify the situation and must adjust the sector to

lation 1612/68 and repealing Directives 64/221, 68/360, 72/194, 73/148, 75/34, 75/35, 90/364, 90/365 and 93/96, *OJ* 2004 L 158/77. See corrigendum in *OJ* 2004 L 229/4.

the economy of the common market. The extent and the timeframe of any derogation given will be determined accordingly. Preference is given to measures that least disturb the functioning of the common market but, again, they may not involve frontier controls.

As seen earlier, such measures are rare and the Commission discretion is broad. The European Commission envisaged this legal basis, for example, to protect the Polish agriculture sector from market disturbances, in the form of systems to monitor trade flows between Poland and all the other Member States.[82] While Poland (or the other CEECs for that matter) did not make up a major part of the Fifteen's imports prior to Poland's accession to the Union, the Fifteen's exports accounted for 43 percent of Polish agriculture imports of which the main products imported were animal feeds, live animals and meat.[83] Of all the CEEC members, Poland has a significant agriculture sector in addition to having nearly five hundred food producing establishments that were excluded from the Internal Market (being restricted to the national market of origin) at the date of accession, under pre-determined transitional arrangements for some years after accession, pending their structural upgrade. This list has changed since, see Chapter 7 on the agri-food *acquis*. Their competitive situation is made no easier by the fact that their full participation in the CAP is staggered over the first decade after the fifth enlargement.

In the case of Slovenia alone, this emergency economic safeguard clause may be resorted to for up to seven years from the date of accession as regards the Slovenian real estate market.[84] Otherwise Slovenia has no restrictions on the purchase of secondary residences or agricultural land.

Emergency economic safeguard clauses were envisaged to cope with unforeseeable difficulties; Article 135 in the first,[85] Article 130 in the second,[86] Article 379 in the third[87] and Article 152 in the fourth Accession Treaties. Only in the case of Spain and Portugal was a special

---

[82] See Declaration 43, Final Act to the Accession Treaty.

[83] See A. Surdej, 'Enlarging the EU Food Safety Regime: Adjustments of Polish Food Safety Regulations to the Requirement of the EU Membership', *Euro-limes czasopismo naukowe*, numer 2(3), czerwiec 2003, to be found at www.eurolimes.ae.krakow.pl/files/el2(3)2003/el2(3)2003.html at p. 21.

[84] See Annex XIII.4., 2003 Act of Accession, p. 909.

[85] *OJ* 1972 L 73/42.

[86] *OJ* 1979 L 297/47.

[87] *OJ* 1985 L 302/135.

sub-paragraph included on workers giving Luxembourg the right to apply to the Commission for protective measures in respect of Spanish workers. This sub-paragraph was in addition to the specific transitional arrangements applicable to workers contained in Articles 56 to 60 of the 1985 Act of Accession Spain and Portugal.[88]

This was always, as it is in the fifth and now sixth Accession Treaties, an economic safeguard clause of reciprocal application. In the cases of the UK and Greece it lasted until the end of the general transitional period of five years. A dumping safeguard was also contained in the Act of Accession with Greece.[89] For Spain and Portugal the safeguard clause remained in force seven years until end 1992, which alone implies a general transitional period of seven years. For Austria, Finland and Sweden it applied for only one year.

Measures adopted on the basis of these clauses include, for example, in the case of the first 1972 Accession Treaty, measures to allow Ireland to levy a charge on imports of processed agricultural produce under specified tariff headings, between March and December 1977, on imports from the UK and to grant payments on exports to the UK.[90] Under the second Accession Treaty the Commission instituted

---

[88] This fourth paragraph reads; '4 . If difficulties rise which are serious and liable to persist in the employment market of the Grand Duchy of Luxembourg, that State may apply for authorisation, in accordance with the procedure set out in the first and second subparagraphs of paragraph 2 and under the conditions defined in paragraph 3, to apply provisionally until 31 December 1995 protective measures within the framework of national provisions governing change in employment, with regard to workers who are nationals of a new Member State allowed to immigrate to the Grand Duchy after the date of that authorisation with a view to taking up employment there.'

[89] Art. 131(1) reads; 'If before the expiry of the period of application of the transitional measures laid down under this Act for each case the Commission, on the application by a Member State or by any other interested party, finds that dumping is being practised between the Community as at present constituted and Greece, it shall address recommendations to the person or persons with whom such practices originate for the purposes of putting an end to them. Should the practices continue, the Commission shall authorise the injured Member State or States to take protective measures, the conditions and details of which the Commission shall determine. (2) For the application of this Article to the products listed in Annex II to the EEC Treaty, the Commission shall evaluate all relevant factors, in particular the level of prices at which these products are imported into the market in question from elsewhere, account being taken of the provisions of the EEC Treaty relating to agriculture and in particular Article 39 thereof.'

[90] Commission Decision of 23 March 1977 authorising Ireland to take protective measures in respect of certain processes agricultural products under Article 135 (first Act of Accession) and allowing Ireland until 31 December 1977 to levy a charge in imports from the UK and grant a payment on exports to the UK of the processed agricultural products under the relevant tariff headings, *OJ* 1977 L 97/29.

measures to authorise France to take protective measures on imports of cotton yard from Greece[91] on the grounds of serious disturbance in the French combined yarns sector. The measures took the form of limiting imports of cotton yarn and were conditional on the restructuring of the French combined yarns sector. Another example was Commission Decision 1831/81 under the ECSC Treaty establishing for undertakings in the iron and steel industry a monitoring system and a new system of production quotas for certain rolled products for the third quarter of 1981.[92] Greece was also enabled to take protective measures in respect of cigarette imports in the form of a monitoring system.[93]

### 3.2 *The broad discretion of the European Commission*

The Commission's discretion is broad in respect of emergency economic safeguard measures, as the European Court of Justice has made clear in cases concerning the same clause contained in previous accession treaties. In particular, in its *Piraiki-Patraiki* judgment[94] the Court held;

> 39. [...] although Article 130 [Act of Accession Greece] lays down two distinct conditions under which the Commission may authorise a protective measure, that does not mean that factors relating to one or other of those conditions may not be taken into account generally in order to arrive at the conclusion that the request for a protective measure made by a Member State is justified.
> 40. Furthermore, in the application of Article 130 the Commission has a wide discretion in determining whether the conditions justifying the adoption of a protective measure are present [...] in cases involving such discretion the Court must restrict itself to considering whether the exercise of that discretion contains a manifest error or constitutes a misuse of power or whether the Commission clearly exceeded the bounds of its discretion.

Thus, as with safeguard measures typically, the Commission's discretion was nevertheless generally confirmed by the Court as being subject to review only in the event of:

---

[91] See Commission Decision 81/988 of 30 October 1981 authorising the French Republic to take protective measures with regard to imports of cotton yarn from Greece, *OJ* 1981 L 362/33.

[92] *OJ* 1981 L 180/1.

[93] See Commission Decision 84/38.

[94] ECJ, Case 11/82 *SA Piraiki-Patrakai and others* v. *Commission* [1985] *ECR* 207.

- manifest error;
- misuse of power, or;
- where the Commission clearly exceeds the bounds of its discretion.

In the same case the ECJ annulled the Commission's decision only in part. This was because the Commission had not taken fully into account the interests of all of the Greek undertakings concerned, more particularly as concerned contracts entered into in good faith prior to instituting the emergency measures[95] but which were due to be performed during the time frame of the emergency measures.[96]

In a case[97] concerning the Commission Decision establishing a monitoring system and production quotas for rolled products, the Court not only refused to consider the arguments of the applicant, *Metallurgiki Halyps A.E.*, concerning the (negative) effects of the measures on Greece's development. The Court also refused to consider whether the quota system as it applied to Greek undertakings was contrary to the general principles of legal certainty, protection of legitimate expectation and the right to property. The Court's reasoning was that in the scheme of the Act of Accession, the emergency economic safeguard clause is subject to precise conditions, substantive and procedural, and that no inferences may be drawn from the safeguard clause if those conditions are not satisfied. As for the principles of legal certainty and legitimate expectation, the Court balanced these considerations with the fact that the new Member States had undertaken to extend the *acquis* throughout their territory and apply it on an equal basis with any other undertakings in the Union.

In other key cases, the ECJ has also confirmed the Commission's discretion to refuse to institute emergency measures. In a case of the same era and also concerning the Greek Accession Treaty,[98] the Court dealt with a situation where a receiving Member State sought compensation because the Commission had refrained from adopting emergency economic safeguard measures to stop imports of Greek new potatoes into Germany, France and the UK. The French and UK

[95] Commission Decision 81/988 op. cit. n. 91.

[96] See the Piraiki judgment in Case 11/82, op. cit., n. 94, at paras. 35 and 35.

[97] See ECJ, Case 258/81, op. cit., n. 42, at para. 8.

[98] ECJ, Case 114/83 *Société d'Initiatives et de Coopération Agricole and Société Interprofessionnelle des Producteurs et Expéditeurs de Fruits, Légumes, Bulbes et Fleurs d'Ille-et-Vilaine* v. *Commission* [1984] *ECR* 2589.

governments requested the use of these protective measures, arguing that the Commission had exceeded its discretion as framed in the emergency economic safeguard clause.

The Court supported the Commission in its findings of fact and predictions of market demand, based upon its experience of preceding years, that the anticipated risks to the German, French and UK potato markets were unfounded. In a subsequent case also involving the Commission's refusal to grant protective measures in respect of the potato market, the Court followed the same reasoning and the applicants again failed in their action for compensation.[99]

Another case concerned the Act of Accession Spain and Portugal in relation to the Commission's refusal to institute economic safeguard measures in respect of pharmaceutical products.[100] The case concerned a patent holder that had filed a patent for a pharmaceutical product in Spain after Spain's accession. However, the product was under a transitional arrangement which meant that the product could not be protected by a patent in Spain. The action was dismissed as inadmissible because the Commission Decision was addressed to a Member State and the applicant was not individually concerned. However, the Court expressly stated that the Commission is under no obligation to hear the views of any undertaking concerned before adopting such emergency measures.

---

[99] ECJ, Case 289/83 *GAARM* v. *Commission* [1984] *ECR* 4295.

[100] See ECJ, Case T-60/96 *Merck & Co. Inc., NV Organon and Glaxo Welcome plc* v. *Commission* [1997] *ECR* II-849.

CHAPTER FIVE

# NEW FLEXIBILITY MECHANISMS IN THE FIFTH AND SIXTH ACCESSION TREATIES

## 1. Differentiated integration: EMU, Schengen, Cyprus and the CAP

The fifth enlargement is noteworthy for the fact that it is the first time that incoming Member States do not enter as full participants in all areas of the Union's activities. The partial or non-participation of the new Member States in EMU, Schengen and the Common Agricultural Policy reflects the readiness of the new members and/or the Union itself to incorporate them into that area of activity. 'Differentiated integration' had been used in the fifth and sixth Accession Treaties to enable the enlargement project to go ahead. While this is new to enlargement practice, neither Schengen nor EMU were really developed at the time of the fourth enlargement.

However, there is no question of any permanent opt-out by the new members nor are they actually excluded from participating in these areas of the Union's activities, even though certain of the Fifteen have done concerning Schengen or EMU. In all cases they have formally undertaken to adopt, implement and comply with the *acquis*. In all three of these areas, the new Member States will be gradually included in the Union's activities. Differentiation between the 'old' and 'new' Member States has been expanded. Before looking at the safeguard clauses and the co-operation and verification mechanism in section 3 below, this first section outlines the situation of EMU, Schengen, Cyprus and the Common Agricultural Policy, in that order.

### 1.1 *Economic and Monetary Union*

In terms of participation in *Economic and Monetary Union*, Article 4 of the 2003 Accession Treaty obliged the new Member States to participate in EMU from the date of accession 'with a derogation within the meaning of [Article 139 TFEU]' alongside Sweden. In other words, upon accession, the new Member States do not transfer their monetary sovereignty.[1] It is mostly a matter of the new members meeting the convergence criteria although there are crucial institutional and decision-making issues to be resolved also. Neither the fifth nor the sixth Accession Treaties answer the questions that enlargement poses the ECB in terms of revision of its decision-making procedures and the status of members of the Eurozone. Uncertainty continues, not least of which is the open-ended gestation period for the ultimate entry of the new Member States into the Euro zone.[2]

The new members were given no possibility for opt-out comparable to that of the UK for example. Much depends on the country-specific characteristics. On 1 January 2007, Slovenia joined the third stage of the EMU, introducing the Euro there, and Cyprus and Malta joined on 1 January 2008 and Slovakia on 1 January 2009. Convergence Reports, of the European Commission and the European Central Bank, examine whether Member States satisfy the conditions for adopting the single currency and form the basis for the decision on whether a Member State may join the Euro zone. They are every two years but more frequently if an aspiring entrant requests one, as was the case for Slovenia and Lithuania in 2007. The most recent Report, issued in May 2008, covers the Czech Republic, Estonia, Latvia, Lithuania, Hungary, Poland, Slovakia and Sweden as well as being the first to consider Bulgaria and Romania since their accession.[3] It contains the Report from the Commission and the accompanying Staff working paper, which provides a more detailed analysis of how well the criteria have been met by all countries assessed. It was on the basis of this report that Slovakia was able to join the Euro.

Since 1 May 2004 therefore, the Euro Zone has functioned despite the many uncertainties that threaten both the credibility of its policy and the external value of its currency.[4] In terms of institutional adjust-

---

[1] See K. Inglis, 'The Union's Fifth Enlargement: new means to make enlargement possible' in CML Rev. (2004) pp. 937–973, at pp. 947–951. On the sequence of events involved in full participation of the new Members and candidates in EMU, see B. Dziechciarz, 'Candidate Countries and Economic and Monetary Union' in *Handbook on European Enlargement*, op. cit. Chapter 1, n. 24, at pp. 709–726.

[2] See M. Lelart, 'The Euro Zone and the Single Currency in an Enlarging European Union', in N. Neuwahl, ed., *European Union Enlargement: Law and Socio-Economic Changes* (Montréal, Editions Thémis 2004) pp. 133–156, at p. 155, quoting the IMF *Bulletin* of 3 June 2002, at p. 172, which in 2002 estimated the catch-up period for Slovenia at 10 to 15 years but 30 to 40 years for those that are least developed.

[3] COM(2008) 248 final of 7 May 2008.

[4] See M. Lelart, op. cit. n. 2.

ments to the European Central Bank (ECB), Article 17 of the 2003 Act of Accession added a new paragraph[5] to Protocol 18 of the Statute of the European System of Central Banks and of the European Central Bank. In the event of one or more countries becoming members, the limit on the foreign reserve assets transferred to the ECB was automatically increased and the method for doing so established. Four different legal regimes can be observed within the EMU and the end to the duration of the monetary division of the Community is dependent on economic and political factors and, of course, no Member State may be forced to introduce the Euro against its will.[6] At the end of 2008, in the wake of the financial crisis, the field for expanding has changed and may adversely affect the aspirations of various new Member States, such as the Czech Republic, Estonia and Latvia.[7] Some previously anti-Euro countries among the old Member States show more support for the Euro.[8]

The intended final solution for the functioning of the Governing Council proposes a rotation system to take account of the economic weight of Member States.[9] Due to a clause that allows EMU enlargement to be postponed until it reaches twenty-one members in the Governing Council, basically, while all central bank governors will participate in decisions of the Governing Council, their rights to vote in interest rate decisions will rotate, resulting in their temporary exclusion from some of these votes. While the proposal was adopted in Council on 21 March 2003 by unanimity,[10] it still has to be 'ratified'. Due to criticisms not only from the Fifteen but also the Commission

[5] The new Paragraph will be numbered 49.3 to said Protocol 18 of the Statute of the European System of Central Banks.

[6] See B. Dziechciarz, 'Impact of European Union Enlargement on EMU: Monetary Split-up into 'Ins' and 'Outs' as a temporary or Permanent Phenomenon?' in Inglis and Ott, eds., *The Constitution for Europe and an enlarging Union: Unity in Diversity?* (Groningen, Europa law Publishing 2005) pp. 135–157.

[7] On the Member States' progress in meeting their obligations under EMU, see European Commission *Convergence Report 2008: European Economy 3/2008*, to be found at http://ec.europa.eu/economy_finance/publications/publication12574_en.pdf.

[8] See 'Denmark re-thinks euro adoption amid financial crisis', www.EUobserver.com visited on 31 October 2008.

[9] European Central bank, Recommendation under Article 10.6 of the Statute of the ESCB and of the ECB, for a Council Decision on the amendment to Article 10.2 of the Statute of the ECB and of the ECB, (ECB/2003/1), 3 February 2003.

[10] See Decision of the Council of 2003/223, *OJ* 2003 L83/66–68.

and the new Member States[11] it is possible that this rotation system will be reopened for discussion before its entry into force.

With the adoption by Slovakia of the Euro, the number of Governing Council members has exceeded twenty-one and there are fifteen voting members in the Governing Council. Rather than agree on a rotation system, what the Governing Council of the ECB has done instead is to postpone the rotating system until there are eighteen voting members.[12]

### 1.2 *Schengen*

In the case of the Schengen *acquis*, the staggered entry of the twelve new Member States is about the readiness of the new members as well as the technical systems necessary for compliance. Differentiation between the new Member States also becomes evident. New members are fully included in Schengen depending on their progress. This also promises differing combinations of countries participating in the implementation and evolution of the *acquis*. The new Member States will have to meet all the provisions which are not directly linked to the lifting of internal border controls.

There was no specified target date for the full incorporation of the new members into the Schengen area at the time of signing the fifth or the sixth Accession Treaties. As at January 2009, twenty-four EU countries are participating in the border-free Schengen area: all of the countries that joined the EU in 2004, except for Cyprus. The UK and Ireland still operate under their opt-outs. Airport check points have been unmanned from March 2008 and visitors to the EU only need one visa to travel throughout the whole of the Schengen area. Norway and Iceland are associate members in Schengen, and were joined by Switzerland on 12 December 2008.[13] Liecthenstein is not an associate member and therefore Switzerland must control that border. Cyprus' entry is delayed while the intended date for Bulgaria and Romania at the moment is 2012.

[11] See W. Paczynski, 'ECB Decision-making and the Status of the Eurogroup in an Enlarged EMU', CASE, Warsaw 2003, ISSN 1506–1701, ISBN: 83–7178–318–3, at pp. 17–21, to be found at www.case.com.pl

[12] See ECB Decision ECB2008/29 (2009/5/EC) to postpone the start of the rotation system in the Governing Council of the ECB, *OJ* 2009 L 3/ 4.

[13] European Council of 27 November 2008. However, participation could be interrupted if Switzerland votes negatively on entry of Bulgarian and Romanian workers in their 2009 referendum. See www.Euobserver.com visited on 27 November 2008.

The procedure in the Accession Treaty[14] provides that each of the new Member States be subject to the evaluation procedure and the unanimous decision in Council of the participating[15] Schengen States and the new Member State concerned. Only a Decision of the participating Schengen Member States (old and new Member State concerned) can lift border controls for a new Member State. This two-stage procedure[16] made the fifth and sixth enlargements possible while the second generation Schengen Information System (SIS II) got up and running. Also the evaluation of the new Member States' ability to implement the Schengen *acquis* as well as the Schengen Information System would take some time after the fifth enlargement.

SIS II is intended to link the new Member States (and the UK and Ireland, plus the non-Member States of Norway and Iceland)[17] technically and replace the existing Schengen Information System. It should have become operational by end 2007. However, the SIS II has been plagued by technical problems with the result that, in January 2009, there is talk of the scrapping the entire project. The May 2009 European Council will be decisive in the future of the SIS II project. The Schengen Facility, set up under Article 35 of the fifth Accession Treaty, will go some way to helping the new Member States to fully implement the Schengen *acquis* and the Schengen Information System, providing EUR 961.45 million in all. These funds were distributed among the new members having an external land or sea border, except Cyprus.

Due to the delays with the SIS, the new members have instead been included into the first generation or the SIS 1+ system, now known as the 'SISone4ALL project'. The November 2004 The Hague European Council requested the Council, the Commission and Member States 'to take all necessary measures to allow the abolition of controls at internal borders as soon as possible, provided all requirements to apply the Schengen *acquis* have been fulfilled (...)'. This was the launch of the *The Hague Programme* which established an ambitious agenda

---

[14] According to Art. 3(2), 2003 Act of Accession and Art. 4(2), 2005 Act of Accession.

[15] The UK and Ireland will participate in the unanimous Council decision only insofar as they participate in the relevant Schengen *acquis*.

[16] On the accession negotiations, Art. 3 of the Accession Treaty and its implications for internal security in an enlarged Union, see W. de Lobkowicz, 'La sécurité intérieure de l'Union européenne élargie', in G. de Kerchove and A. Weyembergh (eds.), *Sécurité et justice: enjeu de la politique extérieure de l'Union européenne*, (Bruxelles, Editions de l'université de Bruxelles 2003) at pp. 31–65.

[17] Since 1998.

for the creation of the Area of Freedom, Security and Justice.[18] They were declared to be ready to be evaluated on non-SIS related *acquis* as of 2006. Evaluation visits on data protection, police co-operation, external borders and visas were started end of January and finalised in December 2006. The weaknesses were ironed out during 2007. The evaluation of application of the first generation SIS in the new Member States was done in 2007 and on 8 and 9 November 2007, the Justice and Home Affairs Council concluded that all preconditions for the lifting of internal border controls with the nine Member States were fulfilled. The Council Decision of 6 December 2007 set 21 December 2007 as the date for lifting of internal border controls at land borders and sea borders and 30 March 2008 for lifting of internal border controls at airports.

Bulgaria submitted its report to the Schengen Evaluation Group on 6 January 2009, which marks the end of the first phase for inspections of implementation. In the course of 2009 reviews will be carried out on personal data protection, police co-operation, the issue of visas, border controls and implementation of the SIS.

### 1.3 *The special case of the Cyprus 'green line'*

Protocol 10 to the 2003 Accession Treaty contains the simplified procedure adapting the terms of accession for Cyprus to cover the eventuality, now a reality, that no comprehensive settlement would be reached by the date of accession. The actual line between the areas where the Government of the Republic of Cyprus does not exercise effective control on the one hand, and the government-controlled areas on the other, was not drawn by the fifth Accession Treaty.

The EU's way of dealing with the *sui generis* situation of Cyprus following enlargement on 1 May 2005 is *sui generis* in itself. The Union has never in its history had to contemplate a regime to deal with such a scenario. Because a comprehensive settlement could not be found to the Cyprus problem in advance of Cyprus' accession, the Union has found an inventive means to provide for the future inclusion of the part of Cyprus that is beyond the effective control of the Government of the Republic of Cyprus.[19]

---

[18] Adopted by Heads of State or Government on 5 November 2004, *OJ* 2005 C 53/1.

[19] See F. Hoffmeister, *Legal Aspects of the Cyprus Problem: Annan Plan and EU Accession*, Leiden/Boston, Matinus Nijhoff Publishers 2006 at p. 196 *et seq*.

While technically speaking the north part of the island is not a third country, outwardly it would seem more that the application of agri-food laws concerning imports of foodstuffs and livestock in particular, the north part of the island is more of a third country than a Member State. Should a solution to the division of the island be found, the Council will then decide the terms that apply to the accession of the Turkish Cypriot Community. In the meantime, the application of the *acquis* is 'suspended', according to Article 1 of Protocol 10, in those areas where the Government of the Republic of Cyprus does not exercise effective control.[20]

The rights of individuals and companies in terms of directly effective rights contained in the agri-food *acquis* are also suspended in those areas of the island where the Government of the Republic of Cyprus does not exercise effective control. However, this regime cannot be thought of as a transitional arrangement because the suspension of the *acquis* is not a derogation from the *acquis*. Council Regulation 866/04[21] on a regime under Article 2 of Protocol 10 on Cyprus to the 2003 Act of Accession, defines the terms under which the provisions of EU law will apply to the line, which is known as the 'green line' Regulation. Council Decision 2004/115 concerns the representation of the people of Cyprus in the European Parliament in case of settlement of the Cyprus problem.[22] This *sui generis* nature of Cyprus made Article 207 TFEU an in appropriate legal basis for the 'green line' Regulation.[23]

The 'green line' does not constitute an external border of the Union.[24] Suspension of the *acquis* applies in the areas of Cyprus that are not under the Government's control together with special rules concerning the crossing of foodstuffs and goods, services and persons.[25]

---

[20] Acting unanimously on the basis of a proposal from the Commission, see Art. 4 of Protocol 10 to the 2003 Act of Accession.

[21] Council Regulation 866/2004 on a regime under Article 2 of Protocol No. 10 of the 2003 Act of Accession, *OJ* 2004 L 161/128 (Corrigendum *OJ* 2004 L 206/51), as previously amended by Regulation 1283/2005, *OJ* 2005 L 203/8 and last amended by Regulation 587/2008, *OJ* 2008 L 163/1.

[22] *OJ* 2004 L 211/22.

[23] Art. 133 would allow the Commission to act on a mandate by majority vote of the Council. The fact that the legal basis is protocol 10 of the Accession Treaty means that the Council must reach unanimity in order to do away with the suspension of the acquis in the north.

[24] See A. Berramdane, 'Chypre entre adhésion à l'Union europêene et réunification', *Revue du Droit de L'Union Européene* (2003) pp. 87–108.

[25] See Regulation 866/2004, as amended, op. cit. n. 21.

Concentrating here on the trade in goods, the regime is designed to foster trade between the two parts of the island. Customs duties do not apply to goods introduced into the areas where the Government of the Republic of Cyprus does exercise effective control, provided those goods:

- have been wholly obtained in the areas where the Government of the Republic of Cyprus does not exercise control, or;
- have undergone – in areas where the Government of the Republic of Cyprus does not exercise control – their last substantial, economically justifiable processing or working in an undertaking equipped for that purpose within the meaning of Articles 23 and 24 of Council Regulation 2913/94, which established the Community Customs Code.[26]

As a result of an amendment in 2008, in the form of Regulation 587/2008, the Council relaxed the rules in order to encourage the provision of services across the line by companies established in the areas of the Republic of Cyprus in which the Government of the Republic of Cyprus does not exercise effective control. Persons and goods have to be declared for temporary introduction. The aim is to facilitate participation by those companies in trade fairs or similar events. It also allows for goods destined to be repaired in the areas of the Republic of Cyprus in which the Government of the Republic of Cyprus exercises effective control to cross the line.[27] Finally also, it increases the total value of goods contained in personal luggage that can cross the line: this is aimed specifically to encourage economic development in the areas of the Republic of Cyprus that are beyond the control of the Government of the Republic of Cyprus. As a result, the quantitative limits for exemptions for turnover tax and excise duty as well as other duties now stands at 40 cigarettes and 1 litre of spirits for personal consumption.

For the purposes of the environment *acquis*, Community laws are suspended in the parts of the island outwith the effective control of

[26] *OJ* 1992 L 302/1, as amended.

[27] Council Regulation 587/2008 amending Regulation 866/2004 on a regime under Art. 2 of Protocol 10 to the Act of Accession concerning rules on goods, services and persons crossing the Green Line in Cyprus, *OJ* 2008 L163/1.

the Government of Cyprus until such time as the suspension is lifted. For the agri-food *acquis*, imports from the non-controlled part of the island will be subject to the special regime. For foodstuffs, goods crossing the green line must meet the EU veterinary and phytosanitary checks. However, the movement of animals and animal products is prohibited outright by virtue of Article 4(9) of Regulation 866/2004, unless the Commission adopts special measures lifting the ban for specific animals or animal products (under Article 58(2) of the 2002 food hygiene Regulation, Reg. 178/2002). In this way, the principle of equivalence that applies – in terms of production and other standards – to imports from third countries, also applies to imports from the part of Cyprus that is beyond the effective control of the Government of Cyprus.

The above Commission procedure for lifting the ban on imports into the EU of specific animals or animal products also applies. It involves the Standing Committee on the Food Chain and Animal Health (SCFCAH) and the Commission adopts detailed implementing rules to ensure the smooth operation of the transitional arrangements contained in the Accession Treaty.[28] This possibility of an exception to this blanket ban was only introduced end February 2005.[29]

From the outset however, as regards the veterinary and phytosanitary and food safety/human health dimension, the *acquis* has not been compromised. Annex II to Regulation 866/2004 lists the applicable EC requirements and checks. The chapter on the agri-food *acquis* mentions the fact that the Cypriot competent authorities are subject to inspection and control by the Food and Veterinary Office (FVO) just like any other Member State, as are establishments being inspected and controlled by the Cypriot competent authorities. There are now seven[30] recognised crossing-points for goods and persons, compared to the two such posts which were originally recognised in 2004.

---

[28] With the repeal and replacement of the measures listed in the country annexes to the fifth Accession Treaty, the provisions cited (Art. 16 Directive 64/433, Art. 21 Directive 71/118, Art. 15 Directive 91/493, Art. 20 Directive 77/99, Art. 31 Directive 92/46 and Art. 20 Directive 94/65) have been replaced by Art. 58 of Regulation 178/2002.

[29] By virtue of an amendment to Art. 4(9) of Regulation 866/2004, op. cit. n. 21, by Commission Regulation 293/2005, *OJ* 2005 L 50/1, which entered into force on 26 February 2005.

[30] As a result of Regulation 1283/2005, *OJ* 2005 L 203/8.

### 1.4 *The Common Agricultural Policy*

Concerning the Common Agricultural Policy, the new members have been obliged to meet the quality, production, processing and hygiene standards and to take full responsibility for third country imports to the Internal Market. However, they have been excluded from the financial benefits in terms of subsidies and direct payments, due to the ongoing reform of the CAP, and are only gradually being integrated into it. Entry into the financial market related aspects of the CAP are staggered over a period of ten years. The December 2002 Copenhagen European Council settled the financial package and enabled the Council to engage in the real negotiations with the future new Member States.[31] How the CAP actually looked after the fifth enlargement, however, was not fully determined until March 2003, after the signature of the 2003 Accession Treaty. Certain key CAP provisions were revised along with the fifth Accession Treaty[32] to take account of that reform. Poland, with its significant agriculture sector, challenged the legality of the measures specified in Article 1.5 of Decision 2004/281, to extend the restricted scope of payments to the new direct payments. The main reforms concern the subsidies for energy crops, nuts and dairy products, staggering these payments until 2013, as was already the case for direct payments.

In the first place, in Case C-273/04, Poland challenged the legality of the measures taken to adapt the 2003 Act of Accession.[33] This dimension to the case was dealt with in Chapter 4. Poland also argued that the contested measure infringes the principle of non-discrimination.

[31] See www.ue.eu.int/eu/Info/eurocouncil/index.htm. See J. Rollo, 'Agriculture, the Structural funds and the Budget after Enlargement', in N. Neuwahl (ed.), op. cit. n. 2, at 117–130. See J. McMahon, *Handbook on European enlargement*, op. cit. Chapter 1, n. 24, at pp. 391–414.

[32] See Council Decision 2004/281 adapting the Act of Accession following the reform of the CAP, *OJ* 2004 L 93/1–17, which entered into force on 1 May 2004, sets out the adaptations to be made to the Act of Accession following the CAP reform: progressive introduction of (new) direct payments; single area payment; complementary national direct payments (topping-up); milk; rural development. Decision 2004/281 amends the following annexes to the Accession Treaty: Annex II (making adaptation to the *acquis*), Chapter 6,A; and the agriculture chapters of the country annexes for Annex VI (Estonia), chapter 4.2 and 4.3, Annex VII (Cyprus), chapter 5, A, Annex VIII (Latvia), chapter 4, A, Annex IX (Lithuania), chapter 5, A, Annex XI (Malta), chapter 4, A and Annex XII (Poland), chapter 6, A.

[33] ECJ, Case C-273/04, *Republic of Poland* v. *Council*, *OJ* 2004 C 239/6. See Chapter 4 at 2.3.

However, to the mind of both the Grand Chamber of the European Court of Justice and Advocate-General Maduro, it was clear to Poland when it signed the 2003 Accession Treaty, that the reform was ongoing and far from finalised. It was also clear at that time that the EU was faced with a considerable task in integrating Poland's agriculture sector, the largest and most backward agricultural sector of all the Central and East European candidates at the time and particularly in comparison to the EU Member States.[34] This took any strength out of Poland's claims of discriminatory treatment. Both the Court and the Advocate General relied on Commission and Council strategy documents and negotiating mandates in order to determine the intentions of the Parties and whether the 2003 CAP reform went further than was allowed for in the fifth Accession Treaty (using the legal basis of Art. 23 Act of Accession).[35]

## 2. New forms of flexibility mechanism

This section looks at how the fifth Accession Treaty applies pre-accession conditionality to new Member States after their accession. The fifth enlargement has heralded a new age in the use of flexibility mechanisms in both pre-accession and post-accession practice. Continued incentives and support for maintaining and improving administrative capacity was extended to the twelve new Member States in the form of the Transition Facility as well as the Cash Flow and Schengen Facility.

The Transition Facility today is provided for in Article 31 of the 2005 Act of Accession (the equivalent under the 2003 Accession Treaty ended at the end of 2006, Art. 34 2003 Act of Accession). It is, effectively, an extension of PHARE funds into the first years of membership and concentrates on institution building in situations that

[34] On this the Court and the Advocate General both agreed, see para. 87 of the Court's judgment and para. 75 of Advocate General Maduro's Opinion in ECJ, Case-273/04, ibid.

[35] Commission Discussion Paper *Enlargement and Agriculture: successfully integrating the new Member States into the CAP,* SEC(2002) 95, 30 January 2002, *Bull. EU* 1 /2, 2002 at 1.5.1., the Common Position of the European Union of 31 October 2002, see Presidency Conclusions 6/12, *Bull. EU* 10, 2002, at 1.7.12., and the outcome of the December 2002 Copenhagen European Council on the closure of the negotiations, *Bull. EU* 12, 2002 at 1.5.1. The Court even took into account 'the intention of the Conference' (where the accession negotiations between the Member States and the incoming members are conducted).

are not eligible for structural funding. A broad, non-exhaustive list of activities covered include:

- justice and home affairs (strengthening of the judicial system, external border controls, anti-corruption strategy, strengthening of law enforcement capacities)
- financial control
- protection of the Communities' financial interests and the fight against fraud
- internal market
- environment
- veterinary services and administrative capacity-building related to food safety
- administrative and control structures for agriculture and rural development, including the integrated administration and control system (IACS)
- nuclear safety
- statistics

For Bulgaria the total allocation for the year after accession was EUR 31.5 million while for Romania the allocation was EUR 46.5 million. The ten countries of the 2004 enlargement wave had three years provision from the Transition Facility.

Also, safeguard clauses were introduced into the fifth and the sixth Accession Treaties specifically to maintain the momentum of reform and compliance in the new Member States with the Internal Market *acquis* and parts of the Justice and Home Affairs *acquis* in the first years of membership, see 2.1 and 2.2 respectively. The only example so far of the use of the safeguard clauses was in respect of the Bulgarian aviation sector, using the Internal Market safeguard clause.[36] They purported to foster trust by the Fifteen old Member States in the abilities of the new Member States to continue to meet their obligations after they had joined, suspecting that the incentive of membership no longer exists once the accession treaty has been signed. However, the very existence of these clauses raises the potential for discrimination by the fifteen against the twelve new members, especially in areas of

[36] See Regulation 1962/2006, *OJ* 2007 L47/8.

the *acquis* where the Fifteen themselves are no angels in meeting their obligations as Member States.

Only the 2005 Accession Treaty provided for the postponement of Bulgaria and Romania's accession on the politically agree date of 1 January 2007 should they prove manifestly unprepared. The European Commission reports on their preparedness, issued in September 2006[37] only a few months before the sixth enlargement, found serious problems in their readiness. This did not stop the European Parliament nor the Member States in Council from proceeding with the sixth enlargement on 1 January 2007, without reverting to the postponement clause. The fact that it was not used is another indication of the Union's political commitment to enlargement. Rather than postpone their entry or make use of the safeguard clauses, the Co-operation and Verification Mechanism was devised to support ongoing reforms in Bulgaria and Romania. Two years after setting up the Co-operation and Verification Mechanism, neither Bulgaria nor Romania have brought their judiciary up to standard or sufficiently progressed in the fight against corruption there, see further at 3.1.

Bulgaria and Romania acceded to the Union on I January 2007 without having been subject to the postponement clause. While just before their accession, the Commission had reported that Bulgaria was ready but Romania was not, the Council and the European Parliament both opted for proceeding with the joint accession on 1 January 2007. Romania's most serious weaknesses were identified in the state aid and competition chapters of the *acquis* as well as in the Schengen *acquis*, the control of external borders, corruption, the co-operation between the gendarmerie and the police as well as the struggle against organised crime. In terms of food law, there were also serious concerns as to the ability of both Bulgaria and Romania to meet the obligations of a Member States, the same problems that had been highlighted in the spring of 2006.[38] For example, problems were identified in compliance with the TSE laws and special measures thereunder, similar to the ban that had endured against UK beef and which had only then been lifted

[37] Comprehensive Monitoring Report, COM(2005) 534 final of 25 October 2005.

[38] Commission Communication Monitoring Report on the state of preparedness of Romania and Bulgaria, COM(2006) (unnumbered), of 16 May 2006. See 'Commission keeps Bulgaria and Romania in limbo', www.EurActiv.com visited on 24 April 2006, in anticipation of the Commission's May 2006 Progress Reports.

in the March of 2006.[39] TSEs are a family of diseases that are characterised by a degeneration of brain tissue such a CJD in humans, scrapie in sheep or BSE in cows. While Romania and Bulgaria are banned from marketing their meat products on the Internal Market, they were nevertheless able to continue to sell on their national market. At least Romania had transposed the agri-food *acquis* into national law, but its ability to guarantee the administrative capacity in order to ensure compliance with the laws was not certain. In the end, these problems have to be sorted out using the legal tools available under the agri-food *acquis* itself, without the added and most significant incentive that accession provides, as illustrated in Chapter 7.

To brush over the legal conditions of the pre-accession strategy in this way can be criticised for setting a dangerous precedent for future enlargements. Choosing to proceed with the enlargement on the pre-agreed date will no doubt be interpreted by many as the precedence given to the political goal of enlargement over the legal and economic conditionality of the pre-accession strategy and weakening the equality of rights and obligations of Member States.

Safeguard and postponement clauses in the 2003 and 2005 Accession Treaties and the new Co-operation and Verification Mechanism are tangible evidence of the importance that the Union gives to the candidate's ability to meet the Copenhagen criteria both before and after their accession. Also relevant will be how the new Member States continue to meet their obligations as Member States and whether the safeguard clauses contained in the accession treaties are used against them. If the pre-accession conditions applied to the country have no meaning becomes a member, the very purpose of the EU enlargement preparations strategy would be negated. The pre-accession strategy and the limited transitional arrangements in the accession treaty have certainly limited the possibility of new members failing in their obligations as Member State. The first and only Internal Market safeguard measures adopted under an accession treaty were those adopted in respect of Bulgaria and concerned its air transport sector.[40] The fact that the safeguard measures have not generally been used to some extent however, also attests to the effectiveness of the pre-accession

[39] See Key Findings of the May 2006 Monitoring Reports on Bulgaria and Romania, Commission MEMO/06/201 of 16 May 2006.

[40] See Commission Regulation 1962/2006 in application of Art. 37, 2003 Act of Accession of Bulgaria to the European Union, *OJ* 2006 L 408/8.

strategy and to the readiness of the incoming countries to become fully fledged Member States.

Then again, the Internal Market and JHA clauses are specifically designed to guard against a protectionist backlash in the form of unilateral national measures against new Member States and to guarantee the integrity of the *acquis*. An informal transitional arrangement would be a legitimate case for the use of safeguard measures. As Cremona puts it,[41] the safeguard clauses give an impressive of being purely technical enforcement mechanisms. After all, the new Member States agreed to close their transitional arrangements for derogations from the *acquis* in December 2002. If the safeguard clauses are not used, governance initiatives at EU level take on a more significant role in the longer term both as a means of ensuring the integrity of the *acquis* but also of preventing rifts between Member States.

However, the very existence of such clauses is very much an indication of issues of mutual trust and confidence of the Fifteen in the Twelve. These clauses cannot be used against the Fifteen and are in addition to the traditional treaty provisions for enforcement of the Ten's obligations. It would have been difficult even to open accession negotiations if such safeguard clauses had not been proposed early on the pre-accession strategy.[42] The fact that such safeguard measures are available in respect of the incoming Member States only is in itself discriminatory. It speaks not only of the mistrust of the receiving Member States in the incoming countries, but also in the ability of the Union's institutions to prepare enlargement as well as in the pre-accession strategy.[43] Thus, the idea of equality of rights and obligations among Member States is called into question by the very existence of such clause in an accession treaty and necessarily undermines solidarity among Member States.

The role of the European Commission has been pivotal throughout pre-accession in applying pre-accession conditionality: in programming and prioritising Community assistance and funds, monitoring and reporting on the progress of each candidate, negotiating the

---

[41] See Cremona, 'EU enlargement: solidarity and conditionality', op. cit. Chapter 1, n. 41 at p. 21.

[42] See House of Lords Report 1997.

[43] See M. Cremona, 'EU enlargement: solidarity and conditionality', op. cit. n. 41, at p. 21, and on the importance of solidarity as a constitutional value of the EU both from an internal and an external stand point see pp. 3–7.

content and limits to the transitional arrangements and evaluating each candidate's readiness for membership. Giving such responsibilities to the Commission was meant to take the political heat out of managing and checking compliance with what is a highly political area of the *acquis*. The Commission has continued in this role in the first years after accession as it also plays a key role in the management of the transitional arrangements and it falls on the Commission to trigger the procedure for instituting safeguard measures and nowadays, in administering the co-operation and verification mechanism.

### 2.1 *Internal Market safeguard measures*

The Internal Market safeguard clause, Article 37 Act of Accession of the sixth Accession Treaty with Bulgaria and Romania, enables the Union to take unspecified action against a new Member State to address any threat to the Internal Market arising as a result of a failed or potential failure to meet their commitments given during the negotiations. The Commission could exclude products from the Internal Market or suspend Community funds. It gave a considerable discretion to the Commission to evaluate whether commitments have been met or not, to decide the form of measures, adapt them or evaluate whether the failing has been remedied to the extent necessary to merit lifting those safeguard measures. The equivalent in the fifth Accession Treaty can be found in Article 38 of the Act of Accession, which expired on 30 April 2007 without having been used.

#### 2.1.1 *Motivation, content and use*

Only in the case of the Bulgarian aviation sector has this clause been used[44] and it has since been revoked.[45] The 'serious deficiencies' identified in the European Aviation Safety Agency and the Joint Aviation Authorities included problems with airworthiness of the craft, maintenance, operations and crew licensing. Bulgaria was refused mutual recognition in safety areas.

Essentially, Bulgaria was not able to ensure compliance with various EC Regulations concerning the Internal Market and safety of

[44] Op. cit. n. 36.
[45] Commission Regulation 875/2008, *OJ* 2008 L 240/3.

the aviation sector.[46] The Commission foresaw that giving the Bulgarian carriers unrestricted access to the Internal Market in aviation could, because of these deficiencies, lead to distortions of competition between Bulgarian carriers and those licensed in other Member States. Moreover, allowing Bulgarian carriers unrestricted access throughout the EU could help the Bulgarian carriers to expand their operations in other Member States, thereby increasing safety risks. The Commission Regulation revoking the safeguard measures followed only two years later following planning and investment by Bulgaria and an exigent series of inspections to verify compliance. In particular, the Commission only proposed revoking the measures once it was convinced that Bulgaria could guarantee the capacity of the Bulgarian Civil Aviation Authority to ensure compliance with the 2008 Regulation on common rules in the field of civil aviation.[47]

Both the Internal Market safeguard clause and the JHA safeguard clause were a considerable political conditionality-stick for pre-accession efforts in the fifth and the sixth enlargements. While in the last years of the enlargement preparations for the fifth enlargement, different Commission sources had expressly said that they intended to use the safeguard clauses in the weeks leading up to the fifth enlargement, Commissioner Verheugen was more cautious about their use, favouring the use of the Article 258 TFEU procedure.[48]

In its guide to the negotiations, the Commission made clear that, after enlargement, it would monitor the new members 'using the same mechanisms as those applied to the existing Member States'.[49] However, Commissioner Verheugen also made clear that the safeguard measures were likely in the food safety *acquis*.[50] The use of these safeguard

---

[46] Regulation 2407/92, *OJ* 1992 L240/1, Regulation 2408/92, *OJ* 1992 L240/8, Regulation 2409/92, L240/9 and Regulation 1592/2002, *OJ* 2002L240/1, as amended.

[47] See Regulation 216/2008, *OJ* 2008 L 79/1.

[48] See 'Zero Tolerance for new Member States', to be found on www.EurActive.com visited on 14 April 2004.

[49] See the Commission *Guide to the Negotiations*, dated 31 December 2002 at p. 22, to be found at www.europa.eu.int/comm/enlargement/negotiations/index.htm

[50] Of course, all twenty-five Member States will be open to make use of the safeguard clauses contained in the secondary EC agri-food legislation, such as Article 53 and 54 of Regulation 178/2002 of the European Parliament and of the Council of 28 January 2002 laying down the general principles and requirements of food law, establishing the European Food Safety Authority and laying down procedures in matters of food safety, *OJ* 2002 L 31/1–24. These provisions provides for emergency measures to be taken by the Commission or a Member State where a serious risk is posed to human health, animal health or the environment. But emergency measures are not

measures had previously been seen as 'inevitable' where legislative tasks such as implementing the *acquis communautaire* and practical preparations such as introducing EU standards and norms, were not met by November 2003.[51]

The Commission in its 2003 comprehensive report, however, had indicated that these '[safeguard measures] may result in temporarily excluding this new Member State or its citizens and economic operators from the benefits of certain Internal Market legislation and from the benefits of membership in specific areas, in order to protect the integrity of the Internal Market and damage to others [...] The Commission will not hesitate to make use of such safeguards when circumstances require.'[52] Thirty-nine areas of serious concern were raised in that same report.[53] The Commission expressly mentioned that measures might be needed to protect the single market in the fisheries sector against Lithuania and Poland.[54] The Commission also mentioned that Malta and Slovakia would not benefit from certain beneficial transitional arrangements concerning their shipbuilding industry (Malta) and aid to the steel sector (Slovakia) if they continued to remain in non-compliance with the *acquis*, thus giving unfair advantages to the companies concerned.

Other areas of serious concern to the functioning of the Internal Market included the workers' *acquis*: in the same Comprehensive Monitoring Report of November 2003, the Commission said it was considering these safeguard clause to address failures in the administrative capacity of the Czech Republic, Estonia, Latvia, Lithuania, Poland and Slovenia to apply the rules on mutual recognition of professional qualifications or social security provision. In particular, it said that: 'professionals from those countries who would, as a result, not meet the minimum requirements, may as a consequence, not be allowed to benefit from the right to exercise their profession in other Member

---

designed to guarantee the overall integrity of any one country's regulatory regime governing the food chain and its general capacity and ability to guarantee it.

[51] See the remarks of the European Commission's Director-General for Enlargement Eneko Landaburu speaking at the joint committee of the Polish and European Parliament meeting in Poland on 29 April 2003.

[52] See Comprehensive Monitoring Report of 5 November 2003, COM(2003) 676, 5 November 2003 at p. 18.

[53] See Comprehensive Monitoring Report of 5 November 2003, ibid. at pp. 14–16.

[54] See Comprehensive Monitoring Report of 5 November 2003, op. cit. n. 52 at p. 15.

States until the gap is filled'.[55] Serious shortcomings were identified in the general system of recognition of training and qualifications in Poland[56] for example, and in the capacity to enforce that recognition of professional qualifications and the co-ordination of social security systems in Cyprus.[57]

While the Commission did not invoke more safeguards, could it refuse a request by a Member State to do so? Politically speaking, it would seem untenable to revert to safeguard measures in respect of the new members if the Fifteen were not themselves fully and correctly implementing the law in question. The Commission has no such fast-track preventive route for managing and enforcing compliance by the old Member States. It is from the viewpoint of solidarity and the necessary fabric of trust among the Member States that the Internal Market clause becomes dubious. The Commission must revert to the comparably limited resort of Article 258 TFEU in the event of failures arising in compliance by the old Member States, see 2.1.3. Even in terms of administrative capacity, the Commission held seminars for the old Member States in 2002 on the correct implementation of particularly complex environmental directives.[58]

However, this may well be a legitimate request. It is foreseeable that a Member State might make a request to the Commission for safeguard measures to be taken under the Accession Treaty against a new member, for example, pending the outcome of proceedings against a new Member State which has been brought before the European Court of Justice for failure to meet its Treaty obligations. Moreover, by taking such action itself, the Commission could defuse any potential protectionist backlash against the new Member States. The safeguard clause would, if used, enable to the Commission to lever immediate legislative revision, administrative capacity improvement and compliance with the *acquis* by the new Member States. While secondary EC legislation provides specific safeguards in various sectors, such as in food safety laws or in the area of road transport, this is not the case in all sectors of the *acquis*. After all, it is something of a technocractic procedure in the hands of the executive and kept at arms reach from

---

[55] See Comprehensive Monitoring Report of 5 November 2003, op. cit. n. 52 at p. 14.
[56] Poland Report, 5 November 2003 at p. 22.
[57] Cyprus Report, 5 November 2003 at p. 16.
[58] Ibid.

political motivations of Member States, whether acting on their own or together in Council.[59] The fact that another Member State is falling behind should not be an excuse for allowing a new Member State to fall behind in its obligations when a legal mechanism exists to resolve the situation quickly. Transposition of the *acquis* was not negotiable during the pre-accession negotiations and the new members committed to correct failings in terms of administrative capacity or lack of criminal sanctions, for example, prior to the date of accession. The fact that the Internal Market safeguard clause has not been used deflates the pre-accession conditionality and sends contradictory signals to candidates and potential candidates.

As is pointed out in the below chapter on the agri-food *acquis*, there are already safeguard and emergency measures and procedures in place to protect against serious risks to the food chain. Commissioner Verheugen at the time of the 2004 enlargement, emphasised[60] that the Commission will take a tough line in respect of the new members' compliance and the Commission could also use safeguard clauses in the Accession Treaty in addition to legal action, to protect the functioning of EU's Internal Market. He is also reported to have said that;

> the safeguard measures are only likely to be invoked concerning food safety. Slaughterhouses and dairy producers could thus be barred from exporting if their standards are not satisfactory.

The then European Commission's Director-General for Enlargement, Eneko Landaburu, said;[61]

> if [legislative tasks such as implementing the *acquis communitaire* and practical preparations such as introducing EU standards and norms] were not met by November, when the Commission has to present the final reports on the 10 applicants' readiness to join the EU, then the introduction of the so-called protective clauses would be inevitable.

Commissioner Byrne, the then Commissioner for Health and Consumer Protection and Food Safety, emphasised that;

[59] See Cremona, op. cit. Chapter 1 at n. 41.

[60] See www.euractiv.com, visited on 14 April 2004.

[61] Speaking at the joint committee of the Polish and European Parliament meeting in Poland on 29 April 2003, see www.EUobserver.com/index.phtml?aid=11053 visited on 30 April 2003.

> Many problems need to be resolved and significant improvements need to be made between now and accession [...]. If deficiencies remain, safeguard measures can be triggered to ensure that standards are maintained and that consumers are not put at risk.[62]

On the other hand, after the signature of the sixth Accession Treaty the Commission continued to threaten Bulgaria and Romania with these clauses if they failed to meet their commitments as they stood at the closure of the accession negotiations.[63]

### 2.1.2 *Procedure*

The safeguard clause is intended as a last resort[64] – a means of ensuring compliance in addition to the traditional Treaty basis of Article 258 TFEU for pursuing a new Member State that has failed to meet its obligations. It is a tool of prevention, designed to anticipate compliance, implementation and enforcement inadequacies and non-compliance. Article 226 EC however, is more reactive in approach in that the breach must already have occurred.

The Commission may take 'appropriate measures' under Article 37 Act of Accession, should a new Member State fail to meet their commitments made during the accession negotiations. The failure must 'cause serious breach of the functioning of the Internal Market' including 'any commitments in all sectoral policies which concern economic activities with cross-border effect or an imminent risk of such breach'. Only the Commission may adopt measures under the safeguard-clause, although any Member State (including a new Member State) may make a request that they be adopted. Preference is given to measures that

---

[62] See Speech/03/329, 'Completion of Farm to Fork Approach Economic and Social Committee Brussels, 27 June 2003.'

[63] See remarks made by Commissioner Kroes (Competition), made at the European Institute of Romania in Bucharest on 12 May 2005, in respect of improving Romania's performance in the competition acquis: 'Of course we all trust that we will not need to use this option. But it is my responsibility and duty to make it very clear, in no uncertain terms, that should Romania's performance not improve, the Commission would have no other option other than to propose postponement.' Commission Rehn (enlargement) made clear at the launch of the 2004 progress reports on Bulgaria and Romania's preparedness for accession in Brussels on 5 October 2005 that the postponement clause 'is not included in the accession treaty just for fun, it is a serious clause and we would not hesitate to use it.' He did so again at the EU-Romania Joint Parliamentary Committee in Brussels on 22 November 2005, see 'Romania's work programme up to accession in the light of the monitoring report', Speach/05/2005, 22 November 2005.

[64] See Comprehensive Monitoring Report of November 2003, op. cit. n. 52 at p. 18.

least disturb the functioning of the common market. The principles of proportionality and non-discrimination are explicitly incorporated in the formulation of safeguard measures and those measures must not act as disguised restrictions on trade.

They must 'be maintained no longer than strictly necessary, and, in any case, will be lifted when the relevant commitment is implemented' and the Commission may only revert to using safeguard measures until end 2009 for Bulgaria and Romania. If they are in place before the end of the three-year period, the Commission will be able to continue their application should the new Member States not have met their pre-accession commitments to which the safeguard measures apply. Once they are in place, however, the Council must be informed 'in good time' before the Commission revokes the measures, and it must take the Council's observations into account. However, the Commission will be able to adapt the safeguard measures in line with progress in meeting pre-accession commitments.

The safeguards could only take effect on the first day of accession and can only be instituted within the first three years of the date of accession. They must 'be maintained no longer than strictly necessary, and, in any case, will be lifted when the relevant commitment is implemented'. However, where such measures are in place before end-December 2009, the Commission will be able to continue their application should the new Member State in question still not have met their commitments. When they are in place, the Council must be informed 'in good time' before the Commission may revoke the measures, and it must take the Council's observations into account – although the Commission will be able to adapt the safeguard measures in line with the new Member State's progress in meeting its commitments.

In an attempt to introduce some legal certainty into the use of this clause, six of the new members of the fifth enlargement wave made a Declaration on this clause. It aimed to restrict the scope of this clause in the fifth Accession Treaty to failures to fulfil Treaty obligations in the same way as under Article 258 TFEU, seeing that both provisions aim to bring about compliance with the *acquis*.[65] There is no equivalent declaration in the sixth Accession Treaty.

[65] The Czech Republic, Estonia, Lithuania, Poland, Slovenia and the Slovak Republic jointly declared (Joint Declaration 22 to the Final Act) that they understand 'the notion 'has failed to implement commitments undertaken in the context of the accession negotiations' only [to cover] the obligations that are arising from the original

The Commission gave no such guarantees and accepted no such restrictions on its discretion under the safeguard clause.[66] The Commission has declared that it will hear the views of Member States directly affected by such measures and will duly take into account these views and positions.[67] The Commission has not limited itself to the fulfilment of Treaty obligations. The safeguard measures may address the commitments made during the negotiations, which include for example, building administrative capacity and making provision for criminal sanctions. This is an extension of the pre-accession conditionality that has been prevalent throughout pre-accession. Just as was the case before accession, the new members must do more than meet the *acquis*. Throughout the first three years after their accession to the Union, they will have to convince the Commission and the 'old' Member States of their willingness and capacity to contribute to the evolution of the *acquis*.

The only certainty for new Member State concerned is when the Commission makes a proposal to revoke the measures. At this point, any of the twenty-five Member States may submit observations, meeting within the Council, not only the Member State subjected to the safeguard measures. Thus, the Internal Market safeguard clause gives broad discretion to the Commission together with seemingly far-reaching powers to sanction action or inaction by the new Members under their pre-determined transitional measures at the final close of the accession negotiations.

### 2.1.3 *A comparison with the Article 258 TFEU infringement procedure*

In theory, this clause could be used to bypass the more lengthy procedures of Article 258 TFEU. For practical purposes, the Internal Market safeguard clause offers advantages over the traditional means available to the European Commission for bringing Member States into compliance with their Treaty obligations.

---

Treaties ... under the conditions laid down in the Act of Accession and the obligations defined in this Act' and that therefore, they 'understand that the Commission will consider application of Article 38 only in cases of alleged violations of the obligations' arising from the original Treaties. These countries also expressly declared, in paragraphs 2 and 3, that Article 38 if without prejudice to jurisdiction of the Court of Justice and insofar as any sanctions might be concerned and that they must be heard before measures are taken against them.

[66] See in particular Final Act to the fifth Accession Treaty, Declaration 43.

[67] Ibid.

Under the Article 258 TFEU procedure, the Commission submits a reasoned opinion and hears the Member State concerned, giving that Member State the opportunity to bring itself into compliance before initiating court action against it. Also here, only the Member State concerned is entitled to submit observations in the pre-litigation phase. Once before the Court, of course, all Member States may submit observations.

The Internal Market safeguard clause however, gives the new Member State no legally established right to submit observations or to be heard on a Commission proposal for a safeguard measure. On the matter of timing and suspension of funds, the Internal Market safeguard clause enables the Commission to take immediately effective action in respect of the new Member States by means of appropriate measures, which may involve the suspension of EC funds. By comparison, the lead-time for the Commission between the issue of the reasoned opinion under Article 258 TFEU and actually bringing a Member State before the Court may take years. In the case of the Article 258 TFEU procedure against the Member States, the procedure lasts 59 months on average. In the past, where the Article 260 TFEU procedure was launched, it took an average nine years, from the issue of the formal notice,[68] to impose fines[69] although the situation is improving.[70] Consequently, the imposition of fines has not always elicited corrective action by those of the Fifteen in default and nor can fines be said to be effective in the short term.

Withholding funds from recalcitrant Member States would seem a more effective and stronger incentive to improving application and enforcement of the *acquis*. The Commission determines whether commitments have been met or not, decides the form of the measures, adapts those measures and evaluates whether compliance with the pre-accession commitments has been sufficient to merit lifting the safeguard measures.

---

[68] See Art. 260 TFEU.

[69] See Commission *20th Annual Report on Monitoring the Application of Community Law (2002)*, COM(2003) 669, 22 November 2003 at pp. 9–11. These three pages give a summary of the compliance by the Member States with Court judgments against them. Of the twenty-eight cases, thirteen concern the environment *acquis*.

[70] See *The 24th Annual Report of the Commission on the Monitoring of the Application of Community Law* for the year 2006, COM(2007) 398, presented on 18 November 2008.

In the past the Commission had attempted to improve its powers to bring the old Member States into compliance with the *acquis*. In 1997 the Commission issued a proposal, following a request from the June 1997 Amsterdam European Council, for a Council Regulation based on Article 235 EC (now Art. 268 TFEU) creating a mechanism whereby the Commission could intervene in order to remove certain obstacles to trade.[71] The proposal was soon dubbed the 'strawberry regulation' because it was made in direct response to French farmer-activists radically opposed to imports of Spanish fruit and vegetables. In the December of 1997 the ECJ had condemned France for failing to take all the necessary and proportionate measures in order to prevent the free movement of fruit and vegetables from being obstructed by actions by private individuals and found this to have contravene Articles 36 TFEU and 5 TEU (in today's Treaties).[72] It was the first time that the ECJ had ruled that a Member State's failure to take measures against the actions of private individuals constitutes a State measure incompatible with Article 36 TFEU. As a result, individuals could then seek redress for losses suffered as a result of hindrances incompatible with Article 36 TFEU.

The Commission designed the proposal to set up an intervention mechanism to allow it to call on a Member State to take whatever measures necessary and appropriate to eliminate certain types of obstacles to trade. A sort of rapid intervention mechanism, it was intended to introduce an accelerated Article 169 EC (now Art. 258 TFEU) procedure, only with teeth by which the Commission could enforce compliance. The Commission proposed that it would be required to take urgent action to tackle the action or inaction by Member States to deal with obstructions to the free movement of goods. The Commission would fix strict time limits for the pre-litigation stage of the Article 258 TFEU procedure, thereby giving the Commission additional powers to those contained in the Treaty on the Functioning of the Union.

To introduce such a Regulation, however, would have required a unanimous decision of the European Council. In the end, a 'toothless' Regulation was adopted instead and issued together with a Resolution of the Council and the Representatives of the Governments

---

[71] See Proposal for a Council Regulation creating a mechanism whereby the Commission can intervene in order to remove certain obstacles to trade, *OJ* 1997 C 10/14.

[72] See ECJ, Case C-265/95 *Commission* v. *France*, [1997] *ECR* I-6959.

of the Member States.[73] Regulation 2678/98[74] spelt out the Member States' obligations to act against obstacles to trade and contained provisions for increased information flow between the Member States on such obstacles arising, including an early warning system. The use of the complementary Resolution was to indicate political commitment among Member States rather than submit to binding measures of the Commission, and consequently also, to relinquish exclusive competence to decide which measures are necessary and proportionate to facilitate the free movement of goods on their territory in a given situation. The Member States objected to giving the Commission such a strong right to decide whether they were in breach of their Treaty obligations, a traditional reserve of the ECJ.

Neither Article 258 TFEU nor Regulation 2678/98 provides a means of rapid reaction in a case where an incoming Member State does in fact meet its accession obligations upon the date of accession.

### 2.2 *The Justice and Home Affairs safeguard clause*

Special safeguard measures could also be adopted in the field of mutual recognition in criminal law and regulations on mutual recognition in civil matters, on the basis of Article 38, 2005 Act of Accession. It will expire end December 2009. The equivalent clause in the fifth Accession Treaty is Article 39, 2003 Act of Accession expired on 30 April 2007. As a result of the Nice Treaty, the title of Justice and Home Affairs *acquis* is no longer correct and reference to the Justice and Home Affairs *acquis* is used here solely for ease of reference. The scope of application of the safeguard clause concerns framework decisions or any other relevant commitments, instruments of co-operation and decisions relating to mutual recognition in the area of criminal law under Title VI of the EU Treaty and Directives and Regulations relating to mutual recognition in civil matters under Title IV of the EC Treaty (currently chapters 1, 3, 4 and 5 of Title V, TFEU on the Area of freedom, security and justice).

These safeguards are intended to address 'serious shortcomings or any imminent risks of such shortcomings in the transposition, state

---

[73] Resolution of the Council and the Representatives of the Governments of the Member States, meeting within the Council, of 7 December 1998 on the free movement of goods, *OJ* 1998 L 337/10.

[74] Council Regulation 2678/98 on the functioning of the Internal Market in relation to the free movement of goods among the Member States, *OJ* 1998 L 337/8.

of implementation, or the application of the laws concerned in a new Member State'.[75] They would involve 'temporary suspension of the application of relevant provisions and decisions in the relations between a new Member State and any other Member State or Member States, without prejudice to the continuation of close judicial co-operation'.

No transitional arrangements as such were agreed at the December 2002 Copenhagen European Council in the field of Justice and Home Affairs, although various Council and Presidency Conclusions singled out administrative and judicial capacity for special attention.[76] The justification for this safeguard clause stems from the sensitive internal security issues that this chapter of the *acquis* raises for the Member States. This is a matter of confidence in the capacity of the new members' courts and judicial systems. The October 2002 country reports all highlighted the need for reinforced administrative and judicial capacity.[77]

Like the transitional safeguard clause relating to the Internal Market, these 'appropriate measures' may be instituted in respect of the new Member States only. They are at the Commission's disposal – either by its own initiative or at the request of a Member State – but the Member States (including the new Member States) must be consulted before their adoption. Again, these measures are limited to the three-year period after accession, may be adapted according to the new Member State's progress in remedying the shortcomings, should be maintained no longer than strictly necessary, must be lifted once the shortcomings have been remedied and may be extended for as long as the shortcomings persist, even after expiry of the three-year period. Finally, the Council must be informed in good time before the measures are revoked and the Council's observations must be duly taken into account. Unlike the provision for temporary Internal Market safeguard measures, the Member States must be consulted before such measures are adopted or

75 'If there are serious shortcomings or any imminent risks of such shortcomings in the transposition, state of implementation, or the application of the framework decisions or any other relevant commitments, instruments of co-operation and decision relating to mutual recognition in the area of criminal law under Title VI of the EU Treaty and Directives and Regulations relating to mutual recognition in civil matters under Title IV of the EC Treaty in a new Member State.'

76 See for example the 2002 Seville Presidency Conclusions, Conclusion 20, or the Council Conclusions of 10 June 2002.

77 See also the 2002 Strategy Paper, SEC(2002) 1400–1412.

before they are adapted and there is no reference to the principles of proportionality or non-discrimination.

As with the Internal Market safeguard clause it would appear politically sensitive to institute safeguard measures in respect of the new Member States in areas where the old Member States also face implementation difficulties. This clause was not used against any of the countries that joined in 2004.

## 3. Romania and Bulgaria: special tools to deal with their 'manifest unpreparedness'

The same Internal Market and JHA safeguard clauses were built into the 2005 Accession Treaty with Bulgaria and Romania. Rather than proceeding directly to instituting a raft of safeguard measures as such, the Commission instead proposed a benchmarking approach in order to keep up the pressure on Bulgaria and Romania after they became Member States, see 3.1 below.

Also in the 2005 Accession Treaty an additional flexibility clause was inserted, Article 39 of the Act of Accession, to allow for the postponement of their accession for up to one year 'if there is a serious risk' that either of these countries is 'manifestly unprepared to meet the requirements of membership by the date of accession', see 3.2 below.

### 3.1 *The Co-operation and Verification Mechanism*

A new 'Co-operation and Verification Mechanism' for the judiciary and the fight against corruption was adopted for the post-accession phase of the 2005 Accession Treaty.[78] It was adopted on the basis of Articles 4(3), Articles 37 and 38 of the 2005 Act of Accession. Therefore, there is a direct link between this mechanism and the safeguard clauses. While throughout pre-accession the safeguard clauses were used as a threat, the Co-operation and Verification Mechanism is a far more nuanced form of post-accession safeguard mechanism than that used for the air transport sector. In particular, it maintains the control and right of direct interference of the European Commission, Council

[78] For the legal basis, see Commission Decisions of 13 December 2006. See M. Spernbauer, 'Benchmarking, Safeguard Clauses and Verification Mechanisms – What's in a Name? Recent Developments in Pre- and Post-accession Conditionality and Compliance with EU Law', (2007) *Croation Yearbook of European Law & Policy*, Vol. 3, pp. 273–306.

and European Parliament, in Bulgaria and Romania's governmental structures and procedures. The Co-operation and Verification Mechanism has become a post-accession governance tool to compensate for the weak application of the legal conditionality of the pre-accession strategy.

The Co-operation and Verification Mechanism sets down benchmarks to be addressed by Bulgaria and Romania were reiterated again by the European Commission in 2007,[79] 2008 and 2009.[80] Each has established their national action plans in order to meet the benchmarks.[81] Their performance is still under observation, with the shadow of safeguard measures still looming.[82] Due to the expiry of this clause in the Accession Treaty, they would have to be put in place before the end of 2009 if they are to be used at all. Once in place there is no deadline for the removal of this mechanism. There is no indication of when this mechanism will become obsolete. The European Council repeatedly confirmed that the Co-operation and Verification Mechanism is the 'appropriate tool' for the job and 'will remain in place pending the results expected'.[83]

However, lack of progress has triggered a massive withdrawal of funding to Bulgaria and Romania.[84] The Commission's autumn 2009 reports show that neither Bulgaria nor Romania are ready to absorb structural funds. In Bulgaria only EUR 1.3 billion of pre-accession funds have been paid out and EUR 109 million remain frozen. Of the EUR 1,03 billion available to Bulgaria under the European Regional Development Fund alone, an EUR 288 million have been committed as advance payments. Of Romania's total eligibility of EUR 8 billion in structural funds, only EUR 2,6 billion has been received. Romania

[79] See Commission MEMO/07/260 *Progress Report on the Co-operation and verification mechanisms – procedural aspects*, of 27 June 2007.

[80] *Progress Reports on the Cooperation and Verification mechanism – procedural aspects*, Commission MEMO/08/523 of 23 July 2008 and *More efforts needed by Bulgaria and Romania to tackle judicial reform and corruption*, Commission Press Release, IP/08/1195 of 23 July 2008. See also COM (2009) 401, 402, 1073 and 1074, all of 22 July 2009.

[81] For Bulgaria see http://www.mvr.bg/en/EUIntegration/plan_BM_1_6_21_10_07_final.htm For Romania, see http://www.just.ro/Portals/0/Right_Panel/Plan%20de%20actiune/plan_actiune_en_21122007[1].pdf

[82] See Council Conclusions of 10 September 2008, *The Mechanism on Co-operation and Verification for Bulgaria and Romania – Adoption of Council conclusions*, Doc. 12678/08 of 10 September 2008. The Council Conclusions of 23 July 2007, 10 March 2008 and 15 September 2008 all reaffirm the Council's 2006 position.

[83] See Council Conclusions 12678/08, ibid.

[84] See www.EurActiv.com visited on 26 November 2008.

has failed to absorb EUR 169 million in pre-accession funds out of a total of 3 billion.

The benchmarks to be addressed by *Bulgaria* were:

1. Adopt constitutional amendments removing any ambiguity regarding the independence and accountability of the judicial system.
2. Ensure a more transparent and efficient judicial process by adopting and implementing a new judicial system act and the new civil procedure code. Report on the impact of these new laws and of the penal and administrative procedure code, notably on the pre-trial phase.
3. Continue the reform of the judiciary in order to enhance professionalism, accountability and efficiency. Evaluate the impact of this reform and publish the results annually.
4. Conduct and report on professional, non-partisan investigations into allegations of high-level corruption. Report internal inspections of public institutions and on the publication of assets of high-level officials.
5. Take further measures to prevent and fight corruption, in particular at the borders and within local government.
6. Implement a strategy to fight organised crime, focussing on serious crime, money laundering as well as on the systematic confiscation of assets of criminals. Report on new and ongoing investigations, indictments and convictions in these areas.

The benchmarks to be addressed by *Romania* were:

1. Ensure a more transparent, and efficient judicial process notably by enhancing the capacity and accountability of the Superior Council of Magistracy. Report and monitor the impact of the new civil and penal procedures codes.
2. Establish, as foreseen, an integrity agency with responsibilities for verifying assets, incompatibilities and potential conflicts of interest, and for issuing mandatory decisions on the basis of which dissuasive sanctions can be taken.
3. Building on progress already made, continue to conduct professional, non-partisan investigations into allegations of high level corruption.
4. Take further measures to prevent and fight against corruption, in particular within the local government.

The Commission's most recent report on progress by Bulgaria[85] in its reform process, finds that the results are not yet sufficient. For example, one paragraph neatly summarises the situation:

> The assessment made points to serious difficulties which the Bulgarian authorities are facing in making real headway in judicial reforms and the fight against corruption and organised crime. Despite good efforts to establish necessary institutions and introduce required procedures and processes, there are few results to demonstrate that the system is actually functioning correctly. It would have been unrealistic to assume that deep seated change would be quick. However, despite the efforts of the Bulgarian government, progress has been slower and more limited than expected and the need for verification and co-operation will continue for some time. The judicial system and the administration need serious strengthening. This is a long haul exercise.

This report attests to the conflict of interest, fraud and financial irregularities in administering EU pre-accession funds (committed pre-accession for the 2007–2013 financial perspective) and structural funds. EU funds earmarked for Bulgaria are the practical expression of the Union's solidarity with the citizens of Bulgaria and aim to foster social cohesion, improving regional development and at enhancing Bulgaria's overall economic performance and stability. The report also speaks of the growing frustration of the Member States and the Commission who have also input technical assistance to help matters, but see poor results.

In an accompanying report specifically on the EU funds and the Co-operation and Verification Mechanism, the Commission noted that the deadlines for allocating pre-accession and structural-funding under the pre-accession and Accession Treaty planning were fast approaching. It emphasised that 'this situation is serious' and that the reforms being taken 'must be followed up with credible, structural corrective actions and a fundamental reform.' Access to the funds would be lost if urgent action cold not be taken to improve administrative capacity of the funds and wipe out conflicts of interest and fraud for example. It goes without saying that loosing such funds will compound the challenge facing Bulgaria in meeting its benchmarks under the Co-operation and Verification Mechanism.

---

[85] COM(2008) 495 of 23 July 2008 at p. 2. A detailed assessment accompanies the report, COM(2008) 2350 of 23 July 2008.

In November 2008, EUR 220 million with of pre-accession funds was withdrawn from Bulgaria. The Commission already hinted at refusing Union funds to Bulgaria in its findings on funds management for 2008. In 2008 the Union froze EUR 500 million to Bulgaria and EUR 142 million to Romania.

In 2009, substantial other EU funds became open to these Member States, in particular structural and agricultural funds. The Commission will ensure that these funds are properly managed. Any improper use of EU funds will lead to financial corrections. These may consist of delayed disbursements, reduction on future payments or recovery of funds.[86] In April 2009 the European Parliament demanded special reports from the Commission on the management of EU funds in both Romania and Bulgaria, and the EP's budgetary control committee even found the situation in Romania to be worsening.[87] The draft EP report even contained a clause threatening censure of the Commission for the situation, which was motivated by complaints that the Commission had misled the European Parliament over the true situation in the final country reports of September 2006. While the final report did not include this formula, such a threat however seems somewhat steep given that the Parliament gave its consent to proceed with the 2007 enlargement in spite of the Commission's far-from-rosy findings in those reports on Bulgaria and Romania. It had the opportunity to vote to invoke the postponement clause but chose not to do so and sided with Commission and Council on the Co-operation and Verification Mechanism approach instead.

The Co-operation and Verification Mechanism was not part of the pre-accession strategies' conditionality tools but was invented to enable the political commitment to enlargement to be maintained. Perhaps in the end, depriving these countries of EU funds will prove a more effective conditionality tool than the safeguard clauses and the postponement clause. In this way, the Co-operation and Verification Mechanism may well prove to be more effective governance mechanism in the post-accession phase in order to guarantee the proper management of

[86] See COM(2008) 496, of 23 July 2008. See also MEMO/08/523 op. cit. n. 81.

[87] See www.EUObserver.com, *MEPs turn screw on Romania and Bulgaria corruption*, 24 April 2009.

Union funds. While the safeguard clauses expire at the end of 2009, the drafting of these clauses allows for any safeguard measures in place before then to continue indefinitely. It could be therefore, that the Co-operation and Verification Mechanism being based on these two safeguard clauses, will simply remain in place.

It may well be then, that the withdrawal of EU funds will be the most effective stick – or carrot – to drive Bulgaria and Romania's continued efforts to meet their pre-accession commitments under the 2005 Accession Treaty. Certainly, the Union has not done either Bulgaria or Romania any favours in allowing this situation to arise. Allowing these two Member States to accede without being ready will be costly for the Union, not least in terms of the threat to effective governance in the Union, as well as for these two countries.

### 3.2 *The postponement clause*

In the cases of Bulgaria and Romania, the sixth Accession Treaty contained an additional flexibility clause. Article 39 of the Act of Accession allowed for the postponement of their accession for up to one year 'if there is a serious risk' that either of these countries is 'manifestly unprepared to meet the requirements of membership by the date of accession', the only qualification to this requirement being that it must be so in 'a number of important areas'. The criteria used to evaluate 'manifestly unprepared' are not specified but, again, the European Commission played a central role in the evaluation and initiation of this clause and the Commission makes its recommendation for invoking this clause to the Council. In such circumstances the Council could have acted by unanimity to postpone accession of either or both countries. However, the two following subparagraphs, Article 39(2) and 39(3), 2005 Act of Accession, would have enabled the Council to act by qualified majority in the event of 'serious shortcomings' of Romania (not Bulgaria) in meeting specific commitments made during the negotiations.

Clause 39 of the sixth Accession Treaty was inserted because of extent of outstanding commitments undertaken by Bulgaria and Romania in the course of their accession negotiations, in which they had to make sufficient progress before their accession, all of which were monitored by the Commission. While Bulgaria had made 'excellent progress', Romania was in a more doubtful circumstance in the weeks before the signature of the sixth Accession Treaty.[88] Moreover, Romania also made a series of 'specific commitments', contained in full within the body of the sixth Accession Treaty, at Annex IX,[89] in relation to:

- the application of the Schengen *acquis* and the control of the future external borders of the Union, the capacity of the judiciary, the fight against corruption, co-operation between the police and the gendarmerie;
- effective government control over potential state aid, strengthening state aid enforcement, the restructuring of the steel sector and the development of adequate financial and human resources within the Competition Council.

During 2005 serious doubts were raised as to Romania's ability to meet the commitments that it gave in the negotiations in time for its accession, particularly its fight against corruption, public procurement legislation, state aid in its outsized steel sector and the preparedness of its judiciary. In January 2005 the Commission published the conditions that could trigger the postponement clause in the Romanian case.[90] Eleven items were listed, four of which related to competition and state aid[91] while the remaining seven relate to Justice and Home Affairs.[92]

[88] See the words of the enlargement Commissioner, Olli Rehn speaking before Members of the European Parliament on 29 March 2005 and reported on in 'MEPs back Bulgaria and Romania to join the EU' www.euractiv.com visited on 31 March 2005.

[89] See sixth Accession treaty at pp. 374–375.

[90] See 'The Conditions to apply the postponement clause; Romanian case', European Commission, Press Information, 5 January 2005.

[91] The four conditions are 1. effective control by the Competition Council of any potential State aid, 2, the strengthening without delay, of Romania's State aid enforcement record, 3. the respect of Romania's commitment not to grant or pay State aid to the steel mills covered by the National Restructuring Strategy from 1 January 2005 to 31 December 2008 and the respect of State aid amounts to be decided in the context of Protocol 2 of the Europe Agreement, 4. the allocation of adequate financial means and qualified human resources to the Competition Council.

[92] 1. The implementation without further delay of the Schengen Action Plan, 2. obtaining a high level of control and surveillance at the future external borders of the EU, 3. the development and the implementation of an updated and integrated Action Plan and Strategy for the reform of the judiciary, 4. the acceleration of the fight against high-level corruption; 5. the conduct of an independent audit of the results and impact of the current National Anti-Corruption Strategy as well as the revision of the protracted criminal procedure by the end of 2005, 6. the adoption by March

The postponement clause on the one hand, is remarkable: it is an indication of the EU's political commitment to enlargement in spite of doubts remaining. The two safeguard clauses on the Internal Market and Justice and Home Affairs are dubious because of their potential to discriminate between the incoming Member States compared to the receiving Member States and to undermine the solidarity between Member States. The postponement clause, does not discriminate between Member States because, technically speaking, membership will only have been postponed. The delay of membership certainly seems less politically untenable and a more effective conditionality tool because of it. The postponement clause would have enabled the Union to meet its political commitment to its planned date of enlargement. It could not be interpreted as weakening the notions of solidarity and reciprocal obligations between Member States because membership will have been postponed. However, this clause could not have extended beyond the one-year postponement clause, and given the lack of progress under the Co-operation and Verification Mechanism above, it is not likely that it would have done much good in any case. In the end, therefore, the postponement clause was clearly more of a pre-accession conditionality stick than an effective post-accession conditionality.

2005 of a clear framework for the respective tasks of, and co-operation between, the gendarmerie and police, 7. the development and implementation of a coherent multi-annual strategy to fight organised crime.

# PART TWO

# CASE STUDIES ON EU ENVIRONMENT AND AGRI-FOOD LAW

CHAPTER SIX

# EU ENVIRONMENT LAW

The Union has drawn up its environment *acquis* according to the needs and priorities of its Member States at the time of adoption of a piece of legislation. This is perhaps to state the obvious but it is not enough to adopt the environment laws of the *acquis communautaire* in order to establish effective environment law and policy at national level. Also, it cannot be assumed that the *acquis* is entirely appropriate to the particular environmental needs and priorities of the new Member States[1] although there are major advantages and benefits involved in approximating to the EU in this important field of the *acquis*. A lot has already been written on the pros and cons of eastwards enlargement for green decision-making at EU level and the governance challenge it poses to the enforcement of the environment *acquis*.[2]

This chapter contributes to that debate, from a legal perspective, with a general introduction to the pre-accession strategy and accession treaties. It draws lessons from the perspective of the pre-accession strategy as concerns the environment *acquis* and how this strategy has been projected into the post-accession phase through the Accession Treaties in the form of transitional arrangements and financing and capacity building in the post-enlargement phase.

This chapter first sets out the challenge that faces the twelve new Member States in approximating to the environment *acquis* still today and gives a more specific insight into the pre-accession strategy for

---

[1] See *Europe's Environment: the Second Assessment*, Denmark, EEA 1998 at p. 4.

[2] See in particular, P. Jehlincka, *Environmental Implications of Eastern European Enlargement of the EU: End of Progressive Environmental Policy?*, Florence, EUI (RSC) Working Paper 2002/23 2002, T. Garvey, 'EU Enlargement: Is it Sustainable?' in S. Crisen and J. Carmin (eds.) *EU Enlargement and Environmental Quality: Central and Eastern Europe & Beyond*, Washington, DC. Woordow Wilson International Center for Scholars, pp. 53–62, I. Von Homeyer, 'Differential Effects of Enlargement on EU Environmental Governance', 2004 *Environmental Politics*, suppl. 1/2004, pp. 52–76, D. Wilkinson, C. Monkhouse and D. Baldock, *The Future of EU Environment Policy: Challenges and Opportunities*, December 2004, Institute for European Environmental Policy, Special Report of the All-part Parliamentary Environment Group, J.B. Skjaerseth and J. Wettestad, EU *Enlargement and Environmental Policy: the Bright Side*, The Fridtjof Nonsens Institute 2006.

that purpose. Briefly drawing the limits to the EU environment *acquis*, the pre-accession and post-accession conditions of approximation on the incoming Member States in policy areas beyond the reach of the environment *acquis* are then explored. It draws on the examples of previous enlargements in order to do so. The approximation of today's Member States is an extension of this approach and is also outlined.

The approach of the fifth and sixth Accession Treaties to transitional arrangements in the environment *acquis* and their content, is explored at 2.2.1. This section also traces the conditionality that these Accession Treaties attach to the new Member States' commitments to fully comply with the *acquis* once these temporary derogations have expired. For readers' ease, all references to the Accession Treaty Bulgaria and Romania are referring to the Act of Accession and annexes thereto rather than the Accession Protocol because of the failure of the Constitutional Treaty.

The final section looks at the performance of the new Member States after their accession in order to comment on whether the transitional arrangements have been feasible benchmarks for compliance by the new Member States. The conclusions consider whether this approach has strengthened the environment *acquis* in an expanding Union.

## 1. The starting point for approximating to the EU environment *acquis*

The environment *acquis* really began in the early Nineteen-seventies[3] and has steadily evolved since then. EU environment law is having to grapple with an ever increasing diversity of environments within the Union's borders as well as the environmental challenges of economic growth in the broader European context. Compared to the Fifteen, a diverse group of countries in itself, the CEECs have dramatically different environments (some land-locked, others with coast lines for

[3] Early 'environmental' (including consumer) provisions can be found in early Community legislation on the approximation of national laws, notably in the form of the 1967 Directive 67/548 on the classification, packaging and labelling of dangerous chemicals, *OJ* 1967 L196/1, as amended, and Directive 76/769 on marketing and use of dangerous substances and preparations, *OJ* 1976 L 262/02, as amended. The first Environmental Action Programme of 1972 was the beginning of a concerted Community approach in environmental policy, covering the period 1973 to 1977.

example), environmental pasts and socio-economic priorities as well as considerable pressures on existing financing and investment resources. A brief outline of the change in geographical boundaries as a result of the fifth and sixth enlargement as well as recent socio-economic trends in the pan-European region, illustrates this.

*Change in geographical boudaries*

Enlargement to the eastern borders of the new Member States has considerably extended the territory of the European Union. The Union now shares common land borders with the Russian Federation and extends its reach to the borders of the NIS and Belarus and Ukraine. Once Romania joined, the Union shares borders with Moldova. The accession of Hungary, Bulgaria and Romania expanded the EU borders shared with Western Balkan countries, in particular having to deal with the reconstruction of Kosovo following the impact of bombing and population migration following the crises that have ensued there during the Nineties.

The EU already shared a presence around the Mediterranean Sea with Turkey (with which it also shares a land border), Syria, Lebanon, Israel[4] and the Palestinian Authority, Egypt, Libya and the Maghreb countries of Morocco, Algeria and Tunisia. The accession of Malta and Cyprus in 2004 expanded the Union's presence in the Mediterranean. The Mediterranean is a region of a fragile environmental situation and a complexity of scarce resources, such as water, which is directly linked to the social and economic development of neighbouring countries. Environmental pressures threaten to heighten political tension and even conflict there.

Accession of Bulgaria and Romania also brought an entirely new presence for the EU around the Black Sea, on to which Turkey also looks, together with Ukraine, the Russian Federation and Georgia. Italy and Slovenia look on to the Adriatic along with the Balkan countries while both Italy and Greece look on to the Aegean with Bulgaria and Turkey.

---

[4] Although water is not the primary reason for Israel's annexation of the West Bank and Gaza strip, it is indisputable that most of the land that Israel has annexed in the past continues to be held for its hydrological significance. See B. Smith, 'Water: a critical resource', in R. King (ed.), *The Mediterranean Environment and Society* (London and New York, Arnold 1997) at p. 243.

Prior to the fifth enlargement, the EU had six biogeographic regions which are distinct in terms of their flora and fauna: Continental, Mediterranean, Alpine, Atlantic, Macaronesian and Boreal. The Pannonian region was been added with the accessions of Hungary, the Czech Republic and Slovakia (although it also covers a tiny part of Austria).

*Socio-economic influences*

In terms of socio-economic trends, as the Union continues to enlarge to the South and East, the European Union is a key regional player in the framing of environment policy in the pan-European region. In 1995 the European environment Agency (EEAg) published the Dobris Assessment, the first report on the state of Europe's environment covering 50 countries, which had been requested by the pan-European ministerial conference on environmental matters held at the Dobris Castle in Prague in June 1991.[5] In 2007 the European Environmental Agency summed up Europe's environment as follows:[6]

> The pan-European region harbours rich cultural and environmental diversity. More than 870 million people live in the region; more than half of them in Western and Central Europe (WCE), making the European Union one of the most densely populated areas of the world with more than 100 people per square kilometre. This is in stark contrast to the relatively sparse populations of Eastern Europe and Central Asia, where the average density is well below 20 people per square metre. Economic recovery in recent years has resulted in an increase, in relative terms, of national income in virtually all countries of the pan-European region. Economic growth rates have been particularly high in South Eastern Europe (SEE) and Eastern European, Caucasus and Central Asian (EECCA) countries.
>
> Increasingly, the economies of EECCA countries are moving away from reliance on agricultural output towards service industries. Nonetheless, the EECCA region is still relatively more dependent on mineral extraction and agriculture, often resulting in major environmental pressures and high volumes of wastes. The number of independent States in the region has increased from 33 in 1990 to 53 in 2007, during which time the EU expanded from 15 to 27 Member States.

The dramatic environmental degradation of Europe's environment is now firmly established to be the direct result of economic devel-

---

[5] See *Europe's environment: the first assessment*, (Denmark, EEAg 1995).

[6] See the executive summary of *Europe's environment: the fourth Assessment*, (Denmark, EEAg 2007), pp. 1–2.

opment.[7] The EEAg's press release launching its 2007 assessment highlighted the continuing trend of unsustainable development: 'consumption and production also place an increasing demand on natural resources, putting our environment at further risk'. The following quote of Domingo Jiménez-Beltrán, the first Director of the EEAg, from 1995 is as pertinent today as it was then: 'in relation to sustainable development, we are all countries in transition'.[8]

### 1.1 *Approximation: appropriateness and environmental benefits?*

#### 1.1.1 *Enlargement: a considerable stick in EU green foreign policy*

The growing external facet to the Union's environment *acquis* is natural given the environmental interdependence of the States in the pan-European region. Enlargement is a considerable foreign policy tool generally speaking and equally important in the environmental ambitions of the Member States.[9] The external dimension is increasingly apparent in policy documents programming the Union's work towards sustainable development not only in its contractual relations with partner countries in the region but also in the conception and design of 'internal' EU legislation. The 1992 European Commission Communication *The State of the Environment in the European Community*[10] was a key document in taking up the flag of the UN Conference on Environment and Development of 1992. In the context of the completion of the Internal Market, the emergence of the transition economies in Central and Eastern Europe, the imminent integration of the EFTA economies in the European Economic Area and the GATT negotiations that would later lead to the establishment of the

[7] In addition to reports of the EEAg, some of the most high profile reference works include: Report of the UN Intergovernmental Panel on Climate Change *Climate Change 2007: The Physical Science Basis*, of 2 February 2007, available at: www.ipcc.ch; Prof. J. Lovelock, *Revenge of the Gaia: Why the Earth is Fighting Back and How We Can Still Save Humanity* (London: Allen Lane, 2006); N. Stern *Review on the Economics of Climate Change*, 30 October 2006 (Cambridge: Cambridge University Press, 2006).

[8] Addressing the Sofia Conference of Ministers of the region of the United Nations Economic Commission for Europe (UNECE), referred to in *Europe's Environment: the Second Assessment*, op. cit. n. 1, p. 7.

[9] See T. Garvey, op. cit. n. 2, and K. Inglis, 'EU Environmental law and its green footprints in the world', in A. Dashwood and M. Maresceau, (eds.), *Law and Practice of EU External Relations: Salient features of a changing landscape*, (Cambridge, CUP 2008), pp. 429–464.

[10] See COM(92) 23 final, Vol. III, 27 March 1992.

World Trade Organisation, this policy document would set the policy ball rolling but was remarkable for its lack of coverage of the international dimension and its focus purely on the state of the environment in the then Community.[11]

The significance of enlargement cannot be underestimated either in terms of maintaining the integrity of the environment *acquis* or in terms of its evolution in an enlarging Union. The fifth and sixth enlargements of the European Union undoubtedly present the EU with greater challenges than any previous enlargement.[12] The CEECs have made momentous progress in tackling the environmental devastation of irresponsible industrialisation during the Communist era and in approximating their environmental policy and laws with those of the European Union. Part of the credit for the improvements in the environmental situation must go however, to the hardships following the painful economic transition that brought an end to out-of-date heavy and polluting industries as well as the transition in the agriculture sector, which ultimately reduced pesticide and fertilizer use. The ten new CEEC Member States need to protect vast areas of virgin territory while also having suffered the acute environmental effects of the Communist era, including the environmental horrors of dumping of obsolete nuclear equipment, nuclear testing and nuclear disasters.[13] Upon their accession, all the CEEC Member States lagged behind the Fifteen in terms of the necessary administrative capacity and infrastructure to comply with the environment chapter of the *acquis communautaire* in full. The new Member States also have new typical and endangered species and habitats. Also, because the environment knows no borders, the behaviour of third countries impacts heavily on the potential and potency of the environment *acquis* in the 'old' Member States.

[11] In the introduction to COM(92) 23, ibid. at p. 8.

[12] Communication from the Commission on *Accession Strategies for Environment*, COM(1998) 294 of 20 May 1998.

[13] On the nature, risks and environmental legacy of state socialism, see P. Pavelínek and J. Pickles, *Environmental Transitions; Transformation and Ecological Defence in Central and Eastern Europe* (London an New York, Routledge 2000) at pp. 37–155. See also J. Klarer and P. Francis, 'Regional overview' in J. Klarer (ed.), *The Environmental Challenge for Central European Economies in Transition* (Chichester, John Wiley & Sons 1997), pp. 1–66.

Today, the Union's *Sixth Environment Action Programme*[14] programming work between 2002 and 2012, expressly provides for the integration of environmental concerns into all external relations: this is also an objective of the 6th EAP. Enlargement is a means to meet these external environmental objectives, by exporting the environment *acquis* through third countries' accession aspirations. Key to achieving sustainable economic development, obviously, is the integration principle: that of building environmental concerns into all areas of activity of the Union at home and abroad, a principle enshrined in the TFEU since 1997. However, the Report of the Former Dutch Prime Minister Wim Kok to the Commission on *Enlarging the EU: Achievements and Challenges* in 2003[15] summed up the challenge a year before the 2004 enlargement:

> To ensure that positive results are achieved, there will need to be effective monitoring and implementation of EU rules and a real effort to take account of the environment in other policies applied in the new Member States, with the aim of sustainable economic development.

With *Agenda 2000* of 1997, the newly revitalised pre-accession strategy reflected these ambitions for its environment policy and insisted on the indivisibility of the *acquis* for any country acceding to the EU: candidates must adopt the entire *acquis*, including the environment chapter. Whether the pre-accession strategy succeeded in its aims of ensuring the maintenance and continued evolution of the environment *acquis* in an enlarging Union arises repeatedly in this Chapter.

#### 1.1.2 *The environment* acquis*: the benefits of a* 'fait accompli'

It was only in October 1972 that the European Council that decided a common environmental policy was essential and the first four Environmental Action Programmes[16] saw the introduction of some 200 pieces

---

[14] Decision 1600/2002 of the European Parliament and of the Council laying down the Sixth Community Environment Action Programme, *OJ* 2002 L 242/1. See Commission Communication on the Sixth Environment Action Programme of the European Community 'Environment 2010: Our future, our choice', COM(2001) 31 of 24 January 2001.

[15] Florence, EUI (RSC) Working Paper 2003 at pp. 55–58.

[16] See Council Declaration of 22 November 1973, *OJ* 1973 C 112/1. The First, ibid. n. 1, Second, *OJ* 1977 C 139/1, and Third Programmes, *OJ* 1983 C 139/1, covered the period from 1972–1986. The Fourth Environmental Action Programme (1987–1992), COM(86) 485 of 9 October 1986, *OJ* 1987 C70/30. The fourth was followed by the fifth (1992–2000): Communication from the Commission on *The global assessment of the*

of EC legislation. The measures adopted were designed to limit pollution by introducing minimum standards in a range of areas, and in particular to tackle waste, air and water pollution. They were adopted on the legal basis for Internal Market measures[17] or on the general legal basis for Community action in the absence of express Community powers, which 'should prove necessary to attain [...] one of the objectives of the Community'. At this stage Community environment policy found itself in direct competition with other policy areas, such as agriculture and the common market.

Originally therefore, protection of the environment and sustainable development were not expressly established as objectives of the Community in its own right, although the European Court of Justice expressly affirmed protection of the environment as an essential objective of the Union early on.[18] Only later Treaty amendments – with the Single European Act 1986, the Maastricht and Amsterdam Treaties (1992 and 1997 respectively) – introduced enabling clauses to provide the necessary competence and scope for Community action that resulted in ambitious (industry-targeted) measures to curb various seriously polluting activities.

The Single European Act of 1986 introduced the first title on Environment Protection into the EC Treaty and this included a specific legal basis for environment protection measures [Arts. 130r-t EEC Treaty, now Arts. 191–193 TFEU]. The SEA also introduced the principle of the integration of environmental concerns into all sectors of Community activity. Protection of the environment was still not formally included among the aims of the Community within the body of the Community Treaty at that time. This new legal basis and the increased use of the co-operation procedure and then the co-decision procedure, meant that the Union would be better able to continue in developing its environment *acquis* as it enlarged.

It was the Amsterdam Treaty of 1997 that introduced the principle of balanced and sustainable development of economic activities, which

---

*European Community programme of policy and action in relation to the environment and sustainable development, Towards Sustainability (Fifth Environmental Action Programme),* COM(1999) 543 of 24 November 1999. The Sixth, op. cit. n. 14.

[17] Art. 100a EEC Treaty and now Art. 114 TFEU, using qualified majority voting.

[18] See F. *Jacobs*, 'The Role of the *European Court of Justice* in the Protection of the *Environment*', (2006) 18 *Journal* of *Environmental Law* p. 201. See also P. Wennerås, 'Towards an ever green Union?', 2008 *CML Rev.* pp. 1645–1685.

became one of the main objectives of the EU [Art. 3(3) TEU].[19] Thereafter, sustainable development has been worked out within the environment *acquis*.[20] The Amsterdam Treaty also introduced into the Treaties the objective of promoting a 'high level of protection and improvement of the quality of the environment'.[21] This is reflected equally in the legal basis for the Community environment policy, which again as a result of the Amsterdam Treaty;

> shall aim at a high level of protection [...] based on the precautionary principle and on the principles of protective action, that environmental damage should as a priority be rectified at source and that the polluter should pay.

The Amsterdam Treaty also brought forward the explicit reference[22] to the need to integrate environmental protection into all sectoral policies from the environmental protection title of the EC Treaty to the very front of the Treaty [Art. 6 EC],[23] underlining the commitment of the Union to achieving sustainable development.[24] In the Final Act the

---

[19] Art. 3(3) TEU reads: 'The Community shall establish an internal market. It shall work for the sustainable development of Europe based on balanced economic growth and price stability, a highly competitive social market economy, aiming at full employment and social progress, and a high level of protection and improvement of the quality of the environment [...]'. Art. 4(2)(e), (f) and (k) establish the Union's shared competence in environment, consumer protection and common safety in public health matter.

[20] See Decision 2179/98 of the European Parliament and of the Council of 24 September 1998 on the review of the European Community programme of policy and action in relation to the environment and sustainable development 'Towards sustainability'. See also the Commissions' 'Global Assessment' in response thereto and in preparation for the Sixth Environmental Action Programme, op. cit. n. 5. The June 2001 Gothenburg European Council agreed elements of the sustainable development strategy and added a sustainable development element to the Lisbon strategy, under review in the course of 2005.

[21] See for example R. Macrory 'The Amsterdam Treaty: an environmental perspective' in D. O'Keeffe and P. Twomey (eds.) in *Legal Issues of the Amsterdam Treaty* (Oxford-Portland Oregon, Hart Publishing 1999) at pp. 171–183.

[22] In Article 130r of the Maastricht version of the EC Treaty.

[23] Art. 11 TEU reads: 'Environmental protection requirements must be read into the definition and implementation of the Union policies and activities, in particular with a view to promoting sustainable development'.

[24] A significant development was the request by the June 1998 Cardiff European Council to the relevant Councils of Ministers to develop integration strategies covering their respective policy areas. The is known as the Cardiff Process and there are nine sectoral strategies in; Transport, Agriculture, Energy, Industry, Internal Market, Fisheries, Economic and Financial Affairs, Trade and Foreign Policy. See Commission Communication, *Partnership for integration – A strategy for Integrating Environment*

Commission undertook to draw up environmental impact studies to assess whether proposals for Community legislation are likely to have serious repercussions for the environment.[25]

Consequently, the building blocks of today's environment *acquis* were laid gradually after the signature of the first Accession Treaty in January 1972 while the heaviest and most expensive legislation in operation today was negotiated with the full participation of the twelve but mostly the fifteen Member States, prior to the fifth and sixth enlargements. Thus, most of the ambitious and costly EU environment legislation has been developed after the accession of Spain and Portugal acceded in 1986 and therefore also with their inclusion throughout consultations, drafting and decision-making. For example, the rules on large combustion plants,[26] integrated pollution prevention and control (IPPC),[27] urban waste water,[28] the air quality framework[29] and its daughter directives, hazardous waste incineration,[30] municipal waste,[31] packaging and packaging waste[32] have all been enacted since that time. A number of amendments and implementing laws have been thrashed out with the participation of the Austria, Finland and Sweden. Also from the point of sustainable economic development and preventing environmental damage, recent initiatives such as that on preventing

*into EU Policies – Cardiff – June 1998*, COM(98) 333, 25 May 1998, not published in the *OJ*. Positive and negative results are outlined in the Commission Communication COM(2004) 394, 1 June 2004, not published in the *OJ*.

[25] See Declaration 12 to the Final Act of the Amsterdam Treaty; 'The Conference notes that the Commission undertakes to prepare environmental impact assessment studies when making proposals which may have significant environmental implications.'

[26] See Council Directive 88/609 on the limitation of emissions of certain pollutants into the air from large combustion plants, *OJ* 1988 L 336/1 ('Large Combustion Plant Directive).

[27] See Council Directive 96/61 concerning integrated pollution prevention and control (IPPC), *OJ* 1996 L 257/26 ('IPPC Directive').

[28] See Council Directive 91/271 concerning urban waste water treatment, *OJ* 1991 L135/40 ('Urban Waste Water Treatment Directive').

[29] Council Directive 96/62 on ambient air quality assessment and management, *OJ* 1996 L 296/55.

[30] See Council Directive 94/67 on incineration of hazardous waste, *OJ* 1994 L 365/34 (Hazardous Waste Directive).

[31] See Council Directive 89/369 on the prevention of air pollution from new municipal waste incineration plants, *OJ* 1989 L 163/32 ('Municipal Waste Directive').

[32] See Council Directive 94/62 on packaging and packaging waste, *OJ* 1994 L 365/10 (Packaging Waste Directive).

and remedying environmental damage, Directive 2004/35,[33] will provide a strong disincentive to further polluting activities, the new Directive only entered into force in April 2007. Moreover, recent judgments of the ECJ have proved daring and further consolidated the environmental benefits of waste legislation for example.[34] Other legislation adopted prior to the fifth enlargement will make significant inroads into specific waste streams. The fact that it was adopted without the new Member States having participated in its adoption does not automatically mean that they will be worse prepared or less willing to enforce that legislation than any of the Fifteen Member States.[35] Take the example of the Directive on waste electronic and electrical equipment (the WEEE Directive),[36] which took effect in August 2005 where a number of the fifteen Member States had not transposed the WEEE Directive on time.[37] These measures were conceived for the purposes of the priorities of the Member States at the time.

The appropriateness for the CEECs' environments cannot be assumed although it seems pointless now to question the logic of the pre-accession strategy demand for wholesale compliance with the *acquis*: this is the approach that has been followed and this approach brings it own benefits for 'new' and 'old' Member States.

Generally speaking, in the absence of adequate and effective means to prevent environmental damage at EU level, relying on the experience and examples of previous enlargements and the development of the Union thereafter, enlargement therefore necessarily implies a further deterioration in the state of Europe's enlarged environment. It also implies a contribution to the deterioration in the state of the environment of countries of proximity to the Union due to increased transboundary pollution from the EU to neighbouring countries. In the Union's *Sixth Environment Action Programme*, adopted in

[33] Environmental liability with regard to the prevention and remedying of environmental damage, COM(2002) 17 of 23 January 2002, and published as Directive 2004/35, *OJ* 2004 L 143/56.

[34] Wenneras, op. cit. n. 18. Jacobs, op. cit. n. 18.

[35] See P. Jehlicka, *Environmental Implications of Eastern European Enlargement of the EU: End of Progressive Environmental Policy?*, Florence, EUI (RSC) (2002), Working Paper 2002/23 at pp. 22–24.

[36] Directive 2002/96, as amended by Directive 2003/108, *OJ* 2003 L 345/106.

[37] The European Commission announced in July 2005 that it was sending warning letters to Estonia, Finland, France, Greece, Italy, Malta, Poland and the UK for failure even to transpose the legislation into national law, IP/05/895, 11 July 2005.

2002,[38] the policy direction and tasks that the Member States and EU institutions have set themselves display the global ambitions of the Union environment policy. It is the strategic programme for the policy direction and content of EC work in the field of the environment between 2002 and 2012, and forms the environment axis of the Union's Sustainable Development Strategy (SDS). The integration of environmental concerns into all aspects of the Union's external relations is an objective of the *Sixth Environment Action Programme* in the pan-European region. Thus for example, the Union's *Thematic Strategy on the Sustainable Use of Natural Resources*[39] foresaw the creation of an International Panel on the subject, which is being set up with the United Nations Environment Programme (UNEP).[40] Also important was the 'Green Diplomacy'[41] initiative of the Barcelona General Affairs Council in March 2002 to integrate environmental concerns into the Union's external policies. The aim was to promote the integration of environment into external relations through the creation of an informal network of environment experts within foreign ministries.

Nevertheless, approximation under the pre-accession process therefore is not *per se* about the state of the environment in candidate countries. While the European Union has developed an impressive body of 'environmental' laws, even raising the overall standards among the Member States,[42] increased external activity and economic development of the Union as it enlarges and reaches to the countries of immediate proximity, presents it with the challenge of an ever greater and more complex environment and consequent environmental challenge. As the Union of twenty-five continues and deepens its integration efforts, the costs to the environment also deepen. EU environment law is not reversing the dramatic trends in environmental degrada-

[38] Op. Cit. n. 14.

[39] COM(2005) 670 of 21 December 2005.

[40] See Commission Communication, *Halting the loss of biodiversity by 2010 – and beyond. Sustaining ecosystem services for human well-being*, COM(2006) 216 of 22 May 2006. The Union also provides support for third countries in implementing the international Convention on Biological Diversity and funds such efforts through contributions to the Global Environmental Facility.

[41] See www.europa.eu.int/comm/environment/international_issues/…

[42] See M. Schreurs 'Environmental protection in an expanding European Community: lessons from past accessions' in J.A. Carmin and S.D. Van Deveer *EU Enlargement and the environment; Institutional change and environmental policy in Central and Eastern Europe*, (Oxon and New York, Routledge 2005), pp. 27–51.

tion that have progressively reduced the qualitative state of Europe's environment as a direct result of increased economic activity of the past half-century. Economic development has impacted negatively, and unrelentingly so, on Europe's environment and has brought about serious degradation[43] in the general state of Europe's environment and an increased burden on the global environment in terms of consumption of natural resources.[44] In an orientation debate held by the European Commission[45] on the seven *Thematic Strategies* for EU environment policy in the future,[46] while the costs of these strategies were criticised by a number of Commissioners, in the end the environment Commissioner Dimas won his argument: that the costs of the Thematic Strategies would prevent higher longer terms costs. The costs of air pollution for example could be as high as EUR 12 billion in a worst case scenario but taking action now would lead to health benefits of EUR 48 billion.

Thus, in the first instance, the aim of the pre-accession strategy is not to improve the quality of the environment in the candidate countries. Indeed, in the early years of the enhanced pre-accession strategy, the Executive Director of the European Environment Agency questioned the appropriateness of the strategy for the CEECs: 'Why is it assumed that Central European countries must follow the western model, may be even making the same mistakes?'[47] To crudely summarise the Second Assessment:

[43] The European Environment Agency *Europe's Environment: the Second Assessment*, op. cit. n. 1 at p. 4, which is confirmed by The European Environment Agency, *Europe's Environment: the Third Assessment* (Copenhagen, EEA 2003), at p. 5. The third reports highlights certain areas where environment policies that have been properly developed and implemented have improved the state of the environment and reduced pressures on it, but also highlights areas of degradation, both in the EU and in the CEECs and beyond, see the latter report at pp. 5–7.

[44] European Environment Agency, *Total Material Requirement of the European Union, Report No 55*, (Copehagen, EEA 2001). No major change to this situation is reported in The European Environment Agency, *Environmental Signals 2002* (Copenhagen, EEA 2002), at p. 3.

[45] See 'Dimas gives green light to present environmental strategies', to be found at www.EurActive.com visited on 29 July 2005.

[46] So far only the air pollution and marine strategies have been issued while the five remaining strategies are due later in the year.

[47] See *Europe's Environment; The Second Assessment*, op. cit. n. 1 at p. 7.

- economic convergence of the CEECs with the West may even reverse the trend in the West to reduce consumption;
- environmental integration into agriculture at national level through to pan-European level is seen as crucial to limiting environmental impacts as a result of growth in both production and consumption and all the more so considering that it is not yet possible to assess the environmental impacts of structural reform, modernisation and diversification of agriculture;
- environmental integration into management processes as in the West is necessary to encourage similar falls in air and water emissions;
- and, in the case of both the EU and the CEECs 'in the transport sector, more than any other, environmental policies are failing to keep up with the pace of growth'.[48]

The need for the protection of untouched bio-diversity was also stressed there, as was the need for national development policies and financial mechanisms as well as adequate provision against its destruction in the pre-accession phase.

Significantly also, NGOs, such as the European Environmental Bureau, have reported instances where national legislation has been 'softened': such as in the case of Slovenia, where the *acquis* has been taken as a ceiling rather than a floor for setting national standards.[49] In the same report, the EEB reported for example also, on a conflict between Polish legislation transposing the environment *acquis* was often 'in conflict' with other national programmes and policies, such as transport, energy and agriculture. As for the integration of environmental concerns into other sectors of legislation, the EEB reported that the most positive trend was to be seen in the agriculture sector in Cyprus, Estonia and Latvia, although the evidence for this findings was not yet complete and reliable. Other research has criticised the pre-accession strategy approach for how passive it makes national officials, assisting a political culture that gives overriding priority to economic growth.[50]

---

[48] See *Europe's Environment; The Second Assessment*, op. cit. n. 1. at p. 20.
[49] See *The Environmental results of the Accession Process*, EEB Special Report, April 2004, p. 8.
[50] See P. Jehlicka, op. cit. n. 35.

On the other hand, it can also be said that the pre-accession strategy stepped in to plug an ostensible vacuum in environmental policies. All this said, while sustainable development itself may not be guaranteed, the benefits of implementing the environment *acquis* promise nevertheless to be enormous.[51] The EU has nevertheless been a world leader in environment legislation for any regional integration and has fostered the development of incoming countries and trading partners. In terms of approximation and compliance with the environment *acquis*, the pre-accession strategy involves considerable benefits for candidate countries. For the CEEC Member States the environmental benefits in terms of human health alone are estimated to have a cumulative value of between EUR 134 and EUR 681 by the year 2020. Hot on the heals of *Agenda 2000*, the Commission's Communication on the 1998 *Accession Strategies for the Environment*[52] aimed expressly to avoid any abstract or blindfold adoption and implementation of the environment *acquis* and insisted that candidates apply the priorities of their Accession Partnerships in such a way as to take account of their own particular environmental needs and priorities when drafting their National Plans for the Adoption of the *Acquis*.[53]

#### 1.1.3 *Limits to the environment* acquis

Obviously, the environmental standards enshrined in EU law are only one dimension in EU-wide efforts to tackle environmental degradation. Environmental standards and restrictions put in place by the EU cannot be enough either in the Union or the world context. Under the TFEU, the most sensitive policy areas are subject to the unanimity voting requirement for Union level actions, so these areas essentially remain the preserve of the Member States to take their own initiatives at national level. Such areas for policy and law include fiscal measures, town and country planning, quantitative management of water resources, land use (except waste management), and measures affecting a Member State's choice between energy sources and the general structure of its energy supply.

---

[51] See 'The benefits of compliance with the environmental *acquis* for the candidate countries and their preparations for accession', a Commission external service contract carried out by Ecotec Research and Consulting Limited, B7–8110/2000/159960/MAR/H1, in 2000 at p. xxxix, to be found on the Europa website at www.europa.eu.int/comm/environment/enlarg/pdf/benefit_long.pdf.

[52] See op. cit. n. 35.

[53] See ibid. at pp. 5 and 16.

To a limited extent, the Lisbon Treaty affects the broader spectrum of the environment *acquis*. In the first place, the environment, Articles become Articles 191 to 193 TFEU. Climate change is expressly included as an objective for international action, although the Member States have already been active on this front for many years, notably through participation in the Kyoto Protocol. However, a new Title on Energy (Art. 194 TFEU) will, like the Titles on Environment and Transport, introduce a legal basis of shared competence in terms of Article 4 TFEU for the purposes of co-ordinated actions in energy policy. Alongside the Internal Market in energy and security of supply issues, Union energy policy will aim to promote: energy efficiency and energy saving and the development of new and renewable forms of energy, and; interconnection of energy networks. While the ordinary legislative procedure is foreseen here, the Member States have been careful to provide that 'such measures shall not affect a Member State's right to determine the conditions for exploiting its energy sources, its choice between different energy sources and the general structure of its energy supply (see also Declaration 35, ToL)' and also to maintain unanimity in any initiatives designed to introduce fiscal measures. As with the Environment Title of the EC Treaty previously therefore, any fiscal measures under the Energy Title will require a unanimous Council vote, making the Commission's hopes of a CO2 tax on energy products – as it proposed again in its 2008 Work Programme – as out of reach as ever.

The Lisbon Treaty would also introduce new Titles on Tourism and on Civil Protection (Arts. 195 and 196 TFEU respectively) provide for supporting, co-ordinating and supplementary Union action in terms of Article 6 TFEU. In both cases, any harmonisation of national laws and regulations is expressly excluded, thus limiting the extent of concerted action at Union level to actions that support, complment or co-ordinate national actions rather than integration by means of Directives. To date, actions in these areas had been cobbled together using Article 308 EC and 208 Euratom, requiring unanimity. These new legal bases will use the ordinary legislative procedure involving the co-decision of Parliament and Council acting by qualified majority. An entirely new Title XVIII on Research and Technological Development would also be introduced, which is intended for support to research and technological development and co-ordination of national efforts for the exploration and exploitation of space. Again the ordinary legislative procedure will apply but the approximation of national laws and regulations is expressly excluded.

The tensions between national sovereignty and other (economic) priorities on the one hand, and EU competences and the goals of an effective environment policy on the other, are particularly strained at policy and law making levels as well as in implementation and enforcement.[54] The environment *acquis* has consistently suffered a serious implementation and enforcement deficit by the Fifteen. At the same time, further evolution in EU environment law is countered by resistance at national/local level, in particular with the introduction by the 1992 Maastricht Treaty of the principle of subsidiarity.

The principle of subsidiarity was first formally introduced into the legal basis for environmental protection by the 1992 Maastricht Treaty [Art. 3b EC Treaty and now numbered Art. 5(3) TEU]. It was supplemented by the 'Protocol on the application of the principles of subsidiarity and proportionality' by the Amsterdam Treaty,[55] which incorporates the approach to applying the subsidiarity principle set out by the 1992 Edinburgh European Council and, importantly, subjected the use of the principle to judicial review.[56] Because Union action in the interests of environmental protection does not fall within the exclusive competence of the Union, the Union may only act:

- where the objectives of the proposed action cannot be sufficiently achieved by the Member States, and;
- that particular action would be better achieved at Community level.

In practice, the edges to the principle of subsidiarity are woolly and this is fundamentally bound up with the principle of proportionality.[57] It does not relate to specific policy fields for action but is functional in nature. Also, Article 352 TFEU may also be used as legal basis to extend Union competences in the interests of environmental protection

[54] See Wenneras and Jacobs, op. cit. n. 18.

[55] See Protocol 7 but also see Declaration 43 of the High Contracting Parties relating to that Protocol.

[56] As a 'principle', subsidiarity cannot be considered a general principle of Community law against which the legality of Community action may be tested. See judgment of the Court of First Instance of the European Communities of 21 February 1995, *ECR* II-289 at para. 331.

[57] See K. Lenearts 'The Principle of Subsidiarity and the Environment in the European Union: Keeping the Balance of Federalism', (1994) *Fordham International Law Journal*, pp. 846–895. See also Jacobs, op. cit. n. 18.

if the action proposed is necessary to pursue Treaty objectives. While the subsidiarity principle can be used to justify Union level action, it also demarcates the limits of that action. Where the Union institutions are restricted from taking action, a Member State cannot be forced to take environmentally protective action in situations where the Union has no competence.[58] Due to lack of political consensus for example, or the subsidiarity 'excuse', the European Commission has faced a political impasse, even withdrawing key proposals, in crucial initiatives designed to improve the state of the environment and prevent the escalation of pollution. A most high profile example of this is the failed proposals for an EU wide energy tax which would removed the need for a raft of other environmental Directives.[59]

Therefore, the environmental benefits of approximation with the environment *acquis* in an enlarging Union will be affected not only by the approximation process. Equally important ingredients in an effective and evolving environment *acquis* will be the continued application and enforcement of existing policy and law, the political commitment of all Member States, including of course the new Member States, to the maintenance and evolution of an environment policy fit-for-purpose and crucially also, by the evolution of national environmental policies. Consequently, the approximation exercise will not complete the circle, so to speak. For progress to be made in environmental protection in such areas, progress in the Member States' own national environment policies are crucial. There is less room for stricter national standards in those provisions of the environment *acquis* that have been adopted on the TFEU legal basis for Internal Market measures than the more generous competence for higher national standards than the Union

[58] See L. Krämer, *EC Treaty and Environmental Law* (London, Sweet & Maxwell 1998) at p. 202; '[...] and nobody has ever invoked the subsidiarity clause to oppose the degradation of the local or regional environment by [Community] financial assistance measures. Nobody arguing that the Community should not, under subsidiarity auspices, tackle issues such as environmental liability, discusses the startling absence of environmental liability provisions at local, regional or national level in most Member States'.

[59] Amended Proposal for a Council Directive introducing a tax on carbon dioxide emissions and energy COM(1995) 172, 10 May 1995. It was withdrawn by the Commission on 11 December 2001. See Answer by Commissioner Bolkestein of 12 July 2001 to Written question P-1725/01 by Alexander de Roo (Verts/ALE) to the Commission. Structure of, and timescale for, a European energy tax on the basis of enhanced co-operation., *OJ* 2001 C 350 E/215.

'minimum' standard provided for in EU laws adopted on the legal basis of environment policy.[60] What emerges is a 'no man's land' – the unoccupied areas between two opposing forces – in terms of the lack of actions in areas that have considerable potential to make sustainable development a reality.

This impression is reinforced by the fact that the most sensitive policy areas of the environment *acquis* remain subject to unanimous voting, which restrains common action at EU level in those fields in an enlarging EU. This has proved a major stumbling block to the development of the environment *acquis* in these areas. Member States, that have traditionally taken the lead in environment law at Union level, find considerable resistance to their pro-active environment measures among their counterpart Member States. With the Sixth Environmental Action Programme, the strategic approach to achieving sustainable development has been redesigned and further worked out through the seven 'thematic strategies'[61] and offers new ways to simplify and enforce the regulatory backdrop to the Union's environment *acquis*. Article 2 of the Sixth Environmental Action Programme sets out its principles and overall aims as follows:

> 1. The Programme constitutes a framework for the [Union's] environmental policy during the period of the Programme with the aim of ensuring a high level of protection, taking into account the principle of subsidiarity and the diversity of situations in the various regions of the [Union's], and of achieving a decoupling between environmental pressures and economic growth. It shall be based particularly on the polluter-pays principle, the precautionary principle and preventive action, and the principle of rectification of pollution at source.
>
> The Programme shall form a basis for the environmental dimension of the European Sustainable Development Strategy and contribute to the integration of environmental concerns into all [Union's] policies, inter alia by setting out environmental priorities for the Strategy.

Only mixed results are reported so far, by the Commission's own findings as well as independent research.[62]

---

[60] Wenneras, op. cit. n. 18 at pp. 1664–1669.

[61] Decision 1600/2002 laying down the Sixth Community Environment Action Programme, OJ 2002 L 242/1.

[62] See Commission Communication on the *Mid-term review of the Sixth Community Environment Action Programme*, COM(2007) 225 of 30 April 2007. See M. Pallemaerts et al., *Drowning in Process of April*, IEEP, 2006.

Section 3 below explores key issues arising in the evolution of the environment *acquis* in an enlarging Union. It also assesses the effectiveness of the Union's pre-accession strategy and in particular, the governance challenge that the Union faces following the 2004 and 2007 enlargements. Certain limited changes to competence in environment policy that are introduced by the Lisbon Treaty, are commented on there.

### 1.2 *The mechanics of the pre-accession strategy for the environment* acquis

The pre-accession process for environmental approximation has to be seen in the global context of the Union's externals relations ambitions on the environmental front. The EU had been active, both internally and externally, in the promotion of environmental protection and sustainable development in the CEECs even before the Union expressed any commitment to enlargement and before the Copenhagen criteria. Initial PHARE and TACIS funding was allocated for environmental projects allocated according to the priorities set by the partner country: it was 'demand driven'. Technical and financial assistance had been provided to the CEECs since 1989 in the form of the PHARE programme,[63] and included significant funding for environment related projects. During the first year of the programme, the then Czechoslovakia even devoted its entire PHARE budget to the environment.[64] Also, environmental funding instruments exist at international level and include the World Bank, the Global Environment Facility, international financing institutions, and bilateral programmes involved the individual EU Member States, the US or Japan. From an EU perspective, considerable regional funding was provided to different environmental themes through the European Investment Bank and the European Bank for Reconstruction and Development or through specific regional programmes such as PHARE, TACIS and the Mediterranean budget lines.

---

[63] Council Regulation 3906/89 on economic aid to the Republic of Hungary and the Polish People's Republic, *OJ* 1989 L 375/11.

[64] See European Commission *Agenda 21 – the first five years: Implementation of Agenda 21 in the European Community*, 1997, at p. 22. [Agenda 21, the Rio Declaration on Environment and Development, and the Statement of principles for the Sustainable Management of Forests were adopted by more than 178 Governments at the United Nations Conference on Environment and Development (UNCED) held in Rio de Janeiro, Brazil, 3 to 14 June 1992.]

Chapter 3 dealt with the strategic approach to pre-accession generally. The *1995 White Paper*,[65] which listed all the legislation pertaining to the Internal Market *acquis*, was read by the aspiring Member States as a goal for their approximation work. It was only with the launch in 1997 of the 'reinforced' pre-accession strategy by the *Agenda 2000* document[66] that 30 percent of PHARE funds was allocated to capacity building for the application and enforcement of the *acquis* generally, the remaining 70 percent being allocated to the transposition and implementation of the *acquis communautaire*.[67] These two themes of approximation and capacity building are explored briefly in the next section. All funding then became 'accession driven' and the first clear signal was given that the adoption of environmental rules and standards was 'essential' despite the fact that full compliance with the environment *acquis* would not be possible upon accession. As the Commission noted in *Agenda 2000*:

> The persistence of a gap between levels of environmental protection in present and new members would distort the functioning of the Single Market and could lead to a protectionist reaction. This situation would affect the Union's capability to develop its environmental policy.[68]

The principle of environmental integration enshrined in Article 11 TFEU also applies to the pre-accession strategy. As part of the Commission's *Agenda 2000* as well as the *Strategy for environmental integration* of 1998,[69] environmental integration is also one of the principles that guides the accession strategy. Candidates were required –as they are today – to adopt plans for incorporating the environmental body of law into their legislation and the Commission also called on applicant countries to integrate the environmental dimension into all their policy areas.

---

[65] Commission White Paper *Preparing the CEECs for integration into the internal market*, *OJ* 1996 C 146/135.

[66] *Agenda 2000*, COM(1997) 2000 of 15 July 1997, based on the Europe Agreements, as re-oriented by among other instruments the Copenhagen Criteria, set out the bones of the strategy, including the legal and economic instruments and institutional mechanisms for the pre-accession phase, including the negotiations.

[67] Ibid. at Vol. I, pp. 49–50.

[68] See *Agenda 2000*, Vol. II, op. cit. n. 66 at p. 56.

[69] Op. cit. n. 12.

The Commission's working document on the achievements and weaknesses of the Cardiff Process[70] specifically calls for a re-launch of the Cardiff initiatives and it is clear here that the problem of environmental degradation and unsustainable development is just as much a problem for the 'old' as well as the 'new' Member States. The Commission put forward a number of strategies under the Cardiff Process, launched in 1998, to build environmental considerations into various key sectors of activity that had been kept from any effective reach of EU environmental policy. They relate, for example, to agriculture, energy, the Internal Market, tourism, transport and into economic and development policy. As regards economic and development policy, in 1999 the Commission emphasised that '[EU] funding to specifically environmental purposes are relatively modest compared to the overall flows of [EU] aid' and illustrated the specific percentage of funding provided to environmental themes that is actually allocated to the environment.[71] The Commission's 2004 review of the Cardiff process[72] made clear the aims of the Union in the promotion of environmental integration into the Union's activities in its relations with third countries as much as within the EU, and called for environmental integration in for example, the Union's new neighbourhood policy (ENP).

The bilateral contractual relations between the Union and the candidates have evolved to take account of the *Agenda 2000* focus on the equivalence of the environment chapter of the *acquis* on a par with all other chapters. The Europe Agreements – reoriented as a result of *Agenda 2000* to focus squarely upon approximation and capacity building efforts – provided for co-operation in the field of the environment and were/are basically the same with only minor textual differences. For example, specific provisions were inserted into or left aside in the Title on Economic Co-operation in the EAs with the Baltic States. Also, the EA with Lithuania was the only EA[73] to contain a provision on housing and construction, which briefly provides for co-operation to modernise and restructure the sector, taking account of health, safety, environment and energy efficiency although the Lithu-

---

[70] Op. cit. n. 12.

[71] Commission Communication *Integrating environment and sustainable development into economic and development co-operation policy*, COM(1999) 499, 20 October 1999. The percentage allocations referred to are contained in Annex IV.

[72] COM(2004) 394 of 28 February 2006.

[73] At Art. 92.

ania Accession Partnership (AP) did not refer to pre-accession objectives in this field.

The EA with Slovenia did contain additional provisions on protection against natural disasters unlike any other EAs. As with all the other country APs however, the emphasis rested on the transposition of EU environment *acquis* and approximation programmes, which included co-operation measures on protection against natural disasters. Thus, the process of alignment of the candidates was reinforced through, for example, the 'Catch-up' facility (worth EUR 100 million for 1998–1999) which targeted Romania, Slovakia, Latvia, Lithuania and Bulgaria specifically to help their progress in economic and social reform in order to attract investment and fight corruption and to align their progress with that of the other candidates at the time.

Again today, the SAAs remain the bilateral legal basis for pre-accession work of the Western Balkans countries. The EP/APs put the meat on the bones of priorities and objectives of the pre-accession efforts of the candidates. Progress in the economic co-operation of the associated partners must be assessed by reference to the EP/APs and the coherence that they introduce into the relations between the EU and the associated partner countries. The programming of EU assistance is now fully accession driven in line with the EP/APs. The programming reflects two clear priorities: institution building and investment support to bring the (potential) candidate countries' industries and major infrastructure up to EU standards.

For the purposes of developing the necessary capacity for the proper implementation of the environment *acquis*, there is also the matter of infrastructure investment, dealt with below at 1.2.2.

### 1.2.1 *Approximation, capacity building and regional co-operation*

All Union and international financial institution funding is now channelled into meeting the goals of the pre-accession strategy, as specified in the Instrument for Pre-accession (IPA).

#### *Approximation*

As is the case for any other chapter of the *acquis*, incoming Member States are required to have transposed and implemented the environment *acquis* in its entirety – subject only to limited derogations/transitional arrangements in the Accesion Treaties – which includes building-up the necessary administrative capacity for enforcement, in order to fully meet their Treaty obligations as Member States of the

European Union.[74] In the broadest sense, this means revising legislation or introducing entirely new laws as well as implementing these changes and enforcing the laws.[75] While approximation of the laws of the Member States is typically a phrase introducing the titles of Internal Market legislation,[76] in the case of the pre-accession process approximation for the candidates is different in that they are third countries that have no say – strictly speaking – in the formulation of the *acquis* and are approximating to an external legal system that does not actually bind them. Building up national capacity continues to be a major challenge for the CEECs after enlargement. The fifth enlargement was, and still is, particularly challenging from the perspective of EU environment law when compared to other chapters of the *acquis communautaire*, especially in terms of securing the necessary financing for infrastructure projects.

*Capacity building*

Lacks or weaknesses in the administrative capacity of the candidates affect their ability to absorb funding and will have a detrimental affect on the leverage potential of EU funds for external investment. The acceding countries have had to build their administrative and judicial capacities from scratch, in parallel with the adoption of the *acquis*.

The Court of Auditors, in a report published on 21 May 2003[77] (examining the years 1995 to 2001) pointed out that the future new Member States did not have sufficient institutional capacity to develop environmental and financing strategies at a sufficiently early stage. This resulted in problems with project preparation and tendering for environmental infrastructure projects. In particular, the Court of Auditors highlighted the need to reduce EU grant levels below the seventy-five percent ceiling, even further than has already been done, in order to

---

[74] See A. Lazowski 'Approximation of laws' in Ott and Inglis, op. cit. Chapter 1, n. 24 at pp. 631–639.

[75] See A. Mayhew *Recreating Europe. The European Union's Policy Towards Central and Eastern Europe* (Cambridge, Cambridge University Press 1998) at p. 221.

[76] See A. Evans 'Voluntary harmonisation in integration between the European Community and Eastern Europe', 22 *EL Rev.* (1997) p. 201.

[77] See Special Report No. 5/2003 *concerning PHARE and ISPA funding of environmental projects in the candidate countries*, together with Commission replies thereto, *OJ* 2003 C 167/1.

cover more projects. The Court of Auditors also criticised the Commission for its 'over-emphasis on twinning'.[78]

This state of affairs could be attributed to various circumstances, including the numerous re-orientations of the approximation exercise undertaken by the CEECs under the Europe Agreements as a result of the pre-accession strategy. The Commission explained,[79] in its response accompanying the Special Reports, such historical and other limitations placed upon it. Significantly, however, the Commission shared the concerns expressed by the Court of Auditors. PHARE funding, inspired by the Priority Environment Programme for Accession (PEPA),[80] concentrated on these concerns during 2003 and the Commission has provided assistance to reduce deficiencies in tendering and contracting. However, the grant rate remained at a 65 per cent ceiling at the time of the fifth enlargement.

Adequacy of administrative capacity is more than a matter of financing. While all (existing and future) Member States are obliged to transpose and comply with the *acquis*, the institutions of the Union have no formal jurisdiction to evaluate the judicial and administrative capacity of the Member States in order to do so.[81] Member States are encouraged to improve their administrative structures through more informal channels to strengthen their capacity. For example, this is underlined in the *2001 Recommendation on Minimum Criteria for Environmental Inspections in Member States*,[82] whereby the Member States are 'urged' to supply information on staffing levels and other resources of environmental inspection authorities.

The pre-accession strategy approach to building-up and reinforcing administrative and judicial capacity in the future new Member States has been to ensure that enough qualified staff are employed and that enough money is made available in order to meet the end goal of implementation and enforcement. Nicolaides points out that this

---

[78] See Court of Auditors, Special Report 6/2003 *concerning PHARE and ISPA funding of environmental projects in the candidate countries* together with Commission replies thereto, *OJ* 2003 C 167/21 at 31.

[79] See the response of the Commission accompanying the Special Reports, op. cit. ns. 77 and 78.

[80] A programme set up by each candidate in accordance with Commission Communication on *Accession Strategies for Environment* (op. cit. n. 12) and subsequently with the Commission Communication on *the Challenge of Environmental Financing in the Candidate Countries*, COM(2001) 304, 8 June 2001.

[81] See P. Nicolaides, in Cremona, op. cit. Chapter 1, n. 24.

[82] Recommendation 2001/331, *OJ* 2001 L 118/48.

approach lacks the necessary ingredient of 'credible commitment' to apply the *acquis* once they have become Member States. He points to the weakness in the eight methods the Union uses to ensure effective implementation of the *acquis* and advises candidates to adopt an institutional approach to building administrative capacity.[83] Through this 'institutional approach', acceding countries will be able:

> to demonstrate to the EU a credible commitment to apply the *acquis communautaire* if they delegate that task to sufficiently empowered and accountable institutions which both have considerable decision-making independence and are subject to specific performance obligations.[84]

*Including aspiring Member States in EU agencies and programmes*

Including the candidates at an operational level in the implementation and application of Union environment policies has been a key aim of the overall pre-accession strategy. Participation of the candidates in the Community programmes, agencies and committees was anticipated by the Copenhagen European Council of 1993. In the later Europe Agreements, provision for such participation was made in the EAs themselves but Protocols had to be added to the earlier EAs.[85] A Commission Communication on the matter outlined the new approach to incorporating the candidates following *Agenda 2000* and the 1997 Luxembourg European Council. Decisions adopting the new generation of programmes under LIFE+[86] for example, automatically included the candidates. LIFE+, the financial instrument for the environment, is the latest programme in a generation of Union funding for the implementation, development and enhancement of EU environment legislation as well as the integration of the environment into other EU policies. Turkey and the countries of the Western Balkans are the focus of LIFE+ alongside the Member States or as third countries.

Thus, EUR 6.5 million of LIFE+ funds were deployed in 2008 in Albania to strengthen key wetland management skills and build

[83] See P. Nicolaides, op. cit. n. 81, at pp. 64–67.

[84] Op. cit. n. 81 at p. 67.

[85] See for example, Additional Protocol to the Europe Agreement establishing an association between the European Communities and their Member States, of the one part, and Romania, of the other part. *OJ* L 317, 30/12/1995 pp. 40–43

[86] The current LIFE+ Regulation 614/2007, *OJ* 2007 L149, covers the period 2007–2013.

resource capacities through a three year project implemented by the European network of Environmental Centres for Administration and Technology.[87] In the earlier LIFE III programme Albania also secured a contribution of EUR 504,545 for a project to build its capacity for sustainable tourism development. The project facilitated 'the transfer of know-how in Sustainable Tourism Development, develop, test, and implement environmental management instruments, support the establishment of a new administrative structure dealing with Sustainable Tourism Development issues, and build and disseminate best practices.'[88]

Participation in Union agencies and programmes typically requires that the (potential) candidates forward part of their financial allocation under the Instrument for Pre-Accession to the programme in question. In return, they receive the full administrative backup of the Union agencies and bodies. Chapter 3.6 has dealt with the inclusion of the (potential) candidates in Union programmes and agencies, which nowadays begins long before formal recognition of official candidate status. As regards participation in Union bodies, this is decided on a case by case basis but is a fundamental step towards familiarising the candidates with the *acquis communautaire*. Again, the EP/AP specifies priorities for reinforcing administrative and judicial capacity in the implementation, compliance and enforcement of the environment *acquis*. This further deepens the overall a process of familiarising the candidates with practical aspects of applying the environment *acquis*.

Already for the fifth enlargement, the twelve new Member States enjoyed associate status under the Sixth Research and Technological Development Framework Programme (2002–2006) for example, and were fully eligible on a par with the Member States. The candidates made a contribution based on the percentage of the GDP and were eligible for a 20% or 30% rebate for the first two years of their participation. Once Member States of course, their contribution would be met by the Union budget. Under the Seventh Research and Technological

[87] See Capacity building on conservation of Albanian wetland ecosystems (ALWET), LIFE03 TCY/AL/000004.

[88] See Commission Press Release 'LIFE-Third Countries 2006: Commission grants €6.5 million to 16 environment projects in neighbouring countries' of 19 October 2006.

Development Framework Programme,[89] Turkey and all the candidates and potential candidates are also associate members.

For the countries of the Western Balkans, the Commission's 2003 Communication, *Preparing for the participation of the Western Balkan countries in Community programmes and agencies*[90] structured the approach. Environment and energy are among the many priorities. A Protocol to the SAA FYROM sets general principles for the FYROM's participation in EU programmes.[91] Framework Agreements were also concluded in June 2005 with the other Western Balkans countries.[92] The advantage of pre-accession participation in Union bodies and programmes familiarises candidates with the practicalities of membership. It also has the 'multiplier effect' that comes with investing EU resources in the region as a whole. Standards of public administration in (potential) candidate countries are therefore being raised to the Union standard. However, the matter of the long-term 'credible commitments' to continuing to meet the administrative and governmental capacity post-accession, will also be a factor in the success of this approach and the future orientation and evolution of such programmes. This challenge is bound up with the matter of attracting the necessary investments and financing. Before moving on to the singular challenge of investment, it is important to mention regional co-operation in the context of the pre-accession strategy for the Western Balkans and Turkey.

---

[89] See http://cordis.europa.eu/fp7/. See the Memorandums of Understanding to this effect signed 1 June 2007 (Turkey), 13 June 2007 (Croatia, FYROM, Serbia), 17 December 2007 (Albania), 25 January 2008 (Montenegro), 1 January 2009 (Bosnia & Herzegovina).

[90] COM(2003) 748, 3 December 2003.

[91] Commission Proposal for a Council Decision concerning the signing of a Protocol to the Stabilisation and Association Agreement between the European Communities and their Member States, of the one part, and the former Yugoslav Republic of Macedonia, of the other part, on a Framework Agreement between the European Community and the former Yugoslav Republic of Macedonia on the general principles for the participation of the former Yugoslav Republic of Macedonia in Community programmes, COM(2004) 729, 27 October 2004. It was adopted by the Justice and Home Affairs Council on 2 June 2005, see Council document 9568/05 of 1 June 2005 (it was adopted as an 'A' point), to be found on the Council website at www.register.consilium.eu.int/pdf/fr/05/st05/st05532.fr05.pdf.

[92] Including Albania, Bosnia and Herzegovina, Croatia and Serbia and Montenegro, all contained in COM(2004) 809, 16 December 2004. These were formally adopted by Council on 2 June 2005, see Council Decision *OJ* 2005 L 92/84. A Protocol to the SAA Montenegro, Protocol 8, has also been adopted and is being implemented on a provisional basis, see Council Decision 2008/127, *OJ* 2008 L 43/9.

*Regional co-operation*
As pointed out in earlier chapters, with the accession aspirations of the Western Balkans, regional co-operation has come into its own as a conditionality tool of the pre-accession strategy. In the broader region, the ripples of that conditionality are felt in the European Neighbourhood and Partnership Instrument (ENPI), in particular through the Cross-Border Co-operation (CBC) instrument.[93] The objective of environment and public health is a key component of that conditionality in cross-border projects between the countries of eastern Europe, the Southern Caucasus and the Southern Mediterranean and the EU's Strategic Relationship with Russia. CBC projects are also key in the Barcelona Process and the Northern Dimension as well as the ENPI.

The renewed Environment for Europe Process of the UN's Economic Commission for Europe is important here also. The latest ministerial meeting in January 2009 set the ground for a reform of the process. This informal multilateral forum was created in 1991 in order to stimulate environmental awareness in the CEECs in transition. Today it comprises 56 countries. While the Union previously had only informal links with the process, it is now pushing for the central role of the Environment for Europe Process to be the implementation of UN multilateral, international conventions throughout the region.[94] The Commission focuses on four themes:

- co-operating with EU neighbours on sustainable development;
- pursuing environmental objectives through partnerships and political dialogue with neighbouring countries;
- improving environmental understanding at pan-European level;
- promoting the role of civil society in the environmental sector through the Regional Environment Centers (RECs), see p. 246.

In parallel the Union pursues it environmental agenda in various countries involved in the Environment for Europe Process.

The pre-accession strategy provides the framework for bilateral relations with the countries of the Western Balkans and Turkey. Two Member States (Bulgaria and Romania) and various candidate and potential

[93] See European Commission, *CBC Strategy Paper 2007–2013*, of November 2006.
[94] See Commission Communication, Commission co-operation with the Environment for Europe Process after the 2007 Ministerial Conference in Belgrade, COM(2007) 262, *OJ* 2007 C191/17.

candidate countries participate in initiatives to protect the Danube and the Black Sea and Forest Law Enforcement.[95] Within the catchment area of the Danube are Austria, the Czech and Slovak Republics, Germany, Hungary, Italy, Poland and Slovenia, the clean-up and protection of the Danube has benefited from PHARE and other EU funding over the last 20 years. Moreover, accession conditionality in the European/Accession Partnerships reflect these continuing concerns. Also, a first EU Danube Strategy is under preparation[96] and EU support is already extended to the Danube corridor within the EU through Trans-European Networks, through two transnational programmes: the 'South-East Europe' and the 'Central Europe' programmes. Both programmes offer assistance for projects in the fields of transport and accessibility, environment and risk prevention as well as socio-economic development. During the 2000–2006 financing period, European regional policy provided support for a number of Danube-related projects, principally in the field of flood prevention.

Relations with Russia have developed independently of the Environment for Europe Process, and have been conducted in the framework of the Russia Strategic Partnership and the Common Economic Spaces. An EU Russia Environmental Dialogue was launched in October 2006 to strengthen bilateral co-operation.

Also, the European Neighbourhood Policy provides the framework for bilateral relations with Armenia, Azerbaijan, Georgia, Moldova and Ukraine. In April 2006, the Ministerial Conference in Almaty brought the representatives if the Central Asian countries together with the EU to enhanced environmental co-operation. Bilateral relations between, the EU and these countries are based on Partnership and Co-operation Agreements with Kazakhstan, Kyrgyzstan, Tajikistan, Turkmenistan and Uzbekistan.

The regional co-operation structure of the South East Europe Co-operation Process (SEECP), with its new Regional Co-operation Coun-

---

[95] Danube-Black Sea (DABLAS) Task Force (set up in November 2001, following Commission Communication *Environmental co-operation in the Danube – Black Sea Region*, COM(2001) 615 of 30 October 2001, see DABLAS website homepage to be found at http://ec.europa.eu/environment/enlarg/dablas/index_en.htm), the International Commission for the Protection of the Danube River (ICPDR), and the Europe and North Asia Forest Law Enforcement Governance (FLEG).

[96] See Commissioner Hübner, 'European Danube Strategy', SPEECH/08/501 of 6 October 2008. See DABLAS news letter 2008, to be found at http://ec.europa.eu/environment/enlarg/dablas/downloads/newsletter08_en.pdf.

cil (RCC) set up in 2007, took over the responsibilities of the Regional Table and the Working Tables of the Stability Pact in 2008.[97] This process was an initiative of the SEE countries themselves. It is therefore seen as a means to 'enhance local ownership in regional co-operation in South East Europe' in areas covered by the Stability Pact.[98] Such strategic governmental approaches project environmental concerns throughout the region and go beyond the approximation and capacity building aims of the pre-accession strategy. Environmental concerns straddle various of the priority areas for SEECP actions, in particular infrastructure and energy.[99]

An example of co-operation projects undertaken include projects to improve the use of inland waterways from Croatia to Turkey and from Moldova to Montenegro where a comparatively large number of rivers converge. The conference was based on the UN convention on transboundary use of inland waterways, which most South Eastern Europe have ratified.

Core to this priority area is implementation of the Treaty establishing the Energy Community between the EU and these Western Balkans countries.[100] Article 2(1)(d) of that Treaty expressly establishes as a task of the Energy Community, the improvement of the environmental situation in relation to Network Energy and related energy efficiency, foster the use of renewable energy and set out the conditions for energy trade in the single regulatory space. Network Energy is defined as electricity and gas sectors as defined in Directives 2003/54 and 2003/55.[101] Chapter III (Arts. 12 to 17) of that Treaty also provides for a timetable for the adoption by the Western Balkan partners of a raft of environment *acquis* measures, a process referred to as the 'extension of the *acquis*'. However, by virtue of Article 17, this requirement applies to Network Energy alone. The measures listed are:

---

[97] See Chapter 2.2.

[98] See Commission Press Release, *Zagreb Summit for more regional cooperation in South-East Europe*, IP/07/622 of 8 May 2007.

[99] Initiatives in this area are outlined at http://www.rcc-see.org/index.php?action=page&id=17&link_id=20%20.

[100] See the website of the Energy Community http://www.energy-community.org/portal/page/portal/ENC_HOME.

[101] Directive 2003/54 concerning common rules for the internal market in electricity and repealing Directive 96/92/EC – Statements made with regard to decommissioning and waste management activities, *OJ* 2003 L 176/1 and Directive 2003/55 concerning common rules for the internal market in natural gas and repealing Directive 98/30, OJ 2003 L 176/57.

- Directive 85/337 – Environmental Impact Assessment;[102]
- Directive 1999/32 – sulphur content of liquid fuel;[103]
- Directive 2001/80 – large combustion plants;[104]
- Directive 79/409 – conservation of wild birds.[105]

Both the Directives on Environmental Impact Assessment and wild birds took effect in these partner countries on the date of entry into effect of the Treaty on 1 July 2006. The Directives on the sulphur content of liquid fuels and large combustion plants must be implemented by 31 December 2011 and 2017 respectively. Chapter VI, Article 35 of the Energy Community Treaty provides a legal basis for further measures on energy sources and efficiency, taking account of their advantages for security supply, environment protection, social cohesion and regional development.

The input of independent, Non-Governmental Organisations (NGOs) is crucial to making development sustainable in Europe. Among them, the Regional Environmental Center for Central and Eastern Europe (REC), created by the EU together with the USA and Hungary in 1990, has been a great success. In addition there are more local Regional Environmental Centers throughout the region. The REC promotes co-operation among governments, non-governmental organisations, businesses and other environmental stakeholders, and by supporting the free exchange of information and public participation in environmental decision making. The EU is a major donor to the work of the REC and at present 29 countries have signed its Charter (1996), including all of the countries of the Western Balkans and recently also, Turkey.[106] It is funded by these countries and by EU Member States individually countries as well as Norway, Switzerland and the United States, together with other intergovernmental and private institutions. Assisting today's actual and potential candidate countries to approximate to the *acquis* and build their capacity in environment law has been the subject of many projects of the REC.

[102] Council Directive 85/337 on the assessment of the effects of certain public and private projects on the environment, *OJ* 1985 L 175/40.

[103] Directive 1999/32 relating to a reduction in the sulphur content of certain liquid fuels, *OJ* 1999 L 121/13.

[104] Op. cit. n. 26.

[105] Council Directive 79/409/EEC of 2 April 1979 on the conservation of wild birds, *OJ 1979 L 103/1, as amended.*

[106] See http://www.rec.org/REC/Introduction/Johannesburg/doc/charter.pdf.

Among its many achievements in the region is the UNECE Aarhus Convention on Access to Information, Public Participation in Decision-Making and Access to Justice in Environmental Matters.[107] Turkey has not yet signed the Aarhus Convention and nor have Serbia or Montenegro or Kosovo, but other of the Western Balkans have now ratified it following Bosnia and Herzegovina's accession on 1 October 2008.

1.2.2 *The singular challenge of investment*

Before looking at the provision for transitional arrangements set out in the fifth and sixth Accession Treaties, it is useful to consider the limitations that external investment and financing present to the environment *acquis*. The single most challenging task facing the new Member States in respect of the environment *acquis* will be to secure the necessary investment for many years to come. The need for the new members to find financing and investment for infrastructure projects will continue for many years after enlargement. This threatens the true potential for implementation of the corner stones of the existing *acquis* by the CEECs. Compliance will involve considerable investment not only in building up the necessary administrative capacity but in the necessary infrastructure upgrade required to implement the environment *acquis* on waste, water, energy and IPPC.

In its original strategy for accession to the environment *acquis*[108] the Commission estimated that implementation would require EUR 120 billion, of which no more than 10 percent could be met by the EU.[109] The more detailed compliance-costing reports of 1997[110] give more of an idea of the magnitude of capital and recurring costs. But these reports are fraught with uncertainties and methodological weaknesses (as noted in the reports themselves) and highlight the need for external financing by the CEECs. In 2001, the Commission published its guide[111] for the future new Member States to follow when developing investment strategies for the implementation of the environment

[107] See http://www.unece.org/env/pp/documents/cep43e.pdf.

[108] Commission Communication, op. cit n. 12.

[109] Ibid.

[110] For more information, see www.europa.eu.int/comm/environment/enlarg/compcos.pdf. A separate report exists for Cyprus, found at www.europa.eu.int/comm/environment/enlarg/cocyp.pdf.

[111] Commission Communication *The Challenge of Environmental Financing in the Candidate Countries*, op. cit. n. 80.

*acquis* and national approximation strategies. New estimates outlined there, lowered the original prediction by 10 to 20 percent but are not based on a common methodology with the 1997 figures. However, the PEPA[112] that had been established in 1999 (designed to develop investment strategies from domestic, foreign and private sources for thirteen of the heaviest Directives[113] in terms of investment) had been devised on the basis of the 1997 estimates.[114]

According to the Commission, in the years 2000 to 2002 the loans signed by international financial institutions (IFIs) with all ten new Member States amounted to EUR 5 billion.[115] If it takes three years to attract EUR 5 billion (EUR 1.666 billion per year), will it take until 2050 to attract the lower estimate of total financing needed to fully apply the *acquis*?[116]

Answering this question is not a matter for this book. However, the apparent limits on financial possibilities not only constrains the ability of the new and future Member States to comply with the *acquis*; it will

---

[112] Op. cit. n. 80.

[113] Council Directive 91/271 Urban Waste Water Treatment Directive, op. cit. n. 28; Council Directive 98/83 on the quality of water intended for human consumption (Drinking Water Directive), *OJ* 1998 L 330/32; Council Directive 76/464 on pollution caused by certain dangerous substances discharged into the aquatic environment of the Community, *OJ* 1976 L 129/23 ('Discharge of Certain Dangerous Substances into Surface Water Directive'); Council Directive 91/676 concerning the protection of waters from pollution caused by nitrates from agricultural sources, *OJ* 1991 L 375/1; Council Directive 1999/31 on the landfill of waste, *OJ* 1999 L182/1 (Landfill Directive'); Council Directive 89/369 Municipal Waste Directive, op. cit. n. 31; Council Directive 94/67 Hazardous Waste Directive, op. cit. n. 30; European Parliament and Council Directive 94/62 on packaging and packaging waste, op. cit. n. 32 ('Packaging Waste Directive'); Council Directive 88/609 Large Combustion Plant Directive, op. cit. n. 26; Directive 98/70 of the European Parliament and the Council relating to the quality of petrol and diesel fuels, *OJ* 1998 L 350/58; Sulphur Content of Liquid Fuels Directive, op. cit. n. 103; Council Directive 96/61, IPPC Directive, op. cit. n. 27; Council Directive 94/63 on the control of volatile organic compound (VOC) emissions resulting from the storage of petrol and its distribution from terminals to service stations, *OJ* 1994 L 365/24 ('VOC Directive'). A complete list is supplied in Annex I to Commission Communication on *The Challenge of Environmental Financing in the Candidate Countries,* op. cit. n. 80.

[114] See Communication from the Commission on *Accession Strategies for Environment,* op. cit. n. 12.

[115] Commission Report, *General report on pre-accession assistance* (*Phare, ISPA, SAPARD*), COM(2003) 844, 5 January 2004 at p. 21.

[116] The original estimate stood at EUR 120 billion. If it is reduced by 20 percent, it will stand at under EUR 96 billion. An EU contribution of EUR 12 billion would mean that EUR 84 billion would have to come from external sources. If it is the case EUR 1.6666 billion external investment is found on an annual basis, it would take approximately 50 years to attract the total investment required.

necessarily also impact upon the behaviour of the new Member Sates at the heart of decision-making in the environment *acquis*.[117] Uncertainties and methodological weakness are inherent in the process and undermine the financial planning not only for external investment but also for EU funding both pre-accession and post-accession. The consequent 'political and financial trap for the Union' identified by Hager,[118] lies in the fact that the headline figure for needed investments is both too high and too low:

- too high in terms of initial investment because they reflect the traditional public planning and pricing context that prevailed in the CEECs at the time of their inception;
- too low in terms of the follow-on costs, especially for public budgets in terms of financial costs, routine operating costs and maintenance.

Uncertainties and weaknesses in investment planning imply uncertainty as to the reliability of timeframes agreed for transitional arrangements in the environment *acquis*.

As is seen below, the transitional arrangements relate to those laws that require the heaviest investment. Financing will influence the political priorities of the new Member States and their willingness to contribute to further raising environmental standards after their accession to the Union. Where investment thresholds have to be revised upwards, the new Member States will have a solid argument for additional EU contributions in order that they may meet their post-accession implementation deadlines. Hager's conclusion is dramatic:[119]

> In sum, while sources of economic intelligence and the instruments for applying such intelligence exist, the Union's governance of the enlargement process is fragmented and lacks an administrative/political focus for any strategy going beyond formal *acquis* compliance. The costs to the candidate countries, the future stability of the euro, the Union's own budget and last, but by no means least, to the environment are significant.

[117] See Jehlicka, op. cit. n. 35.

[118] See W. Hager, *Enlargement: Paying for the Green Acquis* (Brussels, Centre for European Policy Studies 2002) at pp. 9–10

[119] See Hager, ibid at p. 68.

Additional financial burdens will also be an argument for the new members against their participation in future EU environment initiatives that involve additional costs beyond their accession treaty commitments.

In terms of financing, there is also the matter of the capacity to absorb available EU funding. The Instrument for Structural Policy for Pre-Accession (ISPA)[120] was the pre-accession programme for funding large-scale infrastructure projects in the transport and environment sectors. SAPARD[121] was the pre-accession programme for agricultural support and rural development. The Instrument for Pre-Accession (IPA) has replaced these instruments, as well as PHARE, see Chapter 4, although various PHARE, ISPA and SAPARD projects are still running their course. With the focus on accession and enlargement, the input from International Financing Institutions is reigned in through the Memorandum of Understanding of 26 April 2006, taking over from the earlier MoU of 2003. Since 2002, four types of programme have also been developed by the Union in order to encourage and complement IFI inputs: the SME facility, the Municipal Finance Facility, the Municipal Finance Facility and the Energy Efficiency Finance Facility. The Energy Efficiency Finance Facility was introduced in 2006 specifically to stimulate investment in energy efficiency and reductions in CO2 emissions in all types of building and industry sectors, making financing available to end-borrowers.

For the (potential) candidates in today's pre-accession process, the IPA functions in combination with the 2006 MoU and these financing initiatives.

Since their accessions in 2004 and 2007, support for the CEECs from the ISPA and SAPARD type-projects has been succeeded by the Cohesion Fund and the European Agricultural Guidance and Guarantee Fund (EAGGF) respectively. Thus, ISPA and SAPARD projects fall under those budget headings. Since 1 January 2004, the new Member States have been eligible for structural funding under the European Regional Development Fund (ERDF) and the European Social Fund.[122]

---

[120] Council Regulation 1267/99 establishing an Instrument for Structural Policies for Pre-Accession, *OJ* 1999 L 161/73.

[121] Council Regulation 1268/99 on Community support for pre-accession measures for agriculture and rural development in the applicant countries of Central and Eastern Europe in the pre-accession period, *OJ* 1999 L 161/87.

[122] Act of Accession, Art. 32.

The main problem as concerns the structural and cohesion funds, according to the European Commission's November 2003 Comprehensive Monitoring Report[123] and the above reports of the Court of Auditors, has been the lack of a sufficient number of quality projects ready to be launched. The start of the programmes in country is delayed if the legislative framework, including the EU rules on public procurement, State Aid and environment protection, was not in place – only Lithuania did not face this risk according to the Commission's 2003 reports. Malta was singled out for needing to strengthen procedures and institutions to implement the structural funds.

Thus, financial management proved a major and crucial challenge for the CEECs and Malta. In May 2005, the Bulgarian Finance Minister Milen Velchev announced that Bulgaria had used only 17.65% (EUR 237 million) of Bulgaria's ISPA allocation, although it had used 97% of the PHARE allocation.[124] As noted in Chapter 4, the Transition Facilities for the countries of the 2004 enlargement and the for Bulgaria and Romania, are now ended. Such a track record will have to be improved if Bulgaria is not to lose crucial funds and if it is to take full advantage of the post-accession funding available to it once it has acceded to the Union, see Chapter 5.

### 1.2.3 *Nuclear safety: approximation in the absence of* acquis

The demands of the Union during pre-accession in relation to nuclear installations in the CEECs is the subject of this section. The 2003 and 2005 Accession Treaties' conditionality following the fifth and sixth enlargements is dealt with here. The incoming countries have had to approximate with practices and standards of the Member States in the field of nuclear installations, which have not been enshrined in legislation adopted either under the TFEU or the Euratom Treaties but which obviously are motivated by 'environmental' concerns of the Union in the broadest sense. There are a number Directives/Regulations adopted under the Euratom Treaty to which the incoming countries have had to approximate under the general rule of thumb that

---

[123] See Commission *General Report on pre-accession assistance (Phare-ISPA-SAPARD) in 2002*, op. cit. n. 115.

[124] Introductory remarks made by Minister Velchev to a press conference on 'South-Eastern Planning Region on Chapter 21 of EU legislation, Regional Policy and CO-ordination of Structural Instruments', report in 'Poor on ISPA, Good on PHARE', Sofia Echo on 30 May 2005, to be found at www.sofiaecho.com.

applies to all chapters of the *acquis communautaire*: that only limited transitional arrangements from the *acquis* can be negotiated. Thus for example, Poland was entitled to derogate briefly from Article 8 of Directive 97/43/Euratom on ionising radiation in medical exposure[125] and Latvia was entitled to derogate from Articles 8 and 9(1) of that Directive and in both cases the derogations expired at the end of 2006. Significantly, this transitional arrangement concerns exposure during medical treatment rather than nuclear installations.

Nuclear energy is of huge importance to Europe. Each Member State freely decides its own energy policy. In total, 38% of the European Union's electricity is generated by nuclear power.[126] There is no consensus among the Member States on nuclear energy. The European Commission announced in 2000[127] that, of the fifteen receiving Member States, only eight Member States (Belgium, Finland, France, Germany, Greece, Sweden, the Netherlands, United Kingdom) have nuclear installations and five of these have announced a moratorium on nuclear energy.[128] In 2002, France, the United Kingdom and Finland had not decided whether to continue or to stop using nuclear energy. Countries like Germany and Belgium had opted for a policy of progressively phasing out nuclear power production, as had Sweden. Italy renounced nuclear energy after a referendum in 1987 but was openly considering revising its policy in 2005, and Poland too.[129] Finland opted for nuclear power in December 2003 and in spring 2005 France decided to build an EPR (European Pressurized Reactor). Of the new Member States, five intend to remain nuclear power countries: Lithuania, Slovakia, Slovenia, Hungary and the Czech Republic. Finally, Bulgaria decided in May 2004 after signature of the Accession Treaty, to build a new nuclear power plant, scheduled to come into service in 2010. Moreover, under public pressure following the Russia-Ukraine crisis over gas supplies early 2009, Bulgaria seriously

---

[125] *OJ* 1997 L 180/22.

[126] Information obtained from info@ambafrance-us.org, provided by the Embassy of France in the United States. This information is dated 17 May 2005.

[127] See Green Paper of the European Commission *Towards a European Strategy for the Security of Energy Supply* COM(2000) 769 of 29 November 2000.

[128] See European Commission MEMO 'Towards a Community approach to nuclear safety', of 6 November 2002, and also COM(2000) 769 of 29 November 2000, ibid. at p. 19.

[129] See the Speech by Patrick Devedjian, Minister Delegate for Industry at the ICONE 13 Conference held in Beijing on 17 May 2005, the transcript of which can be found at www.ambafrance-us.org/news/statmnts/2005/nuclear_power051705.asp.

reconsidered reopening certain Kozloduy units, which it had committed to closing down permanently, see further.

As for countries preparing their accession today, Turkey has no nuclear power plants in operation today although the Nuclear Energy Agency reports that Turkey's plans for expanding its electricity capacity for the next 15 years, includes nuclear energy in the mix.[130] The Western Balkans countries do not have such plants either although the World Nuclear Association has cited Albania as an 'emerging nuclear country', where the introduction of nuclear energy capacity is seriously under consideration.[131] There have been press reports that Croatia would join Albania in this project at Lake Shkoder.[132] Croatia already owns half of the Krsko nuclear power plant in neighbouring Slovenia.

Various new Member States bowed to Union demands for dismantling, decommissioning and safety standards of unsafe nuclear installations which go beyond the scope of the *acquis* on nuclear matters. This is because so far, the Union has not agreed on basic standards concerning nuclear plants. It is significant that the attempts at EU level to adopt EU-wide legislation on the safety, decommissioning funds and radioactive waste management were not successful in advance of the fifth enlargement. However, there has been some progress at EU level in the verification of environmental radioactivity monitoring facilities following a landmark ruling of the European Court of Justice in December 2002.[133] In that judgment the ECJ basically found that the Member States could not use an artificial distinction between the protection of the health of the general public and the safety of sources of ionizing radiation so as to exclude certain EU competences in the surveillance of levels of radioactivity in the environment (air, water and soil). Nuclear safety became a priority of the European Commission in 2003 and 2004. As a result the practical arrangements for the conduct of safety verification visits in the Member States were updated

[130] See http://www.nea.fr/html/general/profiles/turkey.html#regs#regs, visited January 2009.

[131] See http://world-nuclear.org/info/inf102.html, visited May 2009.

[132] See http://www.world-nuclear-news.org/IT-Albania_and_Croatia_plan_joint_plant-1704095.html.

[133] ECJ, Case C-29/99 Commission v. Council (Accession of the Community to the Convention on Nuclear Safety), see contribution of A. Bouquet to Nuclear Energy Agency legal reporting, to be found at http://www.nea.fr/html/law/nlb/nlb-71/041_056.pdf, at pp. 52–56.

in 2006[134] and certain Euratom provisions concerning Article 36 of the Euratom Treaty were adopted in order to take account of Romania and Bulgaria's accessions, in particular to establish a common basis for the Article 35 verifications in all Member States.[135] Also, in 2007 the Commission reported on the application of Article 35 of the Euratom Treaty Verification of the operation and efficiency of facilities for continuous monitoring of the level of radioactivity in the air, water and soil for the period 1990–2007.[136]

Considerable problems have been faced by a number of the Central and East European Member States as concerns their nuclear installations. The question of how to guarantee continued post-accession performance by the new Member States avoids the pressing underlying issue; that of guaranteeing the standards of performance of nuclear installations throughout the entire EU.

*Pre-accession conditionality under the pre-accession strategy*

Following the Contzen Report of August 1998 of the High Level Group of advisors in nuclear safety in the CEECs and CIS,[137] in June 1999 the Cologne European Council[138] requested the Commission to provide it with regular reports on the situation of nuclear safety in the candidates. At the same time, the Council highlighted the 'urgent need' to adopt high European safety standards in the nuclear field. The Commission duly included the situation of nuclear safety in its country reports on the new Member States (they were candidates at the time of course)

---

[134] *OJ* 2006 C155/2.

[135] See Commission Recommendation 2006/715/Euratom adapting Recommendation 2000/473/Euratom on the application of Article 36 of the Euratom Treaty concerning the monitoring of the levels of radioactivity in the environment for the purpose of assessing the exposure of the population as a whole, by reason of the accession of Bulgaria and Romania, *OJ* 2006 L 293/17. See also Commission Recommendation 2000/473/Euratom on the application of Article 36 of the Euratom Treaty concerning the monitoring of the levels of radioactivity in the environment for the purpose of assessing the exposure of the population as a whole, *OJ* 2000 L 191/37.

[136] See Commission Communication COM(2007) 847 of 20 December 2007.

[137] The Contzen Report, *Point de vue stratégique pour l'avenir des programmes Phare et Tacis de L'Union européenne*, August 1999.

[138] See the Conclusions of the June 1999 Cologne European Council at Conclusion 60; 'The European Council emphasises the importance of high standards of nuclear safety in Central and Eastern Europe. It stresses the importance of this issue in the context of the Union's enlargement and calls on the Commission to examine this issue thoroughly in its next regular progress reports on the applicant countries, due in autumn 1999.'

as well as Bulgaria and Romania in their annual progress reports.[139] As requested by the Council, the Commission also gave high priority to nuclear safety in the Accession Partnerships and in using pre-accession funds to pursue these priorities. Important landmarks were:[140]

- the agreement to close non-upgradeable units in Lithuania, Slovakia and Bulgaria;
- the support that the programme has given to the nuclear regulators;
- the short-term urgent safety improvements made to some reactors;
- the design and operational improvements in upgradeable reactors, and also;
- considerable assistance to tackle the problems related to radioactive waste and spent fuel.

In particular, the Commission's position has remained consistent throughout: that these first-generation reactors of Soviet design are considered inherently unsafe by nuclear experts and cannot be upgraded economically to a required level of safety. This position is in line with the G7 multilateral action programme for improving the safety of all Soviet-designed reactors in Central and Eastern Europe adopted at the Munich G7 summit in 1992.

The approach that applies today is built upon that G7 decision and was set out in *Agenda 2000*. The Bulgarian, Slovak and Lithuanian reactors that have had to be shut down pre- or post-accession are such reactors. The approach has been that:[141]

- where western-designed nuclear plants are in use (Romania and Slovenia), developments should be monitored to ensure that operations comply with the appropriate safety standards and technical assistance is provided if necessary.
- where the safety of Soviet-designed nuclear power stations – whether in operation or under construction – can be upgraded to meet international safety standards, modernisation programmes should be fully implemented over a period of 7–10 years. (This applied to Dukovany and Temelin in the Czech Republic, Paks in Hungary,

[139] See the various progress reports of December 1999.

[140] See Commission Statement 'Nuclear safety fifteen years after Chernobyl' given to the European Parliament in Plenary on 2 May 2001.

[141] At pp. 68–69.

and certain units at Bohunice and Mochovce in Slovakia and at Kozloduy in Bulgaria.)
- the timetables agreed by the governments concerned, subject to certain conditions, for the closure of non-upgradeable units must be respected. (This applies to Bohunice in Slovakia, Ignalina in Lithuania and certain units at Kozloduy in Bulgaria.)

It is also interesting to note that in *Agenda 2000* the Commission had intended full closure of the four of the Kozloduy reactors in Bulgaria by 2002. Also, in Lithuania the Ignalina units had to be closed by 2002 and in Slovakia, both the Bohunice reactors were to close by 2000.

For the countries of the Western Balkans it is useful to mention explicit pre-accession conditionality in the pre-accession strategy concerning nuclear safety and radiation protection. Thus, for example, Albania must adhere to various international standards including the Convention on Nuclear Safety and the Joint Convention on the Safety of Spent Fuel Management and the Safety of Radioactive Waste Management. It also has to give 'proper attention' to the prevention of the illicit trafficking in nuclear and other radioactive materials.[142]

The candidates have achieved a level of nuclear safety comparable to that of the EU as a 'strict condition of accession'.[143] However, as the cases of Lithuania and Bulgaria go to show – see 2.1.3. below – these new Member States have been sorely tempted to set aside their pre-accession commitments after their accession. Therefore, in the interests of guaranteeing nuclear safety, the post-accession conditionality that applies to the new Member States is a short term and not a long-term solution for the lack of a EU approach.

In the run-up to the fifth and now also the sixth enlargements, the basic principles of establishing at EU level a common frame of reference for nuclear safety[144] have been the subject of major contention at

[142] See Commission Staff Working Document, Albania 2008 Progress Report, SEC (2008) 26925 of 5 November 2008 at p. 41.

[143] See European Parliament Resolution on the Commission report to the European Parliament and the Council: Operation of the Euratom Safeguards Office 1999–2000, OJ 2003 C 271 E/173 and European Parliament Briefing 40, 'Nuclear Safety and the applicant countries of Central and Eastern Europe', Part II to be found at www.europarl.eu.int/enlargement/briefings/40a2_en.htm, visited on 9 July 2001. See M. Hattig, 'Candidate countries and energy and nuclear safety' in A. Ott and K. Inglis, Handbook on European Enlargement, op. cit. Chapter 1, n. 26 at pp 962–963.

[144] See Commission proposals known as 'the nuclear package' which were first launched in 2002; Communication from the Commission to the Council and the

national level more from the stand point of the Member States in their concern to guard national competences rather than – it would appear – from the nuclear energy industry.[145] The European Parliament highlighted a range of other radiological issues that could benefit from Union level harmonisation, including uranium extraction waste and its final storage and the handling of materials on contaminated natural radionuclides such as waste, mud from oil extraction, slag, etc.[146] The resistance of the Member States to Union or Euratom or action is obvious given concerns to achieve higher (safety) standards at national level. In spite of the many international agreements in the area, nuclear safety remains the responsibility of the national governments and the lack of any common nuclear safety standard or even any legislative framework defining such a standard is remarkable.[147] The Contzen Report concluded that there should be no great difficulty in the CEECs meeting a comparable level of nuclear safety to the Member States.[148] At the same time it also recognised that a more precise definition of such an EU level or standard would be necessary before a comparison could be made reliably. This debate rages on among the Member States in spite of the European Court of Justice's ruling in December 2002[149] confirming the Community's legislative powers with regard to the safety of nuclear installations. The Court ruled in express terms[150] that the technical competence of national

---

European Parliament on Nuclear Safety in the European Union, COM(2002) 605 of 6 November 2002, Commission proposal for a Council (Euratom) Directive setting out basic obligations and general principles on the safety of nuclear installations and the Commission proposal for a Council Directive (Euratom) on the management of spent nuclear fuel and radioactive waste both contained in COM(2002) 32 of 30 January 2002.

145 See FORATOM, the European Atomic Forum (the trade association for the European Nuclear Industry) positions papers to this effect to be found at www.euronuclear.org

146 See European Parliament Resolution, op. cit. n. 143.

147 The Commission published a Recommendation on voluntary common classifications for radioactive waste in October 1999, *OJ* 1999 L 265/73.

148 The Contzen Report, op. cit. n. 137.

149 Judgment of the Court of Justice of 10 December 2002 in ECJ, Case C-29/99, *Commission* v. *Council*, [2002] *ECR* I-11221.

150 The Court found that the EURATOM Community possess competencies under the Treaty in the fields relating to: the establishment of a legislative and regulatory framework to govern the safety of nuclear installations; measures relating to the assessment and verification of safety; emergency preparedness; the siting of a nuclear installation, and; the design, construction and operation of nuclear installations. The Court refused to draw and 'artificial' distinction between protection of health of the general public and the safety of sources of ionising radiation.

authorities having the responsibility for nuclear safety does not preclude the Community from legislating.

In 2002, Loyola de Palacio, Vice-President of the European Commission at that time, announced in the European Parliament that the time had come for "*common [nuclear] standards and control mechanisms which will guarantee the application of the same criteria and methods in the whole of enlarged Europe*". The Commission proposed a package of measures in 2003, which were watered down in Council.[151] Seven years later – and in spite of the Strategic European Energy Review and more Member States than ever before making public their inclination to bolster their nuclear sectors – the package has made little progress, although the Council did adopt conclusions on the safe management of spent nuclear fuel and radioactive waste in May 2007.[152] In 2008 the European Commission responded to the renewed interest in nuclear power with a proposal for a Council (Euratom) Directive setting up a Community framework for nuclear safety on 26 November 2008[153] which withdraws and replaces the 2003 proposals.

Given that the new Member States have acceded to the Union on condition that they approximate to the EU model, they remain free to act – or not as the case may be – in those areas beyond the reach of the environment *acquis*. The lack of leadership by the Fifteen can be seen as something of a missed opportunity particularly in the field of nuclear safety because the pre-accession conditionality is no longer a carrot for improving the situation in the new Member States. However, the post-accession conditionality applied in the field of nuclear safety does impose certain legal obligations on the new Member States in the interests of human health and the environment. Post-accession conditionality in the nuclear sector is dealt with at 2.1.3.

[151] Since then these proposal have been watered down; see Council (DG CII) Document 5821/04 of 30 January 2004 and Council Document 5585/04 of 30 January 2004. See European Commission Proposal for a Council (Euratom) Directive setting out basic obligations and general principles on the safety of nuclear installations, COM 2003/35 final and also Amended proposal for a Council Directive (Euratom) laying down basic obligations and general principles on the safety of nuclear installations, COM(2004) 526(1) of 8 September 2004. See also amended proposal for a Council Directive (Euratom) on the safe management of the spent nuclear fuel and radioactive waste (presented by the Commission pursuant to Article 119 (2) of the Euratom Treaty) COM(2004) 526(2) of 8 September 2004.

[152] Council Conclusions of 8 May 2007.

[153] See COM(2008) 790 of 26 November 2008.

## 2. The environment *acquis* and the fifth and sixth enlargements: post-accession conditionality and transitional arrangements

### 2.1 *Post-accession incentives*

#### 2.1.1 *EU capacity building actions and incentives*

The carrot of accession that has driven the Union's conditionality during the pre-accession phase, guiding all EU and IFI funding and technical assistance since 1997, is no longer available to the Commission after enlargement. While it has, to all intents and purposes, expired, the 2003 and 2005 Accession Treaties have provided additional financial resources to the new Member States in addition to the Cohesion and other funding instrument of the Unions regional development initiatives.

The Transition Facility was established by the 2003 Accession Treaty to further finance the strengthening and development of administrative capacity and the continued implementation and enforcement of law as well as to foster best practice among peers.[154] Article 34 of the Act of Accession provides for temporary financial assistance to be given to the new Member States: EUR 200 million for 2004, EUR 120 million for 2005, EUR 60 million for 2006. Another Transition Facility was established for Bulgaria and Romania under the sixth Accession Treaty.[155] It has the same purpose. For Bulgaria and Romania, the funds made available amounted to EUR 82 million in the first year after accession to address national horizontal priorities. As with the Transition Facility for the fifth enlargement, the PHARE rules determine the implementation of the Transition Facility assistance.[156] The Commission's 2007 report on pre-accession and post-accession instruments provides a broad picture of the use and operation of the Transition Facility.[157]

Implementation of PHARE projects decided before 1 January 2004 (and their equivalents for Cyprus and Malta) continued for three years into membership. PHARE contracts had to be phased out.

[154] See Transition Facility Programming and Implementation Guide, C(2003) 4884 of 19 December 2003.

[155] See Art. 31 of the sixth Accession Treaty.

[156] See Art. 31(3) of the sixth Accession Treaty.

[157] See Commission Communication (2007) 3 of 12 January 2007.

Being external aid operations, PHARE operations were subject to *ex-ante* approval, unlike Community rules which are approved *ex-post*.[158] Under the PHARE Decentralised Implementation System, the EC delegations control all approval documents before project implementation. After accession, the implementation of contracts and payments for pre-accession assistance will be managed in the new Member States by their National Funds, subject to special *ex-ante* control of the relevant body (or PHARE Implementation Agencies) by the European Commission.[159] Each candidate had to secure the EDIS accreditation of such bodies in charge of allocating and managing the funds. EDIS is the Extended Decentralised Implementation System whereby the programme management of EU pre-accession funds is devolved to candidate country administrations, with the Commission, whilst retaining the final responsibility, exercising no systematic *ex-ante* (or prior approval) control over individual transactions and limiting its role to *ex-post* control. Any country that fails to obtain this '*ex-ante* waiver' could see its portion of the money being either suspended or withdrawn.

The Commission highlighted this as an area of 'serious concern' in its November 2003 Comprehensive Monitoring Report despite its positive predictions in its Report on pre-accession assistance for 2002. The Commission had reported in respect of the year 2003 that none of the ten candidates for the fifth enlargement nor Bulgaria and Romania had gained full accreditation. In the end all the new Member States were fully EDIS-accredited.[160]

---

[158] This way of phasing out PHARE was one of a variety of options considered: see Commission Communication on the phasing out of PHARE, COM(2002) 3303-1 of 6 September 2002.

[159] See Art. 33(1) of the fifth Accession Treaty. See Art. 27(1) of the Sixth Accession Treaty. Art. 33(4), fifth Accession Treaty makes special provision for the use of ISPA funds for the purposes of maintaining the necessary statutory staff in the new Member States for fifteen months after the date of accession. This is important because 'officials assigned to posts in the new Member States before accession and who are required to remain in service in those States after the date of accession shall benefit, as an exception, from the same financial and material conditions as were applied to the Commission before accession – in accordance with Annex X to the Staff Regulations of Officials and the Conditions of Employment of Other Servants of the European Communities (Reg 259/68, as amended). Certain ISPA funds will be used together with the Community Budget (part B – 'Support expenditure for operation'). The equivalent in the sixth Accession Treaty is contained in Art. 27(4).

[160] See Commission *2003 Report on Phare and the pre-accession instruments for Cyprus, Malta and Turkey*, COM(2005) 64, 1 March 2005 at pp. 6–7. An action plan

As for other EU financing initiatives that are ongoing, within the cohesion funding for example, the European Commission approved a cross-border co-operation programme between Romania and Bulgaria in October 2007 for the period 2007–2013.[161] The Bulgaria Romania CBC has a total budget of EUR 262 million, with Community assistance through the ERDF amounting to EUR 218 million. This represents approximately 2.5% of the total EU investment earmarked for the European Territorial Co-operation Objective under the Cohesion Policy 2007–2013. 34.3% is allocated to environment projects, aimed at sustainable use and protection of natural resources and the environment, and promotion of efficient risk management in the cross-border area. The objectives are as follows: to ensure effective protection and use of the area's natural assets through co-ordinated joint management systems; to increase awareness on environmental protection and management in the cross-border area; and to protect the local population, businesses, environment and infrastructure from the potentially disastrous consequences of natural and human-made crises.

#### 2.1.2 *The Internal Market safeguard clause and the environment* acquis

The environment *acquis* spans various chapters of the *acquis*. Core instruments of the environment *acquis* such as conservation measures, are founded upon the legal basis in the EU Treaty for environment policy (Art. 192(1) TFEU). Only a very few transitional arrangements are foreseen in the Accession Treaty for the environment *acquis*. While in both the fifth and sixth Accession Treaties, the safeguard clause is designed to protect the functioning of the Internal Market: no such legal tool has been available to the Commission in respect of the measures of the environment *acquis* adopted on the Treaty legal basis for environment policy. This clause is contained in Article 38 of the 2003 Act of Accession and in Article 37 in the 2005 Act of Accession. The

and follow-up measures was devised in 2004 to improve strategic programming, resources, project designed and more systematic quality control in project management. See also the Commission *General Report on pre-accession assistance (Phare-ISPA-SAPARD) in 2002*, COM(2003) 844, 5 January 2004 at pp. 14–17.

[161] See European Commission Memo, Romania and Bulgaria – Operational Programme 2007–2013: Romania-Bulgaria Cross-border Co-operation Programme, MEMO/08/629 of 16 October 2008.

former expired at the end of 2007 and the latter expires at the end of 2009.

However, theoretically, the Commission would have been able to make use of the safeguard clause in respect of sectoral policies including the environment *acquis*, where it adversely affects the functioning of the Internal Market. The state aid provisions undoubtedly fall within the body of commitments that would be subject to the Internal Market safeguard clause. The safeguard clause exclusively has applied to the new Member States and not to the existing Fifteen, enabling the Commission to take 'appropriate measures' against new Member States that fail to implement their commitments made during the accession negotiations. Such safeguard measures, in theory, could be used to exclude products from the Internal Market or suspend EU funds for example.[162]

Technically speaking, it would be feasible for the Commission to institute the Internal Market safeguard clause contained in the fifth and the sixth Accession Treaties in respect of 'serious breach of the functioning of the Internal Market'. It is useful to recap on the Internal Market safeguard clause for ease of reference. This clause enables the Commission to take unspecified action against a new Member State where it has failed to meet the commitments given during the negotiations. After enlargement, the Commission monitors the new members 'using the same mechanisms as those applied to the existing Member States'.[163] For the first three years after accession, the safeguard clause will be an additional means of ensuring compliance in addition to the traditional Treaty basis of Article 258 TFEU for pursuing a new Member State that has failed to meet its Treaty obligations. Such a failure must, however, 'cause serious breach of the functioning of the Internal Market, including commitments.'[164] The safeguard measures may extend to 'any commitments in all sectoral policies which concern

[162] See Chapter 5.2.

[163] European Commission *Guide to the negotiations*, (no official publication reference), updated and published on the Europa website in December 2002 but since removed therefrom and which included Bulgaria and Romania but the negotiations on the environment chapter had not been closed at that time. It was updated by a later *Report on the results of the negotiations on the accession of Cyprus, Malta, Hungary, Poland, Slovak Republic, Latvia, Estonia, Lithuania, the Czech Republic and Slovenia to the European Union*. This later report was published after the fifth enlargement on the Commission's website but carries no date or reference. It can be found at www.europa.eu.int/comm/enlargement/negotiations/pdf/negotiations_report_to_ep.pdf.

[164] Act of Accession to the fifth Accession Treaty, Art. 38, first paragraph.

economic activities with cross-border effect or an imminent breach of such risk'.

Practice shows that the Internal Market clause was intended more a tool of prevention, designed to anticipate compliance, implementation and enforcement inadequacies. Article 258 TFEU is more reactive in that the breach must already have occurred. Of course, all twenty-seven Member States may revert to national safeguard or emergency measures to protect human health and the environment within the scope of Article 36 TFEU and the safeguard clauses contained in secondary EU legislation. The very existence of the Internal Market safeguard clause is a signal of the political importance given the Internal Market *acquis* compared to policy areas like the environment *acquis*. It reads as an incentive to new Member States to prioritise compliance with the Internal Market *acquis* over other environmental provisions in order to avoid safeguard measures. Thus the fifth and sixth Accession Treaties have stronger conditionality in respect of implementation of the Internal Market *acquis* compared to the environment *acquis*. On the other hand, the political divisiveness of pursuing new Members for failing to comply with laws that the Fifteen apply, has played against the true possibility of this clause being used in reality.

Therefore, the Internal Safeguard clauses in the fifth and sixth Accession Treaties are impotent as post-accession governance tools. The Internal Market safeguard clauses could only have been used to address discrepancies in the transitional arrangements and pre-accession commitments of the new Member States, irrespective of the situation in the Fifteen. It would only address discrepancies in the transitional arrangements and pre-accession commitments that adversely affect the functioning of the Internal Market. Examples of environment *acquis* based on the Internal Market legal basis include: the sulphur content of liquid fuels;[165] Volatile Organic Compounds, and;[166] packaging and packaging waste.[167]

The principle of equal treatment among Member States is expressly referred to in the Communication on *Better Monitoring of the Application of Community Law*. This principle, as noted in Chapter 5, has deterred the Commission from the use of Internal Market safeguard

[165] See Sulphur Contact of Liquid Fuels Directive, op. cit. n. 103.
[166] See VOC Directive, op. cit. n. 113.
[167] See Packaging Waste Directive, Directive 94/62, op. cit. n. 32.

clause in both the 2003 and 2005 Accession Treaties because such safeguard measures are restricted to the new Member States alone. By the same logic, however, there would be fewer such arguments against the use of the Internal Market clause in the 2003 and 2005 Accession Treaties if the fifteen themselves had been in compliance with the law in question.

It is interesting to note that, in its 2005 report on the implementation of the 2003–2006 Internal Market Strategy,[168] there was a 7.1% deficit throughout the twenty-five Member States upon the date of accession. This report concerned all Internal Market rules and not simply those having an environment dimension. While this percentage had fallen to 3.6% in 2005 for the twenty-five Member States, the deficit for the fifteen Member States amounted to 2.9% of Internal Market rules. Over one quarter of some 427 Directives had not been fully transposed in at least one Member State. The Czech Republic was singled out as having failed to transpose over 150 Directives. Moreover, the Commission stated that;

> what is striking is that the performance of almost all [of the Fifteen] has deteriorated significantly since enlargement. Only Germany, France and the Netherlands have reduced their deficits since then. [...] What is equally striking is that the [Ten] have significantly reduced their deficits since their EU accession. Many now have better records than [the Fifteen].[169]

A number of the transitional arrangements in the environment *acquis* for the new Member States are Internal Market measures. In theory – because as we have already seen, the Commission has declined to make use of this clause – the new Member States could fall prey to safeguard measures under the Accession Treaty for failing to comply with a directive or regulation that is based on the Internal Market legal basis, by the deadlines set out in the transitional arrangements. They would also theoretically fall prey to the Internal Market safeguard clause should they fail to comply with other measures of the Internal Market *acquis*.

---

[168] See Commission Communication *Second Implementation Report of the Internal Market Strategy 2003–2006*, which has no official reference but which can be found at www.europa.eu.int/comm/internal_market/en/update/strategy/2nd-impl-report_en.pdf.

[169] Ibid. at p. 19.

In 2003[170] for example, Austria was brought before the ECJ for not meeting its reporting obligations under the Directive on the sulphur content of liquid fuels.[171] The UK was condemned by the ECJ for failure to transpose Directive 1999/13 on the limitations on emissions of VOCs.[172] A number of Member States were condemned for failure to comply with previous ECJ judgments over the non-conformity of national legislation with Directive 76/464 on dangerous substances discharged into the aquatic environment.[173] The Commission also sent letters of formal notice to France and the UK in 2003,[174] for failing to comply with previous ECJ judgments condemning them for having breached, *inter alia*, Article 14 of the packaging waste Directive as concerns their national waste management plans.[175]

Ultimately therefore, the Commission has been obliged to fall back on its traditional enforcement and other governance mechanisms to pursue breaches by the new Member States of their Accession Treaty commitments and Treaty obligations in respect of measures of the *acquis* designed to improve or protect the environment.

#### 2.1.3 *Post-accession conditionality in the nuclear sector*

The fifth Accession Treaty makes express reference to the post-accession obligations of the new Member States concerning nuclear safety and radiation protection. These are not transitional arrangements per se because there are, in fact, no Euratom measures in place in this regard. The new Member States were/are not approximating to specific measures of the *acquis communautaire*. The new Member States concerned are Bulgaria, Lithuania and Slovakia. In the fifth Accession Treaty, the 'transitional arrangement' is set out in Protocols 4 and 9 to the fifth Accession Treaty, 2003, for Lithuania and Slovakia respectively. For Bulgaria the relevant provision is contained in Article 30(1) of the sixth Accession Treaty, 2005.

---

[170] Commission *Staff Working Paper Fifth Annual Survey on the implementation and enforcement of Community environment law* SEC(2004) 1025, 27 July 2005.

[171] See ibid. at p. 12.

[172] See ibid. at p. 11.

[173] See ibid. at p. 14.

[174] See ibid. at p. 20.

[175] Judgements in ECJ Cases C-292/99 *Commission* v. *France* [2002] *ECR* I-4097 and C-35/00 *Commission* v. *UK* [2002] *ECR* I-953.

*The fifth Accession Treaty: the Ignalina and Bohunice power plants in Lithuania and Slovakia* Protocol 4 on the Ignalina Power plant in Lithuania[176] provides for the closure of Unit 1 before 2005 and Unit 2 before 31 December 2009. It also addresses the decommissioning of the plant as well as the consequences of the closure and decommissioning. Lithuania extracted a concession entitling it to revert to the general economic safeguard clause[177] until 2012 should it suffer disruptions in energy supply. So far, no such safeguards have been employed. Lithuania is also expressly entitled to grant state aid purposes of closing Ignalina.[178] EUR 285 million were allocated to Ignalina Programme under Article 2(5) of Protocol 4. The monies were to be used for decommissioning Ignalina but also for the environmental upgrading in line with the *acquis* and modernisation measures of the Lithuanian Thermal Power Plant in Elektrenai, which would replace Ignalina.

In the December of 2006, the Council adopted Regulation 1990/2006,[179] which afforded additional EU assistance of EUR 837 to Lithuania. The possibility for extending the assistance beyond 2006 was already foreseen in Article 3 of the Protocol, which recognises the exceptional financial burden on Lithuania compared to its size and economic strength. The same elements and principles set out in Protocol 4 apply for the 2007 to 2013 commitments. The 2006 Regulation reproduces these elements and principles, but it also adds other elements. The decommissioning must be carried out in line with the Environmental Impact Assessment Directive[180] allowing for public participation in national planning and large scale infrastructure projects. It also specifically provides for the auditing of the assistance to Lithuania by the Commission and the Court of Auditors and the European Anti-Fraud Office also has express auditing powers.[181] To

[176] See Protocol 4 to the fifth Accession Treaty, at p. 944. See P. Van Elsuwege, 'From Soviet Republics to EU Member States. A Legal and Political Assessment of the Baltic States' Accession to the EU', (Leiden, Martinus Nijhoff 2008) at pp. 332–335 and 475–481. See also P. Van Elsuwege, 'The Uncertain Future of the Ignalina Nuclear Power Plant: Lithuania's Obligations under the Treaty of Accession to the U', in *Teise*, (vol. 68) 2008, at pp. 155–162.

[177] See Art. 4 of the Protocol 4 to the fifth Accession Treaty.

[178] See Art. 2(8) of the Protocol 4 to the fifth Accession Treaty.

[179] See Council Regulation 1990/2006, first published in *OJ* 2006 L 411 and then published again in full as a corrigendum in February 2007, in *OJ* 2007 L 27/7.

[180] See Directive 85/337, as amended, op. cit. n. 102.

[181] See Art. 8 of Regulation 1990/2006, op. cit. n. 179.

do this, the Council used the legal basis of Article 56 of the 2003 Act of Accession for implementing adaptations to the *acquis* through the Act of Accession.

Protocol 4 – and Regulation 1990/2006 for that matter – expressly extends the availability of the economic safeguard measures to Lithuania until the end of December 2012 if Lithuania's energy supply is disrupted in that time. This same deadline also applies to Slovakia under Protocol 9 to the fifth Accession Treaty.

For Slovakia, Protocol 9 to the fifth Accession Treaty stipulates that Units I and II of the Bohunice VI nuclear power plant had to be closed by 31 December 2006 and 31 December 2008 respectively.[182] Slovakia was originally allocated EUR 90 million under that Protocol. Article 3 of Protocol 9 envisaged the extension of that funding. It obtained another EUR 423 million under Council Regulation 549/2007[183] which is not based on Article 56 of the 2003 Act of Accession but on Euratom financial Regulations.[184] Protocol 9 was not specific on the issue of the money and the 2007 Regulation added a number of conditions to the use of the money for environmental upgrading in line with the *acquis* and for the modernisation of conventional production capacity to replace Bohunice. It also provides for other measures to contribute to the restructuring, upgrading of the environment and modernisation of energy production, transmission and distribution sectors as well as enhancing security supply and energy efficiency.[185]

Moreover, the neighbouring countries of Germany and Austria declared the importance of continuing to monitor the new Member States' progress in implementing the recommendations for improvements in nuclear safety in Joint Declaration 20 to the fifth Accession Treaty[186] 'until a result is available'.[187] Another Joint Declaration by Austria and the Czech Republic concerning the construction of the Temelin nuclear power plant in the Czech Republic, commits the

---

[182] See the Protocol 5 to the fifth Accession Treaty at p. 954.

[183] See *OJ* 2007 L 131/1.

[184] See Council Regulation (Euratom) 1605/2002, *OJ* 2002 L 248/1 and Commission Regulation (Euratom), *OJ* 2002 L 657/1.

[185] See Regulation 549/2007, *OJ* 2007 L 131/1.

[186] At p. 978.

[187] On 10 December 2002, both Germany and Austria had stressed the importance of continued monitoring after enlargement at the General Affairs and External Relations Council, while the accession conferences were ongoing.

Czech Republic to their bilateral relations under the Melk Process.[188] The dispute between these two Parties over the construction[189] of the Temelin plant proved one of the most controversial negotiating points in the pre-accession negotiations, even after agreement between Austria and the Czech Republic on the Melk Protocol.[190]

*The sixth Accession Treaty: the Kozloduy power plant in Bulgaria*
Under Article 30(1) of the sixth Accession Treaty, Bulgaria was bound to close Units 1 and 2 of Kozloduy before 2003 and Units 3 to 4 by end 2006. This was done. However, in January 2009, public protests in Sofia called for the restart of the Kozloduy Units 3 and 4. Bulgaria was reported to have lost its entire gas supply because of the row between State-owned firms in Ukraine and Russia.[191] Temperatures in Bulgaria were below freezing. Ukraine and Greece delivered gas to Bulgaria, despite both Greece and Ukraine suffering dramatic cuts in their own gas supplies due to the dispute. Indeed the annual report of the IAEA on the Safety of Nuclear Installations (2002) reported that:

> A safety review mission to Kozloduy, in Bulgaria, reviewed the results of more than a decade of safety upgrades and assessments at units 3 and 4, including a series of actions recommended by various Agency review teams. The team concluded that the operational and design safety at Kozloduy now corresponds to the level of improvements seen at plants of similar vintage elsewhere. Many of the safety measures adopted for

[188] Co-operation in the field of radiological impact of severe accidents and emergency preparedness under the Protocol on the negotiations between the Czech and Austrian Governments led by the Prime Minister Zeman and the Federal Chancellor Schüssel with the participation of Commission Verheugen, signed in Melk on 12 December 2000, and known as the Melk Protocol. It is an ongoing process because it provides for road maps for their implementation and future co-operation in the field of emergency measures. The Melk process was based upon bilateral relations between these two countries since the beginning of the 1990s on information exchange in case of a nuclear emergency and national radiation monitoring networks.

[189] In the Melk Process they agree on the installation of an information hotline, the installation of an automatic air monitoring system in Cseke Budejovice with on-line data transmission to the Austrian Early Warning System and Environmental Impact Assessment for the Temelin plant. Various working groups were established for follow-up and future co-operation envisaged.

[190] See various reports on www.EurActiv.com; 'Austrian government in crisis over Czech nuclear plant', 23 January 2002, 'Almost a million Austrians want Czech nuclear plant to close', 22 January 2002, 'Austria's Freedom Party wants to renegotiate closure of Czech nuclear plant' 14 January 2002, 'Austria and the Czech Republic agree on Temelin nuclear plant', 30 November 2001, 'Austria and Czech Republic resolve nuclear dispute', 13 December 2000.

[191] Reported by the BBC, http://news.bbc.co.uk/2/hi/business/4587598.stm.

> these plants in the design, operation and seismic areas exceeded those that were foreseen.[192]

The World Nuclear Association maintains that the Union's conditionality about the closure of such nuclear reactors is more about western standards in western licensing agreements rather than about safety as such.[193]

Theoretically, Article 36 of the sixth Accession Treaty would provide a legal basis for Bulgaria to taking emergency protective measures if 'difficulties arise which are serious and liable to persist in any sector of the economy or which could bring about serious deterioration in the economic situation of a given area'. Bulgaria's Parliament gave the government the go-ahead to start this procedure at the end of January 2009. However, this is an EU level procedure and the measures must be taken by the European Commission – not the Member States in Council and without the European Parliament's involvement – and such measures would only be possible until the end of 2009.[194] There is no express clause in Article 36 to allow for the extension of that emergency procedure beyond the end of 2009. In March 2009 the Commission insisted that any unilateral decision by Bulgaria to reopen Kozloduy Units 3 and 4 would be in breach of the Accession Treaty.[195] Should Bulgaria opt unilaterally to reopen the two Kozloduy units, it would certainly find itself in breach of its obligations under the 2005 Accession Treaty.

Turning to the aftermath of closing the Kozloduy nuclear power plant, Bulgaria also committed itself to addressing certain consequences of the closure and decommissioning. A provision of EUR 210 million has been allocated for 2007–2009 (2004 prices) in commitment appropriations for the years 2007 to 2009. Article 30(2), sixth Accession Treaty, 2005, provides for:

> measures for environmental upgrading in line with the *acquis*; measures for the modernisation of the conventional energy sector, transmission and distribution sectors in Bulgaria; measures to improve energy efficiency, to enhance the use of renewable energy sources and to improve the use of energy supply.

---

[192] http://www.iaea.org/Publications/Reports/Anrep2002/safety_nuclear.pdf.

[193] See Early Soviet Reactors and EU Accession, January 2009, http://www.world-nuclear.org/info/inf44.html.

[194] See Chapter 4.3 of this volume.

[195] See Commission response to EP question put at the Strasbourg session of March 2009.

Indeed, the Transition Facility established for the twelve new Member States also supported measures to strengthen the effectiveness and competence of nuclear safety authorities and their technical support organisations as well as public waste management agencies.

However, in the case of Bulgaria, there is a clear post-accession conditionality mandate for the European Commission. The Commission is expressly entitled to adopt rules for the implementation of the EUR 120 million. In contrast to the approach taken under the 2003 Accession Treaty where the arrangements were contained in Protocols, the finer details of the financial support for Bulgaria under this subparagraph are worked out via the standard management comitology procedure. The total contribution of the EU, as solidarity, amounted to EUR 550 million for the period 2000–2009.[196] These funds are largely managed by the EBRD through the Kozloduy International Decommissioning Support Fund, to which other donors also contribute. Bulgaria also participates in and benefits from Phare-funded multi-country and horizontal programmes, such as the Nuclear Safety Programme.

Thus, the Union's post-accession conditionality as regards nuclear safety is underpinned by considerable financial incentives in addition to state aid derogations and the potential for emergency safeguard measures has been strictly limited.

To conclude, there is a certain contradiction in this conditionality due to the absence of nuclear EU or Euratom measures in the *acquis*. This underlines again the essentially political nature of the Union's conditionality both pre-accession and post-accession. The concerns raised by the Fifteen in respect of nuclear safety in the candidate countries resulted in the establishment of a demanding (and very costly[197] for the EU as much as the candidates/new Member States) pre-accession conditionality in a policy field where the Union's actual possibilities to take action are very restricted. It is an example of the different treatment of the new Member States compared to certain among the Fifteen that have always resisted expanding the scope of Union or

---

[196] See Europa website at http://ec.europa.eu/bulgaria/abc/pre_accession/additional_information/index_en.htm, visited on 31 March 2009.

[197] See Annex I to the Presidency Conclusions, Council Conclusions of the General Affairs and External Relations Council of 10 December 2002, *Bull EU*. 10–2002, in which the overall level of allocations EUR 70 million for each of the years 2004, 2005 and 2006 to Lithuania, EUR 20 million to Slovakia for each of the years 2004, 2005 and 2006. These countries have of course, to provide substantial investments themselves to top up this funding.

Euratom level input into their own legal regimes. The general task of co-operation at Euratom level being that of safety, is marked at the same time by the lack of a common Euratom standard for nuclear reactor safety.

### 2.2 *Transitional arrangements in the 2003 and 2005 Accession Treaties*

It has been apparent since the pre-accession strategy was enhanced in 1997 that transitional arrangements were unavoidable if the political momentum of accession was to be maintained. Before 1 May 2004, the acceding countries of the fifth enlargement had a considerable workload to complete. The fifth and sixth Accession Treaties to a certain extent continue the pre-accession conditionality for the first years after enlargement where the carrot of enlargement no longer exists as the incentive for compliance with the *acquis communautaire*.[198] Governance instruments and initiatives will therefore be vital to implementation and enforcement of the environment *acquis* in an enlarging Union.

#### 2.2.1 *Negotiating transitional arrangements*

Requests for transitional arrangements by the acceding countries were divided into three types by the Commission, as outlined earlier: acceptable, negotiable, and unacceptable.[199] During the negotiations it is made clear to the candidates that transitional arrangements are exceptional, limited in time and scope, and where they are acceptable, they must be accompanied by a plan with clearly defined stages for full application of the *acquis*, they must not involve amendments to the rules or policies of the Union and nor may they disrupt their proper functioning or lead to significant distortions of competition.

Because substantial efforts, including financing of large scale infrastructure projects, are required in order to apply the environment *acquis*, the transitional arrangements in the 2003 Accession Treaty for the environment *acquis* are second only in number to the agriculture chapter. As with any other transition arrangements, transitional arrangements concerning the environment *acquis* have been spread

---

[198] See P. Davies *European Union Environment Law; an Introduction to Key Selected Issues* (Wiltshire, Ashgate 2004) at pp 67–118.

[199] See Part 1 at Chapter 3, section 2.

over a definite period of time and they differ from one new Member State to another. Internal Market rules span various of the thirty-one chapters of the *acquis*, including the environment chapter.

The Commission refused as unacceptable any requests for transitional periods in the transposition of the environment *acquis*. Transposition of the *acquis* in its entirety was ruled out from the beginning of the negotiations and obviously posed fundamental problems for the functioning of the *acquis* in an enlarged Union. A transitional arrangement would be easily acceptable if it concerned only technical matters.

A transitional arrangement would only be negotiable where special circumstances justified them, such as the need for long term significant investment or other concerns. They must always be balanced with, *inter alia*, environmental concerns. The Commission made clear throughout the long negotiations with the twelve new Member States that it would only consider postponing the entry into force of specific legislation subject to a work programme that was properly justified and could feasibly be completed within the deadline of the transitional arrangement. Consequently, transitional derogations were simply not entertained in:

1. the transposition of legislation (as opposed to implementation);
2. framework legislation (air, waste, water, EIA, access to information);
3. nature protection (habitat, birds);
4. essentials of the Internal Market (all product-related legislation), and;
5. compliance by all new installations with the *acquis*.

Part of the incoming countries' pre-accession commitments is to pre-notify national implementing measures after the signature of the Accession Treaty and before its entry into force. For example, Bulgaria and Romania began to notify the European Commission of their national implementing measures at the end of 2005. This is done through the Community wide integrated system for electronic notification of national measures for the transposal of directives.

To illustrate the negotiations of transitional arrangements it is useful to take a few examples. When the Czech Republic was unable to show that it required major investment in order to comply with compliance limits set out in the Directive on the discharge of dangerous substances into water, the request was withdrawn.[200] The Commission refused outright to consider postponing the entry into force of conservation measures and all the horizontal or procedural measures, such as Environmental Impact Assessment Directive and the rules on public access to environmental information.

Estonia had sought a transitional derogations from Directive 92/43 on the conservation of natural habitats and of wild fauna and flora, to allow for the hunting of brown bear,[201] lynx,[202] wolf[203] and beavers,[204] where it had been legal in Estonia.

The Union easily accepted a technical adaptation to Directive 92/43 excluding the wolf, lynx and beaver populations in Estonia from the strict protection rules required for 'priority species' by the Directive under its Article 2.[205] Article 2 requires each Member State to designate special conservation areas to various species. It is designed to protect and conserve those species that are seriously threatened and this is assessed according to the proportion of their natural range within the European territory of the Member States. The technical adaptation frees Estonia from the obligation to designate conservation areas to these species. The temporary derogation was easily acceptable because of the extent of the populations of these animals in Estonia as well the variety of their habitats over a large area.[206]

However, the Union was not prepared to consider Estonia's request to introduce a derogation to allow the age-old practice of hunting and shooting of lynx and brown bears in Estonia. The capture or killing of such species must be banned in the Member States where this might cause the local disappearance of or serious disturbance to populations of such species. Estonia was able to justify a derogation from

---

[200] See Press Release of the Czech Ministry of the Environment, 4 June 2001, reporting on the negotiations on 1 June 2001.

[201] Ursus Arctos.

[202] Lynx lynx.

[203] Canis lupus.

[204] Castor fiber.

[205] Contained in Annex IV(a) of Directive 92/43 on the conservation of natural habitats and of wild fauna and flora, *OJ* 2003 L206/7.

[206] Already before the fifth enlargement Finland and Sweden were not required to establish conservation areas for beavers. For wolves, Finland did not have to have conservation areas and Spain was not required to establish a conservation areas south of the Duero, nor Greece, south of the 39th parallel. Finnish populations of Lynx lynx were also excluded. See Annex II to Directive 92/43, as last amended by Directive 97/62, *OJ* 1997 L 305/42.

Directive 92/43 to allow the continued hunting and shooting of lynx because it could justify these practices in terms of what is acceptable under Directive 92/43. Estonia provided the negotiating conference with scientific data proving the direct connection between the sizes of the lynx population and the roe deer population. The Union accepted that these practices contributed to the natural balance between the two populations, but the transitional arrangement is not open ended in time or scope and does not allow the hunting of lynx into (danger of) extinction. The country annex to the fifth Accession Treaty concerning Estonia provides for the review of the transitional arrangement and its possible revocation by 1 May 2009 with a qualified majority vote of the Member States acting on a proposal from the Commission.[207]

The hunting and shooting of brown bears was rejected as Estonia could not justify the legality of such practices under Directive 92/43. These animals must be strictly protected in Estonia under Article 12 of Directive 92/43, although already under Article 16(1) of the Habitats Directive, a Member State may allow the hunting of brown bears under specified circumstances and subject to the management procedures laid down in Article 16(2) and (3). A joint declaration of the Fifteen and Estonia attaches to the fifth Accession Treaty[208] reiterating the legal situation.

### 2.2.2 *Transitional arrangements in the environment* acquis

In the 2003 Accession Treaty, technical adaptations to various laws in order to apply the transitional arrangements to each of the candidates are provided for in Article 24 of the Act of Accession,[209] referring to

---

[207] By 1 May 2009, the Commission shall provide the Council with a report on the further application of the geographical exception for Lynx lynx under Annex IV of Directive 92/43 op. cit. n. 205, taking especially into account the sustainability of the population of Lynx lynx and its effects of sustainability on other wild species. The Council shall on this basis review the exception and may decide to terminate its further application acting by qualified majority on a proposal from the Commission.

[208] As regards brown bears, Estonia will comply fully with the requirements of Directive 92/43 on the conservation of natural habitats and of wild fauna and flora (Habitats Directive). By the latest upon accession, Estonia will establish a system of strict protection that complies with Article 12 of the said Directive.

While general hunting of brown bears could not be allowed, the Conference notes that under Article 16(1) of the Habitats Directive, Estonia may allow hunting of brown bears under specified circumstances and subject to the procedures laid down in Article 16(2) and (3).

[209] Act of Accession to the fifth Accession Treaty, Art. 54 expressly allows for the application of the time limits set out in Annexes V–XIV.

country Annexes V through to XIV for each of the ten Member States that acceded in 2004.

Each Annex relates to a different new Member State and, as was the procedure with previous enlargements, specifies the extent to which they are entitled to derogate from specified EU laws acts in line with the transitional arrangements agreed at the closure of accession negotiations at the December 2002 Luxembourg European Council. The derogations agreed do not relate to the entirety of a piece of legislation and are not the same for each new Member State. In the case of the sixth Accession Treaty with Bulgaria and Romania, the transitional arrangements for the environment *acquis* are contained in the Annexes VI and VII, A to D respectively.

The 2003 and 2005 Accession Treaties formally set down what was agreed at the close of the accession negotiations. The European Commission's *Guide to the Negotiations*[210] was published almost immediately after the 'closure' of the negotiations in December 2002. The Commission Report on the *Results of the Negotiations on the Accession of Bulgaria and Romania* was published in February 2005.[211] In no circumstances may the enforcement of national rules during the transitional periods lead to border controls between the Member States.[212]

The derogations in the chapter on the free movement of goods are also minimal and do not relate to the environment *acquis*.[213] Bulgaria and Romania have no transitional arrangements concerning the free movement of goods. Other derogations are far longer in duration and will involve considerable continued efforts, including financial. Table 4 on pages 279 to 288 summarises the transitional arrangements in the 2003 and 2005 Accession Treaties concerning the environment *acquis*.

---

[210] See n. 163, op. cit.

[211] See Commission document 5859/05, to be found at www.europa.eu.int/comm/enlargement/docs/pdf/result_of_neg_final_council_version_st05859_en0405.pdf.

[212] An Act of Accession forms an integral part of the Accession Treaty itself and contains the conditions of admission and adjustments to the Treaties on which the Union is founded. Act of Accession to the fifth Accession Treaty, at Article 40, reads: 'In order not to hamper the proper functioning of the internal market, the enforcement of the new Member States' national rules during the transitional periods referred to in Annexes V to XIV shall not lead to border controls between Member States.' This is the same text as in Art. 153 Act of Accession for Austria, Finland and Sweden. Act of Accession Bulgaria and Romania reads the same at Art. 40 with only technical wording differences.

[213] These relate only to licensing of medical equipment and the marketing authorisations for pharmaceutical products, concerning Malta, Cyprus, Poland and Slovenia.

*Exceptional state aid transitional arrangement for the environment* acquis: *Poland* Exceptionally, only Poland has been granted limited derogations from the general State aid rules within the body of the 2003 Act of Accession, in order to support necessary investments in meeting the environment *acquis*.[214] This is in addition to and complementary of Poland's derogation[215] in respect of large combustion plants until 2017. Poland's demands for a transitional period for 'Special Economic Zones' (SEZs) to 2017 proved contentious throughout the negotiations, as various European Parliament Resolutions go to show.[216] In the end, Poland secured limited aid ceilings for regional investments. Poland also secured transitional derogations from Articles 87 and 88 EC for certain state aids for environmental investments (alongside training and research and development). The transitional period only applies for the duration of the environmental transitional arrangement. In any case, reporting published on the Europa website show a dramatic decrease in environmental state aid by Poland.[217]

A regional ceiling applies with a 15 per cent supplement for small and medium-sized enterprises (SMEs). A 30 percent aid intensity is allowed until the end of 2010 for IPPC installations entitled to transitional arrangements and a 30 per cent aid intensity was permitted until 31 October 2007 for IPPC-related investments that were not covered by a transitional arrangement under the environment chapter. Large combustion plants that are subject to transitional arrangements were entitled to a state aid intensity of 50 per cent of investment.

No other Member State has agreed such transitional arrangements concerning the state aid provisions in respect of the environment *acquis*[218] – apart from Lithuania in respect of meeting its obligations

---

[214] See Annex XII ibid, at 5.1.(a)(II)(bb) and 5.2, at pp. 879–880.

[215] See Act of Accession to fifth Accession Treaty, Annex XII, 13.A.-E. at pp. 890–902.

[216] See EP Resolutions of 4 October 2000, 5 September 2001 and 13 June 2002.

[217] See Scoreboards and Date on State Aids, Reports and Studies of the European Commission to be found at http://ec.europa.eu/competition/state_aid/studies_reports/expenditure.html. Poland shows a drop in environmental spending from an annual average of EUR 46.6 million in 2002 to 2004 to EUR 7.5 million: http://ec.europa.eu/competition/state_aid/studies_reports/stat_table_pl.xls between 2005 and 2007. This is considerably less that expenditure in other EU Member States, see http://ec.europa.eu/competition/state_aid/studies_reports/ws3_31.xls.

[218] Bulgaria implements the state aid arm of competition policy on the date of accession. Romania has certain derogations in respect of fiscal aid measures for regional investments and the motor vehicle sector but there is no specific green nature to that aid other than is provided for in the general EC state aid regime.

to shut down the Ignalina power plant. In the sixth Accession Treaty, Bulgaria has not secured any derogations from the state aid rules and while Romania may provide state aids for regional investments and steel restructuring,[219] there is no specific mention of environmental investments as such.

Generally speaking, however, it is consistent with the principle of environmental integration that competition policy integrate environmental concerns and principles. State aid for environmental purposes may be possible by means of a derogation from the general prohibition on State aid, that derogation being provided for in Article 107(3)(b) TFEU. Such aid is subject to important limits and procedural requirements and must be declared compatible with Article 107(3)(b) TFEU by the European Commission.[220] The applicable Commission Guidelines on 'green' State aid at the time of both the fifth and sixth enlargements expired at the end of 2007. The new *Community guidelines on State aid for environmental protection* were issued by the Commission in 2008, following the expiry of the previous Guidelines. The state aid guidelines are one of many instruments designed to help meet the energy, climate change and sustainable development ambitions of the Union under the new Strategic European Energy Review and the Lisbon Agenda to create 'the most dynamic and competitive knowledge-based economy in the world, capable of sustainable economic growth with more and better jobs and greater social cohesion, and respect for the environment by 2010.'

The 2008 Guidelines emphasise that the primary objective of state aid in the field of the environment is:

- to reach a higher level of environmental protection than would occur without the aid, and;
- to ensure that the positive effects of the aid outweigh its negative effects in terms of distortions of competition, taking account of the Polluter Pays Principle.

---

[219] See Annex VII.4. A and B. to the Act of Accession of the sixth Accession Treaty, at pp. 316–318.

[220] See Information from the Commission, *Community guidelines on State aid for environmental protection*, *OJ* 2008 C 82/1. For the rationale underlying these new Guidelines, see the European Commission's *State aid Action Plan 2005–2009*, COM(2005) 107 of 7 June 2005. Prior to these new Guidelines, the situation was set out in the *Community guidelines on State aid for environmental protection*, *OJ* 2001 C 37/3–15, which were valid until 31/12/2007.

The mechanics of this 'balancing test' are set out at initially in Guideline 16 and followed up with further Guidance on putting the balancing test into practice.

*The fifth Accession Treaty: the example of Poland* It is useful to provide an example of the nature of the transitional arrangements set out in the fifth and sixth Accession Treaties. The below sections concentrate on Poland, as concerns the fifth Accession Treaty and then on Bulgaria and Romania as concerns the sixth. The Commission *Guide to the Negotiations* summarises succinctly the entirety of the thirteen countries' transitional arrangements. These are self-explanatory. As Table 4 below shows, the transitional arrangements differ from one country to the next. For example, under the conservation chapter of the environment *acquis*, in the case of the fifth enlargement only Malta had a derogation from Directive 79/409[221] allowing it to continue the trapping of songbirds between June 2005 and 31 December 2008, allowing time for the phase-out of traditional practices.

The thrust of the transitional arrangements are to allow the future new Member State the time to attract the often massive infrastructure investment required for implementing a Directive or to introduce new institutional structures and systems for the enforcement and monitoring of legislation. However, the transitional arrangements do not compensate for lacks in the capacity of the new Member States to maintain compliance and enforce the *acquis* once they have acceded to the Union. Taking the example of Poland, transitional arrangements in the environment *acquis* are fewer than Poland had originally intended. Referring to the country annex to the fifth Accession Treaty concerning Poland,[222] the derogations can be summarised as follows:

- Directive 99/32 on Sulphur Content of Liquid Fuels (until 31st December 2006).[223] The most challenging task for both this directive and the VOC Directive[224] is the introduction of a new institutional structure and systems for the monitoring and enforcement of the legislation. In the case of Poland, in the negotiations it was shown that the application of regular limits would raise specific techni-

[221] Op. cit. n. 104.
[222] See Act of Accession to the fifth Accession Treaty, Annex XII (Poland), 13.A–E.
[223] See Sulphur Contact of Liquid Fuels Directive, op. cit. n. 103.
[224] VOC Directive, op. cit. n. 113.

Table 4. Table of transitional derogations in the 2003 and 2005 Accession Treaties: environment *acquis*

WASTE MANAGEMENT

| Directive concerned | Relevant provision: expiry date for country derogation | Relevant provision: expiry date for country derogation | Relevant provision: expiry date for country derogation |
|---|---|---|---|
| Directive 94/62/EC on packaging and packaging waste, OJ 1994 L 365/2 | Art. 6(1)(a)&(b)<br>Expiry on 31 December 2005: Czech Republic, Cyprus, Hungary | Art. 6(1)(c), (d), (e)(i), (iv) & (v) | Art. 18<br>Expiry 31 December 2007: Malta |
| | Expiry on 31 December 2006: Lithuania | Art. 6(1)(c)<br>Expiry on 31 December 2009: Bulgaria<br>Expiry on 31 December 2011: Romania | |
| | Expiry on 31 December 2007: Latvia, Poland, Slovenia | Art. 6(1)(d)<br>Expiry on 31 December 2013: Romania<br>Expiry on 31 December 2014: Bulgaria | |
| | Art. 6(1)(a)<br>Expiry on 31 December 2007: Slovakia<br>Expiry on 31 December 2011: Bulgaria, Romania | Art. 6(1)(e)(i)&(iv)<br>Expiry on 31 December 2013: Bulgaria, Romania | |
| | Expiry on 31 December 2009: Malta | Art. 6(1)(e)(v)<br>Expiry on 31 December 2011: Romania | |
| | Art. 6(1)(b)<br>Expiry on 31 December 2013: Romania<br>Expiry on 31 December 2014: Bulgaria | | |

Table 4 (*cont.*)

| Directive concerned | Relevant provision: expiry date for country derogation | Relevant provision: expiry date for country derogation | Relevant provision: expiry date for country derogation |
|---|---|---|---|
| Directive 91/271/EC on urban waste water treatment, OJ 1991 L 135/40 | Arts. 3, 5 & 5(2):<br>Expiry on 31 December 2010: Czech Republic | | |
| Directive 1999/31 on landfill of waste, OJ 1999 L 182/1 | Art. 2(g), 2nd indent<br>Expiry on 31 December 2004: Latvia<br>Expiry on 31 December 2009: Romania | Art. 5(3)(a)+(b), Art. 14(d)(i)<br>Expiry on 16 July 2009: Estonia | Art. 14(c) + Annex I at 2, 3, 4 +6<br>Expiry on 30 June 2012: Poland |
| | | Art. 5(3)(a)+(b) & Annex I.2, 2nd indent<br>Expiry on 31 December 2013: Romania<br>Expiry on 31 December 2014: Bulgaria | |
| Regulation 259/93 on waste shipments, OJ 1993 L 30/1 | Art. 7(4)&Annexes II, III + IV<br>Expiry on 30 June 2005: Hungary | Annex II, waste for recovery<br>Final expiry on 31 December 2014: Bulgaria | |
| | Expiry on 31 December 2005: Malta | Final expiry on 31 December 2015: Romania | |
| | Final expiry on 31 December 2009: Bulgaria | | |
| | Expiry on 31 December 2010: Latvia | | |

Table 4 (*cont.*)

| Directive concerned | Relevant provision: expiry date for country derogation | Relevant provision: expiry date for country derogation | Relevant provision: expiry date for country derogation |
|---|---|---|---|
| | Expiry on 31 December 2011: Slovakia | | |
| | Expiry on 31 December 2012: Poland | | |
| | Art. 7(4) &Annex III<br>Expiry on 31 December 2011: Romania (with a possible extension to 31 December 2015) | | |
| Directive 2000/76 on the incineration of waste,<br>OJ 2000 L 332/91 | Arts. 6, 7(1) and 11<br>Final expiry on 31 December 2008: Romania | | |
| Directive 2002/96 on waste electrical and electronic equipment (WEEE),<br>OJ 2003 L 37/24<br>[In respect of the 2004 enlargement, adopted under Art. 55, 2003 Accession Treaty, see Council Decisions 2004/312 and 2004/486,<br>OJ 2004 L 100/3 and L162/114 respectively] | Art. 5(5)&7(2)<br>Expiry on 30 April 2006: Cyprus, Czech Republic, Estonia, Hungary, Latvia, Lithuania, Malta, Poland, Slovenia, Slovakia<br>Possible extension of 12 months: Slovenia<br>Expiry on 31 December 2008: Bulgaria, Romania | | |

Table 4 (*cont.*)

INDUSTRIAL POLLUTION PREVENTION AND CONTROL

| Directive concerned | Relevant provision: expiry date for country derogation | Relevant provision: expiry date for country derogation |
|---|---|---|
| Directive 87/217 on asbestos,<br>OJ 1987 L 85/40 | Art. 8, 2nd indent<br>Expiry on 31 December 2004: Latvia | |
| Directive 2001/80 on emissions from large combustion plants, OJ 2001 L 309/1 | Art. 4(1), Part A Annexes III & VII,<br>Expiry 31 December 2004: Hungary | Art. 4(3), Part A, Annexes III & VII<br>Final expiry on 31 December 2015: Estonia, Lithuania |
| | Art. 4(1), Part A Annexes VII<br>Expiry 31 December 2005: Malta | Art. 4(3), Part A, Annexes III & IV |
| | Art. 4(1), Part A Annex III, Expiry 31 December 2007: Slovakia, (Czech Republic, including Parts A, Annexes IV, V, VI & VII) | Expiry on 31 December 2013: Romania<br>Expiry on 31 December 2015: Poland |
| | | Art. 4(3), Part A, Annexes III, IV& VII<br>Expiry on 31 December 2014: Bulgaria |
| | | Art. 4(3) Part A, Annexes IV&VI<br>Expiry on 31 December 2015: Lithuania<br>Art. 4(3) Part A, Annex VI<br>Expiry on 31 December 2011: Bulgaria<br>Expiry on 31 December 2017: Romania<br>Art. 4(3) Part A, Annex VII<br>Expiry on 31 December 2017: Poland concerning limit values that will apply only in 2016<br>Expiry on 31 December 2013: Romania |
| | | Art. 4(3) Part A, Annexes IV, unspecified expiry date for Cyprus |

Table 4 (*cont.*)

| Directive concerned | Relevant provision: expiry date for country derogation | Relevant provision: expiry date for country derogation |
|---|---|---|
| Directive 1996/61 on integrated pollution prevention and control (IPPC), OJ 1996 L 257/26 | Art. 3<br>Expiry on 30 October 2007: Latvia | Art. 5(1) & Art. 9(3)&(4)<br>Final expiry on 31 December 2008: Latvia<br>Final expiry on 31 December 2010: Poland<br>Final expiry on 30 October 2011: Slovenia<br>Final expiry on 31 December 2011: Bulgaria, Slovakia<br>Final expiry on 31 December 2015: Romania |
| Directive 1994/07 on the incineration of hazardous waste, OJ 1994 L 365/34 | Arts. 7 + 11<br>Expiry on 30 June 2005: Hungary | Arts. 7+11 + Annex III (and Arts. 6, 7(1) and 11 of Directive 2007/76)<br>Expiry on 31 December 2006 |

Table 4 (*cont.*)
AIR QUALITY

| Directive concerned | Relevant provision: expiry date for country derogation | Relevant provision: expiry date for country derogation | Relevant provision: expiry date for country derogation | Relevant provision: expiry date for country derogation |
|---|---|---|---|---|
| Directive 94/63/EC on Volatile Organic Compounds, OJ 1994 L 364/ 24 | Art. 3 + Annex I<br>Expiry on 31 December 2005: Estonia,Poland<br>Final expiry on 31 December 2007: Lithuania, Slovakia<br>Final expiry on 31 December 2008: Latvia, Romania<br>Final expiry on 31 December 2009: Bulgaria | Art. 4 + Annex II<br>Expiry on 31 December 2004: Malta, Poland<br>Expiry on 31 December 2006: Estonia<br>Final expiry on 31 December 2007: Lithuania, Slovakia<br>Final expiry on 31 December 2008: Latvia Final expiry on 31 December 2009: Bulgaria, Romania | Art. 5<br>Expiry on 31 December 2005: Lithuania, Poland<br>Expiry on 31 December 2007: Slovakia<br>Expiry on 31 December 2008: Latvia<br>Final expiry on 31 December 2009: Bulgaria, Romania | Art. 6 + Annex III<br>Expiry on 31 December 2004: Latvia, Malta, Poland<br>Expiry on 31 December 2006: Estonia<br>Final expiry on 31 December 2007: Lithuania, Slovakia<br>Expiry on 31 December 2008: Latvia<br>Expiry on 31 December 2009: Romania |
| Directive 1999/32/EC on the sulphur content of certain liquid fuels, OJ 1999L 121/13 | Art. 3(1)<br>Expiry on 30 April 2005: Cyprus<br>Expiry on 30 December 2006: Poland<br>Expiry 31 December 2011: Bulgaria | Art. 4(1)<br>Expiry on 30 April 2005: Cyprus<br>Expiry on 31 December 2009: Bulgaria | Arts. 3(2), 3(5), 4(2) & 4(4)<br>Potential future derogations possible | |

Table 4 (*cont.*)
WATER QUALITY

| Directive concerned | Relevant provision: expiry date for country derogation | Relevant provision: expiry date for country derogation |
|---|---|---|
| Directive 82/176 on mercury discharges by the chlor-alkali industry, OJ 1982 L 81/29 | Art. 3 + Annex I<br>Expiry on 31 December 2007: Poland, Slovakia | |
| Directive 83/513 on cadmium discharges, OJ 1983 L 291/1 | Art. 3 + Annex I<br>Expiry on 31 December 2007: Poland | |
| | Art. 3 + Annexes I + II<br>Final expiry on 31 December 2007: Malta | |
| Directive 84/156 on cadmium discharges by other sectors, OJ 1984 L 74/49 | Art. 3 + Annex I<br>Expiry on 31 December 2006: Slovakia<br>Expiry on 31 December 2007: Poland<br>Expiry on 31 December 2009: Romania | |
| Directive 84/491 on discharges of hexachlorocyclohexane, OJ 1984 L 274/11 | Art. 3 + Annex I<br>Expiry on 31 December 2009: Romania | |
| Directive 86/280 on discharges of dangerous substances, OJ 1986 L 1811/16 | Art. 3 + Annex II (partial)<br>Expiry on 31 December 2006: Slovakia<br>Final expiry on 31 March 2007: Malta<br>Final expiry on 31 December 2007: Poland, Slovakia<br>Expiry on 31 December 2009: Romania | |

Table 4 (*cont.*)

| Directive concerned | Relevant provision: expiry date for country derogation | Relevant provision: expiry date for country derogation |
|---|---|---|
| Directive 1991/271 on urban waste water treatment,<br>OJ 1991 L 135/40 | Art. 3<br>Expiry on 31 December 2006: Malta<br><br>Art. 4<br>Expiry on 31 December 2007: Malta<br>Arts. 3, 4 & 5(2)<br>Expiry on 31 December 2009: Lithuania<br>Expiry on 31 December 2010: Czech Republic, Estonia,<br>Expiry on 31 December 2012: Cyprus<br>Expiry on 31 December 2014: Bulgaria<br>Expiry on 31 December 2015: Latvia, Hungary, Slovenia, Slovakia<br>Expiry on 31 December 2018: Romania | Art. 13<br>Expiry on 31 December 2008: Hungary<br>Expiry on 31 December 2010: Poland |
| | Arts. 3, 4, 5(2) & 7<br>Expiry on 31 December 2015: Poland | |
| Directive 98/83/EC on the quality of water for human consumption,<br>OJ 1998 L 330/32 | Arts. 5(2) and 8 + Annex I, Part C<br>Expiry on 31 December 2005: Malta<br>Expiry on 31 December 2013: Estonia<br>Expiry on 31 December 2015: Latvia, Romania | Art. 9(1)<br>Expiry on 31 December 2009: Hungary |

Table 4 (*cont.*)

NATURE PROTECTION

| Directive concerned | Relevant provision: expiry date for country derogation |
|---|---|
| Directive 92/43/EC on conservation of natural habitats and wild flora and fauna, OJ 1992 L 206/7 | Annex IV, (Lynx lynx) Expiry on 1 May 2009: Estonia |
| Directive 79/409/EEC on conservation of wild birds, OJ 1979 L 103/1 | Arts. 5(a), (e) 8(1) + Annex IV(a) Final expiry on 31 December 2008: Malta |

NUCLEAR SAFETY

| Directive concerned | Relevant provision: expiry date for country derogation | Relevant provision: expiry date for country derogation |
|---|---|---|
| Directive 97/43/Euratom on ionionising radiation in medical exposure, OJ 1997 L 180/22 | Art. 8 Expiry on 31 December 2006: Poland | Arts. 8+9(1) Expiry on 31 December 2006: Latvia |
| Protocol 4, fifth Accession Treaty, 2003 on the Ignalia nuclear power plant in Lithuania, OJ 2003 L 236/944 | Close unit 1 by 31 December 2004: Lithuania | Close unit 2 by 31 December 2009: Lithuania |

Table 4 (*cont.*)

| Directive concerned | Relevant provision: expiry date for country derogation | Relevant provision: expiry date for country derogation |
|---|---|---|
| Protocol 9, fifth Accession Treaty, 2003 on Unit 1 and Unit 2 of the Bohunice VI nuclear power plant in Slovakia, OJ 2003 L 236/954 | Close unit 1 by 31 December 2006: Slovakia | Close unit 2 by 31 December 2008: Slovakia |
| Article 30(1), sixth Accession Treaty, 2005 Kozloduy nuclear power plant in Bulgaria | Close Units 3 and Unit 4 by 31 December 2006: Bulgaria | |

Tables indicating the acceding countries' temporary derogations from certain provisions of the environment and nuclear safety and radiation protection *acquis*, together with the expiry dates for compliance therewith in accordance with pre-accession commitments.
Note: the derogations mush be read carefully in the Accession Treaty itself as often the derogations from any given provision are further restricted and specified in the relevant country annex and are not wholesale derogations from a given provision of the *acquis*.

cal and economic problems. Moreover, this directive is linked to other directives, notably the Large Combustion Plants Directive,[225] which is also be subject to a transitional arrangement, allowing time to attract the necessary investments. This derogation is designed to draw in the crucial investment and financing required but it must not bring about any negative effects on the market in gas and oil.

- Directive 94/63[226] on Volatile Organic Compound Emissions from Storage and Distribution of Petrol (until 31st December 2005). The most challenging task for this directive is the introduction of a new institutional structure and systems for the monitoring and enforcement of the legislation. It also involves local actors in the new Member States. Operators of petrol terminals, service stations and petrol transports are also involved in the implementation of technical and management requirements to minimise vapour losses from the handling of petrol.
- Directive 94/62 on Packaging Waste[227] (until 31 December 2007). Compliance will require the building of infrastructure for the separation and re-use of waste and the modernisation of existing incineration plants. Among other things, this is due to the lack of EU pre-accession funding for such projects coupled with the limited finances of public finance sources in the regions or local authorities responsible for management and implementation.
- Directive 99/31 on Landfill[228] (until 1 July 2012, with target quantities specified each year until the cut-off date of 2012). The most difficult and costly aspects of implementing this directive relate to the administration and establishment of sufficient facilities for the reduction of biodegradable municipal waste to be land-filled and wastes that may no longer be put in landfills. Unsatisfactory landfills have to be phased out, involving considerable maintenance costs, and restoration and aftercare costs. In a study financed by the Commission, the entire cost for Poland alone for meeting the requirements of this directive was estimated at EUR 3.5 billion, of which 60 per cent would have to be used for the aftercare of the existing landfills and closing down others.[229]

---

[225] Large Combustion Plants Directive, op. cit. n. 26.

[226] VOC Directive, op. cit. n. 113.

[227] Packaging Waste Directive, op. cit. n. 32.

[228] Landfill Directive, op. cit. n. 113.

[229] See DISAE Project POL-101 *Costing and financial Analysis of Approximation*, (Agriconsulting Europe June 1998).

- Directive 93/259[230] on Waste Shipments (until 31 December 2012). Poland has a transitional arrangement because of the problem of disposing of its own waste due to the lack of waste disposal infrastructure and the level of investment required to remedy this.
- Directive 91/271 on Urban Waste Water Treatment (until 31 December 2015).[231] Sewers and wastewater treatment facilities must be built and the timeframe will depend upon the availability of finance and construction engineering resources in Poland, hence the 2015 deadline.
- Directive 76/464 on the Discharge of Certain Dangerous Substances into Surface Water (until 31 December 2007), including the amending legislation on mercury discharges from the chlor-alkali electrolysis and other industries as well as that on cadmium discharges.[232] Full compliance requires investment to bring existing plants up to a level of operation that will allow them to meet the directive's emission limit values or quality objectives – in some cases new plants will have to be built. The thrust of the directive is to establish and enforce systems for the monitoring and measuring of pollution of water by certain dangerous substances throughout the entire country. However, where results are unfavourable the directive envisages that remedial action must be taken, which in turn depends very much on the investment timescale available to construct improvement works at the plants concerned. The Commission agrees to the terms with the operators.
- Directive 96/61 on Integrated Pollution Prevention and Control (until 31 December 2010 instead of 2007 for existing Member States).[233] Costs involved in compliance and proper implementation

[230] Council Regulation 259/93 on the supervision and control of shipments of waste within, into and out of the European Community, *OJ* 1993 L 30/1, as amended.

[231] See Urban Waste Water Treatment Directive, op. cit. n. 28.

[232] See Discharge of Certain Dangerous Substances into Surface Water Directive, op. cit. n. 113. The derogations apply to following Directives, which detail the limits values for discharges of certain chemicals into the waters specified in Directive 76/464, op. cit. n. 113, namely: Council Directive 82/176 on limit values and quality objectives for mercury discharges by the chlor-alkali electrolysis industry, *OJ* 1982 L 081/29, Council Directive 83/513 on limit values and quality objectives for cadmium discharges, *OJ* 1983 L 291/1, Council Directive 84/156 on limit values and quality objectives for mercury discharges by sectors other than the chlor-alkali electrolysis industry, *OJ* 1984 L 74/49 and Council Directive 86/280 on limit values and quality objectives for discharges of certain dangerous substances included in List I of the Annex to Directive 76/464, *OJ* 1986 L 181/16.

[233] See IPPC Directive, op. cit. n. 27.

of the Directive are incurred by operators and the administration. For the administration, the setting up of administrative arrangements for the allocation and implementation of permits is a heavy and costly task and requires that a number of operations are already fully functioning in order that the system can be properly evaluated. Also, compliance requires the negotiation of best available techniques (BAT) with the various industrial sectors to identify the viability of the processes. For operators, considerable capital expenditure is required and, inevitably, the detailed planning, design, permitting and construction of new or upgraded facilities to conform with the new standards will be required. Constructing plants in accordance with BAT, including pollution abatement facilities, at new installations will be required by operators, as will alterations to existing plants to incorporate BAT and pollution abatement facilities. Finally, all new plants must meet the BAT requirements while existing plants normally must meet the requirements of the Directive after 2004.

- Directive 88/609,[234] as amended on Air Pollution from Large Combustion Plants (until 2017). The costs for competent national authorities of compliance with this directive are significant. But the costs involved for operators in complying with the directive and abating emissions will be many times higher. Costs for the competent authorities are to be gathered from operators in line with the polluter pays principle. As for installations and plants, it is the adaptation of existing installations that will prove the greatest stumbling block.
- Directive 97/43/Euratom[235] on nuclear safety (until 31 December 2006). A derogation from Article 8 provides that the provisions on radiological equipment shall not apply in Poland until 31 December 2006. Such equipment shall not be placed on the market of other Member States.

Other environment-related derogations are also contained in other chapters of transitional arrangements. For example, Poland also had a derogation from agriculture legislation concerning certain information

[234] See Large Combustion Plants Directive, op. cit. n. 26.

[235] Council Directive 97/43/Euratom on health protection of individuals against the dangers of ionizing radiation in relation to medical exposure, and repealing Directive 84/466/Euratom, *OJ* 1997 L 180/22.

requirements under the 1991 Directive on Marketing of Plant Protection Products until the end of December 2006.[236] Bulgaria had no transitional period for this Directive while Romania has a transitional period until 31 December 2009 for the use of four active substances (copper compounds, sulphur, acetochlor and dimethoate) contained in plant protection products. Additionally, Romania may use the active substance 2.4-D in plant protection products until end December 2008 if that active substance has been included in Annex I to Directive 91/414.[237]

*The sixth Accession Treaty and the examples of Bulgaria and Romania* The sixth Accession Treaty introduced its own transitional arrangements for the environment *acquis* in Annexes VI and VII for Bulgaria and Romania respectively, which have also been incorporated into Table 4.[238] Again, the transitional arrangements are mainly justified by the financial costs involved in investments in infrastructure and technology and in particular to make up for lacking or insufficient investments. However, these transitional arrangements are exceptional, are intended to have limited transboundary impact, will not lead to significant distortions of competition and are subject to binding intermediate targets so that they may be controlled by the Commission throughout the entire transition period. Moreover, the scope of the transitional arrangements is specified by reference to lists of the installations concerned and detailed financial strategies underpin them.

- Directive 94/63[239] on Volatile Organic Compound Emissions from Storage and Distribution of Petrol for both Bulgaria and Romania with staggered deadlines for compliance between end 2007 and 2009.[240] Priority is given to implementation in terminals and stations with the larger throughput in order to reduce the environmental impact efficiently.

---

[236] Fifth Accession Treaty, Annex XII at 884.
[237] Loc. cit. n. 266.
[238] See Act of Accession Bulgaria and Romania, Annex VI.10.A–D. (Bulgaria), pp. 292–301, and Annex VII. A–D. (Romania), pp. 330–631.
[239] VOC Directive, op. cit. n. 113.
[240] See Annex VI.10 for Bulgaria and Annex VII.9 relating to Romania.

- Directive 99/32[241] on Sulphur Content of Liquid Fuels (end 2011 for heavy fuel oils, and end 2009 for gas oils) Bulgaria is allowed to use these heavy fuels for local use only, having a higher sulphur content that Directive 99/32 permits. This is in line with the intended transition of all Member States to phase-out the sulphur content of liquid fuels referred to earlier.
- Directive 94/62 on Packaging Waste. The transition periods end between end-2009 and to end 2013 for Romania and to 2014 for Bulgaria. The rationale is the same as applies to Poland above.
- Regulation 259/93 on Waste Shipments.[242] Romania has derogations from various provisions from between end December 2011 and 2015. For Bulgaria the derogations run between end 2009 and end 2014. These arrangements are designed to prevent the dumping of waste that does not meet the EU standards. National competent authorities can object to waste shipments under the procedures for shipments of disposal of waste until the EU standards are met. Moreover, waste cannot be imported to Bulgaria until 2009 and Romania until 2011, which should allow these countries the time to build up the necessary recovery and recycling capacity.
- Directive 1999/31 on Landfill of Waste.[243] Staggered deadlines apply to Romania from between end 2006 and end 2016. For Bulgaria, 14 facilities benefit from derogations until end December 2014. These derogations exempt Romania from requirements for the temporary storage of hazardous waste. Full implementation of the municipal waste provisions by Romania will be end 2016 compared to 2009 for other Member States. Certain derogations apply to landfill of non-hazardous liquid wastes (Romania 2013 and Bulgaria 2014) although the general provisions of the waste framework Directive apply as of accession.
- Directive 2002/96 on Waste Electrical and Electronic Equipment (WEEE).[244] Romania and Bulgaria have until end 2008 to reach full compliance with certain collection, recovery and reuse/recycling targets. The same deadline applies for meeting the 4 kg collection rate. This in line with the dates applicable to thirteen of the (twenty-five) Member States.

---

241 Op. cit. n. 103.

242 Regulation 259/93, op. cit. n. 230.

243 *OJ* 1999 L 182/1, as amended. Op. cit. n. 113.

244 Op. cit. n. 36.

- In the field of Water Quality, Directive 83/513[245] on Cadmium Discharges and Directive 84/156[246] on Mercury Discharges. Romania has certain less restrictive limit values for discharges in respect of certain installations.
- Directive 84/491 on Quality Objectives for Hexachlorocyclohexane.[247] Romania has derogations for certain installations for discharges of lindane into certain waters until end 2009.
- Directive 86/280 on Discharges of Dangerous Substances.[248] Romania has derogations until end 2009 for discharged of hexachlorobenzene, hexachlorobutadiene, 1,2 – dichloroethane (EDC), trichloroethylene (TRI) and trichlorobenzene (TCB) for certain installations.
- Directive 91/271 on Urban Waste Water Treatment.[249] The derogations for Romania are various and run to between end 2010 and 2015. Bulgaria has a target of end December 2014 for cull compliance of collecting systems and treatment of urban waste.
- Directive 98/83 on the Quality of Drinking Water.[250] Romania's derogations are various and run between end 2010 and 2015. Bulgaria has no derogation in respect of this Directive.
- In the field of industrial installations, the longest derogation for certain Romanian installations, comparable to derogations given to certain Polish installations, is 2017 for Directive 2001/80[251] on Air Emission from Large Combustion Plants. The deadlines for compliance of Bulgarian installations varies between end 2009 and end 2014.
- Directive 2000/76 on the Incineration of Waste.[252] Romania has a general derogation from emission limit values and requirements for measurements until end 2007 and for medical waste until end 2008.
- Derogations for certain Bulgarian and Romanian installations from full compliance with the IPPC Directive 96/61[253] run from between 30 October 2007 and end 2014. However, Bulgaria and Romania will apply integrated permitting by 31 October 2007.

---

245 Op. cit. n. 232.
246 Op. cit. n. 232.
247 *OJ* 1984 L 274/11, as amended.
248 Op. cit. n. 232.
249 Op. cit. n. 28.
250 *OJ* 1998 L 330/32, as amended. Op. cit. n. 113.
251 Op. cit. n. 104.
252 *OJ* 2000 L 332/91, as amended.
253 Op. cit. n. 27.

### 2.2.3 *Adaptations to the environment* acquis *and new transitional derogations*

Due to the fact that the *acquis* is constantly evolving, the candidates are 'approximating' to a moving target and the references of the *acquis* legislation may well change between signature of an accession treaty and the date of accession, where new *acquis* measures have been adopted between 1 November 2002[254] and signature of the Accession Treaty. Chapter 4 in the first part of this book, at 4.3, deals with 'adaptations 'to the *acquis* after the signature of an accession Treaty. This is more about adapting annexes to the Accession Treaty containing transitional arrangements to take account of evolutions in the *acquis* before accession rather than to add further derogations to the country annexes.

Also as mentioned in Chapter 4, in the fifth and sixth Accession Treaties, Article 55 of the Act of Accession is generally applicable and allows, at the duly substantiated request of a new Member, additional 'temporary derogations' to be added to those agreed in Council during accession negotiations but only in respect of new *acquis* measures that were adopted after the closure of the negotiations. Thus, further transitional derogations may be adopted in respect of specific legislation, such as in the case of the Directive on waste electrical and electronic equipment.[255] The Cyprus, Czech Republic, Estonia, Hungary, Latvia, Lithuania, Malta, Poland and Slovakia have all been given a 24 month extension (i.e. until 31 December 2008) for the separate collection of waste electrical and electronic equipment (WEEE) from private households[256] and also for reaching the minimum targets for the recovery of WEEE for component, material and substances reuse and recycling.[257]

---

[254] This was just after the 2002 Commission Country Reports that formed the basis for the December 2002 negotiations, where the transitional arrangements were agreed.

[255] Directive 2002/96, op. cit. n. 36, as amended by Directive 2003/108, *OJ* 2003 L 345/106. The temporary derogations are contained in Council Decision 2004/312 granting Czech Republic, Estonia, Hungary, Latvia, Lithuania, Slovakia and Slovenia temporary derogations from Directive 2002/96 on waste electrical and electronic equipment, *OJ* 2004 L 100/33. See also Council Decision 2004/486 providing the same derogation to Cyprus, Malta and Poland, *OJ* 2004 L 162/114.

[256] Art. 5(5) Directive 2002/96 requires the separate collection of at least four kilograms on average per inhabitant per year of WEEE equipment from private households.

[257] Art. 7(2) Directive 2002/96 sets these targets.

Bulgaria and Romania have secured the same deadline of 2008. Slovenia was given until 31 December 2007 to do the same. While the Council Decision is based on Article 55 of the Act of Accession, the WEEE Directive in any case specifically allows for such derogations on grounds such as infrastructure deficit, low population density and level of consumption of electrical and electronic equipment and geographical circumstances. These reasons make it all the harder for such countries to meet the recovery and recycling targets. This is also why Ireland and Greece were granted extensions.[258]

In the case of the 2002 Regulation on collecting waste statistics,[259] the regulation itself provides a legal basis for temporary derogations[260] from the obligation upon individual Member States to provide data on the generation, recovery and disposal of waste within the first two to three years of the Directive's life. Again, such derogations have been granted other Member States already.[261]

### 3. Performance of the new Member States in EU environment *acquis* after accession

Due to the fact that so much of the environment *acquis* has been adopted after the accessions of Greece, Spain and Portugal, there was little example in practice of transitional arrangements in the environment *acquis*. Austria, Finland and Sweden, however had higher standards in environment law and policy. Their accession on 1 January 2004 was an opportunity for the twelve Member States to raise certain standards in the environment *acquis* to meet the higher standards of these countries. For completeness' sake it is useful to look at how these transitional arrangements impacted on the evolution of the standards.

---

[258] In fact, application has to be made under Art. 5(2) of Council Directive 1999/312 on the landfill of waste, op. cit. n. 113, for an extension of the deadline up to a maximum of 24 months.

[259] Regulation 2150/2002 on waste statistics. *OJ* 2002 L 332/1.

[260] Art. 4(2) ibid.

[261] Regulation 317/2004 on adopting derogations from the provisions of Regulation 2150/2002 on waste statistics as regards Austria, France and Luxembourg, *OJ* 2004 L 55/43, Commission Regulation 574/2004 amending Annexes I and III to Regulation 2150/2002 on waste statistics *OJ* 2004 L 90/15, Regulation 1829/2004 adopting derogations from the provisions of Regulation 2150/2002 on waste statistics with regard to Belgium, Portugal, Greece and Cyprus, *OJ* 2004 L 321/24.

The Accession Treaty involved transitional arrangements to enable these countries to maintain their higher standards than certain EU environment laws during a four-year review period,[262] beginning the date of accession and lasting until 31 December 1998. The higher standards concerned eleven amendments to nine directives. It was not necessary to amend measures adopted under the legal basis for the environment, Article 191 TFEU, which in any case allows for more stringent national measures. The review clause gave the European Commission and the receiving Member States four years to revise the Community standard upwards to the levels of Austria, Finland or Sweden. However, a literal reading of the review clause gave no guarantees to the new members that the Union standard would indeed be raised: '[a]t the end of the transitional period…the *acquis* will be applicable to the new Member States under the same conditions as in the present Member States.'[263]

It was political pressure that enabled Austria, Finland and Sweden to maintain their higher standards after the review period. The review[264] even went to conciliation between the Council and Parliament in the last months of the transitional period.[265] While four of these Directives[266] were amended by technical amendment[267] in order

[262] Act concerning the conditions of accession of the Kingdom of Norway, the Republic of Austria, the Republic of Finland and the Kingdom of Sweden and the adjustments to the Treaties on which the European Union is founded, Arts. 69, 84 and 112

[263] Ibid., Arts. 69, 84 and 112.

[264] See Commission Communication *The Review Clause: environmental and health standards four years after the accession of Austria, Finland and Sweden to the European Union* COM(1998) 745, 11 December 1998.

[265] Decision 2179/98/EC of the European Parliament and of the Council on the review of the European Community programme of policy and action in relation to the environment and sustainable development 'Towards sustainability', *OJ* 1998 L 275/1–13. See also the European Parliament's Resolution of 4 July 1996 on the review clause, *OJ* 1996 C 211/20.

[266] Directive 67/548 on the classification, packaging and labelling of dangerous substances, as amended, *OJ* 1967 L196/1; Directive 91/414 on the placing on the market of plant protection products, as amended, *OJ* 1991 L 230/1 ('Plant Protection Products Directive'); Directive 76/769 on marketing and use of dangerous substances and preparations, as amended, *OJ* 1976 L 262/02; and Directive 91/157 on batteries and accumulators, as amended, *OJ* 1991 L 78/38.

[267] Derogations were also extended by two years, for example in the case of Directive 67/548 by Directive 1999/33/EC of the European Parliament and of the Council amending Council Directive 67/548 as regards the labelling of certain dangerous substances in Austria and Sweden, *OJ* 1999 L 199/57.

to incorporate the higher standards, the remaining Directives[268] had to be revised substantially according to the full co-decision procedure involving Parliament and Council. Legally speaking, however, in five cases, these new members had their derogations extended – to all intents and purposes – as opposed to raising the overall EU standard.

In the case of cadmium content in fertilisers, the approach was first to extend the transitional derogation for Austria, Finland and Sweden from the relevant measures until December 2001 under the full co-decision procedure.[269] Thereafter, the derogation has, effectively, been extended by means of the notification and authorisation procedure under Article 114(4) TFEU.[270] Moreover, the 2003 Fertilizers Regulation,[271] which repealed and replaced the previous fertilizers law as of 2005, was drafted in such a way as to allow Austria, Finland and Sweden to maintain their standards in accordance with the Commission Decision under Article 114(4) TFEU.

Directives 88/379 and 78/631 on classification, packaging and labelling of dangerous preparations and pesticides were both repealed and replaced in 1999 by Directive 1999/45. That directive effectively extended the derogations that Austria, Finland and Sweden were given under their Accession Treaties in order to allow them to maintain their higher standards.[272] Austria, Finland and Sweden are now subject to

[268] Council Directive 78/631 on the approximation of the laws of the Member States relating to the classification, packaging and labelling of dangerous preparations (pesticides) *OJ* 1978 L 206/13; Council Directive 88/379 on the approximation of the laws, regulations and administrative provisions of the Member States relating to the classification, packaging and labelling of dangerous preparations, *OJ* 1988 L 187/14; Plant Protection Products Directive 91/414, op. cit. n. 266, Council Directive 76/116 on the approximation of the laws of the Member States relating to fertilizers, *OJ* 1976 L24/21; Council Directive 85/210 on the approximation of the laws of the Member States concerning the lead content of petrol, *OJ* 1985 L 096/25 ('Lead Content of Petrol Directive'); op. cit. n. 103.

[269] Directive 98/97 of the European Parliament and of the Council amending Directive 76/116 on the approximation of the laws of the Member States relating to fertilisers, as regards the marketing in Austria, Finland and in Sweden of fertilisers containing cadmium, *OJ* 1999 L18/60–61.

[270] See Commission Decision 2002/398 on the national provisions notified by the Republic of Finland under Article 95(4) of the EC Treaty concerning the maximum admissible content of cadmium in fertilisers, *OJ* 2002 L138/15–23.

[271] Regulation 2003/2003 of the European Parliament and of the Council relating to fertilisers, *OJ* 2003 L304/1–194.

[272] See Annex VIII to Directive 1999/45 of the European Parliament and of the Council concerning the approximation of the laws, regulations and administrative

the Article 114 procedures to maintain their higher standards or further raise these standards.[273] Finally, Directive 1999/45 also introduced new provisions on classification and labelling of pesticide preparations, which incorporated the higher standards contained in the derogations for Austria, Finland and Sweden from Directive 91/414 on the placing on the market of plant protection products.[274]

As for the Directives 93/12 on the sulphur content of certain liquid fuels[275] and 85/210 on the lead content of petrol,[276] Austria, Finland and Sweden had higher standards for gas oils. The overall EU standard was raised but Greece was given a special five-year derogation and Austria's derogation allowing it to maintain stricter standards in respect of the benzene content of petrol, was prolonged until 1 January 2000.[277] In any case, Directive 98/70 introduced a specific provision – (Art. 6) allowing Member States to apply more stringent environmental specifications to the marketing of fuels – but did not raise the average environmental specification. However, Directive 2003/17 was agreed following the success of Sweden and Finland in the tax differentiation on petrol in order to encourage low-sulphur fuels.[278] The tax differentiation relating to the quality of diesel and petrol is allowed EU wide now, so that sulphur-free fuel should be widely available as of 2005 and mandatory as of 2009. There is no obligation to sell sulphur-free fuels although Member States may introduced mandatory requirements to introduce such fuel.

Therefore, already before the 2004 and 2007 enlargements, the Member States proved resistant to raising the EU to that of the highest standards and reverted to building flexibility into the relevant EU laws to enable individual Member States to proceed at different

provisions of the Member States relating to the classification, packaging and labelling of dangerous preparations, *OJ* 1999 L200/1.

[273] See for example Commission Decision 2002/398 on the national provisions notified by the Republic of Finland under Article 95(4) of the EC Treaty concerning the maximum admissible content of cadmium in fertilisers, *OJ* 2002 L138/15.

[274] See Plant Protection Products Directive, op. cit. n. 266.

[275] See Sulphur Content of Certain Liquid Fuels Directive, op. cit. n. 103.

[276] See Lead Content of Petrol Directive, op. cit. n. 268.

[277] See Article 14 of Directive 98/70 of the European Parliament and of the Council relating to the quality of petrol and diesel fuels and amending Council Directive 93/12, *OJ* 1998 L 350/58–68 and subsequent corrigendum, *OJ* 1999 L 40/52–52, which amended the 1993 Directive.

[278] See Directive 2003/17 amending Directive 98/70 relating to the quality of petrol and diesel fuels, *OJ* 2003 L 76/10.

speeds. Moreover, it was more political embarrassment that maintained the flexibility necessary to enable Austria, Finland and Sweden the leeway to keep their higher standards. The actual room left to Member States to pursue higher national standards for the environment has been given a degree of legal certainty as a result of amendment to the Internal Market legal basis by the Amsterdam Treaty. It introduced a notification and approval procedure for such national measures, within Article 114 TFEU, managed by the European Commission – although it in turn introduced new questions, particularly concerning Member States' room to manoeuvre to raise environment standards.[279] Austria, Finland and Sweden have thus limited their scope of manoeuvrability in Internal Market laws to raise their national environmental standards.

So, the Union has sought to allow the incoming Member States to keep their higher environmental standards in spite of the agreement in the Accession Treaty that the higher standards would fall after the transitional period. However, the means found to do so took longer than the transitional period. The higher standards of the newcomers did not raise the EU-wide standard to the higher standard.

Nevertheless, there has been much progress in the construction of the environment *acquis* with the participation of Austria, Finland and Sweden in the European Union. By comparison, section 3.2 briefly explores the implications of the 2004 and 2007 enlargements for the continued evolution of the environment *acquis*.

### 3.1 *The feasibility of the pre-accession commitments*

The benefits of the 2004 and 2007 enlargements in terms of improving legal standards in human health and the environment are considerable and the progress made by the new Member States in these areas is remarkable. The pre-accession commitments of the new Member States were to achieve full approximation with the environment *acquis* with the only exceptions being the provisions for which transitional arrangements applied. Nevertheless, this section highlights the fact that much outstanding work remained to be completed by the twelve new

[279] On the deficiencies in legal certainty as well as the conflict between national measures and EC harmonisation measures and the impact of the control procedure on national law, see N. de Sadeleer, 'Procedures for derogations from the principle of approximation of laws under Article 95 EC', 40 *CML Review* (2003) at pp. 908–913.

Member States between signature and entry into force of the fifth and sixth Accession Treaties beyond the provisions subject to transitional arrangements. Reading the programme of work to be achieved by the candidates in the Commission's 2002 country reports, however, it was clear that the candidates had indeed to be 'vigourous' before the end of April 2004. The fifth and sixth Accession Treaties were signed without transitional arrangements in areas where the incoming countries had even basic tasks to complete in order to apply the *acquis*. It was clear at the time of the closure of accession negotiations in 2002 that the candidates for the fifth enlargement were not fully prepared in those areas where transitional arrangements were precluded. Pre-accession efforts were required of the new Member States in all areas of the *acquis*, not just in the environment *acquis*, including in respect of the laws that could not be derogated from as well as in terms of the adequacy of their administrative and judicial capacity.

In the six months before accession, the Commission's *2003 Comprehensive Monitoring Report*[280] highlighted the need for 'enhanced efforts' even in transposition of legislation (including, to name a few, the EIA Directive - Malta, Cyprus and Poland - or the nature protection rules) and administrative capacities in most fields. In a very brief overview, that same *2003 Comprehensive Monitoring Report* read:

> In the field of environment policy, Estonia in particular must now increase efforts to complete legal alignment with EU rules on air quality, waste management, nature protection, industrial pollution and radiation protection.[281] Other countries must enhance efforts in specific fields: waste management in Malta, nature protection in the Czech Republic, Cyprus, Hungary, Malta and Poland; industrial pollution and risk management in Hungary, Poland and Slovakia; and genetically modified organisms in Cyprus.[282]

Transposition is the easier of these tasks, although some of the Commission's annual monitoring reports on the progress made by the candidate countries highlighted delays in transposition, even of framework legislation.

---

[280] European Commission, *2003 Comprehensive Monitoring Report, 5 November 2003*, without any official publication reference, found at www.europa.eu.int/comm/enlargement/report_2003/index.htm#comprehensive.

[281] Ibid., at 10.

[282] Op. cit. n. 280 at 13.

Slovenia, Lithuania and Latvia were conspicuous by their absence from the above overview because generally they had made satisfactory progress. However, they too had work to complete in the eighteen months remaining until their accession. Slovenia had, in addition to transitional arrangements, still to transpose the Environmental Impact Assessment Directive[283] together with adequate administrative capacity for applying it, to create inventories for discharges of dangerous substances into water, to implement habitats and birds legislation, to complete the transposition and implementation of legislation concerning industrial installations, to introduce new legislation on ambient noise, to establish authorisations for biocides and to adopt a 'significant amount of implementing legislation' in the field of nuclear safety and radiation protection.[284] Lithuania[285] and Latvia[286] too had transposition, implementation and capacity building work to do in a cross section of the categories of the environment *acquis*. This also raises enforcement issues, in particular the need to have the experience and governmental capacity to apply it.

As already note earlier, under the pre-accession rationale and methodology for the accession negotiations, transitional derogations were simply not entertained in:

1. the transposition of legislation (as opposed to implementation);
2. framework legislation (air, waste, water, EIA, access to information);
3. nature protection (habitat, birds);
4. essentials of the Internal Market (all product-related legislation), and;
5. compliance by all new installations with the *acquis*.

However, Commission reporting on the implementation of the *acquis* reveals that the situation has not been as clear cut as this and points at the emergence of 'informal' transitional arrangements for the new Member States where they were not in compliance with their pre-accession commitments on the date of their accession.

---

[283] Council Directive 85/337, op. cit. n. 102.
[284] See the 2003 Country Report on Slovenia at pp. 37–39.
[285] See the 2003 Country Report on Lithuania at pp 42–44.
[286] See the 2003 Country Report on Latvia at pp. 43–45.

*The example of Poland*

It is useful to take the example of Poland – the largest new Member State of the fifth enlargement wave in 2004 – to illustrate the list of outstanding work to be done which was not open to transitional arrangements after accession. Poland had considerable work still to do between December 2002 and its accession in 2004.[287] Referring to the 2002 and 2003[288] progress reports drawn up by the Commission for Poland, by 30 April 2004, the below table gives an indication of the work that Poland must have undertaken before its accession to the EU.

Table 5. Indicative summary of the list of work outstanding by Poland in the eighteen months leading up to its accession on 1 May 2004

- complete transposition for: horizontal legislation, air quality directives; water quality framework *acquis*; biocides; solvents; large combustion plants; nature protection; some waste management, GMOs, ambient noise;
- improve implementation for waste management, water quality including nitrate pollution, industrial pollution control and major industrial accident hazards, nature protection, chemicals, biocides;
- improve environmental integration into the definition and implementation of all other sectoral policies so as to promote sustainable development (specified only in the 2002 report);
- improve administrative capacity for implementing the environmental acquis through additional staff resources, making the Polish voivodships and counties fully operational and completing the creation of the national and 16 regional Environmental Impact Assessment Commissions;
- ensure issuance of and compliance with IPPC integrated permits – a significant challenge for the regional and local authorities as about 70 percent of the installations covered by the IPPC Directive will have to be dealt with at district level;[289]

[287] The Commission's reports on the progress of all the candidate countries were published on 13 December 2002 and was to found at www.europa.eu.int/comm/enlargement/report2002/#report2002 until 2007. A draft of this report can still be found at http://ec.europa.eu/enlargement/5years/documents/background/negotiations_report_to_ep_en.pdf The final report on the conclusion of the accession negotiations in the cases of Bulgaria and Romania of February 2005 can be found at http://ec.europa.eu/enlargement/archives/pdf/result_of_neg_final_council_version_st05859_0405_en.pdf

[288] Ten separate European Commission *Comprehensive Country Reports*, 5 November 2003, for each of the Ten (without official publication reference) can be found at www.europa.eu.int/comm/enlargement/report_2003/index.htm#paper2003.

[289] To do this there is an urgent need for training staff at regional and district level in issuing integrated permits, notably as regards: process-issues and technology; some staff increases; clear guidelines from central authorities on how to implement the new laws, and; the newly established Centre for 'Best Available Techniques' needs of more staff.

Table 5 (*cont.*)

| |
|---|
| – improve environmental planning and programming;[290]<br>– improve monitoring capacity;[291]<br>– improve environmental inspectorates;[292]<br>– agree on improvement programmes for fines and enforcement with the environmental authorities – an important incentive to operators and a source of financing to authorities, and;<br>– improve investments.[293] |

Primary Source: European Commission Reports for 2002 and 2003 on its preparedness for accession

*The examples of Bulgaria and Romania*

For Bulgaria and Romania, the outstanding work in the environment *acquis* before their accession was outlined in the Commission's 2004 reports on their progress in preparing for accession to the Union.[294] Already in 1997, specifically in relation to Bulgaria and Romania the European Commission concluded that:

> compliance with the *acquis* presupposed a positive turn in the economic situation of the CEECs and would require greater consistent emphasis on environmental issues, large-scale investment, together with the development of comprehensive, cost-effective and focused environmental strategy and of adequate implementation and enforcement structure.

[290] While the situation is improving and deadlines have been set to establish plans and programmes required under the *acquis* (preparation of programmes for air quality, the national waste management plan), regional and district plans still need to be improved.

[291] For air, the monitoring capacity needs to be strengthened, in particular as regards particulates (PM10); for water, monitoring of drinking water needs to be extended and all laboratories must be able to measure the full set of parameters under the Drinking Water Directive, op. cit. n. 113.

[292] Referring to the 2002 Report, op. cit. n. 287, although well-established and well-staffed, they needed a transfer of staff from laboratories to monitoring and inspection in some cases. The frequency of inspections also needed to be improved, in particular for small and medium-sized installations. (Nonetheless, large installations were sufficiently inspected and voivodship inspectorates have a good basis for planning and carrying out inspections and for ensuring follow-up to non-compliance.)

[293] See 2002 Commission *Progress Report for Poland*, op. cit. n. 287 at p. 109. 'Poland needs a more strategic approach to environmental investments with clear investment planning and listing of priorities. Considerable investments need to be secured, also in the medium term, to ensure the implementation of the environment *acquis*'.

[294] Commission Regular Report on Bulgaria's progress towards accession, COM(2004) 1199 final, 6 October 2004, not published in the *OJ*. Commission Regular Report on Romania's progress towards accession, COM(2004) 657 final, 6 October 2004, not published in the *OJ*.

> It was estimated that if such a strategy was followed, full transposition of the *acquis* could be expected in the medium to long term [...] however, effective compliance with legislation requiring a sustained high level of investment and considerable administrative effort (e.g. waste water treatment, drinking water, aspects of waste management and air pollution) could be achieved only in the very long term.[295]

The Commission noted[296] Bulgaria's steady progress in transposing and implementing the *acquis* but pointed out that efforts were still needed in particular regarding air and water quality, the management of dangerous substances and chemicals. In the same report the Commission noted that Romania has made good progress in aligning its legislation with the *acquis* but that additional efforts are required to fully implement the legislation in key sectors such as air quality, waste management and water quality. Particular attention also needs to be given to implementation, especially in capacity building by establishing the necessary administrative structures and securing investment.

In the overall assessments for Bulgaria and Romania in 2004, a considerable body of work also remained to be completed before 2007, including:

- transposition of air, waste, water, IPPC, biocides, noise, nuclear safety and radiation protection;
- carry out air assessments regarding air quality and action plans and monitoring systems;
- improve environmental integration into the definition and implementation of all other sectoral policies so as to promote sustainable development;
- improve administrative capacity for implementing the environmental *acquis* through additional staff resources (waste, water, nature protection, IPPC, chemicals and GMOs);
- improve investments, including in the medium term.

Given the amount of work outstanding for the twelve new Member States on the eve of their accessions, two questions arise. Were the pre-accession commitments given by the twelve new Member States realistic? Are the transitional arrangements feasible? The definitive

[295] Quote taken from the two Commission reports on Bulgaria and Romania 2004, ibid. at p. 112 and 120 respectively.
[296] Op. cit. n. 294 at pp. 110–113.

answer to these questions will remain open until all the transitional arrangements in the environment *acquis* have expired, which is some years ahead. It is possible to explore the answers to these questions by looking at the Commission's monitoring reports on the application of the *acquis* in 2005, 2006 and 2007. Exploring the answers to these questions makes it possible to draw conclusions on the strengths and weaknesses of the pre-accession strategy in terms of the application and continued evolution of the environment *acquis* in an enlarging Union.

*Indicators of approximation performance of the new Member States*

The Commissions reports on the application of the *acquis* for 2005, 2006 and 2007 reveal instances where new Member States were clearly not ready to meet the commitments that they gave on the date of their accessions. They also reveal whether the new Member States are continuing to meet their pre-accession commitments to apply the environment *acquis*. Only one Internal Market measure belonging to the environment *acquis* was listed by the European Parliament as not having been transposed on the date of the fifth enlargement:[297] this was Directive 1987/219[298] on the sulphur content of liquid fuels.

Already in 2005, however, the Commission reported[299] that, alongside various infractions found in the cases of the 'old' Member States:

- Slovakia had not transposed the *Strategic Environment Impact Assessment*[300] Directive by July 2004.
- Cyprus, the Czech Republic, Hungary, Malta and Slovakia had not transposed the Directive 2003/35 on *public participation in plans and projects*[301] (this Directive was adopted one month after signature

[297] See Chapter 7 at 3.1, referring to the draft Report of Małgorzata Handzlik MEP, rapporteur to the European Parliament Committee on the Internal Market and Consumer Protection (IMCO), issued her draft report on the Internal Market in the new Member States in December 2004.

[298] *OJ* 1987 L 91/19.

[299] See Commission Communication, *23rd annual report on national implementation of EU law*, COM(2006) 999 of 24 July 2006, pp. 45–61.

[300] Concerning the SEA Directive 2001/42 on the assessment of the effects of certain plans and programmes on the environment, *OJ 2001 L 197/30*, which compliments Directive 85/337, op. cit. n. 102.

[301] Directive 2003/35 providing for public participation in respect of the drawing up of certain plans and programmes relating to the environment and amending with

of the 2003 Accession Treaty but no transitional arrangement was agreed for this Directive).

- Infringement proceedings were initiated against Cyprus, Estonia, Hungary, Malta and Poland concerning failure to report, or inadequate reporting, under the Decision on the *monitoring mechanisms for greenhouse gas emissions* implementing the Kyoto Protocol.[302]
- Malta had failed to transpose the 2003 Directive concerning the reduction *of emissions from new passenger cars*,[303] also adopted after the signature of the 2003 Accession Treaty.
- Under the *PCB/PCTs* Directive,[304] already in 2005 formal letters of notice were sent to various of the new Member States concerning failures in drawing up plans for the safe disposal of equipment containing these substances, as well as outlines for the collection and disposal of equipment not subject to an inventory: Cyprus, Czech Republic, Estonia, Hungary, Latvia, Lithuania, Malta, Poland and Slovakia.
- Malta had not transposed the *WEEE* Directive.[305]
- Hungary had not transposed the 2003 Directive on *access to environmental information*[306] (giving effect, in part, to the Aarhus Convention[307] and adopted before the signature of the 2003 Accession Treaty).
- The Czech Republic was sent a letter of formal notice for non-conformity with the *IPPC* Directive.[308]
- As for the *SEVESO II* Directive concerning the prevention of major industrial accident hazards, Cyprus, Czech Republic, Hungary, Poland and Slovenia had failed to transpose a 2003 amendment to the Directive.

---

regard to public participation and access to justice Council Directives 85/337 and 96/61, *OJ 2003 L 156/17.*

[302] Decision 280/2004 concerning a mechanism for monitoring Community greenhouse gas emissions and for implementing the Kyoto Protocol, *OJ* 2004 L 49/1.

[303] Directive 2003/73 amending Directive 1999/94, *OJ* 2003 L 186/34.

[304] Directive 96/59, *OJ* 1996 L 243/31.

[305] Directive 2002/96, op. cit. n. 36.

[306] Directive 2003/4 on public access to environmental information, *OJ* 2003 L 41/26.

[307] Op. cit. n. 107.

[308] Op. cit. n. 27.

- And the Czech Republic had failed to implement the 2002 Directive on *environmental noise pollution.*[309]

The Commission's monitoring report on the application of the *acquis* for the year 2006 revealed various problems with the new Member States transposition and application of the environment *acquis.* Again, no transitional arrangements were agreed oncerning these provisions in the 2003 and 2005 Accession Treaties. Cases of lacking or poor transposition were reported. Cyprus, the Czech Republic, Hungary, Latvia, Lithuania, Malta, Poland and Slovenia were all the subject of cases launched by the European Commission for bad transposition of the *EIA provisions*[310] (alongside nine of the Fifteen Member States). Poland had shortcomings in its national legislation on *drinking water*[311] (alongside seven of the Fifteen Member States). The new Member States were also reported to have acceded to the ranks of non-compliant 'old' Member States in the case of the Directive on the *energy performance of buildings*, a key measure in the battle against climate change:[312] the Commission launched actions in 2006 against 22 of the 27 Member States for incomplete transposition of the Directive.

In terms of poor implementation or non-compliance various examples also arose in parts of the environment *acquis* for which no transitional arrangements were agreed:

- for the *wild birds Directive*[313] was identified in Cyprus, the Czech Republic, Estonia, Hungary, Latvia, Lithuania, Poland and Slovakia
- As for the *protected habitats Directive,*[314] Cyprus, the Czech Republic, Malta, Poland, Slovakia and Slovenia, national implementing legislation was found not to be in compliance with the Directive
- Poland was sent a final warning letter for not having designated special protected areas under the *wild birds Directive* and had not proposed sites of EU importance under the *habitats Directive.* After its accession, Poland had also launched eight road projects in North

[309] Directive 2002/49 relating to the assessment and management of environmental noise, *OJ* 2002 L 189/12.
[310] Op. cit. n. 102.
[311] Op. cit. n. 113.
[312] Directive 2002/91, *OJ* 2003 L 1/65.
[313] Directive 79/409, op. cit. n. 105.
[314] Directive 92/43, op. cit. n. 205.

East Poland which flouted both the wild birds and habitats Directives and invited a further challenge from the European Commission in 2006. Malta was challenged for illegal bird hunting of migratory birds in the spring.
- Hungary was challenged in respect of its implementation of the *Emissions Trading Scheme Directive*.[315]

Turning to the most recent Commission monitoring report on the application of the *acquis*, reporting for 2007, in the environment *acquis* alone there were 125 new infringement actions brought by the European Commission against the Member States. The year 2007 began with 739 open cases before the European Court of Justice concerning the environment *acquis*.[316] To that number, 461 cases were added to the list in the course of 2007. While traditionally the conservation laws (including the birds and habitats *acquis*) made up for between 20 and 25% of the cases in the environment chapter, various governance initiatives of the Commission have actually reduced this percentage dramatically in spite of the 2004 enlargement to take in the ten new Member States. At the end of 2007, of the total number of cases open in respect of the environment *acquis*, 235 concerned the conservation *acquis*.

For the new Member States, the following actions were reported in 2007. Again these provisions of the environment *acquis* were not open to negotiation for transitional arrangements. In terms of incorrect or lack of transposition, the Commission reported a number of instances of 'informal transitional arrangements':

- The three Baltic States were found to have incorrectly transposed the *WEEE* Directive.[317]
- Lithuania and Malta has not correctly transposed the *RoHS* Directive on the restriction of hazardous substances and electrical and electronic equipment.[318]

---

[315] Directive 2003/87, *OJ* 2003 L 275/32.

[316] See COM(2008) 2854 of 18 November 2008.

[317] Op. cit. n. 36. See Commission Press Release, *Waste: Commission starts legal action against eight Member States over electronic waste and hazardous substances*, IP/07/1513 of 17 October 2007.

[318] See Commission Press Release IP/07/1513, ibid.

- The Commission noted that cases concerning the non-conformity of national implementing measures for the *EIA Directives* now mostly concern the twelve new Member States.[319]
- The Commission services report the need for 'clearer and more complete national implementing provisions of the *drinking water directive*' from the new Member States.
- Nine of the ten new Member States that acceded in 2004 were brought by the Commission before the ECJ because of bad transposition of the *SEVESO II* Directive on the control of major-accident hazards involving dangerous substances.[320]
- Twelve Member States including Cyprus, the Czech Republic and Malta, were also brought before the ECJ for failure to adopt emergency plans for chemicals plants, as required under *SEVESO II* – 8,000 upper tier installations under SEVESO still require emergency plans[321]
- Horizontal legal action concerning non-conform transposition of Directive 90/219 on the contained use of *GMOs*, as amended, (Directive 90/218 on deliberate release of GMOs is commented on in Chapter 7 of this volume)
- As at October 2007, Latvia, together with France, had not notified measures transposing the Directive on the energy performance of buildings.[322]

In terms of bad implementation of and conformity with EU rules, the Commission reported the following for 2007:

- First written warnings were sent to Cyprus, the Czech Republic, Hungary, Latvia, Lithuania, Malta and Slovenia for not designating enough *Special Protected Areas*, while Poland was brought before the ECJ on this same matter. Romania failed to designate any Special

[319] See COM(2008) 2845, op. cit. n. 316.

[320] Directive 96/82 on the control of major-accident hazards involving dangerous substances, *OJ* 1997 L 10/13.

[321] See Commission Press Release, *Major industrial accidents: Commission continues infringement proceedings against 12 Member States over failure to adopt emergency plans for chemical plants*, IP/07/1534 of 17 October 2007.

[322] Directive 2002/91, *OJ* 2003 L 1/65. See Commission Press Release, *Performance énergétique des bâtiments: la Commission intente une action à l'encontre de la France et de la Lettonie*, IP 07/1525 of 17 October 2007.

Protected Areas for migratory and vulnerable wild birds and was already the subject of Court action in October 2007 for this.[323]

- The case against Poland concerning the road project in contravention of various Directives including the EIA Directive, was only dropped in 2007 pending the final judgment of the ECJ in the case.
- The challenge against Malta for *illegal bird hunting* graduated to Court action in 2007[324] and a similar case against Cyprus was closed when such illegal hunting was no longer legal under national law.[325]
- Concerning the *landfill of waste* Directive, first warning letters for incorrect transposition were sent to all of the ten new Member States that joined in 2004, except for Slovakia.[326]
- Bulgaria was sent a first warning letter for failing to provide an adequate system for *domestic waste disposal*, in particular lack of infrastructure.[327]
- Slovenia, which negotiated no transitional derogations from Directive 1999/32 on the *sulphur content of liquid fuels*, is the subject of infringement proceedings concerning sulphur dioxide.[328]
- Twenty-five Member States were reported in 2007 for achieving the binding limit values for *particulate matter (PM10)* concentrations in the air (not including Bulgaria and Romania, for which the reporting obligations only applied from 2007 onwards).[329]
- As for the Ozone Regulation 2037/2000,[330] cases were launched in 2007 against Malta and Cyprus for non-decommissioning of halons used in fire-extinguishers in ships.

---

[323] See Commission Press Release, *Nature protection: Commission takes legal action against Romania for infringement of biodiversity legislation*, IP/07/1508 of 17 October 2007.

[324] See ECJ, Case C-508/06, *Commission* v. *Malta*, [2007] *ECR* I-172.

[325] See Commission Press Release, *Nature protection: Commission takes legal action over spring hunting in Malta, closes Cyprus case*, IP/07/1509 of 17 October 2007.

[326] The Commission's Annual Report for the year 2007, at 6.2.2.3, highlights the fact that landfill accounts for 90% of waste in the twelve new Member States.

[327] See Commission Press Release, *Waste: Commission opens infringement case against Bulgaria over inadequate waste infrastructure in Sofia*, IP/07/1539 of 17 October 2007.

[328] Op. cit. n. 103. See Commission Press Release, *Air pollution: Commission takes action over levels of sulphur dioxide and PM10 in member states* IP/07/1537 of 17 October 2007.

[329] See Commission Press Release, IP/07/1537, ibid.

[330] Regulation 2037/2000 on substances that deplete the ozone layer, *OJ* 2000 L 244/1.

Without attempting an exhaustive survey of the state of transposition of and compliance with the entire environment *acquis* by the new Member States, further instances of infringements of the new Member States with Treaty obligations have since been reported. For example, Slovenia, together with eight 'old' Member States, was taken to court for failing to have transposed the 2004 *environmental liability* Directive,[331] adopted the weak before its accession. Hungary is being taken to task in respect of *illegal logging* in Sajólád Wood in Eastern Hungary.[332] In 2007 the Commission embarked on the preliminary stages of proceedings against Bulgaria for failure to implement the 2006 *Waste Framework Directive* – adopted after signature of the 2005 Accession Treaty but before Bulgaria's accession – and the failings had not been remedied in October 2008.[333] Bulgaria was also taken to task in 2008, for failure to properly apply the *wild birds Directive*.[334]

### 3.2 *Do weaknesses in the pre-accession strategy undermine the application and continued evolution of the environment* acquis *in an enlarging Union?*

*Agenda 2000* sought to ensure both the maintenance and continued evolution of the environment *acquis* in an enlarging Union. Certain conclusions can be drawn from these findings in terms of the strengths and weaknesses of the pre-accession strategy and certain lessons can be learned for the negotiation of future accession treaties. These concluding sections comment on the implications of all of this for the future evolution of the environment *acquis*.

[331] Directive 2004/35 on environmental liability with regard to the prevention and remedying of environmental damage, OJ 2004 L 143/56. See Ends at http://www.endseurope.com/index.cfm?action=main.search&indexTerm=200, visited on 27 June 2008.

[332] Commission Press Release, 'Environment: Commission warns Greece and Hungary over nature protection shortcomings', IP/08/1538 of 16 October 2008. See Directive 2006/12/EC on Waste, of 5 April 2006, *OJ* 2006 L 114/9 and Directive 79/409 on wild birds, op. cit. n. 105.

[333] See Commission Press Release, Environment: Commission warns Bulgaria about poor environmental performance, IP/08/1826 of 27 November 2008.

[334] See Commission Press Release IP/08/1826, ibid.

### 3.2.1 *Transitional arrangements in the environment* acquis*: another governance challenge in an enlarging Union?*

As Table 4 shows, numerous transitional arrangements introduced by the 2003 and 2005 Accession Treaties had not expired at the end of 2007, the last year for which the Commission has published findings on the application of the *acquis* by the Member States. Therefore, it is till too early to fully assess the feasibility of the longer term transitional arrangements concerning the Directives on Large Combustion Plants, Integrated Pollution Prevention and Control, Volatile Organic Compounds, urban waste water treatment and drinking water as well as two wild birds and habitats Directives. This is also the case for the sulphur content of liquid fuels Directive as concerns Bulgaria and certain Directives on water quality in the case of Romania.

More worrying however, is the emergence of 'informal transitional arrangements', which effectively give the new Member States extra time to fully apply different environment laws pending the completion of legal action. The brief synopsis above points out the unfeasibility of a number of the pre-accession commitments made by various of the new Member States and which concern core provisions of the environment *acquis* at the time of closure of accession negotiations. This highlights an important weakness in the pre-accession strategy: that the rationale and methodology for negotiating of transitional arrangements was not entirely fit for the purpose of ensuring that incoming Member States were fully able to take on the rights and obligations of the environment *acquis* on the date of their accession. This puts increased administrative burdens on Commission services in the post-enlargement phase for following up in any failures in transposition and implementation.

The Governance challenge in the case of the environment *acquis* is unique. The issues that arise in the monitoring and enforcement of the environment *acquis* contrast with other chapters of the *acquis communautaire*. The fifteen Member States themselves have long held a poor track record in meeting their Treaty obligations in respect of the environment *acquis*. The governance challenge in the environment *acquis* is about the lack of transposition and implementation of the environment *acquis* as much as the lack of national level governance tools and capacity. For example, the inadequate or a complete lack[335]

[335] The European Commission has published a variety of studies on the various approaches in the Fifteen and the new Member States, as candidate countries,

of criminal penalties and sanctions in national law for the purposes of giving effect to EU environment law motivated the Commission proposed a directive on the protection of the environment through criminal law in 2001,[336] obliging the Member States to adopt a minimum level of criminal penalties for breaches of certain EU environment laws. It led to a dispute as to Community competence in criminal matters before the European Court of Justice, which was only resolved with a combination of two judgments in 2005 and 2007.[337] The ECJ ruled that Community action in criminal matters may be justified where it is necessary in order to combat serious shortcomings in the national implementation of Community common or sectoral policies or the four freedoms. However, that action should be restricted to what is necessary to ensure the full effectiveness of a Community policy or the proper functioning of one of the four freedoms. A Directive was finally adopted only in November 2008.[338]

The environment *acquis* has been bottom of the league in terms of the Member States compliance for decades. The Commission's 1996 findings of a high level of poor application of the environment *acquis* in the Fifteen[339] still applied at the date of the fifth enlargement when compared to the findings of its *2004 Environment Policy Review*[340] One third of all infringement cases investigated by the Commission concerned the environment *acquis*. Of the 129 ECJ judgments against the Member States that remain unimplemented, 59 concerned the envi-

all of which can be found at www.europa.eu.int/comm/environment/crime/index.htm#studies. These studies were carried out by the Maastricht European Institute for Transnational Legal Research, Maastricht University, Maastricht 2002 and are entitled 'Criminal Penalties in EU Member States' Environmental Law – Study I', 'Criminal Penalties in EU Member States' Environmental Law – Study II'. The study 'Criminal Penalties in the Candidate Countries' was carried out by Milieu Ltd and published in 2003. Studies have also been published on organised environmental crime in the Union, which can be found on the same Commission web page.

[336] See COM(2001) 139 of 15 March 2001, *OJ* 2001 C 180/ 238E, as amended by COM(2002) 544 of 30 September 2002, *OJ* 2003 C 20/284E.

[337] Cases ECJ, Case C-176/03, *Commission* v. *Council* [2005] *ECR* I-7879 and ECJ, Case C-440/05, *Commission* v. *Council* [2007] *ECR* I-09097.

[338] Directive 2008/99 on the protection of the environment through criminal law, *OJ 2008 L 328/28. See also* Directive 2005/35/EC of the European Parliament and of the Council of 7 September 2005 on ship-source pollution and on the introduction of penalties for infringements, *OJ 2005 L 255/11.*

[339] See the Commission Twentieth Annual Report monitoring the application of Community law (2002), COM(2003) 669, 21 November 2003, pp. 61–65.

[340] See Commission Communication *2004 Environmental Policy Review*, COM(2005) 17, 27 January 2005.

ronment *acquis*. Moreover, the Commission annual reports on the application of the *acquis* show that various of the Fifteen were failing to comply with provisions of the environment *acquis* for which the new Member States were given no leeway for compliance. To take one important example, in 2002 during the final stages of negotiations of the fifth Accession Treaty, Belgium, France and Luxembourg were all condemned by the ECJ for failure to transpose the 1997 amendment to the Environmental Impact Assessment Directive by its implementation deadline of 14 March 1999.

The implementation deficit in the Fifteen had already inspired work on governance cumulating in the *White Paper on European Governance*[341] in 2001, to improve and encourage the means of redress for citizens and operators, to improve the effectiveness of the pre-litigation stage (of the Article 258 TFEU procedure) seeking compliance by Member State with their Treaty obligations and ultimately to foster trust between Member States. The Fifteen were not setting an example of a properly functioning environment *acquis*.[342] From this stand point, that of overall national compliance with the environment *acquis* and of the deterioration in the state of the environment, enlargements of the European Union – past and future – promise more of the same: cumulative environmental degradation due to economic integration at EU level.

The *White Paper on Governance* was further supplemented in 2002 through the Commission Communication on *Better Monitoring of the Application of Community Law*.[343] Specifically, the Commission concentrated on accelerating on the analysis and processing of infringements and more rigorous compliance by Commission services when handling complaints. A raft of tools were foreseen in order to anticipate and pre-empt implementation problems, concentrating notably by improving the transposition of Directives into national law and taking action against infringements. Already in 2003 the Commission noted that,

> A substantial improvement will require efforts by the Commission to develop new working methods with Member States at all stages of the

[341] *White Paper on European Governance*, COM(2001) 428, 25 July 2001.
[342] See J. Bourrinet 2000, *L'effectivité du droit européen de l'environnement; controle de la mise en oeuvre et sancion de la non-respect*, (Paris, La Documentation Francaise 2000).
[343] COM(2002) 725, *EC Bull* 12/2002 at 1.9.1.

> implementation life cycle. This is particularly relevant in the build up to enlargement to ensure that new Member States transpose and implement correctly the *acquis communautaire* within the agreed timeframes.[344]

Consequently, implementation and enforcement by the existing fifteen Member States is as much a part of the equation as implementation and enforcement by the new Member States. A few months after the fifth enlargement in 2004 the Commission also published a Recommendation on the transposition into national law of directives affecting the Internal Market, which was directed primarily at the implementation of the Internal Market *acquis*.[345]

Ensuring transposition, implementation and enforcement of EU law in advance is an obvious coping mechanism: prevention rather than cure. Such initiatives could already be seen in the Commission's 2002 *Communication on better monitoring of the application of European Community law*[346] and the 2004 Commission *Recommendation on the transposition into national law of Directives affecting the Internal Market*.[347] The Recommendation identified the practices of the Member States that facilitate correct and timely transposition into national law of Directives affecting the Internal Market, under the following headings;

1. Making correct and timely transposition a permanent political and operational priority
2. Ensuring permanent monitoring and co-ordination of the transposition of Internal Market Directives at administrative and political level
3. Ensuring the preparations for transposition take place at an early stage and that they have as their aim correct and timely transposition
4. Working closely with national, regional and devolved Parliaments involved in transposition of Internal Market Directives to ensure correct and timely transposition
5. Taking action quickly, visibly and effectively to transpose directives whose transposition is late.

---

[344] See the European Commission's *Fourth Annual Survey on the implementation and enforcement of European Union environment law*, SEC(2003) 804, 17 July 2003.

[345] Commission Recommendation of 12 July 2004, *OJ* 2005 L 98.

[346] COM(2002) 725 of 11 December 2002.

[347] *OJ* 2005 L 98/47.

Given that all Member States are treated on an equal footing in practice, initiatives in capacity building in all Member States are welcome. Still more room for additional governance initiatives was clear however. The European Parliament Resolution[348] expressly called upon the new Member States to reinforce their administrative capacity in order to reduce the disparity between theory and practice in the application of EU law (draft resolution 6). The European Parliament, as regards all the Member States, also called on the Commission (draft resolution 7) to report more frequently on the state of transposition of EU law in all the Member States. For the moment, the Commission reports only on an annual basis. The reports serve to 'name and shame' errant Member States and congratulate those that meet their obligations as Member States.

To give this approach even more clout the European Parliament proposed that the European Council give political recognition to the Commission's findings as the main reference point for establishing the state of transposition of all Internal Market legislation. This would put legal infringement cases on the political agenda of the European Council. Equally as interesting is the fact that the European Parliament proposed that it – the European Parliament – adopt a preventive approach by taking up its own surveillance over the transposition and implementation of EU laws. It sees this as a means (Resolution 21) of applying pressure on errant Member States to properly transpose EC laws. The Commission had already taken the initiative of drawing up a recommendation on the transposition into national law of Internal Market directives in July 2004.[349] Such practical approaches to reducing the implementation deficit in EU law, being preventive in nature and promising to curb infractions, helps to short circuit the lengthy legal procedures against errant Member States which can take years while consumer and commercial rights are adversely affected.

Three years after the 2004 enlargement however, the Commission report on the application of the environment *acquis* for the year 2007[350] highlighted both that:

---

[348] A resolution based on this draft report was adopted 16 March 2005. Parliament further suggested that the Member States should carry out screening of their existing domestic legislation for compatibility with EU rules in aid of the process of removing market barriers and opening up competition in the Internal Market.

[349] See Recommendation from the Commission, SEC(2004) 918, 12 July 2004.

[350] COM(2008) 733 of 18 November 2008.

- over 20% of enforcement actions brought by the Commission concerning the (twenty-seven) Member States' implementation of the *acquis*, concern the environment chapter;
- pre-accession support in enlargement countries is an important policy tool in preventing breaches of Union environment law, to ensure that new Member States are better able to comply with the *acquis* on the date of their accession.

Where the timetables for the transitional arrangements are not being met or where pre-accession commitments are not being maintained, this obviously accentuates the governance challenge for the environment *acquis* in an enlarging Union. In 2007 the Commission did issue another Communication, this time focusing implementation, including improvements to infringement proceedings against Member States.[351]

Then in 2008 that the Commission issued its plans to improve the implementation of the environment *acquis*.[352] This fitted into the Commission's overall strategy of 2007 and coincided with the publication of findings of the application of Union law in general for the year 2007. The 2008 Communication identifies a number of common implementation problems: insufficient attention to deadlines and correctness during the adoption of national and regional legislation; shortcomings in knowledge and awareness in national and regional administrations; shortcomings in administrative capacities; weak national and regional enforcement policies and practices; under-investment or delayed investment in the necessary infrastructure to reduce pollution.

The Commission's proposals reveal the task it faces due to weaknesses in the pre-accession strategy. To address implementation problems the Commission is combining preventive actions with more environmental rights legislation and action together with more strategic and intensive enforcement work. New preventive actions include better information on practice at local level and more guidance documentation and technical assistance and dialogue together in areas such as water supplies. This is an area where all twelve new Member States had transitional arrangements (only Malta and Hungary's have expired) and where, as noted earlier, the Commission was critical the

[351] Commission Communication, *A Europe of results – Applying Community law*, *Bull EU*, 9–2007 at 1.36.1.

[352] COM(2008) 2852 of 18 November 2008.

unclear and incomplete legislation transposing the Community rules. The Commission also proposes to add to its policy of naming and shaming of recalcitrant Member States by publishing comparative scoreboards of their performance – comparable to the Internal Market Scoreboard – to encourage better efforts.

As for environmental rights, the Convention on Accession to Information, Public Participation in Decision-Making and Access to Justice in Environmental Matters of 1998 has recently been implemented into EU law as well as in the Member States. This convention is remarkable because it involves the recognition by States of the rights of their citizens rather than being an agreement on the reciprocal rights and obligations of States. There is some controversy around the extent to which these measures implement Aarhus,[353] particularly its provisions concerning Access to Justice in Environmental Matters (AJEM) but are definitely another string in the governance bow. Moreover, a trial project of making environmental expertise available in Commission Representations in Madrid, Lisbon, Rome and Warsaw is under way to help national officials as well as citizens with defending their rights. Certainly, implicating the Member States and their local and regional areas in the management and implementation of the environment *acquis* appears an obvious way of improving the implementation deficit.

Finally, the Commission intends to focus on breaches that are fundamental or systemic, such as defects in national implementing rules, widespread tolerance of illegal landfills, serious gaps in permitting for major industries and lack of designation of key nature sites.

Consequently, the Union was still developing the governance tools necessary to manage and maintain the environment *acquis* in a Union of twenty-seven, *after* the fifth and the sixth enlargements. The Fifteen were themselves not ready for the enlargement of the environment *acquis*. However, recent improvements in the governance regimen will undoubtedly assist in guaranteeing the environment *acquis* in future enlargements. The lessons learned from the fifth and sixth Accession Treaties will surely impact on the pre-accession strategy as it is being applied to today's candidates. Certainly cases of incomplete transposition by a candidate could be made a valid reason for 'postponing' the application of an Accession Treaty for example. Even more simple a

[353] Op. cit. n. 107.

solution would be to only close accession negotiations once transposition was complete. Another suggestion would be to include candidates in the system for notifying transposition of provisions of the *acquis* to the Commission and monitoring their behaviour alongside the actual Member States. However, this latter option would involve further resources for already under-resourced Commission services. Another suggestion would be to include a safeguard clause, the like of the Internal Market Safeguard clause that was incorporated into both the 2003 and 2005 Accession Treaties, specifically aimed at enforcing pre-accession commitments of future new Member States in respect of the environment *acquis*.

It is useful to conclude here by mentioning certain constructive developments in green governance which would be introduced by the Lisbon Treaty. From the point of view of access to justice in environmental matters, Article 263 of the consolidated version of the future Treaty on the Functioning of the European Union (TFEU) makes certain changes to Article 230, fourth paragraph EC,[354] apparently opening up access to individuals to challenge laws that are of direct concern to them, without having to show individual concern. A new paragraph will additionally specify the conditions and arrangements for actions brought by individuals against acts taken by bodies, offices or agencies set up by the institutions.[355] This would seem at first glance to be an attempt to fill the vacuum in legal protection and access to justice in environmental matters and to complement EU actions to implement the Aarhus Convention.[356] On closer reading however, this is not so

[354] Art. 263, fourth paragraph, TFEU will read, 'Any natural or legal person may, under the conditions laid down in the first and second paragraphs, institute proceedings against an act addressed to that person or which is of direct and individual concern to them, and against a regulatory act which is of direct concern to them and does not entail implementing measures.'

[355] Art. 263, fifth paragraph will read, 'Acts setting up bodies, offices and agencies of the Union may lay down specific conditions and arrangements concerning actions brought by natural or legal persons against acts of these bodies, offices or agencies intended to produce legal effects in relation to them.'

[356] See B. Dette, 'Access to justice in environmental matters: a fundamental democratic right', in M. Onida ed., *Europe and the environment: legal essays in honour of Ludwig Krämer* (Groningen: Europa Law Publishing, 2004), pp. 3–22 at pp. 7–10; see also J. H. Jans, 'Did Baron von Munchhausen ever Visit Aarhus? Some Critical Remarks on the Proposal for a Regulation on the Application of the Provisions of the Aarhus Convention to EC Institutions and Bodies', in R. Macrory, ed., *Reflections on 30 years of EU environment law: a high level of protection?*, (Groningen, Europa Law Publishing – The Avosetta Series 2005) Vol. 7, pp. 475–490.

clear. Measures of general application (referred to as 'regulatory acts') must be shown to be of direct concern but not individual concern, but the act in question must not entail 'implementing measures' in which case individual concern must be shown. This terminology confuses the true intent of these changes. It remains to be seen whether standing will actually be opened up as a result of the Lisbon Treaty amendment and further input from the Court will no doubt be needed.[357]

Other novelties of the Lisbon Treaty will certainly improve governance aspects of the environment *acquis*. Under Article 260(2) and (3) TFEU (ex-Art. 228(2) EC), if a Member State has not complied with a Court ruling against it for failing to meet its Treaty obligations to properly apply the *acquis*, the Commission will be able to skip the reasoned opinion stage and go straight to asking the Court to impose lump sum or penalty payments. Moreover, an entirely new provision allows the Commission to request a lump sum or penalty payment at the Article 258 TFEU procedure stage in cases of non-transposition of Directives into national law.

Finally, the new Art. 16(8) TEU revised, will make public how the Member States vote in Council when adopting legislation. This should prove a useful yardstick for measuring whether the national governments stand by their green manifesto pledges. It will put the spotlight on those members that hold the majority back from pursuing a truly effective, common European 'green' front at home and abroad.

### 3.2.2 *Continued evolution of the environment* acquis *in an enlarging Union*

Some conclusions are drawn here from the above findings on the pre-accession strategy in the context of the broader debate on the evolution of the environment *acquis* in an enlarging Union. It cannot be denied that considerable human health and environmental benefits can be directly attributed to the 'carrot' of enlargement and the pre-accession strategy for eastwards enlargement, and now also for enlargement to the South East. The progress of the new Member States as well as today's candidates in approximating to the environment *acquis* has to been considered a positive development in many ways: even if it were

[357] See R. Barents, 'The Court of Justice and the Renewed European Treaties', A. Ott and E. Vos, eds., *50 years of European Integration: Foundations and Perspectives*, (The Hague: TMC Asser Press/CUP, 2008).

to be considered only a minimum standard in environment law and policy, this approximation exercise marks a standard throughout the entire region and expands that minimum threshold from fifteen countries to twenty-seven and more countries in the region.

For all its defects and justified criticism of the enlargement process, therefore, the pre-accession strategy is due credit for this remarkable success in such a relatively short time frame, especially given the magnitude of the task facing the central and eastern European Member States in particular. The impact of the vast approximation exercise, driven by political commitment and a strategically designed conditionality, has resulted in the extension of the ambitious body of EU environment laws into the broader European continent. An important part of that conditionality has been to build the necessary governance structures in the new Member States to anchor their practice and commitment to the environment *acquis*. It is true that with the acceding countries of the fifth and sixth or subsequent enlargements, the incoming countries in many cases have had to start from scratch with building environmental policies.[358]

Whether or not the pre-accession strategy's approach is appropriate to the needs of the new members no longer seems to be a relevant question. Simply, the pre-accession strategy has been the route followed. It has been practical and expedient to the political goal of enlargement. To their advantage the new Member States underwent an arduous approximation exercise in preparation for accession and environmental projects were among the first EU projects to be undertaken in the CEECs after the fall of the Berlin wall. They have built up administrative structures and practice in applying the *acquis*, albeit with drawbacks, where previously there was little or nothing in place. The pre-accession strategy is due credit for the role it has played in the massive investment to date by the new Member States – over and above EU and IFI investment – in establishing their compliance with the environment *acquis*. For example, according to Eurostat;

> the Ten new Member States spent 1.6% of GDP on environmental protection in 2000 [...] a higher percentage than many older Member States [...] this is expected to rise to 2–3% in order to comply with *acquis* requirements.[359]

---

[358] See P. Pavlínek and J. Pickles, op. cit. n. 13.

[359] See Eurostat, *Environmental expenditure in accession countries-data 1996–2000*, ISBN 92-8944372-3, published 2002.

Rooting practice in behaviour of complying with the *acquis* is ongoing even now in the post-enlargement phase, evidenced in particular by the Transition Facility to support capacity building and the Cross-Border Co-operation Programme.

By far the biggest fear is that eastwards enlargement will at least inhibit the evolution of the environment *acquis* if not unravel it. Indeed, the *Agenda 2000* document of the European Commission was clear about the threats and consequent challenges. From early on, expansion of the Union from fifteen to twenty-seven Member States has led to predictions not only of a further deterioration in the application of the *acquis* but also that it would inhibit the evolution of the environment *acquis*. Governance of the existing environment *acquis*, even as it stood at the turn of the Twenty-first Century, had already proved inadequate before the fifth and sixth enlargements. The very reason for devising such a detailed preparations strategy for the CEECs was to keep transitional arrangements to a minimum and to ensure that the new Member States would continue to enforce the environment *acquis* after their accessions. This was seen as necessary to avoid compounding the compliance deficit in the environment *acquis* that was already facing the Union as much as to pre-empt the consequent governance challenge that this would involve. The first thing to note is that many of the transitional arrangements legally specified in the 2003 and 2005 Accession Treaties for the environment *acquis*, are ongoing and the progress of the new Member States in meeting the timetables remains to be seen. There are examples where the new Member States are already falling behind in meeting their transitional arrangements.

More worrying is the emergence of 'informal transitional arrangements' in area of the environment *acquis* that were ruled out for transitional arrangements in the pre-accession strategy. While the Commission expressly intended that the candidates adapt the pre-accession priorities to their specific needs, it is clear that the vastness of the approximation exercise with the entire *acquis* in combination with the influences of national interests and priorities, has had an impact on the extent of approximation by the new Member States with the environment *acquis*. Compared to the acceding countries in previous enlargements there is, comparably, a far greater workload for the new members regarding the environment *acquis* for many years after enlargement, as much because of their own lacks in terms of environment policy and law as because of the growth in the environment *acquis* itself. They must continue to comply and enforce the *acquis* like any other Member State. This will necessarily also affect their ability and willingness to participate in raising environment standards any further at the EU level as much as the ability and willingness of the Fifteen to do so.

The European Commission reported on the extent of work outstanding before the signature of the 2003 and 2005 Accession Treaties, the Member States proceeded to sign these Treaties in order to meet their political commitment to the promised dates for these enlargements in May 2004 and January 2007. This, once again, underlines the essentially political nature of enlargement. Because unanimity is required of the Member States in order to proceed with enlargement, it is fair to conclude that the political commitment of the Union to enlarge has taken precedence over the actual state of preparedness of the receiving Union as well as the new Member States. From the point of view of the environment *acquis*, however, this also betrays the political bias towards economic development at the cost of the Treaty objective of sustainable development and the principle of integrating environmental concerns into all policy areas. The drafting of the 2003 and 2005 Accession Treaties with safeguard clauses only in the Internal Market and JHA *acquis* – '(dis)trust mechanisms' – betray the Union's own commitment to preserving integration in these fields first. In the end however, these safeguard clauses have proved toothless as conditionality tools in the pre-accession strategy, which reduces their potency even as a threat in the pre-accession strategy.

Numerous examples exist where the new Member States have not met their pre-accession commitments under the pre-accession strategy – 'informal transitional arrangements' – in core areas of the environment *acquis*, which would not have been eligible for consideration as formal transitional arrangements by the Commission. For the new Member States, the major and enormous challenge of attracting sufficient investment and maintaining the necessary administrative capacity to enforce the environment *acquis* will continue for many years to come. The need for such massive external investment in infrastructure in order to comply with the long-term transitional arrangements in the *acquis* concerning water quality or emissions from large combustion plants, for example, makes these transitional periods look infeasible. Moreover, the fact that informal transitional arrangements have been allowed to arise in the water quality sector, for example, implies that the Commission and the fifteen Member States underestimated, if not failed to appreciate or anticipate, how unfeasible these transitional arrangements would be, before they signed the 2003 Accession Treaty.

This all reveals a lack of rigour in the pre-accession conditionality and sets a dangerous precedent for current pre-accession conditionaltiy and the negotiation of transitional arrangements in future accession treaties. This would be less of a problem if the Fifteen Member States themselves had put in place the necessary governance mechanisms for dealing with such a scenario in advance of the 2004 enlargement. The impact of recent governance initiatives in the environment *acquis* – including innovations of the Lisbon Treaty – remains to be seen. It is still too early to tell: in order to test the effectiveness of these new governance initiatives, the Commission's reporting on the application of the *acquis* following their use will only be published in the future.

These weaknesses in the pre-accession strategy are part of the broader picture of the future evolution of the environment *acquis* in an enlarging Union. In sustainable development terms, the pre-accession strategy involved approximation to an environment *acquis* that was already limited and failing to curb environmental degradation. The ever-growing consumption and polluting-production in an enlarging Union is putting increasing demand on natural resources and putting our environment at further risk. The debate on the nature of the environment *acquis* in the future of an enlarged and enlarging Union has predicted a somewhat bleak future for the environment *acquis*.[360] Some have reported that the EU standard becomes the ceiling for national standards rather than a floor for more ambitious standards that might actually achieve sustainable economic development.[361] While the EU environment *acquis* as it stands today is impressive, the Union's development cannot be called sustainable.

The preceding section emphasised the weaknesses in the pre-accession strategy which have accentuated the governance challenge in a Union of twenty-seven Member States. To raise common environmental standards at Union level will obviously also become more challenging because of the need to reach agreement between twenty-seven rather than fifteen Member States, particularly as concerns those

[360] See, for example, Jehlicka, op. cit. n. 35, D. Wilkinson et al, *The future of EU environment policy, Special Report of the All-party Parliamentary Environment Group*, Institute for European Environment Policy, December 2004. J.B. Skjaerseth and J. Wettestad, *EU Enlargement and Environment Policy: the Bright Side*, Norway, The Fridtjof Nansen Institute 2006.

[361] See *The Environmental results of the Accession Process*, EEB Special Report, April 2004.

decisions in sensitive areas such as fiscal measures and energy, which require unanimity. This is further complicated by the sheer diversity of the environmental and political situations and priorities of so many Member States. However, it cannot be taken as read that the new Member States will be any less green than the other Member States. In relation to the voting in the European Parliament, one NGO survey predicts that:

> the representatives of the new EU countries are not going to become an obstruction for a more progressive environmental policy in the [European Parliament] [...] in total there is a majority among the answers which support that improvements in the environmental policy are necessary.[362]

Nevertheless, the resources of the new Member States and the Union institutions will have to focus on reaching compliance with the *acquis* as it stands today.

A shift towards more framework (and less detailed) legislation is already emerging in order to take account of the diversity of environments and the political/social/economic interests of twenty-seven and more Member States. The prediction of a softening of the *acquis* as a result of a more complex environment and growth and jobs priorities under the Lisbon Agenda is well founded. The 2000 Lisbon European Council adopted the Lisbon Agenda to create the most dynamic and competitive knowledge-based economy in the world capable of sustainable economic growth with more and better jobs and greater social cohesion, and respect for the environment by 2010. The sustainable development and respect for the environment axis of the Lisbon Agenda was only later introduced as the third pillar of the Lisbon Agenda by the 2001 Stockholm European Council and the (June) Gothenburg Summit three months later, which adopted the guiding principles.[363] However, some commentators see the Lisbon priorities as being used to call into question the very legitimacy of EU regulatory

---

[362] See www.EU-votewatch.org, where the European Environmental Bureau, Friends of the Earth Europe, Greenpeace, the European Federation for Transport and the Environment, and Climate Action Network Europe. See Friends of the Earth Denmark, 'Survey on environmental opinions among politicians in the new EU countries', to be found at www.foeeurope.org visited on 6 June 2005. This survey must be treated with caution as the survey was prepared on the basis of questionnaires sent out to political parties in the new Member States and not all questionnaires were returned. 34 of the 76 parties addressed did not reply.

[363] See Council Press Release 10117/06, 9 June 2006.

action in many fields, including the environment.[364] The command and control approach that characterised EU environment law in the last Century has given way to framework legislation and Market Based Instruments (MBIs) and a concentration of efforts on implementation and enforcement through governance instruments.

Past experience with unsuccessful initiatives, such as the eco-tax which promised considerable progress in environmental protection and improvement,[365] highlight the weaknesses of decision-making in politically sensitive areas. Environmental taxes are the most cost-effective instruments for achieving environmental objectives. They encourage actors to allocate their resources more efficiently than would be the case with the command and control approach, which is established in terms of quantifiable results. Revenue tends to go to the general national budget and not for environmental ends. This is an area where the environmental benefits are potentially considerable but where the need for unanimity has served to prevent some Member States from making progress, holding them back to take account of the more 'reluctant' Member States. Generally speaking, there is a potential or perceived risk of damage to a country's competitiveness and price increases. While such fears influence the thinking at national policy level in the use of such instruments,

> there is no evidence that existing economic instruments have a major adverse effect on competitiveness on the macro and sector level [...] competitiveness issues have been given greater weight than is justifiable.

The fourth enlargement highlighted the fact that incoming countries often have a political struggle to maintain their higher standards once

---

[364] See Wilkinson, op. cit. n. 3. See also M. Pallemaerts et al., Drowning in Process: the implementation of the EU's 6th Environment Action Programme, Institute for European Environment Policy, April 2006.on progress under the 6th EAP.

[365] See EEAg Report *Market Based Instruments for environmental policy in Europe*, (EEAg, Denmark 2006) at pp. 40–49. Proposal for a Council Directive introducing a tax on carbon dioxide emissions and energy COM(92) 226, 27 May 1992, *OJ* 1992 C196 and Amended Proposal for a Council Directive introducing a tax on carbon dioxide emissions and energy COM(1995) 172, 10 May 1995. It was withdrawn by the Commission on 11 December 2001. See Answer by Commissioner Bolkestein of 12 July 2001 to Written question P-1725/01 by Alexander de Roo (Verts/ALE) to the Commission, *Structure of, and timescale for, a European energy tax on the basis of enhanced co-operation*, *OJ* 2001 C 350 E/215. For other examples, see the Resolution of the European Parliament on the Communication of 14 November 1996 from the Commission on the review of the Community strategy for waste management and the draft Council resolution on waste policy, *OJ* 1996 C 362/241.

they become a Member State. Traditional 'pusher'[366] countries find themselves restrained from initiating national environment measures that affect trade and therefore also, from leading EU environmental standards and, ultimately, global standards. With the expansion of the EU from fifteen to twenty-seven Member States, the pusher countries are now outnumbered by environmentally-challenged Member States. In this light, the case for the 'decentralisation' of the implementation of EU environmental law gains would seems to make some, a little, sense as the Union enlarges. Apart from threatening to unravel the *environment acquis*, this would also dilute the pusher impetus that the environmental leaders play in raising the Union and global standards. Flexibility mechanisms in the form of intergovernmental instruments or the so-far untapped resource of the enhanced co-operation decision-making procedure, must be criticised for the same reason.

The risks inherent in such decentralisation arose, for example, in the context of the LIFE is the sole Community financing instrument for environmental projects and in place since 1992.[367] The Commission's 2004 proposal for a renewed LIFE instrument for 2007–2013,[368] ended in conciliation between the Member States in Council and the European Parliament. The Parliament was concerned that:

> [i]t is questionable whether, if the Member States have too much freedom to decide on the types of projects to be managed, this will not be detrimental to the effectiveness of the EU's environment policy. At best such a high level of decentralisation risks compromising the guarantee of

[366] See M. Skou Andersen and D. Lieferink, 'Introduction: the impact of the pioneers on EU environmental policy' in M. Skou Andersen and D. Lieferink, *European Environmental Policy: the pioneers* (New York, Manchester University Press 1997), 25, at 43. Pusher countries being those that pursue 'strategies to push environmental issues on to the EU agenda and build the necessary alliances with other Member States in order to push through environmental initiatives'.

[367] See the original Council Regulation 1992/1973 establishing a financial instrument for the environment (LIFE), *OJ* 1992 L 206/1–6.

[368] See Commission Proposal Concerning the Financial Instrument for the Environment (LIFE +), COM(2004) 261, 29 September 2004. Partial agreement was reached between Council and Parliament on 7 June 2005 but some issues remained outstanding, namely: the criteria for allocation of funds, as part of the programming approach, and the percentage of LIFE+ funding available to the Commission and Member States, see Commission Press Release IP/04/1152 of 29 September 2005. See 'Minutes of the 2697th Council Meeting Environment, Brussels, Council Press Release' C/05/315, 2 December 2005.

> EU added value, at worst it risks leading to national interests overriding European-level interests.[369]

To guard against such outcomes, the European Parliament suggested that the Commission specify that projects should provide EU added value, both in the strategic planning and for the purposes of evaluation. It wanted better guarantees that the projects financed would not be a replacement for national budget allocations to environment projects. At second reading, the Parliament was again particularly critical of proposals to decentralise LIFE would create an 'à la carte' European environmental policy leaving Member States free to choose which projects to carry out with EU co-financing.[370]

The final agreement on the LIFE+ Regulation 2007–2013[371] was delayed and in the end, it was adopted with the participation of all 27 Member States. The conciliation compromise reached was to establish a decentralised system of project selection where the Commission, when it selects the projects, has to have regard to:

- national allocations which are pre-established for each Member State on the basis of objective criteria;
- national priorities established by the Member States, and;
- comments by the Member States on whether project applications correspond to national priorities.

Ultimately, it seems, the state of Europe's environment will depend significantly on the continued evolution of progressive environment policies and law at national level, as well as on enforcement and the effectiveness of EU initiatives to integrate the needs of the environment into all EU policy areas.

---

[369] See the Report of the European Parliament's Committee on the Environment, Public Health and Food Safety on the proposal for a regulation of the European Parliament and of the Council concerning the Financial Instrument for the Environment (LIFE+), A6–0131/2005 of 2 May 2005, at p.29. The Legislation Opinion was adopted by the European Parliament in July 2005.

[370] See also the Explanatory Memorandum (second reading) to the EP Resolution of 19 September 2006, A6–0288/2006.

[371] Regulation 614/2007, *OJ* 2007 L149, covers the period 2007–2013. The second phase of LIFE expired in 2000, see Council Regulation 1404/96 of 15 July 1996 amending Regulation 1973/92 establishing a financial instrument for the environment (Life), 1996 *OJ* L 181/1. The third phase expired end 2006, Regulation 1682/2004, *OJ* 2004 L 308/1.

Thus, the gamut of challenges facing the EU Member States today in terms of pursuing a progressive environment *acquis* go far deeper than dealing with the emergence of informal transitional arrangements. It is still too early to tell how the new Member States will actually behave in the adoption of Community environment laws. The transitional arrangements in the environment *acquis* have not all expired. The Commission and European Parliament are entering new terms and the Lisbon Treaty has entered into force. Certainly, making public how the Council votes will enable the general public to identify whether national governments are following their manifesto pledges as concerns their green agendas.

The limits to Union environment policy and law – a shared competence between the EU and national levels – is reflected in the limits of the conditionality in the pre-accession strategy as concerns the environment *acquis*. The absence of common standards in areas of the Euratom *acquis* concerning basic safety standards in nuclear plants, and relied instead on international standards as reference points. It has taken proactive ECJ action to establish the health and environmental interests of the Union to pave the way for such standards.

Various other potential spheres for Union action remain unchartered because of national priorities and sensitivities. It is clear that there is a 'no man's land' where neither Member States nor the Union act, for whatever reason, to introduce environmental standards and sustainable development, whether at national level or at Community level. The area of energy policy is a case in point, where the Member States had never ceded to Community competence as such but acted on an *ad hoc* basis using convenient alternative legal bases.[372] This is important because, since the launch of the Strategic European Energy Review (SEER) on 10 January 2007, energy policy is expressly intended as a core vehicle in both the Lisbon Agenda and the fight against climate change. Common actions in energy are intended to help the Union attain its low carbon economic revolution and achieve

---

[372] On the need for new competences in energy, see L. Krämer, 'Some reflections on the EU mix of instruments on climate change', in M. Peeters and K. Dekettelaere *EU Climate Change Policy: The Challenge of new Regulatory Initiatives*, (Cheltenham and Massachusetts, Edward Elgar 2006), pp. 279–295.

its $CO_2$ emissions reduction targets under the Kyoto Protocol.[373] While the Lisbon Treaty will make some tentative steps to installing a common EU energy policy, unanimity still prevails as concern a Member State's choice between energy sources and the general structure of its energy supply, and makes common action very difficult. Consequently, the advent of ambitious sustainable development initiatives will still rely on the meaningful commitment of the Member States.

[373] See COM(2006) 105 10 January 2007, endorsed by the European Council on 8 and 9 March 2007, paving the way for a central European energy objective for the Union. Part and parcel of the SEER, is an integrated approach to climate change.

# CHAPTER SEVEN

## EU AGRI-FOOD LAW

This chapter focuses on EC agri-food law in the context of pre-accession and the transitional arrangements contained in the fifth and sixth Accession Treaties. The first part introduces the challenge of approximating to the agri-food *acquis* for candidates countries. Then, the transitional arrangements in the fifth and sixth Accession Treaties are outlined in the second part. The third part explores the evolution of EU agri-food law in an enlarging Union, drawing on the experience in the Fifteen and the new Member States making use of a sample of the missions carried out by the Food and Veterinary Office of the European Commission, which report on the implementation of the agri-food *acquis* in-country.

In particular, the third part explores the emergence of 'informal transitional arrangements' in the agri-food *acquis* in some of the new Member States after they acceded on 1 May 2004 (CEEC Member States, Cyprus and Malta) and 1 January 2007 (Bulgaria and Romania). It suggests that the Internal Market safeguard clause in the fifth and sixth Accession Treaties, while obviously discriminatory against the new Member States, may in the end be an (exceptional) appropriate tool for ensuring the integrity of the food chain. For the reader's ease, all references to the Accession Treaty Bulgaria and Romania are referring to the Act of Accession and annexes thereto rather than the Accession Protocol because of the failure of the Constitutional Treaty.

### 1. The starting point for approximating to the EU agri-food *acquis*

As the Union prepared its fifth and sixth enlargements, it undertook a profound and progressive transformation in the regulatory and administrative framework for the entire food chain. To understand the pre-accession efforts of the new and incoming Member States as well as the Union's approach towards the negotiation of transitional arrangements in the EU agri-food *acquis*, it is necessary first to highlight the fact that throughout, the agri-food *acquis* has been under radical legislative and institutional overhaul over the past decade. This chapter concerns the enlargement dimension in terms of the pre-accession strategy and transitional arrangements.

The agri-food *acquis* spans a number of chapters of the *acquis*, notably those on the free movement of goods and on the veterinary and phytosanitary section of the agriculture *acquis* (including the Common Fisheries Policy). The former covers EU legislation that harmonises and approximates national laws and standards concerning products, fundamental to the proper functioning of the Internal Market. At the time of the fifth enlargement, the veterinary and phytosanitary chapter of the *acquis* consisted mostly of directives – requiring transposition and implementation but is increasingly being regulated by means of regulations under the food reform that began in the Nineteen-nineties following the BSE or 'mad cow disease' crisis. This chapter governs animal and plant production methods and quality or animal health standards for example. It also regulates establishments involved in food production as well as animal welfare legislation and the regime applicable to controls on imports from third countries at external borders. A list of the current relevant measures today is contained in Annex I relating to the general food safety rules and the marketing conditions that apply to food, feed and animal by-products, official controls of compliance with the agri-food *acquis*, animal health, animal feed and phytosanitary measures.

The differentiation between 'old' and 'new' Member States and the gradual inclusion of the new Member States in the Common Agricultural Policy does not apply to the hygiene and food safety rules and the nature of the transitional arrangements contained in the Accession Treaties reflect this. For the purposes of this book, outside the agri-food *acquis* therefore are the rules on the Common Market Organisations (CMOs), the financial and market related aspects of agriculture generally speaking, including the rules on direct payments or aid for rural development or the establishment of reference quantities, or the Farm Accountancy Data Network. Likewise, the fisheries CMO is left aside but various of the food hygiene and processing, veterinary and other agri-food laws are included within the agri-food *acquis*.

Until the reform of the agri-food *acquis* in the late 1990s, consumer policy/protection was primarily dealt with in the context only of the environment *acquis*. The human health dimension of EU environment law concentrated on bathing water standards, for example, or waste legislation and food safety as such was not an area of activity of environment law. Food hygiene and quality parameters were established at EU level, in terms of labelling provisions[1] for example or rules on the material and articles that come into contact with foodstuffs[2] or rules on food additives.[3] Such legislative initiatives were very much kept within the policy context of Community legislation concerning agricultural production standards and practices despite the fact that they were based upon the Internal Market legal basis.

Today's EU agri-food law owes its existence to the BSE crisis of the early 1990s.[4] Significantly, the mismanagement crisis at EU level had far reaching governance implications and food law has become, as one commentator puts it, 'the centrepiece in the development of a new administrative landscape built on scientific information networks, that may in the future become a model for other areas of EU governance'.[5] Union agri-food law is now a sophisticated regime in its own right, managed by the European Commission's Directorate General for Health and Consumer Protection. Food safety is now a mainstay of the food chain, based on scientific advice, where risk assessment and scientific consultations are kept separate from the risk management and control of the food chain and where decision-making and

[1] The first law being Directive 79/112 on the approximation of the laws of the Member States relating to the labelling presentation and advertising of foodstuffs, *OJ* 1978 L 33/1, since amended.

[2] Directive 89/109 on the approximation of the laws of the Member States relating to materials and articles intended to come into contact with foodstuffs, *OJ* 1989 L 40/38, since amended.

[3] Horizontal legislation concerned the labelling, materials and articles in contact with foodstuffs, additives, processing aids, water for human consumption, pesticide residues, and various provisions on sampling and analysis, official controls of foodstuffs, geographical indications and designations of origin, certificates of specific character and the hygiene of foodstuffs. Vertical legislation relating to specific types of product was also administered by the agriculture Directorate, namely, cocoa and chocolate, sugars, honey, fruit juices, preserved milk, erucid acid in oils and fats, foodstuffs for particular nutritional purposes, coffee extracts and chicory, fruit jams, natural mineral waters; caseins and caseinates, quick-frozen foodstuffs, spirit drinks, organic products and multi-lingual lists of EC additives (E numbers). This is brief list of the categories of legislation in force in the EU in 1994, taken from Volumes I and II of *Eurofood Monitor; European Community Legislation on Foodstuffs* (Tunbridge Wells, Agra-Europe (London) Ltd. 1995).

[4] See E. Vos, 'EU Food Safety Regulation in the Aftermath of the BSE Crisis', in *Journal of Consumer Policy*, 2000, 227–255.

[5] See K. Vincent, '"Mad Cows" and Eurocrats – Community Responses to the BSE Crisis', 5 *European Law Journal* (2004) pp. 499–517, at p. 517.

inspection are subject to greater transparency than was the case in the pre-BSE climate.

In contrast to the environment *acquis*, the institutional and policy shifts in EU agri-food law is also characterised by a preventive approach and the Member States' willingness to relinquish competence and powers to the EU level in order to ensure not only its effectiveness throughout the (enlarging) Union but actually to prevent risks arising in the food chain. Moreover, the Member States have established their own national bodies for scientific risk analysis, and the institutional and policy changes at EU level have had a knock-on effect national systems for monitoring and controls of compliance with EU and national food laws.

### 1.1 *Approximation during the reform of EU agri-food law*

A brief introduction to the salient dates, policy documents and legislative steps in the progress of the agri-food *acquis* is useful to understanding the approach of the pre-accession strategy and the implications of the transitional arrangements. At a time when the candidates were approximating to the *acquis*, particularly those measures listed in the 1995 White Paper, the agri-food *acquis* was under radical reform. As the BSE crisis unfolded in the mid-Nineties,[6] the Commission's issues paper[7] on the way to proceed with EU agri-food law only came out in the April of 1997.[8] This was only a matter of months before *Agenda 2000* was published, in the July of that year. *Agenda 2000* would emphasise the food safety pre-occupations of the Union in its proposals for CAP reform.[9] In the context of agri-food law generally the Commission was already highlighting the risks involved in the late or inadequate adaptation by the incoming countries to the *acquis* in

[6] For an introduction to the crisis, see S.C. Ratzan, *The Mad Cow Crisis; Health and the Public Good* (London, UC Press 1998). See also M. Hirsch, P. Duneton, P. Baron and F. Noiville, *L'affolante histoire de la vache folle*, (Paris, Editions Balland 1996).

[7] See Commission Communication *The general principles of food law in the European Union – Commission Green Paper* COM(97) 176, 30 April 1997

[8] On food safety in Community legislation, see L. Azoulay, 'La Sécurité alimentaire dans la législation communautaire' in J. Bourrinet and F. Snyder, eds., *La Sécurité alimentaire dans l'Union européenne* (Brussels, Bruylant 2003) at p. 67.

[9] *Agenda 2000* emphasises the food safety and food quality as one of the competitiveness aspects of the policy objectives for the CAP, and as 'a top priority' and treats safety as being bound up with quality. See *Agenda 2000*, COM(97) 2000, 15 July 1997, Vol. 1 at p. 27.

terms not only of the destabilising effects on the Internal Market but also on food safety, and singled out the sensitivity of the veterinary and phytosanitary *acquis* in this respect.[10] The more concrete proposals relating to the future EU agri-food *acquis* were contained in the White Paper on food safety of January 2000,[11] setting out the policy direction and specifics of legislative initiatives.

The overhaul of Community and national rules governing food production from 'the farm to the fork'[12] in the wake of the BSE crisis, notably to incorporate increasingly onerous consumer protection and safety standards, was far reaching and necessary in order to re-establish consumer confidence in the Union's food industry, which had been badly knocked by consumer mistrust.

For example, the Member States adopted Union rules on GMOs in the early Nineteen-nineties[13] only to watch a groundswell of consumer resistance knock all political support for the regime, which effectively shelved the EU rules even before they entered into force.[14] Over a decade later and despite new, upgraded measures having been adopted in the form of Directive 2001/18 on the deliberate release of GMOs into the environment, many Member States had still not given effect to the EC rules in 2001 and Austria, Belgium, France, Germany, the Netherlands and were condemned by the Court for failure to transpose the Directive.[15] For failing to comply with the earlier judgment

---

[10] See *Agenda 2000*, ibid., Vol. 2 at p. 57.

[11] COM(99) 719 of 12 January 2000.

[12] See Commission *Green Paper* COM(97) 176, op. cit. n. 7. On the overhaul generally see J. Bourrinet 'L'Union européenne entre sécurité et insecurité alimentaire' in J. Bourrinet and F. Snyder, op. cit. n. 8, pp. 21–27.

[13] See Directive 90/220 on the deliberate release into the environment of genetically modified organisms, *OJ* 1990 L 117/15, as amended, and Directive 90/219 on the contained use of genetically modified micro-organisms, *OJ* 1990 L 117/1, as amended.

[14] For an introduction to how this has come about see E. Brosset, 'The prior authorisation procedure adopted for the deliberate release into the environment of genetically modified organisms: the complexities of balancing Community and national competences', *European Law Journal* (2004) pp. 555–579 at p. 557 and 570. See in particular, P. Dabrowska, 'The Polish Regulatory System on GMOs: between EU influences and national nuances', in M. Everson and E. Vos (eds.) *Uncertain Risks Regulated: facing the unknown*, (Oxon, Routledge 2009) pp. 207–226.

[15] See Directive 2001/18 on the deliberate release into the environment of GMOs and repealing Council Directive 90/220, *OJ* 2001 L 106/1. For the cases, see ECJ, Case C-422/03 *Commission* v. *the Netherlands*, *OJ* 2005 C 6/16, ECJ, Case C-421/03 *Commission* v. *Austria*, *OJ* 2005 C 6/15; ECJ, Case C-417/03 *Commission* v. *Belgium OJ* 2004 C 284/5, ECJ, Case C-420/03 *Commission* v. *Germany*, *OJ* 2004 C 228/16, ECJ, Case C-419/03 *Commission* v. *France* , *OJ* 2004 C 228/15.

France was fined a lump sum payment of EUR 10 million in case C-217/07, judgment of 9 December 2008.[16]

At the time of the fifth enlargement, these Member States insisted on maintaining national safeguard measures and the European Commission suggested revising the system in order to take account of this political resistance.[17] The ten new Member State have been required to adopt the GM regime in full and without reservation, as part of their pre-accession commitments before they could join the Union. However, the new Member States' continued support for the existing GM regime after their accession was not certain.

As part of its strategy to enforce the EU legal regime for GMOs, the European Commission had proposed the repeal of various national safeguard measures banning or restricting the marketing of GM products at the 24 June 2005 Environment Council. These national safeguard measures ban or restrict the marketing and cultivating or processing of GM products which would otherwise be authorised under the EU regime. The countries concerned are Austria, France, Germany, Greece and Luxembourg. When it acceded, Hungary joined the ranks of those maintaining their national safeguards. Poland has also had attempts at derogating from the 2001 Directive's provisions on experimental release and cultivation of GMOs rejected by the Commission.[18]

These national safeguard measures predate the upgraded rules following the adoption of Directive 2001/18. The GM products concerned have all been successful in clearing the scientific risk assessments in accordance with. Until June 2005, the Council had failed on fourteen successive occasions to reach a qualified majority proposal to block or even approve Commission proposals on the matter of marketing authorisations for GM products. But the Environment Council of 24 June 2005 reached a qualified majority vote *against* the Commission's proposals. This was the first time that it has done so. Commissioner Dimas, Environment Commissioner at that time, interpreted the

[16] ECJ, Case C-121/07 *Commission* v. France, *OJ* 2009 C 44/8, *nyr*.

[17] See Commission Press Release 'GMOs: Commission reaction on Council votes on safeguards and GM maize MON 863' IP/05/793 of 24 June 2005.

[18] Commission Decision of 12 October 2007 relating to Arts. 111 and 172 of the Polish Draft Act on Genetically Modified Organisms, notified by the Republic of Poland pursuant to Article 95(5) of the EC Treaty as derogations from the provisions of Directive 2001/18 of the European Parliament and of the Council on the deliberate release into the environment of genetically modified organisms, *OJ* 2008 L 16/17.

Council vote as 'a political signal that Member States may want to revisit some aspects of the system'.[19]

National safeguard measures are intended, according to Article 23 of the 2001 Directive, only for situations where new or additional scientific knowledge arises to indicate that the placing on the market of the product in question would have adverse effects on human health and the environment. National safeguard measures are intended to be temporary: for 60 days pending a scientific decision on the basis for these national restrictions. Eight separate Commission proposals to have these safeguard measures lifted, fell. The Commission based these proposals on the opinions of Scientific Committees and the European Food Safety Authority in accordance with the Directive. Their advice to the Commission was that the safeguard measures were not based on any grounds that justified the revision of the original scientific risk assessments. The Commission reached this conclusion that these measures cannot be justified under the terms established by the Member States in the 2001 Directive.

In 2006 the Commission proposed a number of practical improvements designed to reassure the Member States, stakeholders and the general public that the authorisation decisions are based on high quality scientific assessments and deliver a high level of protection of human health and the environment. These measures aim at improving the scientific consistency and transparency for risk assessment and decision making procedures under the current legislative framework.[20]

In its 2007 Report[21] on the experience of Member States under Directive 2001/18 – which shows a mixed picture of experiences of national authorities, industry, NGOs and the public – the Commission noted that it was pursuing all six Member States in respect of the maintenance of their national safeguards. For example, France had already lost a case brought against it before the ECJ by European Commission in 2003 for failing to transpose Directive 2001/18,[22] and in December 2008 was fined a lump sum of EUR 10 million for failing to comply with the earlier ruling.[23] Already in the earlier case, in

---

[19] See Commission Press Release, *Commission reaction on Council votes on safeguards and GM maize MON863*, IP/05/793, 24 June 2005.

[20] Adopted as Directive 2008/27, *OJ* 2008 L 81/45.

[21] COM(2007) 81, 5 March 2007.

[22] ECJ, Case C-419/03 *Commission* v. *France*, judgment of the Court of 15 July 2004, unpublished.

[23] ECJ, Case C-121/07, nyr.

respect of its failure to transpose the Directive France had incurred a daily penalty payment of EUR 366, 744 until it fully complied with the ECJ's judgment as well as a one-off fine of EUR 43,660.

The Commission had failed to bring Germany to lift its restrictions on certain GMOs in 2005.[24] It likewise failed in respect of similar such restrictions by Luxembourg,[25] Greece,[26] France[27] and Austria.[28] In January 2009 the European Commission proposed a Council Decision to lift Hungary's safeguard measures[29] following its unsuccessful attempt to bring Hungary into compliance with Directive 2001/18 back in 2006.[30] In February 2009, the European Commission proposed a Council Decision to the Member States to lift Austria's safeguard measures,[31] also where its own Decision failed to bring about compliance with the 2001 Directive.[32]

---

[24] Proposal for a Council Decision concerning the provisional restriction of the use and sale in Germany of genetically modified maize (Zea mays L. line Bt 176) pursuant to Directive 2001/18, COM(2005) 167 final of 26 April 2005.

[25] Proposal for a Council Decision concerning the provisional prohibition of the use and sale in Luxembourg of genetically modified maize (Zea mays L. line Bt 176) pursuant to Directive 2001/18, COM(2005) 165 final of 26 April 2005.

[26] Proposal for a Council Decision concerning the provisional prohibition of the use and sale in Greece of genetically modified spring swede rape (Brassica napus L. ssp. oleifera) derived from transformation event Topas 19/2, pursuant to Directive 2001/18, COM(2005) 164 final of 26 April 2005.

[27] Proposal for a Council Decision concerning the provisional prohibition of the use and sale in France of genetically modified hybrid swede rape (Brassica napus L. ssp. oleifera Metzg. MS1Bn x RF1Bn) pursuant to Directive 2001/18, COM(2005) 162 final of 26 April 2005.

[28] Proposal for a Council Decision concerning the provisional prohibition of the use and sale in Austria of genetically modified maize ( Zea mays L. line T25) pursuant to Directive 2001/18, COM(2005) 161 final of 26 April 2005.

[29] Proposal for a Council Decision concerning the provisional prohibition of the use and sale in Hungary of genetically modified maize (Zea mays L. line MON810) expressing the Bt cry1Ab gene, pursuant to Directive 2001/18, COM(2009) 12 of 21 January 2009.

[30] Proposal for a Council Decision concerning the provisional prohibition of the use and sale in Hungary of genetically modified maize (Zea mays L. line MON810) expressing the Bt cryIA(b) gene, pursuant to Directive 2001/18, COM(2006) 713 final of 23 November 2006.

[31] See Proposal for a Council Decision concerning the provisional prohibition of the use and sale in Austria of genetically modified maize (Zea mays L. line T25) pursuant to Directive 2001/18, COM(2009) 51 and Proposal for a Council Decision concerning the provisional prohibition of the use and sale in Austria of genetically modified maize (Zea mays L. line MON810) pursuant to Directive 2001/18, COM(2009) 56, both of 10 February 2009.

[32] Commission Decision 2008/470 concerning the provisional prohibition of the use and sale in Austria of genetically modified maize (Zea mays L. line T25) pursuant to Directive 2001/18, *OJ* 2008 L162/31. The initial Polish application for national

It is an indication of the sensitivity of food regulation generally and the extent of the lack of trust of the Union's consumers in the Union's legislature, including their own governments, as well as farmers and food industry. Even after the fifth enlargement, the new Member States, like the Fifteen, have been approximating to a moving target in the agri-food *acquis* as the legal instruments of the reform have progressively entered into force. In the long period of gestation of Regulation 178/2002, from conception to adoption and then progressive entry into force, the Commission has emphasised that the candidates have been kept abreast of the policy development.[33] New legislation on the hygiene of foodstuffs entered into force on 1 January 2006, see Annex I.

Moreover, as part of the overall programme of simplification and modernisation of legislation, sectoral directives of agri-food law are being consolidated into regulations. For today's candidate countries the switch to the use of regulations rather than directives should not only reduce the approximation exercise but should facilitate the control of legal compliance by the Member States. This is because a regulation, which is directly applicable, does not as such require to be transposed into national law and then implemented and enforced and therefore, EU membership automatically inserts the regulation into the national legal orders. A directive, has to be transposed or adopted into national law, including approximation of national provisions to the directive where necessary in order to give effect to the results intended to be achieved by the Member States when they adopted that directive: by comparison with a regulation, the provisions of a directive are capable of direct effect.

The Report of the Former Dutch Prime Minister Wim Kok to the Commission on *Enlarging the EU: Achievements and Challenges* in 2003 – while flagging up the many benefits of further enlargements – emphasised the considerable demands on acceding countries in raising their national food safety standards to the Union level and

measures was contained in, Notification pursuant to Article 95, paragraph 5 of the EC Treaty – Polish draft Act on Genetically Modified Organisms, including derogations from the provisions of Directive 2001/18.

[33] See for example, the Explanatory Memorandum introducing Commission proposal for a Regulation on materials and articles intended to come into contact with food COM(2003) 689, 17 November 2003.

that the EU makes no compromise on the safety of the food chain. As concerns food standards in particular, the Kok Report read:

> The importance of food safety issues in the present Member States has been raised by recent crises such as the 'mad cow' disease, which is related to intensive farming practices which are less widespread in the future member countries. The EU launched a reform in 2000 that draws together all aspects of food safety throughout the whole food chain, from the hygiene provisions to the associated animal and plant health requirements. The objective is to deliver a high level of public health and consumer protection throughout the enlarged EU.
>
> The future Member States have accepted to apply all food safety rules, and to have appropriate control mechanisms in place. No exemptions have been allowed in the accession negotiations: food that does not meet full EU rules cannot be marketed in other Member States. The objective is that EU enlargement should not in any way lead to the reduction of the present levels of food safety.
>
> Enlargement will extend a common set of rules to the new members, thereby raising the overall level of safety. It thus will ensure that the new EU borders effectively guard against risks to public, plant and animal health in the enlarged EU. However, alignment to these rules is a demanding task for the future Member States. The EU gives financial assistance, and the Commission is monitoring the situation as regards food safety to check that rules are properly applied.[34]

In the context of the overhaul of the Union's policy and legislative framework for food safety, the following sections set the scene for the pre-accession strategy specifically in respect of the agri-food *acquis*. The challenges that approximation posed the candidates and new Member States are explored. Sections 2 and 3 investigate the transitional arrangements stipulated in the fifth and sixth Accession Treaties and assess the effectiveness of the pre-accession strategy in ensuring that the food safety and the integrity of the agri-food *acquis*, has been guaranteed during the fifth and sixth enlargements.

#### 1.1.1 *The institutional and policy overhaul after the fourth enlargement*

Until the BSE crisis the farming lobby had been very powerful in the formulation of all EU policy relating to the production of food. This was inevitable given that the aim of Common Agricultural Policy envisaged by the original Treaty of Rome was to provide a reason-

[34] Florence, EUI (RSC) Working Paper 2003 at p. 58.

able standard of living for the agricultural population and to encourage productivity and fair prices for consumers. The method chosen, based on the control of market prices within the Community and in particular on price support, made the CAP a highly protective policy where consumers did not benefit from low prices and low-cost producers were prevented from accessing the Community market. Even before the BSE crisis the farming community had begun to lose the support of the EEC taxpayers because of the infamous wine lakes and butter-mountains, amongst others, and the exorbitant costs of maintaining them. The influence of the farming community was further being eroded by the increasing pressure on the EU from the international community, in the context of the General Agreement on Tariffs and Trade (GATT), to move away from the clearly discriminatory (at international level) EU policy of price maintenance under the CAP.

The BSE crisis was to tip the balance[35] in favour of the EU consumer at the heart of food safety and hygiene rules and at EU level in particular. Food safety and hygiene rules at Community level were generally administered by the European Commission's Directorate-General for Agriculture, which also held the reins of the CAP. The relevant provisions on hygiene and quality standards were incorporated within the body of the food regulations on production and marketing standards. Agricultural produce was excluded from the producer liability provisions of the Defective Products Directive,[36] which basically introduced no-fault liability of producers for damage suffered by consumers of their products. However, all primary foodstuffs (as opposed to processed foodstuffs) were free of liability for their defects giving rise to damage under that Directive.[37] It took a crisis on the scale of the BSE crisis to close this 'loophole'. Only on 4 June 1999 was liability under the EU defective products regime extended to primary agricultural

[35] On the implications of food safety on the CAP, see C. Blumann, 'Les implications de la sécurité alimentaire dans l'évolution de la politique agricole commune' in Bourrinet and Snyder, op. cit. n. 8 at pp. 70–93.

[36] Directive 85/374 on the approximation of the laws, regulations and administrative provisions of the Member States concerning liability for defective products, *OJ* 1985 L 210/29.

[37] Excluded from the scope of the Directive 85/374 was, according to Art. 2 thereof, all 'primary agricultural products and game, even though incorporated into another movable or into an immovable product' and 'Primary agricultural products' were defined as meaning any 'products of the soil, of stock-farming and of fisheries, excluding products which have undergone initial processing'.

produce.[38] Only thereafter were operators, including primary producers that participated in the handling, import and packaging of the agricultural products, expressly brought within the remit of the Defective Products Directive.

### 1.1.2 *The legal basis for EU agri-food law*

Consumer concerns became of paramount importance to the Internal Market *acquis*. Health aspects became and remain today the major reason for legislative action in agri-food law at EU level. The consumer protection title of the EC Treaty was contained in Article 153 EC.[39] It was introduced by the Maastricht Treaty[40] but has not been used as the legal basis for agri-food law. Previously the agri-food laws were founded on the legal basis for the CAP, or on the legal basis for the Internal Market, or on the legal basis for the Common Commercial Policy or on a combination of these legal bases.[41] There was no practice of taking the legal basis of Article on public health for adopting agri-food laws.

The agri-food laws of the Union of today are based on a combination of legal bases in the TFEU. The Internal Market legal basis of today, contained in Article 115 TFEU,[42] expressly provides for the adoption of health, safety, environmental and consumer protection legislation, 'taking as a base a high level of protection'. However, the consumer protection legal basis as such is not used and is considered adequately covered by other legal bases. Take as the principal example the mother regulation of the agri-food law reform. Regulation 178/2002 lays down the general principles and requirements of food law, establishing the European Food Safety Authority and laying down procedures in matters of food safety.[43] It is based on the com-

---

[38] As a result of the amendment of Art. 2 of Directive 85/374, by virtue of Directive 1999/34, *OJ* 1999 L 141/20.

[39] Which had not been altered by either the Amsterdam or the Nice Treaties.

[40] It was contained in Art. 129a EC.

[41] See for example the Council Directive 88/344 on the approximation of the laws of the Member States on extraction solvents used in the production of foodstuffs and food ingredients, *OJ* 1988 L157/28.

[42] Prior to the Amsterdam Treaty, Art. 100 and as a result of the Amsterdam Treaty repeal and replacement, it was renumbered Article 95 and its paragraphs 3–5 were replaced while new paragraphs 6–10 were introduced.

[43] See below at n. 49.

bined legal bases of Articles 43, 114, 207 and 168(4)(b)[44] concerning the Common Agricultural Policy (CAP), the Internal Market, Common Commercial Policy (CCP) and public health respectively. Agri-food laws continue to be based on the Internal Market legal basis of Article 114 TFEU, making specific reference to consumer protection concerns in the preambles, either alone or potentially in combination with the legal bases for agriculture, trade and health protection. Take for example the rules on foodstuffs intended for particular nutritional purposes, which dates back to 1989[45] and was amended in 1999. The original Directive was based upon the Internal Market legal basis and made no reference to consumer protection while the amending Directive does so.[46] The codification of this Directive[47] was also based upon the Internal Market legal basis. The codification of the labelling rules[48] was also based on the Internal Market legal basis.

Regulation 178/2002[49] is the corner stone of the new EU-wide regulatory system. While the main tenets of the new EU agri-food regime were established in 2002, key legislative measures entered into force progressively since the end of February 2002.[50] The general requirements of food law (Arts. 14 to 20) took effect on 1 January 2005; these requirements relate to food and feed safety requirements, labelling, advertising and presentation of food and feed as well responsibilities

---

[44] By means of the co-decision procedure.

[45] Directive 89/398 on the approximation of the laws of the Member States relating to foodstuffs intended for particular nutritional uses, *OJ* 1989 L 186/27, which is in the process of being recast, see Commission Proposal COM(2008) 3, 16 January 2008.

[46] See Recital 7 to Directive 1999/41 amending Directive 89/398/EEC on the approximation of the laws of the Member States relating to foodstuffs intended for particular nutritional uses, *OJ* 1999 L 172 /38.

[47] Proposal for a Directive of the European Parliament and of the Council on foodstuffs intended for particular nutritional uses (Codified version), COM(2004) 290, 22 April 2004. The Commission withdrew this proposal on 13 March 2008 because agreement it was not likely to reach agreement among the Member States.

[48] Directive 2000/13 on the approximation of the laws of the Member States relating to the labelling, presentation and advertising of foodstuffs, *OJ* 2000 L 109/29, it codified Directive 79/112 on the approximation of the laws of the Member States relating to the labelling, presentation and advertising of foodstuffs for sale to the ultimate consumer, *OJ* 1979 L 033/1.

[49] Regulation 178/2002 laying down the general principles and requirements of food law, establishing the European Food Safety Authority and laying down procedures in matters of food safety, *OJ* 2002 L 31/1. A general introduction can be found in H. Holland and H. Pope, *EU food law and policy* (The Hague, Kluwer Law International 2004).

[50] Art. 65 of Regulation 178/2002, ibid.

of food and feed operators. A network of supporting bodies (notably the European Food Safety Authority) and programmes[51] foster the further development of EU agri-food law. A package of complementing EU instruments followed, implementing onerous systems for the food sector. In particular, on the eve of the fifth enlargement, four regulations were adopted laying down specific hygiene rules for food and food of animal origin,[52] for official controls on products of animal origin intended for human consumption and for official controls on food and feed law,[53] animal health and animal welfare rules.[54] However, in order to smooth the functioning of entry into effect of these provisions, transitional arrangements were agreed in December 2005 – for all Member States – in respect of certain provisions of these Regulations which present practical difficulties. This particular transitional period lasts until end 2009.[55]

In 2005 Regulation on the requirements for animal feed hygiene was adopted.[56] Emergency measures have been given form and force to deal with risks arising in the food chain, in addition to the Rapid Alert System for Food and Feed Safety.[57] Crisis measures have been introduced for co-ordination at Union level in the event of serious direct or indirect risks to human health and/or perceived or publicised as such or can be perceived or publicised as such.[58] The European Commission can establish a crisis unit especially to co-ordinate any crisis that arises.

#### 1.1.3 *Institutional reform and the elevated status of food safety*

The shift in policy emphasis on consumer safety and health as well as consumer choice issues can be seen in the reorganisation of the EU institutions' internal functioning. The European Parliament's Com-

[51] Food safety initiatives are supported by Research and Development budget lines also.

[52] Regulations 852/2004, *OJ* 2004 L 139/1 and 853/2004, *OJ* 2004 L 139/55.

[53] Regulation 854/2004, *OJ* 2004 L 139/206.

[54] Regulation 882/2004, *OJ* 2004 L 191/1.

[55] See Commission Regulation 2076/2005, *OJ* 2005 L 338/83.

[56] Regulation 183/2005 on requirements for feed hygiene, *OJ* 2005 35/1.

[57] See section 3.2 below.

[58] See section 3.2 below. See J. Vergnettes, 'Les prérogatives communautaires: analyse du risque – nouvelle autorité européenne de sécurité des aliments' in Bourrinet et Snyder, op. cit. n. 8 at pp. 109–121.

mittee of Enquiry on BSE[59] was ferociously critical of the Commission's historical failure to separate food safety and consumer interests from those of agriculture and food production interests.[60] The European Parliament had gained considerably in its legislative powers with the introduction of the co-operation and then co-decision procedures. With the stick of censure[61] to hand, the European Parliament has been able to wield considerable power over the legislative evolution of the new Union agri-food regime. The Commission answered to the Parliament's Environment, Public Health and Consumer Affairs Committee, rising to one of the most powerful of the EP committees alongside the Committees on foreign affairs and monetary policy and legal affairs.

In fact, there was no separate reference to food law or food safety in the titles of Commission or Parliament organisational structures prior to the BSE crisis. In 1993 the EP environment Committee was called Committee on the Environment, Public Health and Consumer Protection. There was no reference to food safety or indeed to the food sector in the European Parliament's committee names. Since the new Parliamentary term 2004–2009, the consumer arm of the environment committee has been transferred to the European Parliament's Internal Market Committee but the food safety portfolio remains with the European Parliament's Environment, Public Health and Food Safety Committee.

The elevated status of food safety has also become apparent in the organisational structure of the European Commission. Until 1997, consumer policy was a policy area within the Commission Directorate responsible for the environment and nuclear *acquis*. A small unit called the Consumer Protection Service, within the European Commission's Internal Market Directorate, was dedicated to consumer protection matters but food safety was treated alongside any other product safety

[59] The Decision to do so was published in *OJ* 1997 C 150/9. It was based on Art. 135(2) of the EP's rules of procedure and it was established pursuant to resolution of 19 February 1997 on the results of the Temporary Committee of Inquiry into BSE, *OJ* 1997 C 85/61.

[60] See in particular the report of the Temporary Committee of Inquiry into BSE, A4-0020/97 in *OJ* 1997 C85/61.

[61] The motion of censure was put forward by Josè Happart MEP on 20 February 1997. Under Article 144 EC, the EP may force the members of the Commission to resign collectively. The motion of censure is a political tool in the hands of Parliament and the use thereof is not subject to any particular basic requirements.

issue. Since 1997, all matters of food hygiene and food safety previously managed by the European Commission's Directorate for Agriculture as well as relevant staff and dossiers from the Internal Market Directorate General, have been transferred to the new Directorate responsible for Consumer Policy and Consumer Health Protection.

As of 1997, when a distinct Directorate General for Consumer Policy and Consumer Health Protection was created, the policy shift in the conception of Union agri-food law has been clear. Today it is called the Directorate General for Health and Consumer Protection. Nowadays food safety is managed by a special Unit within the European Commission's Directorate for Health and Consumer Protection. The Directorate took on a completely new structure of scientific advice and the Food and Veterinary Office (FVO)[62] was created in order to monitor the Member State's and third countries' control systems in the field of veterinary and plant health control. Previously this office was referred to as the Office for Veterinary and Phytosanitary Control and had been part of the Commission's Directorate General for Agriculture. The FVO is an enforcement body, entrusted with the task of ensuring that the Member States apply food and feed safety controls properly. It carries out some 250 inspections and audits in the Member States as well as third countries every year and where weaknesses are found, it agrees action plans with the Member States concerned. In particular it checks up on transposition of EU laws into national legislation. The FVO thus helps to identify systemic weaknesses and to resolve them, failing which it may propose court proceedings against the Member State for failure to transpose a given measure.

Additionally a third unit was created within the Consumer Directorate, DG SANCO, to co-ordinate horizontal issues, particularly the resources of the Directorate and its policies. This Directorate now has over 600 staff compared to the 400 in entire Internal Market Directorate General, although of course, not all are dedicated to food safety and agri-food law as the consumer portfolio is far broader. The management of all the relevant scientific committees falls under this Directorate's responsibility together with the FVO, and a new unit on the assessment of consumer health risks.

---

[62] The FVO's activities and staff were introduced as of 1 April 1997 and its main office is located in Dublin. See *Second Annual Report of the Food and Veterinary Office April 1998–March 1999* to be found at www.europa.eu.int.

The Commission also began reorganising and reinforcing the three complementary instruments for protecting consumer health: scientific advice, risk analysis, and controls. Included in the transfer were all the comitology committees, having executive implementing powers under the agri-food *acquis*.[63] The comitology structures have been revised and rationalised, most recently by Regulation 178/2002.[64] The agri-food *acquis* has steadily been extricated from the CAP and environment realms of the EU activities, and the latter were progressively subordinated to safety issues and consumer needs. There has also been a clearer demarcation between policy and management of the agri-food regime, on the one hand, and risk assessment on the other, including within the latter category of scientific opinion and advice. Last but by no means least, the European Food Safety Authority was established[65] for the purposes of providing an independent source of advice on food safety issues in order to contribute to a high level of consumer health protection in the area of food safety, through which consumer confidence can be restored and maintained.

Accordingly, EFSA is an independent scientific source of advice, information and risk communication in food and feed safety. It has set up a network enabling close collaboration with similar bodies in the European Union Member States. The responsibility for risk assessment is clearly separated from that of risk management. EFSA advises on possible risk related to food safety but the responsibility for risk

---

[63] Although the management committees concerned with the functioning of the Common Market Organisations (COMs) were not included in the transfer being primarily concerned with the functioning of the Common Agricultural Policy.

[64] Op. cit. n. 49. See Recital 62 and Art. 62 thereof. The distinction between scientific committees and the standing or regulatory committees remains. Every reference in Community legislation to the Scientific Committee on Food, the Scientific Committee on Animal Nutrition, the Scientific Veterinary Committee, the Scientific Committee on Pesticides, the Scientific Committee on Plants and the Scientific Steering Committee shall be replaced by a reference to the European Food Safety Authority. In order to ensure a more effective, comprehensive approach to the food chain, the Committee on the Food Chain and Animal Health has been established and replaces the Standing Veterinary Committee, the Standing Committee for Foodstuffs and the Standing Committee for Feedingstuffs. For the same reasons the same Committee on the Food Chain and Animal Health also replaces the Standing Committee on Plant Health in relation to its competences on plant protection products and the setting of maximum residue levels.

[65] By virtue of Regulation 178/2002, op. cit. n. 49 at Arts. 22–49. The missions and tasks of EFSA can be found in Arts. 22 and 23 of Regulation 178/2002. An introduction to EFSA's legal foundation see the official EFSA website can be found at www.efsa.eu.int/about_efsa/legislation/catindex_en.html.

management lies with the EU institutions (European Commission, European Parliament and the Council). The EU institutions take account of EFSA's advice as well as other considerations when proposing and adopting legislation as well as regulatory and control measures. EFSA is a Union body having its own legal personality, is funded from the Union budget but operates independently of the Union Institutions. It is not therefore managed by the Commission but by an Executive Director, who is answerable to a Management Board. Since its creation, EFSA has established key operating principles and rules which have been adopted by its Management Board. They include a commitment to openness and transparency in all of the Authority's work. For example, EFSA undertakes to open up its meetings, to organise consultations with stakeholders and the public, and to ensure full access to all documents.

Thus, EU agri-food law has undergone a profound transformation in the last decade, characterised by a sophisticated legal regime worked out in substantive detail at EU level and leaving increasingly less for the Member States to work out for the purposes of implementation, other than transposition or, for example, establishing criminal/civil sanctions and inspection and control. Over the last ten years the EU has also gained considerable competences from the Member States for the elaboration of hygiene and safety and consumer protection aspects of regulating the food sector, including agricultural production.[66] Union competences reach far into national legal systems and administrative structures. The pre-occupation with the integrity of the food chain jointly with maintaining consumer confidence is now king.

### 1.2 *The mechanics of the pre-accession strategy for the agri-food* acquis

The Europe Agreements listed consumer protection under general provisions on economic co-operation and approximation of laws.[67] The later Europe Agreements for the Baltic States and Slovenia contained more detailed food-safety provisions, reflecting the fact that

[66] See I. Chmitelin, 'Le role des états members dans la securité sanitaire des aliments' in Bourrinet and Snyder, op. cit. n. 8 at pp. 95–107.

[67] See G. Sander 'Consumer protection and public health' in *Handbook on European Enlargement* (The Hague, T.M.C. Asser Press 2002) at pp. 867–880.

they were drawn up as the Union embarked upon the overhaul of the agri-food laws. It was clear from *Agenda 2000* of 1997 that the candidates lagged behind the Fifteen in terms of ensuring the efficient protection of consumers, especially in the light of economic reforms ongoing in the candidate countries.[68] The lack of specific food safety laws was only part of the reason for the overall gap in consumer protection laws in the candidate countries. Consumer protection laws overlap with economic interests. In order for the agri-food *acquis* to be effective, parallel actions are important, including: effective judicial redress mechanisms; producer liability rules; changes in competitive practices and business ethics; the existence of non-governmental consumer organisations, together with; consumer information and educational capacity.

It was the *Agenda 2000* innovations to the pre-accession strategy that gave the impetus to approximation by the candidates with the consumer protection *acquis*. By the end of 2000, some of the candidates had made considerable progress according to the European Commission's progress reports under the pre-accession strategy.[69] In Hungary, for example, consumer protection laws took effect in March 1998 transposing product safety rules amongst others. Poland introduced laws on product safety and liability for defective products in 2000. Latvia and Estonia were reported as having made major inroads into approximation with EU standards in 2000 and Lithuania passed a law on product safety and foodstuffs, also reported on by the Commission in 2000. Malta in particular was lagging behind with approximation.

For Bulgaria and Romania, a matter of days before the votes of the twenty-five Member States and the European Parliament to proceed with their enlargement, the Commission was most critical of Bulgaria and Romania in its September 2006 Opinion on their readiness to implement the agri-food *acquis*.[70] It was clear for both Bulgaria and Romania that while they had continued in their efforts to align to the agri-food *acquis* after their accession, throughout 2007, there were

---

[68] *Agenda 2000*, op. cit. n. 9.

[69] See COM(2000) 701, 702, 703, 704, 705, 706, 707, 708, 709, 710, 711, and 712, all of 8 November 2000. These are summarised at greater length in G. Sander, op. cit. n. 67.

[70] Commission Opinions of 26 September 2006,

still significant discrepancies reported by the FVO in its 2007 Annual Report concerning:

- veterinary public health concerns in both Bulgaria and Romania;
- controls on classical swine fever in Romania;
- preparedness of national competent authorities in avian influenza and New Castle disease in Romania;
- traceability and labelling of GMOs in Romania.

Various means have been used to ensure the safety of the food chain in an enlarged Union.

Preparations for future enlargements also involve upgrading the administrative capacity and legal framework in the incoming countries. Thus the Accession Partnership Turkey provides for the following priority actions in their approximation efforts concerning the agri-food *acquis*:[71]

- adopt a framework law on food, feed and veterinary matters compliant with EU requirements and which allows a complete transposition of the EU *acquis*,
- ensure the operationality of the system for the identification and registration of bovines and registration of their movement in compliance with the EU *acquis*, and start the implementation of an appropriate system for sheep and goats in order to trace movements,
- take the necessary measures to allow the Thrace region to be recognised by the World Organisation on Animal Health as a foot-and-mouth disease-free zone with vaccination,
- classify all agri-food establishments by category based on the EU *acquis* and prepare a National Programme for upgrading those establishments.

The FVO carried out a general review of animal and public health pre-accession in 2008 although the results are not yet published on

[71] See Council Decision 2008/157 on the principles, priorities and conditions contained in the Accession Partnership with the Republic of Turkey and repealing Decision 2006/35, *OJ* 2008 L 051/4, at Chapter 12: Food safety, veterinary and phytosanitary policy.

the Commission's website. All the candidates will be subject to more detailed, sectoral reviews in 2009.[72]

Different priorities have been identified for Turkey, FYROM and Croatia in their Accession Partnerships. The Association Agreement Turkey, has been reoriented to focus on accession and approximation with the *acquis*, reflecting the 1997 pre-accession strategy set down by the *Agenda 2000* document of the Commission including capacity building. However, the Stabilisation and Association Agreements have been drafted as pre-accession vehicles from the outset. Approximation to the *acquis* is an aim of the association and is provided for in Article 1(2). For example, in the SAA Croatia, two articles provide the basis for approximation on the agri-food *acquis*. Article 74 concerning consumer protection sets out an obligation on Croatia to align to the standards of consumer protection of the EU. It also provides that:

> Effective consumer protection is necessary in order to ensure that the market economy functions properly, and this protection will depend on the development of an administrative infrastructure in order to ensure market surveillance and law enforcement in this field.
>
> To that end, and in view of their common interests, the Parties will encourage and ensure:
>
> - the harmonisation of legislation and the alignment of consumer protection in Croatia on that in force in the EU;
> - a policy of active consumer protection including the increase of information and development of independent organisations;
> - effective legal protection for consumers in order to improve the quality of consumer goods and maintain appropriate safety standards.

Article 92 also provides for co-operation in agriculture and the agro-industrial sector. The aim here is:

> the modernisation and restructuring of agriculture and the agro-industrial sector consistent with the [EU] rules and standards, the water management, the rural development, the gradual harmonisation of the veterinary and phytosanitary legislation with [EU] standards and the development of the forestry sector in Croatia.

An FVO general review of FYROM was carried out in 2006[73] and further missions and a general assessment were carried out in 2008.[74]

---

[72] See FVO *Programme of Audits and inspections 2009*, at p. 8, to be found at http://ec.europa.eu/food/fvo/inspectprog/inspect_prog_fvo_2009_en.pdf

[73] FVO Report 8036/2006.

[74] See *Programme of Audits and inspections 2009*, op. cit. n. 72.

Various reports of the FVO on Croatia give specific guidance on work completed and outstanding in different areas[75] and a general review was also conducted there in 2008.[76] For FYROM the priorities currently governing their pre-accession efforts are set out in the Accession Partnership, which includes:[77]

- Continue to align legislation with the veterinary and phytosanitary *acquis*, focusing on framework legislation compatible with the *acquis*.
- Continue to reinforce the capacity of the veterinary service at both central and local levels in order to put in place an EU-compatible control system, particularly for import controls.
- Ensure the operational character of the system for identification of bovines and registration of their movements and start a system of identification of pigs, sheep and goats.
- Further align animal disease and animal health control systems with the EU legislative and institutional requirements and the contingency plans for notifiable diseases.
- Assess the compliance of agri-food establishments with EU requirements, which will serve as a basis for a future upgrading plan of those establishments.

For Croatia, the priorities indicate a lower level of approximation so far compared to FYROM:[78]

- Substantially improve the alignment of legislation in the food safety, veterinary and phytosanitary domain and strengthen the necessary implementing structures including control and inspection services,
- ensure the setting up of compliant regimes in the food safety, veterinary and phytosanitary sectors, including a system for animal identification and registration of movements, treatment of animal

[75] See various FVO Reports, 2007/2354, 2007/7355, 2006/8331, 2005/7586.
[76] See *Programme of Audits and inspections 2009*, op. cit. n. 72.
[77] Council Decision 2008/212 on the principles, priorities and conditions contained in the Accession Partnership with the former Yugoslav Republic of Macedonia and repealing Decision 2006/57, *OJ* 2008 L80/32, at Chapter 12: Food safety, veterinary and phytosanitary policy.
[78] Council Decision 2008/119 on the principles, priorities and conditions contained in the Accession Partnership with Croatia and repealing Decision 2006/145, *OJ* 2008 L42/51, at Chapter 12: Food safety, veterinary and phytosanitary policy.

by-products, upgrading of agri-food establishments, animal welfare and programmes of control of animal diseases, control of animals and animal products at border inspection posts, control of plant health, authorisation of plant protection products and control of their residues as well as quality of seeds and plant propagating material.

As for potential candidates, Albania together with Bosnia and Herzegovina were also subject to general FVO reviews in the second half of 2008[79] although the results are not yet available on the Commission's website either.

### 1.2.1 *The shift from 'equivalence' to full compliance as a Member State*

Under the Europe Agreements (or the association agreements) of the candidates of the fifth and sixth enlargements, Free Trade Areas were established progressively.[80] The approach taken was the asymmetrical opening up of trade based on reciprocal concessions whereby the EU Member States moved faster than their counterparts to lift such duties and tariffs on products originating in the EA countries.[81] As third countries importing foodstuffs into the Union under the Europe Agreements (or in the cases of Cyprus and Malta under their association agreements), the candidate countries held the general status of a third country. Third countries importing into the Union are not required to have in place the full raft of laws and administrative provisions and structures as the Union.[82] However, a principle of equivalence has been established according to which the importing country

---

[79] See See *Programme of Audits and inspections 2009*, op. cit. n. 72.

[80] The general target date for opening up the Free Trade Area to all the CEEC was 1 January 2004. The transitional period starting from the dates of entry into force of the Europe Agreements and the Agreements on Trade-Related Matters with the Baltic States.

[81] See M. Maresceau and E. Montaguti, 'The Relations between the European Union and Central and Eastern Europe: A Legal Appraisal', 32 *CML Rev.* (1995) p. 1327 at pp. 1345–1363 and M. Cremona, 'The New Associations: Substantive Issues of the Europe Agreements with the Central and Eastern European States', in S. Kostantinidis, ed., *The Legal Regulation of the European Community's External Relations after the Completion of the Internal Market* (Aldershot, Dartmouth 1996) p. 141. See also, P. Koutrakos 'Free movement of goods under the Europe Agreements' in *Handbook on European Enlargement*, op. cit. 67, pp. 369–390.

[82] The rules relevant to import are also under revision, see European Commission Guidance Document on certain key questions related to import requirements and the

demonstrates the capability of its inspection and certification systems to meet the same/equivalent objectives as the EU agri-food standards relevant to the product concerned.[83] The FVO inspects third countries' administrative capacity and legislative frameworks to this end and identifies the countries and specific establishments entitled to import food into the Union.[84]

In order to meet the obligations of membership of the Union, the candidate takes on the task of fully approximating with the *acquis*. This involves transposing the *acquis* into national law, of implementing it together with establishing the necessary administrative capacity that this involves, and guaranteeing compliance with the *acquis* thereafter. The FVO inspection reports will trigger Commission court action against Member States that fail to correctly transpose, implement and comply with the agri-food *acquis*. These themes are taken up further below. With the overhaul of Community agri-food law over the last decade, the new Member States were approximating to a moving target.

For the countries waiting in the wings today, the legislative backdrop is more stable.

### 1.2.2 *The aim: food hygiene and safety is paramount*

As will become apparent, the transitional arrangements provided for in the fifth and sixth Accession Treaties relating to EU agri-food law are far shorter than the transitional arrangements for the environment *acquis*. However, the transitional arrangements in both chapters share the fact that the main justification for any derogation from the *acquis* must be structural and expensive. It must simply not be possible to comply with the *acquis* on the day of accession because of the expense involved in upgrading, or even building from scratch, facilities in order that they meet with the structural requirements of

new rules on food hygiene and on official food controls, no official reference, of 29 June 2005.

[83] CODEX guidelines were adopted in 1999 for the development of equivalence agreements regarding food import and export inspection and certification systems. CAC/GL 34–1999. However, the notion and practice of applying the principle of equivalence to imports to the Union long pre-date these CODEX guidelines.

[84] Typically, the Commission adopts a decision establishing the list of the countries and even the specific establishments in those countries which meet the equivalence criteria. See for example Commission Decision 97/20 establishing the list of third countries fulfilling the equivalence conditions for the production and placing on the market of bivalve molluscs, echinoderms, tunicates and marine gastropods, *OJ* 1997 L 6/47, as last modified by Commission Decision 2006/766, *OJ* 2006 L 320/ 53–57.

the agri-food *acquis* (as is also the case for the environment *acquis*), such as upgrading food producing establishments (slaughter houses or fishing boats or handling facilities milk products, for example). Even where transitional arrangements are granted, they are time limited and restricted to only parts of a given directive or regulation. For example, where a particular food processing plant fails to upgrade in order to meet the full requirements of a piece of the agri-food legislation by the specified date, then they must close.

On no account is a transitional arrangement acceptable in respect of the transposition of agri-food laws. As will also become apparent, however, while no transitional arrangements were allowed the new Member States to delay transposition of agri-food legislation, in reality the fact that certain agri-food laws remained un-transposed on the date of accession amounted to the institution of informal transitional arrangements, see Table 7. In the case of the agri-food *acquis*, transitional arrangements may be added in respect of the veterinary and phytosanitary *acquis* – see chapter 4 of Part One. The purpose is specifically to guarantee the integrity/safety of the Union's food chain and to prevent barriers to the free movement of goods. Border controls are expressly forbidden.

The extension of the reach of EU agri-food law from the farm to the fork has considerably increased the number of laws to cover additional areas, including to cover animal feedingstuffs, over recent years. The General Principles of Food Law (contained in Arts. 5 to 10 of Regulation 178/2002)[85] entered into force on 21 February 2002 and must be followed as the Union measures are taken. The existing food law principles and procedures must be adapted by 1 January 2007 in order to comply with the general framework established by Regulation 178/2002. This is the same for all Member States. There have been no exceptions, derogations or otherwise, given the new Member States in respect of the implementation of the food law principles and hygiene rules. Prior to their accession to the EU on 1 May 2004, the new Members were denied any possibility of not transposing EU legislation. Certain transitional arrangements were allowed the new Member States in the implementation of certain provisions of EU agri-food legislation but only as far as necessary to allow these countries to make heavy structural adjustments requiring investment.

[85] Op. cit. n. 49.

### 1.2.3 *Comparative advantage of EFTA members under the EEA Agreement*

Upon their accession, the new Member States also acceded to the EEA Agreement. The EFTA members of the EEA have not been subject to the same food safety and hygiene reform as the candidates, new Member States or even the old Member States.

Under the EU agri-food regime prior to the fifth enlargement, the EFTA countries of the EEA did not have to approximate to the same agri-food *acquis* as applied in the fifteen and nor the twenty-seven Member States. On the same day as the EU enlarged, 1 May 2004, the EEA also enlarged. While most of the EEA contracting parties ratified the EEA Enlargement Agreement on time, a few countries had still not met this requirement at the end of 2004. In order to ensure the parallel entry into force of the extension of the EEA Agreement to the new Member States on the date of enlargement, the parties agreed that the EEA Enlargement Agreement should be applied provisionally until all contracting parties had ratified it. This agreement was signed on 1 April 2004 and the objective of simultaneous enlargement of the EU and the EEA was thus fulfilled.[86]

At the time of the fifth and the sixth enlargements, the EEA Agreement did not extend to Regulation 178/2002, the new regulatory framework for the handling and disposal of animal by-products (ABP);[87] the entire hygiene package,[88] and; the Regulation on food

---

[86] See *Annual Report of the [EEA] Joint Committee for the Year 2004 on the functioning of the EEA Agreement*, of 29 April 2005, Ref: 1051228 at point 23.

[87] Regulation 1774/2002 laying down health rules concerning animal by-products not intended for human consumption, *OJ* 2002 L 273/1. It is a major component of the Commission strategy to combat and eradicate feed-borne food crises such as BSE, foot and mouth disease, swine fever and dioxin contamination. The Regulation has been applicable since 1 May 2003.

[88] The package comprises five parts covering general hygiene, hygiene of food of animal origin, official controls and animal health rules for products of animal origin intended for human consumption, and a directive repealing the previously existing legislation contained in 17 separate Directives. See Regulation 852/2004 on the hygiene of foodstuffs, *OJ* 2004 L 226/3, Regulation 853/2004 laying down specific hygiene rules for food of animal origin, *OJ* 2004 L 139/55, Regulation 854/2004 laying down specific rules for the organisation of official controls on products of animal origin intended for human consumption, *OJ* 2004 L 226/83, Council Directive 2002/99 laying down the animal health rules governing the production, processing, distribution and introduction of products of animal origin for human consumption, *OJ* 2003 L18/11, Directive 2004/41 repealing certain Directives concerning food hygiene and health conditions for the production and placing on the market of certain products of animal origin intended for human consumption and amending Council Directives 89/662/EEC and

and feed control.[89] The EEA Agreement was only extended in 2007 in order to apply Regulation 178/2002[90] and the other provisions of the agri-food law reform. As at 29 March 2009 the extension of the EEA Agreement was still awaiting the fulfilment of national constitutional requirements[91] but the package of EC agri-food laws entered into provisional application on 26 April 2008 in any case, pending fulfilment of the national constitutional requirements in Iceland, Liecthenstein and Norway.[92]

In spite of this the EEA boasted a better track record in transposition of EEA legislation than the EU twenty-five Member States, according to the EEA Joint Committee.[93] From an agri-food law perspective, however, this report gave a false impression because certain key agri-food laws could not be transposed in the EEA until they had been incorporated into the EEA Agreement. Under the heading of *Veterinary, Feedingstuffs and Phytosanitary Matters*, the EEA Joint Committee Report for 2004[94] also made clear that the main tenets of the EU agri-food law reform had not yet been incorporated within the obligations for transposition and implementation by the EEA countries.[95]

Until negotiations were completed on the incorporation of the agri-food reform into the EEA Agreement – negotiations which were ongoing since 2002 – the 'old' agri-food laws continued to apply in the

92/118/EEC and Council Decision 95/408/EC, *OJ* 2004 L 157/33, amended by corrigendum, *OJ* 2004 L 195/12.

[89] See Regulation 882/2004 on official controls performed to ensure the verification of compliance with feed and food law, animal health and animal welfare rules was adopted by the, *OJ* 2004 L 191/1.

[90] See Decision of the EEA Joint Committee, 134/2007 of 26 October 2007, *OJ* 2007 L100/33 and EEA Supplement 19 of 10 April 2008, p. 39.

[91] See official EEA website updated periodically: http://www.efta.int/content/legal-texts/eea/list-awaited-notifications

[92] By virtue of Article 103(2) EEA Agreement.

[93] See EEA Joint Committee Report of 29 April 2005. The ESA claimed that EEA EFTA States kept their transposition deficits (i.e. the number of legislative measures that were not transposed into the national legal order on time) at a very low level in 2004 and were among the best performers in the whole EEA. In January 2005, the EFTA Surveillance Authority Scoreboard showed that Norway had a transposition deficit of only 1 percent, which gave the country the lead among the 28 EEA States. Iceland was fourth, while Liechtenstein slipped from the fourth to the fourteenth place during 2004. See *Annual Report of the [EEA] Joint Committee for the Year 2004 on the functioning of the EEA Agreement*, ibid. at point 12.

[94] Ibid. n. 93 at Annex I, points 2–5.

[95] The legislation on food and veterinary issues in the EEA is laid down in Chapter I of Annex I (Veterinary) and Chapter XII of Annex II (Foodstuffs) to the EEA Agreement.

EFTA members of the EEA.[96] In accordance with the practical application of the principle of mutual recognition, therefore, agri-food products emanating from the EFTA members of the EEA were, technically speaking, entitled to access the Internal Market provided they had been lawfully manufactured and marketed in accordance with the 'old' agri-food laws that had been incorporated into the EEA Agreement.[97]

This implied a certain bias of trust of the Union in the EEA countries compared to the new Member States. The EEA Agreement forms an integral part of the *acquis communautaire* and requires that incoming Member States are obliged to adhere to the EEA Agreement upon their accession to the Union. Accession to the EEA is an accession condition. But the EFTA countries to the EEA Agreement are not required to implement legislation adopted by the Union as a Member State must. They negotiate the updating of the annexes to the EEA Agreement with the Union. Consequently, it is not untypical that a long gestation period is involved in the incorporation of legislative developments into the EEA Agreement.

It is true that the EFTA countries of the EEA do not have the same spectrum of food industry[98] as the twenty-five Member States of the Union, such as wine production for example. However, this could also be said of a number of the smaller new EU Member States. Also, the EFTA members of the EEA did participate in the Rapid Alert System for Food and Feed (RASFF) at that time and in any case they also have national emergency or safeguard provision to deal with food scares as they may arise.

Nevertheless, Regulation 178/2002 sets out the fundamental principles and objectives that govern all EU agri-food laws. The new EU agri-food regime also includes safeguard clauses and seemingly also watertight emergency provisions in order to tackle food scares or crises that may arise,[99] which may be used by the EU Member States in

---

[96] By means of an interview with the Internal Market Affairs unit of the EFTA Surveillance Authority on 14 October 2005.

[97] See for example the Commission interpretative communication on facilitating the access of products to the markets of other Member States: the practical application of mutual recognition, *OJ* 2003 C 265/2, at para. 2.2.

[98] The EEA agreement covers the agri-food *acquis* on animal welfare, border inspection posts, fishery products and live bivalve molluscs, food control systems, fresh meat, meat products/minced meat/meat preparations and casings, milk and milk products, poultry meat, residues in live animals and their products, wild game meat and farmed game meat.

[99] See section 3.2 below

respect of risks arising in food coming from the EFTA members of the EEA. The very purpose of the agri-food reform was to design the regulatory backdrop of the Union's food sector in order to prevent crises arising at any given link throughout the entire food chain from 'farm-to-fork'. The delay in transposition in the EEA highlighted a gap in the Internal Market rules applying to the food (safety) sector and certainly gave a competitive advantage to the EFTA countries of the EEA not only over the EU Member States, as much as for the current candidates approximating with the agri-food *acquis*.

By contrast, neither the incoming Member States of the fifth enlargement, nor Bulgaria and Romania were allowed to put off transposing Regulation 178/2002 and nor were they allowed transitional derogations from compliance therewith in their Accession Treaties. The pre-accession conditionality applied to the candidates has certainly provided the Union with the upper hand in all accession negotiations. Incoming countries have had to fully approximate to the agri-food *acquis* and also to accede to the EEA Agreement.

A final comment is relevant concerning the administrative and governmental capacity of the EEA countries as concerns the application of EU (as opposed to EEA) agri-food law. Inspections of compliance by the Member States, their competent authorities and establishments with the EU agri-food rules is carried out by the Food and Veterinary Office. For the EEA countries, the inspection controls of the relevant governmental offices and competent authorities as well as food establishments are carried out by the EFTA Surveillance Authorities (ESA) Internal Market Affairs Directorate.[100] The FVO inspection programming does not include EEA countries while other third countries, including Switzerland and Turkey, are covered. The FVO only sends observers to accompany the inspection visits of the ESA. The ESA accompanies FVO inspections also in observer capacity. These

[100] The legal basis for the veterinary inspection is laid down in Article 1(e) of Protocol 1 to the Agreement between the EFTA States on the establishment of a Surveillance Authority and a Court of Justice. Detailed provisions regarding veterinary inspections are laid down in points 4(A) and 4(B) of the Introductory Part of Chapter I of Annex I to the EEA Agreement. More than 50 directives contain a legal basis for inspections by the ESA in the EFTA States. Detailed rules concerning on-the-spot checks carried out in the veterinary field are also laid down in a Commission Decision incorporated into the EEA Agreement. As for food inspections in the EFTA countries of the EEA, the legal basis for the inspections carried out by the ESA are the provisions of the EEA acts on the official control of foodstuffs.

two inspection authorities aim to provide a homogeneous approach to their inspections[101] and the ESA carries out 'equivalent' inspections to those conducted by the FVO. The new extension of the EEA Agreement to include the raft of food safety and hygiene rules secures the very legal basis for such 'equivalence', including the EEA partner countries within the safeguard measures and institutional provisions of Regulation 178/2002 on the EFSA and emergency and crisis measures.

## 2. The agri-food *acquis* and the fifth and sixth enlargements: post-accession conditionality and transitional arrangements

In previous enlargements the incoming Member States had less of an approximation exercise to prepare their accessions compared to the CEEC Member States, Malta and Cyprus and the current candidates. The evolution in the *acquis* also puts increasing demands on national competent authorities' inspection and controls on the application of veterinary and phytosanitary laws, as well as on standardisation and certification bodies, customs authorities and Border Inspection Posts (BIPs), bodies responsible for the sampling and analysis of foodstuffs, trading standards organisations and industry federations, and all businesses involved in the food chain. Gradual inclusion of the candidates in the programmes and agencies is an important means of building familiarity with the *acquis* as well as the necessary governmental capacity. For example, the Animal Disease Notification System has included Turkey as an informal member of the ADNS system since 2005, alongside the EEA countries and Switzerland, although the Balkans are not so included.[102]

The June 2002 Seville European Council Conclusions stressed the importance of continued progress in implementation and effective application of the *acquis* generally.[103] The Council was particularly concerned to see progress before it would consider finalising as

---

[101] See the webpage of the EFTA Surveillance authority on 'Food and Veterinary Issues', visited on 21 May 2005, to be found at www.eftasurv.int

[102] See EC Commission DG SANCO, *ADNS Annual Report 2006*, of February 2006.

[103] See *Bull. EU* 6–2002, Conclusion 24.

planned the accession negotiations in the December of that year. In 2002 the Commission issued action plans[104] [the environment chapter of the *acquis* is not so covered by this document] designed to take more decisive action and enable the Commission to monitor the commitments given by the candidates in the accession negotiations. These plans covered all twelve of the new Member States.[105]

The aim was to ensure that on accession, not even two years away at that time, the new Member States would meet adequate levels of administrative and judicial capacity after accession. The plan involved mobilising pre-accession assistance to the tune of EUR 250 million in pre-accession assistance on top of funding available under PHARE and thus extending the overall budgetary allocation for strengthening administrative and judicial capacity to EUR 1 billion in all.

### 2.1 *Post-accession incentives*

Further post-accession funding would be made available through the Transition Facility[106] to the same end. Where the structural funds do not cover capacity building, the Transition Facility expressly covers capacity building of veterinary services and food safety in its budget in the fifth Accession Treaty. In the sixth Accession Treaty administrative capacity for veterinary services and food safety is not specifically mentioned but would in any case be covered where necessary. The overall purpose of the Transition Facility is, after all, to develop and strengthen the administrative and judicial capacity to implement and enforce Community legislation and to foster exchange among peers.

---

[104] See Commission Communication on the *Action Plans for administrative and judicial capacity, and the monitoring of commitments made by the negotiating countries in the accession negotiations*, COM(2002) 256, 5 June 2002, not published in the *Official Journal*. A Food Safety Action Programme dated 23 July 2002 and contained in a Note from Commissioner Byrne to E. Landaburu, the Director General for Enlargement, outlines the joint initiative of DG Enlargement and DG Health and Consumer Protection as part of the last 18 months of the pre-accession effort.

[105] There was no action plan Turkey because accession negotiations had not been opened with Turkey at that time.

[106] To further finance the strengthening and developing administrative capacity and the continued implementation and enforcement of EU law as well as to foster best practice among peers. Art 34 Act of Accession provides for certain temporary financial assistance to be given the new Member States in the form of a 'Transition Facility': EUR 200 million for 2004, EUR 120 million for 2005, EUR 60 million for 2006.

Various other instruments also comprise components of relevance to the capacity building of the administration and the judiciary in the post-accession phase. Thus for example, under the sixth Accession Treaty for both Bulgaria and Romania, temporary rural development measures for Bulgaria and Romania include support for investments to improve processing and marketing of agricultural produce, *inter alia* to enable them to reach the minimum standards regarding the environment, hygiene and animal welfare by the end of the transitional arrangements.

### 2.1.1 *The need for credible commitments*

Certain comments made on the challenge of capacity building for the purposes of complying with the environment *acquis*, also apply in the context of the agri-food *acquis*. The extent of investment required for compliance with the agri-food *acquis* are of course far lower than that required for the environment *acquis*. But the matter of credible commitments by the new Member States to continue to comply with the *acquis* post-accession is also relevant to the agri-food *acquis*.[107] In order to do so the same comment applies; that of the need for an institutional approach by delegating the task to sufficiently empowered and accountable institutions which have both considerable decision-making independence and are subject to specific performance obligations.

### 2.1.2 *EU capacity building actions pre-accession*

Again, the FVO is active in today's candidate countries just as it was in twelve new Member States before they acceded. Among other actions taken to ensure the smooth functioning of the Internal Market *acquis*, the Action Plans targeted various aspects of the agri-food *acquis* and were designed for each candidate according to its needs, also reflecting the finding of the FVO.[108] The actions would establish or reinforce regulatory authorities, horizontal administrative structures and supervisory or administrative bodies. Action envisaged in the field of agriculture concerned the application of EC quality standards. In terms of food safety in particular, the action plans tackled the upgrad-

---

[107] See P. Nicolaides, 'Preparing for Accession to the EU: How to establish capacity for effective and credible application of EU rules', in M. Cremona, *The Enlargement of the European Union*, (Oxford, Oxford University Press 2003) pp. 43–78.

[108] COM(2002) 256, op. cit. n. 104.

ing of food processing establishments and inspection arrangements to enforce the veterinary and phyto-sanitary *acquis* as well as the food safety *acquis* covering the free movement of goods.

The specific measures listed included: the adoption of outstanding legislation; strengthening of relevant structures, including through budget and staff increases; the establishment of inter-ministerial co-ordination groups and scientific committees; the establishment or upgrading of laboratories, border inspection posts (BIPs) and the RASFF; the development of Hazard Analysis Critical Control Point (HACCP) auditing; the development or upgrading of databases and computerised networks; creating training structures for inspectors, for laboratory staff as well as for food operators, including training veterinarians and slaughterhouse personnel on Transmissible Spongiform Encephalopathies (TSE); supplementary assistance was specifically earmarked for Czech Republic, Hungary, Latvia, Poland, Slovakia and Slovenia for twinning on TSE control, for market surveillance in the food chain and for the creation and upgrading of BIPs.

The Commission also set out its plans for 'enhanced monitoring' of the commitments that the candidates made during the negotiations. Administrative structures responsible for food safety were specifically highlighted for attention in the context of the goods chapter of the *acquis*, as well as the agriculture chapter.

#### 2.1.3 *Post-accession capacity building, monitoring and evaluation*

Since enlargement the governmental capacity of the new Member States has continued to be monitored and evaluated by the FVO as it does for any other Member State. The proportion of FVO inspections in the candidate countries was already increasing in the years leading up to enlargement. FVO inspections increased by a third in 2003 compared to the number of inspections in 2002.[109] Also since enlargement, the new Member States have been entitled to funding under a range of Community financed programmes for the eradication and monitoring of animal diseases, for example, on classical swine fever or on rabies.[110] Also, the Commission launched capacity building projects for all twenty-five Member States in 2005.[111] Various proactive means of

[109] See *FVO Annual Report for 2003*, European Commission, at p. 3.
[110] See Commission Decision 2004/840, *OJ* 2004 L 361/41.
[111] Contract Notices for 'Better Training for Safer Food', of 19 July 2005, *OJ* 2005 S 137.

preventing inadequate application of the agri-food *acquis* are in place and 'formal legal proceedings are only resorted to where it is apparent that there is a blatant violation or where a Member State is exhibiting lack of cooperation [with the FVO] to resolve an issue'.[112] Prevention tools include guidance documentation on implementing core legislation[113] and including Directive 91/414 on pesticides or plant protection products (PPP) and their residues on food.[114] The PPD Directive is soon to be replaced by a Regulation.[115] Finally, the rules on technical standards also require that Member States notify the European Commission of draft national technical standards and regulations so that the European Commission may ensure that they are not incompatible with Community law.[116]

The issue of building and guaranteed sufficient administrative capacity remains a challenge after the enlargements. As we see further on in this chapter, when looking at the reality of how ready the new Member States were to accede to the Union in May 2004, the administrative capacity of some of the new members remains a post-accession problem. For example, in an FVO report on Malta carried out in December 2004, the FVO concluded that the Maltese Central Competent Authority was not able to ensure compliance with Community laws on slaughterhouses, cutting premises, milk processing plants, cheese processing plants or farms and also that the food establishments did not comply with EU law.[117] It transpired that in general, the recon-

[112] See European Commission Communication, *25th Annual Report on the Monitoring of the Application of Community law, Situation in the Different Sectors*, SEC (2008) 2854 of 18 November 2008, pp. 219–221.

[113] See European Commission, Conclusions of the Standing Committee on the Food Chain and Animal Health, of 20 December 2004 on *Guidance of the Implementation of Arts. 11, 12, 16, 17, 18, 19 and 20 of Regulation 178/2002*, to be found at http://ec.europa.eu/food/food/foodlaw/guidance/guidance_rev_7_en.pdf. See also DG SANCO Guidance document of 5 January 2006 on certain key questions related to import requirements and the new rules on food hygiene and official controls, to be found at http://ec.europa.eu/food/international/trade/interpretation_imports.pdf

[114] Council Directive 91/414/EEC of 15 July 1991 concerning the placing of plant protection products on the market, *OJ* 1991 L 230/1, as amended. The guidance can be found at http://ec.europa.eu/food/plant/protection/resources/publications_en.htm Three new guidelines were added in 2007.

[115] See Amended Proposal for a Regulation concerning the placing of plant protection products on the market, COM(2008) 93 of 11 March 2008.

[116] See Directive 98/34, *OJ* 1998 L 204/37.

[117] See FVO Report, DG(SANCO)/7182/2004 of 28 April 2005 for the period 14 to 17 December 2004, at p. 14.

struction of such food establishments only began after accession, and that included an establishment that was under a transitional period (until 31 December 2004) in the 2003 Accession Treaty.

### 2.2 *Transitional arrangements contained in the 2003 and 2005 Accession Treaties*

The priority of food safety and the functioning of the Internal Market made widespread use of transitional arrangements out of the question. It is not an area where Member States are able to institute stricter or higher standards outside of the recognised legal channels and conditions. The fact that the agri-food *acquis* essentially concerns the free movement of goods means that transitional arrangements were not really an option. This applies not only to transposition of laws but also to building the necessary administrative capacity giving them effect. Also, the agri-food trade is a sector where standardisation and certification arise in relation to goods and in fields such as the veterinary and phytosanitary *acquis*. Thus, the potential for technical barriers to trade are considerable.

However, the rationale underlying the negotiation of the transitional arrangements in agri-food *acquis* is fundamentally the same as that applied to the negotiation of the transitional arrangements in the environment *acquis*. It is useful to recap on them very briefly here: requests for transitional arrangements by the acceding countries were divided into three types[118] by the Commission: acceptable, negotiable and unacceptable.

Article 24 Act of Accession 2003[119] refers to the country Annexes V through to XIV for each of the ten new Member States. It specifies the temporary derogations for each of the new members in respect of specific laws. The equivalent in the sixth (2005) Accession Treaty is Article 23. Consistent with the inclusive-yet-differentiating approach seen during pre-accession, the transitional derogations take account of the specific situation or readiness of each of the Ten. The pre-determined transitional arrangements that were agreed by the Ten and the

[118] See European Commission, *Enlargement Strategy Paper, Report on progress towards accession by each of the candidate countries* (*for 2000*), pp. 225–28 See Part 1, Chapter 4. The three types break down as acceptable, negotiable, unacceptable.

[119] Art 54, 2003 Act of Accession expressly allows for the application of the time-limits set out in Annexes V–XIV.

Union at the December 2002 Copenhagen European Council, vary in time scale and do not always follow a three-year rule. However, Article 40 of the Act of Accession specifies that the enforcement of the transitional arrangements may on no account lead to border controls between the Member States.

The following table reflects the situation contained in the 2003 and 2005 Accession Treaties. However, the country annexes to the Act of Accession are not the end to the matter because the fifth and sixth Accession Treaties have been revised or new transitional arrangements introduced or amended.

On 29 April 2004, two days before the fifth enlargement, the fifteen Member States adopted a number of Regulations that would repeal and replace various agri-food laws subject to deferred application or derogation under the fifth Accession Treaty:[120]

- Regulation 852/2004 on the hygiene of foodstuffs;[121]
- Regulation 853/2004 laying down specific hygiene rules for food of animal origin;[122]
- Regulation 882/2004 on official controls performed to ensure the verification of compliance with feed and food law, animal health and animal welfare rules;[123]
- Regulation 854/2004 of the European Parliament and of the Council of 29 April 2004 laying down specific rules for the organisation of official controls on products of animal origin intended for human consumption.[124]

As a result, the number of the Directives subject to transitional arrangements for certain food processing plants under the fifth Accession Treaty have since been repealed and replaced by the above new rules, which took effect on 1 January 2006. The provisions of the 2003 Act of Accession that defer the application of various provisions relating to food processing plants list different legislation in force. These are marked with an asterisk. It is important to note that these laws, as published initially in the *Official Journal* did not contain the dates of

[120] A week earlier, to prepare the ground for the new Regulations, on 21 April 2004, the Fifteen adopted Directive 2004/41, op. cit. n. 88.
[121] *OJ* 2004 L139/1.
[122] *OJ* 2004 L139/55.
[123] *OJ* 2004 L165/1.
[124] *OJ* 2004 L13/206.

entry into force and application and were subsequently republished in their entirety by corrigendum.

Also as a result of these new rules, for example, the HACCP Directive 93/43 on the hygiene of foodstuffs was replaced by Regulations 852/2004 and 853/2004, Directive 93/99 on official controls of foodstuffs was replaced by Regulation 882/2004 and Directive 91/494 on third country controls of animal health conditions was replaced by Directive 2004/41. Being Regulations, there is no room for failure to transpose these laws because they are directly applicable in every Member State. Others on the list have also changed: Directive 96/5 on processed cereal-based baby food, has been replaced by Directive 2006/125.

#### 2.2.1 *A summary of transitional arrangements in the agri-food* acquis

The below table summarises the twelve new Member States' temporary derogations specified in the fifth (2003) and sixth (2005) Accession Treaties in respect of certain provisions of the agri-food *acquis*, together with the expiry dates for compliance therewith in accordance with pre-accession commitments.

The details of the derogations from any given provision in the country annexes must be read carefully and can differ from one Member State to another. Cyprus, Estonia, Malta and Slovenia have no transitional arrangements in the Accession Treaty for their food establishments. Cyprus, Estonia, Latvia and Lithuania have no transitional arrangements concerning the laying hens Directive and the restrictions on seed quality do not apply to the Czech Republic, Estonia, Hungary, Lithuania, Poland or Slovakia (although Poland does have the special transitional regime for potatoes).

Taking Poland as an example, the derogations from the veterinary *acquis* relate to fresh meat establishments and minced meat and meat preparations establishments and applied until 31 December 2007. This list of establishments could be updated by the Commission in accordance with the comitology procedure provided in the relevant Directive, in order to add to the lists of these establishments or delete them from the lists in the light of the progress that they make in remedying the short comings.[125] The Commission may also adopt detailed

[125] See XII.6.B(e), 2003 Accession Treaty, p. 883.

Table 6. Table of transitional derogations in the 2003 and 2005 Accession Treaties: agri-food *acquis*

VETERINARY

| Directive concerned | Relevant provision: expiry date for country derogation | Relevant provision: expiry date for country derogation |
|---|---|---|
| Directive 64/433* on health conditions for the production and marketing of fresh meat, consolidated,<br>OJ 1991 L 268/71 | Annex I<br>Expiry on 30 December 2005: Latvia,<br>Expiry on 30 December 2006: Lithuania, Hungary, Slovakia<br>Expiry on 30 December 2007: Poland | Annex I and II<br>(structural requirements for establishments)<br>Expiry on 30 December 2006: Czech Republic, |
| Directive 71/118* on health problems affecting the production and placing on the market of fresh poultry meat,<br>OJ 1971 L 55/23 | Annex I<br>Expiry on 30 December 2005: Latvia,<br>Expiry on 30 December 2006: Lithuania<br>Expiry on 30 December 2007: Poland | Annex I and II<br>(structural requirements for establishments)<br>Expiry on 30 December 2006: Czech Republic |
| Council Directive 77/99* on health problems affecting the production and marketing of meat products and certain other products of animal origin,<br>OJ 1977 L 26/85 | Annex A and B<br>(structural requirements for establishments)<br>Expiry on 30 December 2005: Latvia,<br>Expiry on 30 December 2006: Czech Republic, Lithuania, Slovakia<br>Expiry on 30 December 2007: Poland | |
| Council Directive 89/437* on hygiene and health problems affecting the production and the placing on the market of egg products,<br>OJ 1989 L 212/87 | Annex<br>(structural requirements for establishments)<br>Expiry on 30 December 2006: Czech Republic | |
| Directive 91/493* on production and marketing of fishery products,<br>OJ | Annex<br>Expiry on 30 December 2005: Latvia<br>Expiry on 30 December 2006: Lithuania, Sloakia<br>Expiry on 30 December 2007: Poland | |

Table 6 (*cont.*)

| Directive concerned | Relevant provision: expiry date for country derogation | Relevant provision: expiry date for country derogation |
|---|---|---|
| Directive 92/46* on health rules for the production and placing on the market of raw milk, heat-treated milk and milk-based products,<br>OJ 1992 L 268/1 | Annex A, Chapters I, II & IV<br>Expiry on 30 December 2009: Malta<br>Annex A, Chapter IV, A(1)<br>Expiry on 30 December 2007: Poland | Annex B<br>(structural requirements for establishments)<br>Expiry on 30 December 2005: Latvia,<br>Expiry on 30 December 2006: Czech Republic, Lithuania<br>Expiry on 30 December 2007: Poland |
| Directive 94/65* on production and marketing of minced meat and meat preparations,<br>OJ 1994 L 368/10 | Annex I<br>Expiry on 30 December 2005: Latvia,<br>Expiry on 30 December 2006: Lithuania<br>Expiry on 30 December 2007: Poland | |
| Directive 1999/74 on minimum standards for the protection of laying hens,<br>OJ 1999 L 203/53 | Art. 5(1)(4)<br>Expiry on 30 December 2009: Czech Republic, Hungary, Slovenia | Art. 5(1)(5)<br>Expiry on 30 December 2006: Malta, Poland, Slovenia |
| Regulation 1774/2002 on animal by-products not intended for human consumption,1<br>OJ 2002 L 273/1 | Annex V, Chapter I & Annex VII, Chapter I<br>Expiry on 30 December 2004: Latvia | |
| Regulation 853/2004 on hygiene rules for food of animal origin,<br>OJ 2004 L 139/55 | Annex III, Section IX, Chapter I, subchapters II and III<br>Expiry on 31 December 2009: Bulgaria, Romania | Annex III, Section I, Chapters II & III, Section II<br>Expiry on 31 December 2009: Romania |

Table 6 (*cont.*)

PHYTOSANITARY

| Directive concerned | Relevant provision: expiry date for country derogation | Relevant provision: expiry date for country derogation |
|---|---|---|
| Directive 66/402 on marketing of cereal seed,<br>OJ 1966 P 125/2309 | Annex II<br>(analytical purity of *Hordeum vilgare L.* (barley) sold in Cyprus)<br>Expiry on 30 April 2009: Cyprus | |
| Directive 69/464 on control of Potato Wart Disease<br>OJ 1969 L 323/1 | Art. 9, safeguard measures<br>Expiry on 30 April 2014: Poland | |
| Directive 82/471 on certain products used in animal nutrition,<br>OJ 1982 L 213/8 | Art. 3(1)<br>(feedingstuffs based on yeast *Candida utilis*)<br>Expiry on 30 April 2006: Czech Republic | |
| Directive 91/414 on plant protection products,<br>OJ 1991 L 230/1 | Art. 13(1)<br>Expiry on 30 December 2006: Poland | |
| Directive 93/85 on the control of potato ring rot,<br>OJ 1993 L 259/1 | Art. 7(2) & (4)<br>Expiry on 30 December 2006 | |

Table 6 (*cont.*)

| Directive concerned | Relevant provision: expiry date for country derogation | Relevant provision: expiry date for country derogation |
|---|---|---|
| Regulation 2100/94 on Community plant variety rights,<br>OJ 1994 L227/1 | Art. 14(3), 4th indent,<br>(combined with Art. 14(1))<br>Expiry on 30 December 2010: Lithuania | |
| Directive 99/105 on marketing of forestry reproductive material,<br>OJ 1999 L 11/17 | Art. 28(3)<br>No deadline, exhaustion of stocks, Poland | |
| Directive 2002/53 on the common catalogue of<br>varieties of agricultural<br>plant species,<br>OJ 2002 L 193/1 | (National plants species not recognised under 2002/53)<br>Expiry on 30 April 2009: Cyprus, Latvia, Malta, Slovenia | |
| Directive 2002/55 on the marketing of vegetable seed,<br>OJ 2002 L 193/33 | (National vegetable species not recognised under 2002/55)<br>Expiry on 30 April 2009: Latvia, Malta, Slovenia | |

* Laws marked with an asterisk have been repealed and replaced by Regulations 852/2004, 853/2004, 882/2004 and 854/2004.

implementing rules to ensure the smooth operation of the transitional arrangements under Article 58 of Regulation 178/2002.[126] This is a comitology procedure involving the Standing Committee on the Food Chain and Animal Health (SCFCAH). This is the procedure also used to update the import rules for animals and animal products crossing from the areas of Cyprus out with the control of the government of Cyprus.

Such derogations are structural in nature and do *not* relate to hygiene requirements *per se* – see below. The derogations for specified establishments for fishery products and for raw milk, heat-treated milk and milk-based products applied until 31 December 2006. Again, these derogations applied to the structural requirements only. The products issued from these plants were restricted to the Polish market – to this end requirements for marking the products are also stipulated. In the Polish annex to the Act of Accession, provision is made for the future adoption of implementing rules for these transitional arrangements, in accordance with the procedures set out in the relevant EC legislation.

However, in the case of potatoes, the annex for Poland also specifies a ten-year transitional arrangement, potentially renewable beyond that term if necessary. The purpose is to ensure that Poland applies *stricter standards* than the EU regime in order to eliminate potato wart disease from its potato crops. Poland also had to institute registration and reporting systems concerning this disease, including the traceability of the potatoes.

As concerns laying hens, transitional arrangements lasting up until 31 December 2009 will apply to more than forty establishments in Poland.

A derogation also applies to the plant protection products Directive[127] extending the deadline for the provision of information by companies on three EC restricted pesticides,[128] to 31 December 2006. However, these pesticides must have been produced in Poland, marketed in Poland and the companies concerned must have begun working on the data requirements before 1 January 2003.

[126] With the repeal and replacement of the measures listed in the country annexes to the fifth Accession Treaty, the provisions cited (Art. 16 Directive 64/433, Art. 21 Directive 71/118, Art. 15 Directive 91/493, Art. 20 Directive 77/99, Art. 31 Directive 92/46 and Art. 20 Directive 94/65) have been replaced by Art. 58 of Regulation 178/2002, op. cit. n. 49.

[127] Directive 91/414, concerning the placing of plant protection products on the market, *OJ* 1991 L 230/1, as amended, op. cit. n. 114.

[128] 2,4–D, MCPA, carbendazim or Mecoprop (MCCP).

A final derogation, mentioned above, also applies to the Directive on marketing of forest reproductive material,[129] in order to allow Poland to exhaust non-compliant stocks that were accumulated before 1 January 2004.

Food processing establishments that do not meet the deadline for compliance with the Community legislation will have to close thereafter. Produce from establishments covered by the transitional arrangements can only be placed on the national market, not on the Internal Market bearing the special markings, and if the plants do not meet the structural requirements in full by the deadline given, they are not entitled to place that produce on the national market.

The relevant country annexes contain lists of establishments entitled to temporary derogations. They are updated under the comitology procedures stipulated in the relevant piece of legislation. Thus, the transitional arrangements have changed since the time of signature of the fifth Accession Treaty and this is also the case for the sixth Accession Treaty. The Commission's *Guide to the Negotiations* dated as at December 2002,[130] summarised the pre-determined transitional arrangements for all of the Ten as follows:

> Certain *food establishments* have been granted a transitional period in order to upgrade to fully meet EU requirements. These include 52 premises in the Czech Republic, 44 in Hungary, 117 in Lithuania, 20 in Latvia, 485 in Poland, and 2 in Slovakia. Such transitional periods are limited in time and scope and do not involve any exemption from food hygiene legislation. During the transitional period, products which come from these establishments must be specifically marked and cannot be marketed in any form in other EU countries.
>
> All establishments not subject to a transitional period will have to comply with the *acquis* on accession and their products will be able to be freely marketed within the EU.
>
> Certain establishments have been granted a transitional period in order to upgrade to fully meet *structural requirements for hen cages* (only the slope and height of the cages). Such transitional periods are limited in time and scope and are applicable in the Czech Republic, Hungary, Malta, Poland and Slovenia.

---

[129] Directive 1999/105 on the marketing of forest reproductive material, *OJ* 2000 L 11/17.

[130] Not published but available on the Europa website. This Guide changed in later versions; such as the version of 17 December 2002, can be found at www.europa.eu.int/comm/enlargement/negotiations/chapters/negotiationsguide.pdf

> There are also transitional periods in the field of *phytosanitary* legislation for Lithuania and Poland (potato ring rot and potato wart disease respectively) as well as transitional periods on certain parts of seed quality legislation for Malta, Cyprus, Latvia and Slovenia. Again, these transitional periods are limited in time and scope.

However, a later version of this *Guide to the Negotiations* entitled the *Report on the result of the negotiations on the accession of [the Ten]*[131] is more detailed on the transitional arrangements set out in the country annexes for food establishments in the new Member States. For example, the later version reported that:

- transitional arrangements apply to 332 Polish meat establishments (until December 2007), 113 milk establishments (until December 2006) and 40 fish establishments (three years as of the date of accession)
- transitional arrangements apply to 44 Czech meat establishments, 1 egg establishment, 7 fish establishments (all until December 2006)
- The transitional arrangements for hen cages changed in that Slovenia had until end 2004 to comply with the requirements for the floor area of cages. Otherwise, the deadline of end 2009 applies to the Czech Republic, Hungary, Malta, Poland and Slovenia as regards the height and/or slope of hen cages.

For Bulgaria[132] and Romania[133] certain derogations apply until end December 2009 for structural requirements in respect of food processing establishments working with meat, poultry meat and milk products. The sixth Accession Treaty for Bulgaria and Romania reflect this evolution in the *acquis* in that these transitional arrangements concern Regulation 853/2004 on the specific hygiene rules for food of animal

---

[131] Which is undated but post-dates the earlier document, see ibid., visited in July 2005.

[132] See Annex VII.5.B., 2005 Accession Treaty, at p. 323. The establishments concerned are listed at pp. 302–310. The derogation relates to Regulation 852/2004 on the hygiene of foodstuffs and Regulation 853/2004 laying down specific hygiene rules for food of animal origin, both op. cit. n. 88.

[133] See Annex VI.4.B., 2005 Accession Treaty at p. 28–2843. The derogation relates to Regulation 852/2004 on the hygiene of foodstuffs, op. cit. n. 88, and Regulation 853/2004 laying down specific hygiene rules for food of animal origin, op. cit. n. 88. The establishments concerned are listed at pp. 366–368.

origin. However, it is important to note that the specific derogation relates to:

- the construction, layout and equipment of slaughter houses and cutting plants for meat processing in Romania;
- the construction, layout and equipment of establishments involved in minced meat, meat preparations and Mechanically Separated Meat in Romania, and;
- equipment and premises of milk production plants as well as the collection and transport of milk in both Romania and Bulgaria.

These provisions concerning Bulgaria expressly do not allow food businesses to derogate from the HACCP principles under the food hygiene *acquis*. However, there is no equivalent provision concerning the derogations for Romania concerning certain milk plants. In both cases, however, milk and meat or meat products produced in the establishments are restricted to the national market and cannot near a Community health marking but must be marked with a different health marking. Finally, rather than use the relevant clauses of the Accession Treaty for adapting or amending the arrangements for these food businesses in Bulgaria and Romani, the sixth Accession Treaty expressly allows for the amendment of these arrangements by means of Article 58 of the mother Regulation, Regulation 178/2002.

As with the fifth Accession Treaty this does not apply to the hygiene obligations of food operators and nor does it apply to transposition or compliance with the rest of the provisions of the rules concerned. Again the list of these establishments can be changed by the Commission, depending on the progress of the establishments, under Article 58 of Regulation 178/2002 comitology procedure in involving the SCF-CAH. Again, produce from these establishments can only be placed on the national market, not on the Internal Market.

Romania also has a derogation in respect of certain pesticides under the 1991 Directive on plant protection products[134] until end December 2009 (and end December 2008 for 2,4–D). These products must have already been authorised in Romania and can only be marketed in Romania.

---

[134] Directive 91/414, as amended, op. cit. n. 114.

2.2.2 *Adaptations to the agri-food* acquis: *Article 57 Act of Accession*
Where appropriate the Council or the Commission, under Article 57 Act of Accession in the fifth Accession Treaty, may make additional 'necessary adaptations' to the *acquis*. It refers also to measures that pre-date the agreement reached in the negotiations of December 2002 on the Treaty of Accession. This provision has been used in previous accession treaties.[135] Article 57 allows for technical adaptations to the *acquis* – to take account of the new members' languages in import and export licences in the sugar sector for example[136] – rather than to add further derogations to the country annexes.[137] On this basis, the Commission has been updating the list of approved border inspection posts (BIPs) in the new Member States and deleting BIPs in Austria, Germany and Italy that have become redundant as a result of accession.[138]

The equivalent in the sixth Accession Treaty is Article 56. This was the legal basis for the Commission Regulation 1792/2006 of 23 October 2006 which adapted certain regulations and decisions in various fields of the *acquis*, including veterinary and phytosanitary legislation and the environment.[139] It also adapts the 2003 Act of Accession.

2.2.3 *New transitional derogations*
Beyond the country annexes, three provisions contained in the fifth and sixth Accession Treaties allow for the introduction of new transitional arrangements: Articles 55, 41 and 42 2003 Act of Accession.

---

[135] See Art. 169, 1994 Act of Accession concerning the accession of the Republic of Austria, the Kingdom of Sweden and the Republic of Finland.

[136] Regulation 96/2004, *OJ* 2004 L 15/13. Other such technical adaptations concerning the common organisation of the markets in agriculture include Regulation 498/2004 (products processed from fruit and vegetables), *OJ* 2004 L80/20, Regulation 406/2004 (olive oil), *OJ* 2004 L67/10, Regulation 323/2004 (rice seed and seed other than rice seed), *OJ* 2004 L58/14.

[137] By reference to Art 57 Act of Accession, which stipulates: '(1) Where acts of the institutions prior to accession require adaptation by reason of accession, and the necessary adaptations have not been provided for in this Act or Annexes, those adaptations shall be made in accordance with the procedure laid down in paragraph 2...(2) The Council acting by qualified majority on a proposal from the Commission, or the Commission, according to which of these two institutions adopted the original acts, shall to this end draw up the necessary texts.'

[138] Commission Decision 2004/273, *OJ* 2004 L 86/21. See also Commission Decision 2003/831, *OJ* 2003 L 313/61.

[139] *OJ* 2006 L 362/1.

*Article 55* Article 55 of the 2003 Act of Accession, is generally applicable and allows, at the duly substantiated request of a new Member, additional 'temporary derogations' to be added to those agreed in Council in December 2002 but only in respect of new *acquis* measures that were adopted between 1 November 2002 and the date of signature of the Accession Treaty on 16 April 2003, which took effect upon accession (Article 2(3) of the Accession Treaty). However, further transitional derogations, apart from Article 55, may be adopted in respect of specific legislation, such as in the case of the Directive on waste electrical and electronic equipment.[140]

Initially no transitional arrangements were agreed for the free movement of foodstuffs but only related to the veterinary and phytosanitary chapter of the *acquis*. However, transitional arrangements concerning the free movement of goods were later negotiated after the closure of the negotiations in December 2002, by making use of a special provision for temporary derogations from the *acquis* on the 'duly substantiated request' of one of the Ten under Article 55 of the Acts of Accession, referred to above.[141]

Using the legal basis of Article 55, new transitional arrangements were introduced to the chocolate Directive of 2000[142] and the 2001 Regulation on maximum levels for certain contaminants in foodstuffs.[143] Malta was allowed to use the term 'milk chocolate' where it would not otherwise be able to so,[144] provided that it label the amount of dry milk solids in accordance with the Directive. In any case the UK and Ireland already had the right to do this.

Using Article 55 of the fifth Accession Treaty, Estonia was entitled to exceed the maximum limits for dioxins in Baltic fish until the end of 2006. Certain of the fifteen Member States also have transitional arrangements from the 2001 Regulation.[145] The Estonian transitional arrangement attaches the following conditions:

---

[140] See Chapter 4.2.

[141] These are listed in the fifth accession treaty at pp. 92–96.

[142] Directive 2000/36, *OJ* 2000 L 197/19.

[143] Regulation 466/2001, *OJ* 2001 L 77/1.

[144] Directive 2000/36 expressly extends the derogation that applied before it was repealed (by Directive 2000/36), which was contained in Directive 73/241. But the English designation 'of milk chocolate with high milk content' was replaced by the term 'family milk chocolate' under Directive 2000/36.

[145] Including other Member States giving on to the Baltic, Sweden and Finland, in respect of fish originating in the Baltic region until end 2006. Other Member States

- Estonia must demonstrate that the average level of human exposure to dioxins in Estonia is not higher than the average levels in the current EU;
- Estonia must demonstrate that an information system is in place to fully inform consumers, especially certain vulnerable groups of the population, in order to avoid potential health risks;
- Estonia must implement the necessary measures to ensure that such fish or fish products are not marketed in other Member States;
- Estonia must carry out monitoring of the levels of dioxins in fish from the Baltic and annually report the results to the Commission.

*Articles 41 and 42* In the veterinary and phytosanitary chapter of the *acquis* however, two provisions provide for additional measures to be introduced, during the first three years of enlargement. In the cases of both the fifth and the sixth Accession Treaties, Article 41 Act of Accession concerns transitional measures in relation to the CMO under the CAP.

Unlike in other chapters of the *acquis communautaire*, more transitional measures may be introduced for the common agricultural policy as well as for the veterinary and phytosanitary *acquis*. Again, the same provision was contained in all previous Accession Treaties and rare instances exist where these arrangements have been extended long after this foreseen time limit.[146] The fifth Accession Treaty makes specific provision for more transitional arrangements to add to the list of derogations from the phytosanitary and veterinary *acquis*. The sixth Accession Treaty makes this possible in respect of phytosanitary and veterinary *acquis* but specifically also includes the possibility of transitional measures in the food safety rules.

Article 42 Acts of Accession (in both the fifth and the sixth Accession Treaties) enables the Commission to adopt further transitional arrangements in accordance with the comitology procedure set out in the relevant *acquis* measure. For the first three years after accession the European Commission will be able to introduce additional

(UK and Belgium also have derogations in respect of spinach (nitrate concentrations) until end 2008.

[146] Measures concerning the fat content of milk in Austria and Finland were extended to 30 April 2009, see Council Regulation 2596/1997, *OJ* 1997 L 351/12, last amended by Council Regulation 1805/2003, *OJ* 2003 L 265/5, to extend the transitional arrangement to end April 2009 and the repealed as obsolete by Council Regulation 72/2009, *OJ* 2009 L 30/1.

derogations from the veterinary and phytosanitary *acquis* for the new Member States. Unlike in the case of the Internal Market safeguard clause, measures adopted under Article 42 Acts of Accession may not be extended beyond the first three years after enlargement. From a veterinary and phytosanitary perspective, Article 42 Act of Accession allows the Commission to act through its scientific and advisory committees to counter potential threats to the integrity/safety of the food chain that might arise in the new Member States in the earliest stages of the food chain. The Food and Veterinary Office (FVO) of the European Commission continues to perform the necessary task of monitoring the progress of the new members' in the pre-accession preparations.

While the new Member States are subject to the same mechanisms as the Fifteen for checking the implementation of the veterinary and phytosanitary rules, for the first three years following enlargement, the European Commission is able to institute additional transitional arrangements for the new Member States, depending on the progress made prior to accession.[147] It is not expressly stated that such 'measures' will involve derogations from the *acquis* but it is clear from the wording of Article 42 compared to the wording of the safeguard clauses – see below – that these are not intended to be safeguard measures but are designed 'to facilitate the transition from the existing regime in the new Member States to that resulting from the application of the Community [rules]'. Moreover, unlike the safeguard clauses, these additional transitional arrangements must be adopted, and also end, by 30 April 2007.[148] Therefore, this avenue for introducing such new transitional arrangements expired on 30 April 2007 for the fifth enlargement and will expire on 31 December 2009 in the case of Bulgaria and Romania.

Just before enlargement, in March 2004 the Commission adopted Decision 2004/280, based on Article 42 Act of Accession, in accordance with the opinion of the Standing Committee on the Food Chain and Animal Health, which imposes a restriction on a whole range of food

[147] ...in additional to the traditional Article 258 TFEU procedure for pursuing a Member State that fails to meet its Treaty obligations.

[148] Although Art. 41 Act of Accession foresees the possibility of extending this transitional system beyond the three years, but only in accordance with a decision-making procedure that involves consultation with the European Parliament.

products of animal origin produced before the date of accession.[149] As of 1 May 2004 until 30 April 2005,[150] such food products originating in one of the ten new Member States are under a blanket ban from being traded within the Internal Market and may only be sold in the country of origin.[151] A derogation to this general rule is set out in the Decision 2004/280 which allows that produce to be traded between Member States if it comes from establishments that have been EU-authorised to export (as is the case with third country imports) and it bears the Community export health mark of the establishments concerned, and the fact that it was produced prior to 1 May 2004 has been certified. The country annexes for the sixth Accession Treaty incorporates the same system in respect of Bulgaria and Romania.

Breaches of this cut-off date became apparent in Poland but were controlled by the FVO. The Competent Authority in Poland had allowed operators to use stocks of pre-printed wrapping and packaging material and labels on packaging obtained after 1 May 2004 until 31 December 2004. Following the objections of the FVO, Poland revised the relevant Polish Ordinance.

This is not a safeguard measure per se, despite the fact that it imposes additional restrictions/requirements on the new members' food produce in the first year of enlargement. For Poland, the numerous transitional arrangements relating to health and production and marketing of meat, milk, fishery, etc, products, basically prevented such Polish products from being placed on the EC market (restricting them to the Polish market) and require that they bear special markings. This is the case for all those food establishments in the new Member States that have these limited derogations from the agri-food *acquis*: this produce is prohibited from being put on the Internal Market but must remain within the national territory.

In the first three years after accession the Commission is able to adopt additional arrangements restricting the placing on the market of

---

[149] Including fresh meat, poultrymeat, meat products, egg products; fishery products, rabbit meat, wild game and wild game meat, milk and milk products, minced meat and meat preparations.

[150] Initially Decision 2004/280 provided for this arrangement to end on 31 December 2004 but this date was extended to 30 April 2005 by virtue of Commission Decision 2004/700, *OJ* 2004 L318/21. This gives these countries more time to sell produce in stock that has a long shelf life and is fit for human consumption.

[151] See FVO Report DG(SANCO)/7177/2004 for the period 6 to 17 September 2004 at p. 20 and the response of the Polish authorities annexed thereto at p. 10.

new members' agri-food produce if they fail to meet the veterinary and phytosanitary rules. Given the dramatic food scares that the Community has experienced since the BSE crisis, this provision seems justified, especially given that in the past Member States have instituted national protective measures that are blatant obstructions to intra-Community trade on grounds of health and consumer protection. French measures to prevent British beef from being placed on the market in France are one example, only recently removed, and Swedish measures requiring the prior notification of arrivals of agri-food products (fresh meat products or products containing animal products) from other Member States is another.

## 3. Performance of the new member states in EU agri-food *acquis* after accession

### 3.1 *Informal transitional arrangements: an undergrowth of non-compliance?*

This section attempts to test how realistic the transitional arrangement were. While the new Member States had clearly made remarkable progress in their approximation to and compliance with the agri-food *acquis* before they acceded to the EU,[152] there were a number of problem areas still persisting at the time of the accessions of the twelve new Member States.

Numerous 'informal' transitional arrangements emerged in practice within the agri-food *acquis* after the fifth enlargement. Formal transitional arrangements in terms of not transposing the agri-food *acquis* were simply not entertained, were not even negotiable, and the EU would not have agreed to such requests. Failure to transpose a Directive is especially serious because without actual legislation in place the corporate and consumer sectors are deprived of their rights or alternatively, gain a competitive advantage because they are free of the obligations that apply in other Member States. Also, the longer a law is not enforced, the longer a Member State, operators and consumers will take to gain experience in the application of their rights and/or obliga-

[152] For example, monitoring and testing for TSE has proved successful for new members as well as the Fifteen, see Report on the monitoring and testing of ruminants for the presence of transmissible spongiform encephalopathy (TSE) in the EU in 2004, 13 June 2005.

tions. Transposition is only the first step in enforcement, after implementation and involving of course having the necessary administrative capacity and familiarity of competent authorities to apply these laws. Moreover, between the time of signature and entry into force of the fifth and sixth Accession Treaties, the incoming Member States had a considerable workload to meet their commitments both in terms of administrative capacity as well as transposition and implementation of the *acquis*. Governance issues become all the more important to avoiding an undergrowth of non-compliance, even at the very lowest level of transposition, eroding the agri-food *acquis* and institutional set up that has been so meticulously constructed.

Considerable approximation efforts were still required between signature and entry into force of the fifth and sixth Accession Treaties. On the basis of the Commission's annual reports of November 2002 on the progress of the ten new Member States in transposing and implementing the *acquis*, it seems that most of them made considerable and remarkable progress in aligning to the agri-food *acquis*. Nevertheless, the need to continue and even to step up efforts of future new Member States in the run up to accession was stated over and again by the European Commission.

It was clear from the 2003 Reports[153] that all of the Ten incoming countries of the fifth enlargement had to make 'enhanced efforts by accelerating [the] pace of progress' in the *acquis* on agriculture and fisheries and the paying agencies for agricultural trade mechanisms, foodstuffs and the veterinary and phytosanitary *acquis*. Efforts were needed to improve their administrative capacity for application and enforcement of the agri-food *acquis*. In some cases this was the case for every aspect of the agri-food *acquis*. In the other cases (Czech Republic, Estonia, Hungary, Latvia, Lithuania, Slovakia) efforts had to focus on improving capacity in one or a number of the following areas: market surveillance mechanisms to prevent the circulation of unsafe products in the Internal Market; food safety controls; veterinary; phytosanitary; border inspection posts (BIPs) – see below, and; the Common Fisheries Policy (CFP).

[153] See European Commission *2003 Comprehensive Monitoring Report of the European Commission on the state of preparedness for EU membership*, 5 November 2003, at p. 10.

Poland, was singled out as being is weak in terms of its alignment with the *acquis* in that it was behind even in its transposition of the food safety *acquis*. Slovenia too still had to transpose some foodstuff legislation. The extent of the efforts to be made varied. Thus for example, at one end of the scale Hungary and Slovakia were far ahead of the others in terms of administrative capacity. Poland was generally weak in terms of its overall capacity to apply the *acquis*. Eight of the new Member States of the fifth enlargement wave had still to align with the Common Fisheries Policy *acquis*, excepting only Malta and Slovenia.

> Substantial shortcomings are identified in the veterinary and phytosanitary field, most markedly in the Czech republic, Hungary and Poland, but also in Latvia and Slovakia. All acceding countries need to take measures to put in place the EU's veterinary control system (including import controls and animal identification), measures to deal with transmissible spongiform encephalopathies (such as BSE) and animal by-products (particularly Latvia, Malta and Poland), structural and hygiene standards in meat, milk and fish processing plants (particularly in the Czech republic, Hungary, Poland and Slovakia), common measures in relation to residue monitoring, and phytosanitary control (particularly Poland). Other areas requiring enhanced efforts are: animal disease control measures (Latvia); trade in live animals and animal products; animal welfare (Czech Republic, Latvia, Lithuania and Poland) and animal nutrition (Czech Republic, Estonia, Cyprus, Malta and Poland).[154]

In addition, the Commission identified a number of gaps in the preparation for membership which are of 'serious concern and where, unless immediate and decisive action is taken, the country in question will not be in a position to implement the *acquis* by the date of accession'. All of the Ten were expressly mentioned in this regard. The area of serious concern either affect the Internal Market or they affect the delivery of CAP funds to beneficiaries in the new Member States. Areas of serious concern for the Internal Market also concerned the agri-food *acquis*: Lithuania and Poland were not taking the necessary measures for inspection and control of their fisheries fleets; Czech Republic, Hungary, Latvia, Malta, Poland and Slovakia were all singled out as raising serious concerns in the veterinary and phytosanitary *acquis*.

[154] See ibid. at p. 12.

Different countries had different problems. Taking the specific example of Poland,[155] enhanced efforts were required before accession on 1 May 2004 in:

- trade mechanisms;
- the CMOs for milk, beefmeat, eggs and poultry;
- rural development;
- trade in live animals and animal products;
- common measures;
- animal welfare and animal nutrition;
- state aid, and;
- international fisheries agreements in relation to fisheries policy, and;
- surveillance and non-safety measures in the area of consumer and health protection were also expressly mentioned.

In the veterinary and phytosanitary *acquis* the serious concerns arose in the transmissible spongiform encephalopathies (TSEs), animals by-products, movement controls on animals, the control of potato ring rot and wart disease as well as the areas of resource management and inspection and control and the market policy in the fisheries chapter.

All the efforts in capacity building cannot make up for the lack of transposition of key agri-food laws. Employing and training staff to properly implement and enforce the measures adopted is not effective in hypothetical situations. As at June 2002, Poland had not yet transposed the HACCP rules[156] contained in the hygiene directive, one of the central tenets of the EU agri-food hygiene rules. The HACCP rules involve a system whereby all food business – large or small – are obliged to have put in place a permanent procedure or procedures based upon internationally recognised principles designed to prevent risks arising in the food chain. The European Commission was adamant prior to accession that there should be no derogation in the form of transitional arrangements or any other means for the 1993 HACCP Directive. By the time of accession, Poland had little experience of the

[155] See ibid. at p. 41.

[156] Hazard Analysis of Critical Control Points (HACCP) was contained in the Directive 93/43 on the hygiene of foodstuffs, *OJ* 1993 L 175/1, which will be repealed and replaced on 31 December 2005 by Regulation 852/2004 on the hygiene of foodstuffs, op. cit. n. 88.

application and control of the HACCP rules and the same can be said of other new Member States, such as Malta.[157] By the end of 2005, the EU will raise the standard of the HACCP rules[158] as part of the agri-food reform package. Poland then also had to implement the higher standard in order not to be in breach of its Treaty obligations.

The HACCP Directive was among the thirty-nine EC agri-food laws that had still not been transposed by all the new Member States after their accession on 1 May 2004. In an own-initiative opinion of the European Parliament, Małgorzata Handzlik MEP, acting in her capacity as rapporteur to the European Parliament Committee on the Internal Market and Consumer Protection (IMCO), issued her draft report on the Internal Market in the new Member States in December 2004.[159] The European Parliament report is in response to the Commission's initiation of legal action against certain of the new Member States on 20 October 2004 in the fields of free movement of goods, services and capital as well as of public procurement. As concerns foodstuffs in particular, food legislation accounts for a hefty chunk of the total number of directives that had not been transposed into national law, by 15 November 2004. Transitional arrangements were not negotiated in respect of these laws, which is why the term 'informal transitional arrangements' is used here. Of the ten new Member States, the Małgorzata Handzlik report noted that only Cyprus was not subject to the infringement procedures. The agri-food legislation concerned included some 40 directives – see Table 7 – and thus left serious question marks over the credibility (if not the safety) of the food *acquis*. A number of the Directives listed there were almost immediately repealed and replaced – or 'recast' – by the new legislation adopted on 29 April 2004.

[157] See Final Report of a mission carried out in Malta from 7 to 11 March 2005 in order to evaluate the official foodstuffs control system and in particular the implementation of controls on the hygiene of foodstuffs, DG(SANCO)/7563/2005, 17 June 2005.

[158] HACCP will now encompass the seven Codex HACCP principles (as opposed to the five HACCP principles contained in the earlier Hygiene Directive 93/43, op. cit. n. 117. There is specific provision for these HACCP principles to be extended – potentially – to primary food production.

[159] See provisional Draft Report on the internal market in the new Member States: situation, opportunities and lessons to be learnt, INI/2004/2155 of 16 December 2004 and made public 14 January 2005. The final European Parliament resolution of the same name was adopted 28 April 2005 under the reference P6_TA(2005)0149.

Table 7. List referred to in the Rapporteur's Draft Report on *The Internal Market in the new Member States: situation, opportunities and lessons to be learnt*

- Directive 1999/2 on the approximation of the laws of the Member States concerning foods and food ingredients treated with ionising radiation *OJ* 1999 L 66/16.
- Directive 1999/3 on the establishment of a Community list of foods and food ingredients treated with ionising radiation, *OJ* 1999 L 66/24.
- Directive 93/43 on the hygiene of foodstuffs, *OJ* 1993 L 175/1
- Directive 89/398 on the approximation of the laws of the Member States relating to foodstuffs intended for particular nutritional uses *OJ* 1989 L 186/27
- Directive 1999/41 amending Directive 89/398 on the approximation of the laws of the Member States relating to foodstuffs intended for particular nutritional uses, *OJ* 1999 L 172/38
- Directive 96/5 on processed cereal-based foods and baby foods for infants and young children, *OJ* 1996 L 49/17
- Directive 98/36 amending Directive 96/5 on processed cereal-based foods and baby foods for infants and young children, *OJ* 1998 L 167/23
- Directive 98/83 on the quality of water intended for human consumption, *OJ* 1998 L 330/32
- Directive 80/777 on the approximation of the laws of the Member States relating to the exploitation and marketing of natural mineral waters, *OJ* 1980 L 229/1
- Directive 91/71 completing Council Directive 88/388 on the approximation of the laws of the Member States relating to flavourings for use in foodstuffs and to source materials for their production, *OJ* 1991 L 42/25
- Directive 96/8 on foods intended for use in energy-restricted diets for weight reduction, *OJ* 1996 L 55/22
- Directive 89/107 on the approximation of the laws of the Member States concerning food additives authorised for use in foodstuffs intended for human consumption, *OJ* 1989 L 40/27,
- Directive 76/399 making a fifth amendment to the Council Directive of 23 October 1962 on the approximation of the rules of the Member States concerning the colouring matters authorized for use in foodstuffs intended for human consumption, *OJ* 1976 L 108/19
- Directive 78/144 amending for the sixth time the Council Directive of 23 October 1962 on the approximation of the laws of the Member States concerning the colouring matters authorized for use in foodstuffs intended for human consumption, *OJ* 1978 L 44/20
- Directive 81/20 amending for the seventh time the Directive of 23 October 1962, on the approximation of the rules of the Member States concerning the colouring matters authorized for use in foodstuffs intended for human consumption, *OJ* 1981 L 43/11
- Directive 94/35 on sweeteners for use in foodstuffs, *OJ* 1994 L 237/3

Table 7 (*cont.*)

- Directive 95/2 on food additives other than colours and sweeteners, *OJ* 1995 L 061/1
- Directive 90/496 on nutrition labelling for foodstuffs, *OJ* 1990 L 276/40
- Directive 2001/12 amending Directive 91/440 on the development of the Community's railways, *OJ* 2001 L 75/1
- Directive 2001/114 relating to certain partly or wholly dehydrated preserved milk for human consumption, *OJ* 2002 L 15/19
- Directive 78/663 laying down specific criteria of purity for emulsifiers, stabilizers, thickeners and gelling agents for use in foodstuffs, *OJ* 1979 L11/24
- Directive 90/612 amending Council Directive 78/663 laying down specific purity criteria for emulsifiers, stabilizers, thickeners and gelling agents for use in foodstuffs, *OJ* 1978 L 326/58
- Directive 92/4 amending Council Directive 78/663 laying down specific criteria of purity for emulsifiers, stabilizers, thickeners and gelling agents for use in foodstuffs, *OJ* 1992 L 55/96
- Directive 82/504 amending Directive 78/663 laying down specific criteria of purity for emulsifiers, stabilizers, thickeners and gelling agents for use in foodstuffs, *OJ* 1982 L 230/35
- Directive 81/712 laying down Community methods of analysis for verifying that certain additives used in foodstuffs satisfy criteria of purity, *OJ* 1981 L 257/1
- Directive 87/250 on the indication of alcoholic strength by volume in the labelling of alcoholic beverages for sale to the ultimate consumer, *OJ* 1987 L 113/57
- Directive 76/621 relating to the fixing of the maximum level of erucic acid in oils and fats intended as such for human consumption and in foodstuffs containing added oils or fats, *OJ* 1976 L 202/35
- Directive 1999/4 relating to coffee extracts and chicory extracts, *OJ* 1999 L 66/26
- Directive 93/99 on the subject of additional measures concerning the official control of foodstuffs, *OJ* 1993 L 290/14
- Directive 96/43 amending and consolidating Directive 85/73 in order to ensure financing of veterinary inspections and controls on live animals and certain animal products and amending Directives 90/675 and 91/496, *OJ* 1996 L 162/1
- Directive 97/79 amending Directives 71/118, 72/462, 85/73, 91/67, 91/492, 91/493, 92/45 and 92/118 as regards the organisation of veterinary checks on products entering the Community from third countries, *OJ* 1998 L 24/31
- Directive 91/688 amending Directive 72/462 on health and veterinary inspection problems upon importation of bovine, ovine and caprine animals and swine, fresh meat or meat products from third countries, *OJ* 1991 L 377/18

Table 7 (*cont.*)

- Directive 91/69 amending Directive 72/462 on health and veterinary inspection problems upon importation of bovine animals and swine, fresh meat or meat products from third countries, in order to include ovine and caprine animals, *OJ* 1991 L 46/37
- Directive 96/91 amending Directive 72/462 on health and veterinary inspection problems on importation of animals of the bovine, ovine, caprine and porcine species, fresh meat and meat-based products from third countries, *OJ* 1996 L 13/26
- Directive 92/36 amending, with regard to African horse sickness, Directive 90/426 on animal health conditions governing the movement and import from third countries of equidae, *OJ* 1992 L 157/28 ·
- Directive 90/426 on animal health conditions governing the movement and import from third countries of equidae, *OJ* 1990 L 224/42
- Directive 2002/16 on the use of certain epoxy derivatives in materials and articles intended to come into contact with foodstuffs, *OJ* 2002 L 051/27
- Directive 89/608 on mutual assistance between the administrative authorities of the Member States and cooperation between the latter and the Commission to ensure the correct application of legislation on veterinary and zootechnical matters, *OJ* 1989 L 351/34
- Directive 91/494/EEC on animal health conditions governing intra-Community trade in and imports from third countries of fresh poultrymeat, *OJ* 1991 L 268/35
- Directive 2003/34 amending for the 23rd time Council Directive 76/769 relating to restrictions on the marketing and use of certain dangerous substances and preparations (substances classified as carcinogens, mutagens or substances toxic to reproduction – c/m/r), *OJ* 2003 L 156/14
- Directive 2003/36 of the European Parliament and of the Council of 26 May 2003 amending, for the 25th time, Council Directive 76/769 on the approximation of the laws, regulations and administrative provisions of the Member States relating to restrictions on the marketing and use of certain dangerous substances and preparations (substances classified as carcinogens, mutagens or substances toxic to reproduction – c/m/r), *OJ* 2003 L 156/26
- Directive 2003/53 amending for the 26th time Council Directive 76/769 relating to restrictions on the marketing and use of certain dangerous substances and preparations (nonylphenol, nonylphenol ethoxylate and cement), *OJ* 2003 L 178/24
- Directive 88/344 on the approximation of the laws of the Member States on extraction solvents used in the production of foodstuffs and food ingredients, *OJ* 1988 L 157/28

Source: European Parliament Committee on the Internal Market and Consumer Protection, INI/2004/2155 of 16 December 2004

In its *23rd Annual Monitoring Report on National Implementation of EU law*, reporting for the year 2005, the Commission noted that the number of complaints against the ten new Member States was low. However, it also highlighted the fact that the most of the infringement procedures launched for *incorrect transposition* of Directives in 2005 concerned the Health and Consumer Protection chapter of the *acquis*, and implementation thereof, and the vast majority of these infringements concerned the food safety and zootechnics provisions.[160] [By way of comment, in the Accession Treaties, the transitional arrangements in the country annexes classify these same laws as veterinary and phytosanitary legislation, not as consumer protection legislation]. In July 2005 the Commission reported on the transposition deficit in the *Internal Market Scoreboard 2005*,[161] expressing the percentage of Internal Market legislation not yet introduced into national legislation by Member States. The accompanying breakdown of those statistics[162] shows that 380 of the infringement proceedings initiated in 2005 for non-communication of national transposition measures concerned the whole consumer protection *acquis*. It also showed that 153 of all these procedures had not been closed at the end of 2005. Despite the fact that they had to implement a much greater amount of EU legislation as well as build their administrative capacity to cope with implementation and enforcement, the three leading countries in transposing legislation essential for the functioning of the EU's internal market were Lithuania, Hungary and Slovenia, closely followed by Denmark and Finland. Thirteen infringement proceedings were opened against Poland for the entirety of the Internal Market *acquis*.

From the full Statistical Annex II[163] it can indeed be seen that the cases concerning agri-food measures make up the bulk of all these consumer protection *acquis* infringements in 2005. The vast majority of these procedures concerned new Member States. Of course, this is not to say that all the new Member States were equally problematic. Slovakia was not the subject of any such procedures. Lithuania was the subject of 2 procedures in the consumer protection *acquis*, most of which concerned the agri-food *acquis*. Poland was the subject of 13,

[160] See SEC(2006) 999 of 24 July 2009, Annex, at p. 79.
[161] To be found at www.europa.eu.int/comm/internal_market/score/index_en.htm
[162] See COM(2006) 999, Annex 1, p. 6.
[163] See COM (2006) 416 of 24 July 2006, *Protection des Consommateurs*, pp. 309–387.

Hungary of 20, Slovenia of 26. The Czech Republic, Latvia and Malta scored the highest for 60 or more infringement letters having been sent out and Cyprus and Estonia followed with relatively high scores also of 41 and 49 respectively. Most of these procedures were closed on 5 July 2005 although a few remained open until 13 December 2005.[164] Of the ten files in this chapter of the *acquis* concerning the agri-food *acquis* that remained active at the end of 2005, only the Czech Republic, Cyprus and Estonia were concerned.[165] These last remaining files were closed on 28 June 2006. Such figures give a more reliable impression of informal transitional arrangements that emerged at the time of the fifth enlargement, but which ended, approximately and in the main, within the first year after the fifth enlargement.

As for non-conformity or bad implementation of agri-food laws, the *23rd Annual Monitoring Report on National Implementation of EU law* showed the state of play as at July 2005 and it was too early for the infringement proceedings to reach Court action at that point. The *24th*

[164] Files that were closed on 13 December 2005 concerned Malta (Directive 1994/14 establishing Community methods of analysis for the official control of feedingstuffs, *OJ* 1994 L 94/30, Directive 1996/24 on the marketing of compound feedingstuffs, *OJ* 1996 L 125/33, and Directive 2000/16 amending Council Directive 79/373/EEC on the marketing of compound feedingstuffs and Council Directive 96/25/EC on the circulation of feed materials, *OJ* 2000 L 105/36) and Malta (Directive 2001/37 the manufacture, presentation and sale of tobacco products, *OJ* 2001 L 194/26) and Cyprus (Directive 2002/89 on protective measures against the introduction into the Community of organisms harmful to plants or plant products and against their spread within the Community, *OJ* 2002 L655/45).

[165] Directive 89/608 on mutual assistance between the administrative authorities of the Member States and cooperation between the latter and the Commission to ensure the correct application of legislation on veterinary and zootechnical matters, *OJ* 1989 L 351/34 (Czech Republic); Directive 93/53 introducing minimum Community measures for the control of certain fish diseases *OJ* 1993 L 175/23, (Estonia); Directive 95/70 introducing minimum Community measures for the control of certain diseases affecting bivalve molluscs. *OJ* 1995 L 332/33, (Estonia); Directive 2000/27 introducing minimum Community measures for the control of certain fish diseases, *OJ* 2000 L 114/28, (Estonia); Directive 2000/75 laying down specific provisions for the control and eradication of bluetongue, *OJ* 2000 L 327/ 74 (Estonia); Directive 2003/11 relating to restrictions on the marketing and use of certain dangerous substances and preparations (pentabromodiphenyl ether, octabromodiphenyl ether), *OJ* 2003 L 42/45, (Czech Republic); Directive 2004/1 as regards the suspension of the use of azodicarbonamide as blowing agent, *OJ* 2004 L 7/45, (Cyprus, Czech Republic); Directive 2004/14 relating to materials and articles made of regenerated cellulose film intended to come into contact with foodstuffs, *OJ* 2004 L 27/48 (Cyprus, Czech Republic); Directive 2004/19 relating to plastic materials and articles intended to come into contact with foodstuffs, *OJ* 2004 L 71/8, (Cyprus, Czech Republic), Directive 2004/103 (Czech Republic, Estonia).

*Annual Monitoring Report on National Implementation of EU law* for the year ending 31 December 2006, showed that no cases against the new Member States concerned non-conformity or bad implementation of measures of the food safety *acquis*.

However, in 2006, various of the new Member States of the fifth enlargement wave were identified as failing to meet the deadline for transposing certain legislation[166] on:

- Pesticides – Directive 91/414 – Cyprus, Estonia, Hungary, Malta, Poland;
- Potato ring rot – Directive 93/85 – Cyprus, Estonia, Lithuania, Hungary, Poland, Slovakia, Slovenia;
- Laying hens – Directive 1999/74 – Malta.

These instances can also be considered persistent informal transitional arrangements. However, to put these informal transitional arrangements in a correct light, in the same annex concerning the year 2006, all 27 Member States were noted as having failed to transpose various agri-food laws adopted after (or immediately prior to) the 2004 enlargement.

For both Bulgaria and Romania, having acceded on 1 January 2007, the *26th Annual Monitoring Report on National Implementation of EU law* for the year 2007,[167] shows that Bulgaria was sent 80 letters of formal notice in its first year of membership, and Romania was sent 195. Moreover Bulgaria and Romania were listed as failing to have transposed literally hundreds of Directives of the Public Health and Consumer Protection *acquis* that was in place before their accession, the bulk of which are agri-food laws: DG SANCO opened a total of 428 new cases in the agri-food chapter of the *acquis*[168] although overall, 334 were closed in the same year. This is in addition to the problems of transposing and implementing the Common Agricultural Policy and financial and other regulations of the common organisations of the markets. The 2008 report, due to be published in 2009, will give a truer picture of the state of informal transitional arrangements arising in the cases of Romania and Bulgaria.

---

[166] See p. 157.
[167] See COM(2008) 777 of 18 November 2008.
[168] See ibid., p. 221

This raises the question: Were all of the new Member States truly ready to accede to the entire agri-food *acquis* upon the date of their accession and if not, have they improved since?

The Commission apparently believed so when it adopted its final opinion on readiness of the ten countries of the fifth enlargement, a decision that gave the green light to proceeding to signature of the Accession Treaty itself. The Commission nevertheless maintained the pressure on the new members of the fifth enlargement in its opinion leading to the signature of the fifth Accession Treaty; the Commission did confirm their readiness in its progress reports only a matter of months before the signature of the fifth Accession Treaty.[169] The European Parliament's findings did not inspire the same certainty as to the actual state of readiness of the incoming countries.

The Commission was very critical of Bulgaria and Romania in its September 2006 opinion on their readiness to implement the agri-food *acquis*.[170] The Commission at the same time publicised its various proposals for dealing with the lacks in Bulgaria's and Romania's preparedness, as outlined in Part One, Chapter 2, at 2. In terms of food law, there were serious concerns as to the ability of both Bulgaria and Romania to meet the obligations of a Member State, the same problems that had been highlighted in the spring of 2006.[171] For example, problems were identified in compliance with the TSE laws and special measures thereunder, similar to the ban that had endured against UK beef and which had only then been lifted in the March of 2006.[172] All this highlights the political commitment to a given date for enlargement takes precedence over the reality of the new Member States' readiness to comply with the Community law. However, in 2008 the FVO reported that Bulgaria had made 'very good progress in all areas of the implementation of the hygiene package and the level reached can be considered as satisfactory' in its first year of

[169] Although the Commission did highlight the need for 'enhanced efforts' and singled out certain areas of 'serious concern' to be resolved before accession. See the Commission's Comprehensive Monitoring Report of 16 May 2006.

[170] Commission Opinion of 26 September 2006.

[171] Commission Communication Monitoring Report on the state of preparedness of Romania and Bulgaria, COM(2006) (unnumbered), of 16 May 2006. See 'Commission keeps Bulgaria and Romania in limbo', www.EurActiv.com visited on 24 April 2006, in anticipation of the Commission's May 2006 Progress Reports.

[172] See Key Findings of the May 2006 Monitoring Reports on Bulgaria and Romania, Commission MEMO/06/201 of 16 May 2006.

membership.[173] Following a particularly critical report by the FVO in 2007 on public health controls of food producing establishments in Romania,[174] Romania was reported to have made some improvements but was criticised for significant deficiencies and in particular, the FVO expressed concerns as to raw milk quality.[175]

The subsequent annual monitoring reports compiled by the Commission on the application of the *acquis communaitaire* also show that the new incoming Member States of the fifth and sixth enlargements were not fully prepared when they acceded.

Certain reports of the FVO on the administrative capacity of the new Member States to properly apply the agri-food *acquis* reinforce this impression that the incoming countries were not fully ably to meet their commitment to fully transpose and implement the *acquis* on the date of their accession. Relevant FVO reports on the upgrade of food-processing establishments – where all twelve new Member States had transitional arrangements – show how the new members fared in meeting their accession commitments. Establishments that are not included in the lists incorporated into the Act of Accession had to apply the *acquis* in full. Thus for example, in the Czech Republic, any establishment that was not included on the list of those subject to a transitional arrangement was obliged to close after 31 December 2003 if they had not been inspected and approved under the EU compliant system for doing so. A subsequent mission by the FVO to the Czech Republic resulted in the suspension of approvals where the FVO found that the EU standards had not been met after all.[176] The new food hygiene package adopted in April 2004 had to be given effect in respect of these establishments, i.e. Regulations 852/2004, 853/2004, 882/2004 and 854/2004 when they entered into effect.

The country profiles of each Member State are a good starting point for investigating the actual progress of the new Member States in meeting their pre-accession commitments and ironing out remaining

---

[173] FVO Report, DG(SANCO) 2008–7950, for the period 28 January to 8 February 2008.

[174] FVO Report, DG(SANCO) 2008–7576, for the period 26 February to 9 March 2007.

[175] FVO Report, DG(SANCO) 2008–7820, for the period 21 to 31 October 2008, p. 21.

[176] FVO Report, DG (SANCO) 2750/2004 for the period 12 to 13 September 2005, at p. 6.

work to be done during the time of their transitional arrangements.[177] Reports of the various missions of the FVO, to be found on the Europa website, show mixed results in the success of the new Member States in completing the restructuring of their food establishments under the transitional arrangements set out in their Accession Treaties. An incomplete sample of FVO reports show various weakness and even serious deficiencies in some of the new Member State's food producing or processing establishments and in the governmental or administrative capacity to apply this veterinary chapter of the agri-food *acquis*. While the temporary derogations allowed certain food establishments in the countries that acceded in 2004 have generally expired, there are numerous examples of compliance failures.

For the *Czech Republic*, mixed results for the registration and approval of food-processing establishments and the implementation the hygiene package were also shown in 2008 although improvements had been made.[178]

*Slovakia* and *Cyprus* were recognised as generally being able to guarantee that the Community law was complied with, although a few deficiencies arose in respect of the supervision of food establishments.[179]

*Estonia* was found to be generally in accordance with registration and approval requirements as well as the overall hygiene package of Regulations, and only a few discrepancies were listed.[180]

For other Member States the picture was not so good. *Malta*, for example, had struggled with reaching the necessary standard of compliance of its food processing establishments, associated live animal controls and the capacity of its competent authorities to oversee compliance[181] and it was seriously criticised again in 2007.[182]

The *Slovenian* Central Competent Authority was criticised for not taking remedial action against infringements of the Community laws

---

177 http://ec.europa.eu/food/fvo/country_profiles_en.cfm

178 FVO Report DG(SANCO) 2008–7939 for the period 1 to 12 September 2008.

179 FVO Report, DG(SANCO) 7180/2004 for the period 22 to 26 November 2004. FVO Report, DG(SANCO)/7183/2004 for the period 6 to 10 December 2004, p. 17.

180 See FVO Report, DG (SANCO) 2750/2004 for the period 18 to 22 October 2004 and FVO Report, DG(SANCO) 8194/2006 3 to 7 July 2006.

181 See FVO Report, DG(SANCO) 7182/2004, Report of a Mission to Malta between 14 and 17 December 2004.

182 See FVO Report, DG(SANCO) 2007/7588, Report of a Mission to Malta between 21 and 24 May 2007.

in the December of 2004,[183] and the FVO also found that certain establishments under transitional arrangements provided for in the fifth Accession Treaty, could not be upgraded by the agreed deadline.[184] Serious deficiencies were also found in the standard of operational hygiene of certain meat establishments. A 2007 mission of the FVO found that:

> official control programmes at central and regional levels had not been drawn up taking into consideration the general obligation of Article 3(1) of Regulation 852/2004 and Article 4(9) of Regulation 854/2001, in particular, there was no identification of risks for establishing the nature and intensity of official controls in respect of individual establishments producing food of animal origin.[185]

In 2004 *Lithuania* was found to have the control systems in place for food processing establishments and animal health controls were found to be well developed but deficiencies were highlighted: in particular, Lithuania had failed to meet its targets for the supervision of food plants.[186] However, Lithuania's governmental capacity to apply the food hygiene *acquis* concerning meat and milk production, was found to be in a good state of compliance in 2008.[187]

In the case of *Latvia*, the FVO found that the enforcement by the competent authorities of the transitional period was unsatisfactory and that upgrade of the establishments began only after accession and also that 'the majority of them are unlikely to comply with the relevant Community legislation by the deadline fixed [31 December 2004].'[188] The FVO also questioned the abilities of the competent authorities to ensure compliance with the agri-food laws. The overall level of compliance was described as 'unsatisfactory'. Latvian establishments were found generally compliant in 2005[189] but the 2006 FVO Report highlighted a number of serious deficiencies in application of the hygiene package of Regulations.[190] Latvia also showed mixed results

[183] See FVO Report, DG(SANCO) 7181/2004, for the period 6 to 10 December 2004, p. 7.
[184] Ibid. p. 7.
[185] FVO Report, DG(SANCO) 8195/2006, for the period 30 May to 9 June 2006.
[186] FVO Report, DG(SANCO) 7175/2004, for the period 29 to 3 December 2004.
[187] FVO Report, DG(SANCO) 2008/7940, for the period 2 to 12 September 2008.
[188] FVO Report, DG(SANCO)/7174/2004, for the period 22 to 26 November 2004, at pp. 3–4.
[189] FVO Report DG(SANCO) 7617/2005, for the period 7 to 17 November 2005.
[190] FVO Report DG(SANCO) 2006–8206, for the period 20 to 24 March 2006.

in this area in 2008: in particular, that the action planned in response to the 2006 Report 'did not address adequately the recommendation requiring that all establishments should comply with all EU relevant requirements'.[191]

The FVO findings following a mission to *Poland* in September 2004 painted a very poor picture of Poland's progress in meeting its pre-accession commitments concerning the upgrade of food establishments, animal health controls, and controls of food of animal origin intended for human consumption.[192] A long list of deficiencies was given, ranging from the transposition of laws to weaknesses in the structure, layout and operational hygiene of food establishments. The FVO even recommended the re-evaluation of establishments that have transitional arrangements and insisted that their progress in being upgraded was monitored accurately.[193] It concluded that the recommendations made during previous missions had only partly been taken into account by Poland. Moreover, the action that has been taken was considered unsatisfactory and 'the control systems currently in place cannot guarantee that essential provisions of Community legislation are complied with'.[194] The detailed response of the Polish competent authorities amounted to ten pages and required future verification to establish how quickly Poland responded to such recommendations and therefore also, how well it met its Treaty obligations as a new Member State. In 2006, problems with the official control system for the new hygiene legislation persisted. The introductory conclusions note that:[195]

> efforts are being made to adapt the official control system to the new EU hygiene legislation and although the system may provide a good basis for an efficient control system, some specific points will require further attention. In particular this relates to the limits documented controls of districts veterinarians and appointed veterinarians at local level as well as the continuing production for the national market for establishments not fulfilling basic hygiene requirements.

---

[191] FVO Report DG(SANCO) 2008–7936, for the period 20 to 28 May 2008.
[192] FVO Report, DG(SANCO) 7177/2004, for the period 6 to 17 September 2004.
[193] Ibid. at p. 28.
[194] Ibid. at p. 26.
[195] FVO Report, DG(SANCO) 8210/2006, for the period 4 to 15 September 2006.

A 2007 FVO Report however, shows more reasonable progress by Poland in 2007.[196]

For *Hungary*, still in 2006 it had only started to implement the food hygiene package and 'significant progress still [had] to be made, especially in some counties, before this implementation reaches an acceptable level all over the country'.[197] This situation had improved in 2007 but 'significant deficiencies' persisted in Hungarian food processing establishments.[198]

Various instances of informal transitional arrangements can be found in areas where there were no formal transitional arrangements contained in the fifth and sixth Accession Treaties. For example, only the Czech Republic, Hungary, Malta, Poland and Slovenia had transitional derogations from Article 5(1)(4) and 5(1)(5) of Directive 1999/74 on minimum standards for the protection of laying hens. However, serious problems in applying this Directive were found in Lithuania, which negotiated no transitional arrangement in the fifth Accession Treaty. The FVO noted in 2008, that:[199]

> [...] the system of controls in place did not ensure that deficiencies in laying hen holdings equipped with cages were detected and corrected. Even though some progress was made, serious deficiencies already highlighted during missions in 2004 and 2006, such as insufficient height of enriched cages and the installation of cages with no enrichment after accession were still outstanding.

For Romania, the FVO was very critical of its control system for pesticides in food of plant origin.[200] There is no temporary derogation for Romania in respect of pesticide residues in fruit and vegetables and this was most unlikely to be have been entertained.

Malta was criticised by the FVO for lack of progress in implementing Regulation 1774/2002 on animal by-products (ABPs) for human consumption,[201] noting that certain operators in Malta are still not subject to official controls there. ABPs in animal feed can spread BSE or chemical contaminants, such as dioxin. The Commission notes in the

---

196 FVO Report, DG(SANCO) 7442/2007, for the period 4 to 15 June 2007.

197 FVO Report, DG(SANCO) 8209/2006, for the period 4 to 15 September 2006, p. 23.

198 FVO Report, DG(SANCO) 2007–7432, for the period 4 to 15 June 2007.

199 FVO Report, DG(SANCO) 2008–7689, for the period 19 to 22 February 2008.

200 FVO Report, DG(SANCO) 2008–7859, for the period 10 to 14 March 2008.

201 Op. cit. n. 87. See FVO Report, DG(SANCO) 2008–7738, for the period 3 to 7 March 2008.

25th *Report on the application of Community law*,[202] that both Poland and Malta were found in breach of this law, and were in the process of remedying the situation in 2007.

Problems with BIPs in certain new Member States are another example. This was an area highlighted for enhanced efforts by candidates in the run-up to accession. No transitional arrangements were allowed at the BIPs. However, an FVO visit to Poland for example, in early 2005[203] found that not all the relevant legislation had been transposed, that the competent authorities were criticised for not assuring their co-operation, BIPs were found not to be discharging all their duties under the Community rules, the lack of detailed procedural guidance meant that veterinary checks could not be relied on to reach the EU standard, while staff was sufficient but training was not satisfactory. Other criticisms included certain infrastructure problems. Procedures for veterinary checks were found lacking and hygienic deficiencies in customs warehouses jeopardise the storage and movement of consignments. In response the Polish competent authorities undertook 18 actions to remedy matters. At the top of the list was capacity building actions, such as training BIP staff and veterinarians. Further problems were identified by the FVO in 2006 and the FVO concluded that the import control system for products of animal origin and live animals was compromised.[204] Reporting on the inspection of BIPs in Poland for 2008 is awaited. As for Bulgaria and Romania, the BIPs were also a problem at the time of the accession and problems persisted in 2008.[205]

Again, this is not the case for all of the new Member States having external EU borders and BIPs. For example, in the Czech Republic the FVO found a functioning import control system in place which mostly complied with the relevant *acquis*, although with some deficiencies that did not pose an immediate risk to animal or public health.[206]

---

[202] Op. cit. n. 112 at p. 218.

[203] FVO Report, DG(SANCO)/7594/2005, for the period 31 January to 4 February 2005.

[204] FVO Report, DG(SANCO) 8063/2006, for the period 13 to 14 November 2006.

[205] FVO Report, DG(SANCO) 2008–7747, for the period 4 to 8 February 2008 following up in Report DG(SANCO) 2007–7571, for the period 15 to 26 January 2007.

[206] FVO Report, DG(SANCO) 7727/2005, for the period 7 to 10 November 2005. A second FVO Report, DG(SANCO) 2008–7746 indicated a well organised system, again with some shortcomings.

### 3.2 *Are safeguard and crisis measures under Regulation 178/2002 sufficient?*

We have seen that all food produced in establishments under transitional arrangements from the new Member States cannot enter the Internal Market. We have also seen that any food produced before the date of accession is also restricted from being placed on the Internal Market. Any other foods that are put on the Internal Market must meet the standards set out in the *acquis* on food safety.

There are other mechanisms in the *acquis* for protecting the food chain from products that do not come up to standard. Article 53 of Regulation 178/2002 enables the Commission to adopt EU-wide emergency measures in respect of products that originate in a Member State or third countries. Emergency measures are envisaged for food or feed that is;

> likely to constitute a serious risk to human health, animal health or the environment, and [...] such risk cannot be contained satisfactorily by means of measures taken by the Member State(s) concerned.

The Commission takes action either on its own initiative or at the request of another Member State. The SCFCAH plays a key role in emergency measures. Both the Commission and the SCFCAH act by qualified majority vote. The Commission may immediately adopt provisional emergency measures on consultation with the Member States but it must consult the SCFCAH on the content of the emergency measures within ten working days. Emergency measures may suspend the product from being put on the market, establish special conditions for the food and/or 'any other appropriate measure' may be taken depending on the gravity of the situation.

Until such time as the Union measures are in place, other Member States are allowed to adopt interim protective measures in accordance with Article 54 of Regulation 178/2002.[207] Thus, for example, France first alerted its partner Member States to the risks of Sudan red 1 on 9 May 2003 when it notified available experimental data through the

---

[207] The Member States are also entitled, under Art. 16(1) of Regulation 178/2002, op. cit. n. 49, to adopt safeguard measures to temporarily suspend or restrict the application on its territory of Community laws on specific groups of materials and articles (such as adhesives or cork, to name only a few – see Annex I to Regulation 178/2002). Such measures must be founded upon a risk to human health deriving from the migration of substances from food contact materials and articles in food.

RASFF. France took its own interim emergency measures to restrict imports of the products concerned on 5 June 2003 which applied until the EU measures took effect some weeks later. National interim protective measures must be notified to the Commission and all other Member States and then the Commission has ten working days to refer the national measures to the SCFCAH in order to extend them to all Member States, amend them or repeal them.

Under the Rapid Alert System for Food and Feed (RASFF),[208] where a Member State, the European Commission or the European Food Safety Authority have any information relating to the existence of a serious direct or indirect risk to human health deriving from food or feed, they are under an obligation to notify that risk immediately to the European Commission, which in turn must notify all the other Member States. This is a new version of a previously existing Rapid Alert System for Food (RASF) in that it covers more that the food sector in the EU.[209] It now covers the feed sector as well as imports from third countries into the EU. Member States are specifically under an obligation to notify the Commission under the RASFF of:

a) any measure they adopt which is aimed at restricting the placing on the market or forcing the withdrawal from the market or the recall of food or feed in order to protect human health and requiring rapid action;
b) any recommendation or agreement with professional operators which is aimed, on a voluntary or obligatory basis, at preventing, limiting or imposing specific conditions on the placing on the market or the eventual use of food or feed on account of a serious risk to human health requiring rapid action;

[208] The rules governing the RASFF are contained in Art. 50(1)–(6) of Regulation 178/2002, op. cit. n. 49.

[209] In practice a distinction is made in the RASFF between Rapid Alert Notifications and Rapid Information Notifications: Rapid Alert Notifications are made by a Member States that detects the problem and initiates the recall or withdrawal of products from the market under their own national systems. This enables the other Member States to check whether they have the same products on their markets and withdraw or recall them also. They in turn make an Alert Notification if they then recall a product from the market. Rapid Information Notifications are made by the Member States when a risk has been identified but where other members in the network do not have to take immediate action themselves. These mostly concern products that have been tested and rejected at the external borders of the EU and therefore the products concerned have not reached the EU market.

c) any rejection, related to a direct or indirect risk to human health, of a batch, container or cargo of food or feed by a competent authority at a border post within the European Union.

Notifications have to be accompanied by a detailed explanation of the reasons for the action taken by the competent authorities of the Member State in which the notification was issued. Supplementary information has also to be supplied 'in good time', in particular where the measures on which the notification is based are modified or withdrawn. All Member States have to keep the Commission abreast of the measures they take to follow up the notifications under the RASFF.

Should emergency measures prove inadequate for the purposes of protecting against direct or indirect threats to human health, the crisis provisions of Regulation 178/2002 would kick in to action (Arts. 55–57). Only two days before the fifth enlargement took place, on 29 April 2004, the Commission, the Member States and European Food Safety Authority adopted the General Plan for food/feed crisis management.[210] This crisis plan was then amended by corrigendum on 12 June 2004. This General Plan emphasises at 2.1 that:

> Crisis situations are those where critical factors are involved at such a level that the Commission considers that the management of the risk in question deriving from food or feed will be of such complexity that it cannot be managed adequately by existing provisions or solely by way of application of Articles 53 and 54 [of Regulation 178/2002].'

Critical factors include situations involving serious direct or indirect risks to human health and/or perceived or publicised as such, or can be perceived or publicised as such. Other critical factors include where the risk is spread by a large part of the food chain or it is highly likely that the risk will be spread to several Member States and/or non-EU countries. Where the risk involved is considered to be 'serious', a crisis unit will be set up within the European Commission.

These provisions are thorough and apparently all embracing. As with the food hygiene rules generally speaking, there are no transitional arrangements in either the fifth or sixth Accession Treaties in respect of full participation in the RASFF. It would certainly seem to

[210] See Commission Decision 2004/478 concerning the adoption of a general plan for food/feed crisis management, *OJ* 2004 L 160/98. The plan was subsequently amended by corrigendum, including section 2.1of the General Plan for food/feed crisis management, see *OJ* 2004 L212/60–68.

be the case that any errant Member State, old or new, will fall prey to emergency measures if a 'serious risk' is 'likely' to arise and that the risk concerned cannot be 'satisfactorily contained'. The scope of the emergency measures is therefore very broadly defined and the Commission holds the reins over them. The Food and Veterinary Office, in its findings, advises the Commission not only on the functioning of a country's systems for and participation in the RASFF. The FVO also makes recommendations to the Commission on actions that it should take in respect of breaches of the *acquis* or risks arising and at the same it makes recommendations to the Member States, setting time limits for response and demanding compliance where deficiencies arise.

From an enlargement perspective, during the infancy of the membership, these new emergency provisions of Regulation 178/2002 provide certain advantages over the Internal Market safeguard clause of the Accession Treaties. First, without any political distinction between 'old' or 'new' Member State having to be drawn, emergency measures may be taken by any Member State or by the European Commission where needs demand. Second, this system of emergency measures and crisis provisions provides a sound legal and scientific basis for such measures, which pre-empts any threat of arbitrary national measures or protectionist backlash against the new Member States.

But do these emergency provisions of Regulation 178/2002 apply to the situations of non-transposition of agri-food laws, such as those listed in Table 7? Where a serious risk is presented to the food chain, the answer must surely be 'yes'. It is unlikely from this wording that failure to transpose a law would amount to a 'serious risk' in itself for the purposes of triggering safeguard and crisis measures under Regulation 178/2002. The main advantage of the Accession Treaties' safeguard clauses however, is that the are an executive tool that involves no inter-institutional discussion, could be applied in respect of accession commitments without needing of the 'seriousness' of risks arising, and without involving scientific proof.

*Advantages of safeguard measures under the accession treaties* There are obvious advantages to safeguard measures based on the Internal Market safeguard clause contained in the fifth and sixth Accession Treaties as a means of preventing informal transitional arrangements from arising. While the Internal Market safeguard clause gives the

European Commission an additional stick with which to cajole compliance out of the new Member States, and this could also improve trust between the Member States, the Commission has no such preventive route for managing and enforcing compliance by the 'old' Member States. This is particularly striking when one considers that the Fifteen have been no angels themselves in this field of the *acquis*.[211] Many cases have been brought by the Commission against Member States for serious hygiene and other violations of fundamental Community laws. The Commission must revert to the comparably limited resort of Article 258 TFEU in the event of failures arising in compliance by the Fifteen.

In areas of the agri-food *acquis* where the new Member States do not benefit from transitional arrangements, the Fifteen have not been exemplary in their compliance. For example, the Commission sent reasoned opinions to Greece, Italy and the United Kingdom in 2002 in respect of Directive 2000/75[212] on the eradication of bluetongue. The Commission took infringement proceedings against Belgium, Denmark, Spain, the Netherlands and Finland for failing to notify measures to transpose Council Directive 2001/89[213] on classical swine fever.

The implementation deficit in the EU Member States has inspired work on governance initiatives to improve and encourage the means of redress for citizens and operators, to improve the effectiveness of the pre-litigation stage seeking compliance by Member State with their Treaty obligations and ultimately to foster trust between Member States.[214] The Food and Veterinary Office will dedicate 40 per cent

---

[211] See also the *FVO General Report 2002* for an overview of its inspection findings for the year 2002: www.europa.eu.int/comm/food/fs/inspections/policy_papers/ann_rep_2002_en.pdf

[212] Council Directive 2000/75 laying down specific provisions for the control and eradication of bluetongue, *OJ* 2000 L 327/74 (Bluetongue is an insect-borne viral disease to which all species of ruminants are susceptible, although sheep are most severely affected. However, cattle are the main mammalian reservoir of the virus and are very important in the epidemiology of the disease. It is characterised by changes to the mucous linings of the mouth and nose and the coronary band of the foot. Bluetongue is present when it is confirmed by laboratory tests that the Bluetongue virus (BTV) is circulating in an area.)

[213] Council Directive 2001/89 on Community measures for the control of classical swine fever, *OJ* 2001 L 316/5.

[214] European Commission, *White Paper on European Governance*, COM(2001) 428, 25 July 2001.

of its resources to the compliance of the new Member States. Indeed, it has been heavily involved in the Commission's monitoring programme for evaluating the Ten's compliance with the *acquis*. The FVO continues to work in the same way with the new members as it does with the existing members. The Commission will have to work hard at the pre-litigation stages of the Article 258 TFEU procedure to ensure the coherent transposition and compliance in the existing Member States and to avoid a further decline in the implementation deficit for agri-food law.

In the 2003 report monitoring application of Union law, the Commission served reasoned opinions against Austria, Belgium, Greece, Italy and Portugal for failure to implement the laying hens Directive,[215] one of the principle objectives of which is to phase out the use of conventional battery cages ('unenriched cages') as of 1 January 2003 and provide caged birds with sufficient space. The transitional arrangements for Czech Republic, Hungary, Malta, Poland and Slovenia related only to Article 5 of the laying hens Directive and allowed them to phase out existing cages that did not meet the slope and height requirements. Moreover, for the Fifteen, even in the last months prior to enlargement between January and May 2004,[216] the FVO carried out a series of missions in six Member States and revealed that five of them had not fully transposed key legislation in this area.[217] The FVO found that in some Member States some new un-enriched cages had been introduced after the cut-off date, due to lack of transposition as well as lacks in guidance and training of the national competent authorities. The Commission will follow up compliance with these Member States and ultimately, may initiate formal complaints for failure to meet Treaty obligations.

---

[215] Directive 1999/74 laying down minimum standards for the protection of laying hens, *OJ* 1999 L 203/53. See the *Twentieth Report Monitoring the Application of Community Law* (2002), COM (2003) 669, 21/11/03, pp. 61–63. Certain of the new Member States have temporary derogations under this Directive but are not otherwise exempt from the transposition and implementation of Directive 1999/74 by the date of accession.

[216] Overview of a series of missions carried out in 2004 concerning animal welfare standards on holdings with laying hens, FVO Report, DG(SANCO)/8509/2004–GR, 27/05/05, 21034.

[217] Namely, Directive 1999/74, op. cit. n. 215, and Directive 2002/4 on the registration of establishments keeping laying hens, covered by Directive 1999/74, *OJ* 2002 L 30/44.

Take as another example Directive 64/433 on health conditions for the production and marketing of fresh meat produce. While meat produced at specified Polish establishments are excluded from marketing their produce in the EU,[218] the Commission has had to bring France before the ECJ for refusing to comply with a Food and Veterinary Office (FVO) report requiring that it withdraw health approval for an abattoir that failed to meet the requirements of the same Directive and the UK was criticised in 2002 for infringements by certain of its poultry abattoirs.[219] In 2001, Greece was forced to close a number of slaughterhouses found by the FVO to be of 'extremely poor structural and hygienic standards and expressed very serious concerns on veterinary supervision'.[220] The Fifteen themselves have not proved exemplary in implementing judgments of the ECJ against them for failing to implement laws of the veterinary and phytosanitary *acquis* for which the new members have transitional arrangements.[221]

Border Inspection Posts (BIPs) are an example of the higher demands put on the new Member States compared to the actual level of compliance in the Fifteen. In a report of the FVO reporting for the years 2000–2001 on the state of compliance by the Fifteen's BIPS, 14.8 per cent of BIPs failed to comply with registration requirements, 80.9 per cent non-compliance was identified in product receiving facilities of BIPs and 50 per cent non-compliance was found in live animal handling facilities.[222] While on the whole the relevant import legislation had been transposed, instances of incomplete transposition and/or implementation were found and even cases of non-transposition were found.[223] As for implementation, while the rules on veterinary checks were immediately applicable, the FVO highlighted delays in the applicability of administrative procedures, a lack of national guidelines and instructions in most Member States as well as the lack of a plan

[218] See Annex (Poland) XII.6.B.I. Act of Accession, p. 883.

[219] See *Nineteenth Annual Report on Monitoring the application of Community Law*, COM(2002) 324, 28 June 2002 at p. 67.

[220] See FVO Report, DG(SANCO)/8660/2002, FVO mission of 26 November to 6 December 2002, at p. 14.

[221] See European Commission *Eighteenth Annual Report on Monitoring the application of Community Law*, COM(2001) 309, 16 July 2001, Annex V.

[222] See the *General Review* Report of the FVO for veterinary checks at border inspection posts for 2000–2001, undated but which was published on the europa website in August 2003, at www.europa.eu.int/comm/food/fs/inspections/special_reports/sr_rep_9001-2002_en.pdf

[223] Ibid., at point 5.1.3.

for monitoring for residues, pathogenic organisms or other substances dangerous to humans, animals or the environment in consignments coming from third countries.[224]

The FVO report on BIPs in Austria, following an inspection between 3 and 12 June 2002, found that Austria had failed to remedy criticisms raised in the previous FVO report on its BIPs.[225] In 2005 the UK was criticised for gaps in implementation, enforcement and application of the relevant EU legislation, particularly with regard to identification and selection of consignments and the performance of delivery checks.[226] The FVO found that 'the system for import controls cannot be regarded as fully effective'. In the same report the FVO expressed its dissatisfaction with the actions taken by the UK to address deficiencies uncovered in its previous reports of 1999 and 2004. It even advised the Commission to suspend the approval of the inspection centre in respect of products for (and not for) human consumption at the BIP at Heathrow airport in the absence of sufficient guarantees that the deficiencies would be remedied within six months. The FVO was also critical of import controls and border inspection posts in the Netherlands[227] although it took note of the progress made in monitoring the performance of BIPs. Among the criticisms listed included the lack of staff at inspection centres and gaps in transposition and implementation of the relevant *acquis* in addition to structural problems, such as storage facilities, or organisational problems of veterinary services.

While the number of the BIPs in the Fifteen fell on accession when the BIPs in the new Member States began to operate fully, on 1 May 2004, the Ten were not allowed any transitional arrangements in respect of BIPs, of which there were around seventy in total. Full compliance was required as of the date of accession. Specific funding has been provided the new members in the Accession Treaty from the Transition Facility.[228] The use of safeguard measures against the Romania and Bulgaria remains a theoretical possibility until the end of 2009. If the new members have not brought their BIPs up to scratch

---

[224] Op. cit. n. 222, at point 5.1.4.

[225] To be found at www.europa.eu.int/comm/food/fs/inspections/vi/reports/austria/vi_rep_oste_8562-2002_en.pdf

[226] FVO Report, DG(SANCO)/7526/2005, for the period 31 January to 4 February 2005.

[227] See FVO Report DG(SANCO)/7282/2004, for the period 6 to 15 October 2004.

[228] Op. cit. n. 106.

for example, and this poses a serious threat to the functioning of the Internal Market, surely its use may well be justified? The Internal Market in the agri-food market cannot be seen as divorced from the consumer protection and public health component.

In addition to the emergency and crisis measures available to curb infringements of the agri-food *acquis*, the overall monitoring and evaluation of the *acquis* by means of governance initiatives offers a route to preventing risks to the food chain from arising in the first place. Governance initiatives have already been explored in Chapter 6 at 3.2.1, which are of commensurate importance to the Internal Market *acquis*.

Certain innovations of the Lisbon Treaty promise to improve the situation. Under Article 260(2) and (3) TFEU (ex-Art. 228(2) EC), if a Member State has not complied with a Court ruling against it for failing to meet its Treaty obligations to properly apply the *acquis*, the Commission will be able to skip the reasoned opinion stage and go straight to asking the Court to impose lump sum or penalty payments. Moreover, an entirely new provision allows the Commission to request a lump sum or penalty payment at the earlier procedure stage in cases of non-transposition of Directives into national law.

Having said this, the Internal Market safeguard clause offer the Commission a last resort means of securing swift compliance with the agri-food *acquis* where there is no crisis as such, but where the incoming country is falling behind in transposition and compliance obligations and their pre-accession commitments. The question is: should the Internal Market safeguard clause be used after all? The reluctance of the Commission to revert to the Internal Market safeguard clause was due in the main to the fact that a discriminatory distinction would be made between Member States if a new member could be pursued for a breach of its Treaty obligations while an 'old' member could not be pursued by the same means in respect of the same infringement.

As politically untenable as it may be to employ the Internal Market safeguard clause, in the interests of the integrity of EU agri-food law and the food chain, there is a case for using this tool for the purpose it was intended: to ensure that the new Member States meet their pre-accession commitments in respect of the measures outlined above as well as in respect of the agri-food law reform package. Moreover, this clause in the sixth Accession Treaty expressly provides for safeguards to protect the food safety *acquis*, and is not limited to the Internal

Market chapter only. Measures taken using this clause could remain in place until the problems were resolved.

The possibility of transitional arrangements from transposition, let alone full compliance, from these measures of the *acquis* was not negotiable for the agri-food *acquis*. Transposition, implementation and compliance must be looked on as accession conditions as well as commitments. It would seem acceptable – leaving aside the obvious political weaknesses of the Internal Market safeguard clause in terms of solidarity and discrimination – that the Internal Market safeguard measure could be used both to ensure the integrity of the food chain and to insist that the new Member States meet their accession commitments. The fact that the Fifteen themselves face difficulties in compliance with food laws should be no excuse in itself. If the Fifteen were to find themselves advantaged because of breaches in their own compliance, the political fallout would at least give an added dimension to their 'naming and shaming', with the added potential to threaten consumer confidence in their national food sectors.

Moreover, the programme of approximation to the agri-food reform is demanding for new and old Member States alike. The purpose of the agri-food law reform was designed to establish the regulatory framework for the food sector from the farm and following through to a product's ultimate consumption. The safeguard measures introduced by the new agri-food reform under Regulation 178/2002 are one component in the entire regulatory framework. The Internal Market safeguard clause could be used as one of the enforcement mechanisms in that regulatory framework.

# CONCLUSIONS

Since its inception in the 1950s, the EU has pursued its widening – enlargement – agenda ambitions alongside its deepening – integration – ambitions. Almost continuously from its birth in 1958, the EU has been in a state of pre-accession or of post-accession transition: preparing and negotiating enlargements or else adjusting to the integration of new Member States under the transitional arrangements contained in the Accession Treaties.

The European Union has completed its strategy for enlarging that it embarked upon first with the commitment it made at the 1993 Copenhagen European Council to the CEECs that they could join, and then in earnest with the launch of the *Agenda 2000* strategy in 1997. Twelve new Member States acceded to the Union on 1 May 2004 and 1 January 2007. The Union has achieved what it set out to do but has some important lessons to learn from the exercise.

## New means to make the irreversible process of enlargement possible

Due to the progress already made in its deepening agenda, new means had to be found to deal with the integration of the new Member States into the Common Agricultural Policy, Economic and Monetary Union and Schengen *acquis* as well as to deal with the accession of Cyprus, still a divided island some five years after its accession to the European Union. In order to make eastwards enlargement possible, the full participation of the new members in these areas is staggered over time and the impression of transition persists in all three of these areas still. Moreover, the staggered participation of the twelve new Member States in the Common Agricultural Policy, the Schengen *acquis* and the Eurozone has introduced a level of complexity that compounds the uncertainty and leaves the entire Union in a state of transition for many years to come, even as it continues with its current enlargement strategy to bring in the countries of the Western Balkans and Turkey, which have all been recognized by the Union as actual or potential candidates in an irreversible process of EU enlargement. Croatia is leading, being the only one among them to have opened accession negotiations.

## Some of the uncertainties facing future enlargements

The first half of this book put the general pre-accession strategy in its historical context and traced its evolution and influences. These first five chapters highlighted the particular problems facing today's pre-accession strategy and how to smooth the entry of the incoming countries into the Union post-enlargement. In terms of eligibility and procedural steps for accession, uncertainty arises in various ways. In particular, there is the 'wild card' or unpredictable hurdle of national referendums which are increasingly likely to scupper the ratification of accession treaties at the level of the Member States even if further accession treaties should be concluded.

The 1993 Copenhagen criteria that form the basis of the political, economic and legal conditionality of the pre-accession strategy, were drafted also to include the precondition that the Union has the capacity to absorb new members: the fourth Copenhagen criterion. While this flared up in the aftermath of the 2004 enlargement, the Member States had already committed to the 'irreversibleness' of the process of enlargement when it recognized both Turkey and the countries of the Western Balkans as actual or potential members. To renege on such commitments would certainly have serious consequences for the Union's relations with the countries concerned, for its legal credibility with other world partners and for its conditionality in relations with neighbouring countries in particular.

The opening of accession negotiations has also become increasingly important although it has always indicated the Union's intention to enlarge. Today it marks the graduation from a 'potential' candidate to a 'candidate with which accession negotiations have been opened', but without necessarily having an actual date for their accession recognized by the EU Member States. Moreover, the gestation period from opening accession negotiations to accession is growing. For Turkey in particular, now formally recognized as a candidate since 1999, no date has been fixed for its accession due to failings in progress to meet the Copenhagen political criteria. Since 1993 in particular, the enlargement process has been held-out to be inclusive and irreversible but certain statements by the Council and Parliament in 2004 and 2005 as regards Turkey[1] detract from the inclusive and irreversible nature of the pre-accession process, which obviously undermines the strength of the pre-accession conditionality in relations with Turkey.

Another future source of uncertainty is the Council's 2005 proposals to introduce various transitional arrangements and other flexibility mechanisms and even permanent derogations into future accession treaties in core Community areas, such as the freedom of movement of persons, structural funds and the Common Agricultural Policy, which put increasing strain on the glue of solidarity between the Member States and gnaw away at core principles such as equal treatment and non-discrimination. To do so would go against the grain of previous accession treaty rationale and practice and makes the discussion of the primary law limits – the limits to how 'flexible' the Member States can be in smoothing the entry of incoming Member States – increasingly important.

If the Member States should choose to go down the path of permanently excluding incoming countries from full participation in core areas of Union activities, accession treaties would become inadequate accession instruments in their own right. The current legal basis in the EU Treaty, Article 49 TEU, which provides only for adjustments to the Treaties, may well no longer be appropriate and major treaty revision would no doubt be required, triggering the procedure currently set out in Article 48 TEU. Significantly, this would involve national referendums. Changes to the procedural legal basis for future accession treaties will follow the entry into force of the Lisbon Treaty are discussed, although there would be only minor changes to Article 49 TEU.

In previous enlargements there was no going back once accession negotiations had been opened and the politically agreed timeframe took on a binding effect. This was consistent with the irreversible nature of the project. In previous enlargements, including the fifth and the sixth enlargements, to do otherwise has been considered grossly prejudicial to both the interests of the Member States and the Union, and especially in their international relations with third countries.[2]

---

[1] See Chapter 3.1 and 3.2.

[2] The European Parliament highlighted this fact in its Explanatory Statement accompanying its Resolution of the European Parliament of 14 March 1985 on the results of the negotiations on the enlargement of the European Community, *OJ* 1985 C94/78, see European Parliament Working Documents, A2-20/85, 24 April 1985 at paragraph 21.

Will this still apply to future enlargements? Various statements by the European Council and the European Parliament imply a reticence that weakens the commitment to future enlargements and underlines the overall uncertainty that the candidates and potential candidates face. The second principle of the European Commission's negotiating mandate for Turkey, adopted in October 2005 specifically mentions that, 'these negotiations are an open-ended process, the outcome of which cannot be guaranteed beforehand'.[3] The failure of the Constitutional Treaty emphasises this reticence. Moreover, the new wording of Article 49 TEU under the Lisbon Treaty[4] removes the express reference to the 'openness' of the Union to other European countries under the Constitutional Treaty and which had been the intention of the original Treaty writers.

## Evolution in pre-accession conditionality tools

The pre-accession strategy of today is founded within the pre-accession strategy devised for the 2004 and 2007 enlargements, which is characterized by an inclusive and differentiating approach to the region: inclusive in that all countries are treated on an equal basis; differentiating in that their progress towards membership is dependent on their progress in meeting the Union's pre-accession conditionality. That conditionality is, as it ever was, devised by the Union autonomously and the aspiring members act of their own accord in response to those conditions and requirements. However, the pre-accession strategy today has been further reoriented and refined: the Copenhagen criteria have been worked out in greater and greater detail according to the partner country concerned and in the context of the region as a whole. For the countries of the Western Balkans in particular, the requirement of good neighbourliness and neighbourly relations has come into its own in pre-accession conditionality. Only a few months before, the time of the re-launch of the pre-accession strategy by the *Agenda 2000* document of July 1997, the Council adopted its April

[3] See Commission negotiating mandate adopted by the European Council on 3 October 2005. See Resolution 55 of European Parliament Resolution on the 2004 regular report and the recommendation of the European Commission on Turkey's progress towards accession, contained in European Parliament Report A6-0063/2004 of 3 December 2004.

[4] See Chapter 1 at 2.3.

2007 Conclusions establishing the regional conditionality applicable to the Western Balkans. While there was no talk of the Union's commitment to enlarge to the south east at this time, the pre-accession strategy that is in place now is squarely based on the conditionality established then.

Also for the countries of the Western Balkans, the use of association agreements (the Stabilisation and Association Agreements) as a 'carrot' for reaching the minimum threshold of compliance with the Copenhagen criteria has introduced a new stage in pre-accession in advance of the opening of negotiations on an eventual accession treaty. Other instruments of the pre-accession strategy have also been revised or revamped to suit the different needs of the partners: the Accession Partnerships now have a preparatory phase themselves, in the form of the 'European Partnership' for example; the Instrument for Pre-accession has replaced the mix of funding instruments, including Phare. The pre-accession strategy and its components have been used as templates for strategies in the region, notably the European Neighbourhood Policy (ENP), although without the ultimate carrot of accession.

## Evolutions in accession treaty practice

With the opening of accession negotiations, previously work would begin on the drafting of the accession treaty itself. Being an 'adjustment' instrument only, it contains the transitional arrangements of which, in line with the primary law limits on such arrangements, the rationale is not to allow permanent derogations from the *acquis communautaire*. As such, accession negotiations are negotiations about temporary and exception arrangements, in some cases involving temporary derogations from the *acquis*, within very restrictive boundaries. Chapter 4 set out the typical provisions of accession treaties, while Chapter 5 concentrated on the new flexibility means introduced into the 2003 and 2005 Accession Treaties. The number of acceding countries and growth of the *acquis* since the last enlargement in 1995, had made the transitional arrangements particularly complicated in the 2003 and 2005 Accession Treaties. While the flexibility arrangements concerning the CAP, Schengen, the Euro and Cyprus are not transitional arrangements as such, they add to the overall complexity of the recent enlargement projects.

Various transitional arrangements are used in accession treaties, including temporary derogations and various clauses to adjust or amend the *acquis* or to introduce new temporary derogations from the *acquis* after the signature of the accession treaty. In terms of temporary derogations from the *acquis communautaire* under the 2003 and 2005 Accession Treaties, many of these transitional arrangements have expired. However, various are still running their course, especially in the case of the environment *acquis*. Poland has until 2017 to bring installations classifying as large combustion plants fully into line with the relevant *acquis* for example.

Transitional arrangements have always been the norm in accession treaty practice and it is fair to say that the Union has nearly always been in a state of transition if we count the years spent in pre-accession preparations together with the years after the enlargements that have been spent smoothing the entry of new members. Ultimately, transitional arrangements have a positive integration function as do the flexibility mechanisms for the CAP and Schengen.

The three cases that came before the European Court of Justice dealt with in Chapter 4 at section 2.2, gave useful guidance on the scope for introducing new transitional derogations from the *acquis* or adjusting and adapting the *acquis* after an accession treaty is signed by special legislative procedures. Two of these cases, Cases C-413/04 and C-414/04, give further insight into the scope and limits of standard clauses in accession treaties for such derogations, adaptations and adjustments. These judgments rule out previous practice in using these clauses under previous accession treaties. The third judgment of the ECJ concerned Poland's challenge in Case C-273/04 against certain elements of the CAP reform that the fifteen Member States agreed after signature of the 2003 Accession Treaty. In this case, Poland failed on the substance of its challenge. Most interesting about this case is the reasoning of Advocate-General Maduro in which he calls for access by candidates that have signed an accession treaty, to be able to bring an annulment challenge under the principle of effective judicial protection of community law rights.[5] Such a question could not have arisen of course, if the Member States had been able to meet their own time-

[5] See Chapter 4 at 2.3.3.

table for reform of the CAP in advance of the fifth enlargement. It is a dilemma that would no doubt arise in the context of future accession treaties should the time frame between signature and entry into force be lengthier, if they include postponement clauses akin to that included in the 2005 Accession Treaty that delay their entry into force or should national referendums delay their effect.

The very purpose of the reinforced 1997 *Agenda 2000* pre-accession strategy was to keep the need for such temporary derogations to an absolute minimum. This was the main reason for such a massive and lengthy approximation exercise. *Agenda 2000* established the indivisibility of the *acquis communautaire*, removing any room for approximation to bits and pieces and insisting on the wholesale transposition, implementation and enforcement of the entire *acquis* upon the very date of their accession. Key to such a vast approximation exercise is building up the necessary governmental capacity to make the approximation meaningful in practice. However, the emergence of 'informal transitional arrangements' – situations where the new Member States have not met the commitments they gave at the close of the accession negotiations to be in full compliance with all the *acquis* excepting only for those measures for which transitional arrangements had been formally agreed in the accession treaty – puts the spotlight on the weaknesses of the pre-accession strategy. The fact that such situations have arisen underlines the importance of the Member States' political commitment to enlarge.

## The significance of the political commitment to enlarge

In the case of the fifth and sixth enlargements it would seem that to a certain extent the political will to go ahead with the 'big-bang' enlargement has prioritised the inclusive nature of the project over: the concern of the Union to differentiate between the new Member States in terms of their progress towards membership, and; the actual readiness of the new Member States to meet the legal conditions set out under the pre-accession strategy, and; perhaps most significantly, over the readiness of the Union itself to take in so many new countries.

When fixing the enlargement date, the findings of Chapter 5 shows how the Member States and the European Parliament went ahead with signing the 2005 Accession Treaty with Bulgaria and Romania in spite of their clear lack of preparedness according to the European Commission's progress reports. Only a matter of months after signature of the 2005 Accession Treaty with Bulgaria and Romania, it was made clear by the European Commission that Romania was lacking in various areas of the Justice and Home Affairs *acquis* as well as in competition and state aid matters.[6]

The postponement clause was not under consideration for breaches of other chapters of the *acquis* even though serious lacks were found. One year on, Romania was still having problems. For example, it had still not been able to put in place the full breadth of controls over agricultural spending and at the end of 2007, it faced a 25% cut in EU farm payments as a result,[7] although in the end this did not happen. Chapter 5 (p. 205 and pp. 208–209) showed how problems persist in both countries today.

Rather than postpone the sixth enlargement for a further year to give more time for them to bring themselves into compliance and keep the conditionality-carrot of accession in place, which would have been possible under Article 39, 2005 Act of Accession, the European Parliament decided to proceed with Bulgaria and Romania's accession on 1 January 2007. Again this underlines the significance of the political commitment to a date for enlargement, even at the expense of the legal pre-conditions of the pre-accession strategy. Nearly three years on these countries remain under surveillance – the Cooperation and Verification Mechanism[8] – and are facing a dramatic loss of Community funds due to failings in particular as concerns corruption in local government and the independence of the judiciary. This must mean then that even the postponement clause was not adequate: given that it is three years since Bulgaria and Romania acceded to the EU and that there is no end in sight to the Co-operation and Verification Mechanism, we must conclude not only that the 2005 Accession Treaty was premature. The pre-accession strategy applied to Bulgaria and Romania was unrealistically inclusive; more differentiation was needed to take account of these specific problems in Bulgaria and Romania. It is

[6] See Commission *2005 Comprehensive Monitoring Reports on Bulgaria and Romania*, 25 October 2005.

[7] See Commission Press Release IP/2007/1697, *Farm Payments, Commission asks Romania to make further improvements to control system*, 14 November 2007.

[8] See Chapter 5.3.1.

obvious then to question the logic, the fairness, of going against pre-accession conditionality in order to allow them to accede, being fully aware of such problems, and then to deprive these new Member States of access to Union funds.

## Anticipating new flexibility and trust mechanisms in future accession treaty practice

The '(dis)-trust mechanisms' dealt with in Chapter 5 have not been widely used as had been threatened by high level Commission officials during the pre-accession phases of the 2004 and 2007 enlargements. Such a potential scenario was the very reason for the introduction of the two safeguard clauses in the 2003 and 2005 Accession Treaties to protect specifically the Internal Market *acquis* and the Justice and Home Affairs *acquis*. Without these clauses, the necessary unanimity among the receiving fifteen Member States could not have been reached and would have prevented even the launch of accession negotiations for the fifth and sixth enlargements.

Such safeguard measures could have involved measures, for example, to exclude nationals of the new Member States from practicing certain professions in the event that that country has failed to adopt rules of mutual recognition for other Member States' professionals, which would have given rise to a raft of questions concerning core principles of EC law that could normally be relied upon by individuals. Chapter 5 also explores the potential for the use of these clauses. The only example of use is the Regulation 857/2006[9] excluding Bulgaria's aviation sector from the Internal Market. This Regulation has since been revoked. Such clauses are dubious legally speaking and above all, they are clearly discriminatory in that they are addressed at the 'new' Member States and not the 'old' Member States, even though the latter have themselves been no angels in the application of the *acquis*. The threat of these clauses seems to have been of far more use as a pre-accession threat rather than as a post-accession conditionality tool.

Whether a postponement clause or similar trust mechanisms will actually be inserted in a future accession treaty, and whether their drafting will be tailored for the purposes of actually using them, remains to be seen. However, the European Council, at its summit in

[9] See Chapter 5 at 2.1.

December 2004, already stated that 'long transitional periods, derogations, specific arrangements or permanent safeguard clauses would be considered specifically in respect of Turkey' and that 'transitional arrangements or safeguards should be reviewed regarding their impact on competition or the Internal Market'.[10] The Commission and the European Council have already indicated that any future accession treaty with Turkey may well include a new safeguard clause or clauses in the fields of freedom of movement of persons, structural policies or agriculture. Such a statement bodes of an expansion of entirely new 'flexibility' mechanisms, although again, it is not possible to predict their form.

### Approximating to the environment and agri-food *acquis*

Chapters 6 and 7 explored the starting point for the approximation exercise under the pre-accession strategy. The agri-food law *acquis* was undergoing a root and branch overhaul in the aftermath of the BSE crisis at the time of *Agenda 2000*, the main tenets of which were entering into effect in 2002 and in the first years after the 2004 enlargement. As for the environment *acquis*, some of the most expensive and ambitious laws were adopted with the full participation of the fifteen Member States, which means that enlargement of the environment *acquis* in the cases of the fifth and sixth enlargements cannot be compared to previous enlargement practices really. The very different needs of candidate countries in the pre-accession process required specific policy actions within the overall frame of the pre-accession strategy. Today, the pre-accession strategy continues to evolve to take account of the specificity of the candidates. For example, in the context of the current pre-accession countries, there is an increasingly regional dimension to their activities with the Regional Table and the Working Tables of the Stability Pact.

[10] See Council Press Release, 16238/1/04, *Presidency Conclusions*, of 17 December 2004, under title *Enlargements* at point 7. The same wording appears in the European Commission's negotiating mandate, adopted by the Council on 3 October 2005. See Chapter 3 at 1.2, for context and a full quote.

The enormous health and environmental benefits of eastwards enlargement are undeniable.[11] Moreover, the pre-accession strategy imposed approximation with 'green standards beyond the reach of the environment *acquis* proper. While it is not strictly speaking within the environment chapter of the *acquis*, the pre-accession strategy as well as the 2003 and 2005 Accession Treaties have incorporated a strong conditionality concerning the dismantling, decommissioning and safety standards of nuclear power plants.[12] The new Member States concerned are Bulgaria, the Czech Republic, Lithuania, Slovakia, Slovenia, Hungary.

However, Chapters 6 and 7 revealed various instances of weaknesses in this strategy in the context of the EU agri-food and environment chapters of the *acquis communautaire*. It was also apparent in advance of the fifth enlargement in 2004, at the time of signature of the 2003 Accession Treaty, that the eight CEEC Member States and Cyprus and Malta had a considerable workload to complete in the year before their accession.

For the countries of central and eastern Europe in particular, the legacy of the communist era complicated their starting point for approximation to the environment *acquis*, as much in terms of their administrative capacity to apply and enforce it as the lack of standards. The priorities of the new Member States are necessarily influenced by the daunting task of attracting the necessary investment in order to bring themselves up to the Community level standard in a range of environment measures, such as those concerning large combustion plants, water quality and integrated pollution prevention and control, to name only a few. This fact alone instills much uncertainty into the future of the environment *acquis* not only for the new Member States but also for any Member State seeking to pursue higher national and EU standards.

Chapter 6 at section 3, asks whether the transitional arrangements agreed in the fifth and sixth Accession Treaties were feasible. It was already clear in the first years after the 2004 enlargement that various new Member States had not even transposed core environment legislation. For example, Cyprus, the Czech Republic, Hungary, Latvia, Lithuania, Malta, Poland and Slovenia were all the subject of actions in

[11] See Chapter 6 at 1.1.
[12] See Chapter 6 at 1.2.3 and 2.1.3.

2006 for failure to have transposed the Environmental Impact Assessment Directive, alongside nine of the 'old' Member States. Any request for a transitional arrangement for the transposition of legislation was expressly refused under the rationale of negotiating transitional arrangements. Chapter 6 reveals a lack of rigour in the application of the pre-accession conditionality for the environment *acquis*.

The governance challenge facing the enlarging Union is accentuated in the case of the environment *acquis*. EC environment law has a long history of poor application by the Member States of environment laws and a lack of adequate governance tools at the European Commission's disposal in order to address that problem. The lack of rigour in the pre-accession conditionality is part of the problem. From the Commission's own progress reports on the preparedness of the incoming Member States in the run-up to the signature of the 2003 and 2005 enlargements, it is clear that the extent of work outstanding under the pre-accession strategy was considerable. Chapter 6[13] explored this as well as the governance challenge posed by the transitional arrangements and the emergence of 'informal transitional arrangements' as a result of the 2004 and 2007 enlargements. Soon after the fifth enlargement, the Commission initiated actions[14] against new Member States for failure to have adopted or implemented key environment laws too; Poland for example had only allocated seventy-two protected areas for endangered species whereas it should have identified one hundred and forty and was given no temporary derogation from such conservation measures in the fifth Accession Treaty.

If the track records of the Member States prior to the recent enlargements are anything to go by, innovative governance mechanisms will be crucial to the enforcement of the environment *acquis* in an enlarging Union. It is relevant that the 'old' Member States are themselves no angels in the implementation of and compliance with the environment *acquis*, nor the agri-food *acquis* for that matter.

There is no safeguard clause for the environment *acquis* comparable to those for the Internal Market *acquis* or the Justice and Home Affairs *acquis*. The Union itself was not ready for this accentuated governance challenge at the time of the fifth and sixth enlargements, although in

[13] See section 3.

[14] See Commission Staff Working Document, COM(2007) 487, 30 April 2007, which is an annex to the Commission Communication *2006 Environment Policy Review*, COM(2007) 195 of the same date.

2008, new plans for improving the implementation of the environment *acquis* promise to improve the situation.[15] Should it enter into force, the Treaty of Lisbon will add some welcome innovations to the environmental governance weaponry, such as enabling the Commission to ask the ECJ to impose lump sums and penalty payments on recalcitrant Member States at an earlier stage in infringement proceedings.

As for the evolution of the environment *acquis* in an enlarging Union, Chapter 6 concludes with a comment on the benefits and drawbacks of the pre-accession strategy. This concluding section looks at enlargement of the environment *acquis* in the broader context of achieving economic development that is sustainable from an environmental perspective and notes the need for continued efforts by the EU twenty-seven. The pre-accession strategy demands approximation with the *acquis* and cannot replace national environmental policies and actions. The fact that environment is a shared competence at Union level is a further complicating factor in the mix. Also there are important areas where the Union could well take action but is held back by national political sensitivities, which gives the impression of the 'no man's land' in the environment *acquis*, where the Union and the Member States do not set foot. The examples of energy taxation was given to illustrate this.

In the 2003 and 2005 Accession Treaties, there are few transitional arrangements in the agri-food *acquis* compared to the environment *acquis*. Also, different clauses provide for special legislative procedures to derogate from, adapt or adjust the food safety, veterinary and phytosanitary *acquis*.[16] However, here too there are various examples of informal transitional arrangements arising, which again, like the environment chapter of the *acquis*, highlights a lack of rigour in the pre-accession process. Reports of the Food and Veterinary Office that were researched here show persistent problems in various, although not all, of the new Member States in meeting their pre-accession commitments to comply fully with the agri-food *acquis*.[17]

Chapter 7 shows how important a role the FVO plays in inspection the Member States' capacity to guarantee the proper application of the agri-food *acquis*. Various reports of the FVO help to identify the

[15] See Chapter 6 at 3.2.1, and particularly COM(2008) 2852 of 18 November 2008.
[16] See Chapter 7 at 2.2.3.
[17] See Chapter 7 at 3.1.

extent of approximation problems in the new and old Member States. They also reveal instances of informal transitional arrangements arising in the agri-food *acquis*. Those reports are used as the basis for legal proceedings by the Commission against Member States where appropriate or may trigger safeguard measures under relevant agri-food laws.

Bulgaria and Romania[18] were shown in a very poor light in terms of compliance with the agri-food *acquis* in the first year of their membership, 2007. Bulgaria was sent 80 letters of formal notice in its first year of membership, and Romania was sent 195. Moreover Bulgaria were listed as failing to have transposed literally hundreds of Directives of the Public Health and Consumer Protection *acquis* that was in place before their accession, the bulk of which are agri-food laws: DG SANCO opened a total of 428 new cases in the agri-food chapter of the *acquis*[19] although overall, 334 were closed in the same year. This is in addition to the problems of transposing and implementing the Common Agricultural Policy and financial and other regulations of the common organisations of the markets.

While various provisions of the agri-food *acquis* provide a legal basis for the Union to take safeguard measures to address threats to the food chain – such as Regulation 178/2002 laying down the general principles and requirements of food law, establishing the European Food Safety Authority and laying down procedures in matters of food safety[20] – it is argued that the use of the Internal Market safeguard clause in the fifth and sixth Accession Treaties would have been appropriate in order to stem any threat to the integrity of the agri-food *acquis* and the food chain. Of course the Internal Market safeguard clause should normally become a dead-letter on the date of enlargement itself because the candidate should – under the rigorous pre-accession strategy – be able to take on the full breadth of the rights and obligations of membership. But these trust mechanisms were intended to ensure that a new Member State continue to meet its rights and obligations after their accession not that they continue in pre-accession efforts beyond their accession. It has the potential of bringing about

[18] See Chapter 7 at 3.1, referring to European Commission, *26th Annual Monitoring Report on National Implementation of EU law* for the year 2007, COM(2008) 777 of 18 November 2008.

[19] See ibid., p. 221.

[20] See Chapter 7 at 1.1.2.

speedier compliance compared to standard procedures for addressing such failings by the Member States in enforcing the *acquis*. It would also apply in addition to the standard legal mechanisms available to the European Commission under Article 258 TFEU, together with the European Court of Justice, for ensuring that Member States properly implement and comply with the *acquis*.

The Internal Market clause has not been used in the end for the agri-food *acquis*. Since the 2004 and 2007 enlargements, the Commission has been pursuing the instances of informal transitional arrangements by means of the standard governance mechanisms available to it under the TFEU. However, to keep the problems facing the new Member States in perspective, the Fifteen themselves also face compliance problems in the agri-food *acquis*. As with the environment *acquis*, this is a governance challenge for all Member States.

The fact that these safeguard mechanisms focused on the JHA and the Internal Market *acquis* inevitably implies a priority for these chapters over others, such as the environment chapter. Why not include a safeguard clause to guarantee the integrity of the existing environment *acquis* – and other chapters of the *acquis* for that matter – at the same time, at least to ensure against an undergrowth of 'informal' transitional arrangements? After all, each Accession Treaty states in the very first provisions on Principles, that upon accession the incoming Member State is in the 'same situation' with every other Member State. It is an established point of principle that the provisions of Community law apply *ab initio* and *in toto* to new Member States, derogations being allowed only insofar as they are expressly laid down by transitional measures.[21] This is settled case law and the same applies to the 2003 and 2005 Accession Treaties.[22] Taking safeguard measures to protect the *acquis* would be consistent with the incoming countries commitments when signing the accession treaty: to adopt the entire *acquis*. This would also be consistent with the pre-accession conditionality.

All this said, in both the environment and agri-food law chapters of the *acquis communautaire*, the pre-accession strategy must be given credit for its achievements: of raising the standards of human health

[21] See Chapter 1 at 3, referring in particular to ECJ Case 258/81, *Metallurgiki Halyps A.E.* v. *Commission* [1982] *ECR* 4261.

[22] Latterly in relation to the fourth Accession Treaty, see for example ECJ, Case C-233/97 *KappAhl Oy* [1998] *ECR* I-8069. See Art. 5(3) and 3(2), 2003 and 2005 Accession Treaties respectively.

and environment protection throughout the region and in a relatively short time frame given the enormity of the task that faced the new Member States in approximating to the *acquis communautaire*. It cannot be denied that considerable human health and environmental benefits can be directly attributed to the 'carrot' of enlargement and the pre-accession strategy for eastwards enlargement, and now also for enlargement to the South East. The progress of the new Member States as well as today's candidates in approximating to the environment *acquis* has to been considered a positive development in many ways: even if it were to be considered only a minimum standard in environment law and policy, this approximation exercise marks a standard throughout the entire region and expands that minimum threshold from fifteen countries to twenty-seven and more countries in the region. For all the defects and justified criticism of the enlargement process, therefore, the pre-accession strategy is due credit for this remarkable success in such a relatively short time frame and given the magnitude of the task facing the central and eastern European Member States in particular. The impact of the vast approximation exercise, driven by political commitment and a strategically designed conditionality has resulted in the extension of the ambitious body of EU environment and human health standards into the broader European continent.

## ANNEX I

# CURRENT AGRI-FOOD LEGISLATION IN FORCE

### Food safety

#### 1. *General*

- Regulation 178/2002 laying down the general principles and requirements of food law, establishing the European Food Safety Authority and laying down procedures in matters of food safety

#### 2. *Placing on the market of food, feed and animal by-products*

- Regulation 852/2004 on the hygiene of foodstuffs
- Regulation 853/2004 laying down specific hygiene rules for food of animal origin
- Directive 2004/41 repealing certain Directives concerning food hygiene and health conditions for the production and placing on the market of certain products of animal origin intended for human consumption and amending Directives 89/662 and 92/118 and Decision 95/408
- Directive 92/118 laying down animal health and public health requirements governing trade in and imports into the Community of products not subject to the said requirements laid down in specific Community rules referred to in Annex A (I) to Directive 89/662 and, as regards pathogens, to Directive 90/425
- Directive 2002/99 laying down the animal health rules governing the production, processing, distribution and introduction of products of animal origin for human consumption
- Regulation 1774/2002 laying down health rules concerning animal by-products not intended for human consumption
- Regulation 1523/2007 banning the placing on the market and the import to, or export from, the Community of cat and dog fur, and products containing such fur

#### 3. *Controls*

- Regulation 882/2004 on official controls performed to ensure the verification of compliance with feed and food law, animal health and animal welfare rules
- Regulation 854/2004 laying down specific rules for the organisation of official controls on products of animal origin intended for human consumption
- Directive 2004/41 repealing certain Directives concerning food hygiene and health conditions for the production and placing on the market of certain

products of animal origin intended for human consumption and amending Council Directives 89/662 and 92/118 and Council Decision 95/408
- Directive 90/425 concerning veterinary and zootechnical checks applicable in intra-Community trade in certain live animals and products with a view to the completion of the internal market
- Directive 89/662 concerning veterinary checks in intra-Community trade with a view to the completion of the internal market
- Directive 96/93 on the certification of animals and animal products
- Directive 2002/99 laying down the animal health rules governing the production, processing, distribution and introduction of products of animal origin for human consumption
- Directive 89/608 on mutual assistance between the administrative authorities of the Member States and cooperation between the latter and the Commission to ensure the correct application of legislation on veterinary and zootechnical matters
- Directive 91/496 laying down the principles governing the organization of veterinary checks on animals entering the Community from third countries and amending Directives 89/662, 90/425 and 90/675
- Directive 97/78 laying down the principles governing the organisation of veterinary checks
- Directive 2002/99 laying down the animal health rules governing the production, processing, distribution and introduction of products of animal origin for human consumption
- Directive 91/496 laying down the principles governing the organization of veterinary checks on animals entering the Community from third countries and amending Directives 89/662, 90/425 and 90/675
- Directive 97/78 laying down the principles governing the organisation of veterinary checks on products entering the Community from third countries
- Regulation 882/2004 on official controls performed to ensure the verification of compliance with feed and food law, animal health and animal welfare rules

### 4. *Food Safety*

- Directive 87/250 on the indication of alcoholic strength by volume in the labelling of alcoholic beverages for sale to the ultimate consumer
- Directive 89/396 on indications or marks identifying the lot to which a foodstuff belongs
- Directive 90/496 on nutrition labelling for foodstuffs
- Directive 2000/13 on the approximation of the laws of the Member States relating to the labelling, presentation and advertising of foodstuffs
- Regulation 1924/2006 on nutrition and health claims made on foods
- Directive 89/107 on the approximation of the laws of the Member States concerning food additives authorized for use in foodstuffs intended for human consumption

- Directive 88/344 on the approximation of the laws of the Member States on extraction solvents used in the production of foodstuffs and food ingredients
- Directive 88/388 on the approximation of the laws of the Member States relating to flavourings for use in foodstuffs and to source materials for their production
- Council Decision 88/389 on the establishment, by the Commission, of an inventory of the source materials and substances used in the preparation of flavourings
- Regulation 2232/96 laying down a Community procedure for flavouring substances used or intended for use in or on foodstuffs
- Regulation 2065/2003 on smoke flavourings used or intended for use in or on foods
- Regulation 1935/2004 on materials and articles intended to come into contact with food
- Regulation 2023/2006 on good manufacturing practice for materials and articles intended to come into contact with food
- Directive 2002/46 on the approximation of the laws of the Member States relating to food supplements
- Regulation 1925/2006 on the addition of vitamins and minerals and of certain other substances to foods
- Directive 89/398 on the approximation of the laws of the Member States relating to foodstuffs intended for particular nutritional uses
- Directive 92/52 on infant formulae and follow-on formulae intended for export to third countries
- Directive 89/108 on the approximation of the laws of the Member States relating to quick-frozen foodstuffs for human consumption
- Regulation 315/93 laying down Community procedures for contaminants in food
- Regulation 258/97 concerning novel foods and novel food ingredients
- Regulation 1829/2003 on genetically modified food and feed
- Regulation 1830/2003 concerning the traceability and labelling of genetically modified organisms and the traceability of food and feed products produced from genetically modified organisms and amending Directive 2001/18
- Directive 1999/2 on the approximation of the laws of the Member States concerning foods and food ingredients treated with ionising radiation
- Directive 1999/3 on the establishment of a Community list of foods and food ingredients treated with ionising radiation
- Directive 80/777 on the approximation of the laws of the Member States relating to the exploitation and marketing of natural mineral waters
- Commission Directive 2003/40/EC of 16 May 2003 establishing the list, concentration limits and labelling requirements for the constituents of natural mineral waters and the conditions for using ozone-enriched air for the treatment of natural mineral waters and spring waters

## 5. *Animal health*

- Regulation 1760/2000 establishing a system for the identification and registration of bovine animals and regarding the labelling of beef and beef products and repealing Regulation 820/97
- Directive 64/432 on animal health problems affecting intra-Community trade in bovine animals and swine
- Directive 92/102 on the identification and registration of animals
- Regulation 21/2004 establishing a system for the identification and registration of ovine and caprine animals and amending Regulation 1782/2003 and Directives 92/102 and 64/432
- Directive 90/426 on animal health conditions governing the movement and import from third countries of equidae
- Directive 90/427 on the zootechnical and genealogical conditions governing intra-Community trade in equidae
- Directive 2003/85 on Community measures for the control of foot-and-mouth disease repealing Directive 85/511 and Decisions 89/531 and 91/665 and amending Directive 92/46
- Directive 2001/89 on Community measures for the control of classical swine fever
- Directive 2002/60 laying down specific provisions for the control of African swine fever and amending Directive 92/119 as regards Teschen disease and African swine fever
- Directive 92/35 laying down control rules and measures to combat African horse sickness
- Directive 2005/94 on Community measures for the control of avian influenza and repealing Directive 92/40
- Directive 92/66 introducing Community measures for the control of Newcastle disease
- Directive 2006/88 on animal health requirements for aquaculture animals and products thereof, and on the prevention and control of certain diseases in aquatic animals
- Directive 2000/75 laying down specific provisions for the control and eradication of bluetongue
- Regulation 999/2001 laying down rules for the prevention, control and eradication of certain transmissible spongiform encephalopathies
- Regulation 2160/2003 of salmonella and other specified food-borne zoonotic agents, *OJ* 2003 L 325/1
- Directive 2003/99 on the monitoring of zoonoses and zoonotic agents, amending Council Decision 90/424 and repealing Directive 92/117
- Directive 92/119 introducing general Community measures for the control of certain animal diseases and specific measures relating to swine vesicular disease
- Directive 82/894 on the notification of animal diseases within the Community
- Directive 64/432 on animal health problems affecting intra-Community trade in bovine animals and swine

- Directive 91/68 on animal health conditions governing intra-Community trade in ovine and caprine animals
- Directive 90/426 on animal health conditions governing the movement and import from third countries of equidae
- Directive 90/539 on animal health conditions governing intra-Community trade in, and imports from third countries of, poultry and hatching eggs
- Directive 2006/88/EC on animal health requirements for aquaculture animals and products thereof, and on the prevention and control of certain diseases in aquatic animals [01/08/2008]
- Directive 89/556 on animal health conditions governing intra-Community trade in and importation from third countries of embryos of domestic animals of the bovine species
- Directive 88/407 laying down the animal health requirements applicable to intra-Community trade in and imports of deep-frozen semen of domestic animals of the bovine species
- Directive 90/429 laying down the animal health requirements applicable to intra-Community trade in and imports of semen of domestic animals of the porcine species
- Directive 92/65 laying down animal health requirements governing trade in and imports into the Community of animals, semen, ova and embryos not subject to animal health requirements laid down in specific Community rules referred to in Annex A (I) to Directive 90/425
- Directive 96/22 concerning the prohibition on the use in stockfarming of certain substances having a hormonal or thyrostatic action and of beta-agonists, and repealing Directives 81/602, 88/146 and 88/299
- Decision 1999/879 concerning the placing on the market and administration of bovine somatotrophin BST) and repealing Decision 90/218
- Directive 96/23 on measures to monitor certain substances and residues thereof in live animals and animal products and repealing Directives 85/358 and 86/469 and Decisions 89/187 and 91/664
- Directive 2004/68 laying down animal health rules for the importation into and transit through the Community of certain live ungulate animals, amending Directives 90/426 and 92/65 and repealing Directive 72/462
- Directive 90/426 on animal health conditions governing the movement and import from third countries of equidae
- Directive 90/539 on animal health conditions governing intra-Community trade in, and imports from third countries of, poultry and hatching eggs
- Directive 89/556 on animal health conditions governing intra-Community trade in and importation from third countries of embryos of domestic animals of the bovine species
- Directive 88/407 laying down the animal health requirements applicable to intra- Community trade in and imports of deep-frozen semen of domestic animals of the bovine species
- Directive 90/429 laying down the animal health requirements applicable to intra-Community trade in and imports of semen of domestic animals of the porcine species

- Directive 92/65 laying down animal health requirements governing trade in and imports into the Community of animals, semen, ova and embryos not subject to animal health requirements laid down in specific Community rules referred to in Annex A (I) to Directive 90/425
- Directive 98/58 concerning the protection of animals kept for farming purposes
- Directive 1999/74 laying down minimum standards for the protection of laying hens
- Directive 2007/43 laying down minimum rules for the protection of chickens kept for meat production
- Directive 91/629 laying down minimum standards for the protection of calves
- Directive 91/630 laying down minimum standards for the protection of pigs
- Regulation 1/2005 on the protection of animals during transport and related operations and amending Directives 64/432 and 93/119 and Regulation 1255/97
- Directive 93/119/EC of 22 December 1993 on the protection of animals at the time of slaughter or killing
- Directive 77/504 on pure- bred breeding animals of the bovine species
- Directive 88/661 on the zoo technical standards applicable to breeding animals of the porcine species
- Directive 89/361 concerning pure-bred breeding sheep and goats
- Directive 90/427 on the zootechnical and genealogical conditions governing intra-community trade in equidae
- Directive 90/428 on trade in equidae intended for competitions and laying down the conditions for participation therein
- Directive 91/174 laying down zootechnical and pedigree requirements for the marketing of pure-bred animals and amending Directives 77/504 and 90/425
- Directive 94/28laying down the principles relating to the zootechnical and genealogical conditions applicable to imports from third countries of animals, their semen, ova and embryos, and amending Directive77/504 on purebred breeding animals of the bovine species
- Decision 90/424 on expenditure in the veterinary field

### 6. *Feed*

- Regulation 183/2005 laying down requirements for feed hygiene
- Directive 70/524 concerning additives in feedingstuffs
- Regulation 1831/2003 on additives for use in animal nutrition
- Directive 79/373 on the circulation of compound feedingstuffs
- Directive 96/25 on the circulation of feed materials, amending Directives 70/524, 74/63, 82/471 and 93/74 and repealing Directive 77/101
- Directive 2002/32 on undesirable substances in animal feed
- Directive 93/74 on feedingstuffs intended for particular nutritional purposes
- Directive 82/471 concerning certain products used in animal nutrition

- Directive 90/167 laying down the conditions governing the preparation, placing on the market and use of medicated feedingstuffs in the Community

*7. Phytosanitary*

- Directive 2000/29 on protective measures against the introduction into the Community of organisms harmful to plants or plant products and against their spread within the Community
- Directive 69/464 on control of Potato Wart Disease
- Directive 69/465 on control of Potato Cyst Eelworm (until 01/06/2010)
- Directive 74/647 on control of carnation leaf-rollers
- Directive 93/85 on control of Potato Ring Rot
- Directive 98/57 on the control of *Ralstonia solanacearum* (Smith) Yabuuchi et al.
- Directive 2006/91on control of San José Scale (Codified version)
- Directive 91/414 concerning the placing of plant protection products on the market
- Directive 76/895 relating to the fixing of maximum levels for pesticide residues in and on fruit and vegetables
- Directive 86/362 on the fixing of maximum levels for pesticide residues in and on cereals
- Directive 86/363 on the fixing of maximum levels for pesticide residues in and on foodstuffs of animal origin
- Directive 90/642 on the fixing of maximum levels for pesticide residues in and on certain products of plant origin, including fruit and vegetables
- Regulation 396/2005 on maximum residue levels of pesticides in or on food and feed of plant and animal origin and amending Council Directive 91/414/EEC
- Directive 66/401 on the marketing of fodder plant seed
- Directive 66/402 on the marketing of cereal seed
- Directive 68/193 on the marketing of material for the vegetative propagation of the vine
- Directive 92/33 on the marketing of vegetable propagating and planting material, other than seed
- Directive 92/34 on the marketing of fruit plant propagating material and fruit plants intended for fruit production
- Directive 98/56 on the marketing of propagating material of ornamental plants
- Directive 1999/105 on the marketing of forest
- Directive 2002/53 on the common catalogue of varieties of agricultural plant species
- Directive 2002/54 on the marketing of beet seed
- Directive 2002/55 on the marketing of vegetable seed
- Directive 2002/56 on the marketing of seed potatoes
- Directive 2002/57 on the marketing of seed of oil and fibre plants
- Regulation 2100/94 on Community plant variety rights

# BIBLIOGRAPHY

## Contributions in edited volumes


L. Azoulay, 'La Sécurité alimentaire dans la législation communautaire' in J. Bourrinet and F. Snyder, eds., *La Sécurité alimentaire dans l'Union européenne* (Brussels, Bruylant 2003) at pp. 29–67.

R. Barents, 'The Court of Justice and the Renewed European Treaties', A. Ott and E. Vos, eds., *50 years of European Integration: Foundations and Perspectives*, (The Hague: TMC Asser Press/CUP, 2008), pp. 57–75.

S. Blockmans, 'EU conflict prevention in the Western Balkans' in V. Kronenberger and Jan Wouters, eds., *The European Union and Conflict Prevention: Policy and Legal Aspects* (The Hague, T.M.C. Asser Press 2004), pp. 293–221.

C. Blumann, 'Les implications de la sécurité alimentaire dans l'évolution de la politique agricole commune' in Bourrinet and Snyder, op. cit. pp. 69–93.

J. Bourrinet, 'L'Union européenne entre sécurité et insecurité alimentaire' in J. Bourrinet and F. Snyder, op. cit. pp. 19–27.

F. Cameron, 'The European Union and the Challenge of Enlargement' in Maresceau, ed., *Enlarging of the European Union, Enlarging the European Union; relations between the EU and Central and Eastern Europe* (London and New York, Longman 1997) at pp. 241–251.

J. Charpentier, 'L'est déjà plus? Le cas de l'Allemagne' in Slobodan Milacic, ed., *L'intégration européenne et la révolution de l'europe de l'est* (Luxembourg, Institut Universitaire International Luxembourg 1991) pp. 62–67.

I. Chmitelin, 'Le role des états members dans la securité sanitaire des aliments' in Bourrinet and Snyder, op. cit. pp. 95–107.

M. Cremona, 'The New Associations: Substantive Issues of the Europe Agreements with the Central and Eastern European States', in S. Kostantinidis, ed., *The Legal Regulation of the European Community's External Relations after the Completion of the Internal Market* (Aldershot, Dartmouth 1996) pp. 141–166.

——, 'Enlargement: a Successful Instrument of Foreign Policy?' in Trimidas and Nebbit, eds., *European Law for the Twenty-First Century Vol. II* (Hart Publishing 2004) pp. 397–413.

——, ed., *The Enlargement of the European Union* (New York, Oxford University Press, 2003).

B. Dette, 'Access to justice in environmental matters: a fundamental democratic right', in M. Onida ed., *Europe and the environment: legal essays in honour of Ludwig Krämer* (Groningen: Europa Law Publishing, 2004), pp. 3–22.

W. de Lobkowicz, 'La sécurité intérieure de l'Union européenne élargie', in G. de Kerchove and A. Weyembergh, eds., *Sécurité et justice: enjeu de la politique extérieure de l'Union européenne* (Bruxelles, Editions de l'université de Bruxelles 2003) pp. 31–66.

B. de Witte, 'The Impact of Enlargement and the Constitution of the European Union' in M. Cremona, ed., *The Enlargement of the European Union*, op. cit., pp. 209–252.

B. Dziechciarz, 'Impact of European Union Enlargement on EMU: Monetary Split-up into 'Ins' and 'Outs' as a temporary or Permanent Phenomenon?' in Inglis and Ott, eds., *The Constitution for Europe and an enlarging Union: Unity in Diversity?* (Groningen, Europa Law Publishing 2005) pp. 135–157.

B. Dziechciarz, 'Candidate Countries and Economic and Monetary Union' in Ott and Inglis eds., *Handbook on European Enlargement. A commentary on the Enlargement process* (The Hague, TMC Asser Press 2002) pp. 693–726.

J.-C. Gautron, 'Le problèmatique polique', in J.-C. Gautron, ed., *Les relations communauté européenne europe de l'est* (Paris, Economica 1991), pp. 3–27.

M.-A. Gaudissart and A. Sinnaeve, 'The Role of the white paper in the preparation of the eastern enlargement, in M. Maresceau, ed., *Enlarging the European Union*, op. cit., pp. 41–71.

M. Hattig, 'Candidate countries and energy and nuclear safety' in A. Ott and K. Inglis, eds. *Handbook on European Enlargement*, op. cit. pp. 945–964.

C. Hillion, 'The Copenhagen Criteria and their Progeny', in C. Hillion, ed., *EU Enlargement; a legal appraisal* (Oxford and Portland Oregon 2004) pp. 1–23.

——, 'The EU's Neighbourhood Policy Towards Eastern Europe', in A. Dashwood and M. Maresceau (eds.), *Law and Practice of EU External Relations: Salient Features of a Changing Landscape*, pp. 309–333.

F. Hoffmeister, 'Earlier enlargements' and 'Changing requirements for membership', Ott and Inglis, eds., *Handbook on European Enlargement*, op. cit. pp. 87–102.

K. Inglis on 'Pre-accession and the accession partnerships' in Ott and Inglis, eds., *Handbook on European Enlargement*, op. cit., pp. 103–111.

——, 'Treading the tightrope between flexibility and legal certainty: enlargement and temporary derogations from the workers acquis' in D. Hanf, ed., *La libre circulation 10 ans après '1993'*, not yet in print, 22 pages.

——, 'EU Environmental law and its green footprints in the world', in A. Dashwood and M. Maresceau, (eds.), *Law and Practice of EU External Relations: Salient features of a changing landscape* (Cambridge, CUP 2008), pp. 429–464.

J.H. Jans, 'Did Baron von Munchhausen ever Visit Aarhus? Some Critical Remarks on the Proposal for a Regulation on the Application of the Provisions of the Aarhus Convention to EC Institutions and Bodies', in R. Macrory, ed., *Reflections on 30 years of EU environment law: a high level of protection?* (Groningen, Europa Law Publishing – The Avosetta Series 2005) Vol. 7, pp. 475–490.

J. Klarer and P. Francis, 'Regional overview' in J. Klarer, ed., *The Environmental Challenge for Central European Economies in Transition* (Chichester, John Wiley & Sons 1997), pp. 1–66.

L. Krämer, 'Some reflections on the EU mix of instruments on climate change', in M. Peeters and K. Dekettelaere *EU Climate Change Policy: The Challenge of new Regulatory Initiatives* (Cheltenham and Massachusetts, Edward Elgar 2006), pp. 279–295.

A. Lazowski, 'Approximation of laws' in Ott and Inglis, eds., op. cit. pp. 631–640.

M. Lelart, 'The Euro Zone and the Single Currency in an Enlarging European Union', in N. Neuwahl, ed., *European Union Enlargement: Law and Socio-Economic Changes* (Montréal, Editions Thémis 2004) pp. 133–162.

R. Macrory, 'The Amsterdam Treaty: an environmental perspective' in D. O'Keeffe and P. Twomey, eds., in *Legal Issues of the Amsterdam Treaty* (Oxford-Portland Oregon, Hart Publishing 1999), pp. 171–183.

P. Manin, 'Article I-58' in L. Bourgorgue-Larsen, A. Levade and F. Picod, eds., *Traité établissant un Constitution pour l'Europe* (Bruxelles, Bruylant 2007) at p. 718.

L. Maurer, 'Progress of the negotiations' in Ott and Inglis, eds., *Handbook on European Enlargement*, op. cit. pp. 113–129.

J. Marko and J. Wilhelm, 'The Balkans and the NIS' in Ott and Inglis, *Handbook on European Enlargement*, op. cit. at p. 167.

M. Maresceau, 'Pre-accession' in Cremona, ed., op. cit. at pp. 9–40.

——, 'The EU Pre-accession Strategies: a Political and Legal Analysis' in M. Maresceau and E. Lannon, eds., *The EU's Enlargement and Mediterranean Strategies: a comparative analysis* (Basingstoke, Palgrave 2001) pp. 3–28.

——, 'On Association, Partnership, Pre-accession and Accession' in Maresceau. ed., *Enlarging the European Union*, op. cit. pp. 3–22.

S. Milacic, in S. Milicic, ed., *L'integration européenne et la révolution de l'europe de l'est* op. cit. pp. 11–33.

P.-C. Müller-Graff, ed., *East Central Europe and the European union: from Europe Agreements to a Member Status* (Baden-Baden, Nomos Verlagsgesellschaft, 1997).

——, 'The framework for EU-CEEC relations' in Maresceau, ed., *Enlarging the European Union*, op. cit. p. 34.

P. Nicolaides, 'Preparing for Accession to the EU: How to establish capacity for effective and credible application of EU rules', in M. Cremona, op. cit. pp. 43–78.

M. Onida, 'Europe and the Environment; legal essays in honours of Ludmig Krämer' (Groningen, Europa Law Publishing 2004).

A. Ott, 'The European Union, its Constitution and institutional future' in N. Neuwahl, ed., *European Union Enlargement*, op. cit. pp. 237–254.

I. Pernice, 'Institutional Settlements for an Enlarged EU' in G.A. Bermann and K. Pistor, eds., *Law and Governance in an Enlarged European Union: essays in European Law* (Oxford and Portland, Hart Publishing 2004) pp. 3–36.

G. Sander, 'Consumer protection and public health' in Ott and Inglis, eds., *Handbook on European Enlargement*, op. cit. at pp. 867–880.

M. Schreurs, 'Environmental protection in an expanding European Community: lessons from past accessions' in J.A. Carmin and S.D. Van Deveer, eds., *EU Enlargement and the environment; Institutional change and environmental policy in Central and Eastern Europe* (Oxon and New York, Routledge 2005).

M. Skou Andersen and D. Lieferink, 'Introduction: the impact of the pioneers on EU environmental policy' in M. Skou Andersen and D. Lieferink, eds., *European Environmental Policy: the pioneers* (New York, Manchester University Press 1997) pp. 25.

B. Smith, 'Water: a critical resource', in R. King, ed., *The Mediterranean Environment and Society* (London and New York, Arnold 1997) p. 243.

B. Soret, 'Réforme Institutionelle et Elargissmenet de l'Union Européenne aux PECOs' in Müller-Graff, ed., *East Central Europe and the European Union: from Europe Agreements to a Member Status*, op. cit. n. 24 at pp. 369–376.

P. Van Elsuwege and Vermeersch A., 'Institutional Reform in the European Union: A Difficult Balancing Act', in Inglis and Ott, eds., *The Constitution for Europe and an Enlarging Union: Unity and Diversity?*, Groningen, Europa Law Publishing, 2005, pp. 57–84.

J. Vergnettes, 'Les prérogatives communautaires: analyse du risque – nouvelle autorité européenne de sécurité des aliments' in Bourrinet et Snyder, eds., op. cit. pp. 109–121.

G. Wilkes, ed., *Britain's Failure to enter the European Community 1961–1963: The enlargement negotiations and crises in European, Atlantic and Commonwealth relations* (London-Portland Oregon, Frank Cass 1997).

J. Wouters, 'Constitutional Limits of differentiation: the principle of equality', in B. de Witte, D. Hanf and E. Vos, eds., *The Many Faces of Differentiation in EU law* (Antwerp, Oxford, New York, Intersentia 2001) at p. 326.

G. Zeigler, 'the Accession Negotiations on the free movement of workers' in *Handbook on European Enlargement*, pp. 131–142.

## Books

S. Blockmans, *Tough Love: the European Union's Relations with the Western Balkans*, The Hague, T.M.C. Asser Press 2007.

J. Bourrinet 2000, *L'effectivité du droit européen de l'environnement; controle de la mise en oeuvre et sancion de la non-respect* (Paris, La Documentation Francaise 2000).

J. Burchell and S. Lightfoot, *The Greening of the European Union* (London and New York, Sheffield Academic Press 2001).
F. Comte and L. Krämer, *Environmental Crime in Europe* (Groningen/Amsterdam, Europa Law Publishing 2004).
P. Davies, *European Union Environment Law; an Introduction to Key Selected Issues* (Wiltshire, Ashgate 2004).
F. de La Serre, C. Lequesne, J. Rupnik, *L'Union européenne: ouverture à l'est?* (Paris, Presses Universitaires de Frances, 1994).
W. Hager, *Enlargement: Paying for the Green Acquis* (Brussels, Centre for European Policy Studies 2002).
M. Hirsch, P. Duneton, P. Baron and F. Noiville, *L'affolante histoire de la vache folle* (Paris, Editions Balland 1996).
F. Hoffmeister, *Legal Aspects of the Cyprus Problem: Annan Plan and EU Accession* (Leiden/Boston, Matinus Nijhoff Publishers 2006).
H. Holland and H. Pope, *EU food law and policy* (The Hague, Kluwer Law International 2004).
I. Jalles, *Implications juridico-constitutionelles de l'adhésion aux Communautés européennes; le case de Portugal* (Bruxelles, Bruylant, 1981).
Kapteyn and VerLoren van Themaat on 'Scope and revision of the Treaty' in Gormley, ed., *Introduction to the Law of the European Communities*, (London, The Hague, Boston, Kluwer Law International 1998).
L. Krämer, *European Environmental Law* (Dartmouth, Ashgate 2003).
——, *EC Treaty and Environmental Law* (London, Sweet & Maxwell 1998).
K. Lenaerts and P. Van Nuffel, *Constitutional Law of the European Union* (London, Sweet and Maxwell 2005).
A. Mayhew, *Recreating Europe. The European Union's Policy Towards Central and Eastern Europe* (Cambridge, Cambridge University Press 1998).
J. McCormick, Environmental Policy in the European Union (Hampshire and New York, Palgrave 2001).
W. Nicoll and A. Salmon, *Understanding the European Communities* (Worcester, Philip Allan 1990).
P. Pavelínek and J. Pickles, *Environmental Transitions; Transformation and Ecological Defence in Central and Eastern Europe* (London and New York, Routledge 2000).
C. Preston, *Enlargement and Integration in the European Union* (London and New York, Routledge 1997).
J.-P. Puissochet, *L'élargissement des Communautés européennes* (Paris, Editions techniques et économiques 1974).
S.C. Ratzan, *The Mad Cow Crisis; health and the Public Good* (London, UC Press 1998).
J.I. Torreblanca Payá, *The reuniting of Europe: promises, negotiations and compromises* (Aldershot, Ashgate, 2001).
——, *The European Community and Central and Eastern Europe (1989–1993): Foreign policy and decision-making* (Madrid, Centro de Estudios Avanzados en Ciencias Sociales, 1997).

## Articles and working papers

A. Berramdane, 'Chypre entre adhésion à l'Union européene et réunification', *Revue du Droit de L'Union Européene* (2003) pp. 87–108.
D. Binder, 'The European Court of Justice and the Protection of Fundamental Rights in the European Community; New Developments and Future Possibilities in Expanding Fundamental Rights Review to Member State Action', *Jean Monet Working Paper* 4/1995.

D. Booss and J. Forman, 'Enlargement', 32 *CML Rev.* (1995) at p. 95.

E. Brosset, 'The prior authorisation procedure adopted for the deliberate release into the environment of genetically modified organisms: the complexities of balancing Community and national competences', *European Law Journal* (2004) pp. 555–579.

C. Closa, 'Ratiying the EU Constitution: referendums and their implications', *US-Europe Analysis Series* (November 2004), www.brookings.edu

The Contzen Report, *Point de vue stratégique pour l'avenir des programmes Phare et Tacis de L'Union européenne*, August 1999.

P. Craig, 'The Treaty of Lisbon', 2008 *EL Rev.*, pp. 137–166.

M. Cremona, 'EU Enlargement: solidarity and conditionality', 30 *EL Rev.* (2005) pp. 3–22.

M. Dougan, 'The Treaty of Lisbon', 2008 *CML Rev.*, pp. 617–703.

J.L. Cruz Vilaca and N. Picara, 'Y a-t-il des limites matérielles à la révision des traités instituant les CE?, *Cahiers du droit européen*, 193, p. 29.

Dagtoglou, 'The Southern Enlargement of the European Community', 1984 21 *CML Rev.* 149–162.

N. de Sadeleer, 'Procedures for derogations from the principle of approximation of laws under Article 95 EC', 40 *CML Review* (2003) at pp. 908-913.

C. Delcourt, 'The *acquis communautaire*: has the concept had its day', 38 *CML Rev.* (2001) pp. 829–870.

T. Digneffe, I. Einfeldt, J. Harrison, 'Lobbying in the environmental field, the 'lowest common factor' hypothesis', *News of the College of Europe, Collegium* 17/IX. 1999.

See A. Evans, 'Voluntary harmonisation in integration between the European Community and Eastern Europe', 22 *EL Rev.* (1997).

E.T. Fakiolas and N. Tzifakis, 'Transformation or Accession? Reflecting on the EU's Strategy Towards the Western Balkans', 2008 *European Foreign Affairs Review* pp. 377–398.

*Friends of the Earth Europe Paper*, 'Will the new EU Constitution promote Nuclear energy?', April 2005, to be found at www.foreurope.org

T. Garvey, 'EU Enlargement: Is it Sustainable?' in S. Crisen and J. Carmin (eds.) *EU Enlargement and Environmental Quality: Central and Eastern Europe & Beyond*, Washington, DC. Woodrow Wilson International Center for Scholars, pp. 53–62.

M.A. Gaudissart, 'Cyprus and the European Union. The Long Road to Accession', 8 *The Cyprus Review Spring* 1996 pp. 13–22.

——, 'L'association des pays d'Europe centrale et orientale", Chapter VII of *L'association: un mode de co-opération privilégié et les Etats tiers*, PhD Thesis, Ghent European Institute, University of Gent, Faculteit Rechtsgeleerdheid, 1999–2000.

C. Hillion, 'Enlargement of the European Union – The discrepancy between membership obligations and accession conditions as regards the protection of minorities', 27 *Fordham International Law Journal* (2004) pp. 715–740.

K. Inglis, 'The Union's Fifth Enlargement: New Means to Make Enlargement Possible', 43 *CML Rev.* (2004) pp. 937–973.

——, 'The Europe Agreements Compared in the Light of their Pre-accession Strategy', 37 *CML Rev.* (2002) 1173–1184.

——, 'Anticipating New Union Competences in Energy' in (2008) *Maastricht Journal of European and Comparative Law*, Vol. 15, pp. 125–134.

——, Annotation on ECJ Cases C-413/04, C-414/04 and C-273/04, (2009) *CML Rev.* 641–663.

F. Jacobs, 'The Role of the *European Court of Justice* in the Protection of the *Environment*', (2006) 18 *Journal of Environmental Law* p. 201.

J.-P. Jacqué, 'German unification and the European Community', 94 *Revue générale du droit international public* (1990) pp. 997–1018.

P. Jehlicka, 'Implications of Eastern Enlargement of the EU: The end of Progressive Environmental Policy', *EUI working papers, RSC 2002/23.*

W. Kok, *Enlarging the EU: Achievements and Challenges* Florence, EUI (RSC) Working Paper 2003 at pp. 55–58.

H.G. Krenzler, 'Preparing for the acquis communautaire', *EUI working paper*, 98/6.

K. Lenearts, 'The Principle of Subsidiarity and the Environment in the European Union: Keeping the Balance of Federalism', *Fordham International Law Journal* (1994) pp. 846–895.

M. Maresceau and I. Montaguti, 'The relations between the European Union and central and eastern Europe: a legal appraisal', 32 *CML Rev.* (1995) p. 1328.

A. Ott, 'Unity in Diversity? Differentiation in EU law and policy in an enlarged European Union', Zeszyt 15 EUI *Research Laboratory Centrum Europejskie Natolin* (2004).

——, Unity in Diversity? – *Differentiation in EU Law and policy in an Enlarged European*, EUI Working Paper. 2004/16.

W. Paczy´nski, 'ECB Decision-making and the Status of the Eurogroup in an Enlarged EMU', CASE, Warsaw 2003, ISSN 1506-1701, ISBN: 83-7178-318-3.

M. Pallemaerts et al., Drowning in Process: the implementation of the Eu's 6th Environment Action Programme, Institute for European Environment Policy, April 2006.on progress under the 6th EAP.

D. Phinnemore, 'Stabilisation and Association Agreements: Europe Agreements for the Western Balkans?', 8 *EFA Rev.* (2003) pp. 77–103.

J.B. Skjaerseth and J. Wettestad, EU *Enlargement and Environmental Policy: the Bright Side*, The Fridtjof Nonsens Institute 2006.

M. Spernbauer, 'Benchmarking, Safeguard Clauses and Verification Mechanisms – What's in a Name? Recent Developments in Pre- and Post-accession Conditionality and Compliance with EU Law', (2007) *Croation Yearbook of European Law & Policy*, Vol. 3, pp. 273–306.

A. Surdej, 'Enlarging the EU Food Safety Regime: Adjustments of Polish Food Safety Regulations to the Requirement of the EU Membership', *Euro-limes czasopismo naukowe*, numer 2(3), czerwiec 2003.

C. Timmermans, 'German unification and Community law', 27 *CML Rev.* (1990) at p. 437.

K. Vincent, 'Mad Cows' and Eurocrats – Community Responses to the BSE Crisis', 5 *European Law Journal* (2004) pp. 499–517.

I. Von Homeyer, 'Differential Effects of Enlargement on EU Environmental Governance', 2004 *Environmental Politics*, suppl. 1/2004, pp. 52–76.

N. Walker, 'Constitutionalising Enlargement, Enlarging Constitutionalism', 8 *European Law Journal* (2003) pp. 365–385.

H. Wallace, *Adapting to Enlargement of the European Union: Institutional Practice since May 2004*, TEPSA Conference Paper, 16 November 2007.

P. Wennerås, 'Towards an ever green Union?', 2008 *CML Rev.* pp. 1645–1685.

D. Wilkinson, C. Monkhouse and D. Baldock, *The Future of EU Environment Policy: Challenges and Opportunities*, December 2004, Institute for European Environmental Policy, Special Report of the All-part Parliamentary Environment Group.

# INDEX

# Studies in EU External Relations

Edited by Marc Maresceau

brill.nl/seur

1. Rasch, Maximilian. *The European Union at the United Nations*. The Functioning and Coherence of EU External Representation in a State-centric environment. 2008. ISBN 978 90 04 16714 8.
2. Van Elsuwege, Peter. *From Soviet Republics to EU Member States*. A Legal and Political Assessment of the Baltic States' Accession to the EU. 2008. ISBN 978 90 04 16945 6.
3. Laulhé Shaelou, Stéphanie. *The EU and Cyprus*. Principles and Strategies of Full Integration. 2010. ISBN 978 90 04 17619 5.
4. Inglis, Kirstyn. *Evolving Practice in EU Enlargement*. With Case Studies in Agri-Food and Environment Law. 2010. ISBN 978 90 04 18166 3.